Forgotten Books takes the uppermost care to preserve the entire content of the original book. However, this book has been generated from a scan of the original, and as such we cannot guarantee that it is free from errors or contains the full content of the original. But we try our best!

Truth may seem, but cannot be:
Beauty brag, but 'tis not she;
Truth and beauty buried be.

To this urn let those repair
That are either true or fair;
For these dead birds sigh a prayer.

Bacon

SIXTY YEARS

IN

SOUTHERN CALIFORNIA

CONTAINING THE REMINISCENCES OF

HARRIS NEWMARK

EDITED BY

MAURICE H. NEWMARK
MARCO R. NEWMARK

> Every generation enjoys the use of a vast hoard bequeathed to it by antiquity, and transmits that hoard, augmented by fresh acquisitions, to future ages. In these pursuits, therefore, the first speculators lie under great disadvantages, and, even when they fail, are entitled to praise.—MACAULAY.

WITH 150 ILLUSTRATIONS

NEW YORK
The Knickerbocker Press

In Memoriam

At the hour of high twelve on April the fourth, 1916, the sun shone into a room where lay the temporal abode, for eighty-one years and more, of the spirit of Harris Newmark. On his face still lingered that look of peace which betokens a life worthily used and gently relinquished.

Many were the duties allotted him in his pilgrimage; splendidly did he accomplish them! Providence permitted him the completion of his final task—a labor of love—but denied him the privilege of seeing it given to the community of his adoption.

To him and to her, by whose side he sleeps, may it be both monument and epitaph.

Thy will be done!

M. H. N.
M. R. N.

INTRODUCTION

SEVERAL times during his latter years my friend, Charles Dwight Willard, urged me to write out my recollections of the five or six decades I had already passed in Los Angeles, expressing his regret that many pioneers had carried from this world so much that might have been of interest to both the Angeleño of the present and the future historian of Southern California; but as I had always led an active life of business or travel, and had neither fitted myself for any sort of literary undertaking nor attempted one, I gave scant attention to the proposal. Mr. Willard's persistency, however, together with the prospect of coöperation offered me by my sons, finally overcame my reluctance and I determined to commence the work.

Accordingly in June, 1913, at my Santa Monica home, I began to devote a few hours each day to a more or less fragmentary enumeration of the incidents of my boyhood; of my voyage over the great wastes of sea and land between my ancestral and adopted homes; of the pueblo and its surroundings that I found on this Western shore; of its people and their customs; and, finally, of the men and women who, from then until now, have contributed to the greatness of the Southland, and of the things they have done or said to entitle their names to be recorded. This task I finished in the early fall. During its progress I entered more and more into the distant Past, until Memory conjured before me many long-forgotten faces and happenings. In the end, I found that I had jotted down a mass of notes much greater than I had expected.

Thereupon the Editors began their duties, which were to arrange the materials at hand, to supply names and dates that had escaped me, and to interview many who had been principals in events and, accordingly, were presumed to know the details; and much progress was made, to the enlarging and enrichment of the book. But it was not long before they found that the work involved an amount of investigation which their limited time would not permit; and that if carried out on even the modest plan originally contemplated, some additional assistance would be required.

Fortunately, just then they met Perry Worden, a postgraduate of Columbia and a Doctor of Philosophy of the University of Halle, Germany; a scholar and an author of attainments. His aid, as investigator and adviser, has been indispensable to the completion of the work in its present form. Dr. Worden spent many months searching the newspapers, magazines and books—some of whose titles find special mention in the text—which deal with Southern California and its past; and he also interviewed many pioneers, to each of whom I owe acknowledgment for ready and friendly coöperation. In short, no pains was spared to confirm and amplify all the facts and narratives.

Whether to arrange the matter chronologically or not, was a problem impossible of solution to the complete satisfaction of the Editors; this, as well as other methods, having its advantages and disadvantages. After mature consideration, the chronological plan was adopted, and the events of each year have been recorded more or less in the order of their happening. Whatever confusion, if any, may arise through this treatment of local history as a chronicle for ready reference will be easily overcome, it is believed, through the dating of the chapters and the provision of a comprehensive index; while the brief chapter-heading, generally a reference to some marked occurrence in that period, will further assist the reader to get his bearings. Preference has been given to the first thirty years of my residence in Los Angeles, both on account of my affectionate remembrance of that time and because of the peculiarity of memory in advanced life which enables us to recall remote events when more recent ones are forgotten; and inasmuch as so little has been handed down from the days of the adobe, this partiality will probably find favor.

In collecting this mass of data, many discrepancies were met with, calling for the acceptance or rejection of much long current here as fact; and in all such cases I selected the version most closely corresponding with my own recollection, or that seemed to me, in the light of other facts, to be correct. For this reason, no less than because in my narrative of hitherto unrecorded events and personalities it would be miraculous if errors have not found their way into the story, I shall be grateful if those who discover inaccuracies will report them to me. In these sixty years, also, I have met many men and women worthy of recollection, and it is certain that there are some whose names I have not mentioned; if so, I wish to disclaim any intentional neglect. Indeed, precisely as I have introduced the names of a number for whom I have had no personal liking, but whose services to the community I remember with respect, so there are doubtless others whose activities, past or present, it would afford me keen pleasure to note, but whom unhappily I have overlooked.

With this brief introduction, I give the manuscript to the printer, not with the ambitious hope of enriching literature in any respect, but not without confidence that I have provided some new material for the local historian—perhaps of the future—and that there may be a goodly number of people sufficiently interested to read and enjoy the story, yet indulgent enough to overlook the many faults in its narration.

H. N.

Los Angeles,
    December 31, 1915.

FOREWORD

THE Historian no longer writes History by warming over the pancakes of his predecessors. He must surely know what they have done, and how—and whereby they succeeded and wherein they failed. But his own labor is to find the sidelights they did not have. Macaulay saves him from doing again all the research that Macaulay had to do; but if he could find a twin Boswell or a second Pepys he would rather have either than a dozen new Macaulays. Since history is becoming really a Science, and is no more a closet exploration of half-digested arm-chair books, we are beginning to learn the overwhelming value of the contemporary witness. Even a justice's court will not admit Hearsay Evidence; and Science has been shamed into adopting the same sane rule. Nowadays it demands the eye-witness. We look less for the "Authorities" now, and more for the Documents. There are too many histories already, such as they are—self-satisfied and oracular, but not one conclusive. Every history is put out of date, almost daily, by the discovery of some scrap of paper or some clay tablet from under the ashes of Babylon.

Mere Humans no longer read History—except in school where they have to, or in study clubs where it is also Required. But a plain personal narrative is interesting now as it has been for five thousand years. The world's greatest book is of course compulsory; but what is the *interesting* part of it? Why, the stories—Adam and Eve; Abraham, Isaac and Jacob; Saul and David and Samson and Delilah; Solomon, Job, and Jesus the Christ! And if anyone thinks Moses worked-in a little too much of the Family Tree—he doesn't know what biblical archæology is doing. For it is thanks to these same "petty" details that modern Science, in its excavations and decipherings, has verified the Bible and resolved many of its riddles!

Greece had one Herodotus. America had *four*, antedating the year 1600. All these truly great historians built from all the "sources" they could find. But none of them quite give us the homely, vital picture of life and feeling that one untaught and untamed soldier, Bernal Diaz, wrote for us three hundred years ago when he was past ninety, and toothless—and angry "because the historians didn't get it straight." The student of Spanish America has often to wish there had been a Bernal Diaz for every decade and every province from 1492 to 1800. His unstudied gossip about the conquest of Mexico is less balanced and less authoritative, but far more illuminative, than the classics of his leader, Cortez—a university man, as well as a great conqueror.

For more than a quarter of a century it was one of my duties to study and review (for the *Nation* and other critical journals) all sorts of local chronicles all over Spanish and English America —particularly of frontier times. In this work I have read searchingly many hundreds of volumes; and have been brought into close contact with our greatest students and editors of "History-Material," and with their standards.

I have read no other such book with so unflagging interest and content as these memoirs of Harris Newmark. My personal acquaintance with Southern California for more than thirty years may color my interest in names and incidents; but I am appraising this book (whose proofs I have been permitted to read thoroughly) from the standpoint of the student of history anywhere. Parkman and Fiske and Coues and Hodge and Thwaites would join me in the wish that every American community might have so competent a memorandum of its life and customs and growth, for its most formative half-century.

This is *not* a history. It is two other much more necessary things—for there is no such thing as a real History of Los Angeles, and cannot be for years. These are the frank, naïve, conversational memoirs of a man who for more than sixty years could say of Southern California almost as truly as Æneas of his own time—"All of which I saw, much of which I was." The keen observation, the dry humor, the fireside intimacy of the talk, the equity and accuracy of memory and judgment—all these make it a book which will be much more valued by future generations of readers and students. We are rather too near to it now.

But it is more than the "confessions" of one ripe and noble experience. It is, beyond any reasonable comparison, the most characteristic and accurate composite picture we have ever had of an old, brave, human, free, and distinctive life that has changed incredibly to the veneers of modern society. It is the very mirror of who and what the people were that laid the real foundations for a community which is now the wonder of the historian. The very details which are "not Big enough" for the casual reader (mentally over-tuned to newspaper headlines and moving pictures) are the vital and enduring merits of this unpretentious volume. No one else has ever set down so many of the very things that the final historian of Los Angeles will search for, a hundred years after all our orato- · ries and "literary efforts" have been well forgotten. It is a chronicle indispensable for every public library, every reference library, the shelf of every individual concerned with the story of California.

It is the *Pepys's Diary* of Los Angeles and its tributary domain.

CHARLES F. LUMMIS.

PREFACE

THE Editors wish to acknowledge the coöperation given, from time to time, by many whose names, already mentioned in the text, are not repeated here, and in particular to Drs. Leo Newmark and Charles F. Lummis, and Joseph P. and Edwin J. Loeb, for having read the proofs. They also wish to acknowledge Dr. Lummis's self-imposed task of preparing the generous foreword with which this volume has been favored. Gratitude is also due to various friends who have so kindly permitted the use of photographs—not a few of which, never before published, are rare and difficult to obtain. Just as in the case, however, of those who deserve mention in these memoirs, but have been overlooked, so it is feared that there are some who have supplied information and yet have been forgotten. To all such, as well as to several librarians and the following, thanks are hereby expressed: Frederick Baker, Horace Baker, Mrs. J. A. Barrows, Prospero Barrows, Mrs. R. C. Bartow, Miss Anna McConnell Beckley, Sigmund Beel, Samuel Behrendt, Arthur S. Bent, Mrs. Dora Bilderback, C. V. Boquist, Mrs. Mary Bowman, Allan Bromley, Professor Valentin Buehner, Dr. Rose Bullard, J. O. Burns, Malcolm Campbell, Gabe Carroll, J. W. Carson, Walter M. Castle, R. B. Chapman, J. H. Clancy, Herman Cohn, Miss Gertrude Darlow, Ernest Dawson and Dawson's Bookshop, Louise Deen, George E. Dimitry, Robert Dominguez, Durell Draper, Miss Marjorie Driscoll, S. D. Dunann, Gottlieb Eckbahl, Richard Egan, Professor Alfred Ewington, David P. Fleming, James G. Fowler, Miss Effie Josephine Fussell, A. P. Gibson, J. Sherman Glasscock, Gilbert H. Grosvenor, Edgar J. Hartung, Chauncey Hayes, George H. Higbee, Joseph Hopper, Adelbert Hornung,

Walter Hotz, F. A. Howe, Dr. Clarence Edward Ide, Luther
Ingersoll, C. W. Jones, Mrs. Eleanor Brodie Jones, Reverend
Henderson Judd, D. P. Kellogg, C. G. Keyes, Willis T. Knowl-.
ton, Bradner Lee, Jr., H. J. Lelande, Isaac Levy, Miss Ella
Housefield Lowe, Mrs. Celeste Manning, Mrs. Morris Meyberg,
Miss Louisa Meyer, William Meying, Charles E. Mitchell, R. C.
Neuendorffer, S. B. Norton, B. H. Prentice, Burr Price, Edward
H. Quimby, B. B. Rich, Edward I. Robinson, W. J. Rouse,
Paul P. Royere, Louis Sainsevain, Ludwig Schiff, R. D. Sepúl-
veda, Calvin Luther Severy, Miss Emily R. Smith, Miss
Harriet Steele, George F. Strobridge, Father Eugene Sugranes,
Mrs. Carrie Switzer, Walter P. Temple, W. I. Turck, Judge
and Mrs. E. P. Unangst, William M. Van Dyke, August
Wackerbarth, Mrs. J. T. Ward, Mrs. Olive E. Weston, Pro-
fessor A. C. Wheat and Charles L. Wilde.

CONTENTS

Contents

ILLUSTRATIONS

Illustrations

Illustrations xxvii

SIXTY YEARS

IN

SOUTHERN CALIFORNIA

Sixty Years in Southern California

I WAS born in Loebau, West Prussia, on the 5th of July, 1834, the son of Philipp and Esther, *née* Meyer, Neumark; and I have reason to believe that I was not a very welcome guest. My parents, who were poor, already had five children, and the prospects of properly supporting the sixth child were not bright. As I had put in an appearance, however, and there was no alternative, I was admitted with good grace into the family circle and, being the baby, soon became the pet.

My father was born in the ancient town of Neumark; and in his youth he was apprenticed to a dealer in boots and shoes in a Russian village through which Napoleon Bonaparte marched on his way to Moscow. The conqueror sent to the shop for a pair of fur boots, and I have often heard my father tell, with modest satisfaction, how, shortly before he visited the great fair at Nijni Novgorod, he was selected to deliver them; how more than one ambitious and inquisitive friend tried to purchase the privilege of approaching the great man, and what were his impressions of the warrior. When ushered into the august presence, he found Bonaparte in one of his characteristic postures, standing erect, in a meditative mood, braced against the wall, with one hand to his forehead and the other behind his back, apparently absorbed in deep and anxious thought.

When I was but three weeks old, my father's business affairs called him away from home, and compelled the sacrifice of a more or less continued absence of eight and one half years. During this period my mother's health was very poor. Unfortunately, also, my father was too liberal and extravagantly-inclined for his narrow circumstances; and not being equipped to meet the conditions of the district in which we lived and our economical necessities, we were continually, so to speak, in financial hot water. While he was absent, my father traveled in Sweden and Denmark, remitting regularly to his family as much as his means would permit, yet earning for them but a precarious living. In 1842 he again joined his family in Loebau, making visits to Sweden and Denmark during the summer seasons from 1843 until the middle fifties and spending the long winters at home. Loebau was then, as now, of little commercial importance, and until 1849, when I was fifteen years of age and had my first introduction to the world, my life was very commonplace and marked by little worthy of special record, unless it was the commotion centering in the cobble-paved market-place, as a result of the Revolution of 1848.

With the winter of 1837 had come a change in my father's plans and enterprises. Undergoing unusually severe weather in Scandinavia, he listened to the lure of the New World and embarked for New York, arriving there in the very hot summer of 1838. The contrast in climatic conditions proved most disastrous; for, although life in the new Republic seemed both pleasing and acceptable to one of his temperament and liberal views, illness finally compelled him to bid America adieu.

My father was engaged in the making of ink and blacking, neither of which commodities was, at that time, in such universal demand as it is now; and my brother, Joseph Philipp, later known as J. P. Newmark, having some time before left

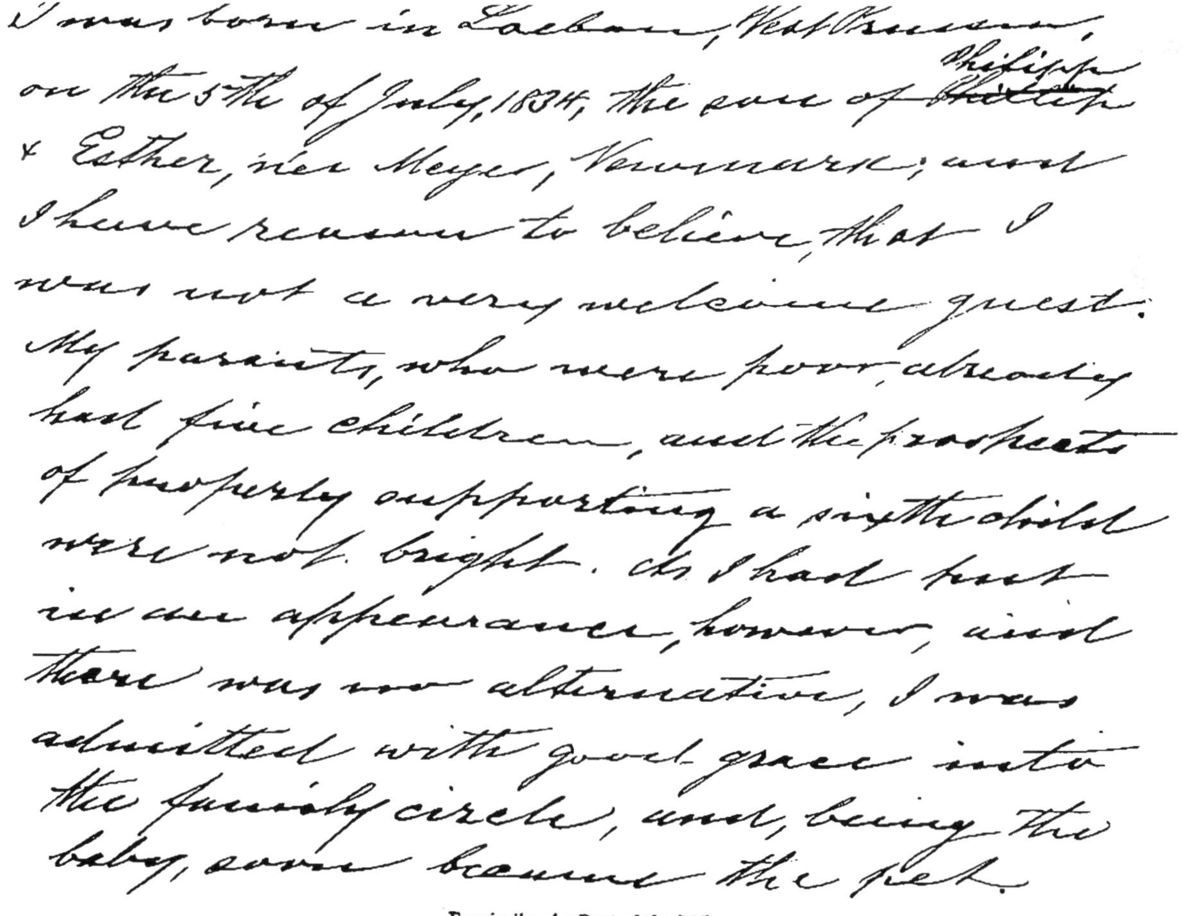

Facsimile of a Part of the MS.

Pris-Courant

öfver

F. NEUMARK$ Fabrikater.

Göttheborg i Augusti 1846.

F. NEUMARK.

unmälsgatan N°/5

		Päls. sk. *köörpris*

CYAN-BLANKSMÖRJA

Spånaskar

1 Dutz. Askar à 12 sk.
1 . . . 8 .
1 . . . 6 .
1 . . . 4 .
1 . . . 2 .

ECONOMIE-BLANKSMÖRJA

i patentäta Carduser à 11 sk.

1 Paket är tillräcklig för bere-
dande af 1 flaska tunnblanksmör-
ja, som utmärker sig genom drygghet
och godhet.

Pr. Contant större partier med
rabatt. Emballage fritt.

BLÄCK för STÅLPENNOR

af utmärkt beskaffenhet p. kanna

"Note.—The 'F' in the above announcement is the abbreviation for Fabian, one of Philipp Neumark's given names, at one time used in business, but seldom employed in social correspondence, and finally abandoned altogether."

Sweden, where he had been assisting him, for England, it was agreed, in 1849, after a family council, that I was old enough to accompany my father on his business trips, gradually become acquainted with his affairs, and thus prepare to succeed him. Accordingly, in April, of that year, I left the family hearth, endeared to me, unpretentious though it was, and wandered with my father out into the world. Open confession, it is said, is good for the soul; hence I must admit that the prospect of making such a trip attracted me, notwithstanding the tender associations of home; and the sorrow of parting from my mother was rather evenly balanced, in my youthful mind, by the pleasurable anticipation of visiting new and strange lands.

Any attempt to compare methods of travel in 1849, even in the countries I then traversed, with those now in vogue, would be somewhat ridiculous. Country roads were generally poor —in fact, very bad; and vehicles were worse, so that the entire first day's run brought us only to Lessen, a small village but twelve miles from home! Here we spent the night, because of the lack of better accommodations, in blankets, on the floor of the wayside inn; and this experience was such a disappointment, failing to realize, as it did, my youthful anticipations, that I was desperately homesick and ready, at the first opportunity, to return to my sorrowing mother. The Fates, however, were against any such change in our plans; and the next morning we proceeded on our way, arriving that evening at the much larger town of Bromberg. Here, for the first time, the roads and other conditions were better, and my spirits revived.

Next day we left for Stettin, where we took passage for Ystad, a small seaport in southern Sweden. Now our real troubles began; part of the trip was arduous, and the low state of our finances permitted us nothing better than exposed deck-quarters. This was particularly trying, since the sea was rough, the weather tempestuous, and I both seasick and longing for home; moreover, on arriving at Ystad, after a voyage of twelve hours or more, the Health Officer came on board our boat and notified us that, as cholera was epidemic in Prussia, we were prohibited from landing! This filled me with mortal fear lest we should be returned to Stettin under the same miserable conditions through which we had just passed; but this state of mind had its compensating influence, for my tears at the discouraging announcement worked upon the charity of the uniformed officials, and, in a short time, to my inexpressible delight, we were permitted to land. With a natural alertness to observe anything new in my experience, I shall never forget my first impressions of the ocean. There seemed no limit to the expanse of stormy waters over which we were traveling; and this fact alone added a touch of solemnity to my first venture from home.

From Ystad we proceeded to Copenhagen, where my father had intimate friends, especially in the Lachmann, Eichel and Ruben families, to whose splendid hospitality and unvarying kindness, displayed whenever I visited their neighborhood, I wish to testify. We remained at Copenhagen a couple of months, and then proceeded to Gothenburg. It was not at this time my father's intention to burden me with serious responsibility; and, having in mind my age, he gave me but little of the work to do, while he never failed to afford me, when he could, an hour of recreation or pleasure. The trip as a whole, therefore, was rather an educational experiment.

In the fall of 1849, we returned to Loebau for the winter. From this time until 1851 we made two trips together, very similar to the one already described; and in 1851, when I was seventeen years of age, I commenced helping in real earnest. By degrees, I was taught the process of manufacturing; and when at intervals a stock had been prepared, I made short trips to dispose of it. The blacking was a paste, put up in small wooden boxes, to be applied with a brush, such a thing as waterproof blacking then not being thought of, at least by us. During the summer of 1851, business carried me to Haparanda, about the most northerly port in Sweden; and from there I took passage, stopping at Luleå, Piteå, Umeå, Hernösand, Sundsvall, Söderhamn and Gefle, all small places along the route. I transacted no business, however, on the trip up the coast because it was my intention to return by land, when I should have more time for trade; accordingly, on my way back to Stockholm, I revisited all of these points and succeeded beyond my expectations.

On my trip north, I sailed over the Gulf of Bothnia which, the reader will recollect, separates Sweden from Finland, a province most unhappily under Russia's bigoted, despotic sway; and while at Haparanda, I was seized with a desire to visit Torneå, in Finland. I was well aware that if I attempted to do so by the regular routes on land, it would be necessary to pass the Russian customhouse, where officers would be sure to examine my passport; and knowing, as the whole liberal world now more than ever knows, that a person of Jewish faith finds the merest sally beyond the Russian border beset with unreasonable obstacles, I decided to walk across the wide marsh in the northern part of the Gulf, and thus circumvent these exponents of intolerance. Besides, I was curious to learn whether, in such a benighted country, blacking and ink were used at all. I set out, therefore, through the great moist waste, making my way without much difficulty, and in due time arrived at Torneå, when I proceeded immediately to the first store in the neighborhood; but there I was destined to experience a rude, unexpected setback. An old man, evidently the proprietor, met me and straightway asked, "Are you a Jew?" and seeing, or imagining that I saw, a delay (perhaps not altogether temporary!) in a Russian jail, I withdrew from the store without ceremony, and returned to the place whence I had come. Notwithstanding this adventure, I reached Stockholm in due season, the trip back consuming about three weeks; and during part of that period I subsisted almost entirely on salmon, bear's meat, milk, and *knäckebröd*, the last a bread usually made of rye flour in which the bran had been preserved. All in all, I was well pleased with this maiden-trip; and as it was then September, I returned to Loebau to spend one more winter at home.

CHAPTER II

WESTWARD, HO!

1853

IN April, 1853, when I had reached the age of nineteen, and was expected to take a still more important part in our business—an arrangement perfectly agreeable to me—my father and I resumed our selling and again left for Sweden. For the sake of economy, as well as to be closer to our field of operations, we had established two insignificant manufacturing plants, the one at Copenhagen, where we packed for two months, the other at Gothenburg, where we also prepared stock; and from these two points, we operated until the middle of May, 1853. Then a most important event occurred, completely changing the course of my life. In the spring, a letter was received from my brother, J. P. Newmark, who, in 1848, had gone to the United States, and had later settled in Los Angeles. He had previously, about 1846, resided in England, as I have said; had then sailed to New York and tarried for a while in the East; when, attracted by the discovery of gold, he had proceeded to San Francisco, arriving there on May 6th, 1851, being the first of our family to come to the Coast. In this letter my brother invited me to join him in California; and from the first I was inclined to make the change, though I realized that much depended on my father. He looked over my shoulder while I read the momentous message; and when I came to the suggestion that I should leave for America, I examined my father's face to anticipate, if possible, his decision. After some reflection, he said he had no doubt that my future would be benefited by such a change; and while reluctant enough to let me go, he decided that as soon as practicable I ought to start. We calculated the amount of blacking likely to be required for our trade to the season's end, and then devoted the necessary time to its manufacture. My mother, when informed of my proposed departure, was beside herself with grief and forthwith insisted on my return to Loebau; but being convinced that she intended to thwart my desire, and having in mind the very optimistic spirit of my brother's letter, I yielded to the influence of ambitious and unreflecting youth, and sorrowfully but firmly insisted on the execution of my plans. I feared that, should I return home to defend my intended course, the mutual pain of parting would still be great. I also had in mind my sisters and brothers (two of whom, Johanna, still alive, and Nathan, deceased, subsequently came to Los Angeles), and knew that each would appeal strongly to my affection and regret. This resolution to leave without a formal adieu caused me no end of distress; and my regret was the greater when, on Friday, July 1st, 1853, I stood face to face with the actual realization, among absolute strangers on the deck of the vessel that was to carry me from Gothenburg to Hull and far away from home and kindred.

With deep emotion, my father bade me good-bye on the Gothenburg pier, nor was I less affected at the parting; indeed, I have never doubted that my father made a great sacrifice when he permitted me to leave him, since I must have been of much assistance and considerable comfort, especially during his otherwise solitary travels in foreign lands. I remember distinctly remaining on deck as long as there was the least vision of him; but when distance obliterated all view of the shore, I went below to regain my composure. I soon installed my belongings in the stateroom, or cabin as it was then called, and began to accustom myself to my new and strange environment.

There was but one other passenger—a young man—and he was to have a curious part in my immediate future. As he also was bound for Hull, we entered into conversation; and following the usual tendency of people aboard ship, we soon became acquaintances. I had learned the Swedish language, and could speak it with comparative ease; so that we conversed without difficulty. He gave Gothenburg as his place of residence, although there was no one at his departure to wish him God-speed; and while this impressed me strangely at the time, I saw in it no particular reason to be suspicious. He stated also that he was bound for New York; and as it developed that we intended to take passage on the same boat, we were pleased with the prospect of having each other's company throughout the entire voyage. Soon our relations became more confidential and he finally told me that he was carrying a sum of money, and asked me to take charge of a part of it. Unsophisticated though I was, I remembered my father's warning to be careful in transactions with strangers; furthermore, the idea of burdening myself with another's responsibility seeming injudicious, I politely refused his request, although even then my suspicions were not aroused. It was peculiar, to be sure, that when we steamed away from land, the young man was in his cabin; but it was only in the light of later developments that I understood why he so concealed himself.

We had now entered the open sea, which was very rough, and I retired, remaining in my bunk for two days, or until we approached Hull, suffering from the most terrible seasickness I have ever experienced; and not until we sailed into port did I recover my sea legs at all. Having dressed, I again met my traveling companion; and we became still more intimate. On Sunday morning we reached Hull, then boasting of no such harbor facilities as the great Humber docks now in course of construction; and having transferred our baggage to the train as best we could, we proceeded almost immediately on our way to Liverpool. While now the fast English express crosses the country in about three hours, the trip then consumed the better part of the night and, being made in the darkness, afforded but little opportunity for observation.

Hardly had we arrived in Liverpool, when I was surprised

in a way that I shall never forget. While attempting to find our bundles as they came from the luggage van—a precaution necessitated by the poor baggage system then in vogue, which did not provide for checking—my companion and I were taken in hand by officers of the law, told that we were under arrest, and at once conducted to an examining magistrate! As my conscience was clear, I had no misgivings on account of the detention, although I did fear that I might lose my personal effects; nor was I at ease again until they were brought in for special inspection. Our trunks were opened in the presence of the Swedish Consul who had come, in the meantime, upon the scene; and mine having been emptied, it was immediately repacked and closed. What was my amazement, however, when my fellow-traveler's trunk was found to contain a very large amount of money with which he had absconded from Gothenburg! He was at once hurried away to police headquarters; and I then learned that, after our departure, messages had been sent to both Hull and Liverpool to stop the thief, but that through confusion in the description, doubtless due to the crude and incomplete information transmitted by telegraph (then by no means as thoroughly developed as now), the Liverpool authorities had arrested the only two passengers arriving there who were known to have embarked at Gothenburg, and I, unfortunately, happened to be one of them.

At the period whereof I write, there was a semimonthly steamer service between Liverpool and New York; and as bad luck would have it, the boat in which I was to travel paddled away while I was in the midst of the predicament just described, leaving me with the unpleasant outlook of having to delay my departure for America two full weeks. The one thing that consoled me was that, not having been fastidious as to my berth, I had not engaged passage in advance, and so was not further embarrassed by the forfeiture of hard-earned and much-needed money. As it was, having stopped at a moderately priced hotel for the night, I set out the next morning to investigate the situation. Speaking no English, I was fortunate, a few days later, in meeting a Swedish emigration agent who informed me that the *Star King*, a three-masted sailing vessel in command of Captain Burland—both ship and captain hailing from Baltimore—was booked to leave the following morning; and finding the office of the company, I engaged one of the six first-class berths in the saloon. There was no second-cabin, or I might have traveled in that class; and of steerage passengers the *Star King* carried more than eight hundred crowded and seasick souls, most of whom were Irish. Even in the first-class saloon, there were few, if any, of the ordinary comforts, as I soon discovered, while of luxuries there were none; and if one had the misfortune to lose even trifling delicacies such as I had, including half a dozen bottles of assorted syrups—put up by good Mrs. Lipman, on my leaving Gothenburg, and dropped by a bungling porter—the inconvenience of the situation was intensified.

We left Liverpool—which, unlike Hull, I have since seen on one of my several visits to Europe—on the evening of the 10th of July. On my way to the cabin, I passed the dining table already arranged for supper; and as I had eaten very sparingly since my seasickness on the way to Hull, I was fully prepared for a square meal. The absence not only of smoke, but of any smell as from an engine, was also favorable to my appetite; and when the proper time arrived, I did full justice to what was set before me. Steamers then were infrequent on the Atlantic, but there were many sailing vessels; and these we often passed, so close, in fact, as to enable the respective captains to converse with each other. In the beginning, we had an ample supply of fresh meat, eggs and butter, as well as some poultry, and the first week's travel was like a delightful pleasure excursion. After that, however, the meat commenced to deteriorate, the eggs turned stale, and the butter became rancid; and as the days passed, everything grew worse, excepting a good supply of cheese which possessed, as usual, the faculty of improving, rather than spoiling, as it aged. Mountain water might justly have shown indignation if the contents of the barrels then on board had claimed relationship;

Philipp Neumark
From a Daguerreotype

Esther Neumark
From a Daguerreotype

J. P. Newmark
From a Daguerreotype

Mr. and Mrs. Joseph Newmark

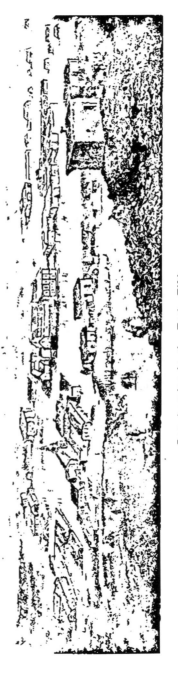

Los Angeles in the Early Fifties

From a drawing of the Pacific Railway Expedition

while coffee and tea, of which we partook in the usual manner at the commencement of our voyage, we were compelled to drink, after a short time, without milk—the one black and the other green. Notwithstanding these annoyances, I enjoyed the experience immensely, once I had recovered from my depression at leaving Europe; for youth could laugh at such drawbacks, none of which, after all, seriously affected my naturally buoyant spirits. Not until I narrowly escaped being shot, through the Captain's careless handling of a derringer, was I roused from a monotonous, half-dreamy existence.

Following this escape, matters progressed without special incident until we were off the coast of Newfoundland, when we had every reason to expect an early arrival in New York. Late one afternoon, while the vessel was proceeding with all sail set, a furious squall struck her, squarely amidships; and in almost as short a time as it takes to relate the catastrophe, our three masts were snapped asunder, falling over the side of the boat and all but capsizing her. The utmost excitement prevailed; and from the Captain down to the ordinary seaman, all hands were terror-stricken. The Captain believed, in fact, that there was no hope of saving his ship; and forgetful of all need of self-control and discipline, he loudly called to us, "Every man for himself!" at the same time actually tearing at and plucking his bushy hair—a performance that in no wise relieved the crisis. In less than half an hour, the fury of the elements had subsided, and we found ourselves becalmed; and the crew, assisted by the passengers, were enabled, by cutting away chains, ropes and torn sails, to steady the ship and keep her afloat. After this was accomplished, the Captain engaged a number of competent steerage passengers to help put up emergency masts, and to prepare new sails, for which we carried material. For twelve weary days we drifted with the current, apparently not advancing a mile; and during all this time the Atlantic, but recently so stormy and raging, was as smooth as a mill-pond, and the wreckage kept close to our ship. It was about the middle of August when this disaster occurred, and not until we had been busy many days rigging up again did a stiff breeze spring up, enabling us to complete our voyage.

On August 28th, 1853, exactly forty-nine days after our departure from Liverpool, we arrived at New York, reaching Sandy Hook in a fog so dense that it was impossible to see any distance ahead; and only when the fog lifted, revealing the great harbor and showing how miraculously we had escaped collision with the numerous craft all about us, was our joy and relief at reaching port complete. I cannot recollect whether we took a pilot aboard or not; but I do know that the peculiar circumstances under which we arrived having prevented a health officer from immediately visiting us, we were obliged to cast anchor and await his inspection the next morning. During the evening, the Captain bought fresh meat, vegetables, butter and eggs, offered for sale by venders in boats coming alongside; and with sharpened appetites we made short work of a fine supper, notwithstanding that various features of shore life, or some passing craft, every minute or two challenged our attention, and quite as amply we did justice, on the following morning, to our last breakfast aboard ship. As I obtained my first glimpse of New York, I thought of the hardships of my father there, a few years before, and of his compulsory return to Europe; and I wondered what might have been my position among Americans had he succeeded in New York. At last, on August 29th, 1853, under a blue and inspiriting sky and with both curiosity and hope tuned to the highest pitch, I first set foot on American soil, in the country where I was to live and labor the remainder of my life, whose flag and institutions I have more and more learned to honor and love.

Before leaving Europe, I had been provided with the New York addresses of friends from Loebau, and my first duty was to look them up. One of these, named Lindauer, kept a boarding-house on Bayard Street near the Five Points, now, I believe, in the neighborhood of Chinatown; and as I had no desire to frequent high-priced hotels, I made my temporary abode with him. I also located the house of Rich Brothers, associated with the San Francisco concern of the same name and through whom

I was to obtain funds from my brother with which to continue my journey; but as I had to remain in New York three weeks until their receipt, I could do little more in furthering my departure than to engage second-cabin passage *via* Nicaragua by a line running in opposition to the Panamá route, and offering cheapness as its principal attraction. Having attended to that, I spent the balance of the time visiting and seeing the city, and in making my first commercial venture in the New World. In my impatience to be doing something, I foolishly relieved Samuel, a brother of Kaspare Cohn, and a nephew of mine, of a portion of his merchandise; but in a single day I decided to abandon peddling—a difficult business for which, evidently, I was never intended. After that, a painful experience with mosquitoes was my only unpleasant adventure. I did not know until later that an excited crowd of men were just then assembled in the neighborhood, in what was styled the Universal Ice-Water Convention, and that not far away a crowd of women, quite as demonstrative, excluded from the councils of men and led by no less a personality than P. T. Barnum, the showman, were clamoring for both Prohibition and Equal Suffrage!

CHAPTER III

NEW YORK—NICARAGUA—THE GOLDEN GATE

1853

ON September 20th, during some excitement due to the fear lest passengers from New Orleans afflicted with yellow-fever were being smuggled into the city despite the vigilance of the health authorities, I left New York for Nicaragua, then popularly spoken of as the Isthmus, sailing on the steamer *Illinois* as one of some eleven or twelve hundred travelers recently arrived from Europe who were hurrying to California on that ship and the *Star of the West*. The occasion afforded my numerous acquaintances a magnificent opportunity to give me all kinds of advice, in the sifting of which the bad was discarded, while some attention was paid to the good. One of the important matters mentioned was the danger from drinking such water as was generally found in the tropics unless it were first mixed with brandy; and this led me, before departing, to buy a gallon demijohn—a bulging bottle destined to figure in a ludicrous episode on my trip from sea to sea. I can recall little of the voyage to the eastern coast of Nicaragua. We kept well out at sea until we reached the Bahama Islands, when we passed near Mariguana, felt our way through the Windward Passage, and steered east of the Island of Jamaica; but I recollect that it became warmer and warmer as we proceeded farther south to about opposite Mosquito Gulf, where we shifted our position in relation to the sun, and that we consumed nine days in covering the two thousand miles or more between New York and San Juan del Norte, or Grey Town.

From San Juan del Norte—in normal times, a hamlet of four or five hundred people clustered near one narrow, dirty street—we proceeded up the San Juan River, nine hundred passengers huddled together on three flat-bottomed boats, until, after three or four days, our progress was interfered with, at Castillo Rapids, by a fall in the stream. There we had to disembark and climb the rough grade, while our baggage was carried up on a tramway; after which we continued our journey on larger boats, though still miserably packed together, until we had almost reached the mouth of Lake Nicaragua, when the water became so shallow that we had to trust ourselves to the uncertain *bongos*, or easily-overturned native canoes, or get out again and walk. It would be impossible to describe the hardships experienced on these crowded little steamboats, which were by no means one quarter as large as the *Hermosa*, at present plying between Los Angeles harbor and Catalina. The only drinking water that we could get came from the river, and it was then that my brandy served its purpose: with the addition of the liquor, I made the drink both palatable and safe. Men, women and children, we were parched and packed like so many herring, and at night there was not only practically no space between passengers sleeping on deck, but the extremities of one were sure to interfere with the body of another. The heat was indeed intense; the mosquitoes seemed omnivorous; to add to which, the native officers in charge of our expedition pestered us with their mercenary proceedings. For a small cup of black coffee, a charge of fifty cents was made, which leaves the impression that food was scarce, else no one would have consented to pay so much for so little. This part of the trip was replete with misery to many, but fortunately for me, although the transportation company provided absolutely no conveniences, the hardships could not interfere with my enjoyment of the delightful and even sublime scenery surrounding us on all sides in this tropical country. As the river had no great width, we were at close range to the changing panorama on both banks; while the neighboring land was covered with gorgeous jungles and vegetation. Here I first saw orange, lemon and cocoanut trees. Monkeys of many kinds and sizes were to be seen; and birds of variegated colors were plentiful, almost innumerable varieties of parrots being visible. All these things were novel to me; and notwithstanding the great discomforts under which we traveled, I repeat that I enjoyed myself.

A walk of a mile or two along the river bank, affording beneficial exercise, brought us to Port San Carlos, from which point a larger boat crossed the lake to Virgin Bay, where we took mules to convey us to San Juan del Sur. This journey was as full of hardship as it was of congeniality, and proved as interesting as it was amusing. Imagine, if you please, nine hundred men, women and children from northern climes, long accustomed to the ways of civilization, suddenly precipitated, under an intensely hot tropical sun, into a small, Central American landing, consisting of a few huts and some cheap, improvised tents (used for saloons and restaurants), every one in search of a mule or a horse, the only modes of transportation. The confusion necessarily following the preparation for this part of the trip can hardly be imagined: the steamship company furnished the army of animals, and the nervous tourists furnished the jumble! Each one of the nine hundred travelers feared that there would not be enough animals for all, and the anxiety to secure a beast caused a stampede.

In the scramble, I managed to get hold of a fine mule, and presently we were all mounted and ready to start. This conglomeration of humanity presented, indeed, a ludicrous sight; and I really believe that I must have been the most grotesque figure of them all. I have mentioned the demijohn of brandy, which a friend advised me to buy; but I have not mentioned another friend who told me that I should be in danger of sunstroke in this climate, and who induced me to carry an umbrella to protect myself from the fierce rays of the enervating sun. Picture me, then, none too short and very lank, astride a mule, a big demijohn in one hand, and a spreading, green umbrella in the other, riding through this southern village, and practically incapable of contributing anything to the course of the mule. Had the animal been left to his own resources, he might have followed the caravan; but in my ignorance, I attempted to indicate to him which direction he should take. My method was evidently not in accordance with the tradition of guiding in just that part of the world; and to make a long story short, the mule, with his three-fold burden, deftly walked into a restaurant, in the most innocent manner and to the very great amusement of the diners, but to the terrible embarrassment and consternation of the rider. After some difficulty (for the restaurant was hardly intended for such maneuvers as were required), we were led out of the tent. This experience showed me the necessity of abandoning either the umbrella or the brandy; and learning that lemonade could be had at points along the route, I bade good-bye to the demijohn and its ex-hilarating contents. From this time on, although I still dis-played inexpertness in control, his muleship and I gradually learned to understand each other, and matters progressed very well, notwithstanding the intense heat, and the fatigue natural to riding so long in such an unaccustomed manner. The lemonade, though warm and, therefore, dear at ten cents a glass, helped to quench my thirst; and as the scenery was wonderful, I derived all the benefit and pleasure possible from the short journey.

All in all, we traversed about twelve miles on mule or horse-back, and finally arrived, about four o'clock in the afternoon of the day we had started, at San Juan del Sur, thus putting behind us the most disagreeable part of this uncomfortable trip. Here it may be interesting to add that on our way across the Isthmus, we met a crowd of disappointed travelers returning from the Golden Gate, on their way toward New York. They were a discouraged lot and loudly declared that California was nothing short of a *fiasco;* but, fortunately, there prevailed that weakness of human nature which impels every man to earn his own experience, else, following the advice of these discomfited people, some of us might have retraced our steps and thus completely altered our destinies. Not until the publication, years later, of the *Personal Memoirs of General W. T. Sherman,* did I learn, with peculiar interest, that the then rising soldier, returning to California with his young wife, infant child and nurse, had actually embarked from New York on the same day that I had, arriving in San Francisco the same day that I arrived, and that therefore the Shermans, whose experience with the mules was none the less trying and ridiculous than my own, must have been members of the same party with me in crossing the mosquito-infested Isthmus.

There was no appreciable variation in temperature while I was in Nicaragua, and at San Juan del Sur (whose older portion, much like San Juan del Norte, was a village of the Spanish-American type with one main street, up and down which, killing time, I wandered) the heat was just as oppressive as it had been before. People often bunked in the open, a hotel-keeper named Green renting hammocks, at one dollar each, when all his beds had been taken. One of these hammocks I engaged; but being unaccustomed to such an aërial lodging, I was most unceremoniously spilled out, during a deep sleep in the night, falling only a few feet, but seeming, to my stirred-up imagination, to be sliding down through limitless space. Here I may mention that this Nicaragua Route was the boom creation of a competitive service generally understood to have been initiated by those who intended, at the first opportunity, to sell out; and that since everybody expected to pack and move on at short notice, San Juan del Sur, suddenly enlarged by the coming and going of adventurers, was for the moment in part a community of tents, presenting a most unstable appearance. A picturesque little creek flowed by the town and into the Pacific; and there a fellow-traveler, L. Harris, and I decided to refresh ourselves. This was no sooner agreed upon than done; but a passer-by having excitedly informed us that the creek was infested with alligators, we were not many seconds in following his advice to scramble out, thereby escaping perhaps a fate similar to that which overtook, only a few years later, a near relative of Mrs. Henry Hancock.

At sundown, on the day after we arrived at San Juan del Sur, the Pacific terminal, we were carried by natives through the surf to small boats, and so transferred to the steamer *Cortez;* and then we started, amidst great rejoicing, on the last lap of our journey. We steamed away in a northerly direction, upon a calm sea and under the most favorable circumstances, albeit the intense heat was most unpleasant. In the course of about a week the temperature fell, for we were steadily approaching a less tropical zone. Finally, on the 16th of October, 1853, we entered the Golden Gate.

Notwithstanding the lapse of many years, this first visit to San Francisco has never been forgotten. The beauty of the harbor, the surrounding elevations, the magnificence of the day, and the joy of being at my journey's end, left an impression of delight which is still fresh and agreeable in my memory. All San Francisco, so to speak, was drawn to the wharf, and enthusiasm ran wild. Jacob Rich, partner of my brother, was there to meet me and, without ceremony, escorted me to his home; and under his hospitable roof I remained until the morning when I was to depart for the still sunnier South.

San Francisco, in 1853, was much like a frontier town, devoid of either style or other evidences of permanent progress; yet it was wide-awake and lively in the extreme. What little had been built, bad and good, after the first rush of gold-seekers, had been destroyed in the five or six fires that swept the city just before I came, so that the best buildings I saw were of hasty and, for the most part, of frame construction. Tents also, of all sizes, shapes and colors, abounded. I was amazed, I remember, at the lack of civilization as I understood it, at the comparative absence of women, and at the spectacle of people riding around the streets on horseback like mad. All sorts of excitement seemed to fill the air; everywhere there was a noticeable lack of repose; and nothing perhaps better fits the scene I would describe than some lines from a popular song of that time entitled, *San Francisco in 1853:*

> City full of people,
>   In a business flurry;
> Everybody's motto,
>   Hurry! hurry! hurry!

> Every nook and corner
> Full to overflowing:
> Like a locomotive,
> Everybody going!

One thing in particular struck me, and that was the un-settled state of the surface on which the new town was being built.   I recall for example, the great quantity of sand that was continually being blown into the streets from sand-dunes uninterruptedly forming in the endless vacant lots, and how people, after a hard wind at night, would find small sand-heaps in front of their stores and residences; so that, in the absence of any municipal effort to keep the thoroughfares in order, the owners were repeatedly engaged in sweeping away the accumu-lation of sand, lest they might be overwhelmed.   The streets were ungraded, although some were covered with planks for pavement, and presented altogether such an aspect of un-certainty that one might well believe General Sherman's testi-mony that, in winter time, he had seen mules fall, unable to rise, and had even witnessed one drown in a pool of mud! Sidewalks, properly speaking, there were none.   Planks and boxes—some filled with produce not yet unpacked—were strung along in irregular lines, requiring the poise of an acrobat to walk upon, especially at night.   As I waded through the sand-heaps or fell over the obstructions designed as pavements, my thoughts reverted, very naturally, to my brother who had preceded me to San Francisco two years before; but it was not until some years later that I learned that my distinguished fellow-country-man, Heinrich Schliemann, destined to wander farther to Greece and Asia Minor, and there to search for ancient Troy, had not only knocked about the sand-lots in the same manner in which I was doing, but, stirred by the discovery of gold and the admission of California to the Union, had even taken on American citizenship. Schliemann visited California in 1850 and became naturalized; nor did he ever, I believe, repudiate the act which makes the greatest explorer of ancient Greece a burgher of the United States!

During my short stay in San Francisco, before leaving for

Los Angeles, I made the usual rounds under the guidance of Jacob Rich. Having just arrived from the tropics, I was not provided with an overcoat; and since the air was chilly at night, my host, who wore a talma or large cape, lent me a shawl, shawls then being more used than they are now. Rich took me to a concert that was held in a one-story wooden shack, whereat I was much amazed; and afterward we visited a number of places of louder revelry. Just as I found it to be a few days later in Los Angeles, so San Francisco was filled with saloons and gambling-houses; and these institutions were in such contrast to the features of European life to which I had been accustomed, that they made a strong impression upon me. There were no restrictions of any sort, not even including a legal limit to their number, and people engaged in these enterprises because, in all probability, they were the most profitable. Such resorts attracted criminals, or developed in certain persons latent propensities to wrong-doing, and perhaps it is no wonder that Walker, but the summer previous, should have selected San Francisco as headquarters for his filibustering expedition to Lower California. By far the most talked-of man of that day was Harry Meiggs—popularly known as "Honest Harry"—who was engaged in various enterprises, and was a good patron of civic and church endeavor. He was evidently the advance guard of the boomer organization, and built the Long Wharf at North Beach, on a spot now at Commercial and Montgomery streets, where later the Australian convict, trying to steal a safe, was captured by the First Vigilance Committee; and so much was Meiggs the envy of the less pyrotechnical though more substantial people, that I repeatedly had my attention called, during my brief stay in San Francisco, to what was looked upon as his prodigious prosperity. But Meiggs, useful as he was to the society of his day, finally ended his career by forging a lot of city scrip (a great deal of which he sold to W. T. Sherman and his banking associates), and by absconding to Peru, where he became prominent as a banker and a developer of mines.

Situated at the Plaza—where, but three years before, on

the admission of California as a State, the meeting of gold-seeking pioneers and lassoing natives had been symbolized with streaming banners, and the thirty-one stars were nailed to a rude pole—was the El Dorado, the most luxurious gambling-place and saloon in the West, despite the existence near by of the Bella Union, the Parker House and the Empire. Music, particularly native Spanish or Mexican airs, played its part there, as well as other attractions; and much of the life of the throbbing town centered in that locality. It is my impression that the water front was then Sansome Street; and if this be correct, it will afford some idea of the large territory in San Francisco that is made ground.

As there was then no stage line between San Francisco and the South, I was compelled to continue my journey by sea; and on the morning of October 18th, I boarded the steamer *Goliah* —whose Captain was Salisbury Haley, formerly a surveyor from Santa Bárbara—bound for Los Angeles, and advertised to stop at Monterey, San Luis Obispo, Santa 'Bárbara and one or two other landings formerly of importance but now more or less forgotten. There were no wharves at any of those places; passengers and freight were taken ashore in small boats; and when they approached shallow water, everything was carried to dry land by the sailors. This performance gave rise, at times, to most annoying situations; boats would capsize and empty their passengers into the water, creating a merriment enjoyed more by those who were secure than by the victims themselves. On October 21st we arrived a mile or so off San Pedro, and were disembarked in the manner above described, having luckily suffered no such mishap as that which befell passengers on the steamship *Winfield Scott* who, journeying from Panamá but a month or so later, at midnight struck one of the Anacapa Islands, now belonging to Ventura County, running dead on to the rocks. The vessel in time was smashed to pieces, and the passengers, several hundred in number, were forced to camp on the island for a week or more.

Almost from the time of the first visit of a steamer to San Pedro, the *Gold Hunter* (a side-wheeler which made the voyage

from San Francisco to Mazatlán in 1849), and certainly from
the day in January of that same year when Temple & Alexander
put on their four-wheeled vehicle, costing one thousand dollars
and the second in the county, there was competition in
transporting passengers to Los Angeles. Phineas Banning,
Augustus W. Timms, J. J. Tomlinson, John Goller, David W.
Alexander, José Rúbio and B. A. Townsend were among the
most enterprising commission men; and their keen rivalry
brought about two landings—one controlled by Banning, who
had come to Los Angeles in 1851, and the other by Timms, after
whom one of the terminals was named. Before I left San
Francisco, Rich provided me with a letter of introduction
to Banning—who was then known, if I remember aright, as
Captain, though later he was called successively Major and
General—at the same time stating that this gentleman
was a forwarding merchant. Now, in European cities where
I had heretofore lived, commission and forwarding merchants
were a dignified and, to my way of thinking, an aristocratic class,
which centuries of business experience had brought to a genteel
perfection; and they would have found themselves entirely
out of their element had their operations demanded their sudden
translation, in the fifties, to the west coast of America. At
any rate, upon arriving at San Pedro I had expected to find a
man dressed either in a uniform or a Prince Albert, with a high
hat and other appropriate appurtenances, and it is impossible to describe my astonishment when Banning was
pointed out to me; for I knew absolutely nothing of the rough
methods in vogue on the Pacific Coast. There stood before
me a very large, powerful man, coatless and vestless, without
necktie or collar, and wearing pantaloons at least six inches
too short, a pair of brogans and socks with large holes; while
bright-colored suspenders added to the picturesque effect of
his costume. It is not my desire to ridicule a gentleman who,
during his lifetime, was to be a good, constant friend of
mine, but rather to give my readers some idea of life in the
West, as well as to present my first impressions of Southern
California. The fact of the matter is that Banning, in his own

way, was even then such a man of affairs that he had bought, but a few months before, some fifteen wagons and nearly five times as many mules, and had paid almost thirty thousand dollars for them. I at once delivered the letter in which Rich had stated that I had but a smattering of English and that it would be a favor to him if Banning would help me safely on my way to Los Angeles; and Banning, having digested the contents of the communication, looked me over from head to foot, shook hands and, in a stentorian voice—loud enough, I thought, to be heard beyond the hills—good-naturedly called out, "*Wie geht's?*" After which, leading the way, and shaking hands again, he provided me with a good place on the stage.

Not a minute was lost between the arrival of passengers and the departure of coaches for Los Angeles in the early fifties. The competition referred to developed a racing tendency that was the talk of the pueblo. The company that made the trip in the shortest time usually obtained, through lively betting, the best of advertising and the largest patronage; so that, from the moment of leaving San Pedro until the final arrival in Los Angeles two and a half hours later, we tore along at breakneck speed, over roads slowly traveled, but a few years before, by Stockton's cannon. These roads never having been cared for, and still less inspected, were abominably bad; and I have often wondered that during such contests there were not more accidents. The stages were of the common Western variety, and four to six broncos were always a feature of the equipment. No particular attention had been given to the harness, and everything was more or less primitive. The stage was provided with four rows of seats and each row, as a rule, was occupied by four passengers, the front row including the oft-bibulous driver; and the fare was five dollars.

Soon after leaving San Pedro, we passed thousands of ground squirrels, and never having seen anything of the kind before, I took them for ordinary rats. This was not an attractive discovery; and when later we drove by a number of ranch houses and I saw beef cut into strings and hung up over fences to dry, it looked as though I had landed on another planet.

I soon learned that dried beef or, as the natives here called it, *carne seca* (more generally known, perhaps, at least among frontiersmen, as "jerked" beef or *jerky*) was an important article of food in Southern California; but from the reminiscences of various pioneers I have known, it evidently astonished others as much as it did me.

Having reached the Half-Way House, we changed horses; then we continued and approached Los Angeles by San Pedro Street, which was a narrow lane, possibly not more than ten feet wide, with growing vineyards bordered by willow trees on each side of the road. It was on a Sunday and in the midst of the grape season that I first beheld the City of the Angels; and to these facts in particular I owe another odd and unfavorable first impression of the neighborhood. Much of the work connected with the grape industry was done by Indians and native Mexicans, or Californians, as they were called, and every Saturday evening they received their pay. During Saturday night and all day Sunday, they drank themselves into hilarity and intoxication, and this dissipation lasted until Sunday night. Then they slept off their sprees and were ready to work Monday morning. During each period of excitement, from one to three or four of these revelers were murdered. Never having seen Indians before, I supposed them to represent the citizenship of Los Angeles—an amusing error for which I might be pardoned when one reflects that nine out of forty-four of the founders of Los Angeles were Indians, and that, according to an official census made the year before, Los Angeles County in 1852 had about thirty-seven hundred domesticated Indians among a population of a little over four thousand whites; and this mistake as to the typical burgher, together with my previous experiences, added to my amazement.

At last, with shouts and yells from the competing drivers, almost as deafening as the horn-blowing of a somewhat later date, and hailed apparently by every inhabitant and dog along the route, we arrived at the only real hotel in town, the Bella Union, where stages stopped and every city function

took place.   This hotel was a one-story, adobe house enlarged
in 1858 to two stories, and located on Main Street above Commercial; and Dr. Obed Macy, who had bought it the previous
spring from Winston & Hodges, was the proprietor.

My friend, Sam Meyer (now deceased, but for fifty years
or more treasurer of Forty-two, the oldest Masonic lodge in
Los Angeles), who had come here a few months in advance of
me, awaited the arrival of the stage and at once recognized
me by my costume, which was anything but in harmony with
Southern California fashions of that time.   My brother, J. P.
Newmark, not having seen me for several years, thought that
our meeting ought to be private, and so requested Sam to show
me to his store.   I was immediately taken to my brother's
place of business where he received me with great affection;
and there and then we renewed that sympathetic association
which continued many years, until his death in 1895.

Bella Union as it Appeared in 1858

From a lithograph

John Goller's Blacksmith Shop

From a lithograph of 1858

CHAPTER IV

FIRST ADVENTURES IN LOS ANGELES

1853

ONCE fairly well settled here, I began to clerk for my brother, who in 1852 had bought out a merchant named Howard. For this service I received my lodging, the cost of my board, and thirty dollars each month. The charges for board at the Bella Union—then enjoying a certain prestige, through having been the official residence of Pio Pico when Stockton took the city—were too heavy, and arrangements were made with a Frenchman named John La Rue, who had a restaurant on the east side of Los Angeles Street, about two hundred feet south of Bell's Row. I paid him nine dollars a week for three more or less hearty meals a day, not including eggs, unless I provided them; in this case he agreed to prepare them for me. Eggs were by no means scarce; but steaks and mutton and pork chops were the popular choice, and potatoes and vegetables a customary accompaniment.

This La Rue, or Leroux, as he was sometimes called, was an interesting personality with an interesting history. Born in France, he sailed for the United States about the time of the discovery of gold in California, and made his way to San Francisco and the mines, where luck encouraged him to venture farther and migrate to Mazatlán, Mexico. While prospecting there, however, he was twice set upon and robbed; and barely escaping with his life, he once more turned northward, this time stopping at San Pedro and Los Angeles. Here, meeting Miss

Bridget Johnson, a native of Ireland, who had just come from New York by way of San Diego, La Rue married her, notwithstanding their inability to speak each other's language, and then opened a restaurant, which he continued to conduct until 1858 when he died, as the result of exposure at a fire on Main Street. Although La Rue was in no sense an eminent citizen, it is certain that he was esteemed and mourned. Prior to his death, he had bought thirty or thirty-five acres of land, on which he planted a vineyard and an orange-orchard; and these his wife inherited. In 1862, Madame La Rue married John Wilson, also a native of Ireland, who had come to Los Angeles during the year that the *restaurateur* died. He was a blacksmith and worked for John Goller, continuing in business for over twenty years, and adding greatly, by industry and wise management, to the dowry brought him by the thrifty widow.

I distinctly recall La Rue's restaurant, and quite as clearly do I remember one or two humorous experiences there. Nothing in Los Angeles, perhaps, has ever been cruder than this popular eating-place. The room, which faced the street, had a mud-floor and led to the kitchen through a narrow opening. Half a dozen cheap wooden tables, each provided with two chairs, stood against the walls. The tablecloths were generally dirty, and the knives and forks, as well as the furniture, were of the homeliest kind. The food made up in portions what it lacked in quality, and the diner rarely had occasion to leave the place hungry. What went most against my grain was the slovenliness of the proprietor himself. Flies were very thick in the summer months; and one day I found a big fellow splurging in my bowl of soup. This did not, however, feaze John La Rue. Seeing the struggling insect, he calmly dipped his coffee-colored fingers into the hot liquid and, quite as serenely, drew out the fly; and although one could not then be as fastidious as nowadays, I nevertheless found it impossible to eat the soup.

On another occasion, however, mine host's equanimity was disturbed. I had given him two eggs one morning, to prepare for me, when Councilman A. Jacobi, a merchant and also a customer of La Rue's, came in for breakfast, bringing one more egg than mine. Presently my meal, unusually generous, was served, and without loss of time I disposed of it and was about to leave; when just then Jacobi discovered that the small portion set before him could not possibly contain the three eggs he had supplied. Now, Jacobi was not only possessed of a considerable appetite, but had as well a definite unwillingness to accept less than his due, while La Rue, on the other hand, was very easily aroused to a high pitch of Gallic excitement; so that in less time than is required to relate the story, the two men were embroiled in a genuine Franco-Prussian dispute, all on account of poor La Rue's unintentional interchange of the two breakfasts. Soon after this encounter, Jacobi, who was an amateur violinist of no mean order, and had fiddled himself into the affections of his neighbors, left for Berlin with a snug fortune, and there after some years he died.

Having arranged for my meals, my brother's next provision was for a sleeping-place. A small, unventilated room adjoining the store was selected; and there I rested on an ordinary cot furnished with a mattress, a pillow, and a pair of *frazadas*, or blankets. According to custom, whatever of these covers I required were taken each evening from stock, and the next morning they were returned to the shelves. Stores as well as houses were then almost without stoves or fireplaces; and as it grew colder, I found that the blankets gave little or no warmth. Indeed they were nothing more or less, notwithstanding their slight mixture of wool, than ordinary horse-blankets, on which account in winter I had to use five or six of them to enjoy any comfort whatever; and since I experienced difficulty in keeping them on the cot, I resorted at last to the device of tacking them down on one side.

In 1853, free-and-easy customs were in vogue in Los Angeles, permitting people in the ordinary affairs of life to do practically as they pleased. There were few if any restrictions; and if circumscribing City ordinances existed—except, perhaps, those of 1850 which, while licensing gaming places, forbade the playing of cards on the street—I do not remember what they were. As was the case in San Francisco, neither saloons nor gambling places were limited by law, and there were no regulations for their management. As many persons as could make a living in this manner kept such establishments, which were conspicuous amid the sights of the town. Indeed, chief among the surprises greeting me during my first few weeks upon the Coast, the many and flourishing gambling dens caused me the greatest astonishment.

Through the most popular of these districts, a newly-found friend escorted me on the evening of my arrival in Los Angeles. The quarter was known by the euphonious title of Calle de los Negros—Nigger Alley; and this alley was a thoroughfare not over forty feet wide which led from Aliso Street to the Plaza, an extent of just one unbroken block. At this period, there was a long adobe facing Los Angeles Street, having a covered platform or kind of veranda, about four feet from the ground, running its entire length. The building commenced at what was later Sanchez Street, and reached, in an easterly direction, to within forty feet, more or less, of the east side of Nigger Alley, then continuing north to the Plaza. This formed the westerly boundary, while a line of adobes on the other side of the street formed the easterly line. The structure first described, and which was demolished many years ago, later became the scene of the beginning of an awful massacre to which I shall refer in due season.

Each side of the alley was occupied by saloons and gambling houses. Men and women alike were to be found there, and both sexes looked after the gaming tables, dealing monte and faro, and managing other contrivances that parted the good-natured and easy-going people from their money. Those in charge of the banks were always provided with pistols, and were ready, if an emergency arose, to settle disputes on the spot; and only rarely did a case come up for adjustment before the properly-constituted authorities, such as that in 1848, which remained a subject of discussion for some time, when counterfeiters, charged with playing at monte with false money, were tried before a special court made up of Abel Stearns and Stephen C. Foster. Time was considered a very important element during the play; and sanguinary verdicts in financial disputes were generally rendered at once.

Human life at this period was about the cheapest thing in Los Angeles, and killings were frequent. Nigger Alley was as tough a neighborhood, in fact, as could be found anywhere, and a large proportion of the twenty or thirty murders a month was committed there. About as plentiful a thing, also, as there was in the pueblo was liquor. This was served generously in these resorts, not only with respect to quantity, but as well regarding variety. In addition to the prodigality of feasting, there was no lack of music of the native sort—the harp and the guitar predominating. These scenes were picturesque and highly interesting. Nigger Alley, for a while the headquarters for gamblers, enjoyed through that circumstance a certain questionable status; but in the course of years it came to be more and more occupied by the Chinese, and given over to their opium-dens, shops and laundries. There, also, their peculiar religious rites were celebrated in just as peculiar a joss house, the hideously-painted gods not in the least becoming a deterrent factor. Juan Apablasa was among those who owned considerable property in Chinatown, and a street in that quarter perpetuates his name.

Having crossed the Plaza, we entered Sonora Town, where my friend told me that every evening there was much indulgence in drinking, smoking and gambling, and quite as much participation in dancing. Some of this life, which continued in full swing until the late seventies, I witnessed on my first evening in Los Angeles.

Returning to Main Street, formerly Calle Principal, we entered the Montgomery, one of the well-known gambling houses—a one-story adobe about a hundred feet in width, in front of which was a shaded veranda—situated nearly opposite the Stearns home, and rather aristocratic, not only in its furnishings but also in its management. This resort was managed by the fearless William C., or Billy Getman, afterward Sheriff of Los Angeles County, whom I saw killed while trying to arrest a lunatic. The Montgomery was conducted in an orderly manner, and catered to the most fastidious people of Los Angeles, supplying liquors of a correspondingly high grade; the charge for a drink there being invariably twenty-five cents. It was provided with a billiard parlor, where matches were often arranged for a stake of hundreds of dollars. Games of chance there were for every requirement, the long and the short purse being equally well accommodated. The ranch owner could bet his hundreds, while he of lowlier estate might tempt the fickle goddess according to his narrower means.

A fraternity of gamblers almost indigenous to California, and which has been celebrated and even, to an extent, glorified by such writers as Mark Twain, Bret Harte and others, was everywhere then in evidence in Los Angeles; and while it is true that their vocation was illegitimate, many of them represented nevertheless a splendid type of man: generous, honest in methods, courageous in operations and respected by everybody. It would be impossible, perhaps, to describe this class as I knew them and at the same time to satisfy the modern ideal; but pioneers will confirm my tribute to these early gamesters (among whom they may recall Brand Phillips) and their redeeming characteristics.

As I have said, my brother, J. P. Newmark, was in partnership with Jacob Rich, the gentleman who met me when I reached San Francisco; their business being dry-goods and clothing. They were established in J. N. Padilla's adobe on the southeast corner of Main and Requena streets, a site so far "out of town" that success was possible only because of their catering to a wholesale clientele rather than to the retail trade; and almost opposite them, ex-Mayor John G. Nichols conducted a small grocery in a store that he built on the Main Street side of the property now occupied by Temple Block. There was an old adobe wall running north and south along the east line of the lot, out of which Nichols cut about fifteen feet, using this property to a depth of some thirty feet, thus forming a rectangular space which he enclosed. Here he carried on a modest trade which, even in addition to his other cares, scarcely demanded his whole time; so that he would frequently visit his neighbors, among whom Newmark & Rich were his nearest friends. Often have I seen him therefore, long and lank, seated in my brother's store tilted back in a chair against the wall or merchandise, a cigar, which he never lighted, in his mouth, exhorting his hearers to be patriotic and to purchase City land at a dollar an acre, thereby furnishing some of the taxes necessary to lubricate the municipal machinery. Little did any of us realize, as we listened to this man, that in the course of another generation or so there would spring into life a prosperous metropolis whose very heart would be situated near where old Mayor Nichols was vainly endeavoring to dispose of thirty-five-acre bargains at thirty-five dollars each—a feature of municipal coöperation with prospective settlers which was inaugurated August 13th, 1852, and repealed through dissatisfaction in 1854. Nichols, who, with J. S. Mallard and Lewis Granger, brought one of the first three American families to settle here permanently, and who married a sister of Mrs. Mallard, was the father of John Gregg Nichols, always claimed to be the first boy born (April 24th, 1851), of American parents, in Los Angeles.   Nichols when Mayor was never neglectful of his official duties, as may be seen from his record in providing Hancock's survey, his construction of the Bath Street School, his encouragement of better irrigation facilities, his introduction of the first fruit grafts—brought, by the way, from far-off New York—and his reëlection as Mayor in 1856, 1857, and 1858. In 1869, another son, Daniel B. Nichols, of whom I shall speak, was a participant in a fatal shooting affray here.

A still earlier survey than that of Hancock was made by Lieutenant Edward O. C. Ord—later distinguished in the Union Army where, singularly enough, he was fighting with Rosecrans, in time a resident of Los Angeles—who, in an effort to bring order out of the pueblo chaos, left still greater confusion. To clear up the difficulty of adobes isolated or stranded in the middle of the streets, the Common Council in 1854 permitted owners to claim a right of way to the thoroughfares nearest their houses. This brings to mind the fact that the *vara*, a

Spanish unit equal to about thirty-three inches, was a standard in real estate measurements even after the advent of Ord, Hancock and Hansen, who were followed by such surveyors as P. J. Virgen (recalled by Virgen Street) and his partner Hardy; and also that the *reata* was often used as a yardstick—its uncertain length having contributed, without doubt, to the chaotic condition confronting Ord.

Graded streets and sidewalks were unknown; hence, after heavy winter rains mud was from six inches to two feet deep, while during the summer dust piled up to about the same extent. Few City ordinances were obeyed; for notwithstanding that a regulation of the City Council called on every citizen to sweep in front of his house to a certain point on Saturday evenings, not the slightest attention was paid to it. Into the roadway was thrown all the rubbish: if a man bought a new suit of clothes, a pair of boots, a hat or a shirt, to replace a corresponding part of his apparel that had outlived its usefulness, he would think nothing, on attiring himself in the new purchase, of tossing the discarded article into the street where it would remain until some passing Indian, or other vagabond, took possession of it. So wretched indeed were the conditions, that I have seen dead animals left on the highways for days at a time, and can recall one instance of a horse dying on Alameda Street and lying there until a party of Indians cut up the carcass for food. What made these street conditions more trying was the fact that on hot days roads and sidewalks were devoid of shade, except for that furnished by a few scattered trees or an occasional projecting veranda; while at night (if I except the illumination from the few lanterns suspended in front of barrooms and stores) thoroughfares were altogether unlighted. In those nights of dark streets and still darker tragedies, people rarely went out unless equipped with candle-burning lanterns, at least until camphine was imported by my brother, after which this was brought into general use. Stores were lighted in the same manner: first with candles, then with camphine and finally with coal-oil, during which period of advancement lamps replaced the cruder contrivances.

Southern California from the first took an active part in State affairs. Edward Hunter and Charles E. Carr were the Assemblymen from this district in 1853; and the following year they were succeeded by Francis Mellus and Dr. Wilson W. Jones. Carr was a lawyer who had come in 1852; Hunter afterward succeeded Pablo de la Guerra as Marshal. Jones was the doctor who just about the time I came, while returning from a professional call at the Lugos at about sunset, nearly rode over the bleeding and still warm body of a cattle-buyer named Porter, on Alameda Street. The latter had been out to the Dominguez *rancho*, to purchase stock, and had taken along with him a Mexican named Manuel Vergara who introduced himself as an experienced interpreter and guide, but who was, in reality, a cutthroat with a record of one or two assassinations. Vergara observed that Porter possessed considerable money; and on their way back to Los Angeles shot the American from behind. Jones quickly gave the alarm; and Banning, Stanley and others of the volunteer mounted police pursued the murderer for eighty-five or ninety miles when, the ammunition of all parties being exhausted, Vergara turned on the one Vigilante who had caught up with him and, with an adroit thrust of his knife, cut the latter's bridle and escaped. In the end, however, some of Major Heintzelman's cavalry at Yuma (who had been informed by a fleet Indian hired to carry the news of the fugitive's flight) overtook Vergara and shot him dead. These volunteer police or Rangers, as they were called, were a company of one hundred or more men under command of Dr. A. W. Hope, and included such well-known early settlers as Nichols, J. G. Downey, S. C. Foster, Agustin Olvera, Juan Sepúlveda, Horace Bell, M. Keller, Banning, Benjamin Hayes, F. L. Guirado, David Alexander, J. L. Brent and I. S. K. Ogier.

Under the new order of things, too, following the adoption in 1849 of a State constitution, County organization in Los Angeles was effected; and by the time I declared myself for American citizenship, several elections had been held. Benjamin Hayes was District Judge in 1853; Agustin Olvera was finishing his term as County Judge; Dr. Wilson W. Jones was

County Clerk and Recorder—two offices not separated for twenty years or until 1873; Lewis Granger was County Attorney; Henry Hancock was Surveyor; Francis Mellus (who succeeded Don Manuel Garfias, once the princely owner but bad manager of the San Pasqual *rancho*), was Treasurer; A. F. Coronel was Assessor; James R. Barton was Sheriff and also Collector of Taxes; and J. S. Mallard, whose name was given to Mallard Street, was Coroner. Russell Sackett was a Justice of the Peace here when I arrived; and after a while Mallard had a court as Justice, near my store on Commercial Street. All in all, a group of rather strong men!

The administrative officials of both the City and the County had their headquarters in the one-story adobe building at the northwest corner of Franklin Alley (later called Jail Street[1]) and Spring Street. In addition to those mentioned, there was a Justice of the Peace, a *Zanjero*, and a Jailer. António Franco Coronel had but recently succeeded Nichols as Mayor; A. S. Beard was Marshal and Tax Collector; Judge William G. Dryden was Clerk; C. E. Carr was Attorney; Ygnácio Coronel was Assessor; and S. Arbuckle was Treasurer.

António Franco Coronel, after whom Coronel Street is named, had just entered upon the duties of Mayor, and was busy enough with the disposal of donation lots when I first commenced to observe Los Angeles' government. He came from Mexico to California with his father, Don Ygnácio F. Coronel; and by 1850 he was the first County Assessor. He lived at what is now Alameda and Seventh streets, and had a brother, Manuel, who was City Assessor in 1858.

Major Henry Hancock, a New Hampshire lawyer and surveyor, came to Los Angeles in 1852, and at the time of my arrival had just made the second survey of the city, defining the boundaries of the thirty-five-acre City lots. I met him frequently, and by 1859 I was well acquainted with him. He then owed Newmark, Kremer & Company some money and offered, toward liquidation of the debt, one hundred and ten acres of land lying along Washington and extending as far as

[1] In April, 1872, officially named Franklin Street.

the present Pico Street. It also reached from Main Street to
what is now Grand Avenue. Newmark, Kremer & Company
did not wish the land, and so arranged with Hancock to take
firewood instead. From time to time, therefore, he brought
great logs into town, to be cut up; he also bought a circular saw,
which he installed, with horse-power and tread-mill, in a vacant
lot on Spring Street, back of Joseph Newmark's second residence. The latter was on Main Street, between First and the
northern junction of Main and Spring; and between this junction
and First Street, it may be interesting to note, there was in
1853 no thoroughfare from Main to Spring. As I was living
there, I acted as his agent for the sale of the wood that was left
after our settlement. The fact is that Hancock was always
land poor, and never out of debt; and when he was particularly
hard up, he parted with his possessions at whatever price they
would bring. The Major (earlier known as Captain Hancock,
who enjoyed his titles through his association with the militia)
retained, however, the celebrated La Brea *rancho*—bought at a
very early date from A. J. Rocha, and lying between the city
and the sea—which he long thought would furnish oil, but
little dreamt would also contain some of the most important
prehistoric finds; and this ranch, once managed by his wife, a
daughter of Colonel Augustin Haraszthy, the San Francisco
pioneer, is now owned by his son, George Allan Hancock.

George Hansen, to whose far-reaching foresight we owe the
Elysian Park of to-day, was another professional man who was
here before I reached Los Angeles, having come to California
in 1850, by way of Cape Horn and Peru. When he arrived at
Los Angeles, in 1853, as he was fond of recounting, he was too
poor to possess even surveying instruments; but he found a
friend in John Temple, who let him have one hundred dollars
at two per cent. interest per month, then a very low rate.
Thereupon Hansen sent to San Francisco for the outfit that
enabled him to establish himself. I met Hansen for the first
time in the last few weeks of 1853, when he came to my brother's
store to buy a suit of clothes, his own being in rags. He had
been out, very probably, on an expedition such as subjected

a surveyor, particularly in the early days, to much hard work and fatigue. Hansen, a good student and fine linguist, was prominent for many years and made more land measurements hereabouts than did any one else; he had the real management, in fact, of Hancock's second survey.

Among others who were here, I might mention the Wheeler brothers. Colonel John Ozias Wheeler, at various times an office-holder, came to California from Florida, and having endured many hardships on the trip along the Mississippi, Arkansas and Gila rivers, arrived at the Chino *rancho* on August 12th, 1849, afterward assisting Isaac Williams in conveying a train of supplies back to the Colorado River. The next year he was joined by his brother, Horace Z. Wheeler, who came by way of the Isthmus, and later rose to be Appraiser-General of the Imperial Customs at Yokohama; and the two young men were soon conducting a general merchandise business in Los Angeles—if I recollect aright, in a one-story adobe at the northeast corner of Main and Commercial streets. Extravagant stories have been printed as to Wheeler's mercantile operations, one narrative crediting him with sales to the extent of five thousand dollars or more a day. In those times, however, no store was large enough to contain such a stock; and two successive days of heavy sales would have been impossible. In 1851 Colonel Wheeler, who had been on General Andrés Pico's staff, served as a Ranger; and in 1853 he organized the first military company in Los Angeles.

Manuel Requena, from Yucatan, was another man of influence. He lived on the east side of Los Angeles Street, north of the thoroughfare opened through his vineyard and named after him—later extended east of Los Angeles Street. As early as June, 1836, Requena, then *Alcalde*, made a census of this district. He was a member of the first, as well as the second, third, fifth and seventh Common Councils, and with David W. Alexander was the only member of the first body to serve out the entire term. In 1852, Requena was elected a Supervisor. Mrs. Requena was a sister of Mrs. Alexander Bell and Mrs. James, or Santiago Johnson, and an aunt of Henry and Francis

Mellus and Mrs. J. H. Lander. Requena died on June 27th, 1876, aged seventy-four years.

Henry N. Alexander appeared in Los Angeles at about the same time that I did—possibly afterward—and was very active as a Ranger. He too occupied positions of trust, in business as well as public life, being both City and County Treasurer—in the latter case, preceding Maurice Kremer. It is not surprising, therefore, that he became Wells Fargo & Company's agent when much uphill work had to be done to establish their interests here. He married a daughter of Don Pedro Dominguez. Alexander moved to Arizona, after which I lost track of him.

John W. Shore, who was here in 1853, was County Clerk from 1854 to 1857, and again from 1860 to 1863. He always canvassed for votes on horseback until, one day, he fell off and broke his leg, necessitating amputation. This terminated his active campaigns; but through sympathy he was reëlected, and by a larger majority. Shore was a Democrat.

Mention of public officials leads me to speak of an interesting personality long associated with them. On the west side of Spring Street near First, where the Schumacher Building now stands, John Schumacher conducted, in a single room, as was then common, a grocery store and bar. A good-hearted, honest German of the old school, and a first-class citizen, he had come from Würtemberg to America, and then, with Stevenson's Regiment, to California, arriving in Los Angeles in 1847 or 1848. From here he went to Sutter's Creek, where he found a nugget of gold worth eight hundred dollars, for which he was offered land in San Francisco later worth millions—a tender which the Würtemberger declined; and the same year that I arrived, he returned to Los Angeles, whose activity had increased considerably since he had last seen it. In 1855, Schumacher married Fräulein Mary Uhrie, from which union six children including two sons, John and Frank G. Schumacher, were born. The eldest daughter became Mrs. Edward A. Preuss. Schumacher established his store, having bought nearly the whole block bounded by Spring and First streets and Franklin Alley for the value of his famous gold nugget; and there he remained until the early seventies, the Schumacher Block being built, as I have said, on a part of the property. Mrs. Schumacher in 1880 met with a tragic death: while at the railway station in Merced, she was jolted from the platform of a car and was instantly killed.

For something else, however, Schumacher was especially known. When he returned in 1853, he put on sale the first lager beer introduced into Los Angeles, importing the same from San Francisco, of which enterprise the genial German was proud; but Schumacher acquired even more fame for a drink that he may be said to have invented, and which was known to the early settlers as *Peach and Honey*. It contained a good mixture with peach brandy, and was a great favorite, especially with politicians and frequenters of the neighboring Courthouse, including well-known members of the Bar, all of whom crowded John's place, "between times," to enjoy his much-praised concoction. Whenever in fact anyone had a cold, or fancied that he was going to be so afflicted, he hastened to John for his reputedly-certain cure. Schumacher, who served as Councilman in 1855, 1856 and 1857, was proficient in languages and, as an interpreter, often gave his time and services freely in assisting his less-gifted neighbors, particularly the poor and unfortunate, to straighten out their affairs. In the fall of 1860, he had a narrow escape through the carelessness of a customer who threw a lighted match into a can of powder. Schumacher owned some acreage in what was known as the Green Meadows, a section located near what is now South Figueroa Street; and this land he held with Jacob Bell, who was assassinated, as I shall relate, by a Frenchman named Lachenais—hanged, in turn, by an exasperated mob.

Most political meetings of that period took place at the Plaza home of Don Ygnácio Del Valle, first County Recorder. From 1841, Don Ygnácio lived for some time on the San Francisco *rancho* granted by the King of Spain to his father and confirmed by patent in 1875. He also owned the more famous Camulos *rancho* on the Santa Clara River, consisting of several thousand acres north and west of Newhall, afterward selected by Helen Hunt Jackson as the setting for some of the scenes in her novel, *Ramona;* and these possessions made him a man of great importance. During his later life, when he had abandoned his town residence, Del Valle dwelt in genteel leisure at the *rancho,* dying there in 1880; and I will not miss this opportunity to attest his patrician bearing and genial qualities.

At the time of my arrival, there was but one voting precinct and the polling place was located at the old municipal and County adobe already spoken of; although later a second polls was established at the Round House. Inside the room, sat the election judges and clerks; outside a window, stood the jam of voters. The window-sill corresponded to the thickness of the adobe wall, and was therefore about three feet deep. This sill served as a table, upon it being placed a soap- or candle-box, into which a hole had been cut for the deposit of the votes.

There was also no register, either great or small, and anyone could vote. Each party printed its own tickets; and so could any candidate. This resulted in great confusion, since there were always many tickets in the field—as many, in fact, as there were candidates; yet the entire proceeding had become legalized by custom. The candidate of one party could thus use the ticket of the other, substituting his own name for his opponent's, and leaving all of the remainder of the ticket unchanged; in addition to which there was such a lack of uniformity in the size and color of the ballots as greatly to add to the confusion in counting.

To make matters worse, the ballot-box was not easily reached because of the crowd which was made up largely of the candidates and their friends. Challenging was the order of the day; yet, after crimination and recrimination, the votes were generally permitted to be cast. Although it is true, of course, that many votes were legitimate, yet aliens such as Mexicans, who had not even considered the question of taking out citizenship papers, were permitted to vote while Indians and half-breeds, who were not eligible to citizenship at all, were irregularly given the franchise. The story is told of an election

not far from Los Angeles at which a whole tribe of Indians
was voted; while on another occasion the names on a steamer's
passenger-list were utilized by persons who had already voted,
that very day, once or twice! Cutting off the hair, shaving
one's beard or mustache, reclothing or otherwise transforming
the appearance of the voter—these were some of the tricks
then practiced, which the new registry law of 1866 only
partially did away with.

Sonorans, who had recently arrived from Mexico, as well as
the aliens I have mentioned, were easy subjects for the political
manipulator. The various candidates, for example, would
round-up these prospective voters like so many cattle, confine
them in corrals (usually in the neighborhood of Boyle
Heights), keep them in a truly magnificent state of intoxication until the eventful morning, and then put them in stages
hired from either Banning or Tomlinson for the purpose; and
from the time the temporary prisoners left the corral until
their votes had been securely deposited, they were closely
watched by guards. On reaching the voting place, the captives
were unloaded from the stage like so much inanimate baggage,
and turned over to friends of the candidate to whom, so to
speak, for the time being they belonged. One at a time, these
creatures were led to vote; and as each staggered to the ballot-
box, a ticket was held up and he was made to deposit it.
Once having served the purpose, he was turned loose and remained free until another election unless, as I have intimated,
he and his fellows were again corralled and made to vote a
second or even a third time the same day.

Nearly all influential Mexicans were Democrats, so that
this party easily controlled the political situation; from which
circumstance a certain brief campaign ended in a most amusing
manner. It happened that Thomas H. Workman, brother of
William H., once ran for County Clerk, although he was not a
Democrat. Billy was naturally much interested in his brother's
candidacy, and did what he could to help him. On the evening
before election, he rented a corral—located near what is now
Macy Street and Mission Road, on property later used by

Charles F., father of Alfred Stern, and for years in partnership with L. J. Rose; and there, with the assistance of some friends, he herded together about one hundred docile though illegal voters, most of whom were Indians, kept them all night and, by supplying fire-water liberally, at length led them into the state of bewilderment necessary for such an occasion. The Democratic leaders, however, having learned of this magnificent *coup*, put their heads together and soon resolved to thwart Billy's plan.   In company with some prominent Mexican politicians led by Tomás Sanchez, they loaded themselves into a stage and visited the corral; and once arrived there, those that could made such flowery stump speeches in the native language of the horde that, in fifteen or twenty minutes, they had stampeded the whole band!   Billy entered a vigorous protest, saying that the votes were *his* and that it was a questionable and even a damnable trick; but all his protests were of no avail: the bunch of corralled voters had been captured in a body by the opposition, deciding the contest.   These were the methods then in vogue in accordance with which it was considered a perfectly legitimate transaction to buy votes, and there was no secret made of the *modus operandi* by either party.

During these times of agitated politics, newspapers (such as they were) played an important part.   In them were published letters written by ambitious candidates to themselves and signed, "The People," "A Disinterested Citizen," or some equally anonymous phrase.   As an exception to the usual maneuver, however, the following witty announcement was once printed by an office-seeker:

George N. Whitman, not having been requested by "Many Friends," or solicited by "Many Voters," to become a candidate for the office of Township Constable, at the end of the ensuing September election, offers himself.

Here I am reminded of an anecdote at the expense of John Quincy Adams Stanley, who in 1856 ran for Sheriff against David W. Alexander, and was County Assessor in the middle seventies. Stanley was a very decent but somewhat over-trusting individual; and ignoring suggestions as to expenditures for votes, too readily believed promises of support by the voters of the county, almost every one of whom gave him a favorable pledge in the course of the campaign. When the ballots were counted, however, and Stanley learned that he had received just about fifty votes, he remarked, rather dryly: "I didn't know that there were so many *damned liars* in the county!"

Another interesting factor in early elections was the vote of Teháchepi, then in Los Angeles County. About thirty votes were cast there; but as communication with Los Angeles was irregular, it was sometimes necessary to wait a week or more to know what bearing the decision of Teháchepi had on the general result.

CHAPTER V

1853

IN the primitive fifties there were but comparatively few reputable lawyers in this neighborhood; nor was there, perhaps, sufficient call for their services to insure much of a living to many more. To a greater extent even than now, attorneys were called "Judge;" and at the time whereof I write, the most important among them were Jonathan R. Scott, Benjamin Hayes, J. Lancaster Brent, Myron Norton, General Ezra Drown, Benjamin S. Eaton, Cameron E. Thom, James H. Lander, Lewis Granger, Isaac Stockton Keith Ogier, Edward J. C. Kewen and Joseph R. Gitchell. In addition to these, there was a lawyer named William G. Dryden, of whom I shall presently speak, and one Kimball H. Dimmick, who was largely devoted to criminal practice.

Scott, who had been a prominent lawyer in Missouri, stood very high, both as to physique and reputation. In addition to his great stature, he had a splendid constitution and wonderful vitality and was identified with nearly every important case. About March, 1850, he came here an overland emigrant, and was made one of the two justices of the peace who formed, with the county judge, on June 24th, the first Court of Sessions. He then entered into partnership with Benjamin Hayes, continuing in joint practice with him until April, 1852, after which he was a member successively of the law firms of Scott & Granger, Scott & Lander, and Scott, Drown & Lander. Practicing law in those days was not without its difficulties, partly because of the lack of law-books; and Scott used to tell in his own vehement style how, on one occasion, when he was defending a French sea captain against charges preferred by a rich Peruvian passenger, he was unable to make much headway because there was but one volume (Kent's *Commentaries*) in the whole pueblo that threw any light, so to speak, on the question; which lack of information induced *Alcalde* Stearns to decide against Scott's client. Although the Captain lost, he nevertheless counted out to Scott, in shining gold-pieces, the full sum of one thousand dollars as a fee. In 1859, a daughter of Scott married Alfred Beck Chapman, a graduate of West Point, who came to Los Angeles and Fort Tejón, as an officer, about 1854. Chapman later studied law with Scott, and for twenty years practiced with Andrew Glassell. In 1863, Chapman succeeded M. J. Newmark as City Attorney; and in 1868, he was elected District Attorney. If I recollect rightly, Scott died in the sixties, survived by Mrs. Scott—a sister of both Mrs. J. S. Mallard and Mrs. J. G. Nichols—and a son, J. R. Scott, admitted in 1880 to practice in the Supreme Court.

Hayes was District Judge when I came, and continued as such for ten or twelve years. His jurisdiction embraced Los Angeles, San Diego, San Luis Obispo and Santa Bárbara counties; and the latter section then included Ventura County. The Judge had regular terms in these districts and was compelled to hold court at all of the County seats. A native of Baltimore, Hayes came to Los Angeles on February 3d, 1850 —followed on St. Valentine's Day, 1852, by his wife whose journey from St. Louis, *via* New Orleans, Havana and Panamá, consumed forty-three days on the steamers. He was at once elected the first County Attorney, and tried the famous case against the Irving party. About the same time Hayes formed his partnership with Scott. In January, 1855, and while District Judge, Hayes sentenced the murderer Brown; and in 1858 he presided at Pancho Daniel's trial. Hayes continued to practice for many years, and was known as a jurist of high standing, though on account of his love for strong drink, court on more than one occasion had to be adjourned. During his residence here, he was known as an assiduous collector of historical data. He was a brother of both Miss Louisa Hayes, the first woman public-school teacher in Los Angeles, later the wife of Dr. J. S. Griffin, and Miss Helena Hayes, who married Benjamin S. Eaton. Judge Hayes died on August 4th, 1877.

Brent, a native of the South, was also a man of attainment, arriving here in 1850 with a fairly representative, though inadequate library, and becoming in 1855 and 1856 a member of the State Assembly. He had such wonderful influence, as one of the Democratic leaders, that he could nominate at will any candidate; and being especially popular with the Mexican element, could also tell a good story or two about fees. When trouble arose in 1851 between several members of the Lugo family and the Indians, resulting finally in an attempted assassination and the narrow escape from death of Judge Hayes (who was associated with the prosecution of the case), several of the Lugos were tried for murder; and Brent, whose defense led to their acquittal, received something like twenty thousand dollars for his services. He was of a studious turn of mind and acquired most of Hugo Reid's Indian library. When the Civil War broke out, Brent went South again and became a Confederate brigadier-general. Brent Street bears his name.

Norton, a Vermonter, who had first practiced law in New York, then migrated west, and had later been a prime mover for, and a member of, the first California Constitutional Convention, and who was afterward Superior Court Judge at San Francisco, was an excellent lawyer, when sober, and a good fellow. He came to the Coast in the summer of 1848, was made First Lieutenant and Chief-of-Staff of the California Volunteers, and drifted in 1852 from Monterey to Los Angeles. He joined Bean's Volunteers, and in 1857 delivered here a flowery Fourth of July oration. Norton was the second County Judge, succeeding Agustin Olvera and living with the latter's family at the Plaza; and it was from Norton's Court of Sessions, in May, 1855, that the dark-skinned Juan Flores was sent to the State prison, although few persons suspected him to be guilty of such criminal tendencies as he later developed.   Norton died in Los Angeles in 1887; and Norton Avenue recalls his life and work.

Judge Hayes' successor, Don Pablo de la Guerra, was born in the *presidio* of Santa Bárbara in 1819, a member of one of the most popular families of that locality.   Although a Spaniard of the Spaniards, he had been educated in an Eastern college, and spoke English fluently.   Four times he was elected State Senator from Santa Bárbara and San Luis Obispo, and was besides a member of the Constitutional Convention of 1849. Late in 1863, he was a candidate for District Judge when a singular opposition developed that might easily have led, in later years at least, to his defeat.   A large part of the population of Santa Bárbara was related to him by blood or marriage; and it was argued that, if elected, De la Guerra in many cases would be disqualified from sitting as judge.   On January 1st, 1864, however, Don Pablo took up the work as District Judge where Hayes surrendered it.   Just as De la Guerra in 1854 had resigned in favor of Hunter, before completing his term as United States Marshal, so now toward the end of 1873, De la Guerra withdrew on account of ill-health from the district judgeship, and on February 5th, 1874, he died.

Drown was a lawyer who came here a few months before I did, having just passed through one of those trying ordeals which might easily prove sufficient to destroy the courage and ambition of any man.   He hailed from Iowa, where he had served as Brigadier-General of Militia, and was bound up the Coast from the Isthmus on the steamer *Independence* when it took fire, off Lower California, and burned to the water's edge. General Drown, being a good swimmer and a plucky fellow, set his wife adrift on a hencoop and then put off for shore with his two children on his back. . Having deposited them safely on the beach, he swam back to get his wife; but a brutal fellow-passenger pushed the fainting woman off when her agonized husband was within a few feet of her; she sank beneath the waves, and he saw his companion go to her doom at the moment she was about to be rescued.   Though broken in spirit, Drown on landing at San Pedro came to Los Angeles with his two boys, and put his best foot forward. He established himself as a lawyer and in 1858 became District Attorney, succeeding Cameron E. Thom; and it was during his term that Pancho Daniel was lynched. In 1855, too, Drown instituted the first Los Angeles lodge of Odd Fellows. Drown was an able lawyer, eloquent and humorous, and fairly popular; but his generosity affected his material prosperity, and he died, at San Juan Capistrano, on August 17th, 1863, none too blessed with this world's goods.

Dimmick, who at one time occupied an office in the old Temple Block on Main Street, had rather an eventful career. Born in Connecticut, he learned the printer's trade; then he studied law and was soon admitted to practice in New York; and in 1846 he sailed with Colonel J. D. Stevenson, in command of Company K, landing, six months later, at the picturesquely-named Yerba Buena, on whose slopes the bustling town of San Francisco was so soon to be founded. When peace with Mexico was established, Dimmick moved to San José; after which with Foster he went to the convention whose mission was to frame a State constitution, and was later chosen Judge of the Supreme Court. In 1852, after having revisited the East and been defrauded of practically all he possessed by those to whom he had entrusted his California affairs, Dimmick came to Los Angeles and served as Justice of the Peace, Notary Public and County Judge. He was also elected District Attorney, and at another time was appointed by the Court to defend the outlaw, Pancho Daniel. Dimmick's practice was really largely criminal, which frequently made him a defender of horse-thieves, gamblers and desperadoes; and in such cases one could always anticipate his stereotyped plea:

Gentlemen of the Jury: The District Attorney prosecuting my client is paid by the County to convict this prisoner, whether he be guilty or innocent; and I plead with you, gentlemen, in the name of Impartial Justice, to bring in a verdict of "Not guilty!"

Through the help of his old-time friend, Secretary William H. Seward, Dimmick toward the end of his life was appointed

Attorney for the Southern District of the United States in California; but on September 11th, 1861, he suddenly died of heart disease.

Eaton, another prominent representative of the Bar, came from New England as early as 1850, while California government was in its infancy and life anything but secure; and he had not been here more than a few months when the maneuvers of António Garra, Agua Caliente's chief, threatened an insurrection extending from Tulare to San Diego and made necessary the organization, under General J. H. Bean, of volunteers to allay the terror-stricken community's fears. Happily, the company's chief activity was the quieting of feminine nerves.   On October 3d, 1853, Eaton was elected District Attorney and in 1857, County Assessor.   Later, after living for a while at San Gabriel, Eaton became a founder of the Pasadena colony; acting as its President for several years; and in 1876 he was one of the committee to arrange for the local Centennial celebration.   Frederick Eaton, several times City Engineer and once—in 1899-1900—Mayor of Los Angeles, is a son of Benjamin Eaton and his first wife, Helena Hayes, who died a few years after she came here, and the brother of Mrs. Hancock Johnston.   He reflects no little credit on his father by reason of a very early, effective advocacy of the Owens River Aqueduct.   Under his administration, the City began this colossal undertaking, which was brought to a happy consummation in the year 1913 through the engineering skill of William Mulholland, Eaton's friend.   In 1861, Judge Eaton married Miss Alice Taylor Clark, of Providence, R. I., who is still living.

While I am upon this subject of lawyers and officialdom, a few words regarding early jurists and court decorum may be in order.   In 1853, Judge Dryden, who had arrived in 1850, was but a Police Justice, not yet having succeeded Dimmick as County Judge; and at no time was his knowledge of the law and things pertaining thereto other than extremely limited. His audacity, however, frequently sustained him in positions that otherwise might have been embarrassing; and this audacity was especially apparent in Dryden's strong opposition to

Henry Mellus
From a Daguerreotype

Francis Mellus
From a Daguerreotype

John G. Downey

Charles L. Ducommun

The Plaza Church

From a photograph, probably taken in the middle eighties

the criminal element.   He talked with the volubility of a Gatling
gun, expressing himself in a quick, nervous manner and was,
besides, very profane.   One day he was trying a case, when
Captain Cameron E. Thom (who had first come to Los Angeles
in 1854, as the representative of the National Government,
to take testimony before Commissioner Burrill) was one of
the attorneys.   During the progress of the case, Thom had
occasion to read a lengthy passage from some statute book.
Interrupting him, the Judge asked to see the weighty volume;
when, having searched in vain for the citation, he said in
his characteristic, jerky way:

"I'll be —— *damned*, Mr. Thom, if I can find that law!"

All of which recalls to me a report, once printed in the *Los
Angeles Star*, concerning this same jurist and an inquest
held by him over a dead Indian:

Justice Dryden and the Jury sat on the body.   The verdict
was: "Death from intoxication, *or* by the visitation of God!"

Dryden, who was possessed of a genial personality, was
long remembered with pleasure for participation in Fourth of
July celebrations and processions.   He was married, I believe,
in 1851, only one year after he arrived here, to Señorita Dolores
Nieto; and she having died, he took as his second wife, in
September, 1868, another Spanish lady, Señorita Anita Dominguez, daughter of Don Manuel Dominguez.   Less than a year
afterward, on September 10th, 1869, Judge Dryden himself
died at the age of seventy years.

Thom, by the way, came from Virginia in 1849 and advanced rapidly in his profession.   It was far from his expectation to remain in Los Angeles longer than was necessary; and
he has frequently repeated to me the story of his immediate
infatuation with this beautiful section and its cheering climate,
and how he fell in love with the quaint little pueblo at first
sight.   Soon after he decided to remain here, he was assigned
as associate counsel to defend Pancho Daniel, after the retirement of Columbus Sims.   In 1856, Thom was appointed both

City and District Attorney, and occupied the two positions at the same time—an odd situation which actually brought it about, during his tenure of offices, that a land dispute between the City and the County obliged Thom to defend both interests! In 1863, he was a partner with A. B. Chapman; and twenty years later, having previously served as State Senator, he was elected Mayor of the city. Captain Thom married two sisters—first choosing Miss Susan Henrietta Hathwell, and then, sometime after her death, leading to the altar Miss Belle Cameron Hathwell whom he had named and for whom, when she was baptized, he had stood godfather. A man ultimately affluent, he owned, among other properties, a large ranch at Glendale.[1]

Another good story concerning Judge Dryden comes to mind, recalling a certain Sheriff. As the yarn goes, the latter presented himself as a candidate for the office of Sheriff; and in order to capture the vote of the native element, he also offered to marry the daughter of an influential Mexican. A bargain was concluded and, as the result, he forthwith assumed the responsibilities and dangers of both shrieval and matrimonial life.

Before the Sheriff had possessed this double dignity very long, however, a gang of horse-thieves began depredations around Los Angeles. A *posse* was immediately organized to pursue the desperadoes, and after a short chase they located the band and brought them into Los Angeles. Imagine the Sheriff's dismay, when he found that the leader was none other than his own brother-in-law whom he had never before seen!

To make the story short, the case was tried and the prisoner was found guilty; but owing to influence (to which most juries in those days were very susceptible) there was an appeal for judicial leniency. Judge Dryden, therefore, in announcing the verdict, said to the Sheriff's brother-in-law, "The jury finds you guilty as charged," and then proceeded to read the prisoner a long and severe lecture, to which he added: "But the jury recommends clemency. Accordingly, I

[1] Thom died on February 2d, 1915.

declare you a free man, and you may go about your business."
Thereupon someone in the room asked: "What *is* his business?"
To which the Judge, never flinching, shouted: "*Horse-stealing*,
sir! *horse-stealing!*"

Lander was here in 1853, having come from the East the
year previous. He was a Harvard College graduate—there
were not many on the Coast in those days—and was known as a
good office-practitioner; he was for some time, in fact, the Bar's
choice for Court Commissioner. I think that, for quite a while,
he was the only examiner of real estate titles; he was certainly
the only one I knew. On October 15th, 1852, Lander had married Señorita Margarita, a daughter of Don Santiago Johnson,
who was said to have been one of the best known business men
prior to 1846. Afterward Lander lived in a cottage on the
northeast corner of Fourth and Spring streets. This cottage
he sold to I. W. Hellman in the early seventies, for four
thousand dollars; and Hellman, in turn, sold it at cost to his
brother. On that lot, worth to-day probably a million dollars,
the H. W. Hellman Building now stands. Lander died on
June 10th, 1873.

Granger was still another lawyer who was here when I
arrived, he having come with his family—one of the first
American households to be permanently established here—in
1850. By 1852, he had formed a partnership with Jonathan
R. Scott, and in that year attained popularity through his
Fourth of July oration. Granger was, in fact, a fluent and
attractive speaker, which accounted, perhaps, for his election
as City Attorney in 1855, after he had served the city as a
member of the Common Council in 1854. If I recollect aright,
he was a candidate for the district judgeship in the seventies,
but was defeated.

Ogier, a lawyer from Charleston, S. C., came to California
in 1849, and to Los Angeles in 1851, forming a partnership on
May 31st of that year with Don Manuel Clemente Rojo, a
clever, genial native of Peru. On September 29th, Ogier
succeeded William C. Ferrell, the first District Attorney; in
1853, he joined the voluntary police; and later served, for

some years, as United States District Judge. He died at Holcombe Valley in May, 1861. Ogier Street, formerly Ogier Lane, was named for him. Rojo, after dividing his time between the law and the Spanish editorial work on the *Star*, wandered off to Lower California and there became a "sub-political chief."

Kewen, a native of Mississippi and a veteran of the Mexican War, came to Los Angeles in 1858 with the title of Colonel, after *fiasco* followed his efforts, in the Southern States, to raise relief for the filibuster Walker, on whose expedition A. L. Kewen, a brother, had been killed in the battle at Rivas, Nicaragua, in June, 1855. Once a practitioner at law in St. Louis, Kewen was elected California's first Attorney-General, and even prior to the delivery of his oration before the Society of Pioneers at San Francisco, in 1854, he was distinguished for his eloquence. In 1858, he was Superintendent of Los Angeles City Schools. In the sixties, Kewen and Norton formed a partnership. Settling on an undulating tract of some four hundred and fifty acres near San Gabriel, including the ruins of the old Mission mill and now embracing the grounds of the Huntington Hotel, Kewen repaired the house and converted it into a cosy and even luxurious residence, calling the estate ornamented with gardens and fountains, *El Molino*—a title perpetuated in the name of the present suburb. Kewen was also a member of the State Assembly and, later, District Attorney. He died in November, 1879.

Gitchell, United States District Attorney in the late fifties, practiced here for many years. He was a jolly old bachelor and was popular, although he did not attain eminence.

Isaac Hartman, an attorney, and his wife, who were among the particularly agreeable people here in 1853, soon left for the East.

Volney E. Howard came with his family in the late fifties. He left San Francisco, where he had been practicing law, rather suddenly, and at a time when social conditions in the city were demoralized, and the citizens, as in the case of the people of Los Angeles, were obliged to organize a vigilance

committee.   William T. Coleman, one of the foremost citizens
of his city, led the Northern movement, and M. J. Newmark,
then a resident of San Francisco, was among those who participated.   Howard, who succeeded William T., afterward General
Sherman in leading the Law and Order contingent, opposed the
idea of mob rule; but the people of San Francisco, fully alive to
the necessity of wiping out the vicious elements, and knowing
how hard it was to get a speedy trial and an honest jury, had
little sympathy with his views. He was accordingly ordered
out of town, and made his way, first to Sacramento, then to the
South.   Here, with Kewen as their neighbor, Howard and his
talented wife, a lady of decidedly blue-stocking tendencies, took
up their residence near the San Gabriel Mission; and he became
one of the most reliable attorneys in Los Angeles, serving once
or twice as County Judge and on the Supreme Court bench, as
well as in the State Constitutional Convention of 1878-1879.

Speaking of the informality of courts in the earlier days, I
should record that jurymen and others would come in coatless
and, especially in warm weather, without vests and collars; and
that it was the fashion for each juryman to provide himself
with a jack-knife and a piece of wood, in order that he might
whittle the time away.   This was a recognized privilege, and
I am not exaggerating when I say that if he forgot his piece of
wood, it was considered his further prerogative to whittle the
chair on which he sat!   In other respects, also, court solemnity
was lacking.   Judge and attorneys would frequently lock horns;
and sometimes their disputes ended violently.   On one occasion, for example, while I was in court, Columbus Sims, an
attorney who came here in 1852, threw an inkstand at his opponent, during an altercation; but this contempt of court did not
call forth his disbarment, for he was later found acting as attorney for Pancho Daniel, one of Sheriff Barton's murderers,
until sickness compelled his retirement from the case.   As to
panel-service, I recollect that while serving as juror in those
early days, we were once locked up for the night; and in order
that time might not hang too heavily on our hands, we
engaged in a sociable little game of poker.   Sims is dead.

More than inkstands were sometimes hurled in the early courts. On one occasion, for instance, after the angry disputants had arrived at a state of agitation which made the further use of canes, chairs, and similar objects tame and uninteresting, revolvers were drawn, notwithstanding the marshal's repeated attempts to restore order. Judge Dryden, in the midst of the *mêlée*, hid behind the platform upon which his Judgeship's bench rested; and being well out of the range of the threatening irons, yelled at the rioters:

"*Shoot away*, damn you! and to *hell* with all of you!"

After making due allowance for primitive conditions, it must be admitted that many and needless were the evils incidental to court administration. There was, for instance, the law's delay, which necessitated additional fees to witnesses and jurors and thus materially added to the expenses of the County. Juries were always a mixture of incoming pioneers and natives; the settlers understood very little Spanish, and the native Californians knew still less English; while few or none of the attorneys could speak Spanish at all. In translating testimony, if the interpreter happened to be a friend of the criminal (which he generally was), he would present the evidence in a favorable light, and much time was wasted in sifting biased translations. Of course, there were interpreters who doubtless endeavored to perform their duties conscientiously. George Thompson Burrill, the first Sheriff, received fifty dollars a month as court interpreter, and Manuel Clemente Rojo translated testimony as well; officials I believe to have been honest and conscientious.

While alluding to court interpreters and the general use of Spanish during at least the first decade after I came to California, I am reminded of the case of Joaquín Carrillo, who was elected District Judge, in the early fifties, to succeed Judge Henry A. Tefft of Santa Bárbara, who had been drowned near San Luis Obispo while attempting to land from a steamer in order to hold court. During the fourteen years when Carrillo held office, he was constantly handicapped by his little knowledge of the English language and the consequent necessity of carrying on all court proceedings in Spanish, to say nothing of the fact that he was really not a lawyer. Yet I am told that Carrillo possessed common sense to such a degree that his decisions were seldom set aside by the higher courts.

Sheriff Burrill had a brother, S. Thompson Burrill, who was a lawyer and a Justice of the Peace. He held court in the Padilla Building on Main Street, opposite the present site of the Bullard Block and adjoining my brother's store; and as a result of this proximity we became friendly. He was one of the best-dressed men in town, although, when I first met him, he could not have been less than sixty years of age. He presented me with my first dog, which I lost on account of stray poison: evil-disposed or thoughtless persons, with no respect for the owner, whether a neighbor or not, and without the slightest consideration for pedigree, were in the habit of throwing poison on the streets to kill off canines, of which there was certainly a superabundance.

Ygnácio Sepúlveda, the jurist and a son of José Andrés Sepúlveda, was living here when I arrived, though but a boy. Born in Los Angeles in 1842, he was educated in the East and in 1863 admitted to the Bar; he served in the State Legislature of the following winter, was County Judge from 1870 to 1873, and District Judge in 1874. Five years later he was elected Superior Judge, but resigned his position in 1884 to become Wells Fargo & Company's representative in the City of Mexico, at which capital for two years he was also American *Chargé d'Affaires*. There to my great pleasure I met him, bearing his honors modestly, in January, 1885, during my tour of the southern republic.[1] Sepúlveda Avenue is named for the family.

Horace Bell was a nephew of Captain Alexander Bell, of Bell's Row; and as an early comer to Los Angeles, he joined the volunteer mounted police. Although for years an attorney and journalist, in which capacity he edited the *Porcupine*, he is

[1] After an absence of thirty years, Judge Sepúlveda returned to Los Angeles, in 1914, and was heartily welcomed back by his many friends and admirers.

best known for his *Reminiscences of a Ranger*, a volume written in rather a breezy and entertaining style, but certainly
containing exaggerations.

This reference to the Rangers reminds me that I was not
long in Los Angeles when I heard of the adventures of Joaquín
Murieta, who had been killed but a few months before I
came.   According to the stories current, Murieta, a nephew of
José María Valdez, was a decent-enough sort of fellow, who
had been subjected to more or less injustice from certain
American settlers, and who was finally bound to a tree and
horsewhipped, after seeing his brother hung, on a trumped-up
charge.   In revenge, Murieta had organized a company of
bandits, and for two or three years had terrorized a good part
of the entire State.   Finally, in August, 1853, while the outlaw
and several of his companions were off their guard near the
Tejón Paso, they were encountered by Captain Harry Love
and his volunteer mounted police organized to get him,
"dead or alive;" the latter killed Murieta and another desperado known as Three-fingered Jack.   Immediately the outlaws were despatched, their heads and the deformed hand of
Three-fingered Jack were removed from the bodies and sent by
John Sylvester and Harry Bloodsworth to Dr. William Francis
Edgar, then a surgeon at Fort Miller; but a flood interfering,
Sylvester swam the river with his barley sack and its gruesome contents.   Edgar put the trophies into whiskey and ar-
senic, when they were transmitted to the civil authorities, as
vouchers for a reward.   Bloodsworth died lately.

Daredevils of a less malicious type were also resident
among us.   On the evening of December 31st, 1853, for example,
I was in our store at eight o'clock when Felipe Rheim—often
called Reihm and even Riehm—gloriously intoxicated and out
for a good time, appeared on the scene, flourishing the ubiquitous weapon.   His celebration of the New Year had apparently
commenced, and he was already six sheets in the wind.   Like
many another man, Felipe, a very worthy German, was good-
natured when sober, but a terror when drunk; and as soon as he
spied my solitary figure, he pointed his gun at me, saying, at the

same time, in his vigorous native tongue, "Treat, or *I shoot!*"
I treated. After this pleasing transaction amid the smoky
obscurity of Ramón Alexander's saloon, Felipe fired his gun
into the air and disappeared. Startling as a demand like
that might appear to-day, no thought of arrest then resulted
from such an incident.

The first New Year's Eve that I spent in Los Angeles was
ushered in with the indiscriminate discharging of pistols and
guns. This method of celebrating was, I may say, a novelty
to me, and no less a surprise; for of course I was unaware of the
fact that, when the city was organized, three years before, a
proposition to prohibit the carrying of firearms of any sort, or
the shooting off of the same, except in defense of self, home
or property, had been stricken from the first constitution by
the committee on police, who reported that such an ordinance
could not at that time be enforced. Promiscuous firing continued for years to be indulged in by early Angeleños, though
frequently condemned in the daily press, and such was its
effect upon even me that I soon found myself peppering away
at a convenient adobe wall on Commercial Street, seeking to
perfect my aim!

CHAPTER VI

MERCHANTS AND SHOPS

1853

TRIVIAL events in a man's life sometimes become indelibly impressed on his memory; and one such experience of my own is perhaps worth mentioning as another illustration of the rough character of the times. One Sunday, a few days after my arrival, my brother called upon a tonsorial celebrity, Peter Biggs, of whom I shall speak later, leaving me in charge of the store. There were two entrances, one on Main Street, the other on Requena. I was standing at the Main Street door, unconscious of impending excitement, when a stranger rode up on horseback and, without the least hesitation or warning, pointed a pistol at me. I was not sufficiently amused to delay my going, but promptly retreated to the other door where the practical joker, astride his horse, had easily anticipated my arrival and again greeted me with the muzzle of his weapon. These maneuvers were executed a number of times, and my ill-concealed trepidation only seemed to augment the diversion of a rapidly-increasing audience. My brother returned in the midst of the fun and asked the jolly joker what in hell he meant by such behavior; to which he replied: "Oh, I just wanted to frighten the boy!"

Soon after this incident, my brother left for San Francisco; and his partner, Jacob Rich, accompanied by his wife, came south and rented rooms in what was then known as Mellus's Row, an adobe building for the most part one-story, standing

alone with a garden in the rear, and occupying about three
hundred feet on the east side of Los Angeles Street, between
Aliso and First.   In this row, said by some to have been built
by Barton & Nordholt, in 1850, for Captain Alexander Bell,
a merchant here since 1842, after whom Bell Street is named,
and by others claimed to have been the headquarters of Frémont, in 1846, there was a second-story at the corner of Aliso,
provided with a large veranda; and there the Bell and Mellus
families lived.   Francis Mellus, who arrived in California in
1839, had married the niece of Mrs. Bell, and Bell having
sold the building to Mellus, Bell's Row became known as
Mellus's Row.   Finally, Bell repurchased the property, retaining it during the remainder of his life; and the name was again
changed.   This famous stretch of adobe, familiarly known as
The Row, housed many early shopkeepers, such as Ferner &
Kraushaar, general merchants, Kalisher & Wartenberg, and
Bachman & Bauman.   The coming to Los Angeles of Mr.
and Mrs. Rich enabled me to abandon La Rue's restaurant, as
I was permitted to board with them.   None the less, I missed
my brother very much.

Everything at that time indicating that I was in for a commercial career, it was natural that I should become acquainted
with the merchants then in Los Angeles.   Some of the tradesmen, I dare say, I have forgotten; but a more or less distinct
recollection remains of many, and to a few of them I shall
allude.

Temple Street had not then been opened by Beaudry and
Potts, although there was a little *cul-de-sac* extending west from
Spring Street; and at the junction of what is now Spring and
Temple streets, there was a two-story adobe building in which
D. W. Alexander and Francis Mellus conducted a general
merchandise business, and at one time acted as agents for
Mellus & Howard of San Francisco.   Mellus, who was born in
Salem, Massachusetts, February 3d, 1824, came to the Coast in
1839, first landing at Santa Bárbara; and when I first met him
he had married Adelaida, daughter of Don Santiago Johnson,
and our fellow-townsman, James J. Mellus—familiarly known

as plain Jim—was a baby. Alexander & Mellus had rather
an extensive business in the early days, bringing goods by sailing
vessel around Cape Horn, and exchanging them for hides and
tallow which were carried back East by the returning merchant-
men. They had operated more or less extensively even some
years before California was ceded to the United States; but
competition from a new source forced these well-established
merchants to retire. With the advent of more frequent,
although still irregular service between San Francisco and the
South, and the influx of more white people, a number of new
stores started here bringing merchandise from the Northern
market, while San Francisco buyers began to outbid Alexander & Mellus for the local supply of hides and tallow. This
so revolutionized the methods under which this tradition-bound
old concern operated that, by 1858, it had succumbed to the
inevitable, and the business passed into the hands of Johnson
& Allanson, a firm made up of Charles R. Johnson, soon to be
elected County Clerk, and Horace S. Allanson.

Most of the commercial activity in this period was carried
on north of First Street. The native population inhabited
Sonora Town, for the most part a collection of adobes, named
after the Mexican state whence came many of our people;
there was a contingent from other parts of Mexico; and a small
sprinkling of South Americans from Chile and Peru. Among
this Spanish-speaking people quite a business was done by
Latin-American storekeepers. It followed, naturally enough,
that they dealt in all kinds of Mexican goods.

One of the very few white men in this district was José
Mascarel (a powerfully-built French sea-captain and master
of the ship that brought Don Luis Vignes to the Southland),
who settled in Los Angeles in 1844, marrying an Indian woman.
He had come with Prudhomme and others; and under Captain
Henseley had taken part in the military events at San Bartolo
and the Mesa. By 1865, when he was Mayor of the city, he had
already accumulated a number of important real estate holdings
and owned, with another Frenchman, Juan Barri, a baker, the
block extending east on the south side of Commercial Street,

from Main to Los Angeles, which had been built in 1861 to take the place of several old adobes. This the owners later divided, Mascarel taking the southeast corner of Commercial and Main streets, and Barri the southwest corner of Commercial and Los Angeles streets. In the seventies, I. W. Hellman bought the Mascarel corner, and in 1883, the Farmers & Merchants Bank moved to that location, where it remained until the institution purchased the southwest corner of Fourth and Main streets, for the erection of its own building.

Andrés Ramirez was another Sonora Town merchant. He had come from Mexico in 1844, and sold general merchandise in what, for a while, was dubbed the Street of the Maids. Later, this was better known as Upper Main Street; and still later it was called San Fernando Street.

Louis Abarca was a tradesman and a neighbor of Ramirez. Prosperous until the advent of the pioneer, he little by little became poorer, and finally withdrew from business.

Juan Bernard, a native of French Switzerland, whose daughter married D. Botiller, now an important landowner, came to California by way of the Horn, in search of the precious metal, preceding me to this land of sunshine. For awhile, he had a brickyard on Buena Vista Street; but in the late seventies, soon after marrying Señorita Susana Machado, daughter of Don Agustin Machado, he bought a vineyard on Alameda Street, picturesquely enclosed by a high adobe or brick wall much after the fashion of a European *château*. He also came to own the site of the Natick House. A clever linguist and a man of attractive personality, he passed away in 1889.

An American by the name of George Walters lived on Upper Main Street, among the denizens of which locality he was an influential person. Born at New Orleans as early as 1809, Walters had trapped and traded in the Rocky Mountains, then teamed for awhile between Santa Fé and neighboring points. Near the end of 1844, he left New Mexico in company with James Waters, Jim Beckwith and other travelers, finally reaching Los Angeles. Walters, who settled in San Bernardino, was at the Chino Ranch, with B. D. Wilson and Louis Robidoux, when so many Americans were made prisoners.

Julian Chavez, after whom Chavez Street is named, was here in 1853. If he was not native-born, he came here at a very early day. He owned a stretch of many acres, about a mile northeast of Los Angeles. He was a good, honest citizen, and is worthy of recollection.

Ramón Alexander, a Frenchman often confused with David Alexander, came to Los Angeles before 1850, while it was still a mere Mexican village. Pioneers remember him especially as the builder of the long-famous Round House, on Main Street, and as one who also for some time kept a saloon near Requena Street. Alexander's wife was a Señorita Valdez. He died in 1870.

Antoine Laborie was another Frenchman here before the beginning of the fifties. He continued to live in Los Angeles till at least the late seventies. A fellow-countryman, B. Dubordieu, had a bakery in Sonora Town.

Philip Rheim, the good-natured German to whom I have referred, had a little store and saloon, before I came, called *Los dos Amigos*, as the proprietor of which he was known as Don Felipe. Nor was this title amiss; for Felipe married a native woman and, German though he had been, he gradually became, like so many others who had mated in the same way, more and more Californian in manners and customs.

A month after I arrived here, John Behn, who had a grocery business at the northeast corner of First and Los Angeles streets, retired. He had come to Los Angeles from Baden in 1848, and, after forming one or two partnerships, had sold out to Lorenzo Leck, a German Dane, who reached here in November, 1849, and whose son, Henry von der Leck, married a daughter of Tom Mott and is living at San Juan Capistrano. Leck opened his own store in 1854, and despite the trials to which he was to be subjected, he was able, in 1868, to pay John Schumacher three thousand dollars for a lot on Main Street. Leck had a liking for the spectacular; and in the November previous to my arrival was active, as I have been told, with

Goller and Nordholt, in organizing the first political procession seen in Los Angeles. The election of Pierce was the incentive, and there were gorgeous transparencies provided for the event. It was on this occasion that a popular local character, George the Baker, burned himself badly while trying to fire off the diminutive cannon borrowed from the Spanish *padre* for the event.

In the one-story adobe of Mascarel and Barri, on the corner of Commercial and Main streets, now the site of the United States National Bank, an Irishman named Samuel G. Arbuckle, who had come here in 1850 and was associated for a short time with S. Lazard, conducted a dry goods store. From 1852 to 1856, Arbuckle was City Treasurer.

In the same building, and adjoining Arbuckle's, John Jones, father of Mrs. J. B. Lankershim and M. G. Jones, carried on a wholesale grocery business. Jones had left England for Australia, when forty-seven years old, and a year later touched the coast of California at Monterey and came to Los Angeles. Twice a year, Jones went north in a schooner, for the purpose of replenishing his stock; and after making his purchases and having the boat loaded, he would return to Los Angeles. Sometimes he traveled with the round-bellied, short and jolly Captain Morton who recalled his illustrious prototype, Wouter van Twiller, so humorously described by Washington Irving as "exactly five feet six inches in height, and six feet five inches in circumference;" sometimes he sailed with Captain J. S. Garcia, a good-natured seaman. During his absence, the store remained closed; and as this trip always required at least six weeks, some idea may be obtained of the Sleepy Hollow methods then prevailing in this part of the West. In 1854 or 1855, Jones, who was reputed to be worth some fifty thousand dollars, went to San Francisco and married Miss Doria Deighton, and it was generally understood that he expected to settle there; but having been away for a couple of years, he returned to the City of the Angels, this being one of the first instances within my observation of the irresistible attraction of Los Angeles for those who have once lived here.

5

It is my recollection that Jones bought from John G. Downey the Cristóbal Aguilar home then occupied by W. H. and Mrs. Perry; a building the more interesting since it was understood to have served, long in the past and before the American occupation, as a *calabozo* or jail, and to have had a whipping-post supposed to have done much service in keeping the turbulently-inclined natives quiet. How many of the old adobes may at times have been used as jails, I am unable to say, but it is also related that there stood on the hill west of the Plaza another *cuartel*, afterward the home of B. S. Eaton, where Fred, later Mayor of Los Angeles, was born. Like Felix Bachman and others, Jones entered actively into trade with Salt Lake City; and although he met with many reverses —notably in the loss of Captain Morton's *Laura Bevan*, which sank, carrying down a shipload of uninsured goods—he retired well-to-do.

John, sometimes called Juan Temple—or Jonathan, as he used to sign himself in earlier years—who paid the debt of Nature in 1866, and after whom Temple Street is named, was another merchant, having a store upon the piece of land (later the site of the Downey Block, and now occupied by the Post Office) which, from 1849 to 1866, was in charge of my friend, Don Ygnácio Garcia, his confidential business agent. Garcia imported from Mexico both *scrapes* and *rebozos;* and as every Mexican man and woman required one of these garments, Temple had a large and very lucrative trade in them alone. Following the death of Temple, Garcia continued under Hinchman, the executor of the estate, until everything had been settled.

It was really far back in 1827 when Temple came to Los Angeles, started the first general merchandise store in town, and soon took such a lead in local affairs that the first Vigilance Committee in the city was organized in his store, in 1836. Toward the fifties, he drifted south to Mexico and there acquired a vast stretch of land on the coast; but he returned here, and was soon known as one of the wealthiest, yet one of the stingiest men in all California. His real estate holdings

in or near Los Angeles were enormous; but the bad judgment
of his executor cost him dear, and valuable properties were
sacrificed. After his death, Temple's wife — who once accompanied her husband to Paris, and had thus formed a
liking for the livelier French capital—returned to France with
her daughter, later Doña Ajuria, to live; and A. F. Hinchman, Temple's brother-in-law, who had been Superintendent of
Santa Bárbara County Schools, was appointed administrator.
Hinchman then resided in San Diego, and was intensely partial
to that place. This may have prejudiced him against Los
Angeles; but whatever the cause, he offered Temple's properties
at ridiculous prices, and some of the items of sale may now be
interesting.

The present site of the Government Building, embracing
as it then did the forty-foot street north of it, was at that time
improved with an adobe building covering the entire front and
running back to New High Street; and this adobe, known after
Temple's death as the Old Temple Block, Hinchman sold for
fifteen thousand dollars. He also disposed of the new Temple
Block, including the improvement at the south end which I
shall describe, for but sixteen thousand dollars. I remember
quite well that Ygnácio Garcia was the purchaser, and that,
tiring of his bargain in a couple of weeks, he resold the property to John Temple's brother, Francisco, at cost.

Hinchman, for fourteen thousand dollars, also disposed of
the site of the present Bullard Block, whereon Temple had
erected a large brick building, the lower part of which was
used as a market while the upper part was a theater. The
terms in each of these three transactions were a thousand
dollars per annum, with interest at ten per cent. He sold
to the Bixbys the Cerritos *rancho*, containing twenty-six
thousand acres, for twenty thousand dollars. Besides these,
there were eighteen lots, each one hundred and twenty by three
hundred and thirty feet, located on Fort Street (now Broadway), some of which ran through to Spring and others to Hill,
which were bought by J. F. Burns and William Buffum for
one thousand and fifty dollars, or fifty dollars each for the

twelve inside and seventy-five dollars each for the six corner lots.

Returning to the Fort Street lots, it may be interesting to know that the property would be worth to-day—at an average price of four thousand dollars per foot—about nine million dollars. Eugene Meyer purchased one of the lots (on the west side of Fort Street, running through to Hill, one hundred and twenty by three hundred and thirty feet in size), for the sum of one thousand dollars; and I paid him a thousand dollars for sixty feet and the same depth. In 1874 I built on this site the home occupied by me for about twelve years, after which I improved both fronts for F. L. Blanchard. These two blocks are still in my possession; the Broadway building is known as Blanchard Hall. Blanchard, by the way, a comer of 1886, started his Los Angeles career in A. G. Bartlett's music store, and has since always been closely identified with art movements. He organized the system of cluster street-lights in use here and was an early promoter of good roads.

Charles L. Ducommun was here in business in 1853, he and John G. Downey having arrived together, three years before. According to the story still current, Ducommun, with his kit and stock as a watchmaker, and Downey, with his outfit as a druggist, hired a *carreta* together, to transport their belongings from San Pedro to Los Angeles; but the *carreta* broke down, and the two pilgrims to the City of the Angels had to finish their journey afoot. Ducommun's first store, located on Commercial Street between Main and Los Angeles, was about sixteen by thirty feet in size, but it contained an astonishing assortment of merchandise, such as hardware, stationery and jewelry. Perhaps the fact that Ducommun came from Switzerland, then even more than now the chief home of watchmaking, explains his early venture in the making and selling of watches; however that may be, it was to Charlie Ducommun's that the bankrupt merchant Moreno—later sentenced to fourteen or fifteen years in the penitentiary for robbing a Frenchman—came to sell the Frenchman's gold watch. Moreno confessed that he had organized a gang of robbers, after his

Pio Pico
From an oil portrait

Juan Bandini

Abel Stearns

Isaac Williams

Store of Felipe Rheim

failure in business, and had murdered even his own lieuten-
ants. Ducommun, pretending to go into a rear room for the
money, slipped out of the back door and gave the alarm. Ducommun's store was a sort of curiosity-shop containing many
articles not obtainable elsewhere; and he was clever enough,
when asked for any rarity, to charge all that the traffic would
bear. I wonder what Charlie Ducommun would say if he could
return to life and see his sons conducting a large, modern wholesale hardware establishment on an avenue never thought of in
his day and where once stretched acres of fruit and vine lands!
Ducommun Street commemorates this pioneer.

Ozro W. Childs, who came to Los Angeles in November,
1850, was for awhile in partnership with J. D. Hicks, the firm
being known as Childs & Hicks. They conducted a tin-shop on
Commercial Street, in a building about twenty by forty feet.
In 1861, H. D. Barrows joined them, and hardware was added
to the business. Somewhat later the firm was known as J. D.
Hicks & Company. In 1871, Barrows bought out the Childs and
Hicks interests, and soon formed a partnership with W. C.
Furrey, although the latter arrived in Los Angeles only in 1872.
When Barrows retired, Furrey continued alone for several years.
The W. C. Furrey Company was next organized, with James W.
Hellman as the active partner of Furrey, and with Simon Maier,
the meat-packer and brother of the brewer, and J. A. Graves
as stockholders. Hellman, in time, succeeded this company
and continued for himself. When Childs withdrew, he went in
for importing and selling exotic trees and plants, and made his
home place, in more modern days known as the Huntington
Purchase and running from Main to Hill and Eleventh to
Twelfth streets, wonderfully attractive to such tourists as then
chanced this way; he also claimed to be the pioneer floricul-
turist of Los Angeles County. Toward the end of his life,
Childs erected on Main Street, south of First, a theater styled
an opera house and later known as the Grand, which was
popular in its time. Childs Avenue bears the family name.

Labatt Brothers had one of the leading dry goods houses,
which, strange as it may seem, they conducted in a part of the

Abel Stearns home, corner of Main and Arcadia streets, now occupied by the Baker Block. Their establishment, while the most pretentious and certainly the most specialized of its day in town, and therefore patronized by our well-to-do people, would nevertheless make but a sorry appearance in comparison with even a single department in any of the mammoth stores of to-day.

Jacob Elias was not only here in 1853, in partnership with his brother under the firm name of Elias Brothers, but he also induced some of his friends in Augusta, Georgia, to migrate to California. Among those who came in 1854 were Pollock, whose given name I forget, and L. C., better known as Clem Goodwin. The latter clerked for awhile for Elias Brothers, after which he associated himself with Pollock under the title of Pollock & Goodwin. They occupied premises at what was then the corner of Aliso Street and Nigger Alley, and the site, some years later, of P. Beaudry's business when we had our interesting contest, the story of which I shall relate in due time. Pollock & Goodwin continued in the general merchandise business for a few years, after which they returned to Augusta. Goodwin, however, came back to California in 1864 a Benedick, and while in San Francisco accidentally met Louis Polaski who was then looking for an opening. Goodwin induced Polaski to enter into partnership with him, and the well-known early clothing house of Polaski & Goodwin was thus established in the Downey Block. In 1867, they bought out I. W. Hellman and moved over to the southeast corner of Commercial and Main streets. Goodwin sold out to Polaski in 1881, when the firm became Polaski & Sons; in 1883 Sam, Isidor and Myer L. Polaski bought out their father, and in time Polaski Brothers also withdrew. Goodwin became Vice-president of the Farmers & Merchants Bank. Polaski died in 1900, Goodwin having preceded him a short time before. Goodwin left his wife some valuable property, and as they were without issue, she so richly endowed the Children's Hospital, at her death, that the present building was made possible.

The Lanfranco brothers—Juan T. and Mateo—came from

Genoa, Italy, by way of Lima, Peru and New York, whence
they crossed the Plains with James Lick the carpenter later so
celebrated, and they were both here in business in 1853; Juan,
a small capitalist or *petit rentier*, living where the Lanfranco
Building now stands, opposite the Federal Building, while
Mateo kept a grocery store on Main Street, not far from Commercial.   In 1854, Juan added to his independence by marrying
Señorita Petra Pilar, one of fourteen children of Don José
Loreto Sepúlveda, owner of the Palos Verdes *rancho;* the celebration of the nuptials, in dancing and feasting, lasting five days.
It was at that ranch that a great stampede of cattle occurred,
due to fright when the pioneer sulky, imported by Juan Lanfranco from San Francisco, and then a strange object, was
driven into their midst.   About 1861, the first Lanfranco Building was erected.   Mateo died on October 4th, 1873, while
Juan passed away on May 20th, 1875.   His wife died in 1877.   A
daughter married Walter Maxwell; a second daughter became
the wife of Walter S. Moore, for years Chief of the Fire Department; and still another daughter married Arthur Brentano,
one of the well-known Paris and New York booksellers.

Solomon Lazard and Maurice Kremer, cousins of about the
same age, and natives of Lorraine, were associated in 1853
under the title of Lazard & Kremer, being located in a
storeroom in Mellus's Row, and I may add that since nearly
all of the country development had taken place in districts
adjacent to San Gabriel, El Monte and San Bernardino,
travel through Aliso Street was important enough to make
their situation one of the best in town.   Lazard had arrived in
San Francisco in 1851, and having remained there about a year,
departed for San Diego, where it was his intention to engage in
the dry goods business.   Finding that there were not enough
people there to maintain such an establishment of even moderate proportions, Lazard decided upon the advice of a seafaring
man whom he met to remove his stock, which he had brought
from the Northern town, to Los Angeles.   He told me that he
paid fifty-six dollars' steamer fare from San Francisco to San
Diego, and that the freight on his merchandise cost him twenty

dollars a ton. Among his native friends, Lazard was always known as Don Solomon, and being popular, he frequently acted as floor-manager at balls and fandangos. Lazard is still living at the good old age of eighty-seven years. Kremer also reached here in 1852. In time, Timoteo Wolfskill, a son of William Wolfskill, bought Kremer's interest, and the firm name became Lazard & Wolfskill. Each of these worthy pioneers in his day rendered signal service to the community —Lazard serving as Councilman in 1862; and I shall have occasion, therefore, to refer to them again. Abe Lazard, a brother of Solomon, who had spent some years in South America, came in the late fifties. Dr. E. M. Lazard is a son of S. Lazard.

While speaking of San Diego, I may remark that it was quite fifteen years before the interesting old Spanish settlement to the South, with which I had no business relations, attracted me; and as I was no exception, the reader may see how seldom the early settlers were inclined to roam about merely for sight-seeing.

In 1853, M. Norton and E. Greenbaum sold merchandise at the southwest corner of Los Angeles and Commercial streets (when Jacob, J. L., an early Supervisor and City Treasurer, 1863–64 and Moritz Morris, Councilman in 1869–70, were competitors). In time, Jacob returned to Germany, where he died. Herman Morris, a brother, was a local newspaper reporter. Jacob Letter was another rival, who removed to Oakland. Still another dealer in general merchandise was M. Michaels, almost a dwarf in size, who emigrated to South America. Casper Behrendt—father-in-law of John Kahn, a man prominent in many movements—who arrived in 1851, was another Commercial Street merchant. Still other early merchants whom I somewhat distinctly recall were Israel Fleishman and Julius Sichel, who had a glassware, crockery and hardware business; and L. Lasky, on Commercial Street.

Thomas D. Mott, father of John Mott, the attorney, who was lured to California by the gold-fever of 1849, and to Los Angeles, three years later, by the climate, I met on the day of my arrival. His room adjoined my brother's store, so that we soon formed an acquaintanceship which ripened, in the course of time, into a friendship that endured until the day of his death. In the early sixties, he was the proprietor of a livery stable on Main Street, opposite the Stearns home. He was very fond of hunting, being an expert at dropping a bird on the wing; and frequently went dove-shooting with his friends.

All of which, insignificant as it may at first appear, I mention for the purpose of indicating the neighborhood of these operations. The hunting-ground covered none other than that now lying between Main and Olive streets from about Sixth Street to Pico, and teeming to-day, as the reader knows, with activity and life. There sportsmen hunted, while more matter-of-fact burghers frequently went with scythes to cut grass for their horses.

Prudent Beaudry, a native of Quebec destined to make and lose several fortunes, was here when I came, having previously been a merchant in San Francisco when staple articles— such as common tacks, selling at sixteen dollars a package!— commanded enormous prices. Two or three times, however, fire obliterated all his savings, and when he reached Los Angeles, Beaudry had only about a thousand dollars' worth of goods and two or three hundred dollars in cash. With these assets he opened a small store on Main Street, opposite the Abel Stearns home; and again favored by the economic conditions of the times, he added to his capital very rapidly. From Main Street Beaudry moved to Commercial, forming partnerships successively with a man named Brown and with one Le Maître. As early as 1854, Beaudry had purchased the property at the northeast corner of Aliso Street and Nigger Alley for eleven thousand dollars, and this he so improved with the additional investment of twenty-five thousand dollars that he made his now elongated adobe bring him in an income of a thousand a month. As stated elsewhere, Beaudry went to Europe in 1855, returning later to Montreal; and it was not until 1861 or later that he came back to Los Angeles and reëngaged in business, this time in his own building where until 1865 he thrived, withdrawing, as I shall soon show, in the beginning of 1866. Beaudry Avenue recalls this early and important man of affairs.

David W. Alexander, Phineas Banning's enterprising partner in establishing wagon-trains, was here when I came and was rather an influential person. An Irishman by birth, he had come to California from Mexico by way of Salt Lake, in the early forties, and lived for awhile in the San Bernardino country. From 1844 to 1849, John Temple and he had a store at San Pedro, and still later he was associated in business with Banning, selling out his interest in 1855. In 1850, Alexander was President of the first Common Council of Los Angeles, being one of the two members who completed their term; in 1852, he visited Europe; and in September, 1855, he was elected Sheriff of the County, bringing to his aid the practical experience of a Ranger. Before keeping store, Alexander had farmed for awhile on the Rincon *rancho;* he continued to hold a large extent of acreage and in 1872 was granted a patent to over four thousand acres in the Providencia, and in 1874 to nearly seventeen thousand acres in the Tejunga *rancho.* George C. Alexander, David's brother, was Postmaster at San Pedro in 1857.

The Hazards arrived in 1853 with a large family of children, Captain A. M. Hazard having made his way with ox-teams from the East, *via* Salt Lake, on a journey which consumed nearly two years. At first they took up a claim about four miles from Los Angeles, which was later declared Government land. The eldest son, Daniel, was employed by Banning as a teamster, traveling between Los Angeles and Yuma; but later he set up in the teaming business for himself. George W. Hazard became a dealer in saddlery in Requena Street; and taking an active interest in the early history of Los Angeles, he collected, at personal sacrifice, souvenirs of the past, and this collection has become one of the few original sources available for research.[1] In 1889, Henry T. Hazard, after having served the City as its Attorney, was elected Mayor, his administration being marked by no little progress in the town's growth and expansion. Henry, who married a daughter of Dr. William Geller, and

[1] George Hazard died on February 8th, 1914.

after whom Hazard Street is named, is the only one of the brothers who survives.

Sam Meyer, who met me, as related, when I alighted from the stage, was another resident of Los Angeles prior to my coming. He had journeyed from Germany to America in 1849, had spent four years in New Orleans, Macon, and other Southern cities, and early in 1853 had come to California. On Main Street, south of Requena, I found him, with Hilliard Loewenstein, in the dry goods business, an undertaking they continued until 1856, when Loewenstein returned to Germany, to marry a sister of Meyer. Emanuel Loewenstein, one of the issue of this marriage, and a jolly, charitable fellow, is well known about town. On December 15th, 1861, Meyer married Miss Johanna,[1] daughter of S. C. and Rosalia Davis, and the same year formed a partnership with Davis in the crockery business. After two and a half years of residence in Germany, Loewenstein returned to Los Angeles. Meyer, so long identified with local freemasonry, died in 1903. A daughter married Max Loewenthal, the attorney.

Baruch Marks, one of the very few people yet living who were here when I arrived, is now about ninety-one years of age, and still[2] a resident of Los Angeles. He was with Louis Schlesinger (who lost his life when the *Ada Hancock* was destroyed) and Hyman Tischler in the general merchandise business in 1853 at Mellus's Row, the firm being known as B. Marks & Company; and having prospered, he went to Berlin. There, after the Franco-Prussian War, when much disaster befell speculators, he lost most of his means; and greatly reduced in resources, he returned to Los Angeles. Since then, however, he has never been able to retrieve his fortune. Luckily he enjoys good health, even being able at his advanced age, as he told me recently, to shave himself.

In 1851, Herman Schlesinger reached Los Angeles and engaged in the dry goods business with Tobias Sherwinsky. In 1855, Moritz Schlesinger, Herman's brother, came here and

---

[1] Mrs. Meyer died on September 4th, 1914.
[2] Marks died on July 9th, 1914.

clerked for the firm.   In 1857, Schlesinger & Sherwinsky, having made, approximately, fourteen thousand dollars, which they divided, sold out to Moritz Schlesinger and returned to Germany.   A few years later Sherwinsky lost his money and, coming back to California, located in San Diego where he died.   Schlesinger remained in Germany and died there, about 1900.

Collins Wadhams had a general store on the northeast corner of Main and Commercial streets—a piece of property afterward bought by Charlie Ducommun.   At another time, Wadhams & Foster were general merchants who, succeeding to the business of Foster & McDougal, were soon followed by Douglass, Foster & Wadhams.   Clerking for this firm when I came was William W. Jenkins, who left for Arizona, years afterward, where he led an adventurous life.

Henry G. Yarrow, often called *Cuatro Ojos* or four eyes, from the fact that he wore a pair of big spectacles on a large hooked nose, was an eccentric character of the fifties and later. He once conducted a store at the southwest corner of Los Angeles and Requena streets, and was the Jevne of his day in so far as he dealt in superior and exceptional commodities generally not found in any other store.   In other respects, however, the comparison fails; for he kept the untidiest place in town, and his stock was fearfully jumbled together, necessitating an indefinite search for every article demanded.   The store was a little low room in an adobe building about twenty feet long and ten feet wide, with another room in the rear where Yarrow cooked and slept.   He was also a mysterious person, and nobody ever saw the inside of this room.   His clothes were of the commonest material; he was polite and apparently well-bred; yet he never went anywhere for social intercourse, nor did he wish anyone to call upon him except for trade.   Aside from the barest necessities, he was never known to spend any money, and so he came to be regarded as a miser.   One morning he was found dead in his store, and for some time thereafter people dug in his backyard searching for the earnings believed to have been secreted there; but not a cent of his horde was ever found. There were all kinds of rumors, however, respecting Yarrow. One was to the effect that he was the scion of a noted English family, and that disappointment in love had soured and driven him from the world; while another report was that his past had been somewhat shady. Nobody, apparently, knew the truth; but I personally believe that Yarrow was honest, and know that when at one time, despite his efforts, he failed in business, he endeavored to settle his debts upon the most honorable basis.

Charles Hale, later associated with M. W. Childs, had a tin-shop just where Stearns's Arcadia Block now stands. This shop stood on elevated ground, making his place of business rather difficult of access; from which the reader will gain some idea of the irregular appearance of the landscape in early days. Hale in time went to Mexico, where he was reported to have made a fortune.

August Ulyard arrived with his wife on the last day of December, 1852, and rented a house near the Plaza. In competition with Joseph Lelong, who had established his Jenny Lind bakery a couple of years previous, Ulyard opened a bake-shop, making his first bread from yeast which Mrs. Ulyard had brought with her across the Plains. There had been nothing but French bread in Los Angeles up to that time, but Ulyard began to introduce both German and American bread and cake, which soon found favor with many; later he added freshly-baked crackers. After a while, he moved to the site of the Natick House, at the southwest corner of Main and First streets; and once he owned the southwest corner of Fifth and Spring streets, on which the Alexandria Hotel now stands. Having no children of their own, Ulyard and his wife adopted first one and then another, until eventually they had a family of seven!

Picturing these unpretentious stores, I recall a custom long prevalent here among the native population. Just as in Mexico a little lump of sugar called a *pilon*, or something equally insignificant, was given with even the smallest purchase, so here some trifle, called a *pilon*, was thrown in to please the buyer. And if a merchant neglected to offer such a gratuity, the customer was almost certain to ask for it.

Among the meat-handlers, there were several Sentous brothers, but those with whom I was more intimately acquainted were Jean and Louis, father of Louis Sentous the present French Consul, both of whom, if I mistake not, came about the middle of the fifties. They engaged in the sheep business; and later Louis had a packing-house of considerable importance located between Los Angeles and Santa Monica, where he also owned over a thousand acres of valuable land which he sold some time before his death. They were very successful; and Sentous Street bears their name. Jean died in 1903, and Louis a few years later.

Refúgio Botello was another wholesale cattle- and meat-dealer.

Arthur McKenzie Dodson, who came here in 1850 and later married Miss Reyes, daughter of Nasário Dominguez, conducted a butcher shop and one of the first grocery stores. He was also the first to make soap here. For a while Dodson was in partnership with John Benner who, during a quarter of a century when in business for himself, in the old Temple adobe on Main Street, built up an important trade in the handling of meat. James H. Dodson is Arthur's son.

Santiago Bollo also kept a small grocery.

"Hog" Bennett was here in the middle fifties. He raised and killed hogs, and cured the ham and bacon which he sold to neighboring dealers.

Possessed as he was of an unusual sense of rectitude, I esteemed Francisco Solano, father of Alfredo Solano, for his many good qualities. He was in the butcher business in Sonora Town, and was prosperous in the early fifties.

An odd little store was that of Madame Salandie, who came to California in 1849, on the same vessel that brought Lorenzo Leck. She had a butcher shop; but, rather curiously, she was also a money-lender.

I believe that Jack Yates was here in 1853. He owned the first general laundry, located on Los Angeles Street between

First and Requena, and conducted it with success and profit for many years, until he succumbed to the competition of the Chinese. Yates's daughter, Miss Mary D., married H. J. Woollacott, at one time a prominent financier.

More than once, in recording these fragmentary recollections, I have had occasion to refer to persons who, at one time or another, were employed in a very different manner than in a later period of their lives. The truth is that in the early days one's occupation did not weigh much in the balance, provided only that he was honorable and a good citizen; and pursuits lowly to-day were then engaged in by excellent men. Many of the vocations of standing were unknown, in fact, fifty or sixty years ago; and refined and educated gentlemen often turned their attention to what are now considered humble occupations.

CHAPTER VII

IN AND NEAR THE OLD PUEBLO

1853

ABOUT the time when I arrived, Assessor António F. Coronel reported an increase in the City and County assessment of over eight hundred and five thousand dollars, but the number of stores was really limited, and the amount of business involved was in proportion. The community was like a village; and such was the provincial character of the town that, instead of indicating the location of a store or office by a number, the advertiser more frequently used such a phrase as "opposite the Bella Union," "near the Express Office," or "*vis-à-vis* to Mr. Temple's." Nor was this of great importance: change of names and addresses were frequent in business establishments in those days—an indication, perhaps, of the restless spirit of the times.

Possibly because of this uncertainty as to headquarters, merchants were indifferent toward many advertising aids considered to-day rather essential. When I began business in Los Angeles, most of the storekeepers contented themselves with signs rudely lettered or painted on unbleached cloth, and nailed on the outside of the adobe walls of their shops. Later, their signs were on bleached cloth and secured in frames without glass. In 1865, we had a painted wooden sign; and still later, many establishments boasted of letters in gold on the glass doors and windows. So too, when I first came here, merchants wrote their own billheads and often did not take the trouble to do that; but within two or three years afterward, they began to have them printed.

People were also not as particular about keeping their places of business open all day. Proprietors would sometimes close their stores and go out for an hour or two for their meals, or to meet in a friendly game of billiards. During the monotonous days when but little business was being transacted, it was not uncommon for merchants to visit back and forth and to spend hours at a time in playing cards. To provide a substitute for a table, the window sill of the thick adobe was used, the visitor seating himself on a box or barrel on the outside, while the host within at the window would make himself equally comfortable. Without particularizing, it is safe to state that the majority of early traders indulged in such methods of killing time. During this period of miserably lighted thoroughfares, and before the arrival of many American families, those who did not play cards and billiards in the saloons met at night at each other's stores where, on an improvised table, they indulged in a little game of draw.

Artisans, too, were among the pioneers. William H. Perry, a carpenter by trade, came to Los Angeles on February 1st, 1853, bringing with him, and setting up here, the first stationary steam engine. In May, 1855, seeing an opportunity to expand, he persuaded Ira Gilchrist to form a partnership with him under the name of W. H. Perry & Company. A brief month later, however—so quickly did enterprises evolve in early Los Angeles—Perry gave up carpentering and joined James D. Brady in the furniture business. Their location was on Main Street between Arcadia and the Plaza. They continued together several years, until Wallace Woodworth—one of Tom Mott's horsemen who went out to avenge the death of Sheriff Barton —bought out Brady's interest, when the firm became Perry & Woodworth. They prospered and grew in importance, their speciality being inside cabinet-work; and on September 6th, 1861, they established a lumber yard in town, with the first regular saw- and planing-mills seen here. They then manufactured beehives, furniture and upholstery, and contracted for building and house-furnishing. In 1863, Stephen H., brother of Tom Mott, joined the firm. Perry & Woodworth were both active in politics, one being a Councilman, the other a Supervisor—the latter, a Democratic leader, going as a delegate to the convention that nominated General Winfield S. Hancock for the presidency. Their political affiliations indeed gave them an influence which, in the awarding of contracts, was sufficient to keep them supplied with large orders. Woodworth's demise occurred in 1883. Perry died on October 30th, 1906.

Nels Williamson, a native of Maine and a clever fellow, was another carpenter who was here when I arrived. He had come across the Plains from New Orleans in 1852 as one of a party of twenty. In the neighborhood of El Paso de Aguila they were all ambushed by Indians, and eighteen members of the party were killed; Williamson, and Dick Johnson, afterward a resident of Los Angeles, being the two that escaped. On a visit to Kern County, Nels was shot by a hunter who mistook him for a bear; the result of which was that he was badly crippled for life. So long as he lived—and he approached ninety years—Nels, like many old-timers, was horribly profane.

Henri Penelon, a fresco-painter, was here in 1853, and was recognized as a decorator of some merit. When the old Plaza Church was renovated, he added some ornamental touches to it. At a later period, he was a photographer as well as a painter.

Among the blacksmiths then in Los Angeles was a well-known German, John Goller, who conducted his trade in his own shop, occupying about one hundred feet on Los Angeles Street where the Los Angeles Saddlery Company is now located. Goller was an emigrant who came by way of the Salt Lake route, and who, when he set up as the pioneer blacksmith and wagon-maker, was supplied by Louis Wilhart, who had a tannery on the west side of the river, with both tools and customers. When Goller arrived, ironworkers were scarce, and he was able to command pretty much his own prices. He charged sixteen dollars for shoeing a horse and used to laugh as he told how he received nearly five hundred dollars for his part in rigging up the awning in front of a neighboring house. When, in 1851, the Court of Sessions ordered the Sheriff to see that fifty lances were made for the volunteer Rangers, Goller secured the contract. Another commission which he filled was the making for the County of a three-inch branding-iron with the letters, *L. A.* There being little iron in stock, Goller bought up old wagon-tires cast away on the plains, and converted them into various utensils, including even horse-shoes. As an early wagon-maker he had rather a discouraging experience, his first wagon remaining on his hands a good while: the natives looked upon it with inquisitive distrust and still clung to their heavy *carretas.* He had introduced, however, more modern methods, and gradually he established a good sale. Afterward he extended his field of operations, the late sixties finding him shipping wagons all over the State. His prosperity increased, and Mullaly, Porter & Ayers constructed for him one of the first brick buildings in Los Angeles. A few years later, Goller met with heavy financial reverses, losing practically all that he had.

I have stated that no care was given to either the streets or sidewalks, and a daily evidence of this was the confusion in the neighborhood of John's shop, which, together with his yard, was one of the sights of the little town because the blacksmith had strewn the footway, and even part of the road, with all kinds of piled-up material; to say nothing of a lot of horses invariably waiting there to be shod. The result was that passers-by were obliged to make a detour into the often muddy street to get around and past Goller's premises.

John Ward was an Angeleño who knew something of the transition from heavy to lighter vehicles. He was born in Virginia and took part in the Battle of New Orleans. In the thirties he went to Santa Fé, in one of the earliest prairie schooners to that point; thence he came to Los Angeles for a temporary stay, making the trip in the first carriage ever brought to the Coast from a Yankee workshop. In 1849, he returned for permanent residence; and here he died in 1859.

D. Anderson, whose daughter married Jerry Newell, a

pioneer of 1856, was a carriage-maker, having previously been in partnership with a man named Burke in the making of pack-saddles. After a while, when Anderson had a shop on Main Street, he commenced making a vehicle somewhat lighter than a road wagon and less elaborate than a carriage. With materials generally purchased from me he covered the vehicle, making it look like a hearse. A newspaper clipping evidences Anderson's activity in the middle seventies—"a little shaky on his pins, but cordial as ever."

Carriages were very scarce in California at the time of my arrival, although there were a few, Don Abel Stearns possessing the only private vehicle in Los Angeles; and transportation was almost entirely by means of saddle-horses, or the native, capacious *carretas*. These consisted of a heavy platform, four or five by eight or ten feet in size, mounted on two large, solid wheels, sawed out of logs, and were exceedingly primitive in appearance, although the owners sometimes decorated them elaborately; while the wheels moved on coarse, wooden axles, affording the traveler more jounce than restful ride. The *carretas* served, indeed, for nearly all the carrying business that was done between the *ranchos* and Los Angeles; and when in operation, the squeaking could be heard at a great distance, owing especially to the fact that the air being undisturbed by factories or noisy traffic, quiet generally prevailed. So solid were these vehicles that, in early wars, they were used for barricades and the making of temporary corrals, and also for transporting cannon.

This sharp squeaking of the *carreta*, however, while penetrating and disagreeable in the extreme, served a purpose, after all, as the signal that a buyer was approaching town; for the vehicle was likely to have on board one or even two good-sized families of women and children, and the keenest expectation of our little business world was consequently aroused, bringing merchants and clerks to the front of their stores. A couple of oxen, by means of ropes attached to their horns, pulled the *carretas*, while the men accompanied their families on horseback; and as the roving oxen were inclined to leave the road, one of the riders (wielding a long, pointed stick) was kept busy moving from side to side, prodding the wandering animals and thus holding them to the highway. Following these *carretas*, there were always from twenty-five to fifty dogs, barking and howling as if mad.

Some of the *carretas* had awnings and other tasteful trimmings, and those who could afford it spent a great deal of money on saddles and bridles. Each *caballero* was supplied with a *reata* (sometimes locally misspelled *riata*) or leathern rope, one end of which was tied around the neck of the horse while the other—coiled and tied to the saddle when not in use—was held by the horseman when he went into a house or store; for hitching posts were unknown, with the natural result that there were many runaways. When necessary, the *reata* was lowered to the level of the ground, to accommodate passers-by. Riders were always provided with one or two pistols, to say nothing of the knife which was frequently a part of the armament; and I have seen even sabers suspended from the saddles.

As I have remarked, Don Abel Stearns owned the first carriage in town; it was a strong, but rather light and graceful vehicle, with a closed top, which he had imported from Boston in 1853, to please Doña Arcadia, it was said. However that may be, it was pronounced by Don Abel's neighbors the same dismal failure, considering the work it would be called upon to perform under California conditions, as these wiseacres later estimated the product of John Goller's carriage shop to be. Speaking of Goller, reminds me that John Schumacher gave him an order to build a spring wagon with a cover, in which he might take his family riding. It was only a one-horse affair, but probably because of the springs and the top which afforded protection from both the sun and the rain, it was looked upon as a curiosity.

It is interesting to note, in passing, that John H. Jones, who was brought from Boston as a coachman by Henry Mellus— while Mrs. Jones came as a seamstress for Mrs. Mellus—and who for years drove for Abel Stearns, left a very large estate when he died, including such properties as the northeast corner of Fifth and Spring streets, the northwest corner of Main and Fifth streets (where, for several years, he resided,) and other sites of great value; and it is my recollection that his wage as coachman was the sole basis of this huge accumulation. Stearns, as I mention elsewhere, suffered for years from financial troubles; and I have always understood that during that crisis Jones rendered his former employer assistance.

Mrs. Frémont, the General's wife, also owned one of the first carriages in California. It was built to order in the East and sent around the Horn; and was constructed so that it could be fitted up as a bed, thus enabling the distinguished lady and her daughter to camp wherever night might overtake them.

Shoemakers had a hard time establishing themselves in Los Angeles in the fifties. A German shoemaker—perhaps I should say a *Schuhmachermeister!*—was said to have come and gone by the beginning of 1852; and less than a year later, Andrew Lehman, a fellow-countryman of John Behn, arrived from Baden and began to solicit trade. So much, however, did the general stores control the sale of boots and shoes at that time, that Lehman used to say it was three years before he began to make more than his expenses. Two other shoemakers, Morris and Weber, came later. Slaney Brothers, in the late sixties, opened the first shoe store here.

In connection with shoemakers and their lack of patronage, I am reminded of the different foot gear worn by nearly every man and boy in the first quarter of a century after my arrival, and the way they were handled. Then shoes were seldom used, although clumsy brogans were occasionally in demand. Boots were almost exclusively worn by the male population, those designed for boys usually being tipped with copper at the toes. A dozen pair, of different sizes, came in a case, and often a careful search was required through several boxes to find just the size needed. At such times, the dealer would fish out one pair after another, tossing them carelessly onto the floor; and as each case contained odd sizes that had proven unsalable, the none too patient and sometimes irascible merchant had to handle and rehandle the slow-moving stock. Some of the boots were highly ornamented at the top, and made a fine exhibit when displayed (by means of strings passing through the boot straps) in front of the store. Boot-jacks, now as obsolete as the boots themselves, are also an institution of that past.

Well out in the country, where the Capitol Milling Company's plant now stands, and perhaps as successor to a still earlier mill built there by an Englishman, Joseph Chapman (who married into the Ortega family—since become famous through Émile C. Ortega who, in 1898, successfully began preserving California chilis),—was a small mill, run by water, known as the Eagle Mills. This was owned at different times by Abel Stearns, Francis Mellus and J. R. Scott, and conducted, from 1855 to 1868, by John Turner, who came here for that purpose, and whose son, William, with Fred Lambourn later managed the grocery store of Lambourn & Turner on Aliso Street. The miller made poor flour indeed; though probably it was quite equal to that produced by Henry Dalton at the Azusa, John Rowland at the Puente, Michael White at San Gabriel, and the Theodore brothers at their Old Mill in Los Angeles. The quantity of wheat raised in Southern California was exceedingly small, and whenever the raw material became exhausted, Turner's supply of flour gave out, and this indispensable commodity was then procured from San Francisco. Turner, who was a large-hearted man and helpful to his fellows, died in 1878. In the seventies, the mill was sold to J. D. Deming, and by him to J. Loew, who still controls the corporation, the activity of which has grown with the city.

Half a year before my coming to Los Angeles, or in April, 1853, nearly twenty-five thousand square miles had been lopped off from Los Angeles County, to create the County of San Bernardino; and yet in that short time the Mormons, who had established themselves there in 1851 as a colony on a tract of land purchased from Diego Sepúlveda and the three Lugos—José del Carmen, José María and Vicente—and consisting of about thirty-five thousand acres, had quite

succeeded in their agricultural and other ventures. Copying
somewhat the plan of Salt Lake City, they laid out a town a
mile square, with right-angled blocks of eight acres and irrigating *zanjas* parallel with the streets. In a short time, they
were raising corn, wheat (some of it commanding five dollars
a bushel), barley and vegetables; and along their route of
travel, by way of the Mormon metropolis, were coming to the
Southland many substantial pioneers. From San Bernardino,
Los Angeles drew her supply of butter, eggs and poultry; and as
three days were ordinarily required for their transportation
across what was then known as the desert, these products
arrived in poor condition, particularly during the summer heat.
The butter would melt, and the eggs would become stale. This
disadvantage, however, was in part compensated for by the
economical advantage of the industry and thrift of the Mormons, and their favorable situation in an open, fertile country;
for they could afford to sell us their produce very reasonably—
fifteen cents a dozen for eggs, and three dollars a dozen for
chickens well satisfying them! San Bernardino also supplied
all of our wants in the lumber line. A lumber yard was then
a prospect—seven or eight years elapsing before the first
yard and planing-mill were established; and this necessary
building material was peddled around town by the Mormon
teamsters who, after disposing of all they could in this manner,
bartered the balance to storekeepers to be later put on sale
somewhere near their stores.

But two towns broke the monotony of a trip between Los
Angeles and San Bernardino, and they were San Gabriel
Mission and El Monte. I need not remind my readers that
the former place, the oldest and quaintest settlement in the
county, was founded by Father Junípero Serra and his associates in 1771, and that thence radiated all of their operations
in this neighborhood; nor that, in spite of all the sacrifice and
human effort, matters with this beautifully-situated Mission
were in a precarious condition for several decades. It may be
less known, however, that the Mission Fathers excelled in the
cultivation of citrus fruits, and that their chief competitors, in

1853, were William Wolfskill and Louis Vignes, who were also raising seedling oranges of a very good quality. The population of San Gabriel was then principally Indian and Mexican, although there were a few whites dwelling some distance away. Among these, J. S. Mallard, afterward Justice of the Peace and father of the present City Assessor, Walter Mallard, carried on a small business; and Mrs. Laura Cecelia Evertsen—mother-in-law of an old pioneer, Andrew J. King, whose wife is the talented daughter, Mrs. Laura Evertsen King—also had a store there.   Still another early storekeeper at the quaint settlement was Max Lazard, nephew of Solomon Lazard, who later went back to France.   Another pioneer to settle near the San Gabriel River was Louis Phillips, a native of Germany who reached California in 1850, by way of Louisiana, and for a while did business in a little store on the Long Wharf at San Francisco. Then he came to Los Angeles, where he engaged in trade; in 1853, he bought land on which, for ten years or until he removed to Spadra (where Mrs. Phillips still survives him), he tilled the soil and raised stock.   The previous year, Hugo Reid, of whom I often heard my neighbors speak in a complimentary way, had died at San Gabriel where he had lived and worked.   Reid was a cultured Scotchman who, though born in the British Isles, had a part, as a member of the convention, in making the first Constitution for California.   He married an Indian woman and, in his leisure hours, studied the Indians on the mainland and Catalina, contributing to the Los Angeles *Star* a series of articles on the aborigines still regarded as the valuable testimony of an eyewitness.

This Indian wife of the scholarly Reid reminds me of Nathan Tuch, who came here in 1853, having formerly lived in Cleveland where he lost his first wife.   He was thoroughly honest, very quiet and genteel, and of an affectionate disposition.   Coming to California and San Gabriel, he opened a little store; and there he soon married a full-blooded squaw. Notwithstanding, however, the difference in their stations and the fact that she was uneducated, Tuch always remained faithful to her, and treated her with every mark of respect.

When I last visited Tuch and his shop, I saw there a home-made sign, reading about as follows:

THIS STORE BELONGS TO NATHAN TUCH,
NOW 73 YEARS OLD.

When he died, his wife permitted his burial in the Jewish Cemetery.

Michael White was another pioneer, who divided his time between San Gabriel and the neighborhood that came to be known as San Bernardino, near which he had the *rancho* Muscupiabe. Although drifting hither as long ago as 1828, he died, in the late eighties, without farm, home or friends.

Cyrus Burdick was still another settler who, after leaving Iowa with his father and other relatives in December, 1853, stopped for a while at San Gabriel. Soon young Burdick went to Oregon; but, being dissatisfied, he returned to the Mission and engaged in farming. In 1855, he was elected Constable; a year later, he opened a store at San Gabriel, which he conducted for eight or nine years. Subsequently, the Burdicks lived in Los Angeles, at the corner of First and Fort streets on the site of the present Tajo Building. They also owned the northeast corner of Second and Spring streets. This property became the possession of Fred Eaton, through his marriage to Miss Helen L. Burdick.

Fielding W. Gibson came early in the fifties. He had bought at Sonora, Mexico, some five hundred and fifty head of cattle, but his *vaqueros* kept up such a regular system of side-tracking and thieving that, by the time he reached the San Gabriel Valley, he had only about one-seventh of his animals left. Fancying that neighborhood, he purchased two hundred and fifty acres of land from Henry Dalton and located west of El Monte, where he raised stock and broom corn.

El Monte—a name by some thought to refer to the adjacent mountains, but actually alluding to the dense willow forests then surrounding the hamlet—the oldest American settlement in the county, was inhabited by a party of mixed emigrants, largely Texans and including Ira W. Thompson who opened the first tavern there and was the Postmaster when its Post Office was officially designated Monte.   Others were Dr. Obed Macy and his son Oscar, of whom I speak elsewhere, Samuel M. Heath and Charlotte Gray, who became John Rowland's second wife; the party having taken possession, in the summer of 1851, of the rich farming tract along the San Gabriel River some eleven or twelve miles east of Los Angeles. The summer before I came, forty or fifty more families arrived there, and among them were A. J. King, afterward a citizen of Los Angeles; Dr. T. A. Hayes, William and Ezekiel Rubottom, Samuel King—A. J. King's father—J. A. Johnson, Jacob Weil, A. Madox, A. J. Horn, Thomas A. Garey, who acquired quite a reputation as a horticulturist, and Jonathan Tibbets, spoken of in another chapter.   While tilling the soil, these farmer folks made it their particular business to keep Whigs and, later, Republicans out of office; and slim were the chances of those parties in El Monte and vicinity, but correspondingly enthusiastic were the receptions given Democratic candidates and their followers visiting there.   Another important function that engaged these worthy people was their part in the lynchings which were necessary in Los Angeles.   As soon as they received the cue, the Monte boys galloped into town; and being by temperament and training, through frontier life, used to dealing with the rougher side of human nature, they were recognized disciplinarians.   The fact is that such was the peculiar public spirit animating these early settlers that no one could live and prosper at the Monte who was not extremely virile and ready for any dare-devil emergency.

David Lewis, a Supervisor of 1855, crossed the continent to the San Gabriel Valley in 1851, marrying there, in the following year, a daughter of the innkeeper Ira Thompson, just referred to.   Thompson was a typical Vermonter and a good, popular fellow, who long kept the Overland Stage station. Sometime in the late fifties, Lewis was a pioneer in the growing of hops. Jonathan Tibbets, who settled at El Monte the year that I came to Los Angeles, had so prospered by 1871 that he

left for the mines in Mohave County, Arizona, to inaugurate a
new enterprise, and took with him some twenty thousand
pounds of cured pork and a large quantity of lard, which had
been prepared at El Monte. Samuel M. Heath was another
El Monte pioneer of 1851; he died in 1876, kindly remembered by many poor immigrants. H. L., J. S. and S. D. Thur-
man were farmers at El Monte, who came here in 1852.
E. C. Parish, who arrived in 1854 and became a Supervisor,
was also a ranchman there. Other El Monte folks, afterward
favorably spoken of, were the Hoyts, who were identified with
early local education.

Dr. Obed Macy, father of Mrs. Sam Foy, came to Los
Angeles from the Island of Nantucket, where he was born, by
way of Indiana, in which State he had practiced medicine,
arriving in Southern California about 1850 and settling in El
Monte. He moved to Los Angeles, a year later, and bought the
Bella Union from Winston & Hodges; where were opened the
Alameda Baths, on the site of the building later erected by
his son Oscar. There Dr. Macy died on July 9th, 1857. Oscar,
a printer on the *Southern Californian*, had set type in San
Francisco, swung a miner's pick and afterward returned to El
Monte where he took up a claim which, in time, he sold to
Samuel King. Macy Street recalls this pioneer family.

The San Fernando and San Juan Capistrano missions, and
Agua Caliente, were the only other settlements in Los Angeles
County then; the former, famous by 1854 for its olives, passing
into history both through the activity of the Mission Fathers
and also the renowned set-to between Micheltorena and Castro when, after hours of cannonading and grotesque swinging
of the would-be terrifying *reata*, the total of the dead was—*a
single mule!* Then, or somewhat subsequently, General
Andrés Pico began to occupy what was the most pretentious adobe in the State, formerly the abode of the *padres*—a
building three hundred feet long, eighty feet wide and with
walls four feet thick.

In 1853, there was but one newspaper in the city—a weekly
known as *La Estrella de los Angeles* or *The Los Angeles Star*,

printed half in Spanish, half in English. It was founded on
May 17th, 1851, by John A. Lewis and John McElroy, who had
their printing office in the lower room of a small wooden house
on Los Angeles Street, near the corral of the Bella Union hotel.
This firm later became Lewis, McElroy & Rand. There was
then no telegraphic communication with the outside world,
and the news ordinarily conveyed by the sheet was anything
but important. Indeed, all such information was known, each
week, by the handful of citizens in the little town long before
the paper was published, and delays in getting mail from a distance—in one case the post from San Francisco to Los Angeles
being under way no less than fifty-two days!—led to Lewis
giving up the editorship in disgust. When a steamer arrived,
some little news found its way into the paper; but even then
matters of national and international moment became known
in Los Angeles only after the lapse of a month or so. The
admission of California to the Union in 1850, for example, was
first reported on the Coast six weeks after Congress had voted
in California's favor; while in 1852, the deaths of Clay and
Webster were not known in the West until more than a month
after they had occurred. This was a slight improvement,
however, over the conditions in 1841 when (it used to be said)
no one west of the Rockies knew of President Harrison's demise
until over three months and a half after he was buried! Our
first Los Angeles newspaper was really more of an advertising
medium than anything else, and the printing outfit was decidedly primitive, though the printers may not have been as
badly off as were the typos of the *Californian*. The latter,
using type picked up in a Mexican cloister, found no *W*'s
among the Spanish letters and had to set double *V*'s until
more type was brought from the Cannibal or Sandwich Islands!
Which reminds me of José de la Rosa, born in Los Angeles
about 1790, and the first journeyman to set type in California,
who died over one hundred years old. But if the *Estrella* made a
poor showing as a newspaper, I have no doubt that, to add to
the editor's misfortunes, the advertising rates were so low that
his entire income was but small. In 1854, the *Star* and its

imprenta, as it was then styled, were sold to a company organized by James S. Waite, who, a year later, was appointed Postmaster of the city. Speaking of the *Star*, I should add that one of its first printers was Charles Meyrs Jenkins, later City *Zanjero*, who had come to California, a mere stripling, with his stepfather, George Dalton, Sr.

The Post Office, too, at this time, was far from being an important institution. It was located in an adobe building on Los Angeles, between Commercial and Arcadia streets, and Dr. William B. Osburn, sometimes known as Osbourn—who came to California from New York in 1847, in Colonel Stevenson's regiment, and who had established a drug store, such as it was, in 1850—had just been appointed Postmaster. A man who in his time played many parts, Osburn had half a dozen other irons in the fire besides politics (including the interests of a floral nursery and an auction room), and as the Postmaster was generally away from his office, citizens desiring their mail would help themselves out of a soap box—subdivided like a pigeon house, each compartment being marked with a letter; and in this way the city's mail was distributed! Indifferent as Dr. Osburn was to the postmastership (which, of course, could not have paid enough to command anyone's exclusive services), he was rather a clever fellow and, somewhat naturally perhaps for a student of chemistry, is said to have made as early as August 9th, 1851, (and in connection with one Moses Searles, a pioneer house and sign painter) the first daguerreotype photographs produced in Los Angeles. For two years or more, Dr. Osburn remained Postmaster, resigning his office on November 1st, 1855. While he was a notary public, he had an office in Keller's Building on Los Angeles Street. J. H. Blond was another notary; he had an office opposite the Bella Union on Main Street. Osburn died in Los Angeles on July 31st, 1867.

No sooner had I arrived in San Francisco, than I became aware of the excitement incidental to the search for gold, and on reaching Los Angeles, I found symptoms of the same fever. That year, as a matter of fact, recorded the highest output of gold, something like sixty-five million dollars' worth being mined; and it was not many months before all was bustle in and about our little city, many people coming and going, and comparatively few wishing to settle, at least until they had first tried their luck with the pick and pan. Not even the discovery of gold in the San Feliciano Cañon, near Newhall, in the early forties—for I believe the claim is made that Southern Californians, while searching for wild onions, had the honor of digging out, in the despised "cow-counties," the first lump of the coveted metal—had set the natives so agog; so that while the rush to the mines claimed many who might otherwise have become permanent residents, it added but little to the prosperity of the town, and it is no wonder that, for a while, the local newspapers refused to give events the notice which they deserved. To be sure, certain merchants—among them dealers in tinware, hardware and groceries, and those who catered especially to miners, carrying such articles as gold-washers, canteens and camp-outfits—increased their trade; but many prospective gold-seekers, on their way to distant diggings, waited until they got nearer the scene of their adventures before buying tools and supplies, when they often exhausted their purses in paying the exorbitant prices which were asked. Barring the success of Francisco Garcia who used gangs of Indians and secured in the one year 1855 over sixty thousand dollars' worth of gold—one nugget being nearly two thousand dollars in value—the placer gold-mining carried on in the San Gabriel and San Francisquito *cañons* was on the whole unimportant, and what gold-dust was produced at these points came to Los Angeles without much profit to the toiling miners; so that it may be safely stated that cattle- and horse-raising, of which I shall speak in more detail, were Southern California's principal sources of income. As for the gold dust secured, San Francisco was the clearing-house for the Coast, and all of the dust ultimately found its way there until sometime later Sacramento developed and became a competitor. Coming, as I did, from a part of the world where gold dust was never seen, at least by the layman, this sudden introduction to sacks and bottles full of the fascinating yellow metal produced upon me, as the reader may imagine, another one of those strange impressions fixing so indelibly my first experiences in the new, raw and yet altogether romantic world.

CHAPTER VIII

ROUND ABOUT THE PLAZA

1853-1854

AT the time of my arrival, the Plaza, long the nucleus of the original settlement, was the center of life in the little community, and around it clustered the homes of many of those who were uppermost in the social scale, although some of the descendants of the finest Spanish families were living in other parts of the city. This was particularly so in the case of José Andrés Sepúlveda, who had a beautiful old adobe on some acreage that he owned northwest of Sonora Town, near the place where he constructed a stone reservoir to supply his house with water. Opposite the old Plaza Church dwelt a number of families of position and, for the most part, of wealth—in many cases the patrons of less fortunate or dependent ones, who lived nearby. The environment was not beautiful, a solitary pepper, somewhat north of the Plaza, being the only shade-tree there; yet the general character of the homes was somewhat aristocratic, the landscape not yet having been seriously disturbed by any utilitarian project such as that of the City Fathers who, by later granting a part of the old square for a prosaic water tank, created a greater rumpus than had the combative soldiers some years before. The Plaza was shaped much as it is at present, having been reduced considerably, but five or six years earlier, by the Mexican authorities: they had planned to improve its shape, but had finished their labors by contracting the object before them. There was no sign of a park; on the contrary, parts of the Plaza itself, which had suffered the same fate as the Plaza in San Francisco, were used as a dumping-ground for refuse. From time to time many church and other festivals were held at this square—a custom no doubt traceable to the Old World and to earlier centuries; but before any such affair could take place—requiring the erecting of booths and banks of vegetation in front of the neighboring houses—all rubbish had to be removed, even at the cost of several days' work.

Among the distinguished citizens of Los Angeles whose residences added to the social prestige of the neighborhood was Don Ygnácio Del Valle, father of R. F. Del Valle. Until 1861, he resided on the east side of the square, in a house between Calle de los Negros and Olvera Street, receiving there his intimate friends as well as those who wished to pay him their respects when he was *Alcalde*, Councilman and member of the State Legislature. In 1861, Del Valle moved to his ranch, Camulos. Ygnácio Coronel was another eminent burgher residing on the east side of the Plaza, while Cristóbal Aguilar's home faced the South.

Not far from Del Valle's—that is, back of the later site of the Pico House, between the future Sanchez Street and Calle de los Negros—lived Don Pio Pico, then and long after a striking figure, not merely on account of his fame as the last of the Mexican governors, but as well because of his physique and personality. I may add that as long as he lived, or at least until the tide of his fortune turned and he was forced to sell his most treasured personal effects, he invariably adorned himself with massive jewelry of much value; and as a further conceit, he frequently wore on his bosom Mexican decorations that had been bestowed upon him for past official services. Don Pio really preferred country life at the *Ranchito*, as his place was called; but official duties and, later, illness and the need of medical care, kept him in town for months at a time. He had three sisters, two of whom married in succession José António Carrillo, another resident at the Plaza and the then owner of the site of the future Pico House; while the third was the wife of Don Juan Forster, in whose comfortable home Don Pio found a retreat when distressing poverty overtook him in old age. Sanchez Street recalls still another don of the neighborhood, Vicente Sanchez, grandfather of Tomás A. Sanchez, who was domiciled in a two-story and rather elaborate dwelling near Carrillo, on the south side of the Plaza. Sanchez Hall stood there until the late seventies.

The Beau Brummel of Los Angeles in the early fifties was Don Vicente Lugo, whose wardrobe was made up exclusively of the fanciest patterns of Mexican type; his home, one of the few two-story houses in the pueblo, was close to Ygnácio Del Valle's. Lugo, a brother of Don José María, was one of the heavy taxpayers of his time; as late as 1860, he had herds of twenty-five hundred head of cattle, or half a thousand more than Pio and Andrés Pico together owned. María Ballestero, Lugo's mother-in-law, lived near him.

Don Agustin Olvera dwelt almost opposite Don Vicente Lugo's, on the north side of the Plaza, at the corner of the street perpetuating his name. Don Agustin arrived from Mexico, where he had been *Juez de Paz*, in 1834, or about the same time that Don Ygnácio Coronel came, and served as Captain in the campaign of Flores against Frémont, even negotiating peace with the Americans; then he joined Dr. Hope's volunteer police, and was finally chosen, at the first election in Los Angeles, Judge of the First Instance, becoming the presiding officer of the Court of Sessions. Five or six years later, he was School Commissioner. He had married Doña Concepción, one of not less than twenty-two children of Don Santiago Arguello, son of a governor of both Californias, and his residence was at the northeast end of the Plaza, in an adobe which is still standing. There, while fraternizing with the newly-arrived Americans, he used to tell how, in 1850, when the movement for the admission of California as a State was under way, he acted as secretary to a meeting called in this city to protest against the proposal, fearing lest the closer association with Northern California would lead to an undue burden of taxes upon the South. Olvera Street is often written by mistake, Olivera.

Francisco O'Campo was another man of means whose home was on the east side of the Plaza. Although he was also a member of the new *Ayuntamiento*, inaugurated in 1849, and although he had occupied other offices, he was very improvident, like so many natives of the time, and died, in consequence, a poor man. In his later years, he used to sit on the curbstone near the Plaza, a character quite forlorn, utterly dejected in appearance, and despondently recalling the by-gone days of his prosperity.

Don Cristóbal Aguilar, several times in his career an *Alcalde*, several times a City Councilman beginning with the first organization of Los Angeles, and even twice or thrice Mayor, was another resident near the Plaza. His adobe on upper Main Street was fairly spacious; and partly, perhaps, for that reason, was used by the Sisters of Charity when they instituted the first hospital in Los Angeles.

A short distance from the Plaza, on Olvera Street, had long stood the home of Don José María Ábila, who was killed in battle in the early thirties. It was there that Commodore Stockton made his headquarters, and the story of how this was brought about is one of the entertaining incidents of this warlike period. The widow Ábila, who had scant love for the Americans, had fled with her daughters to the home of Don Luis[1] Vignes, but not before she placed a native boy on guard, cautioning him against opening either doors or windows. When the young custodian, however, heard the flourishes of Stockton's brass band, he could not resist the temptation to learn what the excitement meant; so he first poked his head out of a window, and finally made off to the Plaza. Some of Stockton's staff, passing by, and seeing the tasteful furniture within, were encouraged to investigate, with the result that they selected the widow Ábila's house for Stockton's abode. Another Ábila—Francisco—had an adobe at the present southeast corner of San Fernando and Alpine streets.

Francisca Gallardo, daughter of one of the Sepúlvedas, lived in the vicinity of the Plaza.

The only church in Los Angeles at this time was that of *Nuestra Señora la Reyna de los Angeles*, known as Our Lady, the

---

[1] Often spoken of as Don Louis.

Queen of the Angels, at the Plaza; and since but few changes were made for years in its exterior, I looked upon the edifice as the original adobe built here in the eighties of the preceding century. When I came to inquire into the matter, however, I was astonished to learn that the Church dated back no farther than the year 1822, although the first attempt at laying a corner-stone was made in 1815, probably somewhat to the east of the old Plaza and a year or two after rising waters frustrated the attempt to build a chapel near the river and the present Aliso Street. Those temporary foundations seem to have marked the spot where later the so-called Woman's Gun—once buried by Mexicans, and afterward dug up by women and used at the Battle of Dominguez Ranch—was long exposed to view, propped up on wooden blocks. The venerable building I then saw, in which all communicants for want of pews knelt on the floor or stood while worshiping, is still admired by those to whom age and sacred tradition, and the sacrifices of the early Spanish Fathers, make appeal. In the first years of my residence here, the bells of this honored old pile, ringing at six in the morning and at eight in the evening, served as a curfew to regulate the daily activities of the town.

Had Edgar Allan Poe lived in early Los Angeles, he might well have added to his poem one more stanza about these old church bells, whose sweet chimes, penetrating the peace and quiet of the sleepy village, not alone summoned the devout to early mass or announced the time of vespers, but as well called many a merchant to his day's labor and dismissed him to his home or the evening's rendezvous. That was a time of sentiment and romance, and the memory of it lingers pleasantly in contrast with the rush and bustle of to-day, when cold and chronometrical exactitude, instead of a careless but, in its time, sufficient measure of the hours, arranged the order of our comings and our goings.

Incidental to the ceremonial activity of the old Church on the Plaza, the *Corpus Christi* festival was one of the events of the year when not the least imposing feature was the opening procession around the Plaza. For all these occasions, the

square was thoroughly cleaned, and notable families, such as
the Del Valles, the Olveras, the Lugos and the Picos erected
before their residences temporary altars, decorated with silks,
satins, laces and even costly jewelry. The procession would
start from the Church after the four o'clock service and
proceed around the Plaza from altar to altar. There the
boys and girls, carrying banners and flowers, and robed
or dressed in white, paused for formal worship, the progress
through the square, small as the Plaza was, thus taking
a couple of hours. Each succeeding year the procession became more resplendent and inclusive, and I have a distinct
recollection of a feature incidental to one of them when
twelve men, with twelve great burning candles, represented
the Apostles.

These midwinter festivities remind me that, on Christmas
Eve, the young people here performed pastoral plays. It was
the custom, much as it still is in Upper Bavaria, to call at the
homes of various friends and acquaintances and, after giving
little performances such as *Los Pastores*, to pass on to the next
house. A number of the Apostles and other characters associated with the life of Jesus were portrayed, and the Devil, who
scared half to death the little children of the hamlet, was never
overlooked. The *buñuelo*, or native doughnut, also added its
delight to these celebrations.

And now a word about the old Spanish Missions in this
vicinity. It was no new experience for me to see religious
edifices that had attained great age, and this feature, therefore,
made no special impression. I dare say that I visited the
Mission of San Gabriel very soon after I arrived in Los Angeles;
but it was then less than a century old, and so was important
only because it was the place of worship of many natives.
The Protestant denominations were not as numerous then as
now, and nearly all of the population was Catholic. With
the passing of the years, sentimental reverence for the Spanish Fathers has grown greater and their old Mission homes
have acquired more and more the dignity of age. Helen
Hunt Jackson's *Ramona*, John S. McGroarty's *Mission Play*

John Jones

Captain F. Morton

Captain and Mrs. J. S. Garcia

Captain Salisbury Haley

El Palacio, Home of Abel and Arcadia Stearns

From a photograph of the seventies

The Lugo Ranch-house, in the Nineties

(in which, by the by, Señorita Lucretia, daughter of R. F. and granddaughter of Don Ygnácio Del Valle, so ably portrays the character of *Doña Josefa Yorba*) and various other literary efforts have increased the interest in these institutions of the past.

The missions and their chapels recall an old Mexican woman who had her home, when I came to Los Angeles, at what is now the southeast corner of San Pedro and First streets. She dwelt in a typical adobe, and in the rear of her house was a vineyard of attractive aspect. Adjoining one of the rooms of her dwelling was a chapel, large enough, perhaps, to hold ten or twelve people and somewhat like those on the Dominguez and Coronel estates; and this chapel, like all the other rooms, had an earthen floor. In it was a gaudily-decorated altar and crucifix. The old lady was very religious and frequently repaired to her sanctuary. From the sale of grapes, she derived, in part, her income; and many a time have I bought from her the privilege of wandering through her vineyard and eating all I could of this refreshing berry. If the grape-season was not on, neighbors were none the less always welcome there; and it was in this quiet and delightful retreat that, in 1856, I proposed marriage to Miss Sarah Newmark, my future wife, such a mere girl that a few evenings later I found her at home playing jackstones—then a popular game—with Mrs. J. G. Downey, herself a child.

But while Catholics predominated, the Protestant churches had made a beginning. Rev. Adam Bland, Presiding Elder of the Methodists in Los Angeles in 1854, had come here a couple of years before, to begin his work in the good, old-fashioned way; and, having bought the barroom, El Dorado, and torn down Hughes's sign, he had transformed the place into a chapel. But, alas for human foresight, or the lack of it: on at least a part of the new church lot, the Merced Theater later stood!

Two cemeteries were in existence at the time whereof I write: the Roman Catholic—abandoned a few years ago—which occupied a site on Buena Vista Street, and one, now long deserted, for other denominations. This cemetery, which we shall see was sadly neglected, thereby occasioning bitter criticism in the press, was on Fort Hill. Later, another burial-ground was established in the neighborhood of what is now Flower and Figueroa streets, near Ninth, many years before there was any thought of Rosedale or Evergreen.

As for my co-religionists and their provision of a cemetery, when I first came to Los Angeles they were without a definite place for the interment of their dead; but in 1854 the first steps were taken to establish a Jewish cemetery here, and it was not very long before the first Jewish child to die in Los Angeles, named Mahler, was buried there. This cemetery, on land once owned and occupied by José Andrés Sepúlveda's reservoir, was beautifully located in a recess or little pocket, as it were, among the hills in the northwest section of the city, where the environment of nature was in perfect harmony with the Jewish ideal—"Home of Peace."

Mrs. Jacob Rich, by the way, had the distinction of being the first Jewess to settle in Los Angeles; and I am under the impression that Mrs. E. Greenbaum became the mother of the first Jewish child born here.

Sam Prager arrived in 1854, and after clerking a while, associated himself with the Morrises, who were just getting nicely established. For a time, they met with much success and were among the most important merchants of their day. Finally they dissolved, and the Morris Brothers bought the large tract of land which I have elsewhere described as having been refused by Newmark, Kremer & Company in liquidation of Major Henry Hancock's account. Here, for several years, in a fine old adobe lived the Morris family, dispensing a bountiful hospitality quite in keeping with the open-handed manner of the times. In the seventies, the Morris Brothers sold this property—later known as Morris Vineyard —after they had planted it to vines, for the insignificant sum of about twenty thousand dollars.

Following Sam Prager, came his brother Charles. For a short time they were associated, but afterward they operated independently, Charles Prager starting on Commercial Street, on May 19th, 1869. Sam Prager, long known as "Uncle Sam," was a good-natured and benevolent man, taking a deep interest in Masonic matters, becoming Master of 42, and a regular attendant at the annual meetings of the Grand Lodge of California. He was also Chairman of the Masonic Board of Relief until the time of his death. Charles Prager and the Morrises have all gone to that

> undiscovered country, from whose bourn
> No traveler returns.

In the summer of 1853, a movement was inaugurated, through the combined efforts of Mayors Nichols and Coronel, aided by John T. Jones, to provide public schools; and three citizens, J. Lancaster Brent, Lewis Granger and Stephen C. Foster, were appointed School Commissioners. As early as 1838, Ygnácio Coronel, assisted by his wife and daughter, had accepted some fifteen dollars a month from the authorities—to permit the exercise of official supervision—and opened a school which, as late as 1854, he conducted in his own home; thereby doubtless inspiring his son António to take marked interest in the education of the Indians. From time to time, private schools, partly subsidized from public funds, were commenced. In May, 1854, Mayor Foster pointed out that, while there were fully five hundred children of school age and the pueblo had three thousand dollars surplus, there was still no school building which the City could call its own. New trustees —Manuel Requena, Francis Mellus and W. T. B. Sanford— were elected; and then happened what, perhaps, has not occurred here since, or ever in any other California town: Foster, still Mayor, was also chosen School Superintendent. The new energy put into the movement now led the Board to build, late in 1854 or early in 1855, a two-story brick schoolhouse, known as School No. 1, on the northwest corner of Spring and Second streets, on the lot later occupied, first by the old City Hall and secondly by the Bryson Block. This structure cost six thousand dollars. Strange as it now seems, the location was then rather "out in the country;" and I dare say the selection was made, in part, to get the youngsters away from the residential district around the Plaza. There school was opened on March 19th, 1855; William A. Wallace, a botanist who had been sent here to study the flora, having charge of the boys' department and Miss Louisa Hayes directing the division for girls. Among her pupils were Sarah Newmark and her sisters; Mary Wheeler, who married William Pridham; and Lucinda Macy, afterward Mrs. Foy, who recalls participating in the first public school examination, in June, 1856. Dr. John S. Griffin, on June 7th, 1856, was elected Superintendent. Having thus established a public school, the City Council voted to discontinue all subsidies to private schools.

One of the early school-teachers was the pioneer, James F. Burns. Coming with an emigrant train in 1853, Burns arrived in Los Angeles, after some adventures with the Indians near what was later the scene of the Mountain Meadow Massacre, in November of the same year. Having been trained in Kalamazoo, Michigan, as a teacher, Burns settled, in 1854, in San Gabriel; and there with Cæsar C. Twitchell, he conducted a cross-roads school in a tent. Later, while still living at San Gabriel, Burns was elected County School Superintendent. Before reaching here — that is, at Provo, Utah, on September 25th—the young schoolmaster had married Miss Lucretia Burdick, aunt of Fred Eaton's first wife. Burns, though of small stature, became one of the fighting sheriffs of the County.

Among others who conducted schools in Los Angeles or vicinity, in the early days, were Mrs. Adam Bland, wife of the missionary; H. D. Barrows and the Hoyts. Mrs. Bland taught ten or twelve poor girls, in 1853, for which the Common Council allowed her about thirty-five dollars. Barrows was one of several teachers employed by William Wolfskill at various times, and at Wolfskill's school not merely were his own children instructed but those of the neighboring families of Carpenter, Rowland and Pleasants as well. Mrs. Gertrude Lawrence Hoyt was an Episcopal clergyman's wife from New York who, being made a widow, followed her son, Albert H.

Hoyt, to Los Angeles in 1853. Young Hoyt, a graduate of Rutgers College and a teacher excited by the gold fever, joined a hundred and twenty men who chartered the bark *Clarissa Perkins* to come around the Horn, in 1849; but failing as a miner, he began farming near Sacramento. When Mrs. Hoyt came to Los Angeles, she conducted a private school in a rented building north of the Plaza, beginning in 1854 and continuing until 1856; while her son moved south and took up seventy or eighty acres of land in the San Gabriel Valley, near El Monte. In 1855, young Hoyt came into town to assist his mother in the school; and the following year Mrs. Hoyt's daughter, Mary, journeyed West and also became a teacher here. Later, Miss Hoyt kept a school on Alameda Street near the site of the Los Angeles & San Pedro Railroad depot. Mrs. Hoyt died in Los Angeles in 1863. Other early teachers were William McKee, Mrs. Thomas Foster and Miss Anna McArthur.

As undeveloped as the pueblo was, Los Angeles boasted, in her very infancy, a number of physicians, although there were few, if any, Spanish or Mexican practitioners. In 1850, Drs. William B. Osburn, W. W. Jones, A. W. Hope, A. P. Hodges and a Dr. Overstreet were here; while in 1851, Drs. Thomas Foster, John Brinckerhoff and James P. McFarland followed, to be reënforced, in 1852, by Dr. James B. Winston and, soon after, by Drs. R. T. Hayes, T. J. White and A. B. Hayward. Dr. John Strother Griffin (General Albert Sidney Johnston's brother-in-law and the accepted suitor of Miss Louisa Hayes) came to Los Angeles in 1848, or rather to San Gabriel—where, according to Hugo Reid, no physician had settled, though the population took drugs by the barrel; being the ranking surgeon under Kearney and Stockton when, on January 8th, they drove back the Mexican forces. He was also one of the hosts to young W. T. Sherman. Not until 1854, however, after Griffin had returned to Washington and had resigned his commission, did he actually settle in Los Angeles. Thereafter, his participation in local affairs was such that, very properly, one of our avenues is named after him. Dr. Richard S. Den antedated all of these gentlemen, having resided and practiced medicine in Los Angeles in 1843, 1844 and again in the early fifties, though he did not dwell in this city permanently until January, 1866. Den I knew fairly well, and Griffin was my esteemed physician and friend. Foster and Griffin were practitioners whom I best recall as being here during my first years, one or two others, as Dr. Osburn and Dr. Winston, having already begun to devote their time to other enterprises.

Dr. Richard S. Den, an Irishman of culture and refinement, having been for awhile with his brother, Nicholas Den, in Santa Bárbara, returned to Los Angeles in 1851. I say, "returned," because Den had looked in on the little pueblo before I had even heard its name. While in the former place, in the winter of 1843–44, Den received a call from Los Angeles to perform one or two surgical operations, and here he practiced until drawn to the mines by the gold excitement. He served, in 1846–47, as Chief Physician and Surgeon of the Mexican forces during the Mexican War, and treated, among others, the famous American Consul Larkin, whose surety he became when Larkin was removed to better quarters in the home of Louis Vignes. Den had only indifferent luck as a miner, but was soon in such demand to relieve the sufferers from malaria that it is said he received as much as a thousand dollars in a day for his practice. In 1854, he returned to Santa Bárbara County, remaining there for several years and suffering great loss, on account of the drought and its effects on his cattle. Nicholas Den, who was also known in Los Angeles, and was esteemed for both his integrity and his hospitality, died at Santa Bárbara in 1862.

Old Dr. Den will be remembered, not only with esteem, but with affection. He was seldom seen except on horseback, in which fashion he visited his patients, and was, all in all, somewhat a man of mystery. He rode a magnificent coal-black charger, and was himself always dressed in black. He wore, too, a black felt hat; and beneath the hat there clustered a mass of wavy hair as white as snow. In addition to all this, his standing collar was so high that he was compelled to hold his head erect; and as if to offset the immaculate linen, he tied around the collar a large black-silk scarf. Thus attired and seated on his richly-caparisoned horse, Dr. Den appeared always dignified, and even imposing. One may therefore easily picture him a friendly rival with Don Juan Bandini at the early Spanish balls, as he was on intimate terms with Don and Doña Abel Stearns, acknowledged social leaders. Dr. Den was fond of horse-racing and had his own favorite race-horses sent here from Santa Bárbara, where they were bred.

Dr. Osburn, the Postmaster of 1853, had two years before installed a small variety of drugs on a few shelves, referred to by the complimentary term of drug store. Dr. Winston also kept a stock of drugs. About the same time, and before Dr. A. W. Hope opened the third drug store in September, 1854, John Gately Downey, an Irishman by birth, who had been apprenticed to the drug trade in Maryland and Ohio, formed a partnership with James P. McFarland, a native of Tennessee, buying some of Winston's stock. Their store was a long, one-story adobe on the northwest corner of Los Angeles and Commercial streets, and was known as McFarland & Downey's. The former had been a gold-miner; and this experience intensified the impression of an already rugged physique as a frontier type. Entering politics, as Osburn and practically every other professional man then did—doubtless as much as anything else for the assurance of some definite income—McFarland secured a seat in the Assembly in 1852, and in the Senate in 1853–54. About 1858, he returned to Tennessee and in December, 1860, revisited California; after which he settled permanently in the East. Downey, in 1859, having been elected Lieutenant-Governor, was later made Governor, through the election of Latham to the United States Senate; but his suddenly-revealed sympathies with the Secessionists, together with his advocacy of a bill for the apprenticing of Indians, contributed toward killing him politically and he retired to private life. Dr. H. R. Myles, destined to meet with a tragic death in a steamboat disaster which I shall narrate, was another druggist, with a partner, Dr. J. C. Welch, a South

Carolinian dentist who came here in the early fifties and died in August, 1869. Their drug store on Main Street, nearly opposite the Bella Union, filled the prescriptions of the city's seven or eight doctors. Considerably later, but still among the pioneer druggists, was Dr. V. Gelcich, who came here as Surgeon to the Fourth California Infantry.

Speaking of druggists, it may be interesting to add that medicines were administered in earlier days to a much greater extent than now. For every little ailment there was a pill, a powder or some other nostrum. The early *botica*, or drug store, kept only drugs and things incidental to the drug business. There was also more of home treatment than now. Every mother did more or less doctoring on her own account, and had her well-stocked medicine-chest. Castor oil, ipecac, black draught and calomel were generally among the domestic supply.

The practice of surgery was also very primitive; and he was unfortunate, indeed, who required such service. Operations had to be performed at home; there were few or none of the modern scientific appliances or devices for either rendering the patient immune or contending with active disease.

Preceded by a brother, Colonel James C. Foy—who visited California in 1850 and was killed in 1864, while in Sherman's army, by the bursting of a shell—Samuel C. Foy started for San Francisco, by way of New Orleans and the Isthmus, when he was but twenty-two years old and, allured by .the gold-fever, wasted a year or two in the mines. In January, 1854, he made his way south to Los Angeles; and seeing the prospect for trade in harness, on February 19th of that year opened an American saddlery, in which business he was joined by his brother, John M. Foy. Their store was on Main Street, between Commercial and Requena. The location was one of the best; and the Foy Brothers offering, besides saddlery, such necessities of the times as tents, enjoyed one of the first chances to sell to passing emigrants and neighboring *rancheros*, as they came into town. Some spurs, exhibited in the County Museum, are a souvenir of Foy's enterprise in those pioneer days. In May, 1856, Sam Foy began operating in cattle and continued in that business until 1865, periodically taking herds north and leaving his brother in charge of the store.

In the course of time, the Foys moved to Los Angeles Street, becoming my neighbors; and while there, in 1882, S. C. Foy, in a quaint advertisement embellished with a blanketed horse, announced his establishment as the "oldest business house in Los Angeles, still at the old stand, 17 Los Angeles Street, next to H. Newmark & Company's." John Foy, who later removed to San Bernardino, died many years ago, and Sam Foy also has long since joined the silent majority; but one of the old signs of the saddlery is still to be seen on Los Angeles Street, where the son, James Calvert Foy, conducts the business. The Foys first lived on Los Angeles Street, and then on Main. Some years later, they moved to the corner of Seventh and Pearl streets, now called Figueroa, and came to control much valuable land there, still in possession of the family. A daughter of Samuel C. Foy is Miss Mary Foy, formerly a teacher and later Public Librarian. Another daughter married Thomas Lee Woolwine, the attorney.

Wells Fargo & Company—formerly always styled Wells, Fargo & Company—were early in the field here. On March 28th, 1854, they were advertising, through H. R. Myles, their agent, that they were a joint stock company with a capital of five hundred thousand dollars!

CHAPTER IX

FAMILIAR HOME-SCENES

1854

MANY of the houses, as I have related, were clustered around and north of the Plaza Church, while the hills surrounding the pueblo to the West were almost bare. These same hills have since been subdivided and graded to accommodate the Westlake, the Wilshire, the West Temple and other sections. Main and Spring streets were laid out beyond First, but they were very sparsely settled; while to the East of Main and extending up to that street, there were many large vineyards without a single break as far south as the Ninth Street of to-day, unless we except a narrow and short lane there. To enable the reader to form an accurate impression of the time spent in getting to a nearby point, I will add that, to reach William Wolfskill's home, which was in the neighborhood of the present Arcade Depot, one was obliged to travel down to Aliso Street, thence to Alameda, and then south on Alameda to Wolfskill's orchard. From Spring Street, west and as far as the coast, there was one huge field, practically unimproved and undeveloped, the swamp lands of which were covered with tules. All of this land, from the heart of the present retail district to the city limits, belonged to the municipality. I incline to the opinion that both Ord and Hancock had already surveyed in this southwestern district; but through there, nevertheless, no single street had as yet been cut.

Not merely at the Plaza, but throughout Los Angeles, most

Jacob Rich

J. P. Newmark
From a vignette of the sixties

O. W. Childs

John O. Wheeler

Benjamin D. Wilson

George Hansen

Dr. Obed Macy

Samuel C. Foy

of the houses were built of adobe, or mud mixed with straw and
dried for months in the sun; and several fine dwellings of this
kind were constructed after I came. The composition was
of such a nature that, unless protected by roofs and verandas, [1]
the mud would slowly wash away. The walls, however, also requiring months in which to dry, were generally three or four
feet thick; and to this as well as to the nature of the material
may be attributed the fact that the houses in the summer
season were cool and comfortable, while in winter they were
warm and cheerful. They were usually rectangular in shape,
and were invariably provided with *patios* and corridors. There
was no such thing as a basement under a house, and floors were
frequently earthen. Conventionality prescribed no limit as to
the number of rooms, an adobe frequently having a sitting-
room, a dining-room, a kitchen and as many bedrooms as were
required; but there were few, if any, "frills" for the mere sake
of style. Most adobes were but one story in height, although
there were a few two-story houses; and it is my recollection that,
in such cases, the second story was reached from the outside.
Everything about an adobe was emblematic of hospitality:
the doors, heavy and often apparently home-made, were
wide, and the windows were deep. In private houses, the
doors were locked with a key; but in some of the stores, they
were fastened with a bolt fitted into iron receptacles on either
side. The windows, swinging on hinges, opened inward and
were locked in the center. There were few curtains or blinds;
wooden shutters, an inch thick, also fastening in the center,
being generally used instead. If there were such conveniences
as hearths and fireplaces, I cannot recollect them, although I
think that here and there the *brasero*, or pan and hot coals, was
still employed. There were no chimneys, and the smoke, as
from the kitchen stove, escaped through the regular stacks
leading out through a pane in the window or a hole in the wall.
The porches, also spoken of as verandas and rather wide,
were supported by equidistant perpendicular posts; and when

[1] Verandas, spoken of locally as *corridors;* from which fact I may use both
terms interchangeably.

8

an adobe had two stories, the veranda was also double-storied. Few if any vines grew around these verandas in early days, largely because of the high cost of water. For the same reason, there were almost no gardens.

The roofs which, as I have intimated, proved as necessary to preserve the adobe as to afford protection from the semi-tropical sun, were generally covered with asphalt and were usually flat in order to keep the tar from running off. As well as I can recollect, Vicente Salsido—or Salcito, as his name was also written—who lived in or somewhere near Nigger Alley, was the only man then engaged in the business of mending pitch-roofs. When winter approached and the first rainfall produced leaks, there was a general demand for Salsido's services and a great scramble among owners of buildings to obtain them. Such was the need, in fact, that more than one family, drowned out while waiting, was compelled to move to the drier quarters of relatives or friends, there to stay until the roofer could attend to their own houses. Under a huge kettle, put up in the public street, Salsido set fire to some wood, threw in his pitch and melted it. Then, after he or a helper had climbed onto the roof, the molten pitch was hauled up in buckets and poured over the troublesome leaks. Much of this tar was imported from the North, but some was obtained in this locality, particularly from so-called springs on the Hancock ranch, which for a long time have furnished great quantities of the useful, if unattractive, substance. This asphalt was later used for sidewalks, and even into the eighties was employed as fuel. To return to Salsido, I might add that in summer the pitch-roofer had no work at all.

Besides the adobes with their asphalt roofs, some houses, erected within the first quarter of the Nineteenth Century, were covered with tiles. The most notable tiled building was the old Church, whose roof was unfortunately removed when the edifice was so extensively renovated. The Carrillo home was topped with these ancient tiles, as were also José María Ábila's residence; Vicente Sanchez's two-story adobe south of the Plaza, and the Alvarado house on First Street, between Main and Los Angeles streets.

It was my impression that there were no bricks in Los Angeles when I first came, although about 1854 or 1855 Jacob Weixel had the first regular brickyard. In conversation with old-timers, however, many years ago, I was assured that Captain Jesse Hunter, whom I recall, had built a kiln not far from the later site of the Potomac Block, on Fort Street, between Second and Third; and that, as early as 1853, he had put up a brick building on the west side of Main Street, about one hundred and fifty feet south of the present site of the Bullard Block. This was for Mayor Nichols, who paid Hunter thirty dollars a thousand for the new and more attractive kind of building material. This pioneer brick building has long since disappeared. Hunter seems to have come to Los Angeles alone, and to have been followed across the plains by his wife, two sons and three daughters, taking up his permanent residence here in 1856. One of the daughters married a man named Burke, who conducted a blacksmith and wagon shop in Hunter's Building on Main Street. Hunter died in 1874. Dr. William A. Hammel, father of Sheriff William Hammel, who came to California during the gold excitement of '49, had one of the first red brick houses in Los Angeles, on San Pedro Street, between Second and Third.

Sometime in 1853, or perhaps in 1854, the first building erected by the public in Los Angeles County was put together here of brick baked in the second kiln ever fired in the city. It was the Town Jail on the site of the present Phillips Block,[1] at the northwest corner of Spring and Franklin streets. This building took the place of the first County Jail, a rude adobe that stood on the hill back of the present National Government Building. In that jail, I have understood, there were no cells, and prisoners were fastened by chains to logs outside.

Zanja water was being used for irrigation when I arrived. A system of seven or eight *zanjas*, or open ditches—originated, I have no doubt, by the Catholic Fathers—was then in operation,

[1] Recently razed.

although it was not placed under the supervision of a *Zanjero*, or Water Commissioner, until 1854. These small surface canals connected at the source with the *zanja madre*, or mother ditch, on the north side of the town, from which they received their supply; the *zanja madre* itself being fed from the river, at a point a long way from town. The *Zanjero* issued permits, for which application had to be made some days in advance, authorizing the use of the water for irrigation purposes. A certain amount was paid for the use of this water during a period of twelve hours, without any limit as to the quantity consumed, and the purchaser was permitted to draw his supply both day and night.

Water for domestic uses was a still more expensive luxury. Inhabitants living in the immediate neighborhood of *zanjas*, or near the river, helped themselves; but their less-fortunate brethren were served by a carrier, who charged fifty cents a week for one bucket a day, while he did not deliver on Sunday at all. Extra requirements were met on the same basis; and in order to avoid an interruption in the supply, prompt settlement of the charge had to be made every Saturday evening. This character was known as Bill the Waterman. He was a tall American, about thirty or thirty-five years old; he had a mustache, wore long, rubber boots coming nearly to his waist, and presented the general appearance of a laboring man; and his somewhat rickety vehicle, drawn by two superannuated horses, slowly conveyed the man and his barrel of about sixty gallons capacity from house to house. He was a wise dispenser, and quite alert to each household's needs.

Bill obtained his supply from the Los Angeles River, where at best it was none too clean, in part owing to the frequent passage of the river by man and beast. Animals of all kinds, including cattle, horses, sheep, pigs, mules and donkeys, crossed and recrossed the stream continually, so that the mud was incessantly stirred up, and the polluted product proved unpalatable and even, undoubtedly, unhealthful. To make matters worse, the river and the *zanjas* were the favorite bathing-places, all the urchins of the hamlet disporting themselves there daily, while most of the adults, also, frequently immersed themselves. Both the yet unbridged stream and the *zanjas*, therefore, were repeatedly contaminated, although common sense should have protected the former to a greater or less extent; while as to the latter there were ordinances drawn up by the Common Council of 1850 which prohibited the throwing of filth into fresh water designed for common use, and also forbade the washing of clothes on the *zanja* banks. This latter regulation was disobeyed by the native women, who continued to gather there, dip their soiled garments in the water, place them on stones and beat them with sticks, a method then popular for the extraction of dirt.

Besides Bill the Waterman, Dan Schieck was a water-vender, but at a somewhat later date. Proceeding to the *zanja* in a curious old cart, he would draw the water he needed, fresh every morning, and make daily deliveries at customers' houses for a couple of dollars a month. Schieck forsook this business, however, and went into draying, making a specialty of meeting Banning's coaches and transferring the passengers to their several destinations. He was a frugal man, and accumulated enough to buy the southwest corner of Franklin and Spring streets. As a result, he left property of considerable value. He died about twenty-five years ago; Mrs. Schieck, who was a sister of John Fröhling, died in 1874.

Just one more reference to the drinking-water of that period. When delivered to the customer, it was emptied into *ollas*, or urn-shaped vessels, made from burned clay or terra cotta. Every family and every store was provided with at least one of these containers which, being slightly porous, possessed the virtue (of particular value at a time when there was no ice) of keeping the water cool and refreshing. The *olla* commonly in use had a capacity of four or five gallons, and was usually suspended from the ceiling of a porch or other convenient place; while attached to this domestic reservoir, as a rule, was a long-handled dipper generally made from a gourd. Filters were not in use, in consequence of which fastidious people washed out their *ollas* very frequently. These wide-mouthed pots recall to me an appetizing Spanish dish, known as *olla-podrida*, a stew consisting of various spiced meats, chopped fine, and an equally varied assortment of vegetables, partaken of separately; all bringing to mind, perhaps, Thackeray's sentimental *Ballad of Bouillabaisse*. Considering these inconveniences, how surprising it is that the Common Council, in 1853, should have frowned upon Judge William G. Dryden's proposition to distribute, in pipes, all the water needed for domestic use.

On May 16th, 1854, the first Masonic lodge—then and now known as 42—received its charter, having worked under special dispensation since the preceding December. The first officers chosen were: H. P. Dorsey, Master; J. Elias, Senior Warden; Thomas Foster, Junior Warden; James R. Barton, Treasurer; Timothy Foster, Secretary; Jacob Rich, Senior Deacon; and W. A. Smith, Tyler.

For about three decades after my arrival, smallpox epidemics visited us somewhat regularly every other year, and the effect on the town was exceedingly bad. The whole population was on such a friendly footing that every death made a very great impression. The native element was always averse to vaccination and other sanitary measures; everybody objected to isolation, and disinfecting was unknown. In more than one familiar case, the surviving members of a stricken family went into the homes of their kinsmen, notwithstanding the danger of contagion. Is it any wonder, therefore, when such ignorance was universal, that the pest spread alarmingly and that the death-rate was high?

The smallpox wagon, dubbed the *Black Maria*, was a frequent sight on the streets of Los Angeles during these sieges. There was an isolated pesthouse near the Chavez Ravine, but the patients of the better class were always treated at home, where the sanitation was never good; and at best the community was seriously exposed. Consternation seized the public mind, communication with the outside world was disturbed, and these epidemics were the invariable signal for business disorder and crises.

This matter of primitive sanitation reminds me of an experience. To accommodate an old iron bath-tub that I wished to set up in my Main Street home in the late sixties, I was obliged to select one of the bedrooms; since, when my adobe was built, the idea of having a separate bathroom in a house had never occurred to any owner. I connected it with the *zanja* at the rear of my lot by means of a wooden conduit; which, although it did not join very closely, answered all purposes for the discharge of waste water. One of my children for several years slept in this combination bath- and bedroom; and although the plumbing was as old-fashioned as it well could be, yet during all that time there was no sickness in our family.

It was fortunate indeed that the adobe construction of the fifties rendered houses practically fireproof since, in the absence of a water-system, a bucket-brigade was all there was to fight a fire with, and this rendered but poor service. I remember such a brigade at work; some years after I came, in the vicinity of the Bell Block, when a chain of helpers formed a relay from the nearest *zanja* to the blazing structure. Buckets were passed briskly along, from person to person, as in the animated scene described by Schiller in the well-known lines of *Das Lied von der Glocke :*

> *Durch der Hände lange Kette*
> *Um die Wette*
> *Fliegt der Eimer;*[1]

a process which was continued until the fire had exhausted itself. Francis Mellus had a little hand-cart, but for lack of water it was generally useless. Instead of fire-bells announcing to the people that a conflagration was in progress, the discharging of pistols in rapid succession gave the alarm and was the signal for a general fusillade throughout the neighboring streets. Indeed, this method of sounding a fire-alarm was used as late

---

[1] Translated by Perry Worden for the centenary of *The Song of the Bell :*

> Through each hand close-joined and waiting,
> Emulating,
> Flies the pail.

as the eighties.   On the breaking out of fires, neighbors and
friends rushed to assist the victim in saving what they could
of his property.

On account of the inadequate facilities for extinguishing
anything like a conflagration, it transpired that insurance
companies would not for some time accept risks in Los Angeles.
If I am not mistaken, S. Lazard obtained the first protection
late in the fifties and paid a premium of four per cent.   The
policy was issued by the Hamburg-Bremen Company, through
Adelsdorfer Brothers of San Francisco, who also imported
foreign merchandise; and Lazard, thereafter, as the Los Angeles
agent for the Hamburg-Bremen Company, was the first
insurance underwriter here of whom I have any knowledge.
Adelsdorfer Brothers, it is also interesting to note, imported
the first Swedish matches brought into California, perhaps having in mind cause and effect with profit at both ends; they
put them on the retail market in Los Angeles at twenty-five
cents a package.

This matter of fires calls to mind an interesting feature of
the city when I first saw it.   When Henry, or Enrique Dalton
sailed from England, he shipped a couple of corrugated iron
buildings, taking them to South America where he used them
for several years.   On coming to Los Angeles, he brought
the buildings with him, and they were set up at the site of
the present corner of Spring and Court streets.   In a sense,
therefore, these much-transported iron structures (one of which,
in 1858, I rented as a storeroom for wool) came to be among
the earliest "fire-proof" buildings here.

As early as 1854, the need of better communication between
Los Angeles and the outside world was beginning to be felt;
and in the summer of that year the Supervisors—D. W.
Alexander, S. C. Foster, J. Sepúlveda, C. Aguilar and S. S.
Thompson—voted to spend one thousand dollars to open a
wagon road over the mountains between the San Fernando
Mission and the San Francisco *rancho*.   A rather broad trail
already existed there; but such was its grade that many a
pioneer, compelled to use a windlass or other contrivance to let

down his wagon in safety, will never forget the real perils of the descent. For years it was a familiar experience with stages, on which I sometimes traveled, to attach chains or boards to retard their downward movement; nor were passengers even then without anxiety until the hill- or mountain-side had been passed.

During 1854, Mr. and Mrs. Joseph Newmark and family, whom I had met, the year before, for a few hours in San Francisco, arrived here and located in the one-story adobe owned by John Goller and adjoining his blacksmith shop. There were six children—Matilda, Myer J., Sarah, Edward, Caroline and Harriet—all of whom had been born in New York City. With their advent, my personal environment immediately changed: they provided me with a congenial home; and as they at once began to take part in local social activities, I soon became well acquainted. My aunt took charge of my English education, and taught me to spell, read and write in that language; and I have always held her efforts in my behalf in grateful appreciation. As a matter of fact, having so early been thrown into contact with Spanish-speaking neighbors and patrons, I learned Spanish before I acquired English.

The Newmarks had left New York on December 15th, 1852, on the ship *Carrington*, T. B. French commanding, to make the trip around the Horn, San Francisco being their destination. After a voyage for the most part pleasant, although not altogether free from disagreeable features and marked by much rough weather, they reached the Golden Gate, having been four months and five days on the ocean. One of the enjoyable incidents *en route* was an old-fashioned celebration in which *Neptune* took part when they crossed the equator. In a diary of that voyage kept by Myer J. Newmark, mention is made that "our Democratic President, Franklin Pierce, and Vice-President, William R. King, were inaugurated March 4th, 1853;" which reminds me that some forty years later Judge H. A. Pierce, the President's cousin, and his wife who was of literary proclivities, came to be my neighbors in Los Angeles. Mr. and Mrs. Newmark and their family remained in San Francisco until 1854.

Joseph Newmark, formerly Neumark, born June 15th, 1799, was, I assume, the first to adopt the English form of the name. He was genuinely religious and exalted in character. His wife, Rosa, whom he married in New York in 1835, was born in London on March 17th, 1808. He came to America in 1824, spent a few years in New York, and resided for a while in Somerset, Connecticut, where, on January 21st, 1831, he joined the Masonic fraternity. During his first residence in New York, he started the Elm Street Synagogue, one of the earliest in America. In 1840, we find him in St. Louis, a pioneer indeed. Five years later he was in Dubuque, Iowa, then a frontier village. In 1846, he once more pitched his tent in New York; and during this sojourn he organized the Wooster Street Congregation. Immediately after reaching Los Angeles, he brought into existence the Los Angeles Hebrew Benevolent Society, which met for some time at his home on Sunday evenings, and which, I think, was the first charitable institution in this city. Its principal objects were to care for the sick, to pay proper respect, according to Jewish ritual, to the dead, and to look after the Jewish Cemetery which was laid out about that time; so that the Society at once became a real spiritual force and continued so for several years. The first President was Jacob Elias. Although Mr. Newmark had never served, as a salaried Rabbi, he had been ordained and was permitted to officiate; and one of the immediate results of his influence was the establishment of worship on Jewish holidays, under the auspices of the Society named. The first service was held in the rear room of an adobe owned by John Temple. Joseph Newmark also inspired the purchase of land for the Jewish Cemetery. After Rabbi Edelman came, my uncle continued on various occasions to assist him. When, in course of time, the population of Los Angeles increased, the responsibilities of the Hebrew Benevolent Society were extended. Although a Jewish organization, and none but Jews could become members of it or receive burial in the Jewish Cemetery, its aim was to give relief, as long as its financial condition would permit, to every worthy person that appeared, whoever he was or whatever his creed. Recalling this efficient organization, I may say that I believe myself to be one of but two survivors among the charter members—S. Lazard being the other.

Kiln Messer was another pioneer who came around the Horn about that time, although he arrived here from Germany a year later than I did; and during his voyage, he had a trying experience in a shipwreck off Cape Verde where, with his comrades, he had to wait a couple of months before another vessel could be signaled. Even then he could get no farther toward his destination—the Golden Gate—than Rio de Janeiro, where he was delayed five or six months more. Finally reaching San Francisco, he took to mining; but, weakened by fever (an experience common among the gold-seekers), he made his way to Los Angeles. After brewing beer for a while at the corner of Third and Main streets, Messer bought a twenty-acre vineyard which, in 1857, he increased by another purchase to forty-five or fifty acres; and it was his good fortune that this property was so located as to be needed by the Santa Fé Railroad, in 1888, as a terminal. Toward the end of the seventies, Messer, moderately well-to-do, was a grocer at the corner of Rose and First streets; and about 1885, he retired.

Joseph Newmark brought with him to Los Angeles a Chinese servant, to whom he paid one hundred dollars a month; and, as far as I know, this Mongolian was the first to come to our city. This domestic item has additional interest, perhaps, because it was but five or six years before that the first Chinese to emigrate from the Celestial Kingdom to California —two men and a lone woman—had come to San Francisco in the ship *Eagle* from Hong Kong. A year later, there were half a hundred Chinamen in the territory, while at the end of still another year, during the gold excitement, nearly a thousand Chinese entered the Golden Gate.

The housekeeping experiences of Mr. and Mrs. Joseph Newmark remind me that it was not easy in the early days to get satisfactory domestic service. Indians, negroes and sometimes Mexicans were employed, until the arrival of more Chinese and the coming of white girls. Joseph Newmark,

when I lived with his family, employed, in addition to the
Chinaman, an Indian named Pedro who had come with his
wife from Temécula and whose remuneration was fifty cents a
day; and these servants attended to most of the household
duties.   The annual *fiesta* at Temécula used to attract Pedro
and his better-half; and while they were absent, the Newmark
girls did the work.

My new home was very congenial, not the least of its attractions being the family associations at meal-time.   The opportunities for obtaining a variety of food were not as good
perhaps as they are to-day, and yet some delicacies were more
in evidence.   Among these I might mention wild game and
chickens.   Turkeys, of all poultry, were the scarcest and most-
prized.   All in all, our ordinary fare has not changed so much
except in the use of mutton, certain vegetables, ice and a
few dainties.

There was no extravagance in the furnishing of pioneer
homes.   Few people coming to Los Angeles expected to locate
permanently; they usually planned to accumulate a small com-
petency and then return to their native heaths.   In consequence, little attention was paid to quality or styles, and it is
hard to convey a comprehensive idea of the prevailing lack of
ordinary comforts.   For many years the inner walls of adobes
were whitewashed—a method of mural finish not the most
agreeable, since the coating so easily "came off;" and only in
the later periods of frame houses, did we have kalsomined and
hard-finished wall surfaces.   Just when papered and tinted
walls came in, I do not remember; but they were long delayed.
Furniture was plain and none too plentiful; and glassware
and tableware were of an inferior grade.

Certain vegetables were abundant, truck-gardening having
been introduced here in the early fifties by Andrew Briswalter, an
Alsatian by birth and an original character.   He first operated
on San Pedro Street, where he rented a tract of land and
peddled his vegetables in a wheelbarrow, charging big prices.
So quickly did he prosper that he was soon able to buy a piece
of land, as well as a horse and wagon.   When he died, in the

eighties, he bequeathed a large estate, consisting of City and County acreage and lots, in the disposition of which he unrighteously cut off his only niece. Playa del Rey was later built on some of this land. Acres of fruit trees, fronting on Main, in the neighborhood of the present Ninth and Tenth streets, and extending far in an easterly direction, formed another part of his holding. It was on this land that Briswalter lived until his last illness. He bought this tract from O. W. Childs, it having originally belonged to H. C. Cardwell, a son-in-law of William Wolfskill—the same Cardwell who introduced here, on January 7th, 1856, the heretofore unknown seedling strawberries.

One Mumus was in the field nearly as soon as Briswalter. A few years later, Chinese vegetable men came to monopolize this trade. Most of their gardens neighbored on what is now Figueroa Street, north of Pico; and then, as now, they peddled their wares from wagons. Wild celery grew in quantities around the *zanjas*, but was not much liked. Cultivated celery, on the other hand, was in demand and was brought from the North, whence we also imported most of our cabbage, cauliflower and asparagus. But after a while, the Chinese also cultivated celery; and when, in the nineties, E. A. Curtis, D. E. Smeltzer and others failed in an effort to grow celery, Curtis fell back on the Chinese gardeners. The Orientals, though pestered by envious workmen, finally made a success of the industry, helping to establish what is now a most important local agricultural activity.

These Chinese vegetable gardeners, by the way, came to practice a trick[1] designed to reduce their expenses, and at which they were sometimes caught. Having bargained with the authorities for a small quantity of water, they would cut the *zanjas*, while the *Zanjero* or his assistants slept, steal the additional water needed, and, before the arrival of the *Zanjero* at daybreak, close the openings!

[1] History repeats itself: in 1915, ranchers at Zelzah were accused of appropriating water from the new aqueduct, under cover of the night, without paying for it.

J. Wesley Potts was an early arrival, having tramped across the Plains all the way from Texas, in 1852, reaching Los Angeles in September. At first, he could obtain nothing to do but haul dirt in a hand-cart for the spasmodic patching-up of the streets; but when he had earned five or six dollars in that way, he took to peddling fruit, first carrying it around in a basket. Then he had a fruit stand. Getting the gold-fever, however, Potts went to the mines; but despairing at last of realizing anything there, he returned to Los Angeles and raised vegetables, introducing, among other things, the first locally-grown sweet potatoes put on the market—a stroke of enterprise recalling J. E. Pleasants's early venture in cultivating garden pease. Later he was widely known as a "weather prophet"—with predictions quite as likely to be worthless as to come true.

The prickly pear, the fruit of the cactus, was common in early Los Angeles. It grew in profusion all over this Southern country, but particularly so around San Gabriel at which place it was found in almost obstructing quantities; and prickly pears bordered the gardens of the Round House where they were plucked by visitors. Ugly enough things to handle, they were, nevertheless, full of juice, and proved refreshing and palatable when properly peeled. Pomegranates and quinces were also numerous, but they were not cultivated for the trade. Sycamore and oak trees were seen here and there, while the willow was evident in almost jungle profuseness, especially around river banks and along the borders of lanes. Wild mustard charmingly variegated the landscape and *chaparral* obscured many of the hills and rising ground. In winter, the ground was thickly covered with burr-clover and the poetically-named *alfilaria*.

Writing of vegetables and fruit, I naturally think of one of California's most popular products, the *sandía* or watermelon, and of its plenteousness in those more monotonous days when many and many a *carreta* load was brought to the indulging town. The melons were sold direct from the vehicles, as well as in stores, and the street seemed to be the principal place for the consumption of the luscious fruit. It was a very common sight to see Indians and others sitting along the roads, their faces buried in the green-pink depths. Some old-timers troubled with diseases of the kidney, believing that there was virtue in watermelon seeds, boiled them and used the tea medicinally.

Fish, caught at San Pedro and peddled around town, was a favorite item of food during the cooler months of the year. The *pescadero*, or vender, used a loud fish horn, whose deep but not melodious tones announced to the expectant house-wife that he was at hand with a load of sea-food. Owing to the poorer facilities for catching them, only a few varieties of deep-water fish, such as barracuda, yellowtail and rockfish were sold.

Somewhere I have seen it stated that, in 1854, O. W. Childs brought the first hive of bees from San Francisco at a cost of one hundred and fifty dollars; but as nearly as I can recollect, a man named Logan owned the first beehives and was, there-fore, the pioneer honey-producer. I remember paying him three dollars for a three-pound box of comb-honey, but I have forgotten the date of the transaction. In 1860, Cyrus Burdick purchased several swarms of bees and had no difficulty in selling the honey at one dollar a pound. By the fall of 1861, the bee industry had so expanded that Perry & Woodworth, as I have stated, devoted part of their time to the making of beehives. J. E. Pleasants, of Santiago Cañon, known also for his Cashmere goats, was another pioneer bee-man and received a gold medal for his exhibit at the New Orleans Exposition.

CHAPTER X

1854

IN June, 1854, my brother sold out, and I determined to establish myself in business and thus become my own master. My lack of knowledge of English was somewhat of a handicap; but youth and energy were in my favor, and an eager desire to succeed overcame all obstacles. Upon computing my worldly possessions, I found that I had saved nearly two hundred and forty dollars, the sum total of my eight months' wages; and this sum I invested in my first venture. My brother, J. P. Newmark, opened a credit for me, which contributed materially to my success; and I rented the store on the north side of Commercial Street, about one hundred feet west of Los Angeles, owned by Mateo Keller and just vacated by Prudent Beaudry. Little did I think, in so doing, that, twelve years later, some Nemesis would cause Beaudry to sell out to me. I fully realized the importance of succeeding in my initial effort, and this requited me for seven months of sacrifices, until January 1st, 1855, when I took an inventory and found a net profit of fifteen hundred dollars. To give some idea of what was then required to attain such success, I may say that, having no assistance at all, I was absolutely a prisoner from early morning until late in the evening —the usual hour of closing, as I have elsewhere explained, being eight o'clock. From sweeping out to keeping books, I attended to all my own work; and since I neither wished to go out and lock up nor leave my stock long unprotected, I remained

Myer J. and Harris Newmark

From a Daguerreotype

George Carson

John G. Nichols

David W. Alexander

Thomas E. Rowan

Matthew Keller

Samuel Meyer

on guard all day, giving the closest possible attention to my little store.

Business conditions in the fifties were necessarily very different from what they are to-day. There was no bank in Los Angeles for some years, although Downey and one or two others may have had some kind of a safe. People generally hoarded their cash in deep, narrow buckskin bags, hiding it behind merchandise on the shelves until the departure of a steamer for San Francisco, or turning it into such vouchers as were negotiable and could be obtained here. John Temple, who had a ranch or two in the North (from which he sent cattle to his agent in San Francisco), generally had a large reserve of cash to his credit with butchers or bankers in the Northern city, and he was thus able to issue drafts against his balances there; being glad enough to make the exchange, free of cost. When, however, Temple had exhausted his cash, the would-be remitter was compelled to send the coin itself by express. He would then take the specie to the company's agent; and the latter, in his presence, would do it up in a sealed package and charge one dollar a hundred for safe transmission. No wonder, therefore, that people found expressing coin somewhat expensive, and were more partial to the other method.

In the beginning of the fifties, too, silver was irregular in supply. Nevada's treasures still lay undiscovered within the bowels of the earth, and much foreign coin was in use here, leading the shrewdest operators to import silver money from France, Spain, Mexico and other countries. The size of coins, rather than their intrinsic value, was then the standard. For example, a five-franc piece, a Mexican dollar or a coin of similar size from any other country passed for a dollar here; while a Mexican twenty-five-cent piece, worth but fourteen cents, was accepted for an American quarter, so that these importers did a "land-office" business. Half-dollars and their equivalents were very scarce; and these coins being in great demand among gamblers, it often happened that they would absorb the supply. This forced such a premium that eighteen dollars in silver would commonly bring twenty dollars in gold.

Most of the output of the mines of Southern California—then rated as the best dust—went to San Francisco assayers, who minted it into octagonal and round pieces known as slugs. Among those issuing privately-stamped coins were. J. S. Ormsby (whose mark, *J. S. O.*, became familiar) and Augustus Humbert, both of whom circulated eight-cornered ingots; and Wass Molitor & Co., whose slugs were always round. Pieces of the value of from one to twenty-five dollars, and even miniature coins for fractional parts of a dollar, were also minted; while F. D. Kohler, the State Assayer, made an oblong ingot worth about fifty dollars. Some of the other important assaying concerns were Moffatt & Co., Kellogg & Co. and Templeton Reid. Baldwin & Co. was another firm which issued coins of smaller denomination; and to this firm belonged David Colbert Broderick, who was killed by Terry.

Usurers were here from the beginning, and their tax was often ruinously exorbitant. So much did they charge for money, in fact, that from two to twelve and a half per cent. *a week* was paid; this brought about the loss of many early estates. I recollect, for example, that the owner of several thousand acres of land borrowed two hundred dollars, at an interest charge of twelve and a half per cent. for each week, from a resident of Los Angeles whose family is still prominent in California; and that when principal and interest amounted to twenty-two thousand dollars, the lender foreclosed and thus ingloriously came into possession of a magnificent property.

For at least twenty years after I arrived in Los Angeles, the credit system was so irregular as to be no system at all. Land and other values were exceedingly low, there was not much ready money, and while the credit of a large rancher was small compared with what his rating would be to-day because of the tremendous advances in land and stock, much longer time was then given on running accounts than would be allowed now. Bills were generally settled after the harvest. The wine-grower would pay his score when the grape crop was sold; and the cattleman would liquidate what he could when he sold his cattle. In other words, there was no credit foundation whatever; indeed, I have known accounts to be carried through three and four dry seasons.

It is true, also, that many a fine property was lost through the mania of the Californian for gambling, and it might be just as well to add that the loose credit system ruined many. I believe, in fact, it is generally recognized in certain lines of business that the too flexible local fiscal practice of to-day is the descendant of the careless methods of the past.

My early experiences as a merchant afforded me a good opportunity to observe the character and peculiarities of the people with whom I had to deal. In those days a disposition to steal was a common weakness on the part of many, especially Indians, and merchants generally suffered so much from the evil that a sharp lookout had to be kept. On one occasion, I saw a native woman deftly abstract a pair of shoes and cleverly secrete them on her person; and at the conclusion of her purchases, as she was about to leave the store, I stepped up to her, and with a "¡Dispense me Vd.!" quietly recovered the zapatos. The woman smiled, each of us bowed, the pilfering patron departed, and nothing further was ever said of the affair.

This proneness to steal was frequently utilized by early and astute traders, who kept on hand a stock of very cheap but gaudy jewelry which was placed on the counter within easy reach—a device which prevented the filching of more valuable articles, while it attracted, at the same time, this class of customers; and as soon as the esteemed customers ceased to buy, the trays of tempting trinkets were removed.

Shyness of the truth was another characteristic of many a native that often had to be reckoned with by merchants wishing to accommodate, as far as possible, while avoiding loss. One day in 1854, a middle-aged Indian related to me that his mother (who was living half a block north on Main Street, and was between eighty and ninety years of age) had suddenly died, and that he would like some candles, for which he was unable to pay, to place around the bed holding the remains of the departed. I could not refuse this filial request, and straightway gave him the wax tapers which were to be used for so holy a purpose. The following day, however, I met the old woman on the street and she was as lively a corpse as one might ever expect to see; leaving me to conclude that she was lighted to her room, the previous night, by one of the very candles supposed to be then lighting her to eternity.

The fact that I used to order straw hats which came telescoped in dozens and were of the same pattern (in the crown of one of which, at the top, I found one morning a litter of kittens tenderly deposited there by the store cat), recalls an amusing incident showing the modesty of the times, at least in the style of ladies' bonnets. S. Lazard & Company once made an importation of Leghorn hats which, when they arrived, were found to be all trimmed alike—a bit of ribbon and a little bunch of artificial flowers in front being their only ornamentation! Practically, all the fair damsels and matrons of the town were limited, for the season, to this supply—a fact that was patent enough, a few days later, at a picnic held at Sainsevain's favorite vineyard and well patronized by the feminine leaders in our little world.

But to return to one or two pioneers. David Workman died soon after he came here, in 1854, with his wife whose maiden name was Nancy Hook. He was a brother of William Workman and followed him to Los Angeles, bringing his three sons, Thomas H.—killed in the explosion of the *Ada Hancock*—Elijah H. and William H., who was for a while a printer and later in partnership with his brother in the saddlery business. Elijah once owned a tract of land stretching from what is now Main to Hill streets and around Twelfth. Workman Street is named after this family.

Henry Mellus, brother of Francis Mellus, to whom I elsewhere more fully refer, who had returned to New England, was among us again in 1854. Whether this was the occasion of Mellus's unfortunate investment, or not, I cannot say; but on one of his trips to the East, he lost a quarter of a million through an unlucky investment in iron.

Jean B. Trudell (a nephew of Damien Marchessault and a cousin of P. Beaudry), for a short time in partnership with

S. Lazard, was an old-timer who married Anita, the widow of Henry Mellus; and through this union a large family resulted. He conducted salt works, from which he supplied the town with all grades of cheap salt; and he stood well in the community. Mrs. Trudell took care of her aunt, Mrs. Bell, during her later years.

With the growth of our little town, newspapers increased, even though they did not exactly prosper. On the 20th of July, 1854, C. N. Richards & Company started the *Southern Californian*, a name no doubt suggested by that of the San Francisco journal, with William Butts as editor; and on November 2d, Colonel John O. Wheeler joined Butts and bought out Richards & Company. Their paper was printed in one of Dalton's corrugated iron houses. The *Southern Californian* was a four-page weekly, on one side of which news, editorials and advertisements, often mere translations of matter in the other columns, were published in Spanish. One result of the appearance of this paper was that Waite & Company, a month or so later, reduced the subscription price of the *Star*—their new rate being nine dollars a year, or six dollars in advance.

In 1853, a number of Spanish-American restaurant keepers plied their vocation, so that Mexican and Spanish cooking were always obtainable. Then came the *cafetería*, but the term was used with a different significance from that now in vogue. It was rather a place for drinking than for eating, and in this respect the name had little of the meaning current in parts of Mexico to-day, where a *cafetería* is a small restaurant serving ordinary alcoholic drinks and plain meals. Nor was the institution the same as that familiarly known in Pacific Coast towns, and particularly in Los Angeles—one of the first American cities to experiment with this departure; where a considerable variety of food (mostly cooked and warm) is displayed to view, and the prospective diner, having secured his tray and napkin, knife, fork and spoons, indicates his choice as he passes by the steam-heated tables and is helped to whatever he selects, and then carries both service and viands to a small table.

The native population followed their own *cuisine*, and the

visitor to Spanish-American homes naturally partook of native food. All the Mexican dishes that are common now, such as *tamales*, *enchiladas* and *frijoles*, were favorite dishes then. There were many saloons in Sonora Town and elsewhere, and *mescal* and *aguardiente*, popular drinks with the Mexicans, were also indulged in by the first white settlers. Although there were imported wines, the wine-drinkers generally patronized the local product. This was a very cheap article, costing about fifteen cents a gallon, and was usually supplied with meals, without extra charge. *Tamales* in particular were very popular with the Californians, but it took some time for the incoming epicure to appreciate all that was claimed for them and other masterpieces of Mexican cooking.

The *tortilla* was another favorite, being a generous-sized maize cake, round and rather thin, in the early preparation of which the grain was softened, cleaned and parboiled, after which it was rolled and crushed between two pieces of flat stone. Deft hands then worked the product into a pancake, which was placed, sometimes on a piece of stoneware, sometimes on a plate of iron, and baked, first on one side and then on the other. A part of the trick in *tortilla*-baking consisted in its delicate toasting; and when just the right degree of parching had been reached, the crisp, tasty *tortilla* was ready to maintain its position even against more pretentious members of the pan-cake family.

Pan de huevos, or bread of eggs, was peddled around town on little trays by Mexican women and, when well-prepared, was very palatable. *Panocha*, a dark Mexican sugar made into cakes, was also vended by native women. *Pinole* was brought in by Indians; and as far as I can remember, it could not have had a very exact meaning, since I have heard the term applied both to ground pinenuts and ground corn, and it may also have been used to mean other food prepared in the same manner. Be this as it may, the value to the Indian came from the fact that, when mixed with water, *pinole* proved a cheap, but nutritious article of diet.

I have told of the old-fashioned, comfortable adobes, broad

and liberal, whose halls, rooms, verandas and *patios* bespoke
at least comfort if not elaborateness. Among the old California families dwelling within these houses, there was much
visiting and entertainment, and I often partook of this proverbial and princely hospitality. There was also much merry-
making, the firing of crackers, bell-ringing and dancing the
fandango, jota and *cachucha* marking their jolly and whole-
souled *fiestas.* Only for the first few years after I came was the
real *fandango*—so popular when Dana visited Los Angeles
and first saw Don Juan Bandini execute the dance—witnessed
here; little by little it went out of fashion, perhaps in part
because of the skill required for its performance. Balls and
hops, however, for a long time were carelessly called by that
name. When the *fandango* really was in vogue, Bandini, António
Coronel, Andrés Pico, the Lugos and other native Californians
were among its most noted exponents; they often hired a hall,
gave a *fandango* in which they did not hesitate to take the leading parts, and turned the whole proceeds over to some church or
charity. On such occasions not merely the plain people
(always so responsive to music and its accompanying pleasures)
were the *fandangueros*, but the flower of our local society turned
out *en masse*, adding to the affair a high degree of *éclat.* There
was no end, too, of good things to eat and drink, which people
managed somehow to pass around; and the enjoyment was
not lessened by the fact that every such dance hall was crowded
to the walls, and that the atmosphere, relieved by but a narrow
door and window or two, was literally thick with both dust and
smoke.

Still living are some who have memories of these old *fandango* days and the journeys taken from suburb to town in
order to participate in them. Doña Petra Pilar Lanfranco used
to tell me how, as a young girl, she came up from the old Palos
Verdes ranch house in a *carreta* and was always chaperoned
by a lady relative. On such occasions, the *carreta* would be
provided with mattresses, pillows and covers, while at the
end, well strapped, was the trunk containing the finery to be
worn at the ball. To reach town even from a point that would

now be regarded as near, a start was generally made by four o'clock in the morning; and it often took until late the same evening to arrive at the Bella Union, where final preparations were made.

One of the pleasant features of a *fandango* or hop was the use of *cascarones*, or egg-shells, filled with one thing or another, agreeable when scattered, and for the time being sealed up. These shells were generally painted; and most often they contained many-colored pieces of paper, or the tinsel, *oropel*, cut up very fine. Not infrequently the shell of the egg was filled with perfume; and in the days when Californians were flush, gold leaf or even gold dust was sometimes thus inclosed, with a wafer, and kept for the *casamiento*, when it would be showered upon the fortunate bride. The greatest compliment that a gentleman could pay a lady was to break one of these *cascarones* over her head, and often the compliment would be returned; the floor, at the termination of such festivities, being literally covered with the bits of paper and egg-shell. When the *fandango* was on in all its mad delight, a gentleman would approach a lady to salute her, upon which she would bow her head slightly and permit him, while he gently squeezed the egg-shell, to let its contents fall gracefully over her head, neck and shoulders; and very often she would cleverly choose the right moment—perhaps when he was not looking—to politely reciprocate the courtesy, under which circumstances he was in duty bound to detect, if he could, among the smiling, blushing ladies, the one who had ventured so agreeably to offend. Such was the courtliness, in fact, among the native population that even at *fandangos*, in which the public participated and the compliment of the *cascarón* was almost universally observed, there was seldom a violation of regard for another's feelings. When such rowdyism did occur, however (prompted perhaps by jealousy), and bad eggs or that which was even less aromatic, were substituted, serious trouble ensued; and one or two fatalities are on record as growing out of such senseless acts. Speaking of *fandangos*, it may be aded that in January, 1861, the Common Council of

Los Angeles passed an ordinance requiring the payment in advance of ten dollars for a one-night license to hold any public dance within the city limits.

The pueblo was so small in the fifties, and the number of white people so limited that, whenever a newcomer arrived, it caused considerable general excitement; and when it infrequently happened that persons of note came for even a single night, a deputation of prominent citizens made their short stay both noisy with cannonading and tiresome with spread-eagle oratory.

A very important individual in early days was Peter Biggs, or Nigger Pete, a pioneer barber who came here in 1852, having previously been sold as a slave to an officer at Fort Leavenworth and freed, in California, at the close of the Mexican War. He was a black-haired, good-natured man, then about forty years of age, and had a shop on Main Street, near the Bella Union. He was, indeed, the only barber in town who catered to Americans, and while by no means of the highest tonsorial capacity, was sufficiently appreciative of his monopoly to charge fifty cents for shaving and seventy-five cents for haircutting. When, however, a Frenchman named Felix Signoret (whose daughter married Ed. McGinnis, the high-toned saloon keeper) appeared, some years later—a barber by trade, of whom we shall hear more later—it was not long before Pete was seriously embarrassed, being compelled, first to reduce his prices and then to look for more humble work. In the early sixties, Pete was advertising as follows:

NEW ORLEANS SHAVING SALOON
OPPOSITE MELLUS' STORE ON MAIN STREET.

PRICES REDUCED!
To Keep Pace with the Times
Shaving   12½c.
Hair-cutting   25c.
Shampooing   25c.

Peter Biggs will always be on hand and ready to attend to all business in his line, such as cleaning and polishing the "understanding" together with an Intelligence Office and City Express. Also washing and ironing done with all neatness and despatch, at reasonable rates.

Recalling Biggs and his barber shop, I may say that, in fitting up his place, he made little or no pretension. He had an old-fashioned, high-backed chair, but otherwise operated much as barbers do to-day. People sat around waiting their turn; and as Biggs called "Next!" he sprinkled the last victim with Florida water, applying to the hair at the same time his *Bear Oil* (sure to leave its mark on walls and pillows), after which, with a soiled towel he put on the finishing touch—for one towel in those days served many customers. But few patrons had their private cups. Biggs served only men and boys, as ladies dressed their own hair. To some extent, Biggs was a maker or, at least, a purveyor of wigs.

Besides Peter Biggs, a number of colored people lived in Los Angeles at an early date—five of whom belonged to the Mexican Veterans—Bob Owens and his wife being among the most prominent. Owens—who came here from Texas in December, 1853—was known to his friends as Uncle Bob, while Mrs. Owens was called Aunt Winnie. The former at first did all kinds of odd jobs, later profiting through dealings with the Government; while his good wife washed clothes, in which capacity she worked from time to time for my family. They lived in San Pedro Street, and invested their savings in a lot extending from Spring to Fort streets, between Third and Fourth. Owens died in 1865. Their heirs are wealthy as a result of this investment; in fact, I should not be surprised if they are among the most prosperous negroes in America.

Another colored man of the sixties was named Berry, though he was popularly known as Uncle George. He was indeed a local character, a kind of popinjay; and when not busy with janitor or other all-around scrubwork, sported among the negroes as an ultra-fashionable.

Elsewhere I have spoken of the versatility of Dr. William B. Osburn, who showed no little commendable enterprise.

In October, 1854, he shipped to an agricultural convention in Albany, New York, the first Los Angeles grapes ever sent to the East; and the next year he imported roses, shrubbery and fruit trees from Rochester.

On October 13th, 1854, a good-for-nothing gambler, Dave Brown—who had planned to rob John Temple on one of his business trips, but was thwarted because Temple changed his route—murdered a companion, Pinckney Clifford, in a livery stable at what was later to become the corner of Main and Court streets; and next day the lawless act created such general indignation that vengeance on Brown would undoubtedly then and there have been wreaked had not Stephen C. Foster, who was Mayor, met the crowd of citizens and persuaded them quietly to disperse. In order to mollify the would-be Vigilantes, Foster promised that, if the case miscarried in the courts and Brown was not given his due, he would resign his office and would himself lead those who favored taking the law into their own hands; and as Foster had been a Lieutenant in the Rangers under Dr. Hope, showing himself to be a man of nerve, the crowd had confidence in him and went its way.

On November 30th, Brown was tried in the District Court, and Judge Benjamin Hayes sentenced him to hang on January 12th, 1855—the same date on which Felipe Alvitre, a half-breed Indian, was to pay the penalty for killing James Ellington at El Monte. Brown's counsel were J. R. Scott, Cameron E. Thom and J. A. Watson; and these attorneys worked so hard and so effectively for their client that on January 10th, or two days before the date set for the execution, Judge Murray of the Supreme Court granted Brown a stay, although apparently no relief was provided for Alvitre. The latter was hanged in the calaboose or jail yard, in the presence of a vast number of people, at the time appointed. Alvitre having been strung up by Sheriff Barton and his assistants, the rope broke, letting the wretch fall to the ground, more dead than alive. This bungling so infuriated the crowd that cries of *"Arriba! Arriba!"* (Up with him! up with him!) rent the air. The executioners sprang forward, lifted the body, knotted the rope together and once more drew aloft the writhing form.   Then the gallows was dismantled and the guards dismissed.

The news that one execution had taken place, while the Court, in the other case, had interfered, was speedily known by the crowds in the streets and proved too much for the patience of the populace; and only a leader or two were required to focus the indignation of the masses.   That leader appeared in Foster who, true to his word, resigned from the office of Mayor and put himself at the head of the mob.   Appeals, evoking loud applause, were made by one speaker after another, each in turn being lifted to the top of a barrel; and then the crowd began to surge toward the jail.   Poles and crowbars were brought, and a blacksmith called for; and the prison doors, which had been locked, bolted and barred, were broken in, very soon convincing the Sheriff and his assistants— if any such conviction were needed—that it was useless to resist.   In a few minutes, Brown was reached, dragged out and across Spring Street, and there hanged to the cross-beam of a corral gateway opposite the old jail, the noose being drawn tight while he was still attempting to address the crowd.

When Brown was about to be disposed of, he was asked if he had anything to say; to which he replied that he had no objection to paying the penalty of his crime, but that he did take exception to a "lot of *Greasers*" shuffling him off!   Brown referred to the fact that Mexicans especially were conspicuous among those who had hold of the rope; and his coarsely-expressed objection striking a humorous vein among the auditors, the order was given to indulge his fancy and accommodate him —whereupon, Americans strung him up!   One of those who had previously volunteered to act as hangman for Brown was Juan Gonzales; but within four months, that is, in May, 1855, Gonzales himself was sent to the penitentiary by Judge Myron Norton, convicted of horse-stealing.

A rather amusing feature of this hanging was the manner in which the report of it was served up to the public.   The lynching-bee seemed likely to come off about three o'clock in the after-

noon, while the steamer for San Francisco was to leave at ten
o'clock on the same morning; so that the schedules did not
agree.   A closer connection was undoubtedly possible—at least
so thought Billy Workman, then a typo on the *Southern Californian*, who planned to print a full account of the execution
in time to reach the steamer. So Billy sat down and wrote
out every detail, even to the confession of the murderer on the
improvised gallows; and several hours before the tragic event
actually took place, the wet news-sheet was aboard the vessel
and on its way north. A few surplus copies gave the lynchers the unique opportunity, while watching the stringing-
up, of comparing the written story with the affair as it actually
occurred.

While upon the subject of lynching, I wish to observe that
I have witnessed many such distressing affairs in Los Angeles;
and that, though the penalty of hanging was sometimes too
severe for the crime (and I have always deplored, as much as
any of us ever did, the administration of mob-justice) yet the
safety of the better classes in those troublous times often demanded quick and determined action, and stern necessity knew
no law.   And what is more, others besides myself who have also
repeatedly faced dangers no longer common, agree with me in
declaring, after half a century of observation and reflection,
that milder courses than those of the vigilance committees of
our young community could hardly have been followed with
wisdom and safety.

Wood was the only regular fuel for many years, and people
were accustomed to buy it in quantities and to pile it carefully in their yards.   When it was more or less of a drug on the
market, I paid as little as three dollars and a half a cord; in
winter I had to pay more, but the price was never high. No tree
was spared, and I have known magnificent oaks to be wanton-
ly felled and used for fuel.   Valuable timber was often destroyed
by squatters guilty of a form of trespassing that gave much
trouble, as I can testify from my own experience.

Henry Dwight Barrows, who had been educated as a Yankee schoolmaster, arrived in Los Angeles in December, 1854, as

private tutor to William Wolfskill. Other parts of Barrows's career were common to many pioneers: he was in business for a while in New York, caught the gold-fever, gave up everything to make the journey across the Isthmus of Panamá, on which trip he was herded as one of seventeen hundred passengers on a rickety Coast vessel; and finally, after some unsuccessful experiences as a miner in Northern California, he made his way to the Southland to accept the proffered tutorship, hoping to be cured of the malarial fever which he had contracted during his adventures. Barrows taught here three years, returned East by steamer for a brief trip in 1857, and in 1859–60 tried his hand at cultivating grapes, in a vineyard owned by Prudent Beaudry. On November 14th, 1860, Barrows was married to Wolfskill's daughter, Señorita Juana; and later he was County School Superintendent. In 1861, President Lincoln appointed Barrows United States Marshal, the duties of which office he performed for four years. In 1864, having lost his wife he married the widow (formerly Miss Alice Woodworth) of Thomas Workman. The same year he formed a partnership with J. D. Hicks, under the firm name of J. D. Hicks & Company, and sold tin and hardware for twelve or fifteen years. In 1868, bereaved of his second wife, Barrows married Miss Bessie Ann Greene, a native of New York. That year, too, he was joined by his brother, James Arnold Barrows,[1] who came by way of Panamá and bought thirty-five acres of land afterward obtained by the University of Southern California. About 1874, Barrows was manufacturing pipe. For years he dwelt with his daughter, Mrs. R. G. Weyse, contributing now and then to the activities of the Historical Society, and taking a keen interest[2] in Los Angeles affairs.

About 1854 or 1855, I. M., Samuel and Herman (who must not be confused with H. W.) Hellman, arrived here, I. M. preceding his brothers by a short period. In time, I. M. Hellman, in San Francisco, married Miss Caroline Adler; and in 1862 her sister, Miss Adelaide, came south on a visit and married

[1] Died, June 9th, 1914.
[2] Died, August 7th, 1914.

Samuel Hellman. One of the children of this union is Maurice
S. Hellman, who, for many years associated with Joseph F.
Sartori, has occupied an important position in banking and
financial circles.

In 1854 or 1855, Bishop & Beale, a firm consisting of Samuel
A. Bishop and E. F. Beale, became owners of an immense tract
of Kern County land consisting of between two and three·
hundred thousand acres. This vast territory was given to
them in payment for the work which they had done in surveying
the Butterfield Route, later incorporated in the stage road
connecting San Francisco with St. Louis. Recently I read an
account of Beale's having been an Indian Agent at the Reservation; but if he was, I have forgotten it. I remember Colonel
James F. Vineyard, an Indian Agent and later Senator from
Los Angeles; one of whose daughters was married, in 1862,
to Congressman Charles De Long, of Nevada City, afterward United States Minister to Japan, and another daughter
to Dr. Hayes, of Los Angeles.

Bishop, after a while, sold out his interest in the land
and moved to San José, where he engaged in street-car operations. He was married near San Gabriel to Miss Frances Young,
and I officiated as one of the groomsmen at the wedding. After
Bishop disposed of his share, Colonel R. S. Baker became
interested, but whether or not he bought Bishop's interest at
once, is not clear in my memory. It is worth noting that
Bakersfield, which was part of this great ranch, took its name
from Colonel Baker. Some time later, Baker sold out to Beale
and then came South and purchased the San Vicente Ranch.
This *rancho* comprised the whole Santa Monica district
and consisted of thirty thousand acres, which Baker stocked
with sheep. On a part of this land, the Soldiers' Home now
stands.

Hilliard P. Dorsey, another typical Western character,
was Register of the Land Office and a leading Mason of early
days. He lived in Los Angeles in 1853, and I met him on the
Goliah in October of that year, on the way south, after a brief
visit to San Francisco, and while I was bound for my new

home. We saw each other frequently after my arrival here; and I was soon on good terms with him. When I embarked in business on my own account, therefore, I solicited Dorsey's patronage.

One day, Dorsey bought a suit of clothes from me on credit. A couple of months passed by, however, without any indication on his part that he intended to pay; and as the sum involved meant much to me at that time, I was on the lookout for my somewhat careless debtor. In due season, catching sight of him on the other side of the street, I approached, in genuine American fashion, and unceremoniously asked him to liquidate his account. I had not then heard of the notches in Friend Dorsey's pistol, and was so unconscious of danger that my temerity seemed to impress him. I believe, in fact, that he must have found the experience novel. However that may be, the next day he called and paid his bill.

In relating this circumstance to friends, I was enlightened as to Dorsey's peculiar propensities and convinced that youth and ignorance alone had saved me from disaster. In other words, he let me go, as it were, on probation. Dorsey himself was killed sometime later by his father-in-law, William Rubottom, who had come to El Monte with Ezekiel Rubottom, in 1852 or 1853. After quarreling with Rubottom, Dorsey, who was not a bad fellow, but of a fiery temper, had entered the yard with a knife in his hand; and Rubottom had threatened to shoot him if he came any nearer. The son-in-law continued to advance; and Rubottom shot him dead. M. J. Newmark, Rubottom's attorney, who had been summoned to El Monte for consultation as to Dorsey's treatment of Rubottom's daughter, was present at the fatal moment and witnessed the shooting affray.

Uncle Billy Rubottom, as he was familiarly called, came to Los Angeles County after losing heavily through the bursting of Yuba Dam and was one of the founders of Spadra. He named the settlement, laid out on a part of the San José *rancho*, after his home town, Spadra Bluffs in Arkansas, and opened a hotel which he made locally famous, during a decade and a half, for barbecues and similar events, giving personal attention (usually while in shirt-sleeves) to his many guests.   In his declining years, Uncle Billy lived with Kewen H. Dorsey, his grandson, who was also prominent in masonic circles.

CHAPTER XI

AS I have already related, I made fifteen hundred dollars in a few months, and in January, 1855, my brother advised me to form a partnership with men of maturer years. In this I acquiesced. He thereupon helped to organize the firm of Rich, Newmark & Company, consisting of Elias Laventhal (who reached here in 1854 and died on January 20th, 1902), Jacob Rich and myself. Rich was to be the San Francisco resident partner, while Laventhal and I undertook the management of the business in Los Angeles. We prospered from the beginning, deriving much benefit from our San Francisco representation which resulted in our building up something of a wholesale business.

In the early fifties, Los Angeles was the meeting-place of a Board of Land Commissioners appointed by the National Government to settle land-claims and to prepare the way for that granting of patents to owners of Southern California ranches which later awakened from time to time such interest here. This interest was largely due to the fact that the Mexican authorities, in numerous instances, had made the same grant to different persons, often confusing matters badly. Cameron E. Thom, then Deputy Land Agent, took testimony for the Commissioners. In 1855, this Board completed its labors. The members were Hiland Hall (later Governor of Vermont,) Harry I. Thornton and Thompson Campbell; and during the season they were here, these Land

Commissioners formed no unimportant part of the Los Angeles legal world.

Thomas A. Delano, whose name is perpetuated in our local geography, was a sailor who came to Los Angeles on January 4th, 1855, after which, for fifteen or sixteen years, he engaged in freighting. He married Señorita Soledad, daughter of John C. Vejar, the well-known Spanish Californian.

Slowness and uncertainty of mail delivery in our first decades affected often vital interests, as is shown in the case of the half-breed Alvitre who, as I have said, was sentenced to be executed. One reason why the Vigilantes, headed by Mayor Foster, despatched Brown was the expectation that both he and Alvitre would get a stay from higher authority; and sure enough, a stay was granted Alvitre, but the document was delayed in transit until the murderer, on January 12th, 1855, had forfeited his life! Curiously enough, another Alvitre—an aged Californian named José Claudio—also of El Monte, but six years later atrociously murdered his aged wife; and on April 28th, 1861, he was hanged. The lynchers placed him on a horse under a tree, and then drove the animal away, leaving him suspended from a limb.

Washington's Birthday, in 1855, was made merrier by festivities conducted under the auspices of the City Guards, of which W. W. Twist—a grocer and commission merchant at Beaudry's Block, Aliso Street, and afterward in partnership with Casildo Aguilar—was Captain. The same organization gave its first anniversary ball in May. Twist was a Ranger, or member of the volunteer mounted police; and it was he who, in March, 1857, formed the first rifle company. In the early sixties, he was identified with the sheriff's office, after which, venturing into Mexico, he was killed.

Henry C. G. Schaeffer came to Los Angeles on March 16th, 1855, and opened the first gunsmith shop in a little adobe on the east side of Los Angeles Street near Commercial, which he soon surrounded with an attractive flower garden. A year after Schaeffer came, he was followed by another gunsmith, August Stoermer. Schaeffer continued, however, to sell and mend guns and to cultivate flowers; and twenty years later found him on Wilmington Street, near New Commercial, still encircled by one of the choicest collections of flowers in the city, and the first to have brought here the night-blooming cereus. With more than regret, therefore, I must record that, in the middle seventies, this warm-hearted friend of children, so deserving of the good will of everyone, committed suicide.

Gold was discovered at Havilah, Kern County, in 1854; and by the early spring of 1855 exaggerated accounts of the find had spread broadcast over the entire State. Yarn after yarn passed from mouth to mouth, one of the most extravagant of the reports being that a Mexican doctor and alchemist suddenly rode into Mariposa from the hills, where he had found a gulch paved with gold, his horse and himself being fairly covered with bags of nuggets. The rush by gold-seekers on their way from the North to Los Angeles (the Southern gateway to the fields) began in January, 1855, and continued a couple of years, every steamer being loaded far beyond the safety limit; and soon miles of the rough highways leading to the mines were covered with every conceivable form of vehicle and struggling animals, as well as with thousands of footsore prospectors, unable to command transportation at any price. For awhile, ten, twelve and even fifteen per cent. interest a month was offered for small amounts of money by those of the prospectors who needed assistance, a rate based on the calculation that a wide-awake digger would be sure of eight to ten dollars a day, and that with such returns one should certainly be satisfied. This time the excitement was a little too much for the Los Angeles editors to ignore; and in March the publisher of the *Southern Californian*, himself losing his balance, issued an "extra" with these startling announcements:

STOP THE PRESS!
GLORIOUS NEWS FROM KERN RIVER!
BRING OUT THE BIG GUN!

There are a thousand gulches rich with gold, and room for ten thousand miners! Miners average $50.00 a day. One man with his own hands took out $160.00 in a day. Five men in ten days took out $4,500.00.

The affair proved, however, a ridiculous failure; and William Marsh, an old Los Angeles settler and a very decent chap, who conducted a store at Havilah, was among those who suffered heavy loss. Although some low-grade ore was found, it was generally not in paying quantities. The dispersion of this adventurous mass of humanity brought to Los Angeles many undesirable people, among them gamblers and desperadoes, who flocked in the wake of the gold-diggers, making another increase in the rough element. Before long, four men were fatally shot and half a dozen wounded near the Plaza, one Sunday night.

When the excitement about the gold-finds along the Kern River was at its height, Frank Lecouvreur arrived here, March 6th, on the steamship *America*, lured by reports then current in San Francisco. To save the fare of five dollars, he trudged for ten hours all the way from San Pedro, carrying on his shoulders forty pounds of baggage; but on putting up at the United States Hotel, then recently started, he was dissuaded by some experienced miners from venturing farther up the country. Soon after, he met a fellow-countryman from Königsberg, named Arnold, who induced him, on account of his needy condition, to take work in his saloon; but disliking his duties and the rather frequent demands upon his nervous system through being shot at, several times, by patrons not exactly satisfied with Lecouvreur's locomotion and his method of serving, the young German quit the job and went to work as a carriage-painter for John Goller. In October, Captain Henry Hancock, then County Surveyor, engaged Lecouvreur as flagman, at a salary of sixty dollars; which was increased twenty-five per cent. on the trip of the surveyors to the Mojave.

March 29th, 1855, witnessed the organization of the first Odd Fellows' lodge—No. 35—instituted here. General Ezra Drown was the leading spirit; and others associated with him were E. Wilson High, Alexander Crabb, L. C. Goodwin, William C. Ardinger, Morris L. Goodman and M. M. Davis.

During the fifties, the Bella Union passed under several successive managements. On July 22d, 1854, Dr. Macy sold it to W. G. Ross and a partner named Crockett. They were succeeded, on April 7th, 1855, by Robert S. Hereford. Ross was killed, some years afterward, by C. P. Duane in San Francisco.

In pursuit of business, in 1855, I made a number of trips to San Bernardino, some of which had their amusing incidents, and most of which afforded pleasure or an agreeable change. Meeting Sam Meyer on one of these occasions, just as I was mounted and ready to start, I invited him to accompany me; and as Sam assured me that he knew where to secure a horse, we started down the street together and soon passed a shop in which there was a Mexican customer holding on to a *reata* leading out through the door to his saddled nag. Sam walked in; and having a casual acquaintance with the man, asked him if he would lend him the animal for a while? People were generous in those days; and the good-hearted Mexican, thinking perhaps that Sam was "just going around the corner," carelessly answered, "*Si, Señor,*" and proceeded with his bartering. Sam, on the other hand, came out of the shop and led the horse away! After some days of minor adventures, when we lost our path near the Old Mission and had to put back to El Monte for the night, we arrived at San Bernardino; and on our return, after watering the horses, Sam found in his unhaltered steed such a veritable Tartar that, in sheer desperation, he was about to shoot the borrowed beast!

On another one of these trips I was entertained by Simon Jackson, a merchant of that town, who took me to a restaurant kept by a Captain Weiner. This, the best eating-place in town, was about ten feet square and had a mud floor. It was a miserably hot day—so hot, in fact, that I distinctly remember the place being filled with flies, and that the butter had run to oil. Nature had not intended Weiner to cater to sensitive stomachs, at least not on the day of which I speak, and to make matters worse, Weiner was then his own waiter. He was wallowing around in his bare feet, and was otherwise unkempt and unclean; and the whole scene is therefore indelibly impressed on my memory. When the slovenly Captain bawled out: "Which will you have—chops or steak?" Jackson straightened up, threw out his chest, and in evidence of the vigor of his appetite, just as vociferously answered: "I want a steak *as big as a mule's foot!*"

Living in San Bernardino was a customer of ours, a celebrity by the name of Lewis Jacobs. He had joined the Mormon Church and was a merchant of worth and consequence. Jacobs was an authority on all matters of finance connected with his town, and anyone wishing to know the condition of business men in that neighborhood had only to apply to him. Once when I was in San Bernardino, I asked him for information regarding a prospective patron who was rather a gay sort of individual; and this was Jacobs's characteristic reply: "A very fine fellow: he plays a little poker, and drinks a little whiskey!" Jacobs became a banker and in 1900 died on shipboard while returning from Europe, leaving a comfortable fortune and the more valuable asset of a good name.

In referring to Alexander & Mellus and their retirement from business, I have said that merchandise required by Southern Californians in the early days, and before the absorption of the Los Angeles market by San Francisco, was largely transported by sailing vessels from the East. When a ship arrived, it was an event worthy of special notice, and this was particularly the case when such sailing craft came less and less often into port. Sometimes the arrival of the vessel was heralded in advance; and when it was unloaded, the shrewd merchants used decidedly modern methods for the marketing of their wares. In 1855, for example, Johnson & Allanson advertised as follows:

NEW GOODS! NEW GOODS!

Direct from the Atlantic States, 112 Days' Passage.

Samples of the Cargo at our Store in the Stearns Building; and the entire Cargo will be disposed of cheap, for cash.

Goods delivered at San Pedro or Los Angeles.

From the above announcement, it must not be inferred that these Los Angeles tradesmen brought to this port the whole shipload of merchandise. Such ships left but a small part of their cargo here, the major portion being generally consigned to the North.

The dependence on San Francisco continued until the completion of our first transcontinental railway. In the meantime, Los Angeles had to rely on the Northern city for nearly everything, live stock being about the only exception; and this relation was shown in 1855 by the publication of no less than four columns of San Francisco advertisements in the regular issue of a Los Angeles newspaper. Much of this commerce with the Southland for years was conducted by means of schooners which ran irregularly and only when there was cargo. They plied between San Francisco and San Pedro, and by agreement put in at Santa Bárbara and other Coast places such as Port San Luis, when the shipments warranted such stops. N. Pierce & Company were the owners. One of these vessels in 1855 was the clipper schooner *Laura Bevan*, captained by F. Morton and later wrecked at sea when Frank Lecouvreur just escaped taking passage on her; and another was the *Sea Serpent*, whose Captain bore the name of Fish.

I have said that in 1849 the old side-wheeler *Gold Hunter* had commenced paddling the waters around here; but so far as I can remember, she was not operating in 1853. The *Goliah*, on the other hand, was making two round trips a month, carrying passengers, mail and freight from San Francisco to San Diego, and stopping at various Coast points including San Pedro. In a vague way, I also remember the mail steamer *Ohio* under one of the Haleys, the *Sea Bird*, at one time commanded by Salisbury Haley, and the *Southerner;* and if I am uncertain about others, the difficulty may be due to the fact that, because of unseaworthiness and miserable service, owners changed the names of ships from time to time in order to allay the popular prejudice and distrust, so that during some years, several names were successively applied to the same vessel. It must have been

about 1855 or 1856 that the *Senator* (brought to the Coast by
Captain Coffin, January 28th, 1853) was put on the Southern run,
and with her advent began a considerably improved service.
As the schooners were even more irregular than the steamers,
I generally divided my shipments, giving to the latter what I
needed immediately, and consigning by the schooners, whose
freight rates were much lower, what could stand delay. One
more word about the *Goliah:* one day in the eighties I heard
that she was still doing valiant service, having been sold to a
Puget Sound company.

Recalling these old-time side-wheelers whose paddles
churned the water into a frothing foam out of all proportion to
the speed with which they drove the boat along her course, I
recall, with a feeling almost akin to sentiment, the roar of the
signal-gun fired just before landing, making the welcome
announcement, as well to the traveler as to his friends
awaiting him on shore, that the voyage had been safely
consummated.

Shortly after my arrival in Los Angeles, the transportation
service was enlarged by the addition of a stage line from San
Francisco which ran along the Coast from the Northern city to
the Old Town of San Diego, making stops all along the road, including San José, San Luis Obispo, Santa Bárbara and San
Buenaventura, and particularly at Los Angeles, where not only
horses, but stages and supplies were kept. The stage to San
Diego followed, for the most part, the route selected later
by the Santa Fé Railroad.

These old-time stages remind me again of the few varieties
of vehicles then in use. John Goller had met with much skepti-
cism and ridicule, as I have said, when he was planning an improvement on the old and clumsy *carreta;* and when his new ideas
did begin to prevail, he suffered from competition. E. L. Scott
& Company came as blacksmiths and carriage-makers in 1855;
and George Boorham was another who arrived about the same
time. Ben McLoughlin was also an early wheelwright. Among
Goller's assistants who afterward opened shops for themselves,
were the three Louis's—Roeder, Lichtenberger and Breer;

Roeder and Lichtenberger[1] having a place on the west side of Spring Street just south of First.

Thomas W. Seeley, Captain of the *Senator*, was very fond of Los Angeles diversions, as will appear from the following anecdote of the late fifties. After bringing his ship to anchor off the coast, he would hasten to Los Angeles, leaving his vessel in command of First Mate Butters to complete the voyage to San Diego and return, which consumed forty-eight hours; and during this interval, the old Captain regularly made his headquarters at the Bella Union. There he would spend practically all of his time playing poker, then considered the gentleman's game of chance, and which, since the mania for Chemical Purity had not yet possessed Los Angeles, was looked upon without criticism. When the steamer returned from San Diego, Captain Seeley, if neither his own interest in the game nor his fellow-players' interest in his pocketbook, had ebbed, would postpone the departure of his ship, frequently for even as much as twenty-four hours, thus adding to the irregularity of sailings which I have already mentioned. Many, in fact, were the inconveniences to which early travelers were subjected from this infrequency of trips and failure to sail at the stated hour; and to aggravate the trouble, the vessels were all too small, especially when a sudden excitement—due, perhaps, to some new report of the discovery of gold—increased the number of intending travelers. It even happened, sometimes, that persons were compelled to postpone their trip until the departure of another boat. Speaking of anchoring vessels off the coast, I may add that high seas frequently made it impossible to reach the steamers announced to leave at a certain time; in which case the officers used to advertise in the newspapers that the time of departure had been changed.

When Captain Seeley was killed in the *Ada Hancock* disaster, in 1863, First Mate Butters was made Captain and continued for some time in command. Just what his real fitness was, I cannot say; but it seemed to me that he did not know the Coast any too well. This impression also existed in

[1] Lichtenberger died some years ago; Roeder died February 20th, 1915.

Louis Sainsevain

Manuel Dominguez

El Aliso, the Sainsevain Winery
From an old lithograph

John T. Lanfranco

Jacob Elias

J. Frank Burns

Henry D. Barrows

the minds of others; and once, when we were supposed to be making our way to San Francisco, the heavy fog lifted and revealed the shore thirty miles north of our destination; whereupon a fellow-passenger exclaimed: "Why, Captain, this isn't at all the part of the Coast where we should be!" The remark stung the sensitive Butters, who probably was conscious enough of his shortcomings; and straightway he threatened to put the offending passenger in irons!

George F. Lamson was an auctioneer who arrived in Los Angeles in 1855. Aside from the sale of live stock, there was not much business in his line; although, as I have said, Dr. Osburn, the Postmaster, also had an auction room. Sales of household effects were held on a Tuesday or a Wednesday; while horses were offered for sale on Saturdays. Lamson had the typical auctioneer's personality; and many good stories were long related, illustrating his humor, wit and amusing impudence by which he often disposed, even to his friends, of almost worthless objects at high prices. A daughter Gertrude, widely known as Lillian Nance O'Neill, never married; another daughter, Lillian, is the wife of William Desmond, the actor.

In 1854, Congress made an appropriation of fifty thousand dollars which went far toward opening up the trade that later flourished between Los Angeles and Salt Lake City. This money was for the survey and location of a wagon-road between San Bernardino and the Utah capital; and on the first of May, 1855, Gilbert & Company established their Great Salt Lake Express over that Government route. It was at first a pony express, making monthly trips, carrying letters and stopping at such stations as Coal Creek, Fillmore City, Summit Creek and American Fork, and finally reaching Great Salt Lake; and early having good Los Angeles connections, it prospered sufficiently to substitute a wagon-service for the pony express. Although this was at first intended only as a means of connecting the Mormon capital with the more recently-founded Mormon settlement at San Bernardino, the extension of the service to Los Angeles eventually made this city the terminus.

Considerable excitement was caused by the landing at San

Pedro, in 1855, of a shipload of Mormons from Honolulu. Though I do not recall that any more recruits came subsequently from that quarter, the arrival of these adherents of Brigham Young added color to his explanation that he had established a Mormon colony in California, as a base of operations and supplies for converts from the Sandwich Islands.

Thomas Foster, a Kentuckian, was the sixth Mayor of Los Angeles, taking office in May, 1855. He lived opposite Masonic Hall on Main Street, with his family, among whom were some charming daughters, and was in partnership with Dr. R. T. Hayes, in Apothecaries' Hall near the Post Office. He was one of the first Masons here and was highly esteemed; and he early declared himself in favor of better school and water facilities.

About the second week of June, 1855, appeared the first Spanish newspaper in Los Angeles under the American *régime*. It was called *El Clamor Público*, and made its appeal, socially, to the better class of native Californians. Politically, it was edited for Republicans, especially for the supporters, in 1856, of Frémont for President. Its editor was Francisco P. Ramirez; but though he was an able journalist and a good typo—becoming, between 1860 and 1862, State Printer in Sonora and, in 1865, Spanish Translator for the State of California—the *Clamor*, on December 31st, 1859, went the way of so many other local journals.

CHAPTER XII

THE GREAT HORSE RACE

1855

FROM all accounts, Fourth of July was celebrated in Los Angeles with more or less enthusiasm from the time of the City's reorganization, although afterward, as we shall see, the day was often neglected; but certainly in 1855 the festivities were worthy of remembrance. There was less formality, perhaps, and more cannonading than in later years; music was furnished by a brass band from Fort Tejón; and Phineas Banning was the stentorian "orator of the day." Two years previously, Banning had provided a three days' celebration and barbecue for the Fourth, attended by my brother; and I once enjoyed a barbecue at San Juan Capistrano where the merriment, continuing for half a week, marked both the hospitality and the leisurely habits of the people. In those days (when men were not afraid of noise) boys, in celebrating American Independence, made all the hullabaloo possible, untrammeled by the nonsense of "a sane Fourth."

On the Fourth of July and other holidays, as well as on Sundays, men from the country came to town, arrayed in their fanciest clothes; and, mounted upon their most spirited and gaily-caparisoned *caballos de silla*, or saddle-horses, they paraded the streets, as many as ten abreast, jingling the metallic parts of their paraphernalia, admired and applauded by the populace, and keenly alive to the splendid appearance they and their outfits made, and to the effect sure to be produced on the fair *señoritas*. The most popular thoroughfare for this purpose was Main Street. On such occasions, the men wore short, very tight-fitting jackets of bright-colored material— blue, green and yellow being the favorite colors—and trimmed with gold and silver lace or fringe. These jackets were so tight that often the wearers put them on only with great difficulty. The *calzoneras*, or pantaloons, were of the same material as the jackets, open on the side and flanked with brass buttons. The openings exposed the *calzoncillos*, or drawers. A fashionable adjunct was the Mexican garter, often costing ten to fifteen dollars, and another was the high-heeled boot, so small that ten minutes or more were required to draw it on. This boot was a great conceit; but though experiencing much discomfort, the victim could not be induced to increase the size.

The *serape*, worn by men, was the native substitute for the overcoat. It was a narrow, Mexican blanket of finest wool, multicolored and provided with a hole near the center large enough to let the wearer's head through; and when not in actual use, it was thrown over the saddle. The head-gear consisted in winter of a broad-rimmed, high-crowned, woolen *sombrero*, usually brown, which was kept in place during fast travel or a race by a ribbon or band fastened under the chin; often, as in the familiar case of Ygnácio Lugo, the hat was ornamented with beads. In summer, the rider substituted a shirt for the *serape* and a Panamá for the *sombrero*. The *caballero's* outfit, in the case of some wealthy dons, exceeded a thousand dollars in value; and it was not uncommon for fancy costumes to be handed down as heirlooms.

The women, on the other hand, wore skirts of silk, wool or cotton, according to their wealth or the season. Many of the female conceits had not appeared in 1853; the grandmothers of the future suffragettes wore, instead of bonnets and hats, a *rebozo*, or sort of scarf or muffler, which covered their heads and shoulders and looked delightfully picturesque. To don this gracefully was, in fact, quite an art. Many of the native California ladies also braided their hair, and wore circular combs around the back of their heads; at least this was so until, with the advent of a greater number of American women, their more modern, though less romantic, styles commenced to prevail, when even the picturesque *mantilla* was discarded.

Noting these differences of dress in early days, I should not forget to state that there were both American and Mexican tailors here; among the former being one McCoy and his son, merry companions whose copartnership carousals were proverbial. The Mexican tailor had the advantage of knowing just what the native requirements were, although in the course of time his *Gringo* rival came to understand the tastes and prejudices of the *paisano*, and to obtain the better share of the patronage. The cloth from which the *caballero's* outfit was made could be found in most of the stores.

As with clothes and tailors, so it was with other articles of apparel and those who manufactured them; the natives had their own shoe- and hat-makers, and their styles were unvarying. The genuine Panamá hat was highly prized and often copied; and Francisco Velardes—who used a grindstone bought of John Temple in 1852, now in the County Museum—was one who sold and imitated Panamás of the fifties. A product of the bootmakers' skill were leathern leggings, worn to protect the trousers when riding on horseback. The *Gringos* were then given to copying the fashions of the natives; but as the pioneer population increased, the Mexican came more and more to adopt American styles.

Growing out of these exhibitions of horsemanship and of the natives' fondness for display, was the rather important industry of making Mexican saddles, in which quite a number of skilled *paisanos* were employed. Among the most expert was Francisco Moreno, who had a little shop on the south side of Aliso Street, not far from Los Angeles. One of these hand-worked saddles often cost two hundred dollars or more, in addition to which expensive bridles, bits and spurs were deemed necessary accessories. António María Lugo had a silver-mounted saddle, bridle and spurs that cost fifteen hundred dollars.

On holidays and even Sundays, Upper Main Street—formerly called the Calle de las Virgenes, or Street of the Maids, later San Fernando Street—was the scene of horse races and their attendant festivities, just as it used to be when money or gold was especially plentiful, if one may judge from the stories of those who were here in the prosperous year, 1850. People from all over the county visited Los Angeles to take part in the sport, some coming from mere curiosity, but the majority anxious to bet. Some money, and often a good deal of stock changed hands, according to the success or failure of the different favorites. It cannot be claimed, perhaps, that the Mexican, like the *Gringo*, made a specialty of developing horse-flesh to perfection; yet Mexicans owned many of the fast horses, such as Don José Sepúlveda's *Sydney Ware* and *Black Swan*, and the Californian *Sarco* belonging to Don Pio Pico.

The most celebrated of all these horse races of early days was that between José Andrés Sepúlveda's *Black Swan* and Pio Pico's *Sarco*, the details of which I learned, soon after I came here, from Tom Mott. Sepúlveda had imported the *Black Swan* from Australia, in 1852, the year of the race, while Pico chose a California steed to defend the honors of the day. Sepúlveda himself went to San Francisco to receive the consignment in person, after which he committed the thoroughbred into the keeping of Bill Brady, the trainer, who rode him down to Los Angeles, and gave him as much care as might have been bestowed upon a favorite child. They were to race nine miles, the *carrera* commencing on San Pedro Street near the city limits, and running south a league and a half and return; and the reports of the preparation having spread throughout California, the event came to be looked upon as of such great importance, that, from San Francisco to San Diego, whoever had the money hurried to Los Angeles to witness the contest and bet on the result. Twenty-five thousand dollars, in addition to five hundred horses, five hundred mares, five hundred heifers, five hundred calves and five hundred sheep were among the princely stakes put up; and the wife of José Andrés was driven to the scene of the memorable contest with a veritable fortune in gold slugs wrapped in a large handkerchief. Upon arriving there, she opened her improvised purse and distributed the shining fifty-dollar pieces to all of her attendants and servants, of whom there were not a few, with the injunction that they should wager the money on the race; and her example was followed by others, so that, in addition to the cattle, land and merchandise hazarded, a considerable sum of money was bet by the contending parties and their friends. The *Black Swan* won easily. The peculiar character of some of the wagers recalls to me an instance of a later date when a native customer of Louis Phillips tried to borrow a wagon, in order to bet the same on a horse race. If the customer won, he was to return the wagon at once; but if he lost, he was to pay Phillips a certain price for the vehicle.

Many kinds of amusements marked these festal occasions, and bull-fights were among the diversions patronized by some Angeleños, the Christmas and New Year holidays of 1854–55 being celebrated in that manner. I dare say that in earlier days Los Angeles may have had its Plaza de Toros, as did the ancient metropolis of the great country to the South; but in the later stages of the sport here, the *toreador* and his colleagues conducted their contests in a gaudily-painted corral, in close proximity to the Plaza. They were usually proclaimed as professionals from Mexico or Spain, but were often engaged for a livelihood, under another name, in a less dangerous and romantic occupation near by. Admission was charged, and some pretense to a grandstand was made; but through the apertures in the fence of the corral those who did not pay might, by dint of hard squinting, still get a peep at the show. In this corral, in the fifties, I saw a fight between a bear and a bull. I can still recollect the crowd, but I cannot say which of the infuriated animals survived. Toward the end of 1858, a bull-fight took place in the Calle de Toros, and there was great excitement when a horse was instantly killed.

Cock-fights were also a very common form of popular entertainment, and sports were frequently seen going around the streets with fighting cocks under each arm. The fights generally took place in Sonora Town, though now and then they were held in San Gabriel. Mexicans carried on quite a trade in game roosters among the patrons of this pastime, of whom M. G. Santa Cruz was one of the best known. Sometimes, too, roosters contributed to still another brutal diversion known as *correr el gallo:* their necks having been well greased, they would be partially buried in the earth alongside a public highway, when riders on fleet horses dashed by at full speed, and tried to seize the fowls and pull them out! This reminds me of another game in which horsemen, speeding madly by a succession of suspended, small rings, would try, by the skillful handling of a long spear, to collect as many of the rings as they could—a sport illustrated in one of the features of the modern merry-go-round. ·

The easy-going temperament of the native gave rise to many an amusing incident. I once asked a woman, as we were discussing the coming marriage of her daughter, whom the dark-eyed *señorita* was to marry; whereupon she replied, "I forget;" and turning to her daughter, she asked: "*¿Como se llama?*" (What did you say was his name?)

George Dalton bought a tract of land on Washington, east of San Pedro Street, in 1855, and set out a vineyard and orchard which he continued to cultivate until 1887, when he moved to Walnut Avenue. Dalton was a Londoner who sailed from Liverpool on the day of Queen Victoria's coronation, to spend some years wandering through Pennsylvania and Ohio. About 1851, he followed to the Azusa district his brother, Henry Dalton, who had previously been a merchant in Peru; but, preferring the embryo city to the country, he returned to Los Angeles to live. Two sons, E. H. Dalton, City Water Overseer, in 1886–87, and Winnall Travelly Dalton, the vineyardist, were offspring of Dalton's first marriage. Elizabeth M., a daughter, married William H. Perry. Dalton Avenue is named after the Dalton family.

In another place I have spoken of the dearth of trees in the town when I came, though the editor of the *Star* and others had advocated tree-planting. This was not due to mere neglect; there was prejudice against such street improvement. The School Trustees had bought a dozen or more black locust-trees, "at eight bits each," and planted them on the school lot at

Second and Spring streets. Drought and squirrels in 1855 attacked the trees, and while the pedagogue went after the "varmints" with a shot-gun, he watered the trees from the school barrel. The carrier, however, complained that drinking-water was being wasted; and only after several rhetorical bouts was the schoolmaster allowed to save what was already invested. The locust-trees flourished until 1884, when they were hewn down to make way for the City Hall.

Two partially-successful attempts were made, in 1855, to introduce the chestnut-tree here. Jean Louis Sainsevain, coming to Los Angeles in that year, brought with him some seed; and this doubtless led Solomon Lazard to send back to Bordeaux for some of the Italian variety. William Wolfskill, who first brought here the persimmon-tree, took a few of the seeds imported by Lazard and planted them near his homestead; and a dozen of the trees later adorned the beautiful garden of O. W. Childs who, in the following year, started some black walnut seed obtained in New York. H. P. Dorsey was also a pioneer walnut grower.

My brother's plans at this time included a European visit, commencing in 1855 and lasting until 1856, during which trip, in Germany, on November 11th, 1855, he was married. After his Continental tour, he returned to San Francisco and was back in Los Angeles some time before 1857. On this European voyage, my brother was entrusted with the care and delivery of American Government documents. From London he carried certain papers to the American Minister in Denmark; and in furtherance of his mission, he was given the following introduction and passport from James Buchanan, then Minister Plenipotentiary to the Court of St. James and later President of the United States:

No. 282   BEARER OF DESPATCHES

LEGATION OF THE UNITED STATES OF AMERICA
AT LONDON.

To all to whom these presents shall come, Greeting;

Know Ye, that the bearer hereof, Joseph P. Newmark, Esq., is proceeding to Hamburgh and Denmark, bearing Despatches from this Legation, to the United States' Legation at Copenhagen.

These are therefore to request all whom it may concern, to permit him to pass freely without let or molestation, and to extend to him such friendly aid and protection, as would be extended to Citizens and Subjects of Foreign Countries, resorting to the United States, bearing Despatches.

In testimony whereof, I, James Buchanan, Envoy Extraordinary and Minister Plenipotentiary, of the United States of America, at London, have hereunto set my hand, and caused the Seal of this Legation to be affixed this Tenth day of July A.D. 1855 and of the Independence of the United States the Eightieth.

(Signed,)

JAMES BUCHANAN.

(Seal of the Legation of the U. S.
of America to Great Britain.)

I have always accepted the fact of my brother's selection to convey these documents as evidence that, in the few years since his arrival in America, he had attained a position of some responsibility. Aside from this, I am inclined to relate the experience because it shows the then limited resources of our Federal authorities abroad, especially as compared with their comprehensive facilities to-day, including their own despatch agents, messengers and Treasury representatives scattered throughout Europe.

A trip of Prudent Beaudry abroad about this time reminds me that specialization in medical science was as unknown in early Los Angeles as was specialization in business, and that persons suffering from grave physical disorders frequently visited even remoter points than San Francisco in search of relief. In 1855, Beaudry's health having become seriously impaired, he went to Paris to consult the famous oculist, Sichel; but he received little or no benefit. While in Europe, Beaudry visited the Exposition of that year, and was one of the first Angeleños, I suppose, to see a World's Fair.

These early tours to Europe by Temple, Beaudry and my brother, and some of my own experiences, recall the changes in the manner of bidding Los Angeles travelers *bon-voyage*. Friends generally accompanied the tourist to the outlying steamer, reached by a tug or lighter; and when the leave-taking came, there were cheers, repetitions of *adiós* and the waving of hats and handkerchiefs, which continued until the steamer had disappeared from view.

The first earthquake felt throughout California, of which I have any recollection, occurred on July 11th, 1855, somewhat after eight o'clock in the evening, and was a most serious local disturbance. Almost every structure in Los Angeles was damaged, and some of the walls were left with large cracks. Near San Gabriel, the adobe in which Hugo Reid's Indian wife dwelt was wrecked, notwithstanding that it had walls four feet thick, with great beams of lumber drawn from the mountains of San Bernardino. In certain spots, the ground rose; in others, it fell; and with the rising and falling, down came chimneys, shelves full of salable stock or household necessities, pictures and even parts of roofs, while water in barrels, and also in several of the *zanjas*, bubbled and splashed and overflowed. Again, on the 14th of April, the 2d of May and the 20th of September of the following year, we were alarmed by recurring and more or less continuous shocks which, however, did little or no damage.

CHAPTER XIII

PRINCELY *RANCHO* DOMAINS

1855

OF the wonderful domains granted to the Spanish dons some were still in the possession of their descendants; some had passed into the hands of the Argonauts; but nothing in the way of subdividing had been attempted. The private ownership of Los Angeles County in the early fifties, therefore, was distinguished by few holders and large tracts, one of the most notable being that of Don Abel Stearns, who came here in 1829, and who, in his early adventures, narrowly escaped exile or being shot by an irate Spanish governor. Eventually, Stearns became the proud possessor of tens of thousands of acres between San Pedro and San Bernardino, now covered with cities, towns and hamlets. The site of the Long Beach of to-day was but a small part of his Alamitos *rancho*, a portion of the town also including some of the Cerritos acres of John Temple. Los Coyotes, La Habra and San Juan Cajón de Santa Ana were among the Stearns ranches advertised for sale in 1869. Later, I shall relate how this Alamitos land came to be held by Jotham Bixby and his associates.

Juan Temple owned the Los Cerritos *rancho*, consisting of some twenty-seven thousand acres, patented on December 27th, 1867, but which, I have heard, he bought of the Nieto heirs in the late thirties, building there the typical ranch-house, later the home of the Bixbys and still a feature of the neighborhood. Across the Cerritos Stockton's weary soldiers dragged their way; and there, or near by, Carrillo, by driving wild horses back and forth in confusion, and so creating a great noise and dust, tricked Stockton into thinking that there were many more of the mounted enemy than he had at first supposed. By 1853, Temple was estimated to be worth, in addition to his ranches, some twenty thousand dollars. In 1860, Los Cerritos supported perhaps four thousand cattle and great flocks of sheep; on a portion of the same ranch to-day, as I have remarked, Long Beach stands.

Another citizen of Los Angeles who owned much property when I came, and who lived upon his ranch, was Francis Phinney Fisk Temple, one of the first Los Angeles supervisors, a man exceptionally modest and known among his Spanish-speaking friends as Templito, because of his five feet four stature. He came here, by way of the Horn, in 1841, when he was but nineteen years of age, and for a while was in business with his brother John. Marrying Señorita Antónia Margarita Workman, however, on September 30th, 1845, Francis made his home at La Merced Ranch, twelve miles east of Los Angeles, in the San Gabriel Valley, where he had a spacious and hospitable adobe after the old Spanish style, shaped something like a *U*, and about seventy by one hundred and ten feet in size. Around this house, later destroyed by fire, Temple planted twenty acres of fruit trees and fifty thousand or more vines, arranging the whole in a garden partly enclosed by a fence—the exception rather than the rule for even a country nabob of that time. Templito also owned other ranches many miles in extent; but misfortune overtook him, and by the nineties his estate possessed scarcely a single acre of land in either the city or the county of Los Angeles; and he breathed his last in a rude sheep herder's camp in a corner of one of his famous properties.

Colonel Julian Isaac Williams, who died some three years after I arrived, owned the celebrated Cucamonga and Chino ranches. As early as 1842, after a nine or ten years' residence in Los Angeles, Williams moved to the Rancho del Chino, which included not merely the Santa Ana del Chino grant—some twenty-two thousand acres originally given to Don António María Lugo, in 1841—but the addition of twelve to thirteen thousand acres, granted in 1843 to Williams (who became Lugo's son-in-law) making a total of almost thirty-five thousand acres. On that ranch Williams built a house famed far and wide for its spaciousness and hospitality; and it was at his *hacienda* that the celebrated capture of B D. Wilson and others was effected when they ran out of ammunition. Williams was liberal in assisting the needy, even despatching messengers to Los Angeles, on the arrival at his ranch of worn-out and ragged immigrants, to secure clothing and other supplies for them; and it is related that, on other occasions, he was known to have advanced to young men capital amounting in the aggregate to thousands of dollars, with which they established themselves in business. By 1851, Williams had amassed personal property estimated to be worth not less than thirty-five thousand dollars. In the end, he gave his *ranchos* to his daughters as marriage-portions: the Chino to Francisca, or Mrs. Robert Carlisle, who became the wife of Dr. F. A. McDougall, Mayor in 1877–78, and, after his death, Mrs. Jesurun; and the Cucamonga to María Merced, or Mrs. John Rains, mother-in-law of ex-Governor Henry T. Gage, who was later Mrs. Carrillo.

Benjamin Davis Wilson, or Benito Wilson, as he was usually called, who owned a good part of the most beautiful land in the San Gabriel Valley and who laid out the trail up the Sierra Madre to Wilson's Peak, was one of our earliest settlers, having come from Tennessee *via* New Mexico, in 1841. In June, 1846, Wilson joined the riflemen organized against Castro, and in 1848, having been put in charge of some twenty men to protect the San Bernardino frontier, he responded to a call from Isaac Williams to hasten to the Chino *rancho* where, with his compatriots, he was taken prisoner. Somewhat earlier—I have understood about 1844—Wilson and Albert Packard formed a partnership, but this was dissolved near the end of 1851. In 1850, Wilson was elected County Clerk; and the following year, he volunteered to patrol the hills and assist in watching for Garra, the outlaw, the report of whose coming was terrorizing the town. In 1853, he was Indian Agent for Southern California. It must have been about 1849 that Wilson secured

Maurice Kremer   Solomon Lazard

Mellus's, or Bell's Row

From a lithograph of 1858

William H. Workman and John King

Prudent Beaudry

James S. Mallard

John Behn

control, for a while, of the Bella Union. His first wife was Ramona Yorba, a daughter of Bernardo Yorba, whom he married in February, 1844, and who died in 1849. On February 1st, 1853, Wilson married again, this time Mrs. Margaret S. Hereford, a sister-in-law of Thomas S. Hereford; they spent many years together at Lake Vineyard, where he became one of the leading producers of good wine, and west of which he planted some twenty-five or thirty thousand raisin grape cuttings, and ten or twelve hundred orange trees, thus founding Oak Knoll. I shall have occasion to speak of this gentleman somewhat later. By the time that I came to know him, Wilson had accumulated much real estate, part of his property being a residence on Alameda Street, corner of Macy; but after a while he moved to one of his larger estates, where stands the present Shorb station named for his son-in-law and associate J. De Barth Shorb, who also had a place known as Mountain Vineyard. Don Benito died in March, 1878.

Colonel Jonathan Trumbull Warner, master of Warner's Ranch, later the property of John G. Downey, and known—from his superb stature of over six feet—both as Juan José Warner and as Juan Largo, "Long John," returned to Los Angeles in 1857. Warner had arrived in Southern California, on December 5th, 1831, at the age of twenty-eight, having come West, from Connecticut, *via* Missouri and Salt Lake, partly for his health, and partly to secure mules for the Louisiana market. Like many others whom I have known, Warner did not intend to remain; but illness decided for him, and in 1843 he settled in San Diego County, near the California border, on what (later known as Warner's Ranch) was to become, with its trail from old Sonora, historic ground. There, during the fourteen years of his occupancy, some of the most stirring episodes of the Mexican War occurred; during one of which— Ensign Espinosa's attack—Don Juan having objected to the forcible searching of his house, he had his arm broken. There, also, António Garra and his lawless band made their assault, and were repulsed by Long John, who escaped on horseback, leaving in his wake four or five dead Indians. For this, and not for military service, Warner was dubbed Colonel; nor was there anyone who cared to dispute his right to the title. In 1837, Juan married Miss Anita Gale, an adopted daughter of Don Pio Pico, and came to Los Angeles; but the following year, Mrs. Warner died. Warner once ran against E. J. C. Kewen for the Legislature but, after an exceedingly bitter campaign, was beaten. In 1874 Warner was a notary public and Spanish-English interpreter. For many years his home was in an orchard occupying the site of the Burbank Theater on Main Street. Warner was a man of character and lived to a venerable age; and after a decidedly arduous life he had more than his share of responsibility and affliction, even losing his sight in his declining years.

William Wolfskill, who died on October 3d, 1866, was another pioneer well-established long before I had even thought of California. Born in Kentucky at the end of the Eighteenth Century—of a family originally of Teutonic stock (if we may credit a high German authority) traced back to a favorite soldier of Frederick the Great—Wolfskill in 1830 came to Los Angeles, for a short time, with Ewing Young, the noted beaver-trapper. Then he acquired several leagues of land in Yolo and Solano counties, sharing what he had with his brothers, John and Mateo. Later he sold out, returned to Los Angeles, and bought and stocked the *rancho* Lomas de Santiago, which he afterward disposed of to Flint, Bixby & Company. He also bought of Corbitt, Dibblee & Barker the Santa Anita *rancho* (comprising between nine and ten thousand acres), and some twelve thousand besides; the Santa Anita he gave to his son, Louis, who later sold it for eighty-five thousand dollars. Besides this, Wolfskill acquired title to a part of the *rancho* San Francisquito, on which Newhall stands, disposing of that, however, during the first oil excitement, to the Philadelphia Oil Company, at seventy-five cents an acre—a good price at that time. Before making these successful realty experiments, this hero of desert hardships had assisted to build, soon after his arrival here, one of the first vessels ever constructed and launched in California—a schooner fitted out at San Pedro to hunt for sea otter. In January, 1841,

Wolfskill married Doña Magdalena Lugo, daughter of Don José Ygnácio Lugo, of Santa Bárbara. A daughter, Señorita Magdalena, in 1865 married Frank Sabichi, a native of Los Angeles, who first saw the light of day in 1842. Sabichi, by the way, always a man of importance in this community, is the son of Mateo and Josefa Franco Sabichi (the mother, a sister of António Franco Coronel), buried at San Gabriel Mission. J. E. Pleasants, to whom I elsewhere refer, first made a good start when he formed a partnership with Wolfskill in a cattle deal.

Concerning Mateo, I recall an interesting illustration of early fiscal operations. He deposited thirty thousand dollars with S. Lazard & Company and left it there so long that they began to think he would never come back for it. He did return, however, after many years, when he presented a certificate of deposit and withdrew the money. This transaction bore no interest, as was often the case in former days. People deposited money with friends in whom they had confidence, not for the purpose of profit but simply for safety.

Elijah T. Moulton, a Canadian, was one of the few pioneers who preceded the Forty-niners and was permitted to see Los Angeles well on its way toward metropolitan standing. In 1844 he had joined an expedition to California organized by Jim Bridger; and having reached the Western country, he volunteered to serve under Frémont in the Mexican campaign. There the hardships which Moulton endured were far severer than those which tested the grit of the average emigrant; and Moulton in better days often told how, when nearly driven to starvation, he and a comrade had actually used a remnant of the Stars and Stripes as a seine with which to fish, and so saved their lives. About 1850, Moulton was Deputy Sheriff under George T. Burrill; then he went to work for Don Louis Vignes. Soon afterward, he bought some land near William Wolfskill's, and in 1855 took charge of Wolfskill's property. This resulted in his marriage to one of Wolfskill's daughters, who died in 1861. In the meantime, he had acquired a hundred and fifty acres or more in what is now East Los Angeles, and was thus one of the first to settle in that section. He had a dairy, for a while, and peddled milk from a can or two carried in a wagon. Afterward, Moulton became a member of the City Council.

William Workman and John Rowland, father of William or Billy Rowland, resided in 1853 on La Puente *rancho*, which was granted them July 22d, 1845, some four years after they had arrived in California. They were leaders of a party from New Mexico, of which B. D. Wilson, Lemuel Carpenter and others were members; and the year following they operated with Pico against Micheltorena and Sutter, Workman serving as Captain, and Rowland as Lieutenant, of a company of volunteers they had organized. The ranch, situated about twenty miles east of Los Angeles, consisted of nearly forty-nine thousand acres, and had one of the first brick residences erected in this neighborhood. Full title to this splendid estate was confirmed by the United States Government in April, 1867, a couple of years before Workman and Rowland, with the assistance of Cameron E. Thom, divided their property. Rowland, who in 1851 was supposed to own some twenty-nine thousand acres and about seventy thousand dollars' worth of personal property, further partitioned his estate, three or four years before his death in 1873, among his nearest of kin, giving to each heir about three thousand acres of land and a thousand head of cattle. One of these heirs, the wife of General Charles Forman, is the half-sister of Billy Rowland by a second marriage.

John Reed, Rowland's son-in-law, was also a large land-proprietor. Reed had fallen in with Rowland in New Mexico, and while there married Rowland's daughter, Nieves; and when Rowland started for California, Reed came with him and together they entered into ranching at La Puente, finding artesian water there, in 1859. Thirteen years before, Reed was in the American army and took part in the battles fought on the march from San Diego to Los Angeles. After his death on the ranch in 1874, his old homestead came into possession of John Rowland's son, William, who often resided there; and Rowland, later discovering oil on his land, organized the Puente Oil Company.

Juan Forster, an Englishman, possessed the Santa Margarita *rancho*, which he had taken up in 1864, some years after he married Doña Ysidora Pico. She was a sister of Pio and Andrés Pico, and there, as a result of that alliance, General Pico found a safe retreat while fleeing from Frémont into Lower California. Forster for a while was a seaman out of San Pedro. When he went to San Juan Capistrano, where he became a sort of local *Alcalde* and was often called Don San Juan or even San Juan Capistrano, he experimented with raising stock and became so successful as a *ranchero* that he remained there twenty years, during which time he acquired a couple of other ranches, in San Diego and Los Angeles counties, comprising quite sixty thousand acres. Forster, however, was comparatively land-poor, as may be inferred from the fact that even though the owner of such a princely territory, he was assessed in 1851 on but thirteen thousand dollars in personal property. Later Don Juan lorded it over twice as much land in the ranches of Santa Margarita and Las Flores. His fourth son, a namesake, married Señorita Josefa del Valle, daughter of Don Ygnácio del Valle.

Manuel, Pedro, Nasário and Victoria Dominguez owned in the neighborhood of forty-eight thousand acres of the choicest land in the South. More than a century ago, Juan José Dominguez received from the King of Spain ten or eleven leagues of land, known as the Rancho de San Pedro; and this was given by Governor de Sola, after Juan José's death in 1822, to his brother, Don Cristóbal Dominguez, a Spanish officer. Don Cristóbal married a Mexican commissioner's daughter, and one of their ten children was Manuel, who, educated by wide reading and fortunate in a genial temperament and high standard of honor, became an esteemed and popular officer under the Mexican *régime*, displaying no little chivalry in the battle of Dominguez fought on his own property. On the death of his father, Don Manuel took charge of the Rancho de San Pedro (buying out his sister Victoria's interest of twelve thousand acres, at fifty cents an acre) until in 1855 it was partitioned between himself, his brother, Don Pedro and two nephews, José António Aguirre and Jacinto Rocha. One daughter, Victoria, married George Carson in 1857. At his death, in 1882, Dominguez bequeathed to his heirs twenty odd thousand acres, including Rattlesnake Island in San Pedro Bay. James A. Watson, an early-comer, married a second daughter; John F. Francis married a third, and Dr. del Amo married a fourth.

Henry Dalton, who came here sometime before 1845, having been a merchant in Peru, owned the Azusa Ranch of over four thousand acres, the patent to which was finally issued in 1876, and also part of the San Francisquito Ranch of eight thousand acres, allowed him somewhat later. Besides these, he had an interest, with Ygnácio Palomares and Ricardo Vejar, in the San José *rancho* of nearly twenty-seven thousand acres. As early as the twenty-first of May, 1851, Dalton, with keen foresight, seems to have published a plan for the subdivision of nine or ten thousand acres into lots to suit limited ranchers; but it was some time before Duarte and other places, now on the above-mentioned estates, arose from his dream. On a part of his property, Azusa, a town of the Boom period, was founded some twenty-two miles from Los Angeles, and seven or eight hundred feet up the Azusa slope; and now other towns also flourish near these attractive foothills. One of Dalton's daughters was given in marriage to Louis, a son of William Wolfskill. Dalton's brother, George, I have already mentioned as having likewise settled here.

Of all these worthy dons, possessing vast landed estates, Don António María Lugo, brother of Ygnácio Lugo, was one of the most affluent and venerable. He owned the San António *rancho*, named I presume after him; and in 1856, when he celebrated his seventy-fifth birthday, was reputed to be the owner of fully twenty-nine thousand acres and personal property to the extent of seventy-two thousand dollars. Three sons, José María, José del Carmen and Vicente Lugo, as early as 1842 also acquired in their own names about thirty-seven thousand acres.

Louis Robidoux, a French-American of superior ability who, like many others, had gone through much that was exciting

Louis Robidoux

Julius G. Weyse

John Behn

Louis Breer

William J. Brodrick

Isaac R. Dunkelberger

Frank J. Carpenter

Augustus Ulyard

and unpleasant to establish himself in this wild, open country, eventually had an immense estate known as the Jurupa *rancho,* from which on September 26th, 1846, during the Mexican War, B. D. Wilson and others rode forth to be neatly trapped and captured at the Chino; and where the outlaw Irving later encamped. Riverside occupies a site on this land; and the famous Robidoux hill, usually spoken of as the Roubidoux mountain, once a part of Louis's ranch and to-day a Mecca for thousands of tourists, was named after him.

Many of the *rancheros* kept little ranch stores, from which they sold to their employees. This was rather for convenience than for profit. When their help came to Los Angeles, they generally got drunk and stayed away from work longer than the allotted time; and it was to prevent this, as far as possible, that these outlying stores were conducted.

Louis Robidoux maintained such a store for the accommodation of his hands, and often came to town, sometimes for several days, on which occasions he would buy very liberally anything that happened to take his fancy. In this respect he occasionally acted without good judgment, and if opposed would become all the more determined. Not infrequently he called for so large a supply of some article that I was constrained to remark that he could not possibly need so much; whereupon he would repeat the order with angry emphasis. I sometimes visited his ranch and recall, in particular, one stay of two or three days there in 1857 when, after an unusually large purchase, Robidoux asked me to assist him in checking up the invoices. The cases were unpacked in his ranchhouse; and I have never forgotten the amusing picture of the numerous little Robidoux, digging and delving among the assorted goods for all the prizes they could find, and thus rendering the process of listing the goods much more difficult. When the delivery had been found correct, Robidoux turned to his Mexican wife and asked her to bring the money. She went to the side of the room, opened a Chinese trunk such as every well-to-do Mexican family had (and sometimes as many as half a dozen), and drew therefrom the customary buckskin, from which she extracted the required and rather large amount. These trunks were made of cedar, were gaudily painted, and had the quality of keeping out moths. They were, therefore, displayed with pride by the owners. Recently on turning the pages of some ledgers in which Newmark, Kremer & Company carried the account of this famous *ranchero*, I was interested to find there full confirmation of what I have elsewhere claimed—that the now renowned Frenchman spelled the first syllable of his name *Ro-*, and not *Ru-*, nor yet *Rou-*, as it is generally recorded in books and newspapers.

I should refrain from mentioning a circumstance or two in Robidoux's life with which I am familiar but for the fact that I believe posterity is ever curious to know the little failings as well as the pronounced virtues of men who, through exceptional personality or association, have become historic characters; and that some knowledge of their foibles should not tarnish their reputation. Robidoux, as I have remarked, came to town very frequently, and when again he found himself amid livelier scenes and congenial fellows, as in the late fifties, he always celebrated the occasion with a few intimates, winding up his befuddling bouts in the arms of Chris Fluhr, who winked at his weakness and good-naturedly tucked him away in one of the old-fashioned beds of the Lafayette Hotel, there to remain until he was able to transact business. After all, such celebrating was then not at all uncommon among the best of Southern California people, nor, if gossip may be credited, is it entirely unknown to-day. Robert Hornbeck, of Redlands, by the way, has sought to perpetuate this pioneer's fame in an illustrated volume, *Roubidoux's Ranch in the 70's*, published as I am closing my story.

Robidoux's name leads me to recur to early judges and to his identification with the first Court of Sessions here, when there was such a sparseness even of *rancherías*. Robidoux then lived on his Jurupa domain, and not having been at the meeting of township justices which selected himself and Judge Scott to sit on the bench, and enjoying but infrequent communication with the more peopled districts of Southern California, he

knew nothing of the outcome of the election until sometime
after it had been called.   More than this, Judge Robidoux never
actually participated in a sitting of the Court of Sessions until
four or five weeks after it had been almost daily transacting
business!

Speaking of ranches, and of the Jurupa in particular, I may
here reprint an advertisement—a miniature tree and a house
heading the following announcement in the *Southern Californian* of June 20th, 1855:

> The Subscriber, being anxious to get away from Swindlers,
> offers for sale one of the very finest *ranchos*, or tracts of land,
> that is to be found in California, known as the Rancho de
> Jurupa, Santa Ana River, in the County of San Bernardino.

Bernardo Yorba was another great landowner; and I am
sure that, in the day of his glory, he might have traveled fifty
to sixty miles in a straight line, touching none but his own
possessions.   His ranches, on one of which Pio Pico hid from
Santiago Arguello, were delightfully located where now stand
such places as Anaheim, Orange, Santa Ana, Westminster,
Garden Grove and other towns in Orange County—then a
part of Los Angeles County.

This leads me to describe a shrewd trick.   Schlesinger &
Sherwinsky, traders in general merchandise in 1853, when
they bought a wagon in San Francisco, brought it here by
steamer, loaded it with various attractive wares, took it out
to good-natured and easy-going Bernardo Yorba, and wheedled
the well-known *ranchero* into purchasing not only the contents,
but the wagon, horses and harness as well.   Indeed, their in-
genuity was so well rewarded, that soon after this first lucky
hit, they repeated their success, to the discomfiture of their
competitors; and if I am not mistaken, they performed the
same operation on the old don several times.

The Verdugo family had an extensive acreage where such
towns as Glendale now enjoy the benefit of recent suburban
development, Governor Pedro Fages having granted, as early
as 1784, some thirty-six thousand acres to Don José María

12

Verdugo, which grant was reaffirmed in 1798, thereby affording the basis of a patent issued in 1882, to Julio Verdugo *et al*, although Verdugo died in 1858. To this Verdugo *rancho*, Frémont sent Jesus Pico—the Mexican guide whose life he had spared, as he was about to be executed at San Luis Obispo— to talk with the Californians and to persuade them to deal with Frémont instead of Stockton; and there on February 21st, 1845, Micheltorena and Castro met. Near there also, still later, the celebrated Casa Verdugo entertained for many years the epicures of Southern California, becoming one of the best-known restaurants for Spanish dishes in the State. Little by little, the Verdugo family lost all their property, partly through their refusal or inability to pay taxes; so that by the second decade of the Twentieth Century the surviving representatives, including Victoriano and Guillermo Verdugo, were reduced to poverty.[1]

Recalling Verdugo and his San Rafael Ranch let me add that he had thirteen sons, all of whom frequently accompanied their father to town, especially on election day. On those occasions, J. Lancaster Brent, whose political influence with the old man was supreme, took the Verdugo party in hand and distributed, through the father, fourteen election tickets, on which were impressed the names of Brent's candidates.

Manuel Garfias, County Treasurer a couple of years before I came, was another land-baron, owning in his own name some thirteen or fourteen thousand acres of the San Pasqual Ranch. There, among the picturesque hills and valleys where both Pico and Flores had military camps, now flourish the cities of Pasadena and South Pasadena, which include the land where stood the first house erected on the ranch. It is my impression that beautiful Altadena is also on this land.

Ricardo Vejar, another magnate, had an interest in a wide area of rich territory known as the San José Ranch. Not less than twenty-two thousand acres made up this *rancho* which, as early as 1837, had been granted by Governor Alvarado to Vejar

[1] Julio Chrisostino Verdugo died early in March, 1915, supposed to be about one hundred and twelve years old.

and Ygnácio Palomares who died on November 25th, 1864. Two or three years later, Luis Arenas joined the two, and Alvarado renewed his grant, tacking on a league or two of San José land lying to the West and nearer the San Gabriel mountains. Arenas, in time, disposed of his interest to Henry Dalton; and Dalton joined Vejar in applying to the courts for a partitioning of the estate. This division was ordered by the Spanish *Alcalde* six or seven years before my arrival; but Palomares still objected to the decision, and the matter dragged along in the tribunals many years, the decree finally being set aside by the Court. Vejar, who had been assessed in 1851 for thirty-four thousand dollars' worth of personal property, sold his share of the estate for twenty-nine thousand dollars, in the spring of 1874. It is a curious fact that not until the San José *rancho* had been so cut up that it was not easy to trace it back to the original grantees, did the authorities at Washington finally issue a patent to Dalton, Palomares and Vejar for the twenty-two thousand acres which originally made up the ranch.

The Machados, of whom there were several brothers—Don Agustin, who died on May 17th, 1865, being the head of the family—had title to nearly fourteen thousand acres. Their ranch, originally granted to Don Ygnácio Machado in 1839 and patented in 1873, was known as La Ballona and extended from the city limits to the ocean; and there, among other stock, in 1860, were more than two thousand head of cattle.

The Picos acquired much territory. There were two brothers—Pio, who as Mexican Governor had had wide supervision over land, and Andrés, who had fought throughout the San Pasqual campaigns until the capitulation at Cahuenga, and still later had dashed with spirit across country in pursuit of the murderers of Sheriff Barton. Pio Pico alone, in 1851, was assessed for twenty-two thousand acres as well as twenty-one thousand dollars in personal property. Besides controlling various San Fernando ranches (once under B. H. Lancaro's management), Andrés Pico possessed La Habra, a ranch of over six thousand acres, for which a patent was granted in 1872, and the ranch Los Coyotes, including over forty-eight thousand acres, patented three years later; while Pio Pico at one time owned the Santa Margarita and Las Flores *ranchos*, and had, in addition, some nine thousand acres known as Paso de Bartolo.   In his old age the Governor—who, as long as I knew him, had been strangely loose in his business methods, and had borrowed from everybody—found himself under the necessity of obtaining some thirty or forty thousand dollars, even at the expense of giving to B. Cohn, W. J. Brodrick and Charles Prager, a blanket mortgage covering all of his properties. These included the Pico House, the Pico Ranch on the other side of the San Gabriel River—the homestead on which has for some time been preserved by the ladies of Whittier—and property on Main Street, north of Commercial, besides some other holdings.   When his note fell due Pico was unable to meet it; and the mortgage was foreclosed.   The old man was then left practically penniless, a suit at law concerning the interpretation of the loan-agreement being decided against him.

Henry C. Wilcy must have arrived very early, as he had been in Los Angeles some years before I came.   He married a daughter of Andrés Pico and for a while had charge of his San Fernando Ranch.   Wiley served, at one time, as Sheriff of the County.   He died in 1898.

The *rancho* Los Nietos or, more properly speaking, perhaps, the Santa Gertrudis, than whose soil (watered, as it is, by the San Gabriel River) none more fertile can be found in the world, included indeed a wide area extending between the Santa Ana and San Gabriel rivers, and embracing the ford known as Pico Crossing.   It was then in possession of the Carpenter family, Lemuel Carpenter having bought it from the heirs of Manuel Nieto, to whom it had been granted in 1784.   Carpenter came from Missouri to this vicinity as early as 1833, when he was but twenty-two years old.   For a while, he had a small soap-factory on the right bank of the San Gabriel River, after which he settled on the ranch; and there he remained until November 6th, 1859, when he committed suicide.   Within the borders of this ranch to-day lie such places as Downey and Rivera.

Francisco Sanchez was another early *ranchero*—probably the same who figured so prominently in early San Francisco; and it is possible that J. M. Sanchez, to whom, in 1859, was re-granted the forty-four hundred acres of the Potrero Grande, was his heir.

There were two large and important landowners, second cousins, known as José Sepúlveda; the one, Don José Andrés, and the other, Don José Loreto. The father of José Andrés was Don Francisco Sepúlveda, a Spanish officer to whom the San Vicente Ranch had been granted; and José Andrés, born in San Diego in 1804, was the oldest of eleven children. His brothers were Fernando, José del Carmen, Dolores and Juan María; and he also had six sisters. To José Andrés, or José as he was called, the San Joaquín Ranch was given, an enormous tract of land lying between the present Tustin, earlier known as Tustin City, and San Juan Capistrano, and running from the hills to the sea; while, on the death of Don Francisco, the San Vicente Ranch, later bought by Jones and Baker, was left to José del Carmen, Dolores and Juan María. José, in addition, bought eighteen hundred acres from José Antónío Yorba, and on this newly-acquired property he built his ranchhouse, al-though he and his family may be said to have been more or less permanent residents of Los Angeles. Fernando Sepúlveda married a Verdugo, and through her became proprietor of much of the Verdugo *rancho*. The fact that José was so well provided for, and that Fernando had come into control of the Verdugo acres, made it mutually satisfactory that the San Vicente Ranch should have been willed to the other sons. The children of José Andrés included Miguel, Maurício, Bernabé, Joaquín, Andró-nico and Ygnácio, and Francisca, wife of James Thompson, Tomása, wife of Frank Rico, Ramona, wife of Captain Salis-bury Haley of the *Sea Bird*, Ascención, wife of Tom Mott, and Tranquilina. The latter, with Mrs. Mott and Judge Ygnácio, are still living here.

Don José Loreto, brother of Juan and Diego Sepúlveda, father of Mrs. John T. Lanfranco, and a well-known resident of Los Angeles County in early days, presided over the destinies of thirty-one thousand acres in the Palos Verdes *rancho*, where Flores had stationed his soldiers to watch the American ship *Savannah*. Full patent to this land was granted in 1880.

There being no fences to separate the great ranches, cattle roamed at will; nor were the owners seriously concerned, for every man had his distinct, registered brand and in proper season the various herds were segregated by means of *rodeos*, or round-ups of strayed or mixed cattle. On such occasions, all of the *rancheros* within a certain radius drove their herds little by little into a corral designated for the purpose, and each selected his own cattle according to brand. After segregation had thus been effected, they were driven from the corral, followed by the calves, which were also branded, in anticipation of the next *rodeo*.

Such round-ups were great events, for they brought all the *rancheros* and *vaqueros* together. They became the *raison d'être* of elaborate celebrations, sometimes including horse-races, bull-fights and other amusements; and this was the case particularly in 1861, because of the rains and consequent excellent season.

The enormous herds of cattle gathered at *rodeos* remind me, in fact, of a danger that the *rancheros* were obliged to contend with, especially when driving their stock from place to place: Indians stampeded the cattle, whenever possible, so that in the confusion those escaping the *vaqueros* and straggling behind might the more easily be driven to the Indian camps; and sometimes covetous ranchmen caused a similar commotion among the stock in order to make thieving easier.

While writing of ranches, one bordering on the other, un-fenced and open, and the enormous number of horses and cattle, as well as men required to take care of such an amount of stock, I must not forget to mention an institution that had flourished, as a branch of the judiciary, in palmier Mexican days, though it was on the wane when I arrived here. This was the Judgeship of the Plains, an office charged directly with the interests of the ranchman. Judges of the Plains were officials delegated to arrange for the *rodeos*, and to hold informal court, in the saddle or on the open hillside, in order to settle

disputes among, and dispense justice to, those living and working beyond the pales of the towns. Under Mexican rule, a
Judge of the Plains, who was more or less a law unto himself,
served for glory and dignity (much as does an English Justice
of the Peace); and the latter factor was an important part of the
stipulation, as we may gather from a story told by early Angeleños of the impeachment of Don António María Lugo. Don
António was then a Judge of the Plains, and as such was
charged with having, while on horseback, nearly trampled upon
Pedro Sanchez, for no other reason than that poor Pedro had
refused to "uncover" while the Judge rode by, and to keep his
hat off until his Honor was unmistakably out of sight! When,
at length, Americans took possession of Southern California,
Judges of the Plains were given less power, and provision was
made, for the first time, for a modest *honorarium* in return for
their travel and work.

For nearly a couple of decades after the organization of Los
Angeles under the incoming white pioneers, not very much was
known of the vast districts inland and adjacent to Southern
California; and one can well understand the interest felt by
our citizens on July 17th, 1855, when Colonel Washington, of the
United States Surveying Expedition to the Rio Colorado, put
up at the Bella Union on his way to San Francisco. He was
bombarded with questions about the region lying between the
San Bernardino Mountain range and the Colorado, hitherto
unexplored; and being a good talker, readily responded with
much entertaining information.

In July, 1855, I attained my majority and, having by this
time a fair command of English, I took a more active part in
social affairs. Before he married Margarita, daughter of Juan
Bandini, Dr. J. B. Winston, then interested in the Bella Union,
organized most of the dances, and I was one of his committee
of arrangements. We would collect from the young men of our
acquaintance money enough to pay for candles and music; for
each musician—playing either a harp, a guitar or a flute—
charged from a dollar to a dollar and a half for his services.
Formal social events occurred in the evening of almost any day

of the week. Whenever Dr. Winston or the young gallants of that period thought it was time to have a dance, they just passed around the hat for the necessary funds, and announced the affair. Ladies were escorted to functions, although we did not take them in carriages or other vehicles but tramped through the dust or mud. Young ladies, however, did not go out with gentlemen unless they were accompanied by a chaperon, generally some antiquated female member of the family.

These hops usually took place at the residence of Widow Blair, opposite the Bella Union and north of the present Post Office. There we could have a sitting-room, possibly eighteen by thirty feet square; and while this was larger than any other room in a private house in town, it will be realized that, after all, the space for dancing was very limited. We made the best, however, of what we had; the refreshments, at these improvised affairs, were rarely more than lemonade and *olla* water.

Many times such dances followed as a natural termination to another social observance, transmitted to us, I have no doubt, by the romantic Spanish settlers here, and very popular for some time after I came. This good old custom was serenading. We would collect money, as if for dancing; and in the evening a company of young men and chaperoned young ladies would proceed in a body to some popular girl's home where, with innocent gallantry, the little band would serenade her. After that, of course, we were always glad to accept an invitation to come into the house, when the ladies of the household sometimes regaled us with a bit of cake and wine.

Speaking of the social life of those early days, when warm, stimulating friendships and the lack of all foolish caste distinctions rendered the occasions delightfully pleasant, may it not be well to ask whether the contrast between those simple, inexpensive pleasures, and the elaborate and extravagant demands of modern society, is not worth sober thought? To be sure, Los Angeles then was exceedingly small, and pioneers here were much like a large family in plain, unpretentious circumstances. There were no such ceremonies as now; there were no four hundred, no three hundred, nor even one hundred. There was, for example, no flunky at the door to receive the visitor's card; and for the very good reason that visiting cards were unknown. In those pastoral, pueblo days it was no indiscretion for a friend to walk into another friend's house without knocking. Society of the early days could be divided, I suppose, into two classes: the respectable and the evil element; and people who were honorable came together because they esteemed each other and liked one another's company. The "gold fish" of the present age had not yet developed. We enjoyed ourselves together, and without distinction were ready to fight to the last ditch for the protection of our families and the preservation of our homes.

In the fall of 1855, Dr. Thomas J. White, a native of St. Louis and Speaker of the Assembly in the first California Legislature convened at San José, in December, 1849, arrived from San Francisco with his wife and two daughters, and bought a vineyard next to Dr. Hoover's ten-acre place where, in three or four years, he became one of the leading wine-producers. Their advent created quite a stir, and the house, which was a fine and rather commodious one for the times, soon became the scene of extensive entertainments. The addition of this highly-accomplished family was indeed quite an accession to our social ranks. Their hospitality compared favorably even with California's open-handed and open-hearted spirit, and soon became notable. Their evening parties and other receptions were both frequent and lavish, so that the Whites quickly took rank as leaders in Los Angeles. While yet in Sacramento, one of the daughters, who had fallen in love with E. J. C. Kewen when the latter was a member of the White party in crossing the great Plains, married the Colonel; and in 1862, another daughter, Miss Jennie, married Judge Murray Morrison. A son was T. Jeff White, who named his place *Casalinda*. In the late fifties, Dr. White had a drug-store in the Temple Building on Main Street.

It was long before Los Angeles had anything like a regular theater, or even enjoyed such shows as were provided by itinerant companies, some of which, when they did begin to come, stayed here for weeks; although I remember having heard of one ambitious group of players styling themselves *The Rough and Ready Theater*, who appeared here very early and gave sufficient satisfaction to elicit the testimony from a local scribe, that "when Richmond was conquered and laid off for dead, the enthusiastic auditors gave the King a smile of decided approval!" Minstrels and circuses were occasionally presented, a minstrel performance taking place sometime in the fifties, in an empty store on Aliso Street, near Los Angeles. About the only feature of this event that is now clear in my memory is that Bob Carsley, played the bones; he remained in Los Angeles and married, later taking charge of the foundry which Stearns established when he built his Arcadia Block on Los Angeles Street. An Albino also was once brought to Los Angeles and publicly exhibited; and since anything out of the ordinary challenged attention, everybody went to see a curiosity that to-day would attract but little notice. Speaking of theatrical performances and the applause bestowed upon favorites, I must not forget to mention the reckless use of money and the custom, at first quite astounding to me, of throwing coins— often large, shining slugs—upon the stage or floor, if an actor or actress particularly pleased the spendthrift patron.

In October, 1855, William Abbott, who was one of the many to come to Los Angeles in 1853, and who had brought with him a small stock of furniture, started a store in a little wooden house he had acquired on a lot next to that which later became the site of the Pico House. Abbott married Doña Merced Garcia; and good fortune favoring him, he not only gradually enlarged his stock of goods, but built a more commodious building, in the upper story of which was the Merced Theater, named after Abbott's wife, and opened in the late sixties. The vanity of things mundane is well illustrated in the degeneration of this center of early histrionic effort, which entered a period of decay in the beginning of the eighties and, as the scene of disreputable dances, before 1890 had been pronounced a nuisance.

During the first decade under the American *régime*, Los Angeles gradually learned the value of reaching toward the outside world and welcoming all who responded. In 1855, as I have said, a brisk trade was begun with Salt Lake, through the opening up of a route—leading along the old Spanish trail to Santa Fé. Banning & Alexander, with their usual enterprise, together with W. T. B. Sanford, made the first shipment in a heavily-freighted train of fifteen wagons drawn by one hundred and fifty mules. The train, which carried thirty tons, was gone four months; having left Los Angeles in May, it returned in September. In every respect the experiment was a success, and naturally the new route had a beneficial effect on Southern California trade. It also contributed to the development of San Bernardino, through which town it passed. Before the year was out, one or two express companies were placarding the stores here with announcements of rates "To Great Salt Lake City." Banning, by the way, then purchased in Salt Lake the best wagons he had, and brought here some of the first vehicles with spokes to be seen in Los Angeles.

The school authorities of the past sometimes sailed on waters as troubled as those rocking the Educational Boards to-day. I recall an amusing incident of the middle fifties, when a new set of Trustees, having succeeded to the control of affairs, were scandalized, or at least pretended to be, by an action of their predecessors, and immediately adopted the following resolution:

Resolved, that page seven of the School Commissioners' Record be pasted down on page eight, so that the indecorous language written therein by the School Commissioners of 1855, can never again be read or seen, said language being couched in such terms that the present School Commissioners are not willing to read such record.

Richard Laugh'in died at his vineyard, on the east side of Alameda Street, in or soon after 1855. Like William Wolfskill, Ewing Young—who fitted out the Wolfskill party—and Moses Carson, brother of the better-known Kit and at one time a trader at San Pedro, Laughlin was a trapper who made his way to Los Angeles along the Gila River. This was a waterway of the savage Apache country traversed even in 1854— according to the lone ferryman's statistics—by nearly ten thousand persons. In middle life, Laughlin supported himself by carpentry and hunting.

With the increase in the number and activity of the Chinese in California, the prejudice of the masses was stirred up violently. This feeling found expression particularly in 1855, when a law was passed by the Legislature, imposing a fine of fifty dollars on each owner or master of a vessel bringing to California anyone incapable of becoming a citizen; but when suit was instituted, to test the act's validity, it was declared unconstitutional. At that time, most of the opposition to the Chinese came from San Franciscans, there being but few coolies here.

Certain members of the same Legislature led a movement to form a new State, to be called Colorado and to include all the territory south of San Luis Obispo; and the matter was repeatedly discussed in several subsequent sessions. Nothing came of it, however; but Kern County was formed, in 1866, partly from Los Angeles County and partly from Tulare. About five thousand square miles, formerly under our County banner, were thus legislated away; and because the mountainous and desert area seemed of little prospective value, we submitted willingly. In this manner, unenlightened by modern science and ignorant of future possibilities, Southern California, guided by no clear and certain vision, drifted and stumbled along to its destiny.

Los Angeles in the Late Fifties

From a contemporary sketch

Myer J. Newmark

Edward J. C. Kewen

Dr. John S. Griffin

William C. Warren

CHAPTER XIV

ORCHARDS AND VINEYARDS

1856

DURING 1856, I dissolved with my partners, Rich and Laventhal, and went into business with my uncle, Joseph Newmark, J. P. Newmark and Maurice Kremer, under the title of Newmark, Kremer & Company. Instead of a quasi wholesale business, we now had a larger assortment and did more of a retail business. We occupied a room, about forty by eighty feet in size, in the Mascarel and Barri block on the south side of Commercial Street (then known as Commercial Row), between Main and Los Angeles streets, our modest establishment being almost directly opposite the contracted quarters of my first store and having the largest single storeroom then in the city; and there we continued with moderate success, until 1858.

To make this new partnership possible, Kremer had sold out his interest in the firm of Lazard & Kremer, dry goods merchants, the readjustment providing an amusing illustration of the manner in which business, with its almost entire lack of specialization, was then conducted. When the stock was taken, a large part of it consisted, not of dry goods, as one might well suppose, but of—cigars and tobacco!

About the beginning of 1856, Sisters of Charity made their first appearance in Los Angeles, following a meeting called by Bishop Amat during the preceding month, to provide for their coming, when Abel Stearns presided and John G. Downey acted as Secretary. Benjamin Hayes, Thomas Foster, Ezra Drown,

Louis Vignes, Ygnácio del Valle and António Coronel co-
operated, while Manuel Requena collected the necessary funds.
On January 5th, Sisters María Scholastica, María Corzina,
Ana, Clara, Francisca and Angela arrived—three of them
coming almost directly from Spain; and immediately they
formed an important adjunct to the Church in matters pertaining to religion, charity and education. It was to them that
B. D. Wilson sold his Los Angeles home, including ten acres of
fine orchard, at the corner of Alameda and Macy streets, for
eight thousand dollars; and there for many years they conducted
their school, the Institute and Orphan Asylum, until they sold
the property to J. M. Griffith, who used the site for a lumber-
yard. Griffith, in turn, disposed of it to the Southern Pacific
Railroad Company. Sister Scholastica, who celebrated in
1889 her fiftieth anniversary as a sister, was long the Mother
Superior.

The so-called First Public School having met with popular
approval, the Board of Education in 1856 opened another
school on Bath Street. The building, two stories in height, was
of brick and had two rooms.

On January 9th, John P. Brodie assumed charge of the
Southern Californian. Andrés Pico was then proprietor; and
before the newspaper died, in 1857, Pico lost, it is said, ten
thousand dollars in the venture.

The first regular course of public lectures here was given in
1856 under the auspices of a society known as the Mechanics'
Institute, and in one of Henry Dalton's corrugated iron
buildings.

George T. Burrill, first County Sheriff, died on February
2d, his demise bringing to mind an interesting story. He was
Sheriff, in the summer of 1850, when certain members of
the infamous Irving party were arraigned for murder, and
during that time received private word that many of the
prisoners' friends would pack the little court room and attempt
a rescue. Burrill, however, who used to wear a sword and had
a rather soldierly bearing, was equal to the emergency. He
quickly sent to Major E. H. Fitzgerald and had the latter

come post-haste to town and court with a detachment of soldiers; and with this superior, disciplined force he overawed the bandits' *compañeros* who, sure enough, were there and fully armed to make a demonstration.

Thomas E. Rowan arrived here with his father, James Rowan, in 1856, and together they opened a bakery. Tom delivered the bread for a short time, but soon abandoned that pursuit for politics, being frequently elected to office, serving in turn as Supervisor, City and County Treasurer and even, from 1893 to 1894, as Mayor of Los Angeles. Shortly before Tom married Miss Josephine Mayerhofer in San Francisco in 1862—and a handsome couple they made—the Rowans bought from Louis Mesmer the American Bakery, located at the southwest corner of Main and First streets and originally established by August Ulyard. When James Rowan died about forty years ago, Tom fell heir to the bakery; but as he was otherwise engaged, he employed Maurice Mauricio as manager, and P. Galta, afterward a prosperous business man of Bakersfield, as driver. Tom, who died in 1899, was also associated as cashier with I. W. Hellman and F. P. F. Temple in their bank. Rowan Avenue and Rowan Street were both named after this early comer.

The time for the return of my brother and his European bride now approached, and I felt a natural desire to meet them. Almost coincident, therefore, with their arrival in San Francisco, I was again in that growing city in 1856, although I had been there but the year previous.

On April 9th, occurred the marriage of Matilda, daughter of Joseph Newmark, to Maurice Kremer. The ceremony was performed by the bride's father. For the subsequent festivities, ice, from which ice cream was made, was brought from San Bernardino; both luxuries on this occasion being used in Los Angeles, as far as I can remember, for the first time.

To return to the Los Angeles *Star*. When J. S. Waite became Postmaster, in 1855, he found it no sinecure to continue even such an unpretentious and, in all likelihood, unprofitable news-sheet and at the same time attend to Uncle Sam's mail-bags; and early in 1856 he offered "the entire establishment at one thousand dollars less than cost." Business was so slow at that time, in fact, that Waite—after, perhaps, ruefully looking over his unpaid subscriptions—announced that he would "take wood, butter, eggs, flour, wheat or corn" in payment of bills due.   He soon found a ready customer in William A. Wallace, the Principal of the boys' school who, on the twelfth of April, bought the paper; but Waite's disgust was nothing to that of the schoolteacher who, after two short months' trial with the editorial quill, scribbled a last doleful *adiós*. "The flush times of the pueblo, the day of large prices and pocket-books, are past," Wallace declared; and before him the editor saw "only picayunes, bad liquor, rags and universal dullness, when neither pistol-shots nor dying groans" could have any effect, and "when earthquakes would hardly turn men in their beds!"   Nothing was left for such a destitute and discouraged quillman "but to wait for a *carreta* and get out of town."   Wallace sold the paper, therefore, in June, 1856, to Henry Hamilton, a native of Ireland who had come to California in 1848 an apprenticed printer, and was for some years in newspaper work in San Francisco; and Hamilton soon put new life into the journal.

In 1856, the many-sided Dr. William B. Osburn organized a company to bore an artesian well west of the city; but when it reached a depth of over seven hundred feet, the prospectors went into bankruptcy.

George Lehman, early known as George the Baker (whose shop at one time was on the site of the Hayward Hotel), was a somewhat original and very popular character who, in 1856, took over the Round House on Main Street, between Third and Fourth, and there opened a pleasure-resort extending to Spring Street and known as the Garden of Paradise.   The grounds really occupied on the one hand what are now the sites of the Pridham, the Pinney and the Turnverein, and on the other the Henne, the Breed and the Lankershim blocks.   There was an entrance on Main Street and one, with two picket gates, on Spring.   From the general shape and appearance of the building, it was always one of the first objects in town to attract attention; and Lehman (who, when he appeared on the street, had a crooked cane hanging on his arm and a lemon in his hand), came to be known as "Round House George." The house had been erected in the late forties by Raimundo, generally called Ramón, or Raymond Alexander, a sailor, who asserted that the design was a copy of a structure he had once seen on the coast of Africa; and there Ramón and his native California wife had lived for many years. Partly because he wished to cover the exterior with vines and flowers, Lehman nailed boards over the outer adobe walls and thus changed the cylinder form into that of an octagon.   An ingenious arrangement of the *parterre* and a peculiar distribution of some trees, together with a profusion of plants and flowers—affording cool and shady bowers, somewhat similar to those of a typical beer or wine garden of the Fatherland—gave the place great popularity; while two heroic statues—one of *Adam* and the other of *Eve*—with a conglomeration of other curiosities, including the *Apple Tree* and the *Serpent*—all illustrating the world-old story of Eden—and a moving panorama made the Garden unique and rather famous.   The balcony of the house provided accommodation for the playing of such music, perhaps discordant, as Los Angeles could then produce, and nearby was a framework containing a kind of swing then popular and known as "flying horses."   The bar was in the Garden, near a well-sweep; and at the Main Street entrance stood a majestic and noted cactus tree which was cut down in 1886.   The Garden of Paradise was opened toward the end of September, 1858, and so large were the grounds that when they were used, in 1876, for the Fourth of July celebration, twenty-six hundred people were seated there.

This leads me to say that Arthur McKenzie Dodson, who established a coal- and wood-yard at what was later the corner of Spring and Sixth streets, started there a little community which he called Georgetown—as a compliment, it was said, to the famous Round House George whose bakery, I have remarked, was located on that corner.

On June 7th, Dr. John S. Griffin, who had an old fashioned,

classical education, and was a graduate, in medicine, of the University of Pennsylvania, succeeded Dr. William B. Osburn as Superintendent of the Los Angeles City Schools.

In these times of modern irrigation and scientific methods, it is hard to realize how disastrous were climatic extremes in an earlier day: in 1856, a single electric disturbance, accompanied by intense heat and sandstorms, left tens of thousands of dead cattle to tell the story of drought and destruction.

During the summer, I had occasion to go to Fort Tejón to see George C. Alexander, a customer, and I again asked Sam Meyer if he would accompany me. Such a proposition was always agreeable to Sam; and, having procured horses, we started, the distance being about one hundred and fifteen miles.

We left Los Angeles early one afternoon, and made our first stop at Lyons's Station, where we put up for the night. One of the brothers, after whom the place was named, prepared supper. Having to draw some thick blackstrap from a keg, he used a pitcher to catch the treacle; and as the liquid ran very slowly, our sociable host sat down to talk a bit, and soon forgot all about what he had started to do. The molasses, however, although it ran pretty slowly, ran steadily, and finally, like the mush in the fairy-tale of the enchanted bowl, overflowed the top of the receptacle and spread itself over the dirt floor. When Lyons had finished his chat, he saw, to his intense chagrin, a new job upon his hands, and one likely to busy him for some time.

Departing next morning at five o'clock we met Cy Lyons, who had come to Los Angeles in 1849 and was then engaged with his brother Sanford in raising sheep in that neighborhood. Cy was on horseback and had two pack animals, loaded with provisions. "Hello, boys! where are you bound?" he asked; and when we told him that we were on our way to Fort Tejón, he said that he was also going there, and volunteered to save us forty miles by guiding us over the trail. Such a shortening of our journey appealed to us as a good prospect, and we fell in behind the mounted guide.

It was one of those red-hot summer days characteristic of

that region and season, and in a couple of hours we began to get very thirsty. Noticing this, Cy told us that no water would be found until we got to the Rancho de la Liebre, and that we could not possibly reach there until evening. Having no *bota de agua* handy, I took an onion from Lyons's pack and ate it, and that afforded me some relief; but Sam, whose decisions were always as lasting as the fragrance of that aromatic bulb, would not try the experiment. To make a long story short, when we at last reached the ranch, Sam, completely fagged out, and unable to alight from his horse, toppled off into our arms. The chewing of the onion had refreshed me to some extent, but just the same the day's journey proved one of the most miserable experiences through which I have ever passed.

The night was so hot at the ranch that we decided to sleep outdoors in one of the wagons; and being worn out with the day's exposure and fatigue, we soon fell asleep. The soundness of our slumbers did not prevent us from hearing, in the middle of the night, a snarling bear, scratching in the immediate neighborhood. A bear generally means business; and you may depend upon it that neither Sam, myself nor even Cy were very long in bundling out of the wagon and making a dash for the more protecting house. Early next morning, we recommenced our journey toward Fort Tejón, and reached there without any further adventures worth relating.

Coming back, we stopped for the night at Gordon's Station, and the next day rode fully seventy miles—not so inconsiderable an accomplishment, perhaps, for those not accustomed to regular saddle exercise.

A few months later, I met Cy on the street. "Harris," said he, "do you know that once, on that hot day going to Fort Tejón, we were within three hundred feet of a fine, cool spring?" "Then why in the devil," I retorted, "didn't you take us to it?" To which Cy, with a chuckle, answered: "Well, I just wanted to see what would happen to you!"

My first experience with camp meetings was in the year 1856, when I attended one in company with Miss Sarah Newmark, to whom I was then engaged, and Miss Harriet, her

sister—later Mrs. Eugene Meyer. I engaged a buggy from
George Carson's livery stable on Main Street; and we rode to
Ira Thompson's grove at El Monte, in which the meeting was
held. These camp meetings supplied a certain amount of social
attraction to residents, in that good-hearted period when
creeds formed a bond rather than a hindrance.

It was in 1856 that, in connection with our regular business,
we began buying hides. One day a Mexican customer came
into the store and, looking around, said: "*¿Compra cueros?*"
(Do you buy hides?) "*Si, señor,*" I replied, to which he then
said: "*Tengo muchos en mi rancho*" (I have many at my ranch).
"Where do you live?" I asked. "Between Cahuenga and San
Fernando Mission," he answered. He had come to town in his
carreta, and added that he would conduct me to his place, if I
wished to go there.

I obtained a wagon and, accompanied by Samuel Cohn,
went with the Mexican. The native jogged on, *carreta*-fashion,
the oxen lazily plodding along, while the driver with his
ubiquitous pole kept them in the road by means of continual
and effective prods, delivered first on one side, then on the other.
It was dark when we reached the ranch; and the night being
balmy, we wrapped ourselves up in blankets, and slept under
the adobe veranda.

Early in the morning, I awoke and took a survey of the
premises. To my amazement, I saw but one little kipskin
hanging up to dry! When at length my Mexican friend
appeared on the scene, I asked him where he kept his hides?
(*¿Donde tiene usted los cueros?*) At which he pointed to the
lone kip and, with a characteristic and perfectly indifferent
shrug of the shoulders, said: "*¡No tengo más!*" (I have no
more!)

I then deliberated with Sam as to what we should do;
and having proceeded to San Fernando Mission to collect
there, if possible, a load of hides, we were soon fortunate
in obtaining enough to compensate us for our previous trouble and disappointment. On the way home, we came to a
rather deep ditch preventing further progress. Being obliged,

however, to get to the other side, we decided to throw the
hides into the ditch, placing one on top of the other, until the
obstructing gap was filled to a level with the road; and then
we drove across, if not on dry land, at least on dry hides,
which we reloaded onto the wagon. Finally, we reached
town at a late hour.

In this connection, I may remind the reader of Dana's
statement, in his celebrated *Two Years before the Mast*, that San
Pedro once furnished more hides than any other port on the
Coast; and may add that from the same port, more than forty
years afterward, consignments of this valuable commodity
were still being made, I myself being engaged more and more
extensively in the hide trade.

Colonel Isaac Williams died on September 13th, having
been a resident of Los Angeles and vicinity nearly a quarter of
a century. A Pennsylvanian by birth, he had with him in the
West a brother, Hiram, later of San Bernardino County.
Happy as was most of Colonel Williams' life, tragedy entered
his family circle, as I shall show, when both of his sons-in-law,
John Rains and Robert Carlisle, met violent deaths at the
hands of others.

Jean Louis Vignes came to Los Angeles in 1829, and set out
the Aliso Vineyard of one hundred and four acres which derived
its name, as did the street, from a previous and incorrect application of the Castilian *aliso*, meaning alder, to the sycamore
tree, a big specimen of which stood on the place. This tree,
possibly a couple of hundred years old, long shaded Vignes'
wine-cellars, and was finally cut down a few years ago to make
room for the Philadelphia Brew House. From a spot about
fifty feet away from the Vignes adobe extended a grape arbor
perhaps ten feet in width and fully a quarter of a mile long,
thus reaching to the river; and this arbor was associated with
many of the early celebrations in Los Angeles. The northern
boundary of the property was Aliso Street; its western boundary
was Alameda; and part of it was surrounded by a high adobe
wall, inside of which, during the troubles of the Mexican War,
Don Louis enjoyed a far safer seclusion than many others.

On June 7th, 1851, Vignes advertised El Aliso for sale, but it was not subdivided until much later, when Eugene Meyer and his associates bought it for this purpose.   Vignes Street recalls the veteran viticulturist.

While upon the subject of this substantial old pioneer family, I may give a rather interesting reminiscence as to the state of Aliso Street at this time.   I have said that this street was the main road from Los Angeles to the San Bernardino country; and so it was.   But in the fifties, Aliso Street stopped very abruptly at the Sainsevain Vineyard, where it narrowed down to one of the willow-bordered, picturesque little lanes so frequently found here, and paralleled the noted grape-arbor as far as the river-bank.   At this point, Andrew Boyle and other residents of the Heights and beyond were wont to cross the stream on their way to and from town.   The more important travel was by means of another lane known as the Aliso Road, turning at a corner occupied by the old Aliso Mill and winding along the Hoover Vineyard to the river.   Along this route the San Bernardino stage rolled noisily, traversing in summer or during a poor season what was an almost dry wash, but encountering in wet winter raging torrents so impassable that all intercourse with the settlements to the east was disturbed.   For a whole week, on several occasions, the San Bernardino stage was tied up, and once at least Andrew Boyle, before he had become conversant with the vagaries of the Los Angeles River, found it impossible for the better part of a fortnight to come to town for the replenishment of a badly-depleted larder. Lovers' Lane, willowed and deep with dust, was a narrow road now variously located in the minds of pioneers; my impression being that it followed the line of the present Date Street, although some insist that it was Macy.

Pierre Sainsevain, a nephew of Vignes, came in 1839 and for a while worked for his uncle.   Jean Louis Sainsevain, another nephew, arrived in Los Angeles in 1849 or soon after, and on April 14th, 1855, purchased for forty-two thousand dollars the vineyard, cellars and other property of his uncle. This was the same year in which he returned to France for his son Michel and remarried, leaving another son, Paul, in school there.   Pierre joined his brother; and in 1857 Sainsevain Brothers made the first California champagne, first shipping their wine to San Francisco.   Paul, now a resident of San Diego, came to Los Angeles in 1861.   The name endures in Sainsevain Street.

The activity of these Frenchmen reminds me that much usually characteristic of country life was present in what was called the city of Los Angeles, when I first saw it, as may be gathered from the fact that, in 1853, there were a hundred or more vineyards hereabouts, seventy-five or eighty of which were within the city precincts.   These did not include the once famous "mother vineyard" of San Gabriel Mission, which the *padres* used to claim had about fifty thousand vines, but which had fallen into somewhat picturesque decay.   Near San Gabriel, however, in 1855, William M. Stockton had a large vineyard nursery.   William Wolfskill was one of the leading vineyardists, having set out his first vine, so it was said, in 1838, when he affirmed his belief that the plant, if well cared for, would flourish a hundred years!   Don José Serrano, from whom Dr. Leonce Hoover bought many of the grapes he needed, did have vines, it was declared, that were nearly a century old.   When I first passed through San Francisco, *en route* to Los Angeles, I saw grapes from this section in the markets of that city bringing twenty cents a pound; and to such an extent for a while did San Francisco continue to draw on Los Angeles for grapes, that Banning shipped thither from San Pedro, in 1857, no less than twenty-one thousand crates, averaging forty-five pounds each. It was not long, however, before ranches nearer San Francisco began to interfere with this monopoly of the South, and, as, a consequence, the shipment of grapes from Los Angeles fell off. This reminds me that William Wolfskill sent to San Francisco some of the first Northern grapes sold there; they were grown in a Napa Valley vineyard that he owned in the middle of the fifties, and when unloaded on the Long Wharf, three or four weeks in advance of Los Angeles grapes, brought at wholesale twenty-five dollars per hundred weight!

With the decline in the fresh fruit trade, however, the making and exportation of wine increased, and several who had not ventured into vineyarding before, now did so, acquiring their own land or an interest in the establishments of others. By 1857, Jean Louis Vignes boasted of possessing some white wine twenty years old—possibly of the same vintage about which Dr. Griffin often talked, in his reminiscences of the days when he had been an army surgeon; and Louis Wilhart occasionally sold wine which was little inferior to that of Jean Louis. Dr. Hoover was one of the first to make wine for the general market, having, for a while, a pretty and well-situated place called the Clayton Vineyard; and old Joseph Huber, who had come to California from Kentucky for his health, began in 1855 to make wine with considerable success. He owned the Foster Vineyard, where he died in July, 1866. B. D. Wilson was also soon shipping wine to San Francisco. L. J. Rose, who first entered the field in January, 1861, at Sunny Slope, not far from San Gabriel Mission, was another producer, and had a vineyard famous for brandy and wine. He made a departure in going to the foothills, and introduced many varieties of foreign grapes. By the same year, or somewhat previously, Matthew Keller, Stearns & Bell, Dr. Thomas J. White, Dr. Parrott, Kiln Messer, Henry Dalton, H. D. Barrows, Juan Bernard and Ricardo Vejar had wineries, and John Schumacher had a vineyard opposite the site of the City Gardens in the late seventies. L. H. Titus, in time, had a vineyard, known as the Dewdrop, near that of Rose. Still another wine producer was António María Lugo, who set out his vines on San Pedro Street, near the present Second, and often dwelt in the long adobe house where both Steve Foster, Lugo's son-in-law, and Mrs. Wallace Woodworth lived, and where I have been many times pleasantly entertained.

Dr. Leonce Hoover, who died on October 8th, 1862, was a native of Switzerland and formerly a surgeon in the army of Napoleon, when his name—later changed at the time of naturalization—had been Huber. Dr. Hoover in 1849 came to Los Angeles with his wife, his son, Vincent A. Hoover,

then a young man, and two daughters, the whole family
traveling by ox-team and prairie schooner. They soon discovered rich *placer* gold-beds, but were driven away by hostile
Indians. A daughter, Mary A., became the wife of Samuel
Briggs, a New Hampshire Yankee, who was for years Wells
Fargo's agent here. For a while the Hoovers lived on the
Wolfskill Ranch, after which they had a vineyard in the neighborhood of what is now the property of the Cudahy Packing
Company. Vincent Hoover was a man of prominence in his
time; he died in 1883. Mrs. Briggs, whose daughter married
the well-known physician, Dr. Granville MacGowan, sold
her home, on Broadway between Third and Fourth streets,
to Homer Laughlin when he erected the Laughlin Building.
Hoover Street is named for this family.

Accompanied by his son William, Joseph Huber, Sr., in
1855 came to Los Angeles from Kentucky, hoping to improve his
health; and when the other members of his family, consisting
of his wife and children, Caroline, Emeline, Edward and
Joseph, followed him here, in 1859, by way of New York and the
Isthmus, they found him settled as a vineyardist, occupying
the Foster property running from Alameda Street to the river,
in a section between Second and Sixth streets. The advent of
a group of young people, so well qualified to add to what has
truthfully been described by old-time Angeleños as our family
circle, was hailed with a great deal of interest and satisfaction.
In time, Miss Emeline Huber was married to O. W. Childs, and
Miss Caroline was wedded to Dr. Frederick Preston Howard, a
druggist who, more than forty years ago, bought out Theodore
Wollweber, selling the business back to the latter a few years
later. The prominence of this family made it comparatively
easy for Joseph Huber, Jr., in 1865, to secure the nomination
and be elected County Treasurer, succeeding M. Kremer, who
had served six years. Huber, Sr., died about the middle sixties.
Mrs. Huber lived to be eighty-three years old.

José de Rúbio had at least two vineyards when I came—
one on Alameda Street, south of Wolfskill's and not far from
Coronel's, and one on the east side of the river. Rúbio came

here very early in the century, after having married Juana, a daughter of Juan María Miron, a well-known sea captain, and built three adobe houses. The first of these was on the site of the present home of William H. Workman, on Boyle Heights; the second was near what was later the corner of Alameda and Eighth streets, and the third was on Alameda Street near the present Vernon Avenue. One of his ranches was known as "Rúbio's," and there many a barbecue was celebrated. In 1859, Rúbio leased the Sepúlveda Landing, at San Pedro, and commenced to haul freight, to and fro. Señor and Señora Rúbio[1] had twenty-five children, of whom five are now living. Another Los Angeles vineyardist who lived near the river when I came was a Frenchman named Clemente.

Julius Weyse also had a vineyard, living on what is now Eighth Street near San Pedro. A son, H. G. Weyse, has distinguished himself as an attorney and has served in the Legislature; another, Otto G., married the widow of Edward Naud, while a third son, Rudolf G., married a daughter of H. D. Barrows.

The Reyes family was prominent here; a daughter married William Nordholt. Ysidro had a vineyard on Washington Street; and during one of the epidemics, he died of smallpox. His brother, Pablo, was a rancher.

While on the subject of vineyards, I may describe the method by which wine was made here in the early days and the part taken in the industry by the Indians, who always interested and astounded me. Stripped to the skin, and wearing only loin-cloths, they tramped with ceaseless tread from morn till night, pressing from the luscious fruit of the vineyard the juice so soon to ferment into wine. The grapes were placed in elevated vats from which the liquid ran into other connecting vessels; and the process exhaled a stale acidity, scenting the surrounding air. These Indians were employed in the early fall, the season of the year when wine is made and when the thermometer as a rule, in Southern California, reaches its

---

[1] Señora de Rúbio survived her husband many years, dying on October 27th, 1914, at the age of one hundred and seven, after residing in Los Angeles ninety-four years.

highest point; and this temperature coupled with incessant
toil caused the perspiration to drip from their swarthy bodies
into the wine product, the sight of which in no wise increased
my appetite for California wine.

A staple article of food for the Indians in 1856, by the
way, was the acorn. The crop that year, however, was very
short; and streams having also failed, in many instances, to
yield the food usually taken from them, the tribes were in a
distressed condition. Such were the aborigines' straits, in
fact, that *rancheros* were warned of the danger, then greater
than ever, from Indian depredations on stock.

In telling of the Sisters of Charity, I have forgotten to add
that, after settling here, they sent to New York for a portable
house, which they shipped to Los Angeles by way of Cape
Horn. In due time, the house arrived; but imagine their vex-
ation on discovering that, although the parts were supposed
to have been marked so that they might easily be joined together, no one here could do the work. In the end, the Sisters
were compelled to send East for a carpenter who, after a long
interval, arrived and finished the house.

Soon after the organization of a Masonic lodge here, in
1854, many of my friends joined, and among them my brother,
J. P. Newmark, who was admitted on February 26th, 1855, on
which occasion J. H. Stuart was the Secretary; and through their
participation in the celebration of St. John's Day (the twenty-
fourth of June,) I was seized with a desire to join the order.
This I did at the end of 1856, becoming a member of Los Angeles
Lodge No. 42, whose meetings were held over Potter's store on
Main Street. Worshipful Master Thomas Foster initiated me,
and on January 22d, 1857, Worshipful Master Jacob Elias offi-
ciating, I took the third degree. I am, therefore, in all probability, the oldest living member of this now venerable Masonic
organization.

CHAPTER XV

1857

IN the beginning of 1857, we had a more serious earthquake than any in recent years. At half-past eight o'clock on the morning of January 9th, a tremor shook the earth from North to South; the first shocks being light, the quake grew in power until houses were deserted, men, women and children sought refuge in the streets, and horses and cattle broke loose in wild alarm. For perhaps two, or two and a half minutes, the *temblor* continued and much damage was done. Los Angeles felt the disturbance far less than many other places, although five to six shocks were noted and twenty times during the week people were frightened from their homes; at Temple's *rancho* and at Fort Tejón great rents were opened in the earth and then closed again, piling up a heap or dune of finely-powdered stone and dirt. Large trees were uprooted and hurled down the hillsides; and tumbling after them went the cattle. Many officers, including Colonel B. L. Beall—well known in Los Angeles social circles—barely escaped from the barracks with their lives; and until the cracked adobes could be repaired, officers and soldiers lived in tents. It was at this time, too, that a so-called tidal wave almost engulfed the *Sea Bird*, plying between San Pedro and San Francisco, as she was entering the Golden Gate. Under the splendid seamanship of Captain Salisbury Haley, however, his little ship weathered the wave, and he was able later to report her awful experience to the scientific world.

This year also proved a dry season; and, consequently, times became very bad. With two periods of adversity, even the richest of the cattle-kings felt the pinch, and many began to part with their lands in order to secure the relief needed to tide them over. The effects of drought continued until 1858, although some good influences improved business conditions.

Due to glowing accounts of the prospects for conquest and fortune given out by Henry A. Crabb, a Stockton lawyer who married a Spanish woman with relatives in Sonora, a hundred or more filibusters gathered in Los Angeles, in January, to meet Crabb at San Pedro, when he arrived from the North on the steamer *Sea Bird*. They strutted about the streets here, displaying rifles and revolvers; and this would seem to have been enough to prevent their departure for Sonita, a little town a hundred miles beyond Yuma, to which they finally tramped. The filibusters were permitted to leave, however, and they invaded the foreign soil; but Crabb made a mess of the undertaking, even failing in blowing up a little church he attacked; and those not killed in the skirmish were soon surrounded and taken prisoners. The next morning, Crabb and some others who had paraded so ostentatiously while here, were tied to trees or posts, and summarily executed. Crabb's body was riddled with a hundred bullets and his head cut off and sent back in *mescal;* only one of the party was spared—Charley Evans, a lad of fifteen years, who worked his way to Los Angeles and was connected with a somewhat similar invasion a while later.

In January, also, when threats were made against the white population of Southern California, Mrs. Griffin, the wife of Dr. J. S. Griffin, came running, in all excitement, to the home of Joseph Newmark, and told the members of the family to lock all their doors and bolt their windows, as it was reported that some of the outlaws were on their way to Los Angeles, to murder the white people. As soon as possible, the ladies of the Griffin, Nichols, Foy, Mallard, Workman, Newmark and other families were brought together for greater safety in Armory Hall, on Spring Street near Second, while the men took their places in line with the other citizens to patrol the hills and streets.

A still vivid impression of this startling episode recalls an Englishman, a Dr. Carter, who arrived here some three years before. He lived on the east side of Main Street near First, where the McDonald Block now stands; and while not prominent in his profession, he associated with some estimable families. When others were volunteering for sentry-work or to fight, the Doctor very gallantly offered his services as a Committee of One to care for the ladies—far from the firing line!

On hearing of these threats by native *bandidos*, James R. Barton, formerly a volunteer under General S. W. Kearny and then Sheriff, at once investigated the rumors; and the truth of the reports being verified, our small and exposed community was seized with terror.

A large band of Mexican outlaws, led by Pancho Daniel, a convict who had escaped from San Quentin prison, and including Luciano Tapía and Juan Flores, on January 22d had killed a German storekeeper named George W. Pflugardt, in San Juan Capistrano, while he was preparing his evening meal; and after having placed his body on the table, they sat around and ate what the poor victim had provided for himself. On the same occasion, these outlaws plundered the stores of Manuel Garcia, Henry Charles and Miguel Kragevsky or Kraszewski; the last named escaping by hiding under a lot of wash in a large clothes-basket. When the news of this murder reached Los Angeles, excitement rose to fever-heat and we prepared for something more than defense.

Jim Barton, accompanied by William H. Little and Charles K. Baker, both constables, Charles F. Daley, an early blacksmith here, Alfred Hardy and Frank Alexander—all volunteers—left that evening for San Juan Capistrano, to capture the murderers, and soon arrived at the San Joaquín Ranch, about eighteen miles from San Juan. There Don José Andrés Sepúlveda told Barton of a trap set for him, and that the robbers outnumbered his *posse*, two to one; and urged him to send back to Los Angeles for more volunteers. Brave but reckless Barton, however, persisted in pushing on the next day, and so encountered some of the marauders in Santiago Canyon. Barton, Baker, Little and Daley were killed; while Hardy and Alexander escaped.

When Los Angeles was apprised of this second tragedy, the frenzy was indescribable, and steps were taken toward the formation of both a Committee of Safety and a Vigilance Committee—the latter to avenge the foul deed and to bring in the culprits. In meeting this emergency, the El Monte boys, as usual, took an active part. The city was placed under martial law, and Dr. John S. Griffin was put in charge of the local defenses. Suspicious houses, thought to be headquarters for robbers and thieves, were searched; and forty or fifty persons were arrested. The State Legislature was appealed to and at once voted financial aid.

Although the Committee of Safety had the assistance of special foot police in guarding the city, the citizens made a requisition on Fort Tejón, and fifty soldiers were sent from that post to help pursue the band. Troops from San Diego, with good horses and plenty of provisions, were also placed at the disposition of the Los Angeles authorities. Companies of mounted Rangers were made up to scour the country, American, German and French citizens vying with one another for the honor of risking their lives; one such company being formed at El Monte, and another at San Bernardino. There were also two detachments of native Californians; but many Sonorans and Mexicans from other States, either from sympathy or fear, aided the murdering robbers and so made their pursuit doubly difficult. However, the outlaws were pursued far into the mountains; and although the first party sent out returned without effecting anything (reporting that the desperadoes were not far from San Juan and that the horses of the pursuers had given out) practically all of the band, as will be seen, were eventually captured.

Not only were vigorous measures taken to apprehend and punish the murderers, but provision was made to rescue the bodies of the slain, and to give them decent and honorable burial. The next morning, after nearly one hundred mounted and armed men had set out to track the fugitives, another party, also on horseback, left to escort several wagons filled with coffins, in which they hoped to bring back the bodies of Sheriff Barton and his comrades. In this effort, the *posse* succeeded; and when the remains were received in Los Angeles on Sunday about noon, the city at once went into mourning. All business was suspended, and the impressive burial ceremonies, conducted on Monday, were attended by the citizens *en masse*. Oddly enough, there was not a Protestant clergyman in town at the time; but the Masonic Order took the matter in hand and performed their rites over those who were Masons, and even paid their respects, with a portion of the ritual, to the non-Masonic dead.

General Andrés Pico, with a company of native mounted Californians, who left immediately after the funeral, was especially prominent in running down the outlaws, thus again displaying his natural gift of leadership; and others fitted themselves out and followed as soon as they could. General Pico knew both land and people; and on capturing Silvas and Ardillero, two of the worst of the *bandidos*, after a hard resistance, he straightway hung them to trees, at the very spot where they had tried to assassinate him and his companions.

In the pursuit of the murderers, James Thompson (successor, in the following January, to the murdered Sheriff Getman) led a company of horsemen toward the Tejunga; and at the Simi Pass, high upon the rocks, he stationed United States soldiers as a lookout. Little San Gabriel, in which J. F. Burns, as Deputy Sheriff, was on the watch, also made its contribution to the restoration of order and peace; for some of its people captured and executed three or four of Daniels's and Flores's band. Flores was caught on the top of a peak in the Santiago range; all in all, some fifty-two culprits were brought to Los Angeles and lodged in jail; and of that number eleven were lynched or legally hung.

When the Vigilance Committee had jailed a suspected murderer, the people were called to sit in judgment. We met near the veranda of the Montgomery, and Judge Jonathan R. Scott having been made Chairman, a regular order of procedure, extra-legal though it was, was followed; after announcing the capture, and naming the criminal, the Judge called upon the crowd to determine the prisoner's fate. Thereupon some one would shout: "*Hang him!*" Scott would then put the question somewhat after the following formula: "Gentlemen, you have heard the motion; all those in favor of hanging So-and-So, will signify by saying, Aye!"

And the citizens present unanimously answered, *Aye!* .

Having thus expressed their will, the assemblage proceeded to the jail, a low, adobe building behind the little Municipal and County structure, and easily subdued the jailer, Frank J. Carpenter, whose daughter, Josephine, became Frank Burns's second wife. The prisoner was then secured, taken from his cell, escorted to Fort Hill—a rise of ground behind the jail—where a temporary gallows had been constructed, and promptly despatched; and after each of the first batch of culprits had there successively paid the penalty for his crime, the avengers quietly dispersed to their homes to await the capture and dragging in of more cutthroats.

Among those condemned by vote at a public meeting in the way I have described, was Juan Flores, who was hanged on February 14th, 1857, well up on Fort Hill, in sight of such a throng that it is hardly too much to say that practically every man, woman and child in the pueblo was present, not to mention many people drawn by curiosity from various parts of the State who had flocked into town. Flores was but twenty-one years of age; yet, the year previous he had been sent to prison for horse-stealing. At the same time that Flores was executed, Miguel Blanco, who had stabbed the militiaman, Captain W. W. Twist, in order to rob him of a thousand dollars, was also hanged.

Espinosa and Lopez, two members of the robber band, for a while eluded their pursuers. At San Buenaventura, however, they were caught, and on the following morning, Espinosa was hung. Lopez again escaped; and it was not until February 16th that he was finally recaptured and despatched to other realms.

Two days after Juan Flores was sent to a warmer clime, Luciano Tapía and Thomas King were executed. Tapía's case was rather regrettable, for he had been a respectable laborer at San Luis Obispo until Flores, meeting him, persuaded him to abandon honest work. Tapía came to Los Angeles, joined the robber band and was one of those who helped to kill Sheriff Barton.

· In 1857, the Sisters of Charity founded the Los Angeles Infirmary, the first regular hospital in the city, with Sister Ana, for years well known here, as Sister Superior. For a while, temporary quarters were taken in the house long occupied by Don José María Aguilar and family, which property the Sisters soon purchased; but the next year they bought some land from Don Luis Arenas, adjoining Don José Andrés Sepúlveda's, and were thus enabled to enlarge the hospital. Their service being the best, in time they were enabled to acquire a good-sized, two-story building of brick, in the upper part of the city; and there their patients enjoyed the refreshing and health-restoring environment of garden and orchard.

It was not until this year that, on the corner of Alameda and Bath streets, Oscar Macy, City Treasurer in 1887–88, opened the first public bath house, having built a water-wheel with small cans attached to the paddles, to dip water up from the Alameda *zanja*, as a medium for supplying his tank. He provided hot water as well as cold. Oscar charged fifty cents a bath, and furnished soap and towels.

In 1857, the steamship *Senator* left San Francisco on the fifth and twentieth of each month and so continued until the people wanted a steamer at least once every ten days.

Despite the inconvenience and expense of obtaining water for the home, it was not until February 24th that Judge W. G. Dryden—who, with a man named McFadden, had established the nucleus of a system—was granted a franchise to distribute water from his land, and to build a water-wheel in the *zanja madre*. The Dryden, formerly known as the Ábila Springs and later the source of the Beaudry supply, were near the site selected for the San Fernando Street Railway Station; and from these springs water was conveyed by a *zanja* to the Plaza. There, in the center, a brick tank, perhaps ten feet square and fifteen feet high, was constructed; and this was filled by means of pumps, while from the tank wooden pipes distributed water to the consumer.

So infrequently did we receive intelligence from the remoter parts of the world throughout the fifties that sometimes a report, especially if apparently authentic, when finally it reached here, created real excitement. I recall, more or less vividly, the arrival of the stages from the *Senator*, late in March, and the stir made when the news was passed from mouth to mouth that Livingstone, the explorer, had at last been heard from in far-off and unknown Africa.

Los Angeles schools were then open only part of the year, the School Board being compelled, in the spring, to close them for want of money. William Wolfskill, however, rough pioneer though he was, came to the Board's rescue. He was widely known as an advocate of popular education, having, as I have said, his own private teachers; and to his lasting honor, he gave the Board sufficient funds to make possible the reopening of one of the schools.

In 1857, I again revisited San Francisco. During the four years since my first visit a complete metamorphosis had taken place. Tents and small frame structures were being largely replaced with fine buildings of brick and stone; many of the sand dunes had succumbed to the march of improvement; gardens were much more numerous, and the uneven character of streets and sidewalks had been wonderfully improved. In a word, the spirit of Western progress was asserting itself, and the city by the Golden Gate was taking on a decidedly metropolitan appearance.

Notwithstanding various attempts at citrus culture in Southern California, some time elapsed before there was much of an orange or lemon industry in this vicinity. In 1854, a Dr. Halsey started an orange and lime nursery, on the Rowland place, which he soon sold to William Wolfskill, for four thousand dollars; and in April, 1857, when there were not many more than a hundred orange trees bearing fruit in the whole county, Wolfskill planted several thousand and so established what was to be, for that time, the largest orange orchard in the United States. He had thrown away a good many of the lemon trees received from Halsey, because they were frost-bitten; but he still had some lemon, orange and olive trees left. Later, under the more scientific care of his son, Joseph Wolfskill, who extended the original Wolfskill grove, this orchard was made to yield very large crops.

In 1857, a group of Germans living in San Francisco bought twelve hundred acres of waste, sandy land, at two dollars an acre, from Don Pacífico Onteveras, and on it started the town of Anaheim—a name composed of the Spanish *Ana*, from Santa Ana, and the German *Heim*, for home; and this was the first settlement in the county founded after my arrival. This land formed a block about one and a quarter miles square, some three miles from the Santa Ana River, and five miles from the residence of Don Bernardo Yorba, from whom the company received special privileges. A. Langenberger, a German, who married Yorba's daughter, was probably one of the originators of the Anaheim plan; at any rate, his influence with his father-in-law was of value to his friends in completing the deal. There were fifty shareholders, who paid seven hundred and fifty dollars each, with an Executive Council composed of Otmar Caler, President; G. Charles Kohler, Vice-President; Cyrus Beythien, Treasurer; and John Fischer, Secretary; while John Fröhling, R. Emerson, Felix Bachman, who was a kind of Sub-treasurer, and Louis Jazyinsky, made up the Los Angeles Auditing Committee. George Hansen, afterward the colony's Superintendent, surveyed the tract and laid it out in fifty twenty-acre lots, with streets and a public park; around it a live fence of some forty to fifty thousand willow cuttings, placed at intervals of a couple of feet, was planted. A main canal, six to seven miles long, with a fall of fifteen to twenty feet, brought abundant water from the Santa Ana

River, while some three hundred and fifty miles of lateral ditches distributed the water to the lots. On each lot, some eight or ten thousand grape vines were set out, the first as early as January, 1858. On December 15th, 1859, the stock-holders came south to settle on their partially-cultivated land; and although but one among the entire number knew anything about wine-making, the dream of the projectors—to establish there the largest vineyard in the world—bade fair to come true. The colonists were quite a curious mixture—two or three carpenters, four blacksmiths, three watchmakers, a brewer, an engraver, a shoemaker, a poet, a miller, a book-binder, two or three merchants, a hatter and a musician; but being mostly of sturdy, industrious German stock, they soon formed such a prosperous and important little community that, by 1876, the settlement had grown to nearly two thousand people. A peculiar plan was adopted for investment, sale and compensation: each stockholder paid the same price at the beginning, and later all drew for the lots, the apportionment being left to chance; but since the pieces of land were conceded to have dissimilar values, those securing the better lots equal-ized in cash with their less lucky associates. Soon after 1860, when Langenberger had erected the first hotel there, Anaheim took a leading place in the production of grapes and wine; and this position of honor it kept until, in 1888, a strange disease suddenly attacked and, within a single year, killed all the vines, after which the cultivation of oranges and walnuts was under-taken. Kohler and Fröhling had wineries in both San Francisco and Los Angeles, the latter being adjacent to the present corner of Central Avenue and Seventh Street; and this firm purchased most of Anaheim's grape crop, although some vine-yard owners made their own wine. Morris L. Goodman, by the way, was here at an early period, and was one of the first settlers of Anaheim.

Hermann Heinsch, a native of Prussia, arrived in Los Angeles in 1857 and soon after engaged in the harness and saddlery business. On March 8th, 1863, he was married to Mary Haap. Having become proficient at German schools in both music and languages, Heinsch lent his time and efforts to the organization and drill of Germans here, and contributed much to the success of both the Teutonia and the Turnverein. In 1869, the Heinsch Building was erected at the corner of Commercial and Los Angeles streets; and as late as 1876 this was a shopping district, a Mrs. T. J. Baker having a dressmaking establishment there. After a prosperous career, Heinsch died on January 13th, 1883; his wife followed him on April 14th, 1906. R. C. Heinsch, a son, survives them.

Major Walter Harris Harvey, a native of Georgia once a cadet at West Point, but dismissed for his pranks (who about the middle of the fifties married Eleanor, eldest full sister of John G. Downey, and became the father of J. Downey Harvey, now living in San Francisco), settled in California shortly after the Mexican War. During the first week in May, 1857, or some four years before he died, Major Harvey arrived from Washington with an appointment as Register of the Land Office, in place of H. P. Dorsey. At the same time, Don Agustin Olvera was appointed Receiver, in lieu of General Andrés Pico. These and other rotations in office were due, of course, to national administration changes, President Buchanan having recently been inaugurated.

One of the interesting legal inquiries of the fifties was conducted in 1857 when, in the District Court here, António María Lugo, crowned with the white of seventy-six winters, testified, at a hearing to establish certain claims to land, as to what he knew of old *ranchos* hereabouts, recalling many details of the pueblo and incidents as far back as 1785. He had seen the San Rafael Ranch, for example, in 1790, and he had also roamed, as a young man, over the still older Dominguez and Nietos hills.

Charles Henry Forbes, who was born at the Mission San José, came to Los Angeles County in 1857 and, though but twenty-two years old, was engaged by Don Abel Stearns to superintend his various *ranchos*, becoming Stearns's business manager in 1866, with a small office on the ground-floor of the Arcadia Block. In 1864, Forbes married Doña Luisa

Olvera, daughter of Judge Agustin Olvera, and a graduate of the Sisters' school. On the death of Don Abel, in 1871, Forbes settled up Stearns's large estate, retaining his professional association with Doña Arcadia, after her marriage to Colonel Baker, and even until he died in May, 1894.

As I have intimated, the principal industry throughout Los Angeles County, and indeed throughout Southern California, up to the sixties, was the raising of cattle and horses—an undertaking favored by a people particularly fond of leisure and knowing little of the latent possibilities in the land; so that this entire area of magnificent soil supported herds which provided the whole population in turn, directly or indirectly, with a livelihood. The live stock subsisted upon the grass growing wild all over the county, and the prosperity of Southern California therefore depended entirely upon the season's rainfall. This was true to a far greater extent than one might suppose, for water-development had received no attention outside of Los Angeles. If the rainfall was sufficient to produce feed, dealers came from the North and purchased our stock, and everybody thrived; if, on the other hand, the season was dry, cattle and horses died and the public's pocket-book shrank to very unpretentious dimensions. As an incident in even a much later period than that which I here have in mind, I can distinctly remember that I would rise three or four times during a single meal to see if the overhanging clouds had yet begun to give that rain which they had seemed to promise, and which was so vital to our prosperity.

As for rain, I am reminded that every newspaper in those days devoted much space to weather reports or, rather, to gossip about the weather at other points along the Coast, as well as to the consequent prospects here. The weather was the one determining factor in the problem of a successful or a disastrous season, and became a very important theme when ranchers and others congregated at our store.

And here I may mention, *à propos* of this matter of rainfall and its general effects, that there were millions of ground-squirrels all over this country that shared with other animals the ups and downs of the season. When there was plenty of rain, these squirrels fattened and multiplied; but when evil days came, they sickened, starved and perished. On the other hand, great overflows, due to heavy rainfalls, drowned many of these troublesome little rodents.

The raising of sheep had not yet developed any importance at the time of my arrival; most of the mutton then consumed in Los Angeles coming from Santa Cruz Island, in the Santa Bárbara Channel, though some was brought from San Clemente and Santa Catalina islands. On the latter, there was a herd of from eight to ten thousand sheep in which Oscar Macy later acquired an interest; and L. Harris, father-in-law of H. W. Frank, the well- and favorably-known President and member of the Board of Education, also had extensive herds there. They ran wild and needed very little care, and only semi-yearly visits were made to look after the shearing, packing and shipping of the wool. Santa Cruz Island had much larger herds, and steamers running to and from San Francisco often stopped there to·take on sheep and sheep-products.

Santa Catalina Island, for years the property of Don José María Covarrúbias—and later of the eccentric San Francisco pioneer James Lick, who crossed the plains in the same party with the Lanfranco brothers and tried to induce them to settle in the North—was not far from San Clemente; and there, throughout the extent of her hills and vales, roamed herd after herd of wild goats. Early seafarers, I believe it has been suggested, accustomed to carry goats on their sailing vessels, for a supply of milk, probably deposited some of the animals on Catalina; but however that may be, hunting parties to this day explore the mountains in search of them.

Considering, therefore, the small number of sheep here about 1853, it is not uninteresting to note that, according to old records of San Gabriel for the winter of 1828-29, there were then at the Mission no less than fifteen thousand sheep; while in 1858, on the other hand, according to fairly accurate reports, there were fully twenty thousand sheep in Los Angeles County. Two years later, the number had doubled.

George Carson, a New Yorker who came here in 1852, and after whom Carson Station is named, was one of the first to engage in the sheep industry. Soon after he arrived, he went into the livery business, to which he gave attention even when in partnership successively with Sanford, Dean and Hicks in the hardware business, on Commercial Street. On July 30th, 1857, Carson married Doña Victoria, a daughter of Manuel Dominguez; but it was not until 1864 that, having sold out his two business interests (the livery to George Butler and the hardware to his partner), he moved to the ranch of his father-in-law, where he continued to live, assisting Dominguez with the management of his great property. Some years later, Carson bought four or five hundred acres of land adjoining the Dominguez acres and turned his attention to sheep. Later still, he became interested in the development of thoroughbred cattle and horses, but continued to help his father-in-law in the directing of his ranch. When rain favored the land, Carson, in common with his neighbors, amassed wealth; but during dry years he suffered disappointment and loss, and on one occasion was forced to take his flocks, then consisting of ten thousand sheep, to the mountains, where he lost all but a thousand head. It cost him ten thousand dollars to save the latter, which amount far exceeded their value. In this movement of stock, he took with him, as his lieutenant, a young Mexican named Martin Cruz whom he had brought up on the *rancho*. Carson was one of my cronies, while I was still young and single; and we remained warm friends until he died.

Almost indescribable excitement followed the substantiated reports, received in the fall of 1857, that a train of emigrants from Missouri and Arkansas, on their way to California, had been set upon by Indians, near Mountain Meadow, Utah, on September 7th, and that thirty-six members of the party had been brutally killed. Particularly were the Gentiles of the Southwest stirred up when it was learned that the assault had been planned and carried through by one Lee, a Mormon, whose act sprang rather from the frenzy of a madman than from the deliberation of a well-balanced mind. The attitude of Brigham Young toward the United States Government, at that time, and his alleged threat to "turn the Indians loose" upon the whites, added color to the assertion that Young's followers were guilty of the massacre; but fuller investigation has absolved the Mormons, I believe, as a society, from any complicity in the awful affair. Some years later the two Oatman girls were rescued from the Indians (by whom they had been tattooed), and for a while they stayed at Ira Thompson's, where I saw them.

In 1857, J. G. Nichols was reëlected Mayor of Los Angeles, and began several improvements he had previously advocated, especially the irrigating of the plain below the city. By August 2d, *Zanja* No. 2 was completed; and this brought about the building of the Aliso Mill and the further cultivation of much excellent land.

One of the passengers that left San Francisco with me for San Pedro on October 18th, 1853, who later became a successful citizen of Southern California, was Edward N. McDonald, a native of New York State. We had sailed from New York together, and together had finished the long journey to the Pacific Coast, after which I lost track of him. McDonald had intended proceeding farther south, and I was surprised at meeting him on the street, some weeks after my arrival, in Los Angeles. Reaching San Pedro, he contracted to enter the service of Alexander & Banning, and remained with Banning for several years, until he formed a partnership with John O. Wheeler's brother, who later went to Japan. McDonald, subsequently raised sheep on a large scale and acquired much ranch property; and in 1876, he built the block on Main Street bearing his name. Sixteen years later, he erected another structure, opposite the first one. When McDonald died at Wilmington, on June 10th, 1899, he left his wife an estate valued at about one hundred and sixty thousand dollars which must have increased in value, since then, many fold.

N. A. Potter, a Rhode Islander, came to Los Angeles in 1855, bringing with him a stock of Yankee goods and opening a store; and two years later he bought a two-story brick building on Main Street, opposite the Bella Union. Louis Jazynsky was a partner with Potter, for a while, under the firm name of Potter & Company; but later Jazynsky left Los Angeles for San Francisco. Potter died here in 1868.

Possibly the first instance of an Angeleño proffering a gift to the President of the United States—and that, too, of something characteristic of this productive soil and climate—was when Henry D. Barrows, in September, called on President Buchanan, in Washington and, on behalf of William Wolfskill, Don Manuel Requena and himself, gave the Chief Executive some California fruit and wine.

I have before me a Ledger of the year 1857; it is a medium-sized volume bound in leather, and on the outside cover is inscribed, in the bold, old-fashioned handwriting of fifty-odd years ago, the simple legend,

NEWMARK, KREMER & COMPANY

Each page is headed with the name of some still-remembered worthy of that distant day who was a customer of the old firm; and in 1857, a customer was always a friend. According to the method of that period the accounts are closed, not with balancing entries and red lines but, in the blackest of black ink, with the good, straightforward and positive inscription, *Settled.*

The perusal of this old book carries me back over the vanished years. As the skull in the hand of the ancient monk, so does this antiquated volume recall to me how transitory is this life and all its affairs. A few remain to tell a younger generation the story of the early days; but the majority, even as in 1857 they carefully balanced their scores in this old Ledger, have now closed their accounts in the great Book of Life. They have settled with their heaviest Creditor; they have gone before Him to render their last account. With few or no exceptions, they were a manly, sterling race, and I have no doubt that He found their assets far greater than their liabilities.

CHAPTER XVI

MARRIAGE—THE BUTTERFIELD STAGES

1858

IN January, 1858, I engaged, in the sheep business. After some investigation, I selected and purchased for an insignificant sum, just west of the present Hollenbeck Home on Boyle Avenue, a convenient site, which consisted of twenty acres of land, through which a ditch conducted water to Don Felipe Lugo's San António *rancho*—a flow quite sufficient, at the time, for my herd. These sheep I pastured on adjacent lands belonging to the City; and as others often did the same, no one said me Nay. Everything progressed beautifully until the first of May, when the ditch ran dry. Upon making inquiry, I learned that the City had permitted Lugo to dig a private ditch across this twenty-acre tract to his ranch, and to use what water he needed during the rainy season; but that in May, when the authorities resumed their irrigation service, the privilege was withdrawn. I was thus deprived of water for the sheep.

Despite the fact that there was an adobe on the land, I could not dispose of the property at any price. One day a half-breed known as the Chicken Thief called on me and offered a dozen chickens for the adobe, but—not a chicken for the land! Stealing chickens was this man's profession; and I suppose that he offered me the medium of exchange he was most accustomed to have about him.

Sheriff William C. Getman had been warned, in the tragic days of 1858, to look out for a maniac named Reed; but almost courting such an emergency, Getman (once a dashing Lieutenant of the Rangers and bearing grapeshot wounds from his participation in the Siege of Mexico) went, on the seventh of January, with Francis Baker to a pawnbroker, whose establishment, near Los Angeles and Aliso streets, was popularly known as the Monte Pio. There the officers found Reed locked and barricaded in a room; and while the Sheriff was endeavoring to force an entrance, Reed suddenly threw open the door, ran out and, to the dismay of myself and many others gathered to witness the arrest, pulled a pistol from his pocket, discharged the weapon, and Getman dropped on the spot. The maniac then retreated into the pawnbroker's from which he fired at the crowd. Deputy Baker—later assistant to Marshal Warren, who was shot by Dye—finally killed the desperado, but not before Reed had fired twenty to thirty shots, four or five of which passed through Baker's clothing. When the excited crowd broke into the shop, it was found that the madman had been armed with two derringers, two revolvers and a bowie knife—a convenient little arsenal which he had taken from the money-lender's stock. The news of the affray spread rapidly through the town and everywhere created great regret. Baker, who had sailed around the Horn a couple of years before I arrived, died on May 17th, 1899, after having been City Marshal and Tax Collector.

Such trouble with men inclined to use firearms too freely was not confined to maniacs or those bent on revenge or robbery. On one occasion, for example, about 1858, while passing along the street I observed Gabriel Allen, known among his intimates as Gabe Allen, a veteran of the War with Mexico—and some years later a Supervisor—on one of his jollifications, with Sheriff Getman following close at his heels. Having arrived in front of a building, Gabe suddenly raised his gun and aimed at a carpenter who was at work on the roof. Getman promptly knocked Allen down; whereupon the latter said, "You've got me, Billy!" Allen's only purpose, it appeared, was to take a shot at the innocent stranger and thus test his marksmanship.

This Gabe Allen was really a notorious character, though not altogether bad. When sober, he was a peaceable man; but when on a spree, he was decidedly warlike and on such occasions always "shot up the town." While on one of these jamborees, for example, he was heard to say, "I'll shoot, if I only kill six of them!" In later life, however, Allen married a Mexican lady who seems to have had a mollifying influence; and thereafter he lived at peace with the world.

During the changing half-century or more of which I write, Los Angeles has witnessed many exciting street scenes, but it is doubtful if any exhibition here ever called to doors, windows and the dusty streets a greater percentage of the entire population than that of the Government camels driven through the town on January 8th, 1858, under the martial and spectacular command of Ned, otherwise Lieutenant, and later General and Ambassador E. F. Beale, and the forbear of the so-called hundred million dollar McLean baby; the same Lieutenant Beale who opened up Beale's Route from the Rio Grande to Fort Tejón. The camels had just come in from the fort, having traveled forty or more miles a day across the desert, to be loaded with military stores and provisions. As early as the beginning of the fifties, Jefferson Davis, then in Congress, had advocated, but without success, the appropriation of thirty thousand dollars for the purchase of such animals, believing that they could be used on the overland routes and would prove especially serviceable in desert regions; and when Davis, in 1854, as Secretary of War, secured the appropriation for which he had so long contended, he despatched American army officers to Egypt and Arabia to make the purchase. Some seventy or seventy-five camels were obtained and transported to Texas by the storeship *Supply;* and in the Lone Star State the herd was divided into two parts, half being sent to the Gadsden Purchase, afterward Arizona, and half to Albuquerque. In a short time, the second division was put in charge of Lieutenant Beale who was assisted by native camel-drivers brought from abroad. Among these was Philip Tedro, or Hi Jolly— who had been picked up by Commodore Dave Porter—and

Greek George, years afterward host to bandit Vasquez; and camels and drivers made several trips back and forth across the Southwest country. Once headquartered at Fort Tejón, they came to Los Angeles every few weeks for provisions; each time creating no little excitement among the adult population and affording much amusement, as they passed along the streets, to the small boy.

To return to Pancho Daniel, the escaped leader of the Barton murderers. He was heard from occasionally, as foraging north toward San Luis Obispo, and was finally captured, after repeated efforts to entrap and round him up, by Sheriff Murphy, on January 19th, 1858, while hiding in a haystack near San José. When he was brought to Los Angeles, he was jailed, and then released on bail. Finally, Daniel's lawyers secured for him a change of venue to Santa Bárbara; and this was the last abuse that led the public again to administer a little law of its own. Early on the morning of November 30th, Pancho's body was found hanging by the neck at the gateway to the County Jail yard, a handful of men having overpowered the keeper, secured the key and the prisoner, and sent him on a journey with a different destination from Santa Bárbara.

On February 25th, fire started in Childs & Hicks's store, on Los Angeles Street, and threatened both the Bella Union and *El Palacio*, then the residence of Don Abel Stearns. The brick in the building of Felix Bachman & Company and the volunteer bucket-brigade prevented a general conflagration. Property worth thousands of dollars was destroyed, Bachman & Company alone carrying insurance. The conflagration demonstrated the need of a fire engine, and a subscription was started to get one.

Weeks later workmen, rummaging among the *débris*, found five thousand dollars in gold, which discovery produced no little excitement. Childs claimed the money as his, saying that it had been stolen from him by a thieving clerk; but the workmen, undisturbed by law, kept the treasure.

A new four-page weekly newspaper appeared on March 24th, bearing the suggestive title, the *Southern Vineyard*, and the name of Colonel J. J. Warner, as editor. By December, it had become a semi-weekly. Originally Democratic, it now favored the Union party; it was edited with ability, but died on June 8th, 1860.

On March 24th, I married Sarah, second daughter of Joseph Newmark, to whom I had been engaged since 1856. She was born on January 9th, 1841, and had come to live in Los Angeles in 1854. The ceremony, performed by the bride's father, took place at the family home, at what is now 501 North Main Street, almost a block from the Plaza, on the site of the Brunswig Drug Company; and there we continued to live until about 1860.

At four o'clock, a small circle of intimates was welcomed at dinner; and in the evening there was a house-party and dance, for which invitations printed on lace-paper, in the typography characteristic of that day, had been sent out. Among the friends who attended, were the military officers stationed at Fort Tejón, including Major Bell, the commanding officer, and Lieutenant John B. Magruder, formerly Colonel at San Diego and later a Major General in the Civil War, commanding Confederate forces in the Peninsula and in Texas, and eventually serving under Maximilian in Mexico. Other friends still living in Los Angeles who were present are Mr. and Mrs. S. Lazard, Mrs. S. C. Foy, William H. Workman, C. E. Thom and H. D. Barrows. Men rarely went out unarmed at night, and most of our male visitors doffed their weapons—both pistols and knives—as they came in, spreading them around in the bedrooms. The ladies brought their babies with them for safe-keeping, and the same rooms were placèd at their disposal. Imagine, if you can, the appearance of this nursery-arsenal!

It was soon after we were married that my wife said to me one day, rather playfully, but with a touch of sadness, that our meeting might easily have never taken place; and when I inquired what she meant, she described an awful calamity that had befallen the Greenwich Avenue school in New York City, which she attended as a little girl, and where several hun-

Sarah Newmark, when (about) Twenty-four Years of Age

Harris Newmark, when (about) Thirty-four Years Old

Mr. and Mrs. J. Newmark
Request the pleasure of your company
to celebrate the nuptials of their Daughter
Sarah, to Mr. Harris Newmark,
Wednesday Evening, the 24th instant,
at 8 o'clock.
Los Angeles, March 16, 1858.

Facsimile of Harris and Sarah Newmark's Wedding Invitation

dred pupils were distributed in different classrooms. The building was four stories in height; the ground floor paved with stones, was used as a playroom; the primary department was on the second floor; the more advanced pupils occupied the third; while the top floor served as a lecture-room.

On the afternoon of November 20th, 1851, Miss Harrison, the Principal of the young ladies' department, suddenly fell in a faint, and the resulting screams for water, being misunderstood, led to the awful cry of *Fire!* It was known that the pupils made a dash for the various doors and were soon massed around the stairway, yet a difference of opinion existed as to the cause of the tragedy. My wife always said that the staircase, which led from the upper to the first floor, *en caracole*, gave way, letting the pupils fall; while others contended that the bannister snapped asunder, hurling the crowded unfortunates over the edge to the pavement beneath. A frightful fatality resulted. Hundreds of pupils of all ages were precipitated in heaps on to the stone floor, with a loss of forty-seven lives and a hundred or more seriously crippled.

My wife, who was a child of but eleven years, was just about to jump with the rest when a providential hand restrained and saved her.

News of the disaster quickly spread, and in a short time the crowd of anxious parents, kinsfolk and friends who had hastened to the scene in every variety of vehicle and on foot, was so dense that the police had the utmost difficulty in removing the wounded, dying and dead.

From Geneva, Switzerland, in 1854, a highly educated French lady, Mlle. Theresa Bry, whose oil portrait hangs in the County Museum, reached Los Angeles, and four years later married François Henriot, a gardener by profession, who had come from *la belle France* in 1851. Together, on First Street near Los Angeles, they conducted a private school which enjoyed considerable patronage; removing the institution, in the early eighties, to the Arroyo Seco district. This matrimonial transaction, on account of the unequal social stations of the respective parties, caused some little flurry: in contrast to her own beauty and ladylike accomplishments, François's manners were unrefined, his stature short and squatty, while his full beard (although it inspired respect, if not a certain feeling of awe, when he came to exercise authority in the school) was scraggy and unkempt. Mme. Henriot died in 1888, aged eighty-seven years, and was followed to the grave by her husband five years later.

In 1858, the outlook for business brightened in Los Angeles; and Don Abel Stearns, who had acquired riches as a *ranchero*, built the Arcadia Block, on the corner of Los Angeles and Arcadia streets, naming it after his wife, Doña Arcadia, who, since these memoirs were commenced, has joined the silent majority. The structure cost about eighty thousand dollars, and was talked of for some time as the most notable business block south of San Francisco. The newspapers hailed it as an ornament to the city and a great step toward providing what the small and undeveloped community then regarded as a fireproof structure for business purposes. Because, however, of the dangerous overflow of the Los Angeles River in rainy seasons, Stearns elevated the building above the grade of the street and to such an extent that, for several years, his store-rooms remained empty. But the enterprise at once bore some good fruit; to make the iron doors and shutters of the block, he started a foundry on New High Street and soon created some local iron-casting trade.

On April 24th, Señora Guadalupe Romero died at the age, it is said, of one hundred and fifteen years. She came to Los Angeles, I was told, as far back as 1781, the wife of one of the earliest soldiers sent here, and had thus lived in the pueblo about seventy-seven years.

Some chapters in the life of Henry Mellus are of more than passing interest. Born in Boston, he came to California in 1835, with Richard Henry Dana, in Captain Thompson's brig *Pilgrim* made famous in the story of *Two Years before the Mast;* clerked for Colonel Isaac Williams when that Chino worthy had a little store where later the Bella Union stood; returned to the East in 1837 and came back to the Coast the second time as supercargo. Settling in San Francisco, he formed with Howard the well-known firm of Howard & Mellus, which was wiped out, by the great fire, in 1851. Again Mellus returned to Massachusetts, and in 1858 for a third time came to California, at length casting his fortune with us in growing Los Angeles. On Dana's return to San Pedro and the Pacific Coast in 1859, Mellus—who had married a sister of Francis Mellus's wife and had become a representative citizen—entertained the distinguished advocate and author, and drove him around Los Angeles to view the once familiar and but little-altered scenes. Dana bore all his honors modestly, apparently quite oblivious of the curiosity displayed toward him and quite as unconscious that he was making one of the memorable visits in the early annals of the town. Dana Street serves as a memorial to one who contributed in no small degree to render the vicinity of Los Angeles famous.

Just what hotel life in Los Angeles was in the late fifties, or about the time when Dana visited here, may be gathered from an anecdote often told by Dr. W. F. Edgar, who came to the City of the Angels for the first time in 1858. Dr. Edgar had been ordered to join an expedition against the Mojave Indians which was to start from Los Angeles for the Colorado River, and he put up at the old Bella Union, expecting at least one good night's rest before taking to the saddle again and making for the desert. Dr. Edgar found, however, to his intense disgust, that the entire second story was overcrowded with lodgers. Singing and loud talking were silenced, in turn, by the protests of those who wanted to sleep; but finally a guest, too full for expression but not so drunk that he was unable to breathe hoarsely, staggered in from a Sonora Town ball, tumbled into bed with his boots on, and commenced to snort, much like a pig. Under ordinary circumstances, this infliction would have been grievous enough; but the inner walls of the Bella Union were never overthick, and the rhythmic snoring of the late-comer made itself emphatically audible and proportionately obnoxious. Quite as emphatic, however, were the objections soon raised by the fellow-guests, who not only raised them but threw them, one after another—boots, bootjacks and sticks striking, with heavy thud, the snorer's portal; but finding that even these did not avail, the remonstrants, in various forms of deshabille, rushed out and began to kick at the door of the objectionable bedroom. Just at that moment the offender turned over with a grunt; and the excited army of lodgers, baffled by the unresisting apathy ·of the sleeper, retreated, each to his nest. The next day, breathing a sigh of relief, Edgar forsook the heavenly regions of the Bella Union and made for Cajón Pass, eventually reaching the Colorado and the place where the expedition found the charred remains of emigrants' wagons, the mournful evidence of Indian treachery and atrocity.

Edgar's nocturnal experience reminds me of another in the good old Bella Union. When Cameron E. Thom arrived here in the spring of 1854, he engaged a room at the hotel which he continued to occupy for several months, or until the rains of 1855 caused both roof and ceiling to cave in during the middle of the night, not altogether pleasantly arousing him from his slumbers. It was then that·he moved to Joseph Newmark's, where he lived for some time, through which circumstance we became warm friends.

Big, husky, hearty Jacob Kuhrts, by birth a German and now living here at eighty-one years of age, left home, as a mere boy, for the sea, visiting California on a vessel from China as early as 1848, and rushing off to Placer County on the outbreak of the gold-fever. Roughing it for several years and narrowly escaping death from Indians, Jake made his first appearance in Los Angeles in 1858, soon after which I met him, when he was cking out a livelihood doing odd jobs about town, a fact leading me to conclude that his success at the mines was hardly commensurate with the privations endured. It was just about that time, when he was running a dray, that, attracted by a dance among Germans, Jake dropped in as he was; but how sorry an appearance he made may perhaps be fancied when I say that the door-keeper, eyeing him suspiciously, refused him admission and advised him to go home and put on his Sunday go-to-meetings. Jake went and, what is more important, fortunately returned; for while spinning around on the knotty floor, he met, fell in love with and ogled Fräulein Susan Buhn, whom somewhat later he married. In 1864, Kuhrts had a little store on Spring Street near the adobe City Hall; and there he prospered so well that by 1866 he had bought the northwest corner of Main and First streets, and put up the building he still owns. For twelve years he conducted a grocery in a part of that structure, living with his family in the second story, after which he was sufficiently prosperous to retire. Active as his business life has been, Jake has proved his patriotism time and again, devoting his efforts as a City Father, and serving, sometimes without salary, as Superintendent of Streets, Chief of the Fire Department and Fire Commissioner.

In 1858, John Temple built what is now the south wing of the Temple Block standing directly opposite the Bullard Building; but the Main Street stores being, like Stearns's Arcadia Block, above the level of the sidewalk and, therefore, reached only by several steps, proved unpopular and did not rent, although Tischler & Schlesinger, heading a party of grain-buyers, stored some wheat in them for a while or until the grain, through its weight, broke the flooring, and was precipitated into the cellar; and even as late as 1859, after telegraph connection with San Francisco had been completed, only one little space on the Spring Street side, in size not more than eight by ten feet, was rented, the telegraph company being the tenants. One day William Wolfskill, pointing to the structure, exclaimed to his friends: "What a pity that Temple put all his money there! Had he not gone into building so extravagantly, he might now be a rich man." Wolfskill himself, however, later commenced the construction of a small block on Main Street, opposite the Bella Union, to be occupied by S. Lazard & Company, but which he did not live to see completed.

Later on, the little town grew and, as this property became more central, Temple removed the steps and built the stores flush with the sidewalk, after which wide-awake merchants began to move into them. One of Temple's first important tenants on Main Street was Daniel Desmond, the hatter. His store was about eighteen by forty feet. Henry Slotterbeck, the well-known gunsmith, was another occupant. He always carried a large stock of gunpowder, which circumstance did not add very much to the security of the neighborhood.

On the Court Street side, Jake Philippi was one of the first to locate, and there he conducted a sort of *Kneipe*. His was a large room, with a bar along the west side. The floor was generously sprinkled with sawdust, and in comfortable arm-chairs, around the good, old-fashioned redwood tables, frequently sat many of his German friends and patrons, gathered together to indulge in a game of *Pedro*, *Skat* or whist, and to pass the time pleasantly away. Some of those who thus met together at Jake Phillippi's, at different periods of his occupancy, were Dr. Joseph Kurtz, H. Heinsch, Conrad Jacoby, Abe Haas, C. F. Heinzeman, P. Lazarus, Edward Pollitz, A. Elsaesser and B. F. Drackenfeld, who was a brother-in-law of Judge Erskine M. Ross and claimed descent from some dwellers on the Rhine. He succeeded Frank Lecouvreur as bookkeeper for H. Newmark & Company, and was in turn succeeded, on removing to New York, by Pollitz; while the latter was followed by John S. Stower, an Englishman now residing in London, whose immediate predecessor was Richard Altschul. Drackenfeld attained prominence in New York, and both Altschul and Pollitz in San Francisco. Of these, Drackenfeld and Pollitz are dead.

Most of these convivial frequenters at Phillipi's belonged to a sort of *Deutscher Klub* which met, at another period, in a little room in the rear of the corner of Main and Requena streets, just over the cool cellar then conducted by Bayer & Sattler. A stairway connected the two floors, and by means of that communication the *Klub* obtained its supply of lager beer. This fact recalls an amusing incident. When Philip Lauth and Louis Schwarz succeeded Christian Henne in the management of the brewery at the corner of Main and Third streets, the *Klub* was much dissatisfied with the new brew and forthwith had Bayer & Sattler send to Milwaukee for beer made by

Philip Best. Getting wind of the matter, Lauth met the competition by at once putting on the market a brand more wittily than appropriately known as "Philip's Best." Sattler left Los Angeles in the early seventies and established a coffee-plantation in South America where, one day, he was killed by a native wielding a *machete.*

The place, which was then known as Joe Bayer's, came to belong to Bob Eckert, a German of ruddy complexion and auburn hair, whose good-nature brought him so much patronage that in course of time he opened a large establishment at Santa Monica.

John D. Woodworth, a cousin, so it was said, of Samuel Woodworth, the author of *The Old Oaken Bucket,* and father of Wallace Woodworth who died in 1883, was among the citizens active here in 1858, being appointed Postmaster, on May 19th of that year, by President Buchanan. Then the Post Office, for a twelvemonth in the old Lanfranco Block, was transferred north on Main Street until, a year or two later, it was located near Temple and Spring streets.

In June, the Surveyor-General of California made an unexpected demand on the authorities of Los Angeles County for all the public documents relating to the County history under Spanish and Mexican rule. The request was at first refused; but finally, despite the indignant protests of the press, the invaluable records were shipped to San Francisco.

I believe it was late in the fifties that O. W. Childs contracted with the City of Los Angeles to dig a water-ditch, perhaps sixteen hundred feet long, eighteen inches wide and about eighteen inches deep. As I recollect the transaction, the City allowed him one dollar per running foot, and he took land in payment. While I cannot remember the exact location of this land, it comprised in part the wonderfully important square beginning at Sixth Street and running to Twelfth, and taking in everything from Main Street as far as and including the present Figueroa. When Childs put this property on the market, his wife named several of the streets. Because of some grasshoppers in the vicinity, she called the extension of Pearl Street (now Figueroa) Grasshopper or Calle de los Chapules¹; her Faith Street has been changed to Flower; for the next street to the East, she selected the name of Hope; while as if to complete the trio of the Graces, she christened the adjoining roadway —since become Grand—Charity. The old Childs home place sold to Henry E. Huntington some years ago, and which has been subdivided, was a part of this land.

None of the old settlers ever placed much value on real estate, and Childs had no sooner closed this transaction than he proceeded to distribute some of the land among his own and his wife's relatives. He also gave to the Catholic Church the block later bounded by Sixth and Seventh streets, between Broadway and Hill; where, until a few years ago, stood St. Vincent's College, opened in 1855 on the Plaza, on the site now occupied by the Pekin Curio Store. In the Boom year of 1887, the Church authorities sold this block for one hundred thousand dollars and moved the school to the corner of Charity and Washington streets.

Andrew A. Boyle, for whom the eastern suburb of Los Angeles, Boyle Heights, was named by William H. Workman, arrived here in 1858. As early as 1848, Boyle had set out from Mexico, where he had been in business, to return to the United States, taking with him some twenty thousand Mexican dollars, at that time his entire fortune, safely packed in a fortified claret box. While attempting to board a steamer from a frail skiff at the mouth of the Rio Grande, the churning by the paddle-wheels capsized the skiff, and Boyle and his treasure were thrown into the water. Boyle narrowly escaped with his life; but his treasure went to the bottom, never to be recovered. It was then said that Boyle had perished; and his wife, on hearing the false report, was killed by the shock. Quite as serious, perhaps, was the fact that an infant daughter was left on his hands—the same daughter who later became the wife of my friend, William H. Workman. Confiding this child to an aunt, Boyle went to the Isthmus where he opened a shoe store;

¹A Mexican corruption of the Aztec *chapollin*, grasshopper. *Cf.* Chapulte-pec, Grasshopper Hill.—CHARLES F. LUMMIS.

and later coming north, after a San Francisco experience in the wholesale boot and shoe business, he settled on the bluff which was to be thereafter associated with his family name. He also planted a small vineyard, and in the early seventies commenced to make wine, digging a cellar out of the hill to store his product.

The brick house, built by Boyle on the Heights in 1858 and always a center of hospitality, is still standing, although recently remodeled by William H. Workman, Jr. (brother of Boyle Workman, the banker), who added a third story and made a cosy dwelling; and it is probably, therefore, the oldest brick structure in that part of the town.

Mendel was a younger brother of Sam Meyer, and it is my impression that he arrived here in the late fifties. He originally clerked for his brother, and for a short time was in partnership with him and Hilliard Loewenstein. In time, Meyer engaged in business for himself. During a number of his best years, Mendel was well thought of socially, with his fiddle often affording much amusement to his friends. All in all, he was a good-hearted, jovial sort of a chap, who too readily gave to others of his slender means. About 1875, he made a visit to Europe and spent more than he could afford. At any rate, in later life he did not prosper. He died in Los Angeles a number of years ago.

Thomas Copley came here in 1858, having met with many hardships while driving an ox-team from Fort Leavenworth to Salt Lake and tramped the entire eight hundred miles between the Mormon capital and San Bernardino. On arriving, he became a waiter and worked for a while for the Sisters' Hospital; subsequently he married a lady of about twice his stature, retiring to private life with a competence.

Another arrival of the late fifties was Manuel Ravenna, an Italian. He started a grocery store and continued the venture for some time; then he entered the saloon business on Main Street. Ravenna commissioned Wells Fargo & Company to bring by express the first ice shipped to Los Angeles for a commercial purpose, paying for it an initial price of twelve and a half cents per pound. The ice came packed in blankets; but the loss by melting, plus the expense of getting it here, made the real cost about twenty-four cents a pound. Nevertheless, it was a clever and profitable move, and brought Ravenna nearly all of the best trade in town.

John Butterfield was originally a New York stage-driver and later the organizer of the American Express Company, as well as projector of the Morse telegraph line between New York and Buffalo. As the head of John Butterfield & Company, he was one of my customers in 1857. He contracted with the United States, in 1858, as President of the Overland Mail Company, to carry mail between San Francisco and the Missouri River. To make this possible, sections of the road, afterward popularly referred to as the Butterfield Route, were built; and the surveyors, Bishop and Beale, were awarded the contract for part of the work. It is my recollection that they used for this purpose some of the camels imported by the United States Government, and that these animals were in charge of Greek George to whom I have already referred.

Butterfield chose a route from San Francisco coming down the Coast to Gilroy, San José and through the mountain passes; on to Visalia and Fort Tejón, and then to Los Angeles, in all some four hundred and sixty-two miles. From Los Angeles it ran eastward through El Monte, San Bernardino, Temécula and Warner's Ranch to Fort Yuma, and then by way of El Paso to St. Louis. In this manner, Butterfield arranged for what was undoubtedly the longest continuous stage-line ever established, the entire length being about two thousand, eight hundred and eighty miles. The Butterfield stages began running in September, 1858; and when the first one from the East reached Los Angeles on October 7th, just twenty days after it started, there was a great demonstration, accompanied by bon-fires and the firing of cannon. On this initial trip, just one passenger made the through journey—W. L. Ormsby, a reporter for the New York *Herald*. This stage reached San Francisco on October 10th, and there the accomplishment was the occasion, as we soon heard, of almost riotous enthusiasm.

Stages were manned by a driver and a conductor or messenger, both heavily armed. Provender and relief stations were established along the route, as a rule not more than twenty miles apart, and sometimes half that distance. The schedule first called for two stages a week, then one stage in each direction, every other day; and after a while this plan was altered to provide for a stage every day. There was little regularity, however, in the hours of departure, and still less in the time of arrival, and I recollect once leaving for San Francisco at the unearthly hour of two o'clock in the morning.

So uncertain, indeed, were the arrival and departure of stages, that not only were passengers often left behind, but mails were actually undelivered because no authorized person was on hand, in the lone hours of the night, to receive and distribute them. Such a ridiculous incident occurred in the fall of 1858, when bags of mail destined for Los Angeles were carried on to San Francisco, and were returned by the stage making its way south and east, fully six days later! Local newspapers were then more or less dependent for their exchanges from the great Eastern centers on the courtesy of drivers or agents; and editors were frequently acknowledging the receipt of such bundles, from which, with scissors and paste, they obtained the so-called news items furnished to their subscribers.

George Lechler, here in 1853, who married Henry Hazard's sister, drove a Butterfield stage and picked up orders for me from customers along the route.

B. W. Pyle, a Virginian by birth, arrived in Los Angeles in 1858, and became, as far as I can recall, the first exclusive jeweler and watchmaker, although Charley Ducommun, as I have said, had handled jewelry and watches some years before in connection with other things. Pyle's store adjoined that of Newmark, Kremer & Company on Commercial Street, and I soon became familiar with his methods. He commissioned many of the stage-drivers to work up business for him on the Butterfield Route; and as his charges were enormous, he was enabled, within three or four years, to establish himself in

New York. He was an exceedingly clever and original man and a good student of human affairs, and I well remember his prediction that, if Lincoln should be elected President, there would be Civil War. When the United States Government first had under consideration the building of a trans-isthmian canal, Pyle bought large tracts of land in Nicaragua, believing that the Nicaraguan route would eventually be chosen. Shortly after the selection of the Panamá survey, however, I read one day in a local newspaper that B. W. Pyle had shot himself, at the age of seventy years.

In 1857, Phineas Banning purchased from one of the Dominguez brothers an extensive tract some miles to the North of San Pedro, along the arm of the sea, and established a new landing which, in a little while, was to monopolize the harbor business and temporarily affect all operations at the old place. Here, on September 25th, 1858, he started a community called at first both San Pedro New Town and New San Pedro, and later Wilmington—the latter name suggested by the capital of Banning's native State of Delaware. Banning next cultivated a tract of six hundred acres, planted with grain and fruit where, among other evidences of his singular enterprise, there was soon to be seen a large well, connected with a steam pump of sufficient force to supply the commercial and irrigation wants of both Wilmington and San Pedro. Banning's founding of the former town was due, in part, to heavy losses sustained through a storm that seriously damaged his wharf, and in part to his desire to outdo J. J. Tomlinson, his chief business rival. The inauguration of the new shipping point, on October 1st, 1858, was celebrated by a procession on the water, when a line of barges loaded with visitors from Los Angeles and vicinity, and with freight, was towed to the decorated landing. A feature of the dedication was the assistance rendered by the ladies, who even tugged at the hawser, following which host and guests liberally partook of the sparkling beverages contributing to enliven the festive occasion.

In a short time, the shipping there gave evidence of Banning's wonderful go-ahead spirit. He had had built, in San

Francisco, a small steamer and some lighters, for the purpose of carrying passengers and baggage to the large steamships lying outside the harbor.   The enterprise was a shrewd move, for it shortened the stage-trip about six miles and so gave the new route a considerable advantage over that of all competitors. Banning, sometimes dubbed "the Admiral," about the same time presented town lots to all of his friends (including Eugene Meyer and myself), and with Timms Landing, the place became a favorite beach resort; but for want of foresight, most of these same lots were sold for taxes in the days of long ago.   I kept mine for many years and finally sold it for twelve hundred dollars; while Meyer still owns his.   As for Banning himself, he built a house on Canal Street which he occupied many years, until he moved to a more commodious home situated half a mile north of the original location.

At about this period, three packets plied between San Francisco and San Diego every ten days, leaving the Commercial Street wharf of the Northern city and stopping at various intermediate points including Wilmington.   These packets were the clipper-brig *Pride of the Sea*, Captain Joseph S. Garcia; the clipper-brig *Boston*, Commander W. H. Martin; and the clipper-schooner *Lewis Perry*, then new and in charge of Captain Hughes.

In the fall of 1858, finding that our business was not sufficiently remunerative to support four families, Newmark, Kremer & Company dissolved.   In the dissolution, I took the clothing part of the business, Newmark & Kremer retaining the dry goods.

In November or December, Dr. John S. Griffin acquired San Pasqual *rancho*, the fine property which had once been the pride of Don Manuel Garfias.   The latter had borrowed three thousand dollars, at four per cent. per month, to complete his manorial residence, which cost some six thousand dollars to build; but the ranch proving unfavorable for cattle, and Don Manuel being a poor manager, the debt of three thousand dollars soon grew into almost treble the original amount.   When Griffin purchased the place, he gave Garfias an additional two thousand dollars to cover the stock, horses and ranch-tools; but even at that the doctor drove a decided bargain. As early as 1852, Garfias had applied to the Land Commission for a patent; but this was not issued until April 3d, 1863, and the document, especially interesting because it bore the signature of Abraham Lincoln, brought little consolation to Garfias or his proud wife, *née* Ábila, who had then signed away all claim to the splendid property which was in time to play such a *rôle* in the development of Los Angeles, Pasadena and their environs.

On November 20th, Don Bernardo Yorba died, bequeathing to numerous children and grandchildren an inheritance of one hundred and ten thousand dollars' worth of personal property, in addition to thirty-seven thousand acres of land.

Sometime in December, 1858, Juan Domingo—or, as he was often called, Juan Cojo or "Lame John," because of a peculiar limp—died at his vineyard on the south side of Aliso Street, having for years enjoyed the esteem of the community as a good, substantial citizen. Domingo, who successfully conducted a wine and brandy business, was a Hollander by birth, and in his youth had borne the name of Johann Groningen; but after coming to California and settling among the Latin element, he had changed it, for what reason will never be known, to Juan Domingo, the Spanish for John Sunday. The coming of Domingo, in 1827, was not without romance; he was a ship's carpenter and one of a crew of twenty-five on the brig *Danube* which sailed from New York and was totally wrecked off San Pedro, only two or three souls (among them Domingo) being saved and hospitably welcomed by the citizens. On February 12th, 1839, he married a Spanish woman, Reymunda Feliz, by whom he had a large family of children. A son, J. A. Domingo, was living until at least recently. A souvenir of Domingo's lameness, in the County Museum, is a cane with which the doughty sailor often defended himself. Samuel Prentiss, a Rhode Islander, was another of the *Danube's* shipwrecked sailors who was saved. He hunted and fished for a living and, about 1864 or 1865, died on Catalina Island; and there, in a secluded spot, not far from the seat of his labors, he was buried.   As the result of a complicated lumber deal, Captain Joseph S. Garcia, of the *Pride of the Sea*, obtained an interest in a small vineyard owned by Juan Domingo and Sainsevain; and through this relation Garcia became a minor partner of Sainsevain in the Cucamonga winery.   Mrs. Garcia is living in Pomona; the Captain died some ten years ago at Ontario.

A propos of the three Louis, referred to—Breer, Lichtenberger and Roeder—all of that sturdy German stock which makes for good American citizenship, I do not suppose that there is any record of the exact date of Breer's arrival, although I imagine that it was in the early sixties.   Lichtenberger, who served both as a City Father and City Treasurer, arrived in 1864, while Roeder used to boast that the ship on which he sailed to San Francisco, just prior to his coming to Los Angeles, in 1856 brought the first news of Buchanan's election to the Presidency.   Of the three, Breer—who was known as Iron Louis, on account of his magnificent physique, suggesting the poet's smith, "with large and sinewy hands," and muscles as "strong as iron bands,"—was the least successful; and truly, till the end of his days, he earned his living by the sweat of his brow.   In 1865, Lichtenberger and Roeder formed a partnership which, in a few years, was dissolved, each of them then conducting business independently until, in comfortable circumstances, he retired.   Roeder, an early and enthusiastic member of the Pioneers, is never so proud as when paying his last respects to a departed comrade: his unfeigned sorrow at the loss apparently being compensated for, if one may so express it, by the recognition he enjoyed as one of the society's official committee.   Two of the three Louis are dead.[1]   Other early wheelwrights and blacksmiths were Richard Maloney, on Aliso Street, near Lambourn & Turner's grocery, and Page & Gravel, who took John Goller's shop when he joined F. Foster at his Aliso Street forge.

[1] Louis Roeder died on February 20, 1915

CHAPTER XVII

ADMISSION TO CITIZENSHIP

1859

IN 1858, my brother, to whom the greater opportunities of San Francisco had long appealed, decided upon a step that was to affect considerably my own modest affairs. This was to remove permanently to the North, with my sister-in-law; and in the Los Angeles *Star* of January 22d, 1859, there appeared the following:

Mr. Joseph P. Newmark has established a commission-house in San Francisco, with a branch in this city. From his experience in business, Mr. Newmark will be a most desirable agent for the sale of our domestic produce in the San Francisco market, and we have no doubt will obtain the confidence of our merchants and shippers.

This move of my brother's was made, as a matter of fact, at a time when Los Angeles, in one or two respects at least, seemed promising. On September 30th, the building commenced by John Temple in the preceding February, on the site of the present Bullard Block, was finished. Most of the upper floor was devoted to a theater, and I am inclined to think that the balance of the building was leased to the City, the court room being next to the theater, and the ground floor being used as a market. To the latter move there was considerable opposition, affecting, as the expenditures did, taxes and the public treasury; and one newspaper, after a spirited attack on the "Black Republicans," concluded its editorial with this patriotic appeal:

Citizens! Attend to your interests; guard your pocket-books!

This building is one of the properties to which I refer as sold by Hinchman, having been bought by Dr. J. S. Griffin and B. D. Wilson who resold it in time to the County.

A striking feature of this market building was the town clock, whose bell was 'pronounced "fine-toned and sonorous." The clock and bell, however, were destined to share the fate of the rest of the structure which, all in all, was not very well constructed. At last, the heavy rains of the early sixties played havoc with the tower, and toward the end of 1861 the clock had set such a pace for itself regardless of the rest of the universe that the newspapers were full of facetious jibes concerning the once serviceable timepiece, and many were the queries as to whether something could not be done to roof the mechanism? The clock, however, remained uncovered until Bullard demolished the building to make room for the present structure.

Elsewhere I have referred to the attempt, shortly after I arrived here, or during the session of the Legislature of 1854-55, to divide California into two states—the proposition, be it added of a San Bernardino County representative. A committee of thirteen, from different sections of the commonwealth, later substituted a bill providing for three states: Shasta, in the North; California, at the middle; Colorado, in the South; but nothing evolving as a result of the effort, our Assemblyman, Andrés Pico, in 1859 fathered a measure for the segregation of the Southern counties under the name of Colorado, when this bill passed both houses and was signed by the Governor. It had to be submitted to the people, however, at the election in September, 1859; and although nearly twenty-five hundred ballots were cast in favor of the division, as against eight hundred in the negative, the movement was afterward stifled in Washington.

Damien Marchessault and Victor Beaudry having enthusiastically organized the Santa Anita Mining Company in 1858, H. N. Alexander, agent at Los Angeles for Wells Fargo & Company, in 1859 announced that the latter had provided scales for weighing gold-dust and were prepared to transact a general exchange business. This was the same firm that had come through the crisis with unimpaired credit when Adams & Company and many others went to the wall in the great financial crash of 1855.

I have mentioned the Mormon Colony at San Bernardino and its connection, as an offshoot, with the great Mormon city, Salt Lake; now I may add that each winter, for fifteen or twenty years, or until railroad connection was established, a lively and growing trade was carried on between Los Angeles and Utah. This was because the Mormons had no open road toward the outside world, except in the direction of Southern California; for snow covered both the Rockies and the Sierra Nevadas, and closed every other highway and trail. A number of Mormon wagon-trains, therefore, went back and forth every winter over the seven hundred miles or more of fairly level, open roadways, between Salt Lake and Los Angeles, taking back not only goods bought here but much that was shipped from San Francisco to Salt Lake *via* San Pedro. I remember that in February, 1859, these Mormon wagons arrived by the Overland Route almost daily.

The third week in February witnessed one of the most interesting gatherings of *rancheros* characteristic of Southern California life I have ever seen. It was a typical *rodeo*, lasting two or three days, for the separating and re-grouping of cattle and horses, and took place at the residence of William Workman at La Puente *rancho*. Strictly speaking, the *rodeo* continued but two days, or less; for, inasmuch as the cattle to be sorted and branded had to be deprived for the time being of their customary nourishment, the work was necessarily one of despatch. Under the direction of a Judge of the Plains—on this occasion, the polished cavalier, Don Felipe Lugo—they were examined, parted and branded, or re-branded, with hot irons impressing a mark (generally a letter or odd monogram) duly registered at the Court House and protected by the County Recorder's certificate. Never have I seen finer horsemanship than was there displayed by those whose task it was to pursue the animal and throw the lasso around the head or leg; and as often as most of those present had probably seen the feat performed, great was their enthusiasm when each *vaquero* brought down his victim.   Among the guests were most of the *rancheros* of wealth and note, together with their attendants, all of whom made up a company ready to enjoy the unlimited hospitality for which the Workmans were so renowned.

Aside from the business in hand of disposing of such an enormous number of mixed-up cattle in so short a time, what made the occasion one of keen delight was the remarkable, almost astounding ability of the horseman in controlling his animal; for lassoing cattle was not his only forte.   The *vaquero* of early days was a clever rider and handler of horses, particularly the bronco—so often erroneously spelled broncho—sometimes a mustang, sometimes an Indian pony.   Out of a drove that had never been saddled, he would lasso one, attach a halter to his neck and blindfold him by means of a strap some two or three inches in width fastened to the halter; after which he would suddenly mount the bronco and remove the blind, when the horse, unaccustomed to discipline or restraint, would buck and kick for over a quarter of a mile, and then stop only because of exhaustion.   With seldom a mishap, however, the *vaquero* almost invariably broke the mustang to the saddle within three or four days.   This little Mexican horse, while perhaps not so graceful as his American brother, was noted for endurance; and he could lope from morning till night, if necessary, without evidence of serious fatigue.

Speaking of this dexterity, I may add that now and then the early Californian *vaquero* gave a good exhibition of his prowess in the town itself.   Runaways, due in part to the absence of hitching posts but frequently to carelessness, occurred daily; and sometimes a clever horseman who happened to be near would pursue, overtake and lasso the frightened steed before serious harm had been done.

Among the professional classes, J. Lancaster Brent was always popular, but never more welcomed than on his return from Washington on February 26th, 1859, when he brought the United States patent to the Dominguez *rancho*, dated December 18th, 1858, and the first document of land conveyance from the American Government to reach California.

In mercantile circles, Adolph Portugal became somewhat prominent, conducting a flourishing business here for a number of years after opening in 1854, and accumulating, before 1865, about seventy-five thousand dollars. With this money he then left Los Angeles and went to Europe, where he made an extremely unprofitable investment. He returned to Los Angeles and again engaged in mercantile pursuits; but he was never able to recover, and died a pauper.

Corbitt, who at one time controlled, with Dibblee, great ranch areas near Santa Bárbara, and in 1859 was in partnership with Barker, owned the Santa Anita *rancho*, which he later sold to William Wolfskill. From Los Angeles, Corbitt went to Oregon, where he became, I think, a leading banker.

Louis Mesmer arrived here in 1858, then went to Fraser River and there, in eight months, he made twenty thousand dollars by baking for the Hudson Bay Company's troops. A year later he was back in Los Angeles; and on Main Street, somewhere near Requena, he started a bakery. In time he controlled the local bread trade, supplying among others the Government troops here. In 1864, Mesmer bought out the United States Hotel, previously run by Webber & Haas, and finally purchased from Don Juan N. Padilla the land on which the building stood. This property, costing three thousand dollars, extended one hundred and forty feet on Main Street and ran through to Los Angeles, on which street it had a frontage of about sixty feet. Mesmer's son Joseph is still living and is active in civic affairs.

William Nordholt, a Forty-niner, was also a resident of Los Angeles for some time. He was a carpenter and worked in partnership with Jim Barton; and when Barton was elected Sheriff, Nordholt continued in business for himself. At length, in 1859, he opened a grocery store on the northwest corner of Los Angeles and First streets, which he conducted for many years. Even in 1853, when I first knew him, Nordholt had made a good start; and he soon accumulated considerable real estate on First Street, extending from Los Angeles to Main. He shared his possessions with his Spanish wife, who attended to his grocery; but after his death, in perhaps the late seventies, his children wasted their patrimony.

Notwithstanding the opening of other hotels, the Bella Union continued throughout the fifties to be the representative headquarters of its kind in Los Angeles and for a wide area around. On April 19th, 1856, Flashner & Hammell took hold of the establishment; and a couple of years after that, Dr. J. B. Winston, who had had local hotel experience, joined Flashner and together they made improvements, adding the second story, which took five or six months to complete. This step forward in the hostelry was duly celebrated, on April 14th, 1859, at a dinner, the new dining-room being advertised, far and wide, as "one of the finest in all California."

Shortly after this, however, Marcus Flashner (who owned some thirty-five acres at the corner of Main and Washington streets, where he managed either a vineyard or an orange orchard), met a violent death. He used to travel to and from this property in a buggy; and one day—June 29th, 1859—his horse ran away, throwing him out and killing him. In 1860, John King, Flashner's brother-in-law, entered the management of the Bella Union; and by 1861, Dr. Winston had sole control.

Strolling again, in imagination, into the old Bella Union of this time, I am reminded of a novel method then employed to call the guests to their meals. When I first came to Los Angeles the hotel waiter rang a large bell to announce that all was ready; but about the spring of 1859 the fact that another meal had been concocted was signalized by the blowing of a shrill steam-whistle placed on the hotel's roof. This brought together both the "regulars" and transients, everyone scurrying to be first at the dining-room door.

About the middle of April, Wells Fargo & Company's rider made a fast run between San Pedro and Los Angeles, bringing all the mail matter from the vessels, and covering the more than twenty-seven miles of the old roundabout route in less than an hour.

The Protestant Church has been represented in Los Angeles since the first service in Mayor Nichols' home and the missionary work of Adam Bland; but it was not until May 4th, 1859, that any attempt was made to erect an edifice for the Protestants in the community. Then a committee, including Isaac S. K. Ogier, A. J. King, Columbus Sims, Thomas Foster, William H. Shore, N. A. Potter, J. R. Gitchell and Henry D. Barrows began to collect funds. Reverend William E. Boardman, an Episcopalian, was invited to take charge; but subscriptions coming in slowly, he conducted services, first in one of the school buildings and then in the Court House, until 1862 when he left.

Despite its growing communication with San Francisco, Los Angeles for years was largely dependent upon sail and steamboat service, and each year the need of a better highway to the North, for stages, became more and more apparent. Finally, in May, 1859, General Ezra Drown was sent as a commissioner to Santa Bárbara, to discuss the construction of a road to that city; and on his return he declared the project quite practicable. The Supervisors had agreed to devote a certain sum of money, and the Santa Barbareños, on their part, were to vote on the proposition of appropriating fifteen thousand dollars for the work. Evidently the citizens voted favorably; for in July of the following year James Thompson, of Los Angeles, contracted for making the new road through Santa Bárbara County, from the Los Angeles to the San Luis Obispo lines, passing through Ventura—or San Buenaventura, as it was then more poetically called—Santa Bárbara and out by the Gaviota Pass; in all, a distance of about one hundred and twenty-five miles. Some five or six months were required to finish the rough work, and over thirty thousand dollars was expended for that alone.

Winfield Scott Hancock, whom I came to know well and who had been here before, arrived in Los Angeles in May, 1859, to establish a depot for the Quartermaster's Department

which he finally located at Wilmington, naming it Drum
Barracks, after Adjutant-General Richard Coulter Drum, for
several years at the head of the Department of the West.
Hancock himself was Quartermaster and had an office in a
brick building on Main Street near Third; and he was in charge
of all Government property here and at Yuma, Arizona Territory, then a military post. He thus both bought and sold;
advertising at one time, for example, a call for three or four
hundred thousand pounds of barley, and again offering for sale,
on behalf of poor Uncle Sam, the important item of a lone,
braying mule! Hancock invested liberally in California
projects, and became interested, with others, in the Bear
Valley mines; and at length had the good luck to strike a rich
and paying vein of gold quartz.

Beaudry & Marchessault were among the first handlers of
ice in Los Angeles, having an ice-house in 1859, where, in the
springtime, they stored the frozen product taken from the
mountain lakes fifty miles away. The ice was cut into cubes
of about one hundred pounds each, packed down the *cañons*
by a train of thirty to forty mules, and then brought in wagons
to Los Angeles. By September, 1860, wagon-loads of San
Bernardino ice—or perhaps one would better say compact
snow—were hawked about town and bought up by saloon-
keepers and others, having been transported in the way I have
just described, a good seventy-five miles. Later, ice was shipped
here from San Francisco; and soon after it reached town, the
saloons displayed signs soliciting orders.

Considering the present popularity of the silver dollar
along the entire Western Coast, it may be interesting to recall
the stamping of these coins, for the first time in California, at
the San Francisco mint. This was in the spring of 1859, soon
after which they began to appear in Los Angeles. A few years
later, in 1863, and for ten or fifteen years thereafter, silver
half-dimes, coined in San Francisco, were to be seen here
occasionally; but they were never popular. The larger silver
piece, the dime, was more common, although for a while it
also had little purchasing power. As late as the early seventies

it was not welcome, and many a time I have seen dimes thrown into the street as if they were worthless. This prejudice against the smaller silver coins was much the same as the feeling which even to-day obtains with many people on the Coast against the copper cent. When the nickel, in the eighties, came into use, the old Californian tradition as to coinage began to disappear; and this opened the way for the introduction of the one-cent piece, which is more and more coming into popular favor.

In the year 1859, the Hellman brothers, Isaias W. and Herman W., arrived here in a sailing-vessel with Captain Morton. I. W. Hellman took a clerkship with his cousin, I. M. Hellman, who had arrived in 1854 and was established in the stationery line in Mellus's Row, while H. W. Hellman went to work in June, 1859, for Phineas Banning, at Wilmington. I. W. Hellman immediately showed much ability and greatly improved his cousin's business. By 1865, he was in trade for himself, selling dry-goods at the corner of Main and Commercial streets as the successor to A. Portugal; while H. W. Hellman, father of Marco H. Hellman, the banker, and father-in-law of the public-spirited citizen, Louis M. Cole, became my competitor, as will be shown later, in the wholesale grocery business.

John Philbin, an Irishman, arrived here penniless late in the fifties, but with my assistance started a small store at Fort Tejón, then a military post necessary for the preservation of order on the Indian Reservation; and there, during the short space of eighteen months, he accumulated twenty thousand dollars. Illness compelled him to leave, and I bought his business and property. After completing this purchase, I engaged a clerk in San Francisco to manage the new branch. As John Philbin had been very popular, the new clerk also called himself "John" and soon enjoyed equal favor. It was only when Bob Wilson came into town one day from the Fort and told me, "That chap John is gambling your whole damned business away; he plays seven-up at twenty dollars a game, and when out of cash, puts up blocks of merchandise," that I investigated and discharged him, sending Kaspare Cohn, who had recently arrived from Europe, to take his place.

It was in 1859, or a year before Abraham Lincoln was elected President, that I bought out Philbin, and at the breaking out of the War, the troops were withdrawn from Fort Tejón, thus ending my activity there as a merchant. We disposed of the stock as best we could; but the building, which had cost three thousand dollars, brought at forced sale just fifty. Fort Tejón, established about 1854, I may add, after it attained some fame as the only military post in Southern California where snow ever fell, and also as the scene of the earthquake phenomena I have described, was abandoned altogether as a military station on September 11th, 1864. Philbin removed to Los Angeles, where he invested in some fifty acres of vineyard along San Pedro Street, extending as far south as the present Pico; and I still have a clear impression of the typical old adobe there, so badly damaged by the rains of 1890.

Kaspare remained in my employ until he set up in business at Red Bluff, Tehama County, where he continued until January, 1866. In more recent years, he has come to occupy an enviable position as a successful financier.

Somewhat less than six years after my arrival (or, to be accurate, on the fifteenth day of August, 1859, about the time of my mother's death at Loebau), and satisfying one of my most ardent ambitions, I entered the family of Uncle Sam, carrying from the District Court here a red-sealed document, to me of great importance; my newly-acquired citizenship being attested by Ch. R. Johnson, Clerk, and John O. Wheeler, Deputy.

On September 3d, the Los Angeles *Star* made the following announcement and salutation:

CALLED TO THE BAR—At the present term of the District Court for the First Judicial District, Mr. M. J. Newmark was called to the bar. We congratulate Mr. Newmark on his success, and wish him a brilliant career in his profession.

This kindly reference was to my brother-in-law, who had read law in the office of E. J. C. Kewen, then on Main Street, opposite the Bella Union, and had there, in the preceding January, when already eleven attorneys were practicing here, hung out his shingle as Notary Public and Conveyancer— an office to which he was reappointed by the Governor in 1860, soon after he had been made Commissioner for the State of Missouri to reside in Los Angeles. About that same time he began to take a lively interest in politics; being elected, on October 13th, 1860, a delegate to the Democratic County Convention. A. J. King was also admitted to the Bar toward the end of that year.

We who have such praise for the rapid growth of the population in Los Angeles must not forget the faithful midwives of early days, when there was not the least indication that there would ever be a lying-in hospital here. First, one naturally recalls old Mrs. Simmons, the *Sarah Gamp* of the fifties; while her professional sister of the sixties was Lydia Rebbick, whose name also will be pleasantly spoken by old-timers. A brother of Mrs. Rebbick was James H. Whitworth, a rancher, who came to Los Angeles County in 1857.

Residents of Los Angeles to-day have but a faint idea, I suppose, of what exertion we cheerfully submitted to, forty or fifty years ago, in order to participate in a little pleasure. This was shown at an outing in 1859, on and by the sea, made possible through the courtesy of my hospitable friend, Phineas Banning, details of which illustrate the social conditions then prevailing here.

Banning had invited fifty or sixty ladies and gentlemen to accompany him to Catalina; and at about half-past five o'clock on a June morning the guests arrived at Banning's residence where they partook of refreshments. Then they started in decorated stages for New San Pedro, where the host (who, by the way, was a man of most genial temperament, fond of a joke and sure to infuse others with his good-heartedness) regaled his friends with a hearty breakfast, not forgetting anything likely to both warm and cheer. After ample justice had been done to this feature, the picknickers boarded Banning's little steamer *Comet* and made for the outer harbor.

There they were transferred to the United States Coast Survey ship *Active*, which steamed away so spiritedly that in two hours the passengers were off Catalina; nothing meanwhile having been left undone to promote the comfort of everyone aboard the vessel. During this time Captain Alder and his officers, resplendent in their naval uniforms, held a reception; and unwilling that the merrymakers should be exposed without provisions to the wilds of the less-trodden island, they set before them a substantial ship's dinner. Once ashore, the visitors strolled along the beach and across that part of the island then most familiar; and at four o'clock the members of the party were again walking the decks of the Government vessel. Steaming back slowly, San Pedro was reached after sundown; and, having again been bundled into the stages, the excursionists were back in Los Angeles about ten o'clock.

I have said that most of the early political meetings took place at the residence of Don Ygnácio del Valle. I recall, however, a mass meeting and barbecue, in August, 1859, in a grove at El Monte owned by inn-keeper Thompson. Benches were provided for the ladies, prompting the editor of the *Star* to observe, with characteristic gallantry, that the seats "were fully occupied by an array of beauty such as no other portion of the State ever witnessed."

On September 11th, Eberhard & Koll opened the Lafayette Hotel on Main Street, on the site opposite the Bella Union where once had stood the residence of Don Eulógio de Celis. Particular inducements to families desiring quiet and the attraction of a table "supplied with the choicest viands and delicacies of the season" were duly advertised; but the proprietors met with only a moderate response. On January 1st, 1862, Eberhard withdrew and Frederick W. Koll took into partnership Henry Dockweiler—father of two of our very prominent young men, J. H. Dockweiler, the civil engineer and, in 1889, City Surveyor, and Isidore B. Dockweiler, the attorney —and Chris Fluhr. In two years, Dockweiler had withdrawn, leaving Fluhr as sole proprietor; and he continued as such until, in the seventies, he took Charles Gerson into partnership with him. It is my recollection, in fact, that Fluhr was associated with this hotel in one capacity or another until its name was changed, first to the Cosmopolitan and then to the St. Elmo.

Various influences contributed to causing radical social changes, particularly throughout the county. When Dr. John S. Griffin and other pioneers came here, they were astonished at the hospitality of the ranch-owners, who provided for them, however numerous, shelter, food and even fresh saddle-horses; and this bounteous provision for the wayfarer continued until the migrating population had so increased as to become something of a burden and economic conditions put a brake on unlimited entertainment. Then a slight reaction set in, and by the sixties a movement to demand some compensation for such service began to make itself felt. In 1859, Don Vicente de la Osa advertised that he would afford accommodation for travelers by way of his ranch, *El Encino;* but that to protect himself, he must consider it "an essential part of the arrangement that visitors should act on the good old rule and—pay as one goes!"

In 1859, C. H. Classen, a native of Germany, opened a cigar factory in the Signoret Building on Main Street, north of Arcadia; and believing that tobacco could be successfully grown in Los Angeles County, he sent to Cuba for some seed and was soon making cigars from the local product. I fancy that the plants degenerated because, although others experimented with Los Angeles tobacco, the growing of the leaf here was abandoned after a few years. H. Newmark & Company handled much tobacco for sheep-wash, and so came to buy the last Southern California crop. When I speak of sheep-wash, I refer to a solution made by steeping tobacco in water and used to cure a skin disease known as scab. It was always applied after shearing, for then the wool could not be affected and the process was easier.

Talking of tobacco, I may say that the commercial cigarette now for sale everywhere was not then to be seen. People rolled their own cigarettes, generally using brown paper, but sometimes the white, which came in reams of sheets about six by ten inches in size: Kentucky leaf was most in vogue; and the first brand of granulated tobacco that I remember was known as *Sultana*. Clay pipes, then packed in barrels, were used a good deal more than now, and brier pipes much less. There was no duty on imported cigars, and their consequent cheapness brought them into general consumption. Practically all of the native female population smoked cigarettes, for it was a custom of the country; but the American ladies did not indulge. While spending an enjoyable hour at the County Museum recently, I noticed a cigarette-case of finely-woven matting that once belonged to António María Lugo, and a bundle of cigarettes, rolled up, like so many matches, by Andrés Pico; and both the little *cigarillos* and the holder will give a fair understanding of these customs of the past.

Besides the use of tobacco in cigar and cigarette form, and for pipes, there was much consumption of the weed by chewers. *Peachbrand*, a black plug saturated with molasses and packed in caddies—a term more commonly applied to little boxes for tea—was the favorite chewing tobacco fifty years or more ago. It would hardly be an exaggeration to say that nine out of ten Americans in Los Angeles indulged in this habit, some of whom certainly exposed us to the criticism of Charles Dickens and others, who found so much fault with our manners.

The pernicious activity of rough or troublesome characters brings to recollection an aged Indian named Polonia, whom pioneers will easily recollect as having been bereft of his sight, by his own people, because of his unnatural ferocity. He was six feet four inches in height, and had once been endowed with great physical strength; he was clad, for the most part, in a tattered blanket, so that his mere appearance was sufficient to impress, if not to intimidate, the observer. Only recently, in fact, Mrs. Solomon Lazard told me that to her and her girl playmates Polonia and his fierce countenance were the terror of their lives. He may thus have deserved to forfeit his life for many crimes; but the idea of cutting a man's eyes out for any offense whatever, no matter how great, is revolting in the extreme. The year I arrived, and for some time thereafter, Polonia slept by night in the corridor of Don Manuel Requena's house.

With the aid of only a very long stick, this blind Indian was able to find his way all over the town.

Sometime in 1859, Daniel Sexton, a veteran of the battles of San Bartolo and the Mesa, became possessed of the idea that gold was secreted in large sacks near the ruins of San Juan Capistrano; and getting permission, he burrowed so far beneath the house of a citizen that the latter, fearing his whole home was likely to cave in, frantically begged the gold-digger to desist. Sexton, in fact, came near digging his own grave instead of another's, and was for a while the good-natured butt of many a pun.

Jacob A. Moerenhout, a native of Antwerp, Belgium, who had been French Consul for a couple of years at Monterey, in the latter days of the Mexican *régime*, removed to Los Angeles on October 29th, 1859, on which occasion the Consular flag of France was raised at his residence in this city. As early as January 13th, 1835, President Andrew Jackson had appointed Moerenhout "U. S. Consul to Otaheite and the Rest of the Society Islands," the original Consular document, with its quaint spelling and signed by the vigorous pen of that President, existing to-day in a collection owned by Dr. E. M. Clinton of Los Angeles; and the Belgian had thus so profited by experience in promoting trade and amicable relations between foreign nations that he was prepared to make himself *persona grata* here. Salvos of cannon were fired, while the French citizens, accompanied by a band, formed in procession and marched to the Plaza. In the afternoon, Don Louis Sainsevain in honor of the event set a groaning and luxurious table for a goodly company at his hospitable residence. There patriotic toasts were gracefully proposed and as gracefully responded to. The festivities continued until the small hours of the morning, after which Consul Moerenhout was declared a duly-initiated Angeleño.

Surrounded by most of his family, Don Juan Bandini, a distinguished Southern Californian and a worthy member of one of the finest Spanish families here, after a long and painful illness, died at the home of his daughter and son-in-law, Doña Arcadia

San Pedro Street, near Second, in the Early Seventies

Commercial Street, Looking East from Main, about 1870

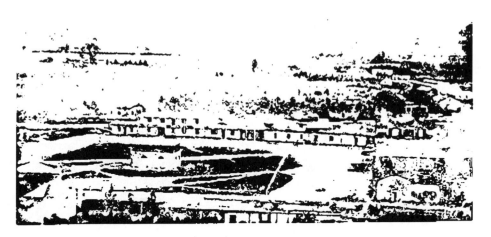

View of Plaza, Showing the Reservoir

Old Lanfranco Block

and Don Abel Stearns, in Los Angeles, on November 4th, 1859. Don Juan had come to California far back in the early twenties, and to Los Angeles so soon thereafter that he was a familiar and welcome figure here many years before I arrived.

It is natural that I should look back with pleasure and satisfaction to my association with a gentleman so typically Californian, warm-hearted, genial and social in the extreme; and one who dispensed so large and generous a hospitality. He came with his father—who eventually died here and was buried at the old San Gabriel Mission—and at one time possessed the Jurupa *rancho*, where he lived. Don Juan was a lawyer by profession, and had written the best part of a history of early California, the manuscript of which went to the State University. The passing glimpse of Bandini, in sunlight and in shadow, recorded by Dana in his classic *Two Years before the Mast*, adds to the fame already enjoyed by this native Californian.

Himself of a good-sized family, Don Juan married twice. His first wife, courted in 1823, was Dolores, daughter of Captain José Estudillo, a *comandante* at Monterey; and of that union were born Doña Arcadia, first the wife of Abel Stearns and later of Colonel R. S. Baker; Doña Ysidora, who married Lieutenant Cave J. Coutts, a cousin of General Grant; Doña Josefa, later the wife of Pedro C. Carrillo (father of J. J. Carrillo, formerly Marshal here and now Justice of the Peace at Santa Monica), and the sons, José María Bandini and Juanito Bandini. Don Juan's second wife was Refúgio, a daughter of Santiago Arguello and a granddaughter of the governor who made the first grants of land to *rancheros* of Los Angeles. She it was who nursed the wounded Kearny and who became a friend of Lieutenant William T. Sherman, once a guest at her home; and she was also the mother of Doña Dolores, later the wife of Charles R. Johnson, and of Doña Margarita whom Dr. James B. Winston married after his rollicking bachelor days. By Bandini's second marriage there were three sons: Juan de la Cruz Bandini, Alfredo Bandini and Arturo Bandini.

The financial depression of 1859 affected the temperament of citizens so much that little or no attention was paid to holidays, with the one exception, perhaps, of the Bella Union's poorly-patronized Christmas dinner; and during 1860 many small concerns closed their doors altogether.

I have spoken of the fact that brick was not much used when I first came to Los Angeles, and have shown how it soon after became more popular as a building material. This was emphasized during 1859, when thirty-one brick buildings, such as they were, were put up.

In December, Benjamin Hayes, then District Judge and holding court in the dingy old adobe at the corner of Spring and Franklin streets, ordered the Sheriff to secure and furnish another place; and despite the fact that there was only a depleted treasury to meet the new outlay of five or six thousand dollars, few persons attempted to deny the necessity. The fact of the matter was that, when it rained, water actually poured through the ceiling and ran down the court-room walls, spattering over the Judge's desk to such an extent that umbrellas might very conveniently have been brought into use; all of which led to the limit of human patience if not of human endurance.

In 1859, one of the first efforts toward the formation of a Public Library was made when Felix Bachman, Myer J. Newmark, William H. Workman, Sam Foy, H. S. Allanson and others organized a Library Association, with John Temple as President; J. J. Warner, Vice-President; Francis Mellus, Treasurer; and Israel Fleishman, Secretary. The Association established a reading-room in Don Abel Stearns's Arcadia Block. An immediate and important acquisition was the collection of books that had been assembled by Henry Mellus for his own home; other citizens contributed books, periodicals and money; and the messengers of the Overland Mail undertook to get such Eastern newspapers as they could for the persual of the library members. Five dollars was charged as an initiation fee, and a dollar for monthly dues; but insignificant as was the expense, the undertaking was not well patronized by the public, and the project, to the regret of many, had to be abandoned.

This effort to establish a library recalls an Angeleño of the fifties, Ralph Emerson, a cousin, I believe, though somewhat distantly removed, of the famous Concord philosopher. He lived on the west side of Alameda Street, in an adobe known as Emerson's Row, between First and Aliso streets, where Miss Mary E. Hoyt, assisted by her mother, had a school; and where at one time Emerson, a strong competitor of mine in the hide business, had his office. Fire destroyed part of their home late in 1859, and again in the following September. Emerson served as a director on the Library Board, both he and his wife being among the most refined and attractive people of the neighborhood.

It must have been late in November that Miss Hoyt announced the opening of her school at No. 2 Emerson Row, in doing which she followed a custom in vogue with private schools at that time and published the endorsements of leading citizens, or patrons.

Again in 1861, Miss Hoyt advertised to give "instruction in the higher branches of English education, with French, drawing, and ornamental needlework," for five dollars a month; while three dollars was asked for the teaching of the common branches and needlework, and only two dollars for teaching the elementary courses. Miss Hoyt's move was probably due to the inability of the Board of Education to secure an appropriation with which to pay the public school teachers. This lack of means led not only to a general discussion of the problem, but to the recommendation that Los Angeles schools be graded and a high school started.

Following a dry year, and especially a fearful heat wave in October which suddenly ran the mercury up to one hundred and ten degrees, December witnessed heavy rains in the mountains inundating both valleys and towns. On the fourth of December the most disastrous rain known in the history of the Southland set in, precipitating, within a single day and night, twelve inches of water; and causing the rise of the San Gabriel and other rivers to a height never before recorded and such a cataclysm that sand and *débris*

were scattered far and wide.   Lean and weakened from
the ravaging drought through which they had just passed,
the poor cattle, now exposed to the elements of cold rain
and wind, fell in vast numbers in their tracks.   The bed of
the Los Angeles River was shifted for, perhaps, a quarter of a
mile.   Many houses in town were cracked and otherwise
damaged, and some caved in altogether.   The front of the old
Church, attacked through a leaking roof, disintegrated, swayed
and finally gave way, filling the neighboring street with
impassable heaps.

I have spoken of the Market House built by John Temple
for the City.   On December 29th, there was a sale of the
stalls by Mayor D. Marchessault; and all except six booths
were disposed of, each for the term of three months.   One
hundred and seventy-three dollars was the rental agreed
upon; and Dodson & Company bid successfully for nine out of
thirteen of the stalls.   By the following month, however,
complaints were made in the press that, though the City Fathers
had "condescended to let the suffering public" have another
market, they still prevented the free competition desired;
and by the end of August, it was openly charged that the
manner in which the City Market was conducted showed "a
gross piece of favoritism," and that the City Treasury on this
account would suffer a monthly loss of one hundred dollars in
rents alone.

About 1859, John Murat, following in the wake of Henry
Kuhn, proprietor of the New York Brewery, established the
Gambrinus in the block bounded by Los Angeles, San Pedro
and First and what has become Second streets.   The brewery,
notwithstanding its spacious yard, was anything but an
extensive institution, and the quality of the product dispensed
to the public left much to be desired; but it was beer, and
Murat has the distinction of having been one of the first
Los Angeles brewers.   The New York's spigot, a suggestive
souvenir of those convivial days picked up by George W.
Hazard, now enriches a local museum.

These reminiscences recall still another brewer—Christian

Henne—at whose popular resort on Main Street, on the last evening of 1859, following some conferences in the old Round House, thirty-eight Los Angeles Germans met and formed an association which they called the Teutonia-Concordia. The object was to promote social intercourse, especially among Germans, and to further the study of German song. C. H. Classen was chosen first President; H. Hammel, Vice-President; H. Heinsch, Secretary; and Lorenzo Leck, Treasurer.

How great were the problems confronting the national government in the development of our continent may be gathered from the strenuous efforts—and their results—to encourage an overland mail route. Six hundred thousand dollars a year was the subsidy granted the Butterfield Company for running two mail coaches each way a week; yet the postal revenue for the first year was but twenty-seven thousand dollars, leaving a deficit of more than half a million! But this was not all that was discouraging: politicians attacked the stage route administration, and then the newspapers had to come to the rescue and point out the advantages as compared with the ocean routes. Indians, also, were an obstacle; and with the arrival of every stage, one expected to hear the sensational story of ambushing and murder rather than the yarn of a monotonous trip. When new reports of such outrages were brought in, new outcries were raised and new petitions, calling on the Government for protection, were hurriedly circulated.

CHAPTER XVIII

FIRST EXPERIENCE WITH THE TELEGRAPH

1860

IN 1860, Maurice Kremer was elected County Treasurer, succeeding H. N. Alexander who had entered the service of Wells Fargo & Company; and he attended to this new function at his store on Commercial Street, where he kept the County funds. I had my office in the same place; and the salary of the Treasurer at the time being but one hundred and twenty-five dollars a month, with no allowance for an assistant, I agreed to act as Deputy Treasurer without pay. As a matter of fact, I was a sort of Emergency Deputy only, and accepted the responsibility as an accommodation to Kremer, in order that when he was out of town there might be some-one to take charge of his affairs. It is very evident, however, that I did not appreciate the danger connected with this little courtesy, since it often happened that there were from forty to fifty thousand dollars in the money-chest. An expert burglar could have opened the safe without special effort, and might have gone scot-free, for the only protector at night was my nephew, Kaspare Cohn, a mere youth, who clerked for me and slept on the premises.

Inasmuch as no bank had as yet been established in Los Angeles, Kremer carried the money to Sacramento twice a year; nor was this transportation of the funds, first by steamer to San Francisco, thence by boat inland, without danger. The State was full of desperate characters who would cut a throat or scuttle a ship for a great deal less than the amount involved.

At the end of five or six years, Kremer was succeeded as County Treasurer by J. Huber, Jr. I may add, incidentally, that the funds in question could have been transported north by Wells Fargo & Company, but their charges were exorbitant. At a later period, when they were better equipped and rates had been reduced, they carried the State money.

On January 2d, Joseph Paulding, a Marylander, died. Twenty-seven years before, he came by way of the Gila, and boasted having made the first two mahogany billiard tables constructed in California.

The same month, attention was directed to a new industry, the polishing and mounting of *abalone* shells, then as now found on the coast of Southern California. A year or so later, G. Fischer was displaying a shell brooch, colored much like an opal and mounted in gold. By 1866, the demand for *abalone* shells had so increased that over fourteen thousand dollars' worth was exported from San Francisco, while a year later consignments valued at not less than thirty-six thousand dollars were sent out through the Golden Gate. Even though the taste of to-day considers this shell as hardly deserving of such a costly setting, it is nevertheless true that these early ornaments, much handsomer than many specimens of quartz jewelry, soon became quite a fad in Los Angeles. Natives and Indians, especially, took a fancy to the *abalone* shell, and even much later earrings of that material were worn by the Crow scout Curley, a survivor of the Custer Massacre. In 1874, R. W. Jackson, a shell-jeweler on Montgomery Street, San Francisco, was advertising here for the rarities, offering as much as forty and fifty dollars for a single sound red, black or silver shell, and from fifty to one hundred dollars for a good green or blue one. Incidentally, it is interesting to note that the Chinese consumed the *abalone* meat in large quantities.

Broom-making was a promising industry in the early sixties, the Carpenters of Los Nietos and F. W. Gibson of El Monte being among the pioneers in this handiwork. Several thousand brooms were made in that year; and since they brought three dollars a dozen, and cost but eleven cents each for the handles and labor, exclusive of the corn, a good profit was realized.

Major Edward Harold Fitzgerald, well known for campaigns against both Indians and bandits, died on January 9th and was buried with military honors.

On January 10th, Bartholomew's Rocky Mountain Circus held forth on the Plaza, people coming in from miles around to see the show. It was then that the circus proprietor sought to quiet the nerves of the anxious by the large-lettered announcement, "A strict Police is engaged for the occasion!"

The printing of news, editorials and advertisements in both English and Spanish recalls again not only some amusing incidents in court activities resulting from the inability of jurists and others to understand the two languages, but also the fact that in the early sixties sermons were preached in the Catholic Church at Los Angeles in English and Spanish, the former being spoken at one mass, the latter at another. English proper names such as John and Benjamin were Spanished into Juan and Benito, and common Spanish terms persisted in English advertisements, as when Don Juan Ávila and Fernando Sepúlveda, in January, announced that they would run the horse *Coyote* one thousand *varas*, for three thousand dollars. In 1862, also, when Syriaco Arza was executed for the murder of Frank Riley, the peddler, and the prisoner had made a speech to the crowd, the Sheriff read the warrant for the execution in both English and Spanish. Still another illustration of the use of Spanish here, side by side with English, is found in the fact that in 1858 the Los Angeles assessment rolls were written in Spanish, although by 1860 the entries were made in English only.

A letter to the editor of the *Star*, published on January 28th, 1860, will confirm my comments on the primitive school conditions in Los Angeles in the first decade or two after I came. The writer complained of the filthy condition of the Boys' Department, School No. 1, in which, to judge by the mud, "the floor did not seem to have been swept for months!" The editor then took up the cudgel, saying that the Board formerly paid a man for keeping the schoolroom clean, but that the Common Council had refused any longer to pass the janitor's bills; adding that, in his opinion, the Council had acted wisely! If the teacher had really wished the schoolroom floor to be clean, contended the economical editor, he should have appointed a pupil to swing a broom each day or, at least, *each week*, and otherwise perform the necessary duties on behalf of the health of the school.

The year 1860 witnessed the death of Don António María Lugo—brother of Don José Ygnácio Lugo, grandfather of the Wolfskills—uncle of General Vallejo and the father-in-law of Colonel Isaac Williams, who preceded Lugo to the grave by four years. For a long time, Lugo lived in a spacious adobe built in 1819 near the present corner of East Second and San Pedro streets, and there the sons, for whom he obtained the San Bernardino *rancho*, were born. In earlier days, or from 1813, Don António lived on the San António Ranch near what is now Compton; and so well did he prosper there that eleven leagues were not enough for the support of his cattle and flocks. It was a daughter of Lugo who, having married a Perez and being made a widow, became the wife of Stephen C. Foster, her daughter in turn marrying Wallace Woodworth and becoming María Antónia Perez de Woodworth; and Lugo, who used to visit them and the business establishments of the town, was a familiar figure as a sturdy *caballero* in the streets of Los Angeles, his ornamental sword strapped in Spanish-soldier fashion to his equally-ornamental saddle. Don António died about the first of February, aged eighty-seven years.

About the middle of February, John Temple fitted up the large hall over the City Market as a theater, providing for it a stage some forty-five by twenty feet in size—in those days considered an abundance of platform space—and a "private box" on each side, whose possession became at once the ambition of every Los Angeles gallant. Temple brought an artist from San Francisco to paint the scenery, Los Angeles then boasting of no one clever enough for the work; and the same genius supervised the general decoration of the house. What was considered a record-breaking effort at making the public comfortable was undertaken in furnishing the parquet with armchairs and in filling the gallery with two tiers of raised benches, guaranteeing some chance of looking over any broad *sombreros* in front; and to cap the enterprise, Temple brought down a company of players especially to dedicate his new house. About February 20th, the actors arrived on the old *Senator;* and while I do not recall who they were or what they produced, I believe that they first held forth on Washington's Birthday when it was said: "The scenery is magnificent, surpassing anything before exhibited in this city."

The spring of 1860 was notable for the introduction of the Pony Express as a potent factor in the despatch of transcontinental mail; and although this new service never included Los Angeles as one of its terminals, it greatly shortened the time required and, naturally if indirectly, benefited the Southland. Speed was, indeed, an ambition of the new management, and some rather extraordinary results were attained. About April 20th, soon after the Pony Express was started, messages were rushed through from St. Louis to San Francisco in eight and a half days; and it was noised about that the Butterfields planned a rival pony express, over a route three hundred miles shorter, that would reach the Coast in seven days. About the end of April, mail from London and Liverpool reached Los Angeles in twenty or twenty-one days; and I believe that the fastest time that the Pony Express ever made was in March, 1861, when President Lincoln's message was brought here in seven days and seventeen hours. This was somewhat quicker than the passage of the report about Fort Sumter, a month afterward, which required twelve days, and considerably faster than the transmission, by the earlier methods of 1850, of the intelligence that California had been admitted to the Union—a bit of news of the greatest possible importance yet not at all known here, I have been told, until six weeks after Congress enacted the law! Which reminds me that the death of Elizabeth Barrett Browning, the poet, although occurring in Italy on June 29th, 1861, was first announced in Los Angeles on the seventeenth of the following August!

In February or March, the sewer crossing Los Angeles Street and connecting the Bella Union with the *zanja* (which passed through the premises of Francis Mellus) burst, probably as the result of the recent rains, discharging its contents into the common yard; and in short order Mellus found himself minus two very desirable tenants. For a while, he thought of suing the City; and then he decided to stop the sewer effectually. As soon as it was plugged up, however, the Bella Union found itself cut off from its accustomed outlet, and there was soon a great uproar in that busy hostelry. The upshot of the matter was that the Bella Union proprietors commenced suit against Mellus. This was the first sewer—really a small, square wooden pipe—whose construction inaugurated an early chapter in the annals of sewer-building and control in Los Angeles.

Competition for Government trade was keen in the sixties, and energetic efforts were made by merchants to secure their share of the crumbs, as well as the loaves, that might fall from Uncle Sam's table. For that reason, Captain Winfield Scott Hancock easily added to his popularity as Quartermaster, early in 1860, by preparing a map in order to show the War Department the relative positions of the various military posts in this district, and to emphasize the proximity of Los Angeles.

One day in the Spring a stranger called upon me with the interesting information that he was an inventor, which led me to observe that someone ought to devise a contrivance with which to pluck oranges—an operation then performed by climbing into the trees and pulling the fruit from the branches. Shortly after the interview, many of us went to the grove of Jean Louis Sainsevain to see a simple, but ingenious appliance for picking the golden fruit. A pair of pincers on a light pole were operated from below by a wire; and when the wire was pulled, the fruit, quite unharmed by scratch or pressure, fell safely into a little basket fastened close to the pincers. In the same year, Pierre Sainsevain established the first California wine house in New York and bought the Cucamonga vineyard, where he introduced new and better varieties of grapes.

But bad luck overtook him. In 1870, grasshoppers ate the leaves and destroyed the crop.

Small as was the population of Los Angeles County at about this time, there was nevertheless for a while an exodus to Texas, due chiefly to the difficulty experienced by white immigrants in competing with Indian ranch and vineyard laborers.

Toward the middle of March, much interest was manifested in the welfare of a native Californian named Serbo—sometimes erroneously given as Serbulo and even Cervelo—Varela who, under the influence of bad whiskey, had assaulted and nearly killed a companion, and who seemed certain of a long term in the State prison. It was recalled, however, that when in the fall of 1846, the fiendish Flores, resisting the invasion of the United States forces, had captured a number of Americans and condemned them to be dragged out and shot, Varela, then a soldier under Flores, and a very brave fellow, broke from the ranks, denounced the act as murder, declared that the order should never be carried out except over his dead body, and said and did such a number of things more or less melodramatic that he finally saved the lives of the American prisoners. Great sympathy was expressed, therefore, when it was discovered that this half-forgotten hero was in the toils; and few persons, if any, were sorry when Varela was induced to plead guilty to assault and battery, enabling the court to deal leniently with him. Varela became more and more addicted to strong drink; and some years later he was the victim of foul play, his body being found in an unfrequented part of the town.

A scrap-book souvenir of the sixties gives us an idyllic view of contemporaneous pueblo life, furnishing, at the same time, an idea of the newspaper English of that day. It reads as follows:

With the exception of a little legitimate shooting affair last Saturday night, by which some fellow had well-nigh the top of his head knocked off, and one or two knock-downs and drag-outs, we have had a very peaceful week indeed. Nothing has occurred to disturb the even tenor of our way, and our good people seem to be given up to the quiet enjoyment of delicious fruits and our unequalled climate,—each one literally under his own vine and fig tree, revelling in fancy's flights, or luxuriating among the good things which he finds temptingly at hand.

The demand for better lighting facilities led the Common Council to make a contract, toward the end of March, with Tiffany & Wethered, who were given a franchise to lay pipes through the streets and to establish gas-works here; but the attempt proved abortive.

In this same year, the trip east by the Overland Stage Route, which had formerly required nearly a month, was accomplished in eighteen or nineteen days; and toward the end of March, the Overland Company replaced the "mud-wagons" they had been using between Los Angeles and San Francisco with brightly-painted and better-upholstered Concord coaches. Then the Los Angeles office was on Spring Street, between First and second—on the lot later bought by Louis Roeder for a wagon-shop, and now the site of the Roeder Block; and there, for the price of two hundred dollars, tickets could be obtained for the entire journey to St. Louis.

Foreign coin circulated in Los Angeles, as I have said, for many years, and even up to the early sixties Mexican money was accepted at par with our own. Improved facilities for intercourse with the outside world, however, affected the markets here, and in the spring of that year several merchants refused to receive the specie of our southern neighbor at more than its actual value as silver. As a result, these dealers, though perhaps but following the trend elsewhere, were charged openly with a combination to obtain an illegitimate profit.

In 1860, while Dr. T. J. White was Postmaster, a regulation was made ordering all mail not called for to be sent to the Dead Letter Office in Washington, within a week after such mail had been advertised; but it was not until the fall of 1871 that this order was really put into operation in our neighborhood. For some time this worked great hardship on many people living in the suburbs who found it impossible to call promptly for their mail, and who learned too late that letters intended for them had been returned to the sender or destroyed.

Political enthusiasm was keen in early days, as is usual in small towns, and victorious candidates, at least, knew how to celebrate. On Monday, May 7th, 1860, Henry Mellus was elected Mayor; and next day, he and the other City officers paraded our streets in a four-horse stagecoach with a brass band. The Mayor-elect and his *confrères* were stuffed inside the hot, decorated vehicle, while the puffing musicians bounced up and down on the swaying top outside, like pop-corn in a frying-pan.

More than a ripple of excitement was produced in Los Angeles about the middle of May, when Jack Martin, Billy Holcomb and Jim Ware, in from Bear Valley, ordered provisions and paid for the same in shining gold dust. It was previously known that they had gone out to hunt for bear, and their sudden return with this precious metal, together with their desire to pick up a few appliances such as are not ordinarily used in trapping, made some of the hangers-on about the store suspicious. The hunters were secretly followed, and were found to return to what is now Holcomb Valley; and then it was learned that gold had been discovered there about the first of the month. For a year or two, many mining camps were formed in Holcomb and Upper Holcomb valleys, and in that district the town of Belleville was founded; but the gold, at first apparently so plentiful, soon gave out, and the excitement incidental to the discovery subsided.

While some men were thus digging for treasure, others sought fortune in the deep. Spearing sharks, as well as whales, was an exciting industry at this period; sharks running in large numbers along the coast, and in the waters of San Pedro Bay. In May, Orin Smith of Los Angeles, with the aid of his son, in one day caught one hundred and three sharks, from which he took only the livers; these, when boiled, yielding oil which, burned fairly well, even in its crude state. During the next year, shark-hunting near Rattlesnake Island continued moderately remunerative.

Sometime in the spring, another effort was made to establish a tannery here and hopes were entertained that an important trade might thus be founded. But the experiment came to naught, and even to-day Los Angeles can boast of no tannery such as exists in several other California cities.

With the approach of summer, Elijah and William H. Workman built a brick dwelling on Main Street, next to Tom Rowan's bakery, and set around it trees of several varieties. The residence, then one of the prettiest in town, was built for the boys' mother; and there, with her, they dwelt.

That sectarian activity regarding public schools is nothing new in Los Angeles may be shown from an incident, not without its humorous side, of the year 1860. T. J. Harvey appeared with a broadside in the press, protesting against the reading of the Bible in schoolrooms, and saying that he, for one, would "never stand it, come what may." Some may still remember his invective and his pyrotechnical conclusion: "*Revolution! War!! Blood!!!*"

During Downey's incumbency as Governor, the Legislature passed a law, popularly known as the Bulkhead Bill, authorizing the San Francisco Dock and Wharf Company to build a stone bulkhead around the water-front of the Northern city, in return for which the company was to have the exclusive privilege of collecting tolls and wharfage for the long period of fifty years, a franchise the stupendous value of which even the projectors of that date could scarcely have anticipated. Downey, when the measure came before him for final action, vetoed the bill and thus performed a judicious act—perhaps the most meritorious of his administration.

Whether Downey, who on January 9th had become Governor, was really popular for any length of time, even in the vicinity of his home, may be a question; but his high office and the fact that he was the first Governor from the Southland assured him a hearty welcome whenever he came down here from the capital. In June Downey returned to Los Angeles, accompanied by his wife, and took rooms at the Bella Union hotel, and besides the usual committee visits, receptions and speeches from the balcony, arranged in honor of the distinguished guests, there was a salute of thirteen guns, fired with all ceremony, which echoed and re-echoed from the hillsides.

In 1860, a number of delegates, including Casper Behrendt and myself, were sent to San Francisco to attend the laying of the corner-stone, on the twenty-fifth of June, of the Masonic Temple at the corner of Post and Montgomery streets. We made the trip when the weather was not only excessively hot, but the sand was a foot deep and headway very slow; so that, although we were young men and enjoyed the excursion, we could not laugh down all of the disagreeable features of the journey. It was no wonder, therefore, that when we arrived at Visalia, where we were to change horses, Behrendt wanted a shave. While he was in the midst of this tonsorial refreshment, the stage started on its way to San Francisco; and as Behrendt heard it passing the shop, he ran out—with one side of his face smooth and clean, while the other side was whiskered and grimy—and tried to stop the disappearing vehicle. Despite all of his yelling and running, however, the stage did not stop; and finally, Behrendt fired his pistol several times into the air. This attracted the attention of the sleepy driver, who took the puffing passenger on board; whereupon the rest of us chaffed him about his singular appearance. Behrendt[1] did not have much peace of mind until we reached the Plaza Hotel at San Juan Bautista ("a relic," as someone has said," of the distant past, where men and women played billiards on horseback, and trees bore human fruit"), situated in a sweet little valley, mountain-girdled and well watered; where he was able to complete his shave and thus restore his countenance to its normal condition.

In connection with this anecdote of the trip to San Francisco, I may add another story. On board the stage was Frederick J. McCrellish, editor of the *Alta California*—the principal Coast paper, bought by McCrellish & Company in 1858—and also Secretary of the telegraph company at that time building its line between San Francisco and Los Angeles.

[1] Died November 19th, 1913.

When we reached a point between Gilroy and Visalia, which was the temporary terminus of the telegraph from San Francisco, McCrellish spoke with some enthusiasm of the Morse invention and invited everybody on the stage to send telegrams, at his expense, to his friends.   I wrote out a message to my brother in San Francisco, telling him about the trip as far as I had completed it, and passed the copy to the operator at the clicking instrument.   It may be hard for the reader to conceive that this would be an exciting episode in a man's life; but since my first arrival in the Southland there had been no telegraphic communication between Los Angeles and the outside world, and the remembrance of this experience at the little wayside station was never to be blotted from my mind.   I may also add that of that committee sent to the Masonic festivities in San Francisco, Behrendt and I are now the only surviving members.

It has been stated that the population of Los Angeles in 1850 was but sixteen hundred and ten.   How true that is I cannot tell.   When I came to the city in 1853, there were some twenty-six hundred people.   In the summer of 1860 a fairly accurate census was made, and it was found that our little town had four thousand three hundred and ninety-nine inhabitants.

Two distinguished military men visited Los Angeles in the midsummer of 1860.   The first was General James Shields who, in search of health, arrived by the Overland Route on the twenty-fourth of July, having just finished his term in the Senate.   The effect of wounds received at the battle of Cerro Gordo, years before, and reports as to the climate of California started the General westward; and quietly he alighted from the stage at the door of the Bella Union.   After a while, General Shields undertook the superintending of a Mexican mine; but at the outbreak of the Civil War, although not entirely recovered, he hastened back to Washington and was at once appointed a Brigadier-General of volunteers.   The rest of his career is known.

A week later, General, or as he was then entitled, Colonel

John C. Frémont drew up at the Plaza. His coming to this locality in connection with the Temescal tin mine and Mariposa forestry interests had been heralded from Godey's ranch some days before; and when he arrived on Tuesday, July 31st, in company with Leonidas Haskell and Joseph C. Palmer, the Republicans were out in full force and fired a salute of twenty-five guns. In the evening, Colonel Frémont was waited upon in the parlors of the Bella Union by a goodly company, under the leadership of the Republican Committee, although all classes, irrespective of politics, united to pay the celebrated California pioneer the honors due him.

Alexander Godey, to whose *rancho* I have just referred, was a man of importance, with a very extensive cattle-range in Kern County not far from Bakersfield, where he later lived. He occasionally came to town, and was an invariable visitor at my store, purchasing many supplies from me. These and other provisions, which Godey and his neighbors sent for, were transported by burro- or mule-train to the ranches in care of Miguel Ortiz, who had his headquarters in Los Angeles. Loading these so-called pack-trains was an art: by means of ropes and slats of wood, merchandise was strapped to the animal's sides and back in such a fashion that it could not slip, and thus a heavy, well-balanced load was conveyed over the plain and the mountain trails.

By 1860, the Germans were well-organized and active here in many ways, a German Benevolent Society, called the Ein-tracht, which met Tuesday and Friday evenings in the Arcadia Block for music drill under Director Heinsch, affording stimulating entertainment and accomplishing much good. The Turnverein, on the other hand, took an interest in the success of the Round House, and on March 12th put up a liberty pole on top of the oddly-shaped building. Lager beer and other things deemed by the Teutonic brethren essential to a Garden of Paradise and to such an occasion were freely dispensed; and on that day Lehman was in all his glory.

A particular feature of this Garden of Paradise was a cab-bage, about which have grown up some traditions of the Brobdingnagian sort that the reader may accept *in toto* or with a grain of salt. It was planted when the place was opened, and is said to have attained, by December, 1859, a height of twelve feet, "with a circumference" (so averred an ambiguous chronicler of the period, referring doubtless to crinolines) "equal to that of any fashionably-attired city belle measuring eight or ten feet." By July, 1860, the cabbage attained a growth, so the story goes, of fourteen feet four inches although, George always claimed, it had been cropped twenty or more times and its leaves used for *Kohlslau, Sauerkraut* and goodness knows what. I can afford the modern reader no better idea of Lehman's personality and resort than by quoting the following contemporaneous, if not very scholarly, account:

THE GARDEN OF PARADISE. Our friend George of the Round House, who there keeps a garden with the above captivating name, was one of the few who done honor to the Fourth. He kept the National Ensign at the fore, showed his fifteen-foot cabbage, and dealt *Lager* to admiring crowds all day.

Among the popular pleasure-resorts of 1860 was the Tivoli Garden on the Wolfskill Road, conducted by Charles Kaiser, who called his friends together by placarding the legend, "Hurrah for the Tivoli!" Music and other amusements were provided every Sunday, from two o'clock, and dancing could be enjoyed until late in the night; and as there was no charge for admission, the place was well patronized.

When the Fourth of July, 1859, approached and no preparation had been made to observe the holiday, some children who were being instructed in calisthenics by A. F. Tilden began to solicit money, their childish enthusiasm resulting in the appointing of a committee, the collecting of four hundred dollars, and a picnic in Don Luis Sainsevain's enclosed garden. A year later, Tilden announced that he would open a place for gymnastic exercises in "Temple's New Block;" charging men three dollars for the use of the apparatus and the privilege of a shower-bath, and training boys at half rates. This was the origin of systematic physical culture in Los Angeles.

CHAPTER XIX

STEAM-WAGON—ODD CHARACTERS

1860

EARLY in 1860, Phineas Banning and J. J. Tomlinson, the energetic rivals in lighterage and freighting at San Pedro, embarked as lumber merchants, thereby anticipating the enormous trade that has flowed for years past from the North through Los Angeles to Southern California and Arizona. Having many teams, they hauled lumber, when traffic was not sufficient to keep their wagon-trains busy, from the harbor to the city or even, when there was need, to the *ranchos*. It must have been in the same year that F. P. F. Temple, at a cost of about forty thousand dollars for lumber alone, fenced in a wide acreage, at the same time building large and substantial barns for his stock. By the summer of that year, Banning was advertising lumber, delivered in Los Angeles; and from October 1st, Banning & Hinchman had an office near the northern junction of Main and Spring streets. A couple of years before, Banning in person had directed the driving of seventeen mule teams, from San Pedro to Fort Yuma, covering, in twelve or thirteen days, the two hundred and thirty miles of barely passable road. The following March, Banning and Tomlinson, who had so often opposed each other even in the courts, came to an understanding and buried the hatchet for good.

At this time, Joseph Everhardt, who, with Frederick W. Koll, had conducted the Lafayette Hotel, sold out and moved to San Francisco, marrying Miss R. Mayer, now John Lang's widow, sister-in-law of Kiln Messer. Later, Everhardt went to Sonoma and then to Victoria, B. C., in each place making his mark; and in the latter city he died.

Like both Messer and Lang, Everhardt had passed through varied and trying experiences. The owner of the Russ Garden restaurant in 1849, in lively San Francisco, he came to Los Angeles and took hold of the hotel Lafayette. With him was a partner named Fucht; but a free fight and display of shooting irons, such as often enlivened a California hotel, having sent the guests and hangers-on scurrying to quarters, induced Fucht to sell out his interests in very short order, whereupon Everhardt took in with him Frederick W. Koll, who lived on a site now the southeast corner of Seventh and Spring streets where he had an orange-grove.

Pursuing Indians was dangerous in the extreme, as Robert Wilburn found when he went after some twenty head of cattle stolen from Felix Bachman by Pi-Ute or Paiute Indians in January, 1860, during one of their marauding expeditions into California. Wilburn chased the red men but he never came back; and when his body was found, it was pierced with three or four arrows, probably shot at him simultaneously by as many of the cattle-thieves.

Don Tomás A. Sanchez, Sheriff from 1860 to 1867, had a record for physical courage and prowess, having previously been an officer under Pico in the Mexican War days, and having later aided Pico in his efforts to punish Barton's murderers. Sanchez had property; and in 1887 a patent was granted his estate for four thousand or more acres in the ranch known as *Ciénega ó Paso de la Tijera.*

Destructive fires in the open country, if not as common as now, still occasionally stirred our citizens. Such a fire broke out in the San Fernando Valley in the middle of July, and spread so rapidly that a square mile and a half of territory was denuded and charred. Not only were there no organized means to fight such fires, but men were compelled to sound the alarm through couriers on horseback; and if the wind happened to be blowing across the plains, even the fleetest horseman had all he could do to avoid the flames and reach in time the widely-separated *rancheros.* Here I may add that as late as the sixties all of the uninhabited parts of Los Angeles, especially to the west of Main Street, were known as plains, and "crossing the plains" was an expression commonly used with a peculiarly local significance.

So wretched were the roads in the early decades after my arrival, and so many were the plans proposed for increasing the rapidity of travel, that great curiosity was excited in 1860 when it was announced that Phineas Banning had bought a "steam-wagon" and would soon introduce a kind of vehicle such as Los Angeles, at least, had never before seen. This steam-wagon was a traction engine built by J. Whitman & Sons, at Leeds, England, and was already on its way across the ocean. It had been ordered by Richard A. Ogden, of San Francisco, for the Patagonia Copper Mining Company, a trial before shipping having proved that, with a load of thirty-eight tons, the engine could attain a speed of five miles an hour; and Banning paid handsomely for the option of purchasing the vehicle, on condition that it would ultimately prove a success.

The announcement was made in April, and by early June the engine had reached San Francisco where it made the run to Mission Dolores in three-quarters of an hour. All the San Francisco papers told of "the truly wonderful machine," one reporter averring that "the engineer had so perfect control that a visit was made to various parts of the city, to the astonishment and gratification of the multitude;" and since these accounts were immediately copied by the Los Angeles papers (which added the official announcement that Captain Hughes had loaded the engine on board his schooner, the *Lewis Perry*, and was bringing it south as fast as he could), popular excitement rose like the mercury in summer, and but one more report was needed to make it the absorbing talk of the hour. That came on the twenty-eighth of July, when the *Star* announced: "The steam-wagon has arrived at San Pedro;" and it was not long before many persons went down to the port to get a sight of the wonderful object.

And wait they did. Although the *Star* said that "all our citizens were anxiously, hourly, expecting to see Major Banning heave in sight at the foot of Main Street," no Banning hove!

Instead, on the fourth of August, the same *Star* broke forth with this lament: "The steam-wagon is at San Pedro, and we regret to learn that it is likely to remain there. So far, all attempts to reach this city with freight have failed." And that was the end of the steam-wagon experiment here.

In every community there are characters who, for one reason or another, develop among their fellows a reputation for oddity. We have all seen the good-natured, rather stout old gentleman, whose claim to dignity is his old-fashioned Prince Albert and rather battered-looking silk hat, but who, although he boasts many friends, is never successful in the acquisition of this world's goods. We have seen, too, the vender of ice-cream, *tamales* or similar commodity, who in his youth had been an opera singer or actor, but whose too intensive thirst rendered him impossible in his profession and brought him far down in the world. Some were dangerous criminals; some were harmless, but obnoxious; others still were harmless and amusing. Many such characters I have met during my sixty years in Los Angeles; and each filled a certain niche, even those whose only mission was to furnish their fellows with humor or amusement having thus contributed to the charm of life.

Viejo Cholo, or Old Half-breed, a Mexican over sixty years of age who was never known by any other name, was such an eccentric character. He was half blind; wore a pair of white linen pantaloons, and for a mantle used an old sheet. This he threw over his shoulders; and thus accoutered, he strutted about the streets like a Spanish cavalier. His cane was a broom-handle; his lunch-counter, the swill-bucket; and when times were particularly bad, Viejo begged. The youngsters of the pueblo were the bane of Cholo's existence and the torment of his infirmity and old age.

Cholo was succeeded by Pinikahti, who was half Indian and half Mexican. He was not over four feet in height and had a flat nose, a stubby beard and a face badly pockmarked; and he presented, altogether, as unkempt and obnoxious an appearance as one might imagine. Pinikahti was generally attired in a well-worn straw hat, the top of which was missing, and his long, straight hair stuck out in clumps and snarls.   A woolen under-shirt and a pair of overalls completed his costume, while his toes, as a rule, protruded from his enormous boots.   Unlike Viejo Cholo, Pinikahti was permitted to go unmolested by the juvenile portion of the population, inasmuch as, though half-witted, he was somewhat of an entertainer; for it was natural for him to play the flute and—what was really interesting—he made his own instruments out of the reed that grew along the river banks.   Pinikahti cut just the holes, I suppose, that produced what seemed to him proper harmony, and on these home-made flutes performed such airs as his wandering fancy suggested. He always played weird tunes and danced strange Indian dances; and through these crude gifts he became, as I have said, suf-ficiently popular to enjoy some immunity.   Nevertheless, he was a professional beggar; and whatever he did to afford amusement, was done, after all, for money.   This was easily explained, for money alone would buy *aguardiente*, and Pinikahti had little use for anything else.   *Aguardiente*, as the word was commonly used in Southern California, was a native brandy, full of hell fire; and so the poor half-breed was always drunk. One day Pinikahti drank a glass too much, and this brought about such a severance of his ties with beautiful Los Angeles that his absorption of one spirit released, at last, the other.

Sometime in the eventful sixties, a tall, angular, muscular-looking woman was here, who went by the singular *sobriquet* of Captain Jinks, a title which she received from a song then very popular, the first couplet of which ran something like this:

> I'm Captain Jinks of the Horse Marines,
> I feed my horse on pork and beans!

She half strode, half jerked her way along the street, as though scanning the lines of that ditty with her feet.   She was strong for woman's rights, she said; and she certainly looked it.

Chinamen were not only more numerous by 1860, but they had begun to vary their occupations, many working as servants, laundrymen or farm hands.   In March, a Chinese company was also organized to compete for local fish trade.

In 1860, Émile Bordenave & Company opened the Louisiana Coffee Saloon as a French restaurant. Roast duck and oysters were their specialty, and they charged fifty cents a meal. But they also served "a plate at one bit."[1] Some years later, there was a two-bit restaurant known as Brown's on Main Street, near the United States Hotel, where a good, substantial meal was served.

James, often called Santiago Johnson, who, for a short time prior to his death about 1860 or 1861, was a forwarder of freight at San Pedro, came to Los Angeles in 1833 with a cargo of Mexican and Chinese goods, and after that owned considerable ranch property. In addition to ranching, he also engaged extensively in cattle-raising.

Peter, popularly known as Pete or Bully Wilson, a native of Sweden, came to Los Angeles about 1860. He ran a one horse dray; and as soon as he had accumulated sufficient money, he bought, for twelve hundred dollars, the southeast corner of Spring and First streets, where he had his stable. He continued to prosper; and his family still enjoy the fruits of his industry.

The same year, George Smith started to haul freight and baggage. He had four horses hitched to a sombre-looking vehicle nicknamed the *Black Swan*.

J. D. Yates was a grocer and provision-dealer of 1860, with a store on the Plaza.

I have referred to Bishop Amat as presiding over the Diocese of Monterey and Los Angeles; but Los Angeles was linked with Monterey, for a while, even in judicial matters. Beginning with 1860 or 1861 (when Fletcher M. Haight, father of Governor H. H. Haight, was the first Judge to preside), the United States Court for the Southern District of California was held alternately in the two towns mentioned, Colonel J. O. Wheeler serving as Clerk and the Court for the Southern term occupying seven rooms of the second story of John Temple's Block. These alternate sessions continued to be held until about 1866 when the tribunal for the Southern District ceased to exist and Angeleños were compelled to apply to the court in San Francisco.

[1] Twelve and one-half cents.

For years, such was the neglect of the Protestant burial ground that in 1860 caustic criticism was made by each newspaper discussing the condition of the cemetery: there was no fence, headstones were disfigured or demolished, and there was little or no protection to the graves. As a matter of fact, when the cemetery on Fort Hill was abandoned, but few of the bodies were removed.

By 1860, the New England Fire Insurance Company, of Hartford, Connecticut, was advertising here through its local agent, H. Hamilton—our friend of the Los Angeles *Star*. Hamilton used to survey the applicants' premises, forward the data to William Faulkner, the San Francisco representative, who executed the policy and mailed the document back to Los Angeles. After a while, Samuel Briggs, with Wells Fargo & Co., represented the Phœnix Insurance Company.

H. Newmark & Company also sold insurance somewhat later, representing the Commercial Union Insurance Company. About 1880, however, they disposed of their insurance interests to Maurice Kremer, whose main competitor was W. J. Brodrick; and from this transaction developed the firm of Kremer, Campbell & Company, still in that business. Not only in this connection but elsewhere in these memoirs it may be noted how little specialization there was in earlier days in Los Angeles; in fact it was not until about 1880 that this process, distinctive of economic progress, began to appear in Los Angeles. I myself have handled practically every staple that makes up the very great proportion of merchandising activity, whereas my successors of to-day, as well as their competitors, deal only in groceries and kindred lines.

Two brothers, Émile and Théophile Vaché, in the fall of 1860, started what has become the oldest firm—Vaché Frères— in the local wine business, at first utilizing the Bernard residence at Alameda and Third streets, in time used by the Government as a bonded warehouse. Later, they removed to the building on Aliso Street once occupied by the Medical College, where the cellars proved serviceable for a winery. There they attempted the manufacture of cream of tartar from wine-crystals, but the venture was not remunerative. In 1881, the Vachés, joined by their brother Adolphe, began to grow grapes in the Barton Vineyard in San Bernardino County, and some time afterward they bought near-by land and started the famous Brookside Vineyard. Émile is now dead; while Théophile, who retired and returned to Europe in 1892, retaining an interest in the firm of T. Vaché & Company, passes his hours pleasantly on the picturesque island of St. George d'Oléron, in the Charente Inférieure, in his native France.

On September 21st, Captain W. S. Hancock, who first came to Los Angeles in connection with the expedition against the Mojave Indians in 1858, sought to establish a new kind of express between Los Angeles and Fort Mojave, and sent out a camel in charge of Greek George to make the trial trip. ·When they had been gone two and a half days, the regular express messenger bound for Los Angeles met them at Lane's Crossing, apparently in none too promising a condition; which later gave rise to a report that the camel had died on the desert. This occasioned numerous newspaper squibs *à propos* of both the speed and the staying powers of the camel as contrasted with those of the burro; and finally, in October, the following cement appeared placarded throughout the town:

BY POULTERER, DE RO &·ELDRIDGE

OFFICE AND SALESROOM, CORNER CALIFORNIA & FRONT STREETS, SAN FRANCISCO.

PEREMPTORY SALE
OF
BACTRIAN CAMELS
IMPORTED FROM THE AMOOR RIVER
EX CAROLINE E. FOOTE.

ON WEDNESDAY, OCT. 10, 1860,
WE WILL SELL AT PUBLIC AUCTION }
IN LOTS TO SUIT PURCHASERS,
FOR CASH,
13 BACTRIAN CAMELS,

From a cold and mountainous country, comprising 6 males and 7 females, (5 being with young,) all in fine health and condition.
* * * For further particulars, inquire of the Auctioneers.

In 1858, Richard Garvey came to Los Angeles and entered the Government service as a messenger, between this city and New Mexico, for Captain W. S. Hancock. Later, he went to the Holcomb Valley mines, where he first met Lucky Baldwin; and by 1872 he had disposed of some San Bernardino mine properties at a figure which seemed to permit his retirement and ease for the rest of his life. For the next twenty years, he was variously employed, at times operating for Baldwin. Garvey is at present living in Los Angeles.

What was one of the last bullfights here, toward the end of September, when a little child was trodden upon in the ring, reminds me not only of the succeeding sports, including horse-racing, but as well that Francis Temple should be credited with encouraging the importation and breeding of good horses. In 1860 he paid seven thousand dollars, then considered an enormous sum, for *Black Warrior;* and not long afterward he bought *Billy Blossom* at a fancy figure.

A political gathering or two enlivened the year 1860. In July, when the local sentiment was, to all appearances, strongly in favor of Breckenridge and Lane, the Democratic candidates for President and Vice-President, one hundred guns were fired in their honor; and great was the jubilation of the Democratic hosts. A later meeting, under the auspices of the Breckenridge Club, was held in front of the Montgomery saloon on Main Street. Judge Dryden presided, and Senator Milton S. Latham was the chief speaker. A number of ladies graced the occasion, some seated in chairs near by and others remaining in their vehicles drawn up in a semicircle before the speaker's stand. As a result of all this effort, the candidates in question did lead in the race here, but only by four votes. On counting the ballots the day after election, it was found that Breckenridge had two hundred and sixty-seven votes, while Douglas, the Independent Democratic nominee, had polled two hundred and sixty-three. Of permanent interest, perhaps, as showing the local sentiment on other questions of the time, is that Lincoln received in Los Angeles only one hundred and seventy-nine votes.

Generally, a candidate persuaded his friends to nominate and endorse him, but now and then one came forward and addressed the public directly. In the fall of 1860, the following announcement appeared in the *Southern News:*

To the Voters of Los Angeles Township:

I am a candidate for the office of Justice of the Peace, and I desire to say to you, frankly, that I want you all to vote for me on the 6th of November next. I aspire to the office for two reasons,—first, because I am vain enough to believe that I am capable of performing the duties required, with credit to myself and to the satisfaction of all good citizens; second, because I am poor, and am desiring of making an honest living thereby.

WILLIAM G. STILL.

During my first visit to San Francisco, in the fall of 1853, and while *en route* to Los Angeles, my attention was called to a line of electric telegraph, then just installed between the Golden Gate and the town, for use in reporting the arrival of vessels. About a month later a line was built from San Francisco to Sacramento, Stockton and around to San José. Nothing further, however, was done toward reaching Southern California with the electric wire until the end of May or the beginning of June, 1860, when President R. E. Raimond and Secretary Fred. J. McCrellish (promoters of the Pacific & Atlantic Telegraph Company, organized in 1858 to reach San António, Texas, and Memphis, Tennessee) came to Los Angeles to lay the matter before our citizens. Stock was soon subscribed for a line through the city and as far as Fort Yuma, and in a few days Banning had fifty teams ready to haul the telegraph poles, which were deposited in time along the proposed route. In the beginning, interest was stimulated by the promise that the telegraph would be in operation by the Fourth of July; but Independence Day came and went, and the best that the telegraph company could do was to make the ambiguous report that there were so and so many "holes in the ground." Worse than that, it was announced, toward the end of July, that the stock of wire had given out; and still worse, that no more could be had this side of the Atlantic States! That news was indeed discouraging; but by the middle of August, twenty tons of wire were known to be on a clipper bound for San Francisco, around the Horn, and five tons were being hurried here by steamer. The wire arrived, in due season, and the most energetic efforts were made to establish telegraphic communication between Los Angeles and San Francisco. It was while McCrellish was slowly returning to the North, in June, that I met him as narrated in a previous chapter.

Finally, at eight o'clock on October 8th, 1860, a few magic words from the North were ticked out in the Los Angeles office of the telegraph company. Two hours later, as those familiar with our local history know, Mayor Henry Mellus sent the following memorable message to H. F. Teschemacher, President of the San Francisco Board of Supervisors:

Allow me, on behalf of the citizens of Los Angeles, to send you greeting of fellowship and good-feeling on the completion of the line of telegraph which now binds the two cities together.

Whereupon, the next day, President Teschemacher (who, by the way, was a well-known importer, having brought the first almond seed from the Mediterranean in the early fifties) replied to Mayor Mellus:

, Your despatch has just been received. On behalf of the citizens of San Francisco, I congratulate Los Angeles, trusting that the benefit may be mutual.

A ball in Los Angeles fittingly celebrated the event, as will be seen from the following despatch, penned by Henry D. Barrows, who was then Southern California correspondent of the *Bulletin:*

Los Angeles, October 9, 1860,
10.45 A. M.

Here is the maiden salutation of Los Angeles to San Francisco by lightning! This despatch—the first to the press from this point—the correspondent of the *Bulletin* takes pleasure in communicating in behalf of his fellow-citizens. The first intelligible communication by the electric wire was received here last night at about eight o'clock, and a few hours later, at a grand and brilliant ball, given in honor of the occasion, despatches were received from San Francisco announcing the complete working of the entire line. Speeches were made in the crowded ball-room by E. J. C. Kewen and J. McCrellish. News of Colonel Baker's election in Oregon to the United States Senate electrified the Republicans, but the Breckenridges doubted it at first. Just before leaving yesterday, Senator Latham planted the first telegraph pole from this point east, assisted by a concourse of citizens.

Barrows' telegram concluded with the statement, highly suggestive of the future commercial possibilities of the telegraph, that the steamer *Senator* would leave San Pedro that evening with three thousand or more boxes of grapes.

On October 16th, the steamer *J..T. Wright*, named after the boat-owner and widely advertised as "new, elegant, and fast," arrived at San Pedro, in charge of Captain Robert Haley; and many persons professed to see in her appearance on the scene new hope for beneficial coastwise competition. After three or four trips, however, the steamer was withdrawn.

Leonard John Rose, a German by birth, and brother-in-law of H. K. S. O'Melveny, arrived with his family by the Butterfield Stage Route in November, having fought and conquered, so to speak, every step of his way from Illinois, from which State, two years before, he had set out. Rose and other pioneers tried to reach California along the Thirty-fifth parallel, a route surveyed by Lieutenant Beale but presenting terrific hardships; on the sides of mountains, at times, they had to let down their wagons by ropes, and again they almost died of thirst. The Mojave Indians, too, set upon them and did not desist until seventeen Indians had been killed and nine whites were slain or wounded, Rose himself not escaping injury. With

the help of other emigrants, Rose and his family managed to
reach Albuquerque, where within two years in the hotel business he acquired fourteen thousand dollars.   Then, coming to
Los Angeles, he bought from William Wolfskill one hundred
and sixty acres near the old Mission of San Gabriel, and so
prospered that he was soon able to enlarge his domain to over
two thousand acres.   He laid out a splendid vineyard and
orange grove, and being full of ambition, enterprise and taste,
it was not long before he had the show-place of the county.

Apparently, Temple really inaugurated his new theater
with the coming to Los Angeles in November of that year of
"the Great Star Company of Stark & Ryer," as well as with
the announcement made at the time by their management:
"This is the first advent of a theatrical company here."   Stark
& Ryer were in Los Angeles for a week or two; and though I
should not vouch for them as stars, the little hall was crowded
each night, and almost to suffocation.   There were no fire
ordinances then as to filling even the aisles and the window-
sills, nor am I sure that the conventional fire-pail, more often
empty than filled with water, stood anywhere about; but
just as many tickets were sold, regardless of the seating capacity.   Tragedy gave way, alternately, to comedy, one of
the evenings being devoted to *The Honeymoon;* and as this
was not quite long enough to satisfy the onlookers, who had
neither trains nor boats to catch, there was an after-piece.
In those days, when Los Angeles was entirely dependent on
the North for theatrical and similar talent, it sometimes
happened that the steamer was delayed or that the "star"
failed to catch the ship and so could not arrive when expected;
as a result of which patrons, who had journeyed in from the
ranches, had to journey home again with their curiosity and
appetite for the histrionic unsatisfied.

Prisoners, especially Indians, were employed on public works.
As late as November, 1860, the Water Overseer was empowered
to take out any Indians who might be in the calaboose, and
to use them for repairing the highways and bridges.

About 1860, Nathan Jacoby came to Los Angeles, on my

invitation, as I had known him in Europe; and he was with me about a year. When I sold out, he entered the employ of M. Kremer and later went into business for himself. As the senior partner of Jacoby Brothers, he died suddenly in 1911. Associated with Nathan at different periods were his brothers, Herman, Abraham, Morris, Charles and Lesser Jacoby, all of them early arrivals. Of this group, Charles and Lesser, both active in business circles in their day, are also dead.

Toward the end of 1860, Solomon Lazard returned to France, to visit his mother; but no sooner had he arrived at his old home and registered, according to law, with the police, than he was arrested, charged with having left his fatherland at the age of seventeen, without having performed military duty. In spite of his American citizenship, he was tried by court-martial and sentenced to a short imprisonment; but through the intervention of the United States Minister, Charles J. Faulkner—the author of the Fugitive Slave Law of 1850—and the clemency of the Emperor Napoleon III., he was finally released. · He had to furnish a substitute, however, or pay a fine of fifteen hundred francs; and he paid the fine. At length, notwithstanding his unpleasant experience, Lazard arrived in Los Angeles about the middle of March, 1861.

Tired of the wretched sidewalks, John Temple, in December, 1860, set to work to introduce an improvement in front of his Main Street block, an experiment that was watched with interest. Bricks were covered with a thick coating of asphalt brought from La Brea Ranch, which was smoothed while still warm and then sprinkled with sand; the combination promising great durability. In the summer season, however, the coating became soft and gluey, and was not comfortable to walk upon.

I have already spoken of the effect of heat and age on foodstuffs such as eggs and butter, when brought over the hot desert between San Bernardino and Los Angeles. This disadvantage continued for years; nor was the succeeding plan of bringing provisions from San Francisco and the North by way of the ocean without its obstacles. A. Ulyard, the baker, realized the situation, and in December advertised "fresh crackers, baked in Los Angeles, and superior to those half spoiled by the sea voyage."

Previous to the days of warehouses, and much before the advent of railroads, the public hay-scale was an institution, having been constructed by Francis Mellus in the dim past. Exposed to the elements, it stood alone out in the center of Los Angeles Street, somewhat south of Aliso; and in the lawless times of the young town was a silent witness to the numerous crimes perpetrated in the adjacent Calle de Los Negros. Onto its rough platform the neighboring farmers drove their heavy loads, often waiting an hour or two for the arrival of the owner, who alone had the key to its mysterious mechanism. Speaking of this lack of a warehouse brings to my mind the pioneer of 1850, Edouard Naud, who first attracted attention as a clever pastryman with a little shop on Commercial Street where he made a specialty of lady-fingers— selling them at fifty cents a dozen. Engaging in the wool industry, he later become interested in wool and this led him in 1878 to erect Naud's warehouse on Alameda Street, at present known as the Union Warehouse.[1] Naud died in 1881. His son, Edward, born in Los Angeles, is famous as an amateur *chef* who can prepare a French dinner that even a professional might be proud of.

In May, as elsewhere stated, Henry Mellus was elected Mayor of Los Angeles; and on the twenty-sixth of December he died—the first to yield that office to the inexorable demands of Death. The news of his demise called forth unfeigned expressions of regret; for Mellus was not only a man of marked ability, but he was of genial temperament and the soul of honor.

[1] Destroyed by fire on September 22d, 1915.

CHAPTER XX

THE RUMBLINGS OF WAR

1861

THE year 1861 dawned dark and foreboding. On the twentieth of the preceding December, South Carolina had seceded, and along the Pacific, as elsewhere, men were anxiously wondering what would happen next. Threats and counter-threats clearly indicated the disturbed state of the public mind; and when, near Charleston Harbor, a hostile shot was fired at the *Star of the West*, the certainty of further trouble, particularly with the coming inauguration of Lincoln, was everywhere felt.

Aside, however, from these disturbing events so much affecting commercial life, the year, sandwiched between two wet seasons, was in general a prosperous one. There were evil effects of the heavy rains, and business in the spring was rather dull; but cattlemen, upon whose success so many other people depended, took advantage of the favoring conditions and profited accordingly.

During the period of the flood in 1859–60, the river, as we have seen, was impassable, and for months there was so much water in the bed, ordinarily dry, that foot-passage was interrupted. In January, 1861, therefore, the Common Council, under the influence of one of its members, E. Moulton, whose dairy was in East Los Angeles, provided a flimsy foot-bridge in his neighborhood. If my memory serves me, construction was delayed, and so the bridge escaped the next winter's flood, though it went down years later.

On January 9th, the schooner *Lewis Perry* arrived at anchorage, to be towed across the bar and to the wharf by the little steamer[1] *Comet*. This was the first sea-going vessel that had ever visited New San Pedro with a full cargo, and demonstrated, it was thought by many, that the port was easily navigable by vessels drawing eleven feet of water or less! Comments of all kinds were made upon this event, one scribe writing:

We expect to see coasting steamers make their regular trips to New Town, discharging freight and loading passengers on the wharf, safe from the dangers of rough weather, instead of lying off at sea, subjecting life and property to the perils of southeast gales and the breakers. The *Senator* even, in the opinion of experienced persons, might easily enter the channel on the easterly side of Dead Man's Island, and thence find a safe passage in the Creek. *It will yet happen!*

John M. Griffith came to Los Angeles in 1861, having four years previously married a sister of John J. Tomlinson. With the latter he formed a partnership in the passenger and freight-carrying business, their firm competing with Banning & Company until 1868, when Tomlinson died.

This same year, at the age of about eighteen, Eugene Meyer arrived. He first clerked for Solomon Lazard, in the retail dry-goods business; and in 1867 he was admitted into partnership. On November 20th of that year Meyer married Miss Harriet, the youngest daughter of Joseph Newmark—who officiated.

Felix Bachman, who came in 1853, was at various times in partnership with Philip Sichel (after whom Sichel Street is named, and Councilman in 1862), Samuel Laubheim and Ben Schloss, the firm being known as Bachman & Company; and on Los Angeles Street near Commercial they carried on the largest business in town. Bachman secured much Salt Lake trade and in 1861 opposed high freight rates; but although well off when he left here, he died a poor man in San Francisco, at the age of nearly one hundred years.

In 1861, Adolph Junge arrived and established a drug-

[1] A term locally applied to tugs.

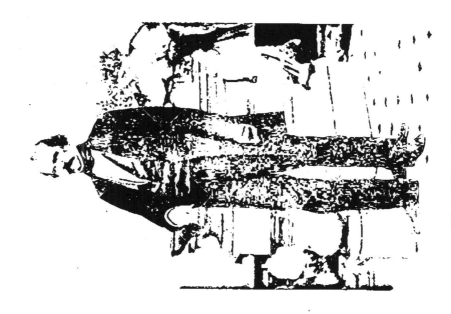

Albert Sidney Johnston

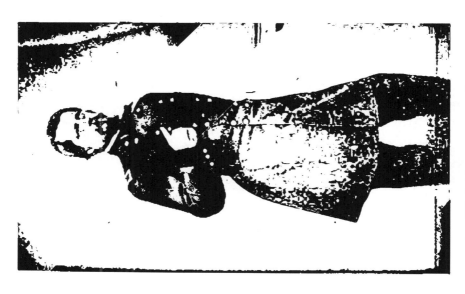

Winfield Scott Hancock

Los Angeles County in 1854

From a contemporary map

The Morris Adobe, once Frémont's Headquarters

store in the Temple Block, his only competitor being Theodore
Wollweber; and there he continued for nearly twenty years, one
of his prescription books, now in the County Museum, evidencing his activity.   For a while, F. J. Gieze, the well-known
druggist for so many years on North Main Street, and an
arrival of '74, clerked for Junge.   At the beginning of the
sixties, Dr. A. B. Hayward practiced medicine here, his office
being next to Workman Brothers' saddlery, on Main Street.
Wollweber's name recalls a practical joke of the late sixties,
when some waggish friend raised the cry that there was a bear
across the river, and induced my Teutonic neighbor to go in
hot pursuit.   After bracing himself for the supreme effort,
Wollweber shot the beast dead; only to learn that the bear,
a blind and feeble animal, was a favorite pet, and that
it would take just twenty-five dollars to placate the irate
owner!

The absence in general of shade trees was so noticeable that
when John Temple, on January 31st, planted a row facing
Temple Building there was the usual town gossip.   Charley
Ducommon followed Temple's example.   Previously, there had
been several wide-spreading trees in front of the Bella Union
hotel, and it came to pass within the next five years that many
pepper-trees adorned the streets.

In 1861, the Post Office was removed from North Spring
Street to a frame building on Main Street, opposite Commercial.   About the same time when, owing to floods, no mail
arrived for three or four weeks and someone facetiously hung
out a sign announcing the office "To Let!" the Washington
postal authorities began issuing stamped envelopes, of the
values of twelve and twenty-four cents, for those business men
of Los Angeles and the Pacific Coast who were likely to use the
recently-developed Pony Express.

Matthew Keller, or Don Mateo, as he was called, who died
in 1881, was a quaint personality of real ability, who had a
shop on the northwest corner of Los Angeles and Commercial
streets, and owned the adjoining store in which P. Beaudry had
been in business.   His operations were original and his adver-

tising unique, as will be seen from his announcement in the
Star in February:

M. KELLER, TO HIS CUSTOMERS

You are hereby notified that the time has at last arrived
when you must pay up, without further delay, or I shall be
obliged to invoke the aid of the law and the lawyers.

Your most ob't servant,
M. KELLER.

Which warning was followed, in the next issue, by this:

M. KELLER, TO HIS CUSTOMERS

The Right of Secession Admitted!

You are hereby notified that the time has arrived when
you must pay up, without further delay, or I shall be obliged
to invoke the aid of the law and the lawyers.

After such settlement, slow-payers are requested to secede.

M. KELLER.

(to be augmented next week)

This later advertisement, with the line in parenthesis,
continued to be printed, week after week, without change,
for at least twelve months.

The following year, Keller, in flaring headlines, offered for
sale the front of his Los Angeles vineyard, facing on Aliso
Street, in building lots of twenty by one hundred feet, saying,
in his prospectus:

Great improvements are on the *tapis* in this quarter.
Governor Downey and the intrepid Beaudry propose to open a
street to let the light of day shine in upon their dark domains.
On the Equerry side of Aliso Street, "what fine legs your master
has," must run to give way for more permanent fixtures.
Further on, the Prior estates are about to be improved by the
astute and far-seeing Templito; and Keller sells lots on the
sunny side of Aliso Street.   The map is on view at my office;
come in and make your selections,—first come, first served!
Terms will be made handy!

· M. KELLER.

Nathaniel Pryor—sometimes known as Don Miguel N. Pryor or Prior—is the pioneer referred to by Keller. At the age of thirty, it is said, in 1828, he came here, and fifteen or twenty years later, about the time that he was a *Regidor* or Councilman, was one of eight or ten Easterners who had farms within the pueblo district. His property, in part a vineyard, included what is now Commercial to First streets and possibly from Los Angeles Street to the river; on it was an adobe which is still standing on Jackson Street, and is the only mud-brick structure in that section. For a while, and probably because he had loaned Pryor some money, F. P. F. Temple had an interest in the estate. Pryor was twice married, having a son, Charles, by his first wife, and a son, Nathaniel, Jr., by his second. Pablo Pryor of San Juan was another son. The first Mrs. Pryor died about 1840, and is one of the few—with the mother of Pio Pico—buried inside of the old church at the Plaza. The second Mrs. Pryor, who inherited the property, died about 1857. A granddaughter, Mrs. Lottie Pryor, is a surviving member of this family.

During the administration of Padre Blas Raho, a genial, broad-minded Italian, several attempts were made, beginning with 1857 or 1858, to improve the old church at the Plaza; and in 1861, the historic edifice, so long unchanged, was practically rebuilt. The front adobe wall, which had become damaged by rains, was taken down and reconstructed of brick; some alterations were made in the tower; and the interesting old tiled roof was replaced—to the intense regret of later and more appreciative generations—with modern, less durable shingles. A fence was provided, and trees, bushes and plants were set out. The church was also frescoed, inside and out, by Henri Penelon, the French pioneer artist and photographer, who painted upon the wall the following inscription:

Los Fieles de Esta Parroquia á la Reina de los Angeles, 1861.[1]

Early in March, Sanchez Street was opened by the Common Council. It was opposite the northern section of Arcadia

[1] "The Faithful of this Parish, to the Queen of the Angels."

Block, passed through the properties of Sanchez, Pico, Coronel and others, and terminated at the Plaza. ·

The Los Angeles Mounted Rifles, part of the five thousand militia wanted by California, was organized on March 6th at a meeting in the Court House presided over by George W. Gift, with M. J. Newmark, who became an officer in the company, as Secretary.

Late in March, John Fröhling rented from the City Fathers a space under the Temple Market building for a wine cellar; and in December, 1860, at the close of his vintage, when he had conducted a hearty harvest-home celebration, he filled the vault with pipes and other casks containing twenty thousand or more gallons of native wines. In a corner, a bar was speedily built; and by many Angeleños that day not associated with at least one pilgrimage to Fröhling's cool and rather obscure recesses was considered incomplete.

Few who witnessed the momentous events of 1861 will forget the fever-heat of the nation. The startling news of the attack on Fort Sumter took twelve days by Pony Express to reach the Coast, the overland telegraph not being completed until six months later; but when, on the twenty-fourth of April, the last messenger in the relay of riders dashed into San Francisco with the story, an excited population was soon seething about the streets. San Francisco instantly flashed the details south, awakening here much the same mingled feelings of elation and sorrow.

When the war thus broke out, Albert Sidney Johnston, a fellow-townsman who had married a sister of Dr. J. S. Griffin, and who, in 1857, had successfully placed Utah under Federal control, resigned from his command as head of the Department of the Pacific—General Edwin V. Sumner succeeding him—and, being a Southerner, left for the South, by way of Warner's Ranch and the Overland Route, with about a hundred companions, most of whom were intercepted at Fort Yuma through the orders of Captain W. S. Hancock. According to Senator Cornelius Cole, Sumner arrived at Johnston's headquarters in San Francisco after dark; and in spite of Johnston's protest, insisted on assuming command at once. Johnston took up arms for the Confederacy, and was made a Brigadier-General; but at Shiloh he was killed, the news of his death causing here the sincerest regret. I shall speak of the loss of one of General Johnston's sons in the disaster to the *Ada Hancock;* another son, William Preston, became President of Tulane University.

Others of our more enthusiastic Southerners, such as Cameron E. Thom and J. Lancaster Brent, also joined the Rebellion and proceeded to the seat of war. Thom, who has since attained much distinction, returned to Los Angeles, where he is still living[1]. Brent never came back here, having settled near New Orleans; and there I again met him, while I was attending the Exposition. He had fought through the War, becoming a General before its close; and he told me that he had been arrested by Federal officers while on his way to the South from Los Angeles, but had made his escape.

Among the very few who went to the front on the Union side and returned here was Charles Meyrs Jenkins, already referred to as a city *Zanjero*. Owing to the possible need of troops here, as well as to the cost of transportation, volunteers from the Pacific slope were not called for and Jenkins joined an Eastern cavalry battalion organized in October, 1862. Even then, he and his comrades were compelled to pay their own way to the Atlantic seaboard, where they were incorporated into the Second Massachusetts Cavalry. Jenkins engaged in twenty battles, and for fifteen months was a prisoner of war confined at both Andersonville and Libby; suffering such terrible hardships that he was but one of three, out of a hundred and fifty of his battalion, who came out alive.

Not everyone possibly even among those familiar with the building of the Los Angeles & San Pedro Railroad, knows that an effort was made, as far back as 1861, to finance a railroad here. About the middle of February in that year, Murray Morrison and Abel Stearns, Assemblymen, learned of the willingness of Eastern capitalists to build such a road within eighteen months, providing the County would subscribe one

[1] Captain Thom died on February 2d, 1915.

hundred thousand dollars toward the undertaking, and the City fifty thousand. The Legislature therefore on May 17th, 1861, granted the franchise; but important as was the matter to our entire district, nothing further was done until 1863 to give life to the movement.

For almost a decade after I came here, St. Valentine's Day was seldom observed in Los Angeles; but about 1861 or 1862, the annual exchange of decorated cards, with their sentimental verses, came to be somewhat general.

Phineas Banning was a staunch Republican and an ardent Abolitionist; and it was not extraordinary that on May 25th, at a grand Union demonstration in Los Angeles, he should have been selected to present to the Union Club, in his characteristically vigorous manner, an American flag made for the occasion. Columbus Sims, as President, accepted the emblem, after which there was a procession, led by the First Dragoons' band, many participants being on horseback. In those days such a procession had done its duty when it tramped along Main Street and around the Plaza and back, by way of Spring Street, as far as First; and everyone was in the right frame of mind to hear and enjoy the patriotic speeches made by Captain Winfield Scott Hancock, General Ezra Drown and Major James Henry Carleton, while in the distance was fired a salute of thirty-four guns—one for each State in the Union.

Senator William McKendree Gwin was another man of prominence. Following his search for gold with the Forty-niners—due, he used to say, to advice from John C. Calhoun, who, probably taking his cue from Dana's prophecy in *Two Years Before the Mast*, one day put his finger on the map and predicted that, should the bay now called San Francisco ever be possessed by Americans, a city rivaling New York would spring up on its shores—Gwin came to Los Angeles occasionally, and never forgot to visit me at my home. In 1861, he was arrested by the Federal Government for his known sympathy with the South, and was kept a prisoner for a couple of years; after which he went to France and there planned to carry through, under force of arms, the colonization of Sonora,

Mexico, depending in vain on Napoleon III. and Maximilian for support. Notwithstanding this futile effort, Gwin became a leader in national Democratic councils, and was an intimate adviser of Samuel J. Tilden in his historic campaign.

Oscar Macy, son of Dr. Obed Macy, having as a newspaper man enthusiastically advocated the election of Frémont in 1856, was appointed, on Lincoln's inauguration, to the Collectorship of Customs at San Pedro; a post which he continued to fill even after the office had been reduced to an inspectorship, later resigning in favor of George C. Alexander. This recalls another appointment by Lincoln—that of Major António María Pico, a nephew of Pio Pico, to the Receivership of Public Moneys at Los Angeles. Pico lived at San José; and finding that his new duties exiled him from his family, he soon resigned the office.

Old-time barbers, as the reader may be aware, were often surgeons, and the arrival in Commercial Street, in the early sixties, of J. A. Meyer, "late of San Francisco," was announced in part as follows:

Gentlemen will be waited on and have Shaving, Hair-Dressing, and Shampooing prepared in the most luxurious manner, and in the finest style of the art; while Cupping, Bleeding, and Teeth-Extracting will also be attended to!

Fort Tejón had been pretty well broken up by June, when a good deal of the army property was moved to Los Angeles. Along with Uncle Sam's bag and baggage, came thirty or more of the camels previously mentioned, including half a dozen "young uns." For some months they were corralled uncomfortably near the genial Quartermaster's Main Street office; but in October they were removed to a yard fixed up for them on D. Anderson's premises, opposite the Second Street schoolhouse.

Starting with the cook brought to Los Angeles by Joseph Newmark, the Chinese population in 1861 had increased to twenty-one men and eight women—a few of them cooks and

servants, but most of them working in five or six laundries.
About the middle of June of that year, Chun Chick arrived
from San Francisco and created a flurry, not merely in Chinatown, but throughout our little city, by his announcement that
he would start a store here; and by the thirteenth of July, this
pioneer Chinese shop, a veritable curiosity shop, was opened.
The establishment was on Spring Street, opposite the Court
House; and besides a general assortment of Chinese goods,
there was a fine display of preserves and other articles hitherto
not obtainable in town.   Chun Chick was clever in his appeals
of "A Chinese Merchant to the Public;" but he nevertheless
joined the celebrities advertised for delinquent taxes.   Chun
Chick—or, as he appeared on the tax collector's list, Chick
Chun—was down for five hundred dollars in merchandise, with
one dollar and twenty-five cents for City, and the same
amount for school taxes.   Sing Hop, Ching Hop and Ah
Hong were other Chinamen whose memory failed at the critical
tax time of that year.

For years, until wharves made possible for thousands the
pleasures of rod and reel, clams, since used for bait, were almost
a drug on the market, being hawked about the streets in 1861
at a dollar a bucket—a price not very remunerative considering that they came from as far north as San Buenaventura.

CHAPTER XXI

HANCOCK—LADY FRANKLIN—THE DELUGE

1861

WHEN the Civil War began, California and the neighboring territory showed such pronounced Southern sympathies that the National Government kept both under close surveillance, for a time stationing Major, afterward General James Henry Carleton—in 1862 sent across the Colorado River when the Government drove out the Texans—with a force at Camp Latham, near Ballona, and dispatching another force to Drum Barracks, near Wilmington. The Government also established a thorough system of espionage over the entire Southwest. In Los Angeles and vicinity, many people, some of whom I mention elsewhere, were arrested; among them being Henry Schaeffer who was taken to Wilmington Barracks but through influential friends was released after a few days. On account of the known political views of their proprietors, some of the hotels also were placed under watch for a while; but beyond the wrath of the innkeepers at the sentinels pacing up and down their verandas, nothing more serious transpired. Men on both sides grew hot-headed and abused one another roundly, but few bones were broken and little blood was shed. A policy of leniency was adopted by the authorities, and sooner or later persons arrested for political offenses were discharged.

The ominous tidings from beyond the Colorado, and their effect, presaging somewhat the great internecine conflict, recalls an unpublished anecdote of Winfield Scott Hancock, who was a graduate of West Point, an intense patriot and a "natural born" fighter. One day in 1861, coincident with the Texan invasion, and while I was visiting him in his office on Main Street near Third (after he had removed from the upstairs rooms adjoining the Odd Fellows' Hall in the Temple Building), John Goller dropped in with the rumor that conspirators, in what was soon to become Arizona, were about to seize the Government stores. Hancock was much wrought up when he heard the report, and declared, with angry vehemence, that he would "treat the whole damned lot of them as common thieves!" In the light of this demonstration and his subsequent part as a national character of great renown, Hancock's speech at the Fourth of July celebration, in 1861, when the patriotic Angeleños assembled at the Plaza and marched to the shady grove of Don Luis Sainsevain, is worthy of special note. Hancock made a sound argument for the preservation of the Union, and was heartily applauded; and a few days afterward one of the local newspapers, in paying him a deserved tribute, almost breathed an augury in saying:

Captain Hancock's loyalty to the Stars and Stripes has never for a moment been doubted, and we hope he may be advanced in rank and honors, and live to a green old age, to see the glorious banner of our country yet waving in peaceful glory over a united, prosperous, and happy people.

Few of us, however, who heard Hancock speak on that occasion, dreamed to what high position he would eventually attain.

Soon after this episode, that is, in the early part of August, 1861, Hancock left for the front, in company with his wife; and taking with him his military band, he departed from San Pedro on the steamer *Senator*. Some of my readers may know that Mrs. Hancock—after whom the ill-fated *Ada Hancock* was named—was a Southern woman, and though very devoted to her husband, had certain natural sympathies for the South; but none, I dare say, will have heard how she perpetrated an amusing joke upon him on their way north. When once out upon the briny deep, she induced the musicians to play *Dixie*, to the great amusement of the passengers.   Like many Southerners, Mrs. Hancock was an Episcopalian and frequently contributed her unusual musical talent to the service of the choir of St. Athanasius Church, the little edifice for a while at the foot of Pound Cake Hill—first the location of the Los Angeles High School and now of the County Courthouse—and the forerunner of the Episcopal Pro-Cathedral, on Olive Street opposite Central Park.

Having in mind the sojourn in Los Angeles for years of these representative Americans, the following editorial from the Los Angeles *Star* on the departure of the future General and Presidential nominee, seems to me now of more than passing significance:

While resident here, Captain Hancock took great interest in our citizens, the development of our resources, and the welfare of this section of the country; and as a public-spirited, enterprising gentleman, he will be missed from among us, and his most estimable lady will long live in the hearts of her many friends.   We desire their prosperity, happiness, and long life, wherever their lot may be cast.

The establishing of Drum Barracks and Camp Drum at Wilmington was a great contribution to the making of that town, for the Government not only spent over a million dollars in buildings and works there, and constantly drew on the town for at least part of its supplies, but provisions of all kinds were sent through Wilmington to troops in Southern California, Utah, Yuma, Tucson and vicinity, and New Mexico.

P. H., popularly known as Major Downing, was employed by Banning for some time during the War to take charge of the great wagon-trains of Government supplies sent inland; and later he opened a general merchandise store in Wilmington, after which he transacted a large volume of business with H. Newmark & Company.

At the breaking out of the War, the Southern Overland Mail Route was discontinued and a contract was made with Butterfield for service along a more central course, by way of Great Salt Lake.   There was then a stage six times a week; and a branch line ran to Denver, the terminus having been changed from St. Joseph to Omaha.   Twenty days was the time allowed the company to get its stages through during eight months of the year, and twenty-three days for the more uncertain winter months.   This contract was made for three years, and one million dollars a year was the compensation allowed the Butterfields.   After the War, the old route was resumed.

J. De Barth Shorb came to Los Angeles at the commencement of the War, as Assistant Superintendent of the Philadelphia & California Oil Company; and in 1867 he bought the Temescal grant and began to mine upon the property.   The same year he married a daughter of B. D. Wilson, establishing a relationship which brought him a partnership in the San Gabriel Wine Company, of which he eventually became manager. His position in this community, until he died in 1895, was important, the little town of Shorb testifying to one of his activities.

Not only were the followers of the indefatigable *padres* rather tardy in taking up the cultivation of olives, but the olive-oil industry hereabouts was a still later venture.   As an illustration, even in 1861 somewhat less than five hundred gallons of olive oil was made in all Los Angeles County, and most of that was produced at the San Fernando Mission.

How important was the office of the *Zanjero*, may be gathered from the fact that in 1861 he was paid twelve hundred dollars a year, while the Mayor received only eight hundred dollars and the Treasurer two hundred dollars less than the Mayor. At the same time, the Marshal, owing to the hazardous duties of his office, received as much as the Mayor; the City Attorney one hundred dollars less than the Treasurer; and the Clerk but three hundred and fifty.

By 1861, there were serious doubts as to the future of cattle-raising in Southern California, but Banning & Company came forward proposing to slaughter at New San Pedro and contracted with John Temple, John Rains and others, to do their killing. For a while, the enterprise was encouraged; Temple alone having six hundred head so disposed of and sold.

In September, Columbus Sims, the popular attorney of unique personality who from 1856 to 1860 had been Clerk of the United States District Court, was appointed Lieutenant-Colonel in the United States Army and placed in charge of Camp Alert, at the Pioneer Race Course, San Francisco, where twelve companies were soon assembled; and a month or two later he was made Colonel in the Second Cavalry. Late in December of that year, however, he had an altercation with D. D. Colton, in San Francisco, when blows were exchanged and Sims drew "a deadly weapon." For this, the doughty Colonel was arrested and held to await the action of the Grand Jury; but I am under the impression that nothing very serious befell the belligerent Sims as a result.

On September 11th, H. Stassforth, after having bought out A. W. Schulze, announced a change in the control of the United States Hotel, inviting the public, at the same time, to a "free lunch," at half-past four o'clock the following Sunday. Stassforth was an odd, but interesting character, and stated in his advertisement that guests were at liberty, when they had partaken of the collation, to judge if he could "keep a hotel." Whether successful or otherwise, Stassforth did not long continue in control, for in November, 1862, he disposed of the business to Webber & Haas, who in turn sold it to Louis Mesmer.

In the fall, an atrocious murder took place here, proving but the first in a series of vile deeds for which, eventually, the culprit paid with his own life at the hands of an infuriated populace. On Sunday evening, September 30th, some Frenchmen were assembled to sit up with the body of one of their recently-deceased countrymen; and at about eleven o'clock a quarrel arose between two of the watchers, A. M. G., or Michel Lachenais—a man once of good repute, who had cast some slurs at the French Benevolent Society—and Henry Delaval, a respected employee of the Aliso Mills who spiritedly defended the organization. Lachenais drew a weapon, approached Delaval and tried to shoot him; but the pistol missed fire. Thereupon

Lachenais, enraged, walked toward a lamp, adjusted two other caps, and deliberately shot Delaval through the body. The next day his victim died. Lachenais made his escape and so eluded the authorities that it was not until the middle of February, 1866, that he surrendered himself to Deputy Sheriff Henderson. Then he was tried, but was acquitted.

About October, Remi Nadeau, a Canadian, after whom Nadeau Street is named and father of George A. Nadeau, came across the Plains to Los Angeles, having spent the previous winter, *en route*, in Salt Lake City; and for a while he teamed between here and Montana. Within the year, believing that San Francisco offered a larger field, he moved to that city and continued his operations there.

In the front part of a little building on Main Street, between Second and Third, Lorenzo Leck, whom I have already mentioned, conducted a grocery, living with his family in the rear. He was a plain, unassuming, honest Dane of the old school, who attended scrupulously to his business and devoted his Sundays and holidays to modest amusements. On such days, he would put his wife, Caroline, and their children on a little wagon that he owned and take them to his vineyard on the outskirts of the town; and there he would enjoy with them those rural pastimes to which he had been accustomed in the Fatherland, and which to many early-comers here were a source of rest and delight.

On the afternoon of Saturday, October 17th, Francisco Cota, a Mexican boy fifteen years of age, entered Leck's store while he was out, and, taking advantage of the fact that Frau Leck was alone, whipped out a knife, stabbed her to death, stole what cash was in sight and then escaped to a vineyard, where he hid himself. John W. Henderson, the son of A. J. Henderson, a Deputy Sheriff here still living in Los Angeles, came in soon after and finding Mrs. Leck horribly disfigured, he gave the alarm. Neighbors and friends at once started in pursuit and caught Cota; and having tied a rope around the murderer's neck during the excitement they dragged him down to Alameda Street, where I witnessed the uproar. As they proceeded by

way of Aliso Street, the mob became more and more infuriated, so that before it reached the spot which had been
selected for his execution, the boy had been repeatedly stabbed
and was nearly dead. At length, he was strung up as a warning
to other malefactors.

A short time after this melancholy event, I was driving with
my wife to the Cerritos *rancho* and, missing our road, we
stopped at a Mexican home to inquire the way. The woman
who answered our summons proved to be one who knew, and
was known by all Los Angeles merchants on account of her
frequent excursions to town; she was, in fact, the mother
of the Mexican boy who had been mobbed and hung for the
murder of poor·Leck's wife! The sight of *Gringos* kindled
anew her maternal wrath; and she set up such a hue and cry
as to preclude any further intelligible conversation.

California being so far removed from the seat of war did
not awake to its full significance until the credit of the Government began to decline. Four weeks were required, it is well
to remember, to complete the trip from New York to San
Francisco *via* Panamá, and our knowledge of events in the
East was far from perfect. Until the completion of the continental telegraph in October, 1861, the only immediate news
that reached the Coast came privately and we were, therefore,
pretty much in the dark until the arrival of Eastern papers,
and even after that telegraphing was so expensive that our
poorly-patronized little news-sheets could not afford the outlay. A few of us therefore made up a purse of one hundred
dollars a month, which small sum enabled us to allay our
anxiety at least in the case of very important happenings.

It must not be forgotten, though, that we then had a little
relief from San Francisco, whose newspapers, containing some
telegraphic despatches, arrived in town perhaps three to four
days after their publication. I may add, in fact, that it was
not until about the beginning of the eighties that Los Angeles
dailies could afford the luxury of regular direct telegrams.

In other respects as well, editing a local newspaper during
the War was apt to entail financial loss. The Los Angeles

News, for instance, was outspoken for the Union and so escaped the temporary eclipse suffered by the *Star* through Government censorship; but the Unionists being in a decided minority in the community, pickings for the *News* were mighty poor. Perhaps this want of patronage suggested the advisability, in 1863 (when that paper was published by C. R. Conway and Alonzo Waite, on Main Street, opposite the express office), of reducing the subscription rate to five dollars a year.

Probably one of the most interesting visits to Los Angeles ever made by a well-known personage was the sudden call with which Lady Franklin, the wife of the eminent, lost Arctic explorer, honored our little town far back in 1861. The distinguished lady, accompanied by Mrs. Cracroft, her niece, Commodore and Madame Watkins and Collector and Mrs. Rankin, arrived at San Pedro on the *Golden State* during the first week in November and was driven, with her companions, to the Bella Union hotel, from which she made such short excursions about the city as were then possible; and as sympathy for her in her sorrow, and admiration for her long years of plucky though vain search for her husband were still general, every courtesy possible was afforded her. During Lady Franklin's stay Benjamin D. Wilson arranged a delightful garden party at his hospitable mansion at Lake Vineyard in her ladyship's honor, and Phineas Banning also entertained her with a reception and collation at his San Pedro home; and these receptions and collations were as enjoyable as they were notable. After a day or two, Lady Franklin and her party left on the *Senator* for San Francisco, being accorded, as the vessel weighed anchor, a marked ovation.

For many years funerals were attended by men on horseback and by women on foot, as hacks were unknown in early days; and while the good citizens were doubtless then conducted to their last resting-place in a manner just as satisfactory to themselves as are their descendants who are buried according to present-day customs, those who followed in the train were very seriously inconvenienced by the melancholy, dusty processions to the old and now-forgotten burial-grounds; for in those days the trip, in summer exceedingly hot and in winter through rain and mud, was a long, fatiguing one.

Speaking of funerals, a strange sight was witnessed in our streets about the end of November, 1861, attending the burial of a child. The father and mother, both native Californians, were seated in a wagon, in which was also placed the strikingly plain little coffin or box containing the dead. Beside the wagon walked an old man, playing a fiddle. Two or three persons followed in the deep mud; the whole forming a weird picture, said to be the relic of an almost obsolete back-woods custom.

Banning & Hinchman's *Comet* proving insufficient, the *Gondolier* was put on in the fall of 1861 and became a familiar craft in the conveying of passengers and freight between New San Pedro and the ships lying off the harbor.

Two years previous to the completion of the telegraph from San Francisco to Los Angeles—that is, in 1858—the first continental telegraph was undertaken; and by October, 1861, Governor Downey of California sent a congratulatory message to President Lincoln. On November 7th, the line was open to the public. Several months before, all the companies in the State had consolidated into the California State Telegraph Company. Banning & Hinchman having succeeded, for a short season, Phineas Banning, the sub-contractor for the building of the first telegraph, they made an effort, following the establishment of communication between the Atlantic and the Pacific, to secure a line to New San Pedro; and at the end of October, 1861, the first telegraph pole in the long row from Los Angeles to the harbor was formally set. About the middle of November, this line was completed; and though it was widely proclaimed as "working like a charm," the apparatus soon got out of order and by the following January there were many complaints that both poles and wire had fallen to the ground, blocking the thoroughfares and entangling animals in such a way as to become a nuisance. Indeed, there was soon a public demand either to repair the telegraph or to remove it altogether and throw the equipment away. Soon after the first of February,

1862, the line was working again; but by that time the telegraph to San Francisco had gotten out of order! And so great were the difficulties in repairing that line, that Los Angeles was not again talking uninterruptedly over the wire with its neighbor until July.

On November 15th, the first number of *El Amigo del Pueblo*, printed in Spanish, appeared from the shop of José E. Gonzales & Company; but native support being withheld, "The Friend of the People" starved to death in the following May.

Whaling, like shark-hunting, continued brisk in 1861 and 1862, and many vessels were fitted out at San Pedro; Los Angeles merchants selling them most of their supplies. The sea-monsters usually moved up the coast about the first of the year, the males keeping in toward the shore going up, and the females hugging the coast, coming down; and small boats such as Captain W. Clark's *Ocean*, used to take from four hundred and fifty to five hundred barrels of oil in five or six weeks. For six days, in March, 1862, San Pedro whalers harpooned a whale a day, bringing to the landing over two hundred barrels of oil as a result of the week's labor.

The bitter fight between Abolitionists and Southern sympathizers was immediately reflected in the public schools. Defenders of the Union worked for a formal oath of allegiance to the National Government, as a preliminary to granting teachers' certificates; while the Confederates, incensed at what they deemed a violation of personal rights, assailed the institutions. The result was that attendance at the public schools gradually fell off until, in the winter of 1865–66, only about three hundred and fifty children of school age were being instructed by public teachers; another third of a thousand was in private schools, while some three hundred and sixty-nine were not on any roster.

The gloom naturally caused by the outbreak of war was sometimes penetrated by the brightness of social life, and among the happier occasions of the winter of 1861 was the marriage, on December 23d, in the presence of a large circle of friends, of Tom D. Mott to Ascención, daughter of Don José Andrés and Doña Francisca Ábila Sepúlveda.

The winter of 1861–62 recorded the greatest of all floods, especially in the North where, in December and January, something like thirty-five inches of rain was precipitated. In Los Angeles County the rivers soon rose and overflowed the lowlands; but the rise was gradual, causing the loss of but few or no lives and permitting the stock to reach the neighboring hills in safety. In Anaheim the water was four feet deep in the streets and people had to seek flight to the uplands or retreat to the roofs of their little houses. Vineyards were sometimes half-ruined with the layers of deep sand; banks of streams were lined for miles with driftwood; and ranchers saw many a clod of their farms carried off and deposited to enrich their neighbors, miles away. For a month it rained so steadily that the sun peeped out for scarcely an hour.

I witnessed this inundation in Los Angeles, where much damage was done to business buildings, especially to Mellus's Row, and saw merchants in water up to their waists, trying to save their goods. The wall of the room occupied by Sam Meyer fell first, whereupon Hellman & Brother became intensely interested in the removal of their stock, while poor Sam, knee-deep in water, sadly contemplated his losses. Before the Hellmans had made much headway, they observed a tendency on the part of their walls to crumble, and their exit was neither graceful nor delayed. After that the store occupied by Meyer & Breslauer caved in, smashing show cases and shelves, and ruining a large amount of merchandise. The ludicrous picture of this rush for "safety first" is not a fit reflection of the feelings of those pioneers who saw the results of years of labor obliterated in a moment. Friends and neighbors lent assistance to the unfortunate, and helped to save what they could. After this flood, Hellman & Brother and Sam Meyer removed to the Arcadia Block, while Meyer & Breslauer secured accommodations north of the Plaza Church.

CHAPTER XXII

DROUGHTS—THE *ADA HANCOCK* DISASTER

1862-1863

ON the first of January, 1862, after an experience of about five years, I retired from the selling of clothing, which was never congenial to me; and as I had been buying hides and wool on a small scale since the middle of the fifties, I forthwith devoted myself to the commission business. Frenchmen from the Basque country, among whom were Miguel Leonis, Gaston Oxarart, Domingo Amestoy and Domingo Bastanchury, had commenced to appear here in 1858 and to raise sheep; so that in 1859 large flocks were brought into Southern California, the sheep commanding a price of three dollars and a half per head. My own operations, exceedingly small in the beginning, increased in importance, and by 1862 I was fairly equipped for this venture. Corn, barley and wheat were also then being raised, and I busied myself with these commodities as well.

Most of the early sheepmen prospered and in time bought large tracts of land for their flocks, and with all of them I had dealings of more or less importance. Amestoy's career is worthy of particular mention as exemplifying the three cardinal virtues of business: honesty, application and frugality. He and his wife took in washing; and while the husband went from house to house, leading a horse with a large basket strapped to either side, to collect and deliver the clothes, the wife toiled at the tub. In the end, what they together had

310

Eugene Meyer

Jacob A. Moerenhout

Frank Lecouvreur

Thomas D. Mott

Leonard J. Rose

H. K. S. O'Melveny

Remi Nadeau

John M. Griffith

saved became the foundation of their important investments in sheep and land. Pedro Larronde, another early sheepman, married the widow of his Basque fellow-countryman, Etchemendy, the tippling baker.

Having regularly established a commission business, I brought consignments of varied merchandise from San Francisco on the semi-monthly steamer *Goliah*, whose Captain at one time was Robert Haley, and at another his brother Salisbury Haley, a brother-in-law of Tom Mott; and I disposed of them to small dealers with whom I thus became pretty well acquainted. These consignments were sold almost as soon as they arrived. I was careful to bring in only staple articles in the grocery line, and it was long before I appreciated the advantage of carrying sufficient stock to supply a regular demand. On the return trips of the steamer to San Francisco I forwarded such produce as I had accumulated.

I do not recall any important changes in 1862, the declining months of which saw the beginning of the two years' devastating drought. The Civil War was in progress, but we were so far from the scene of strife that we were not materially affected. Sympathy was very general here for the Confederate cause, and the Government therefore retained in Wilmington both troops and clerks who were paid in a badly-depreciated currency, which they were obliged to discount at exorbitant rates, to get money at all; while other employees had to accept vouchers which were subject to a still greater discount. Notwithstanding these difficulties, however, pay-day increased the resources of the pueblo considerably.

Hellman & Brother, a partnership consisting of I. M. and Samuel Hellman, dissolved, on January 2d, I. M. continuing in the dry goods business while Sam took the books and stationery. Another brother and associate, H. M. Hellman, a couple of years before had returned to Europe, where he died. If my memory is accurate, I. W. remained with I. M. Hellman until the former, in 1865, bought out A. Portugal. Samuel A. Widney, who later had a curio store, was for a while with Sam Hellman in a partnership known as Hellman & Widney.

On January 17th, Don Louis Vignes passed away in Los Angeles, at the age of ninety-one years.

January also witnessed one of those typical scenes, in the fitting out of a mule- and wagon-train, never likely to be seen in Los Angeles again. Two hundred wagons and twelve hundred mules, mostly brought from San Francisco on steamers, were assembled for a trip across the desert to convey Government stores.

M. J. Newmark became a partner, on February 1st, in the firm of Howard, Butterworth & Newmark, Federal and State Attorneys with offices in the Temple Building, Los Angeles, and Armory Hall, San Francisco; and it was considered at the time a rapid advance for a man of but twenty-three years of age. The Los Angeles *Star* of that date, in fact, added a word of good fellowship: "We congratulate friend Newmark on the association."

The intimate relations characteristic of a small community such as ours, and the much more general effect then than nowadays of any tragical occurrence have already been described. Deep sympathy was therefore awakened, early in February, on the arrival of the steamer *Senator* and the rapid dissemination of the report that Dr. Thomas Foster, the ex-Mayor, had been lost overboard, on January 29th, on the boat's trip northward. Just what happened to Foster will never be known; in San Francisco it was reported that he had thrown himself into the sea, though others who knew him well looked upon the cause of his death as accidental.

But slight attention was paid to the report, brought in by horsemen from San Bernardino on February 4th, that an earthquake had occurred there in the morning, until Captain Tom Seeley returned with the *Senator* to San Pedro and told about a seismic disturbance at sea, during which he struck the wildest storm off Point Concepción, in all his sea-faring experience. Sailors were then better all-round seamen than now; yet there was greater superstition in Jack Tar's mind, and such a storm made a deep impression upon his imagination.

I have alluded to the dependence of Los Angeles on the

outside world, no better evidence of which, perhaps, can be cited than that on the twenty-second of February George W. Chapin & Company of San Francisco advertised here to furnish servants and other help to anyone in the Southland. About the same time, San Bernardino parties, wishing to bore a little artesian well, had to send to the Northern metropolis for the necessary machinery.

In October, 1860, as I have intimated, Phineas Banning took A. F. Hinchman into partnership, the firm being known as Banning & Hinchman, and they seemed to prosper; but on February 12th, 1862, the public was surprised at the announcement of the firm's dissolution. Banning continued as proprietor, and Hinchman became Banning's Los Angeles agent.

Although cattle-raising was the mainstay of Southern California for many years, and gold-mining never played a very important part here, Wells Fargo & Co., during the spring, frequently shipped thousands of dollars' worth of gold at a time, gathered from Santa Anita, San Gabriel and San Fernando *placers*, while probably an equally large amount was forwarded out through other channels.

I have already pointed to the clever foresight shown by Abel Stearns when he built the Arcadia Block and profited by the unhappy experience of others, with rain that flooded their property; but I have not stated that in elevating his new building considerably above the grade of the street, somewhat regardless of the rights of others, he caused the surplus water to run off into neighboring streets and buildings. Following the great storm of 1861–62, the City sued Stearns for damages, but he won his case. More than that, the overflow was a Godsend to him, for it induced a number of people to move from Mellus's Row to Arcadia Block at a time when the owner of vast ranches and some of the best town property was already feeling the pinch of the alternate dry and over-wet seasons. The fact is, as I shall soon make clear, that before Stearns had seen the end of two or three successive dry seasons yet to come, he was temporarily bankrupt and embarrassed to the utmost.

By April, the walls and roof for the little Protestant Church at Temple and New High streets had been built, and there the matter rested for two years, when the structure, on which the taxes were unpaid, was advertised for sale.

We have seen that the first Jewish services here were held soon after the arrival of Joseph Newmark in 1854; under the same disadvantageous conditions as had hampered the Protestant denominations, Mr. Newmark volunteered to officiate on the principal holidays until 1862, when the Reverend Abraham Wolf Edelman arrived. Born at Warsaw in 1832, Rabbi Edelman came to America in 1851, immediately after he was married to Miss Hannah Pessah Cohn, and settled successively in New York, Paterson and Buffalo. Coming to California in 1859, he resided in San Francisco until 1862, when he was chosen Rabbi of the orthodox Congregation B'nai B'rith of Los Angeles, and soon attained distinction as a Talmudic scholar and a preacher. The first services under Rabbi Edelman were held in Stearns's, or Arcadia Hall; next, the Congregation worshipped in Leck's Hall on Main Street between Second and Third; and finally, through the courtesy of Judge Ygnácio Sepúlveda, the court room was used. In 1873 the Jews of Los Angeles erected their first synagogue, a brick building entered by a steep stairway leading to a platform, and located on the east side of Fort Street between Second and Third, on what is now the site of the Copp Building next to the City Hall. In 1886, when local Jewry instituted a much more liberal ritual, Rabbi Edelman's convictions induced him to resign. The purchase of a lot for a home on the corner of Sixth and Main streets proved a fortunate investment, later enabling him to enjoy a well-deserved comfort and to gratify his charitable inclinations. It is a strange coincidence that Reverend Edelman's first marriage ceremony was that which blessed Samuel Prager; while the last occasion on which he performed the solemn rites for the dead—shortly before his own death in 1907—was for the same friend. A. M. Edelman, the architect, and Dr. D. W. Edelman, both well-known here, are sons of the Rabbi.

As late in the season as April, hail and snow fell in and near

Los Angeles. To the North of the city, the white mantle quite hid the mountains and formed a new and lower snow-line; while within the city, the temperature so lowered that at several intervals during the day, huge hail-stones beat against the window-panes—a very unusual experience for Angeleños.

Because of political charges preferred against A. J. King, then Under Sheriff of the County, the latter, on April 10th, was arrested by Henry D. Barrows, United States Marshal, who had been appointed by President Lincoln, the year previous. Colonel Carleton, Commander of the Southern Military Division, however, soon liberated King. On the last day of the year, the Under Sheriff married the estimable Miss Laura C. Evertsen.

Travelers to Europe have often suffered much annoyance through safe-conduct regulations, but seldom have Americans had their liberty thus restricted by their own authorities. Toward the middle of June, word was received in Los Angeles that, owing to the suspicion lest disloyalists were embarking for Aspinwall, all passengers for California *via* the Isthmus would be required to take out passports.

Anticipating, by forty years or more, Luther Burbank's work, attention was directed, as early as 1862, to the possibility of eating the cactus and thus finding, in this half-despised plant of the desert, relief from both hunger and thirst. Half a century later, in 1913, Los Angeles established the cactus candy industry through which the boiled pulp of the *bisnaga*, often spoken of as the fishhook, barrel and nigger-head variety, is made deliciously palatable when siruped from ten to thirty days.

Ygnácio Sepúlveda, declared by the Los Angeles *Star* "a young gentleman of liberal education, and good, natural endowments, already versed in legal studies," on September 6th was admitted to the District Court Bar.

On January 18th, 1860, the first number of the *Semi-Weekly Southern News* appeared, containing advertisements in both English and Spanish. It was issued by C. R. Conway and Alonzo Waite, who charged twenty-five cents a copy, or seven dollars a year. On October 8th, 1862, the title was changed to the *Los Angeles Semi-Weekly News.*

In 1860, the Bella Union, as I have said, was under the management of John King, who came here in 1856; while in 1861 J. B. Winston & Company, who were represented by Henry Reed, controlled the hotel. In 1862 or 1863, John King and Henry Hammel were the managers.

I have told of the purchase of the San Pasqual *rancho* by Dr. J. S. Griffin. On December 11th, Dr. and Mrs. Griffin for five hundred dollars sold to B. D. Wilson and wife some six hundred and forty acres of that property; and a few hours afterward the Wilsons disposed of two hundred and sixty-two acres for one thousand dollars. The purchaser was Mrs. Eliza G. Johnston, wife of General Albert Sidney Johnston. Mrs. Johnston at once built a neat residence on the tract and called it *Fair Oaks,* after the plantation in Virginia on which she had been born; and from this circumstance the name of the now well-known Fair Oaks Avenue in Pasadena is derived. At the time of her purchase Mrs. Johnston had hoped to reside there permanently; but the tragic fate of her son in the *Ada Hancock* disaster, following the untimely death of her husband at Shiloh, and the apparent uselessness of the land, led her to sell to Judge B. S. Eaton what to-day would be worth far more than thousands of acres in many parts of the Southern States. A curious coincidence in the relations of General Sumner, who superseded General Johnston, to the hero of Shiloh is that, later in the War, Sumner led a corps of Union troops at Fair Oaks, Virginia!

Don Ygnácio Coronel, father of António Franco Coronel, and the early school patron to whom I have referred, died in Los Angeles on December 19th, aged seventy years. He had come to California in 1834, and had long been eminent in political councils and social circles. I recall him as a man of strong intellect and sterling character, kind-hearted and popular.

Another effort, without success, to use camels for transportation over the California and adjacent sands, was made in

January, 1863, when a camel express was sent out from New San Pedro to Tucson.

Elsewhere I have indicated the condition of the public cemetery. While an adobe wall enclosed the Roman Catholic burial-place, and a brick wall surrounded the Jewish resting-place for the dead, nothing was done until 1863 to improve the Protestant cemetery, although desecration went so far that the little railing around the grave of poor Mrs. Leck, the grocer's wife who had been murdered, was torn down and burned. Finally, the matter cried to Heaven so audibly that in January Los Angeles Masons appropriated one hundred and fifty dollars, to be added to some five hundred dollars raised by popular subscription; and the Common Council having appointed a committee to supervise the work, William H. Perry put up the fence, making no charge for his services.

About the middle of January word was received in Los Angeles of the death, at Baltimore, of Colonel B. L. Beall, commander for years of the Fort Tejón garrison, and active in the Mojave and Kern River campaigns.

Death entered our home for the first time, when an infant daughter, less than a month old, died this year on February 14th.

In February, the editor of the *News* advised the experiment of growing cotton as an additional activity for the Colorado Indians, who were already cultivating corn, beans and melons. Whether this suggestion led William Workman into cotton culture, I do not know; at any rate, late in November of the same year F. P. F. Temple was exhibiting about town some well-matured bolls of cotton raised on Workman's ranch, and the next spring saw in El Monte a number of fields planted with cotton seed. A year later, J. Moerenhout sent Los Angeles cotton to an exhibition in France, and received from across the water official assurance that the French judges regarded our product as quite equal to that grown in the Southern States. This gave a slight impetus to cotton-culture here and by January, 1865, a number of immigrants had arrived, looking for suitable land for the production of this staple. They soon went to work, and in August of that year many fields gave promise of good crops, far exceeding the expectations of the experimenters.

In the month of March a lively agitation on behalf of a railroad began in the public press, and some bitter things were said against those who, for the sake of a little trade in horses or draying, were opposed to such a forward step; and under the leadership of E. J. C. Kewen and J. A. Watson, our Assemblymen at that session, the Legislature of 1863 passed an act authorizing the construction of the Los Angeles & San Pedro Railroad. A public meeting was called to discuss the details and to further the project; but once more no railroad was built or even begun. Strange as it seems, the idea of a railroad for Los Angeles County in 1863 was much too advanced for the times.

Billed as one who had "had the honor of appearing before King William IV. and all the principal crowned heads of Europe," Professor Courtier held forth with an exhibition of magic in the Temple Theatre; drawing the usual crowd of— royalty-haters!

In 1863, Santa Catalina was the scene of a gold-mining boom which soon came to naught, and through an odd enough occurrence. About April, Martin M. Kimberly and Daniel E. Way staked out a claim or two, and some miners agreed on a code of laws for operations in what was to be known as the San Pedro Mining District, the boundaries of which were to include all the islands of the County. Extensive claims, chiefly in Cherry and Joly valleys and on Mineral Hill, were recorded, and streets were laid out for a town to be known as Queen City; but just as the boom seemed likely to mature, the National Government stepped in and gave a quietus to the whole affair. With or without foundation, reports had reached the Federal authorities that the movement was but a cloak to establish there well-fortified Confederate headquarters for the fitting out and repair of privateers intended to prey upon the coast-wise traders; and on February 5th, 1864, Captain B. R. West, commanding the Fourth California Infantry, ordered practically all of the miners and prospectors to leave the island at once. The following September the National troops were withdrawn, and after the War the Federal authorities retained control of a point on the island deemed serviceable for lighthouse purposes.

In the spring of 1863, feeling ill, I went to San Francisco to consult Dr. Toland, who assured me that there was nothing serious the matter with me; but wishing to satisfy myself more thoroughly, I resorted to the same means that I dare say many others have adopted—a medical examination for life insurance! Bernhard Gattel, general agent of the Germania Life Insurance Company, at 315 Montgomery Street, wrote out my application; and on March 20th, a policy, numbered 1472, was issued, making me, since the fall of 1913, the oldest living policy-holder in the Southwest, and the twentieth oldest of the Germania's patrons in the world.

Californians, during that period of the War when the North was suffering a series of defeats, had little use for greenbacks. At one time, a dollar in currency was worth but thirty-five cents, though early in April it was accepted at sixty-five, late in August at ninety, and about the first of October at seventy-five cents; even interest-bearing gold notes being worth no more. This condition of the money market saw little change until some time in the seventies; and throughout the War greenbacks were handled like any other commodity. Frank Lecouvreur, in one of these periods, after getting judgment in a suit against Deputy Surveyor William Moore, for civil engineering services, and being paid some three hundred and eighty-three dollars in greenbacks, was disconcerted enough when he found that his currency would command but one hundred and eighty dollars in gold. San Francisco merchants realized fortunes when a decline occurred, as they bought their merchandise in the East for greenbacks and sold it on the Coast for gold. Los Angeles people, on the other hand, enjoyed no such benefit, as they brought their wares from San Francisco and were therefore obliged to liquidate in specie.

Among the worst tragedies in the early annals of Los Angeles, and by far the most dramatic, was the disaster on April 27th to the little steamer *Ada Hancock*. While on a second trip, in the harbor of San Pedro, to transfer to the *Senator* the remainder of the passengers bound for the North, the vessel careened, admitting cold water to the engine-room and exploding the boiler with such force that the boat was demolished to the water's edge; fragments being found on an island even half to three-quarters of a mile away. Such was the intensity of the blast and the area of the devastation that, of the fifty-three or more passengers known to have been on board, twenty-six at least perished. Fortunate indeed were those, including Phineas Banning, the owner, who survived with minor injuries, after being hurled many feet into the air. Among the dead were Thomas W. Seeley, Captain of the *Senator;* Joseph Bryant, Captain of the *Ada Hancock;* Dr. H. R. Myles, the druggist, who had been in partnership, opposite the Bella Union, with Dr. J. C. Welch, an arrival of the early fifties who died in 1869; Thomas H. Workman, Banning's chief clerk; Albert Sidney Johnston, Jr.; William T. B. Sanford, once Postmaster; Louis Schlesinger and William Ritchie, Wells Fargo's messenger, to whom was entrusted ten thousand dollars, which, as far as my memory goes, was lost. Two Mormon missionaries, *en route* to the Sandwich Islands, were also killed. Still another, who lost not only his treasure but his life, was Fred E. Kerlin of Fort Tejón: thirty thousand dollars which he carried with him, in greenbacks, disappeared as mysteriously as did the jewelry on the persons of others, and from these circumstances it was concluded that, even in the presence of Death, these bodies had been speedily robbed. Mrs. Banning and her mother, Mrs. Sanford, and a daughter of B. D. Wilson were among the wounded; while Miss M. Hereford, Mrs. Wilson's sister and the *fiancée* of Dr. Myles, was so severely injured that, after long suffering, she also died. Although the accident had happened about five o'clock in the afternoon, the awful news, casting a general and indescribable gloom, was not received in town until nearly eight o'clock; when Drs. Griffin and R. T. Hayes, together with an Army surgeon named Todd, hastened in carriages to the harbor where soldiers from Camp Drum had already asserted their authority. Many of the victims were buried near the beach at New San Pedro. While I was calling upon Mrs. Johnston to express my sympathy, the body of her son was brought in; and words cannot describe the pathos of the scene when she addressed the departed as if he were but asleep.

In June the Government demanded a formal profession of loyalty from teachers, when Miss Mary Hoyt and Miss Eliza Madigan took the oath, but Mrs. Thomas Foster and William McKee refused to do so. The incident provoked bitter criticism, and nothing being done to punish the recalcitrants, the Los Angeles Board of Education was charged with indifference as to the allegiance of its public servants.

During 1863 sectional feeling had grown so bitter on account of the War that no attempt was made to celebrate the Fourth of July in town. At Fort Latham, however, on the Ballona Ranch, the soldiers observed the day with an appropriate demonstration. By the end of July, troops had been sent from Drum Barracks to camp in the city—for the protection, so it was asserted, of Union men whose lives were said to be in danger, although some people claimed that this movement was rather for the purpose of intimidating certain leaders with known sympathy for the South. This military display gave Northerners more backbone; and on the twenty-sixth of September a Union mass-meeting was held on Main Street in front of the Lafayette Hotel.

Eldridge Edwards Hewitt, a Mexican War veteran who came to California in 1849 to search for gold, arrived in Los Angeles on July 31st and soon went on a wild-goose chase to the Weaver Diggings in Arizona, actually tramping with luggage over five hundred miles of the way! After his return, he did odd jobs for his board, working in a stationery and toy store on Main Street, kept by the Goldwater Brothers, Joe and Mike, who had arrived in the early sixties; and later he entered the employ of Phineas Banning at Wilmington, with whom he remained until the completion of the Los Angeles & San Pedro

Railroad in 1870, when he became its Superintendent. When
the Southern Pacific obtained control of that road in 1873,
Hewitt was made Agent, and after the extension of the line
from San Francisco he was appointed Division Superintendent.
In that capacity he brought Senator Leland Stanford to me, as
I shall elsewhere relate, to solicit H. Newmark and Company's
patronage.

It was in 1863 that Dr. J. S. Griffin, father of East Los
Angeles, purchased two thousand acres in that section, at fifty
cents an acre; but even at that price he was only induced to
buy it by necessity. Griffin wanted sheep-pasture, and had
sought to secure some eight hundred acres of City land along the
river; but as this would prevent other cattle or sheep from
approaching the water to drink, the Common Council refused
Griffin's bid on the smaller area of land and he was compelled to buy the *mesa* farther back. It seems to me that B.
D. Wilson, J. G. Downey and Hancock M. Johnston, General
Johnston's son, also had something to do with this transaction.
Both Downey and Griffin avenues derived their names from
the association of these two gentlemen with that section.

A smallpox epidemic which had started in the previous
fall spread through Los Angeles in 1863, and owing possibly
to the bad sanitary and climatic conditions much vigilance
and time were required to eradicate it; compulsory vaccination
not having been introduced (as it finally was at the suggestion
of Dr. Walter Lindley) until the summer of 1876. The dread
disease worked its ravages especially among the Mexicans and
Indians, as many as a dozen of them dying in a single day; and
these sufferers and their associates being under no quarantine,
and even bathing *ad libitum* in the *zanjas,* the pest spread alarmingly. For a time fatalities were so frequent and the nature of
the contagion so feared that it was difficult to persuade under-
takers to bury the dead, even without funeral or other ceremony.

Following the opening of the Owens River Mines this year,
Los Angeles merchants soon established a considerable trade
with that territory. Banning inaugurated a system of wagon-
trains, each guarded by a detachment of soldiers. The San

Fernando mountains, impassable for heavy teaming, were an obstacle to regular trade with the new country and compelled the use of a circuitous route over poor roads.   It became necessary, therefore, to consider a means of overcoming the difficulty, much money having already been spent by the County in an abortive attempt to build a tunnel.   This second plan likewise came to naught, and it was in fact more than a decade before the Southern Pacific finally completed the famous bore.

Largely because of political mistakes, including a manifestation of sympathy for the Southern Confederacy that drew against him Northern resentment and opposition, John G. Downey, the Democratic nominee for Governor, was defeated at the election in September; Frederick F. Low, a Republican, receiving a majority of over twenty thousand votes.

In October, a peddler named Brun was murdered near Chino.   Brun's brother, living at San Bernardino and subsequently a merchant of prominence there, offered two hundred dollars of his slender savings as a reward for the capture of the slayer; but nothing ever came of the search.

In November the stern necessities of war were at last driven home to Angeleños when, on the ninth of that somber month, Don Juan Warner, Deputy Provost Marshal, appeared with his big blank books and began to superintend the registering of all able-bodied citizens suitable for military service.   To many, the inquisition was not very welcome and, had it not been for the Union soldiers encamped at Drum Barracks, this first step toward compulsory enrollment would undoubtedly have resulted in riotous disturbances.

I have frequently named Tom Mott, but I may not have said that he was one of the representative local Democratic politicians of his day.   He possessed, indeed, such influence with all classes that he was not only elected Clerk of Los Angeles County in 1863, but succeeded himself in 1865, 1867 and 1869, afterward sitting in the State Assembly; and in 1876, he was appointed a delegate to the National Convention that nominated Samuel J. Tilden for the Presidency.   His relations in time with Stanford, Crocker, Huntington and Hopkins were very close, and for at least twenty-five years he acted as their political adviser in all matters appertaining to Southern California. Tall, erect and dignified, scrupulously attired and distinguished by his flowing beard, Tom was for more than half a century a striking figure in Los Angeles.

A most brutal murder took place on November 15th on the desert not far from Los Angeles, but few days passing before it was avenged. A poor miner, named R. A. Hester, was fatally attacked by a border ruffian known as Boston Daimwood, while some confederates, including the criminals Chase, Ybarra and Olivas, stood by to prevent interference. In a few hours officers and citizens were in the saddle in pursuit of the murderous band; for Daimwood had boasted that Hester was but the first of several of our citizens to whom he intended to pay his respects. Daimwood and his three companions were captured and lodged in jail, and on the twenty-first of November two hundred or more armed Vigilantes forced the jail doors, seized the scoundrels and hung them to the *pórtico* of the old City Hall on Spring Street. Tomás Sanchez, the Sheriff, talked of organizing a *posse comitatus* to arrest the committee leaders; but so positive was public sentiment, as reflected in the newspapers, in support of the summary executions, that nothing further was heard of the threat.

An incident of value in the study of mob-psychology accentuated the day's events. During the lynching, the clattering of horses' hoofs was heard, when the cry was raised that cavalry from Drum Barracks was rushing to rescue the prisoners; and in a twinkling those but a moment before most demonstrative were seen scurrying to cover in all directions. Instead, however, of Federal soldiers, the horsemen were the usual contingent of El Monte boys, coming to assist in the neck-tie party.

Besides the murderers lynched, there was an American boy named Wood of about eighteen years; and although he had committed no offense more vicious than the theft of some chickens, he paid the penalty with his life, it having been the verdict of the committee that while they were at it, the jail might as well be cleared of every malefactor.   A large empty case was secured as a platform on which the victim was to stand; and I shall never forget the spectacle of the youth, apparently oblivious of his impending doom, as he placed his hands upon the box and vaulted lightly to the top (just as he might have done at an innocent gymnastic contest), and his parting salutation, "I'm going to die a game *hen-chicken!*"   The removal of the case a moment later, after the noose had been thrown over and drawn about the lad's head, left the poor victim suspended beyond human aid.

On that same day, a sixth prisoner barely escaped.   When the crowd was debating the lynchings, John P. Lee, a resident of El Monte who had been convicted of murder, was already under sentence of death; and the Vigilantes, having duly considered his case, decided that it would be just as well to permit the law to take its course.   Some time later, J. Lancaster Brent, Lee's attorney, appealed the case and obtained for his client a new trial, finally clearing Lee of the charges against him, so that, in the end, he died a natural death.

I frequently saw Lee after this episode, and vividly recall an unpleasant interview years later.   The regularity of his visits had been interrupted, and when he reappeared to get some merchandise for a customer at El Monte, I asked him where he had been.   He explained that a dog had bitten a little girl, and that while she was suffering from hydrophobia she had in turn attacked him and so severely scratched his hands and face that, for a while, he could not show himself in public.   After that, whenever I saw Lee, I was aware of a lurking, if ridiculous, suspicion that the moment might have arrived for a new manifestation of the rabies.

Speaking of the Civil War and the fact that in Southern California there was less pronounced sentiment for the Union than in the Northern part of the State, I am reminded of a relief movement that emphasized the distinction.   By the middle of November San Francisco had sent over one hundred and thirty thousand dollars to the United States Sanitary

Commission, and an indignant protest was voiced in some quarters that Los Angeles, up to that date, had not participated. In time, however, the friends of the Union here did make up a small purse.

In 1863 interest in the old San Juan Capistrano Mission was revived with the reopening of the historic structure so badly damaged by the earthquake of 1812, and a considerable number of townspeople went out to the first services under the new roof. When I first saw the Mission, near Don Juan Forster's home, there was in its open doors, windows and cut-stone and stucco ruins, its vines and wild flowers, much of the picturesque.

On November 18th, 1862, our little community was greatly stirred by the news that John Rains, one of Colonel Isaac Williams' sons-in-law and well known in Los Angeles, had been waylaid and killed on the highway near the Azusa *rancho* the night before. It was claimed that one Ramón Carrillo had hired the assassins to do the foul deed; and about the middle of February, 1863, a Mexican by the name of Manuel Cerradel was arrested by Thomas Trafford, the City Marshal, as a participant. In time, he was tried and sentenced to ten years in San Quentin Prison. On December 9th, Sheriff Tomás Sanchez started to take the prisoner north, and at Wilmington boarded the little steamer *Cricket* to go out to the *Senator*, which was ready to sail. A goodly number of other passengers also boarded the tugboat, though nothing in particular was thought of the circumstance; but once out in the harbor, a group of Vigilantes, indignant at the light sentence imposed, seized the culprit at a prearranged signal, threw a noose about his neck and, in a jiffy, hung him to the flagstaff. When he was dead, the body was lowered and stones—brought aboard in packages by the committee, who had evidently considered every detail —were tied to the feet, and the corpse was thrown overboard before the steamer was reached. This was one of the acts of the Vigilantes that no one seemed to deprecate.

Toward the end of 1861, J. E. Pleasants, while overseeing one of Wolfskill's ranches, hit the trail of some horse thieves and, assisted by City Marshal William C. Warren, pursued and captured several, who were sent to the penitentiary.   One, however, escaped.   This was Charles Wilkins, a veritable scoundrel who, having stolen a pistol and a knife from the Bella Union and put the same into the hands of young Wood (whose lynching I have described), sent the lad on his way to the gallows.   A couple of years later Wilkins waylaid and murdered John Sanford, a rancher iving near Fort Tejón and a brother of Captain W. T. B. Sanford, the second Postmaster of Los Angeles; and when the murderer had been apprehended and was being tried, an exciting incident occurred, to which I was an eye-witness. On November 16th, 1854, Phineas Banning had married Miss Rebecca Sanford, a sister of the unfortunate man; and as Banning caught sight of Wilkins, he rushed forward and endeavoured to avenge the crime by shooting the culprit.   Banning was then restrained; but soon after, on December 17th, 1863, he led the Vigilance Committee which strung up Wilkins on Tomlinson & Griffith's corral gateway where nearly a dozen culprits had already forfeited their lives.

CHAPTER XXIII

ASSASSINATION OF LINCOLN

1864–1865

OF all years of adversity before, during or since the Civil War, the seemingly interminable year of 1864 was for Southern California the worst. The varying moves in the great struggle, conducted mostly by Grant and Lee, Sherman and Farragut, buoyed now one, now the other side; but whichever way the tide of battle turned, business and financial conditions here altered but little and improved not a whit. The Southwest, as I have already pointed out, was more dependent for its prosperity on natural conditions, such as rain, than upon the victory of any army or fleet; and as this was the last of three successive seasons of annihilating drought, ranchman and merchant everywhere became downhearted. During the entire winter of 1862–63 no more than four inches of rain had fallen, and in 1864 not until March was there a shower, and even then the earth was scarcely moistened. With a total assessment of something like two million dollars in the County, not a cent of taxes (at least in the city) was collected. Men were so miserably poor that confidence mutually weakened, and merchants refused to trust those who, as land and cattle-barons, but a short time before had been so influential and most of whom, in another and more favorable season or two, were again operators of affluence. How great was the depreciation in values may be seen from the fact that notes given by Francis Temple, and bearing heavy interest, were peddled about at fifty cents on the dollar and even then found few purchasers.

As a result of these very infrequent rains, grass started up only to wither away, a small district around Anaheim independent of the rainfall on account of its fine irrigation system, alone being green; and thither the lean and thirsty cattle came by thousands, rushing in their feverish state against the great willow-fence I have elsewhere described. This stampede became such a menace, in fact, that the Anaheimers were summoned to defend their homes and property, and finally they had to place a mounted guard outside of the willow enclosures. Everywhere large numbers of horses and cattle died, as well as many sheep, the plains at length being strewn with carcasses and bleached bones. The suffering of the poor animals beggars description; and so distressed with hunger were they that I saw famished cattle (during the summer of 1864 while on a visit to the springs at Paso de Robles) crowd around the hotel veranda for the purpose of devouring the discarded matting-containers which had held Chinese rice. I may also add that with the approach of summer the drought became worse and worse, contributing in no small degree to the spread of small-pox, then epidemic here. Stearns lost forty or fifty thousand head of live stock, and was much the greatest sufferer in this respect; and as a result, he was compelled, about June, 1865, to mortgage Los Alamitos *rancho*, with its twenty-six thousand acres, to Michael Reese of San Francisco, for the almost paltry sum of twenty thousand dollars. Even this sacrifice, however, did not save him from still greater financial distress.

In 1864, two Los Angeles merchants, Louis Schlesinger and Hyman Tischler, owing to the recent drought foreclosed a mortgage on several thousand acres of land known as the Ricardo Vejar property, lying between Los Angeles and San Bernardino. Shortly after this transaction, Schlesinger was killed while on his way to San Francisco, in the *Ada Hancock* explosion; after which Tischler purchased Schlesinger's interest in the ranch and managed it alone.

In January, Tischler invited me to accompany him on one of the numerous excursions which he made to his newly-acquired possession, but, though I was inclined to go, a business engagement interfered and kept me in town. Poor Edward Newman, another friend of Tischler's, took my place. On the way to San Bernardino from the *rancho*, the travelers were ambushed by some Mexicans, who shot Newman dead. It was generally assumed that the bullets were intended for Tischler, in revenge for his part in the foreclosure; at any rate, he would never go to the ranch again, and finally sold it to Don Louis Phillips, on credit, for thirty thousand dollars. The inventory included large herds of horses and cattle, which Phillips (during the subsequent wet season) drove to Utah, where he realized sufficient from their sale alone to pay for the whole property. Pomona and other important places now mark the neighborhood where once roamed his herds. Phillips died some years ago at the family residence which he had built on the ranch near Spadra.

James R. Toberman, after a trying experience with Texan Redskins, came to Los Angeles in 1864, President Lincoln having appointed him United States Revenue Assessor here, an office which he held for six years. At the same time, as an exceptional privilege for a Government officer, Toberman was permitted to become agent for Wells Fargo & Company.

Again the Fourth of July was not celebrated here, the two factions in the community still opposing each other with bitterness. Hatred of the National Government had increased through an incident of the previous spring which stirred the town mightily. On the eighth or ninth of May, a group stood discussing the Fort Pillow Massacre, when J. F. Bilderback indiscreetly expressed the wish that the Confederates would annihilate every negro taken with arms, and every white man, as well, who might be found in command of colored troops; or some such equally dangerous and foolish sentiment. The indiscretion was reported to the Government authorities, and Bilderback was straightway arrested by a lieutenant of cavalry, though he was soon released.

Among the most rabid Democrats, particularly during the Civil War period, was Nigger Pete the barber. One hot day in August, patriotic Biggs vociferously proclaimed his ardent attachment to the cause of Secession; whereupon he was promptly arrested, placed in charge of half a dozen cavalrymen, and made to foot it, with an iron chain and ball attached to his ankle, all the way from Los Angeles to Drum Barracks at Wilmington. Not in the least discouraged by his uncertain position, however, Pete threw his hat up into the air as he passed some acquaintances on the road, and gave three hearty cheers for Jeff Davis, thus bringing about the completion of his difficulty.

For my part, I have good reason to remember the drought and crisis of 1864, not alone because times were miserably hard and prosperity seemed to have disappeared forever, or that the important revenue from Uncle Sam, although it relieved the situation, was never sufficient to go around, but also because of an unfortunate investment. I bought and shipped many thousands of hides which owners had taken from the carcasses of their starved cattle, forwarding them to San Francisco by schooner or steamer, and thence to New York by sailing vessel. A large number had commenced to putrefy before they were removed, which fact escaped my attention; and on their arrival in the East, the decomposing skins had to be taken out to sea again and thrown overboard, so that the net results of this venture were disastrous. However, we all met the difficulties of the situation as philosophically as we could.

There were no railroads in California until the late sixties and, consequently, there was no regular method of concentration, nor any systematic marketing of products; and this had a very bad economic effect on the whole State. Prices were extremely high during her early history, and especially so in 1864. Barley sold at three and a half cents per pound; potatoes went up to twelve and a half cents; and flour reached fifteen dollars per barrel, at wholesale. Much flour in wooden barrels was then brought from New York by sailing vessels; and my brother imported a lot during a period of inflation, some of which he sold at thirteen dollars. Isaac Friedlander, a San Francisco pioneer, who was not alone the tallest man in that city but was as well a giant operator in grain and its products, practically monopolized the wheat and flour business of the town; and when he heard of this interference, he purchased all the remainder of my brother's flour at thirteen dollars a barrel, and so secured control of the situation.

Just before this transaction, I happened to be in San Francisco and noticing the advertisement of an approaching flour auction, I attended the sale. This particular lot was packed in sacks which had been eaten into by rats and mice and had, in consequence, to be resacked, sweepings and all. I bought one hundred barrels and shipped the flour to Los Angeles, and B. Dubordieu, the corpulent little French baker, considered himself fortunate in obtaining it at fifteen dollars per barrel.

Speaking of foodstuffs, I may note that red beans then commanded a price of twelve and a half cents per pound, until a sailing vessel from Chile unexpectedly landed a cargo in San Francisco and sent the price dropping to a cent and a quarter; when commission men, among them myself, suffered heavy losses.

In 1864, F. Bachman & Company sold out. Their retirement was ascribed in a measure to the series of bad years, but the influence of their wives was a powerful factor in inducing them to withdraw. The firm had been compelled to accept large parcels of real estate in payment of accounts; and now, while preparing to leave, Bachman & Co. sacrificed their fine holdings at prices considered ridiculous even then. The only one of these sales that I remember was that of a lot with a frontage of one hundred and twenty feet on Fort Street, and a one-story adobe house, which they disposed of for four hundred dollars.

I have told of Don Juan Forster's possessions—the Santa Margarita *rancho*, where he lived until his death, and also the Las Flores. These he obtained in 1864, when land was worth but the merest song, buying the same from Pio Pico, his brother-in-law. The two ranches included over a hundred and forty thousand acres, and pastured some twenty-five thousand cattle, three thousand horses and six or seven thousand sheep;

yet the transaction, on account of the season, was a fiscal operation of but minor importance.

The hard times strikingly conduced to criminality and, since there were then probably not more than three or four policemen in Los Angeles, some of the desperadoes, here in large numbers and not confined to any particular nationality or color, took advantage of the conditions, even making several peculiar nocturnal assaults upon the guardians of the peace. The methods occasionally adopted satisfied the community that Mexican *bandidos* were at work. Two of these worthies on horseback, while approaching a policeman, would suddenly dash in opposite directions, bringing a *reata* (in the use of which they were always most proficient) taut to the level of their saddles; and striking the policeman with the hide or hair rope, they would throw him to the ground with such force as to disable him. Then the ingenious robbers would carry out their well-planned depredations in the neighborhood and disappear with their booty.

J. Ross Browne, one of the active Forty-niners in San Francisco and author of *Crusoe's Island* and various other volumes dealing with early life in California and along the Coast, was on and off a visitor to Los Angeles, first passing through here in 1859, *en route* to the Washoe Gold fields, and stopping again in 1864.

Politics enlivened the situation somewhat in the fall of this year of depression. In September, the troops were withdrawn from Catalina Island, and the following month most of the guard was brought in from Fort Tejón; and this, creating possibly a feeling of security, paved the way for still larger Union meetings in October and November. Toward the end of October, Francisco P. Ramirez, formerly editor of *El Clamor Público*, was made Postmaster, succeeding William G. Still, upon whose life an attempt had been made while he was in office.

As an illustration of how a fortunate plunger acquired property now worth millions, through the disinclination on the part of most people here to add to their taxes in this time of drought,

I may mention two pieces of land included in the early Ord survey, one hundred and twenty by one hundred and sixty-five feet in size—one at the southwest corner of Spring and Fourth streets, the other at the southeast corner of Fort and Fourth— which were sold on December 12th, 1864, for *two dollars and fifty-two cents*, delinquent taxes. The tax on each lot was but one dollar and twenty-six cents, yet only one purchaser appeared!

About that very time, there was another and noteworthy movement in favor of the establishment of a railroad between Los Angeles and San Pedro. In December, committees from outside towns met here with our citizens to debate the subject; but by the end of the several days' conference, no real progress had been made.

The year 1865 gave scant promise, at least in its opening, of better times to come. To be sure, Northern arms were more and more victorious, and with the approach of Lincoln's second inauguration the conviction grew that under the leadership of such a man national prosperity might return. Little did we dream that the most dramatic of all tragedies in our history was soon to be enacted. In Southern California the effects of the long drought continued, and the certainty that the cattle-industry, once so vast and flourishing, was now but a memory, discouraged a people to whom the vision of a far more profitable use of the land had not yet been revealed.

For several years my family, including three children, had been shifting from pillar to post owing to the lack of residences such as are now built to sell or lease, and I could not postpone any longer the necessity of obtaining larger quarters. We had occupied, at various times, a little shanty on Franklin Street, owned by a carpenter named Wilson; a small, one-story brick on Main Street near First, owned by Henne, the brewer; and once we lived with the Kremers in a one-story house, none too large, on Fort Street. Again we dwelt on Fort Street in a little brick house that stood on the site of the present Chamber of Commerce building, next door to Governor Downey's, before he moved to Main Street. The nearest approach to convenience

was afforded by our occupancy of Henry Dalton's two-story
brick on Main Street near Second. One day a friend told me
that Jim Easton had an adobe on Main Street near Third,
which he wished to sell; and on inquiry, I bought the place,
paying him a thousand dollars for fifty-four feet, the entire
frontage being occupied by the house. Main Street, beyond
First, was practically in the same condition as at the time of
my arrival, no streets running east having been opened south
of First.

After moving in, we were inconvenienced because there was
no driveway, and everything needed for housekeeping had to be
carried, in consequence, through the front door of the dwelling.
I therefore interviewed my friend and neighbor, Ygnácio Garcia,
who owned a hundred feet adjoining me, and asked him if he
would sell or rent me twenty feet of his property; whereupon he
permitted me the free use of twenty feet, thus supplying me with
access to the rear of my house. A few months later, Alfred
B. Chapman, Garcia's legal adviser (who, by the way, is still
alive)[1] brought me a deed to the twenty feet of land, the only
expense being a fee of twenty-five dollars to Chapman for
making out the document; and later Garcia sold his remaining
eighty feet to Tom Mott for five dollars a foot. This lot is
still in my possession. In due time, I put up a large, old-
fashioned wooden barn with a roomy hay-loft, stalls for a
couple of horses or mules, and space for a large flat-truck, the
first of the kind for years in Los Angeles. John Simmons had
his room in the barn and was one of my first porters. I had
no regular driver for the truck, but John usually served in that
capacity.

Incidentally to this story of my selecting a street on which
to live, I may say that during the sixties Main and San Pedro
streets were among the chief residential sections, and Spring
Street was only beginning to be popular for homes. The fact
that some people living on the west side of Main Street built
their stables in back-yards connecting with Spring Street, retarded the latter's growth.

[1] Died, January 22d, 1915.

Here I may well repeat the story of the naming of Spring Street, particularly as it exemplifies the influence that romance sometimes has upon affairs usually prosaic. Ord, the surveyor, was then more than prepossessed in favor of the delightful Señorita Trinidad de la Guerra, for whose hand he was, in fact, a suitor and to whom he always referred as *Mi Primavera*—"My Springtime;" and when asked to name the new thoroughfare, he gallantly replied, "Primavera, of course! Primavera!"

On February 3d, a wind-storm, the like of which the proverbial "oldest inhabitant" could scarcely recall, struck Los Angeles amidships, unroofing many houses and blowing down orchards. Wolfskill lost heavily, and Banning & Company's large barn at the northeast corner of Fort and Second streets, near the old schoolhouse, was demolished, scarcely a post remaining upright. A curious sight, soon after the storm began to blow, was that of many citizens weighing down and lashing fast their roofs, just as they do in Sweden, Norway and Switzerland, to keep them from being carried to unexpected, not to say inconvenient, locations.

In early days, steamers plying up and down the Pacific Coast, as I have pointed out, were so poor in every respect that it was necessary to make frequent changes in their names, to induce passengers to travel on them at all. As far back as 1860, one frequently heard the expression, "the old tubs;" and in 1865, even the best-known boat on the Southern run was publicly discussed as "the rotten old *Senator*," "the old hulk" and "the floating coffin." At this time, there was a strong feeling against the Steam Navigation Company for its arbitrary treatment of the public, its steamers sometimes leaving a whole day before the date on which they were advertised to depart; and this criticism and dissatisfaction finally resulted in the putting on of the opposition steamer *Pacific* which for the time became popular.

In 1865, Judge Benjamin S. Eaton tried another agricultural experiment which many persons of more experience at first predicted would be a failure. He had moved into the cottage

at *Fair Oaks*, built by the estimable lady of General Albert
Sidney Johnston, and had planted five thousand or more grape-
vines in the good though dry soil; but the lack of surface
water caused vineyardists to shake their heads incredulously.
The vines prospered so well that, in the following year,
Eaton planted five or six times as many more. He came to
the conclusion, however, that he must have water; and so
arranged to bring some from what is now known as Eaton's
Cañon.   I remember that, after his vines began to bear,
the greatest worry of the Judge was not the matter of irrigation,
but the wild beasts that preyed upon the clustering fruit.
The visitor to Pasadena and Altadena to-day can hardly realize
that in those very localities both coyotes and bears were
rampant, and that many a night the irate Judge was roused
by the barking dogs as they drove the intruders out of the
vineyard.

Tomlinson & Company, always energetic competitors in
the business of transportation in Southern California, began
running, about the first of April, a new stage line between Los
Angeles and San Bernardino, making three trips a week.

On the fifteenth of April, my family physician, Dr. John S.
Griffin, paid a professional visit to my house on Main Street,
which might have ended disastrously for him.   While we were
seated together by an open window in the dining-room, a man
named Kane ran by on the street, shouting out the momentous
news that Abraham Lincoln had been shot!   Griffin, who was a
staunch Southerner, was on his feet instantly, cheering for Jeff
Davis.   He gave evidence, indeed, of great mental excitement,
and soon seized his hat and rushed for the door, hurrahing for
the Confederacy.   In a flash, I realized that Griffin would be in
awful jeopardy if he reached the street in that unbalanced condition, and by main force I held him back, convincing him at
last of his folly.   In later years the genial Doctor frankly
admitted that I had undoubtedly saved him from certain
death.

This incident brings to mind another, associated with
Henry Baer, whose father, Abraham, a native of Bavaria and

one of the earliest tailors here, had arrived from New Orleans in 1854. When Lincoln's assassination was first known, Henry ran out of the house, singing *Dixie* and shouting for the South; but his father, overtaking him, brought him back and gave him a sound whipping—an act nearly breaking up the Baer family, inasmuch as Mrs. Baer was a pronounced Secessionist.

The news of Lincoln's assassination made a profound impression in Los Angeles, though it cannot be denied that some Southern sympathizers, on first impulse, thought that it would be advantageous to the Confederate cause. There was, therefore, for the moment, some ill-advised exultation; but this was promptly suppressed, either by the military or by the firm stand of the more level-headed members of the community. Soon even radically-inclined citizens, in an effort to uphold the fair name of the town, fell into line, and steps were taken fittingly to mourn the nation's loss. On the seventeenth of April, the Common Council passed appropriate resolutions; and Governor Low having telegraphed that Lincoln's funeral would be held in Washington on the nineteenth, at twelve o'clock noon, the Union League of Los Angeles took the initiative and invited the various societies of the city to join in a funeral procession.

On April 19th all the stores were closed, business was suspended and soldiers as well as civilians assembled in front of Arcadia Block. There were present United States officers, mounted cavalry under command of Captain Ledyard; the Mayor and Common Council; various lodges; the Hebrew Congregation B'nai-B'rith; the Teutonia, the French Benevolent and the Junta Patriotica societies, and numerous citizens. Under the marshalship of S. F. Lamson the procession moved slowly over what to-day would be regarded as an insignificantly short route: west on Arcadia Street to Main; down Main Street to Spring as far as First; east on First Street to Main and up Main Street, proceeding back to the City Hall by way of Spring, at which point the parade disbanded.

Later, on the same day, there were memorial services in the

upper story of the old Temple Court House, where Rev. Elias Birdsall, the Episcopal clergyman, delivered a splendid oration and panegyric; and at the same time, the members of the Hebrew Congregation met at the house of Rabbi A. W. Edelman. Prayers for the martyred President were uttered, and supplication was made for the recovery of Secretary of State Seward. The resolutions presented on this occasion concluded as follows:

RESOLVED, that with feelings of the deepest sorrow we deplore the loss our country has sustained in the untimely end of our late President; but as it has pleased the Almighty to deprive this Country of its Chief and great friend, we bow with submission to the All-wise Will.

I may add that, soon after the assassination of the President, the Federal authorities sent an order to Los Angeles to arrest anyone found rejoicing in the foul deed; and that several persons, soon in the toils, were severely dealt with. In San Francisco, too, when the startling news was flashed over the wires, Unionist mobs demolished the plants of the *Democratic Press*, the *News Letter* and a couple of other journals very abusive toward the martyred Emancipator; the editors and publishers themselves escaping with their lives only by flight and concealment.

Notwithstanding the strong Secessionist sentiment in Los Angeles during much of the Civil War period, the City election resulted in a Unionist victory. José Mascarel was elected Mayor; William C. Warren, Marshal; J. F. Burns, Treasurer; J. H. Lander, Attorney; and J. W. Beebe, Assessor. The triumph of the Federal Government doubtless at once began to steady and improve affairs throughout the country; but it was some time before any noticeable progress was felt here. Particularly unfortunate were those who had gone east or south for actual service, and who were obliged to make their way, finally, back to the Coast. Among such volunteers was Captain Cameron E. Thom who, on landing at San Pedro, was glad to have J. M. Griffith advance him money enough to reach Los Angeles and begin life again.

Outdoor restaurant gardens were popular in the sixties. On April 23d, the Tivoli Garden was reopened by Henry Sohms, and thither, on holidays and Sundays, many pleasure-lovers gravitated.

Sometime in the spring and during the incumbency of Rev. Elias Birdsall as rector, the Right Reverend William Ingraham Kip, who had come to the Pacific Coast in 1853, made his first visit to the Episcopal Church in Los Angeles, as Bishop of California, although really elevated to that high office seven years before. Bishop Kip was one of the young clergy who pleaded with the unresponsive culprits strung up by the San Francisco Vigilance Committee of 1856; and later he was known as an author. The Reverend Birdsall, by the way, was Rector of St. Paul's School on Olive Street, between Fifth and Sixth, as late as 1887.

John G. Downey subdivided the extensive Santa Gertrudis *rancho* on the San Gabriel River in the spring, and the first deed was made out to J. H. Burke, a son-in-law of Captain Jesse Hunter. Burke, a man of splendid physique, was a blacksmith whose Main Street shop was next to the site of the present Van Nuys Hotel. Downey and he exchanged properties, the ex-Governor building a handsome brick residence on Burke's lot, and Burke removing his blacksmith business to Downey's new town where, by remaining until the property had appreciated, he became well-to-do.

I have alluded to the Dominguez *rancho*, known as the San Pedro, but I have not said that, in 1865, some four thousand acres of this property were sold to Temple & Gibson at thirty-five cents an acre, and that on a portion of this land G. D. Compton founded the town named after him and first called Comptonville. . It was really a Methodist Church enterprise, planned from the beginning as a pledge to teetotalism, and is of particular interest because it is one of the oldest towns in Los Angeles County, and certainly the first "dry" community. Compton paid Temple & Gibson five dollars an acre.

Toward the end of the War, that is, in May, Major-General Irwin McDowell, the unfortunate commander of the Army of the Potomac who had been nearly a year in charge of the Department of the Pacific, made Los Angeles a long-announced visit, coming on the Government steamer *Saginaw*. The distinguished officer, his family and suite were speedily whirled to the Bella Union, the competing drivers shouting and cursing themselves hoarse in their efforts to get the General or the General's wife, in different stages, there first. As was customary in those simpler days, most of the townsfolk whose politics would permit called upon the guest; and Editor Conway and other Unionists were long closeted with him. After thirty-six hours or more, during which the General inspected the local Government headquarters and the ladies were driven to, and entertained at, various homes, the party, accompanied by Collector James and Attorney-General McCullough, boarded the cutter and made off for the North.

Anticipating this visit of General McDowell, due preparations were made to receive him. It happened, however, as I have indicated, that José Mascarel was then Mayor; and since he had never been able to express himself freely in English, though speaking Spanish as well as French, it was feared that embarrassment must follow the meeting of the civil and military personages. Luckily, however, like many scions of early well-to-do American families, McDowell had been educated in France, and the two chiefs were soon having a free and easy talk in Mascarel's native tongue.

An effort, on May 2d, better to establish St. Vincent's College as the one institution of higher learning here was but natural at that time. In the middle of the sixties, quite as many children attended private academies in Los Angeles County as were in the public schools, while three-fifths of all children attended no school at all. At the beginning of the Twentieth Century, two-thirds of all the children in the county attended public schools.

CHAPTER XXIV

1865–1866

FROM 1862 I continued for three years, as I have told, in the commission business; and notwithstanding the bad seasons, I was thus pursuing a sufficiently easy and pleasant existence when a remark which, after the lapse of time, I see may have been carelessly dropped, inspired me with the determination to enter again upon a more strenuous and confining life.

On Friday, June 18th, 1865, I was seated in my little office, when a Los Angeles merchant named David Solomon, whose store was in the Arcadia Block, called upon me and, with much feeling, related that while returning by steamer from the North, Prudent Beaudry had made the senseless boast that he would drive every Jew in Los Angeles out of business. Beaudry, then a man of large means, conducted in his one-story adobe building on the northeast corner of Aliso and Los Angeles streets the largest general merchandise establishment this side of San Francisco. I listened to Solomon's recital without giving expression to my immediately-formed resolve; but no sooner had he left than I closed my office and started for Wilmington.

During the twelve years that I had been in California the forwarding business between Los Angeles and the Coast had seen many changes. Tomlinson & Company, who had bought out A. W. Timms, controlled the largest tonnage in town, including that of Beaudry, Jones, Childs and others; while

M. A. Newmark

Kaspare Cohn

H. Newmark & Co.'s Store, Arcadia Block, about 1875, Including (left) John Jones's
Former Premises

H. Newmark & Co.'s Building, Amestoy Block, about 1884

Banning & Company, although actively engaged in the transportation to Yuma of freight and supplies for the United States Government, were handicapped for lack of business into Los Angeles. I thought, therefore, that Phineas Banning would eagerly seize an opportunity to pay his score to the numerous local merchants who had treated him with so little consideration. Besides, a very close intimacy existed between him and myself, which may best be illustrated by the fact that, for years past when short of cash, Banning used to come to my old sheet-iron safe and help himself according to his requirements.

Arriving in Wilmington, I found Banning loading a lot of teams with lumber. I related the substance of Solomon's remarks and proposed a secret partnership, with the understanding that, providing he would release me from the then existing charge of seven dollars and a half per ton for hauling freight from Wilmington to Los Angeles, I should supply the necessary capital, purchase a stock of goods, conduct the business without cost to him and then divide the profits if any should accrue. Banning said, "I must first consult Don David," meaning Alexander, his partner, promising at the same time to report the result within a few days. While I was at dinner, therefore, on the following Sunday, Patrick Downey, Banning's Los Angeles agent, called on me and stated that "the Chief" was in his office in the Downey Block, on the site of Temple's old adobe, and would be glad to see me.

Without further parleying, Banning accepted my proposition; and on the following morning, or June 21st, I rented the last vacant store in Stearns's Arcadia Block on Los Angeles Street, which stands to-day, by the way, much as it was erected in 1858. It adjoined John Jones's, and was nearly opposite the establishment of P. Beaudry. There I put up the sign of H. Newmark, soon to be changed to H. Newmark & Company; and it is a source of no little gratification to me that from this small beginning has developed the wholesale grocery firm of M. A. Newmark & Company.[1]

[1] Fifty years after this unpretentious venture in Arcadia Block, that is, in the summer of 1915, the half-centenary of M. A. Newmark & Company and their pre-

At that time, Stearns's property was all in the hands of the Sheriff, Tomás Sanchez, who had also been appointed Receiver; and like all the other tenants, I rented my storeroom from Deputy A. J. King. Rents and other incomes were paid to the Receiver, and out of them a regular monthly allowance of fifty dollars was made to Stearns for his private expenses. The stock on Stearns's ranches, by the way, was then in charge of Pierre Domec, a well-known and prosperous man, who was here perhaps a decade before I came.

My only assistant was my wide-awake nephew, M. A. Newmark, then fifteen years of age, who had arrived in Los Angeles early in 1865. At my request Banning & Company released their bookkeeper, Frank Lecouvreur, and I engaged him. He was a thoroughly reliable man and had, besides, a technical knowledge of wagon materials, in which, as a side-line, I expected to specialize. While all of these arrangements were being completed, the local business world queried and buzzed as to my intentions.

Having rented quarters, I immediately telegraphed my brother, J. P. Newmark, to buy and ship a quantity of flour, sugar, potatoes, salt and other heavy staples; and these I sold, upon arrival, at cost and steamer freight plus seven dollars and a half per ton. Since the departure of my brother from Los Angeles for permanent residence in San Francisco (where he entered into partnership with Isaac Lightner, forming J. P. Newmark & Company), he had been engaged in the commission business; and this afforded me facilities I might

---

decessors was celebrated with a picnic in the woodlands belonging to Universal City, the holiday and its pleasures having been provided by the firm as a compliment to its employees. On that occasion, a loving-cup was presented by the employees to M. A. Newmark, who responded feelingly to the speech by M. H. Newmark. Another, but somewhat differently inscribed cup was tendered Harris Newmark in an address by Herman Flatau, bringing from the venerable recipient a hearty reply, full of genial reminiscence and natural emotion, in which he happily likened his commercial enterprise, once the small store in Los Angeles Street, to a snowball rolling down the mountain-side, gathering in momentum and size and, fortunately, preserving its original whiteness. Undoubtedly, this Fifty-Year Jubilee will take its place among the pleasantest experiences of a long and varied career.—THE EDITORS.

otherwise not have had.   Inasmuch also, as all of my neighbors were obliged to pay this toll for hauling, while I was not, they were forced to do business at cost.   About the first of July, I went to San Francisco and laid in a complete stock paralleling, with the exception of clothing and dry goods, the lines handled by Beaudry.   Banning, who was then building prairie schooners for which he had ordered some three hundred and fifty tons of iron and other wagon materials, joined me in chartering the brig *Tanner* on which I loaded an equal tonnage of general merchandise, wagon parts and blacksmith coal.   The very important trade with Salt Lake City, elsewhere described, helped us greatly, for we at once negotiated with the Mormon leaders; and giving them credit when they were short of funds, it was not long before we were brought into constant communication with Brigham Young and through his influence monopolized the Salt Lake business.

Thinking over these days of our dealings with the Latter-day Saints, I recall a very amusing experience with an apostle named Crosby, who once brought down a number of teams and wagons to load with supplies.   During his visit to town, I invited him and several of his friends to dinner; and in answer to the commonplace inquiry as to his preference for some particular part of a dish, Crosby made the logical Mormonite reply that *quantity* was what appealed to him most—a flash of wit much appreciated by all of the guests.   During this same visit, Crosby tried hard to convert me to Mormonism; but, after several ineffectual interviews, he abandoned me as a hopeless case.

At another time, while reflecting on my first years as a wholesale grocer, I was led to examine a day-book of 1867 and to draw a comparison between the prices then current and now, when the high cost of living is so much discussed.   Raw sugar sold at fourteen cents; starch at sixteen; crushed sugar at seventeen; ordinary tea at sixty; coal oil at sixty-five cents a gallon; axle-grease at seventy-five cents per tin; bluing at one dollar a pound; and wrapping paper at one dollar and a half per ream.   Spices, not yet sold in cans, cost three dollars for a

dozen bottles; yeast powders, now superseded by baking
powder, commanded the same price per dozen; twenty-five
pounds of shot in a bag cost three dollars and a half; while in
October of that year, blacksmith coal, shipped in casks holding
fifteen hundred and ninety-two pounds each, sold at the rate
of fifty dollars a ton.

The steamers *Oriflamme, California, Pacific* and *Sierra
Nevada* commenced to run in 1866 and continued until about
the middle of the seventies.   The *Pacific* was later sunk in the
Straits of San Juan de Fuca; and the *Sierra Nevada* was lost
on the rocks off Port Harford.   The *Los Angeles*, the *Ventura*
and the *Constantine* were steamers of a somewhat later date,
seldom going farther south than San Pedro and continuing
to run until they were lost.

To resume the suggestive story of I. W. Hellman, who
remained in business with his cousin until he was able in 1865
to buy out Adolph Portugal and embark for himself, at the
corner of Main and Commercial streets: during his association
with large landowners and men of affairs, who esteemed
him for his practicality, he was fortunate in securing their
confidence and patronage; and being asked so often to op-
erate for them in financial matters, he laid the foundation for
his subsequent career as a banker, in which he has attained such
success.

The Pioneer Oil Company had been organized about the
first of February, with Phineas Banning, President; P. Downey,
Secretary; Charles Ducommon, Treasurer; and Winfield S.
Hancock, Dr. John S. Griffin, Dr. J. B. Winston, M. Keller,
B. D. Wilson, J. G. Downey and Volney E. Howard among the
trustees; and the company soon acquired title to all *brea*, petroleum or rock oil in San Pasqual *rancho*.   In the early summer,
Sackett & Morgan, on Main Street near the Post Office,
exhibited some local kerosene or "coal-oil;" and experimenters
were gathering the oil that floated on Pico Spring and refining
it, without distillation, at a cost of ten cents a gallon.   Coming
just when Major Stroble announced progress in boring at la
Cañada de Brea, these ventures increased here the excitement

about oil and soon after wells were sunk in the Camulos *rancho*.

On Wednesday afternoon, July 5th, at four o'clock, occurred one of the pleasant social occasions of the mid-sixties—the wedding of Solomon Lazard and Miss Caroline, third daughter of Joseph Newmark. The bride's father performed the ceremony at M. Kremer's residence on Main Street, near my own adobe and the site on which, later, C. E. Thom built his charming residence, with its rural attractions, diagonally across from the pleasant grounds of Colonel J. G. Howard. The same evening at half-past eight a ball and dinner at the Bella Union celebrated the event.

While these festivities were taking place, a quarrel, ending in a tragedy, began in the hotel office below. Robert Carlisle, who had married Francisca, daughter of Colonel Isaac Williams, and was the owner of some forty-six thousand acres comprising the Chino Ranch, fell into an altercation with A. J. King, then Under Sheriff, over the outcome of a murder trial; but before any further damage was done, friends separated them.

About noon on the following day, however, when people were getting ready to leave for the steamer and everything was life and bustle about the hotel, Frank and Houston King, the Under Sheriff's brothers, passing by the bar-room of the Bella Union and seeing Carlisle inside, entered, drew their six-shooters and began firing at him. Carlisle also drew a revolver and shot Frank King, who died almost instantly. Houston King kept up the fight, and Carlisle, riddled with bullets, dropped to the sidewalk. There King, not yet seriously injured, struck his opponent on the head, the force of the blow breaking his weapon; but Carlisle, a man of iron, put forth his little remaining strength, staggered to the wall, raised his pistol with both hands, took deliberate aim and fired. It was his last, but effective shot, for it penetrated King's body.

Carlisle was carried into the hotel and placed on a billiard-table; and there, about three o'clock, he expired. At the first exchange of shots, the people nearby, panic-stricken, fled, and only a merciful Providence prevented the sacrifice of other lives.   J. H. Lander was accidentally wounded in the thigh; some eight or ten bystanders had their clothes pierced by stray bullets; and one of the stage-horses dropped where he stood before the hotel door.   When the first shot was fired, I was on the corner of Commercial Street, only a short distance away, and reached the scene in time to see Frank King expire and witness Carlisle writhing in agony—a death more striking, considering the murder of Carlisle's brother-in-law, John Rains. Carlisle was buried from the Bella Union at four o'clock the next day.   King's funeral took place from A. J. King's residence, two days later, at eight o'clock in the morning.

Houston King having recovered, he was tried for Carlisle's murder, but was acquitted; the trial contributing to make the affair one of the most mournful of all tragic events in the early history of Los Angeles, and rendering it impossible to express the horror of the public.   One feature only of the terrible contest afforded a certain satisfaction, and that was the splendid exhibition of those qualities, in some respects heroic, so common among the old Californians of that time.

July was clouded with a particularly gruesome murder. George Williams and Cyrus Kimball of San Diego, while removing with their families to Los Angeles, had spent the night near the Santa Ana River, and while some distance from camp, at sunrise next morning, were overtaken by seven armed desperadoes, under the leadership of one Jack O'Brien, and without a word of explanation, were shot dead.   The women, hearing the commotion, ran toward the spot, only to be commanded by the robbers to deliver all money and valuables in their possession.   Over three thousand dollars—the entire savings of their husbands—was secured, after which the murderers made their escape.   *Posses* scoured the surrounding country, but the cutthroats were never apprehended.

Stimulated, perhaps, by the King–Carlisle tragedy, the Common Council in July prohibited everybody except officers and travelers from carrying a pistol, dirk, sling-shot or sword; but the measure lacked public support, and little or no attention was paid to the law.

Some idea of the modest proportion of business affairs in the early sixties may be gathered from the fact that, when the Los Angeles Post Office, on August 10th, was made a money-deposit office, it was obligatory that all cash in excess of five hundred dollars should be despatched by steamer to San Francisco.

In 1865, W. H. Perry, having been given a franchise to light the city with gas, organized the Los Angeles City Gas Company, five years later selling out his holdings at a large profit. A promise was made to furnish free gas for lamps at the principal crossings on Main Street and for lights in the Mayor's office, and the consumers' price at first agreed upon was ten dollars a thousand cubic feet.

The history of Westlake Park is full of interest. About 1865, the City began to sell part of its public land, in lots of thirty-five acres, employing E. W. Noyes as auctioneer. Much of it went at five and ten dollars an acre; but when the district now occupied by the park and lake was reached, the auctioneer called in vain for bids at even a dollar an acre; nobody wanted the alkali hillocks. Then the auctioneer offered the area at twenty-five cents an acre, but still received no bids, and the sale was discontinued. In the late eighties, a number of citizens who had bought land in the vicinity came to Mayor Workman and promised to pay one-half of the cost of making a lake and laying out pleasure grounds on the unsightly place; and as the Mayor favored the plan, it was executed, and this was the first step in the formation of Westlake Park.

On September 2d, Dr. J. J. Dyer, a dentist from San Francisco, having opened an office in the Bella Union hotel, announced that he would visit the homes of patrons and there extract or repair the sufferers' teeth. The complicated equipment of a modern dentist would hardly permit of such peripatetic service to-day, although representatives of this profession and also certain opticians still travel to many of the small inland towns in California, once or twice a year, stopping in each for a week or two at a time.

I have spoken of the use, in 1853, of river water for drinking, and the part played by the private water-carrier. This system was still largely used until the fall when David W. Alexander leased all the public water-works for four years, together with the privilege of renewing the lease another four or six years. Alexander was to pay one thousand dollars rental a year, agreeing also to surrender the plant to the City at the termination of his contract. On August 7th, Alexander assigned his lease to Don Louis Sainsevain, and about the middle of October Sainsevain made a new contract. Damien Marchessault associated himself with Don Louis and together they laid pipes from the street now known as Macy throughout the business part of the city, and as far (!) south as First Street. These water pipes were constructed of pine logs from the mountains of San Bernardino, bored and made to join closely at the ends; but they were continually bursting, causing springs of water that made their way to the surface of the streets.

Conway & Waite sold the *News*, then a "tri-weekly" supposed to appear three times a week, yet frequently issued but twice, to A. J. King & Company, on November 11th; and King, becoming the editor, made of the newspaper a semi-weekly.

To complete what I was saying about the Schlesingers: In 1865, Moritz returned to Germany. Jacob had arrived in Los Angeles in 1860, but disappearing four years later, his whereabouts was a mystery until, one fine day, his brother received a letter from him dated, "Gun Boat *Pocahontas*." Jake had entered the service of Uncle Sam! The *Pocahontas* was engaged in blockade work under command of Admiral Farragut; and Jake and the Admiral were paying special attention to Sabine Pass, then fortified by the Confederacy.

On November 27th, Andrew J. Glassell and Colonel James G. Howard arrived together in Los Angeles. The former had been admitted to the California Bar some ten or twelve years before; but in the early sixties he temporarily abandoned his profession and engaged in ranching near Santa Cruz. After the War, Glassell drifted back to the practice of law; and having soon cast his lot with Los Angeles, formed a partnership with Alfred B. Chapman. Two or three years later, Colonel George H. Smith, a Confederate Army officer who in the early seventies lived on Fort Street, was taken into the firm; and for years Glassell, Chapman and Smith were among the leading attorneys at the Los Angeles Bar. Glassell died on January 28th, 1901.

To add to the excitement of the middle sixties, a picturesque street encounter took place, terminating almost fatally. Colonel, the redoubtable E. J. C. Kewen, and a good-natured German named Fred Lemberg, son-in-law to the old miller Bors, having come to blows on Los Angeles Street near Mellus's Row, Lemberg knocked Kewen down; whereupon friends interfered and peace was apparently restored. Kewen, a Southerner, dwelt upon the fancied indignity to which he had been subjected and went from store to store until he finally borrowed a pistol; after which, in front of John Jones's, he lay in wait. When Lemberg, who, because of his nervous energy, was known as the Flying Dutchman, again appeared, rushing across the street in the direction of Mellus's Row, the equally excited Colonel opened fire, drawing from his adversary a retaliatory round of shots. I was standing nearly opposite the scene and saw the Flying Dutchman and Kewen, each dodging around a pillar in front of The Row, until finally Lemberg, with a bullet in his abdomen, ran out into Los Angeles Street and fell to the ground, his legs convulsively assuming a perpendicular position and then dropping back. After recovering from what was thought to be a fatal wound, Lemberg left Los Angeles for Arizona or Mexico; but before he reached his destination, he was murdered by Indians.

I have told of the trade between Los Angeles and Salt Lake City, which started up briskly in 1855, and grew in importance until the completion of the transcontinental railroad put an end to it. Indeed, in 1865 and 1866 Los Angeles enterprise pushed forward until merchandise was teamed as far as Bannock, Idaho, four hundred and fifty miles beyond Salt Lake, and Helena, Montana, fourteen hundred miles away. This indicates to what an extent the building of railroads ultimately affected the early Los Angeles merchants.

The Spanish drama was the event of December 17th, when Señor Don Guirado L. del Castillo and Señora Amelia Estrella del Castillo played *La Trenza de sus Cabellos* to an enthusiastic audience.

In 1865 or 1866, William T. Glassell, a younger brother of Andrew Glassell, came to Los Angeles on a visit; and being attracted by the Southwest country, he remained to assist Glassell & Chapman in founding Orange, formerly known as Richland. No doubt pastoral California looked good to young Glassell, for he had but just passed eighteen weary months in a Northern military prison. Having thought out a plan for blowing up the United States ironclads off Charleston Harbor, Lieutenant Glassell supervised the construction of a cigar-shaped craft, known as a *David*, which carried a torpedo attached to the end of a fifteen-foot pole; and on October 5th, 1863, young Glassell and three other volunteers steamed out in the darkness against the formidable new *Ironsides*. The torpedo was exploded, doing no greater damage than to send up a column of water, which fell onto the ship, and also to hurl the young officers into the bay. Glassell died here at an early age.

John T. Best, the Assessor, was another pioneer who had an adventurous life prior to, and for a long time after, coming to California. Having run away to sea from his Maine home about the middle fifties, Best soon found himself among pirates; but escaping their clutches, he came under the domination of a captain whose cruelty, off desolate Cape Horn, was hardly preferable to death. Reaching California about 1858, Best fled from another captain's brutality and, making his way into the Northern forests, was taken in and protected by kind-hearted woodmen secluded within palisades. Successive Indian outbreaks constantly threatened him and his comrades, and for years he was compelled to defend himself against the savages. At last, safe and sound, he settled within the pale of civilization, at the outbreak of the Civil War enlisting as a

Union officer in the first battalion of California soldiers. Since then Best has resided mostly in Los Angeles.

The year 1866 is memorable as the concluding period of the great War. Although Lee had surrendered in the preceding April, more than fifteen months elapsed before the Washington authorities officially proclaimed the end of the Titanic struggle which left one-half of the nation prostrate and the other half burdened with new and untold responsibilities. By the opening of the year, however, one of the miracles of modern history—the quiet and speedy return of the soldier to the vocations of peace—began, and soon some of those who had left for the front when the War broke out were to be seen again in our Southland, starting life anew. With them, too, came a few pioneers from the East, harbingers of an army soon to settle our valleys and seasides. All in all, the year was the beginning of a brighter era.

Here it may not be amiss to take up the tale of the mimic war in which Phineas Banning and I engaged, in the little commercial world of Los Angeles, and to tell to what an extent the fortunes of my competitors were influenced, and how the absorption of the transportation charge from the seaboard caused their downfall. O. W. Childs, in less than three months, found the competition too severe and surrendered "lock, stock and barrel;" P. Beaudry, whose vain-glorious boast had stirred up this rumpus, sold out to me on January 1st, 1866, just a few months after his big talk. John Jones was the last to yield.

In January, 1866, I bought out Banning, who was soon to take his seat in the Legislature for the advancing of his San Pedro Railroad project, and agreed to pay him, in the future, seven dollars and a half per ton for hauling my goods from Wilmington to Los Angeles, which was mutually satisfactory; and when we came to balance up, it was found that Banning had received, for his part in the enterprise, an amount equal to all that would otherwise have been charged for transportation and a tidy sum besides.

Sam, brother of Kaspare Cohn, who had been in Carson

City, Nevada, came to Los Angeles and joined me. We grew rapidly, and in a short time became of some local importance. When Kaspare sold out at Red Bluff, in January, 1866, we tendered him a partnership. We were now three very busy associates, besides M. A. Newmark, who clerked for us.

Several references have been made to the trade between Los Angeles and Arizona, due in part to the needs of the Army there. I remember that early in February not less than twenty-seven Government wagons were drawn up in front of H. Newmark & Company's store, to be loaded with seventy to seventy-five tons of groceries and provisions for troops in the Territory.

Notwithstanding the handicaps in this wagon-train traffic, there was still much objection to railroads, especially to the plan for a line between Los Angeles and San Pedro, some of the strongest opposition coming from El Monte where, in February, ranchers circulated a petition, disapproving railroad bills introduced by Banning into the Legislature. A common argument was that the railroad would do away with horses and the demand for barley; and one wealthy citizen who succeeded in inducing many to follow his lead, vehemently insisted that two trains a month, for many years, would be all that could be expected! By 1874, however, not less than fifty to sixty freight cars were arriving daily in Los Angeles from Wilmington.

Once more, in 1866, the Post Office was moved, this time to a building opposite the Bella Union hotel. There it remained until perhaps 1868, when it was transferred to the northwest corner of Main and Market streets.

In the spring of 1866, the Los Angeles Board of Education was petitioned to establish a school where Spanish as well as English should be taught—probably the first step toward the introduction into public courses here of the now much-studied *castellano*.

In noting the third schoolhouse, at the corner of San Pedro and Washington streets, I should not forget to say that Judge Dryden bought the lot for the City, at a cost of one hundred dollars. When the fourth school was erected, at the corner of Charity and Eighth streets, it was built on property secured for three hundred and fifty dollars by M. Kremer, who served on the School Board for nine years, from 1866, with Henry D. Barrows and William Workman. There, a few years ago, a brick building replaced the original wooden structure. Besides Miss Eliza Madigan, teachers of this period or later were the Misses Hattie and Frankie Scott, daughters of Judge Scott, the Misses Maggie Hamilton, Eula P. Bixby, Emma L. Hawkes, Clara M. Jones, H. K. Saxe and C. H. Kimball; a sister of Governor Downey, soon to become Mrs. Peter Martin, was also a public school teacher.

Piped gas as well as water had been quite generally brought into private use shortly after their introduction, all pipes running along the surface of walls and ceilings, in neither a very judicious nor ornamental arrangement. The first gas-fixtures consisted of the old-fashioned, unornamented drops from the ceiling, connected at right angles to the cross-pipe, with its two plain burners, one at either end, forming an inverted T (⊥); and years passed before artistic bronzes and globes, such as were displayed in profusion at the Centennial Exposition, were seen to any extent here.

In September, Leon Loeb arrived in Los Angeles and entered the employ of S. Lazard & Company, later becoming a partner. When Eugene Meyer left for San Francisco on the first of January, 1884, resigning his position as French Consular Agent, Loeb succeeded him, both in that capacity and as head of the firm. After fifteen years' service, the French Government conferred upon Mr. Loeb the decoration of an Officer of the Academy. As Past Master of the Odd Fellows, he became in time one of the oldest members of Lodge No. 35. On March 23d, 1879, Loeb married my eldest daughter, Estelle; and on July 22d, 1911, he died. Joseph P. and Edwin J. Loeb, the attorneys and partners of Irving M. Walker, (son-in-law of Tomás Lorenzo Duque),[1] are sons of Leon Loeb.

In the summer there came to Los Angeles from the North-

[1] Died on April 6th, 1915.

ern part of California an educator who already had established there and in Wisconsin an excellent reputation as a teacher. This was George W. Burton, who was accompanied by his wife, a lady educated in France and Italy. With them they brought two assistants, a young man and a young woman, adding another young woman teacher after they arrived. The company of pedagogues made quite a formidable array; and their number permitted the division of the school—then on Main near what is now Second Street—into three departments: one a kind of kindergarten, another for young girls and a third for boys. The school grew and it soon became necessary to move the boys' department to the vestry-room of the little Episcopal Church on the corner of Temple and New High streets.

Not only was Burton an accomplished scholar and experienced teacher, but Mrs. Burton was a linguist of talent and also proficient in both instrumental and vocal music. Our eldest children attended the Burton School, as did also those of many friends such as the Kremers, Whites, Morrises, Griffiths, the Volney Howards, Kewens, Scotts, Nichols, the Schumachers, Joneses and the Bannings.

Daniel Bohen, another watchmaker and jeweler, came after Pyle, establishing himself, on September 11th, on the south side of Commercial Street. He sold watches, clocks, jewelry and spectacles; and he used to advertise with the figure of a huge watch. S. Nordlinger, who arrived here in 1868, bought Bohen out and continued the jewelry business during forty-two years, until his death in 1911, when, as a pioneer jeweler, he was succeeded by Louis S. and Melville Nordlinger, who still use the title of S. Nordlinger & Sons.

Charles C. Lips, a German, came to Los Angeles from Philadelphia in 1866 and joined the wholesale liquor firm of E. Martin & Company, later Lips, Craigue & Company, in the Baker Block. As a volunteer fireman, he was a member of the old Thirty-Eights; a fact adding interest to the appointment, on February 28th, 1905, of his son, Walter Lips, as Chief of the Los Angeles Fire Department.

On October 3d, William Wolfskill died, mourned by many. Though but sixty-eight years of age, he had witnessed much in the founding of our great Southwestern commonwealth; and notwithstanding the handicaps to his early education, and the disappointments of his more eventful years, he was a man of marked intelligence and remained unembittered and kindly disposed toward his fellow-men.

A good example of what an industrious man, following an ordinary trade, could accomplish in early days was afforded by Andrew Joughin, a blacksmith, who came here in 1866, a powerful son of the Isle of Man, measuring over six feet and tipping the beam at more than two hundred pounds. He had soon saved enough money to buy for five hundred dollars a large frontage at Second and Hill streets, selling it shortly after for fifteen hundred. From Los Angeles, Joughin went to Arizona and then to San Juan Capistrano, but was back here again in 1870, opening another shop. Toward the middle seventies, Joughin was making rather ingenious plows of iron and steel which attracted considerable attention. As fast as he accumulated a little money, he invested it in land, buying in 1874, for six thousand dollars, some three hundred and sixty acres comprising a part of one of the Ciénega *ranchos*, to which he moved in 1876. Seven years later, he purchased three hundred and five acres once called the Tom Gray Ranch, now known by the more pretentious name of Arlington Heights. In 1888, three years after he had secured six hundred acres of the Palos Verdes *rancho* near Wilmington, the blacksmith retired and made a grand tour of Europe, revisiting his beloved Isle of Man.

Pat Goodwin was another blacksmith, who reached Los Angeles in 1866 or 1867, shoeing his way, as it were, south from San Francisco, through San José, Whisky Flat and other picturesque places, in the service of A. O. Thorn, one of the stage-line proprietors. He had a shop first on Spring Street, where later the Empire Stables were opened, and afterward at the corner of Second and Spring streets, on the site in time bought by J. E. Hollenbeck.

Still another smith of this period was Henry King (brother of John King, formerly of the Bella Union), who in 1879–80 served two terms as Chief of Police.   Later, A. L. Bath was a well-known wheelwright who located his shop on Spring Street near Third.

In 1866, quite a calamity befell this pueblo: the abandonment by the Government of Drum Barracks.   As this had been one of the chief sources of revenue for our small community, the loss was severely felt, and the immediate effect disastrous.   About the same time, too, Samuel B. Caswell (father of W. M. Caswell, first of the Los Angeles Savings Bank and now of the Security), who had come to Los Angeles the year before, took into partnership John F. Ellis, and under the title of Caswell & Ellis, they started a good-sized grocery and merchandise business; and between the competition that they brought and the reduction of the circulating medium, times with H. Newmark & Company became somewhat less prosperous.   Later, John H. Wright was added to the firm, and it became Caswell, Ellis & Wright.   On September 1st, 1871, the firm dissolved.

CHAPTER XXV

1867–1868

THE reader may already have noted that more than one important move in my life has been decided upon with but little previous deliberation. During August, 1866, while on the way to a family picnic at La Ballona, my brother suggested the advisability of opening an office for H. Newmark & Company in New York; and so quickly had I expressed my willingness to remove there that, when we reached the *rancho*, I announced to my wife that we would leave for the East as soon as we could get ready. Circumstances, however, delayed our going a few months.

My family at this time consisted of my wife and four children; and together on January 29th, 1867, we left San Pedro for New York, by way of San Francisco and Panamá, experiencing frightfully hot weather. Stopping at Acapulco, during Maximilian's revolution, we were summarily warned to keep away from the fort on the hill; while at Panamá yellow fever, spread by travelers recently arrived from South America, caused the Captain to beat a hasty retreat. Sailing on the steamer *Henry Chancey* from Aspinwall, we arrived at New York on the sixth of March; and having domiciled my family comfortably, my next care was to establish an office on the third floor at 31 and 33 Broadway, placing it in charge of M. J. Newmark, who had preceded me to the metropolis a year before. In a short time, I bought a home on Forty-ninth Street, between Sixth and Seventh avenues, then an agreeable residence district. An

359

intense longing to see my old home next induced me to return
to Europe, and I sailed on May 16th for Havre on the steam-
propeller *Union;* the band playing *The Highland Fling* as the
vessel left the pier.   In mid-ocean, the ship's propeller broke,
and she completed the voyage under sail.   Three months later,
I returned on the *Russia.*   The recollection of this journey
gives me real satisfaction; for had I not taken it then, I should
never again have seen my father.   On the twenty-first of the
following November, or a few months after I last bade him
good-bye, he died at Loebau, in the seventy-fifth year of his
age.   My mother had died in the summer of 1859.

It was during this visit that, tarrying for a week in the
brilliant French capital, I saw the Paris Exposition, housed
to a large extent in one immense building in the Champ de
Mars.   I was wonderfully impressed with both the city and the
fair, as well as with the enterprising and artistic French people
who had created it, although I was somewhat disappointed
that, of the fifty thousand or more exhibitors represented, but
seven hundred were Americans.

One little incident may be worth relating.   While I was
standing in the midst of the machinery one day, the *gendarmes*
suddenly began to force the crowd back, and on retreating with
the rest, I saw a group of ladies and gentlemen approaching.
It was soon whispered that they were the Empress Eugénie
and her suite, and that we had been commanded to retire in
order to permit her Majesty to get a better view of a new railroad coach that she desired to inspect.

Not long ago I was reading of a trying ordeal in the life
of Elihu B. Washburne, American Minister to France, who,
having unluckily removed his shoe at a Court dinner, was
compelled to rise with the company on the sudden appearance
of royalty, and to step back with a stockinged foot!   The
incident recalled an experience of my own in London.   I had
ordered from a certain shoemaker in Berlin a pair of patent-
leather gaiters which I wore for the first time when I went to
Covent Garden with an old friend and his wife.   It was a very
warm evening and the performance had not progressed far

before it became evident that the shoes were too small. I was, in fact, nearly overcome with pain, and in my desperation removed the gaiters (when the lights were low), quietly shoved them under the seat and sat out the rest of the performance with a fair degree of comfort and composure. Imagine my consternation, however, when I sought to put the shoes on again and found the operation almost impossible! The curtain fell while I was explaining and apologizing to my friends; and nearly every light was extinguished before I was ready to emerge from the famous opera house and limp to a waiting carriage.

A trifling event also lingers among the memories of this revisit to my native place. While journeying towards Loebau in a stage, I happened to mention that I had married since settling in America; whereupon one of my fellow-passengers inquired whether my wife was white, brown or black?

Major Ben C. Truman was President Johnson's private secretary until he was appointed, in 1866, special agent for the Post Office department on the Pacific Coast. He came to Los Angeles in February, 1867, to look after postal matters in Southern California and Arizona, but more particularly to reëstablish, between Los Angeles and points in New Mexico, the old Butterfield Route which had been discontinued on account of the War. Truman opened post offices at a number of places in Los Angeles County. On December 8th, 1869, the Major married Miss Augusta Mallard, daughter of Judge J. S. Mallard. From July, 1873, until the late summer of 1877, he controlled the Los Angeles *Star*, contributing to its columns many excellent sketches of early life in Southern California, some of which were incorporated in one or more substantial volumes; and of all the pioneer journalists here, it is probable that none have surpassed this affable gentleman in brilliancy and genial, kindly touch. Among Truman's books is an illustrated work entitled *Semi-Tropical California*, dedicated, with a *Dominus vobiscum*, to Phineas Banning and published in San Francisco, 1874; while another volume, issued seven years later, is devoted to *Occidental Sketches*.

A fire, starting in Bell's Block on Los Angeles Street, on July 13th, during my absence from the city, destroyed property to the value of sixty-four thousand dollars; and the same season, S. Lazard & Company moved their dry goods store from Bell's Row to Wolfskill's building on Main Street, opposite the Bella Union hotel.

Germain Pellissier, a Frenchman from the Hautes-Alpes, came to Los Angeles in August, and for twenty-eight years lived at what is now the corner of Seventh and Olive streets. Then the land was in the country; but by 1888, Pellissier had built the block that bears his name.   On settling here, Pellissier went into sheep-raising, scattering stock in Kern and Ventura counties, and importing sheep from France and Australia in order to improve his breed; and from one ram alone in a year, as he demonstrated to some doubting challengers, he clipped sixty-two and a half pounds of wool.

P. Beaudry began to invest in hill property in 1867, at once improving the steep hillside of New High Street, near Sonora Town, which he bought in, at sheriff's sale, for fifty-five dollars. Afterward, Beaudry purchased some twenty acres between Second, Fourth, Charity and Hill streets, for which he paid five hundred and seventeen dollars; and when he had subdivided this into eighty lots, he cleared about thirty thousand dollars. Thirty-nine acres, between Fourth and Sixth, and Pearl and Charity streets, he finally disposed of at a profit, it is said, of over fifty thousand dollars.

John G. Downey having subdivided Nieto's *rancho*, Santa Gertrudis, the little town of Downey, which he named, soon enjoyed such a boom that sleepy Los Angeles began to sit up and take notice.   Among the early residents was E. M. Sanford, a son-in-law of General John W. Gordon, of Georgia.   A short time before the founding of Downey, a small place named Galatin had been started near by, but the flood of 1868 caused our otherwise dry rivers to change their courses, and Galatin was washed away.   This subdividing at once stimulated the coming of land and home-seekers, increased the spirit of enterprise and brought money into circulation.

Soon afterward, Phineas Banning renewed the agitation to connect Los Angeles with Wilmington by rail. He petitioned the County to assist the enterprise, but the larger taxpayers, backed by the over-conservative farmers, still opposed the scheme, tooth and nail, until it finally took all of Banning's influence to carry the project through to a successful termination.

George S. Patton, whose father, Colonel Patton of the Confederate Army, was killed at Winchester, September 19th, 1864, is a nephew of Andrew Glassell and the oldest of four children who came to Los Angeles with their mother and her father, Andrew Glassell, Sr., in 1867. Educated in the public schools of Los Angeles, Patton afterward attended the Virginia Military Institute, where Stonewall Jackson had been a professor, returning to Los Angeles in September, 1877, when he entered the law firm of Glassell, Smith & Patton. In 1884, he married Miss Ruth, youngest daughter of B. D. Wilson, after which he retired to private life. One of Patton's sisters married Tom Brown; another sister became the wife of the popular physician, Dr. W. Le Moyne Wills. In 1871, his mother, relict of Colonel George S. Patton, married her kinsman, Colonel George H. Smith.

John Moran, Sr., conducted a vineyard on San Pedro Street near the present Ninth, in addition to which he initiated the soda-water business here, selling his product at twenty-five cents a bottle. Soda water, however, was too "soft" a drink to find much favor and little was done to establish the trade on a firm basis until 1867, when H. W. Stoll, a German, drove from Colorado to California and organized the Los Angeles Soda Water Works. As soon as he began to manufacture the aerated beverages, Stevens & Wood set up the first soda-water fountain in Los Angeles, on North Spring Street near the Post Office. After that, bubbling water and strangely-colored syrups gained in popularity until, in 1876, quite an expensive fountain was purchased by Preuss & Pironi's drug store, on Spring Street opposite Court. And what is more, they brought in hogsheads from Saratoga what would be difficult to find in all Los Angeles to-day: Congress, Vichy and Kissingen waters. Stoll, by the way, in 1873, married Fräulein Louisa Behn, daughter of John Behn.

An important industry of the late sixties and early seventies was the harvesting of castor beans, then growing wild along the *zanjas*. They were shipped to San Francisco for manufacturing purposes, the oil factories there both supplying the ranchmen with seed and pledging themselves to take the harvest when gathered. In 1867, a small castor-oil mill was set up here.

The *chilicothe*—derived, according to Charles F. Lummis, from the Aztec, *chilacayote*, the wild cucumber, or *echinocystes fabacea*—is the name of a plaything supplied by diversified nature, which grew on large vines, especially along the slope leading down to the river on what is now Elysian Park, and in the neighborhood of the hills adjacent to the Mallard and Nichols places. Four or five of these *chilicothes*, each shaped much like an irregular marble, came in a small burr or gourd; and to secure them for games, the youngsters risked limb, if not life, among the trees and rocks. Small circular holes were sometimes cut into the nuts; and after the meat, which was not edible, had been extracted, the empty shells were strung together like beads and presented, as necklaces and bracelets, to sisters and sweethearts.

Just about the time when I first gazed upon the scattered houses of our little pueblo, the Pacific Railway Expedition, sent out from Washington, prepared and published a tinted lithograph sketch of Los Angeles, now rather rare. In 1867, Stephen A. Rendall, an Englishman of Angora goat fame, who had been here, off and on, as a photographer, devised one of the first large panoramas of Los Angeles, which he sold by advance subscription. It was made in sections; and as the only view of that year extant, it also has become notable as an historical souvenir.

Surrounded by his somewhat pretentious gallery and his mysterious darkroom on the top floor of Temple's new block, V. Wolfenstein also took good, bad and indifferent photographs, having arrived here, perhaps, in the late sixties, and remaining a decade or more, until his return to his native Stockholm where I again met him. He operated with slow wet-plates, and pioneers will remember the inconvenience, almost tantamount to torture, to which the patron was subjected in sitting out an exposure. The children of pioneers, too, will recall his magic, revolving stereoscope, filled with fascinating views at which one peeped through magnifying glasses.

Louis Lewin must have arrived here in the late sixties. Subsequently, he bought out the stationery business of W. J. Brodrick, and P. Lazarus, upon his arrival from Tucson in 1874, entered into partnership with him; Samuel Hellman, as was not generally known at the time, also having an interest in the firm which was styled Louis Lewin & Company. When the Centennial of the United States was celebrated here in 1876, a committee wrote a short historical sketch of Los Angeles; and this was published by Lewin & Company. Now the firm is known as the Lazarus Stationery Company, P. Lazarus[1] being President. Lewin and Lazarus married into families of pioneers: Mrs. Lewin is a daughter of S. Lazard, while Mrs. Lazarus is a daughter of M. Kremer. Lewin died at Manilla on April 5th, 1905.

On November 18th, the Common Council contracted with Jean Louis Sainsevain to lay some five thousand feet of two- and three-inch iron pipe at a cost of about six thousand dollars in scrip; but the great flood of that winter caused Sainsevain so many failures and losses that he transferred his lease, in the spring or summer of 1868, to Dr. J. S. Griffin, Prudent Beaudry, and Solomon Lazard, who completed Sainsevain's contract with the City.

Dr. Griffin and his associates then proposed to lease the water-works from the City for a term of fifty years, but soon changed this to an offer to buy. When the matter came up before the Council for adoption, there was a tie vote, whereupon Murray Morrison, just before resigning as President of the Council, voted in the affirmative, his last official act being

[1] Died on September 30th, 1914.

to sign the franchise. Mayor Aguilar, however, vetoed the ordinance, and then Dr. Griffin and his colleagues came forward with a new proposition. This was to lease the works for a period of thirty years, and to pay fifteen hundred dollars a year in addition to performing certain things promised in the preceding proposition.

At this stage of the negotiations, John Jones made a rival offer, and P. McFadden, who had been an unsuccessful bidder for the Sainsevain lease, tried with Juan Bernard to enter into a twenty-year contract. Notwithstanding these other offers, however, the City authorities thought it best, on July 22d, 1868, to vote the franchise to Dr. Griffin, S. Lazard and P. Beaudry, who soon transferred their thirty-year privileges to a corporation known as the Los Angeles City Water Company, in which they became trustees. Others associated in this enterprise were Eugene Meyer, I. W. Hellman, J. G. Downey, A. J. King, Stephen Hathaway Mott— Tom's brother—W. H. Perry and Charles Lafoon. A spirited fight followed the granting of the thirty-year lease, but the water company came out victorious.

In the late sixties, when the only communities of much consequence in Los Angeles County were Los Angeles, Anaheim and Wilmington, the latter place and Anaheim Landing were the shipping ports of Los Angeles, San Bernardino and Arizona. At that time, or during some of the especially prosperous days of Anaheim, the slough at Anaheim Landing (since filled up by flood) was so formed, and of such depth, that heavily-loaded vessels ran past the warehouse to a considerable distance inland, and there unloaded their cargoes. At the same time the leading Coast steamers began to stop there. Not many miles away was the corn-producing settlement, Gospel Swamp.

I have pointed out the recurring weakness in the wooden pipes laid by Sainsevain and Marchessault. This distressing difficulty, causing, as it did, repeated losses and sharp criticism by the public, has always been regarded as the motive for ex-Mayor Marchessault's death on January 20th, when he committed suicide in the old City Council room.

Jacob Loew arrived in America in 1865 and spent three years in New York before he came to California in 1868. Clerking for a while in San Francisco, he went to the Old Town of San Diego, then to Galatin, and in 1872 settled in Downey; and there, in conjunction with Jacob Baruch, afterward of Haas, Baruch & Company, he conducted for years the principal general merchandise business of that section. On coming to Los Angeles in 1883, he bought, as I have said, the Deming Mill now known as the Capitol Mills. Two years later, on the second of August, he was married to my daughter Emily.

Dr. Joseph Kurtz, once a student at Giessen, arrived in Los Angeles on February 3d, with a record for hospital service at Baltimore during the Civil War, having been induced to come here by the druggist, Adolf Junge, with whom for a while he had some association. Still later he joined Dr. Rudolph Eichler in conducting a pharmacy. For some time prior to his graduation in medicine, in 1872, Dr. Kurtz had an office in the Lanfranco Building. For many years, he was surgeon to the Southern Pacific Railroad Company and consulting physician to the Santa Fé Railroad Company, and he also served as President of the Los Angeles College Clinical Association. I shall have further occasion to refer to this good friend. Dr. Carl Kurtz is distinguishing himself in the profession of his father.

Hale fellow well met and always in favor with a large circle, was my Teutonic friend, Lewis Ebinger, who, after coming to Los Angeles in 1868, turned clay into bricks. Perhaps this also recalled the days of his childhood when he made pies of the same material; but be that as it may, Lewis in the early seventies made his first venture in the bakery business, opening shop on North Spring Street. In the bustling Boom days when real estate men saw naught but the sugar-coating, Ebinger, who had moved to elaborate quarters in a building at the southwest corner of Spring and Third streets, was dispensing cream puffs and other baked delicacies to an enthusiastic and unusually large clientele. But since everybody then had money, or thought that he had, one such place was not enough to satisfy the ravenous speculators; with the result that John Koster was soon conducting a similar establishment on Spring Street near Second, while farther north, on Spring Street near First, the Vienna Bakery ran both Lewis and John a merry race.

Dr. L. W. French, one of the organizers of the Odontological Society of Southern California, also came to Los Angeles in 1868 —so early that he found but a couple of itinerant dentists, who made their headquarters here for a part of the year and then hung out their shingles in other towns or at remote ranches.

One day in the spring of 1868, while I was residing in New York City, I received a letter from Phineas Banning, accompanied by a sealed communication, and reading about as follows:

DEAR HARRIS:
Herewith I enclose to you a letter of the greatest importance, addressed to Miss Mary Hollister (daughter, as you know, of Colonel John H. Hollister), who will soon be on her way to New York, and who may be expected to arrive there by the next steamer.

This letter I beg you to deliver to Miss Hollister personally, immediately upon her arrival in New York, thereby obliging
Yours obediently,
(Signed)   PHINEAS BANNING.

The steamer referred to had not yet arrived, and I lost no time in arranging that I should be informed, by the company's agents, of the vessel's approach, as soon as it was sighted. This notification came, by the by, through a telegram received before daylight one bitterly cold morning, when I was told that the ship would soon be at the dock; and as quickly as I could, I procured a carriage, hastened to the wharf and, before any passengers had landed, boarded the vessel. There I sought out Miss Hollister, a charming lady, and gave her the mysterious missive.

I thought no more of this matter until I returned to Los Angeles when, welcoming me back, Banning told me that the letter I had had the honor to deliver aboard ship in New York contained nothing less than a proposal of marriage, his solicitation of Miss Hollister's heart and hand!

One reason why the Bella Union played such an important *rôle* in the early days of Los Angeles, was because there was no such thing as a high-class restaurant; indeed, the first recollection I have of anything like a satisfactory place is that of Louis Vielle, known by some as French Louis and nicknamed by others Louis *Gordo*, or Louis the Fat. Vielle came to Los Angeles from Mexico, a fat, jolly little French caterer, not much over five feet in height and weighing, I should judge, two hundred and fifty pounds; and this great bulk, supported as it was by two peg-like legs, rendered his appearance truly comical. His blue eyes, light hair and very rosy cheeks accentuated his ludicrous figure. Louis, who must have been about fifty-four years of age when I first met him, then conducted his establishment in John Lanfranco's building on Main Street, between Commercial and Requena; from which fact the place was known as the Lanfranco, although it subsequently received the more suggestive title, the What Cheer House. Louis was an acknowledged expert in his art, but he did not always choose to exert himself. Nevertheless his lunches, for which he charged fifty or seventy-five cents, according to the number of dishes served, were well thought of, and it is certain that Los Angeles had never had so good a restaurant before. At one time, our caterer's partner was a man named Frederico Guiol, whom he later bought out. Louis could never master the English language, and to his last day spoke with a strong French accent. His florid cheeks were due to the enormous quantity of claret consumed both at and between meals. He would mix it with soup, dip his bread into it and otherwise absorb it in large quantities. Indeed, at the time of his fatal illness, while he was living with the family of Don Louis Sainsevain, it was assumed that over-indulgence in wine was the cause. Be that as it may, he sickened and died, passing away at the Lanfranco home in 1872. Vielle had prospered, but during his sickness he spent largely of his means. After his death, it was discovered that he had been in the habit of hiding his coin in little niches in the wall of his room and in other secret places; and only a small amount of the money was found.

A few of the real pioneers recollect Louis *Gordo* as one who added somewhat to the comfort of those who then patronized restaurants; while others will associate him with the introduction here of the first French dolls, to take the place of rag-babies.

Both Judge Robert Maclay Widney and Dr. Joseph P. Widney, the surgeon, took up their residence in Los Angeles in 1868. R. M. Widney set out from Ohio about 1855 and, having spent two years in exploring the Rockies, worked for a while in the Sacramento Valley, where he chopped wood for a living, and finally reached Los Angeles with a small trunk and about a hundred dollars in cash. Here he opened a law and real-estate office and started printing the *Real Estate Advertiser*. Dr. Widney crossed the Continent in 1862, spent two years as surgeon in the United States Army in Arizona, after which he proceeded to Los Angeles and soon became one of the charter members of the Los Angeles Medical Society, exerting himself in particular to extend Southern California's climatic fame.

I have spoken of the ice procured from the San Bernardino mountains in rather early days, but I have not said that in summer, when we most needed the cooling commodity, there was none to be had. The enterprising firm of Queen & Gard, the first to arrange for regular shipments of Truckee River ice in large quantities by steamer from the North, announced their purpose late in March, 1868, of building an ice house on Main Street; and about the first of April they began delivering daily, in a large and substantial wagon especially constructed for that purpose and which, for the time being, was an object of much curiosity. Liberal support was given the enterprise; and perhaps it is no wonder that the perspiring editor of the *News*, going into ecstasies because of a cooling sample or two deposited in his office, said, in the next issue of his paper:

The founding of an ice depot is another step forward in the progress that is to make us a great City. We have Water and Gas, and now we are to have the additional luxury of Ice!

Banning's fight for the Los Angeles & San Pedro Railroad has been touched upon more than once. Tomlinson, his rival,

Dr. Truman H. Rose

Andrew Glassell

Dr. Vincent Gelcich

Charles E. Miles, in Uniform of 38's

Facsimile of Stock Certificate, Pioneer Oil Co.

American Bakery, Jake Kuhrts's Building, about 1880

opposed the project; but his sudden death, about two weeks before the election in 1868, removed one of the serious obstacles. When the vote was taken, on March 24th, as to whether the City and County should bond themselves to encourage the building of the railroad, seven hundred votes were cast in favor of, and six hundred and seventy-two votes against, the undertaking, leaving Banning and his associates ready to go ahead. By the way, as a reminder of the quondam vogue of Spanish here, it may be noted that the proclamation regarding the railroad, published in 1868, was printed in both English and Spanish.

On May 16th, Henry Hamilton, whose newspaper, the *Star*, during part of the War period had been suspended through the censorship of the National Government, again made his bow to the Los Angeles public, this time in a half-facetious leader in which he referred to the "late unpleasantness" in the family circle. Hamilton's old-time vigor was immediately recognized, but not his former disposition to attack and criticize.

Dr. H. S. Orme, once President of the State Board of Health of California, arrived in Los Angeles on July 4th and soon became as prominent in Masonic as in medical circles. Dr. Harmon, an early successor to Drs. Griffin and Den, first settled here in 1868, although he had previously visited California in 1853.

Carl Felix Heinzeman, at one time a well-known chemist and druggist, emigrated from Germany in 1868 and came direct to Los Angeles, where after succeeding J. B. Saunders & Company, he continued, in the Lanfranco Building, what grew to be the largest drug store south of San Francisco. Heinzeman died on April 29th, 1903. About the same period, a popular apothecary shop on Main Street, near the Plaza, was known as Chevalier's. In the seventies, when hygiene and sanitation were given more attention, a Welshman named Hughes conducted a steam-bath establishment on Main Street, almost opposite the Baker Block, and the first place of its kind in the city.

Charles F. Harper[1] of Mississippi, and the father of ex-

[1] Died on September 13th, 1915.

Mayor Harper, in 1868 opened with R. H. Dalton a hardware store in the Allen Block, corner of Spring and Temple streets, thus forerunning Coulter & Harper, Harper & Moore, Harper, Reynolds & Company and the Harper-Reynolds Company.

Michel Lèvy, an Alsatian, arrived in San Francisco when but seventeen years of age, and after various experiences in California and Nevada towns, he came to Los Angeles in 1868, soon establishing, with Joe Coblentz, the wholesale liquor house of Lèvy & Coblentz. The latter left here in 1879, and Lèvy continued under the firm name of M. Lèvy & Company until his death in 1905.

Anastácio Cárdenas, a dwarf who weighed but one and a half pounds when born, came to Los Angeles in 1867 and soon appeared before the public as a singer and dancer. He carried a sword and was popularly dubbed "General." A brother, Ruperto, long lived here.

When the Canal & Reservoir Company was organized with George Hansen as President and J. J. Warner as Secretary, P. Beaudry contributed heavily to construct a twenty-foot dam across the *cañon*, below the present site of Echo Park, and a ditch leading down to Pearl Street. This first turned attention to the possibilities in the hill-lands to the West; and in return, the City gave to the company a large amount of land, popularly designated as canal and reservoir property.

In 1868, when there was still not a three-story house in Los Angeles, James Alvinza Hayward, a San Franciscan, joined John G. Downey in providing one hundred thousand dollars with which to open, in the old Downey Block on the site of the Temple adobe, the first bank in Los Angeles, under the firm name of Hayward & Company. The lack of business afforded this enterprise short shrift and they soon retired. In July of the same year, I. W. Hellman, William Workman, F. P. F. Temple and James R. Toberman started a bank, with a capital of one hundred and twenty-five thousand dollars, under the title of Hellman, Temple & Company, Hellman becoming manager.

I do not remember when postal lock-boxes were first brought into use, but I do recollect that in the late sixties Postmaster

Clarke had a great deal of trouble collecting quarterly rents, and that he finally gave notice that boxes held by delinquents would thereafter be nailed up.

A year or two after the Burtons had established themselves here, came another pedagogue in the person of W. B. Lawlor, a thick-set, bearded man with a flushed complexion, who opened a day-school called the Lawlor Institute; and after the Burtons left here to settle at Portland, Oregon, where Burton became headmaster of an academy for advanced students, many of his former pupils attended Lawlor's school. The two institutions proved quite different in type: the Burton training had tended strongly to languages and literature, while Lawlor, who was an adept at short-cut methods of calculation, placed more stress on arithmetic and commercial education. Burton, who returned to Los Angeles, has been for years a leading member of the *Times* editorial staff, and *Burton's Book on California and its Sunlit Skies* is one of this author's contributions to Pacific Coast literature; his wife, however, died many years ago. Lawlor, who was President of the Common Council in 1880, is also dead.

The most popular piano-teacher of about that time was Professor Van Gilpin.

William Pridham came to Los Angeles in August, having been transferred from the San Francisco office of Wells Fargo & Company, in whose service as pony rider, clerk at Austin, Nevada, and at Sacramento, and cashier in the Northern metropolis he had been for some ten years. Here he succeeded Major J. R. Toberman, when the latter, after long service, resigned; and with a single office-boy, at one time little Joe Binford, he handled all the business committed to the company's charge. John Osborn was the outside expressman. Then most of the heavy express matter from San Francisco was carried by steamers, but letters and limited packages of moment were sent by stage. With the advent of railroads, Pridham was appointed by Wells Fargo & Company Superintendent of the Los Angeles district. On June 12th, 1880, he married Miss Mary Esther, daughter of Colonel John O. Wheeler, and later moved to Alameda. Now, after fifty-one years of association with the express business, Pridham still continues to be officially connected with the Wells Fargo company.

Speaking of that great organization, reminds me that it conducted for years a mail-carrying business. Three-cent stamped envelopes, imprinted with Wells Fargo & Company's name, were sold to their patrons for ten cents each; and to compensate for this bonus, the Company delivered the letters entrusted to them perhaps one to two hours sooner than did the Government.

This recalls to me a familiar experience on the arrival of the mail from the North. Before the inauguration of a stage-line, the best time in the transmission of mail matter between San Francisco and Los Angeles was made by water, and Wells Fargo messengers sailed with the steamers. Immediately upon the arrival of the boat at San Pedro, the messenger boarded the stage, and as soon as he reached Los Angeles, pressed on to the office of the Company, near the Bella Union, where he delivered his bagful of letters. The steamer generally got in by five o'clock in the morning; and many a time, about seven, have I climbed Signal or Pound Cake Hill—higher in those days than now, and affording in clear weather a view of both ocean and the smoke of the steamer—upon whose summit stood a house, used as a signal station, and there watched for the rival stages, the approach of which was indicated by clouds of dust. I would then hurry with many others to the Express Company's office where, as soon as the bag was emptied, we would all help ourselves unceremoniously to the mail.

In August, General Edward Bouton, a Northern Army officer, came to Los Angeles and soon had a sheep ranch on Boyle Heights—a section then containing but two houses; and two years later he camped where Whittier now lies. In 1874, he bought land for pasture in the San Jacinto Valley, and for years owned the ocean front at Alamitos Bay from Devil's Gate to the Inlet, boring artesian wells there north of Long Beach.

Louis Robidoux, who had continued to prosper as a *ranchero*, died in 1868 at the age of seventy-seven years.

With the usual flourish of spades, if not of trumpets, ground was broken for the Los Angeles & San Pedro Railroad at Wilmington on September 19th, and toward the end of November, the rails had been laid about a mile out from Wilmington.

The last contract for carrying the Overland Mail was given to Wells Fargo & Company on October 1st and pledged a round remuneration of one million, seven hundred and fifty thousand dollars per annum, while it also permitted passengers and freight to be transported; but the Company came to have a great deal of competition. Phineas Banning, for example, had a stage-line between Los Angeles and Yuma, in addition to which mail and passengers were carried in buckboards, large wagons and jerkies. Moreover there was another stage-line between Tucson and El Paso, and rival stage-lines between El Paso and St. Louis; and in consequence, the Butterfield service was finally abandoned.

This American vehicle, by the by, the jerky, was so named for the very good reason that, as the wagon was built without springs, it *jerked* the rider around unmercifully. Boards were laid across the wagon-box or bed for seats, accommodating four passengers; and some space was provided in the back for baggage. To maintain one's position in the bumping, squeaking vehicle at all, was difficult; while to keep one's place on the seat approached the impossible.

Of the various Los Angeles roadways in 1868, West Sixth Street was most important in its relation to travel. Along this highway the daily Overland stages entered and departed from the city; and by this route came all the Havilah, Lone Pine, Soledad and Owens River trade, as well as that of the Ballona and Ciénega districts. Sixth Street also led to the Fair Grounds, and over its none too even surface dashed most of the sports and gallants on their way to the race course.

I have said that I returned to New York, in 1867, presumably for permanent residence. Soon after I left Los Angeles, however, Samuel Cohn became desperately ill, and the sole management of H. Newmark & Company suddenly devolved

on Sam's brother Kaspare.   This condition of affairs grew so
bad that my return to Los Angeles became imperative.   Accordingly, leaving my family, I took passage on October 31st,
1868, for San Francisco, and returned to Los Angeles without
delay.   Then I wired my wife to start with the children for the
Coast, and to have the furniture, including a Chickering grand
piano, just purchased, shipped after them; and when they
arrived, we once more took possession of the good old adobe
on Main Street, where we lived contentedly until 1874.   This
piano, by the way, which came by freight around Cape Horn,
was one of the first instruments of the kind seen here, John
Schumacher having previously bought one.   While we were
living in New York, Edward J. Newmark, my wife's brother,
died here on February 17th, 1868.

Before I left for New York, hardly anything had been done,
in subdividing property, save perhaps by the Lugos and
Downey, and at Anaheim and Wilmington.   During the time
that I was away, however, newspapers and letters from home
indicated the changes going on here; and I recall what an
impression all this made upon me.   On my way down from
San Francisco on Captain Johnson's *Orizaba* in December—
about the same time that the now familiar locomotive *San
Gabriel* reached Wilmington—land-agents were active and
people were talking a great deal about these subdivisions; and
by the time I reached Los Angeles I, too, was considerably
stirred up over the innovations and as soon as possible
after my return hastened out to see the change.   The improvements were quite noticeable, and among other alterations
surprising me were the houses people had begun to build on the
approaches to the western hills.   I was also to learn that
there was a general demand for property all over the city,
Colonel Charles H. Larrabee, City Attorney in 1868, especially
having bought several hundred feet on Spring and Fort streets.
Later, I heard of the experiences of other Angeleños aboard
ship who were deluged with circulars advertising prospective
towns.

To show the provincial character of Los Angeles fifty years

ago, I will add an anecdote or two. While I was in New York, members of my family reported by letter, as a matter of extraordinary interest, the novelty of a silver name-plate on a neighboring front door; and when I was taken to inspect it, a year later, I saw the legend, still novel:

Mr. and Mrs. Eugene Meyer

In the metropolis I had found finger-bowls in common use, and having brought back with me such a supply as my family would be likely to need, I discovered that it had actually fallen to my lot to introduce these desirable conveniences into Los Angeles.

William Ferguson was an arrival of 1868, having come to settle up the business of a brother and remaining to open a livery stable on North Main Street near the Plaza, which he conducted for ten years. Investing in water company stock, Ferguson abandoned his stable to make water-pipes, a couple of years later, perhaps, than J. F. Holbrook had entered the same field. Success enabled Ferguson to build a home at 303 South Hill Street, where he found himself the only resident south of Third.

This manufacture here of water pipe recalls a cordial acquaintance with William Lacy, Sr., an Englishman, who was interested with William Rowland in developing the Puente oil fields. His sons, William, Jr., and Richard H., originators of the Lacy Manufacturing Company, began making pipe and tanks a quarter of a century ago.

C. R. Rinaldi started a furniture business here in 1868, opening his store almost opposite the Stearns's home on North Main Street. Before long he disposed of an interest to Charles Dotter, and then, I think, sold out to I. W. Lord and moved to the neighborhood of the San Fernando Mission. About the same time, Sidney Lacey, who arrived in 1870 and was a popular clerk with the pioneer carpet and wall-paper house of Smith & Walter, commenced what was to be a long association with this establishment. In 1876, C. H. Bradley bought out Lord, and the firm of Dotter & Bradley, so well known to householders of forty years ago, came into existence.   In 1884, H. H. Markham (soon to be Congressman and then Governor of the State), with General E. P. Johnson bought this concern and organized the Los Angeles Furniture Company, whose affairs since 1910, (when her husband died), have been conducted by the President, Mrs. Katherine Fredericks.

Conrad Hafen, a German-Swiss, reached Los Angeles in December, 1868, driving a six-horse team and battered wagon with which he had braved the privations of Death Valley; and soon he rented a little vineyard, two years later buying for the same purpose considerable acreage on what is now Central Avenue.   Rewarded for his husbandry with some affluence, Hafen built both the old Hafen House and the new on South Hill Street, once a favorite resort for German arrivals.   He retired in 1905.

CHAPTER XXVI

THE CERRO GORDO MINES

1869

IT was early in 1869 that I was walking down Spring Street one day and saw a crowd at the City Hall. On a large box stood Mayor Joel H. Turner, and just as I arrived a man leaning against the adobe wall called out, "Seven dollars!" The Mayor then announced the bid—for an auction was in progress—"Seven dollars once, seven dollars twice, seven dollars three times!" and as he raised his hand to conclude the sale, I called out, "A half!" This I did in a spirit of fun; in fact, I did not even know what was being offered! "Seven dollars fifty once, seven dollars fifty twice, seven dollars fifty three times, and sold—to Harris Newmark!" called the Mayor. I then inquired what I had bought, and was shown the location of about twenty acres, a part of nine hundred being sold by the City at prices ranging from five to ten dollars an acre.

The piece purchased was west of the city limits, and I kept it until 1886 when I had almost forgotten that I was the owner. Then George Williamson, one of the first salesmen of H. Newmark & Company, who became a boomer of the period, bought it from me for ten thousand dollars and resold it within two weeks for fourteen thousand, the Sunset Oil Company starting there, as the land was within what was known as the oil district. Since the opening of streets in all directions, I have lost trace of this land, but incline to the belief that it lies in the immediate vicinity of the Wilshire district.

My experience reminds me of Colonel John O. Wheeler's

investment in fifty or sixty acres at what is now Figueroa and Adams streets. Later, going to San Francisco as a Customs officer, he forgot about his purchase until one day he received a somewhat surprising offer.

On January 1st, A. J. King and R. H. Offutt began to publish a daily edition of the *News*, hitherto a semi-weekly, making it strongly Democratic. There was no Sunday issue and twelve dollars was the subscription. On October 16th, Offutt sold his interest to Alonzo Waite, and the firm became King & Waite. In another year King had retired.

How modest was the status of the Post Office in 1869 may be gathered from the fact that the Postmaster had only one assistant, a boy, both together receiving fourteen hundred dollars in greenbacks, worth but a thousand dollars in gold.

Henry Hammel, for years connected with the Bella Union, and a partner named Bremerman leased the United States Hotel on February 1st from Louis Mesmer; and in March, John King succeeded Winston & King as manager of the Bella Union. King died in December, 1871.

In the winter of 1868–69, when heavy rains seriously interfered with bringing in the small supply of lumber at San Pedro, a coöperative society was proposed, to insure the importation each summer of enough supplies to tide the community over during the wintry weather. Over one hundred persons, it was then estimated, had abandoned building, and many others were waiting for material to complete fences and repairs.

Thanks to Contractor H. B. Tichenor's vigor in constructing the Los Angeles & San Pedro Railroad, public interest in the venture, by the beginning of 1869, had materially increased. In January, a vessel arrived with a locomotive and a steam pile-driver; and a few days later a schooner sailed into San Pedro with ties, sleepers and rails enough for three miles of the track. Soon, also, the locomotive was running part of the way. The wet winter made muddy roads, and this led to the proposal to lay the tracks some eight or ten miles in the direction of Los Angeles, and there to transfer the freight to wagons.

Stearns Hall and the Plaza were amusement places in 1869. At the latter, in January, the so-called *Paris Exposition Circus* held forth; while Joe Murphy and Maggie Moore, who had just favored the passengers on the *Orizaba*, on coming south from San Francisco, with a show, trod the hall's more classic boards.

Ice a quarter of an inch thick was formed here for several days during the third week in January, and butchers found it so difficult to secure fat cattle that good beef advanced to sixteen and a quarter cents a pound.

On January 20th, I purchased from Eugene Meyer the southern half of lots three and four in block five, fronting on Fort Street between Second and Third, formerly owned by William Buffum and J. F. Burns. Meyer had paid one thousand dollars for one hundred and twenty feet front and three hundred and thirty feet depth; and when I bought half of this piece for one thousand dollars, it was generally admitted that I had paid all that it was worth.

Isaac Lankershim—father of J. B. Lankershim and Mrs. I. N. Van Nuys—who first visited California in 1854, came from San Francisco in 1869 and bought, for one hundred and fifteen thousand dollars, part of Andrés Pico's San Fernando *rancho*, which he stocked with sheep. Levi Strauss & Company, Scholle Brothers, L. and M. Sachs & Company of San Francisco and others, were interested in this partnership, then known as the San Fernando Farm Association; but Lankershim was in control until about one year later, when Isaac Newton Van Nuys arrived from Monticello, where he had been merchandising, and was put permanently in charge of the ranch. At this period Lankershim lived there, for he had not yet undertaken milling in Los Angeles. A little later, Lankershim and Van Nuys successfully engaged in the raising of wheat, cultivating nearly sixty thousand acres, and consigning some of their harvests to Liverpool. This fact recalls a heavy loss in the spring of 1881, when the *Parisian*, which left Wilmington under Captain Reaume, foundered at sea with nearly two hundred and fifty tons of wheat and about seventy-five tons of flour belonging to them.

J. B. Lankershim, owner of the well-known hotel bearing his name, after the death of his father made some very important investments in Los Angeles real estate, including the northwest corner of Broadway and Seventh Street, now occupied by the building devoted to Bullock's department store.

M. N. Newmark, a nephew of mine and President of the Newmark Grain Company, arrived in 1869, and clerked for H. Newmark & Company until 1871, in which year he established a partnership with S. Grand in Compton, selling general merchandise. This partnership lasted until 1878, when Newmark bought out Grand. He finally disposed of the business in 1889 and, with D. K. Edwards, organized the firm of Newmark & Edwards. In 1895 Edwards sold out his interest.

Victor Ponet, a native of Belgium, and once Belgian Consul here, while traveling around the world, landed in California in 1867 and two years later came to Los Angeles. Attracted by the climate and Southern California's possible future, Ponet settled here, engaging first in the pioneer manufacture and importation of mirrors and picture frames; and before his retirement to live in Sherman, he had had experience both as undertaker and banker. [1]

In 1869, General W. S. Rosecrans came south in the interest of the proposed San Diego & Gila Railroad, never constructed. The General, as a result, took up land around Sausal Redondo, and there by the summer of 1869 so many people (who insisted that Rosecrans had appropriated public land) had squatted, that he was put to no end of trouble in ejecting them.

Though I have witnessed most of the progress in Southern California, it is still difficult to realize that so much could have been accomplished within the life-time of one man. During 1868–69 only twenty-two hundred boxes of oranges were shipped from Los Angeles, while the Southern counties' crop of oranges and lemons for 1913–14 is estimated, I am told, at about twelve million boxes!

Due to the eight-day shindy marking the celebration of the Chinese New Year, demand for a more concentrated rumpus

[1] Died, February 9th, 1914.

was voiced in February, 1869, threatening an agitation against John Chinaman.

The same month, residents, wishing a school in which German should be taught, and a gymnasium, petitioned the Common Council to acquire a lot in New High Street for the purpose.

About 1869, the Los Angeles Social Club which, to the best of my recollection, was the first of its kind in the city, was organized, with headquarters in the earliest building erected by I. W. Hellman, at the northwest corner of Los Angeles and Commercial streets. Among other pioneer members were Captain Cameron E. Thom, Tom Mott, Eugene Meyer, Sam and Charles Prager, Tom Rowan, I. W. and H. W. Hellman, S. Lazard, W. J. Brodrick, John Jones, Kaspare Cohn, A. C. Chauvin, M. and J. L. Morris, Leon Loeb, Sam Meyer, Dr. F. A. McDougal, B. Cohn and myself. Somewhat later, the Club moved to the east side of Los Angeles Street, between Commercial and Aliso. Still later, it dissolved; and although it did not become the direct ancestor of any of the several well-known social organizations in the Los Angeles of to-day, I feel that it should be mentioned as having had the honor of being their precursor and model.

Speaking of social organizations, I may say that several Los Angeles clubs were organized in the early era of sympathy, tolerance and good feeling, when the individual was appreciated at his true worth and before the advent of men whose bigotry has sown intolerance and discord, and has made a mockery of both religion and professed ideals.

It must have been early in the sixties that Alexander Bell sold the southern end of his property to H. Heinsch, the saddler. On February 23d, 1869, the directors of the San Pedro Railroad selected the Mike Madigan lot on Alameda Street, on a part of which the owner was conducting a livery-stable, as the site for the depot in Los Angeles; and Heinsch having allowed the authorities to cut through his property, the extension of Commercial and Requena streets eastward from Los Angeles to Alameda was hastened.

Late on February 14th, the news was circulated of a shocking tragedy in the billiard saloon of the Lafayette Hotel, and at once aroused intense regret, affecting, as the affair did, the standing and happiness of two well-known Los Angeles families. About eight o'clock, Charles Howard, a young lawyer of prominence and a son of Volney E. Howard, met Daniel B. Nichols, son of the ex-Mayor; and some dispute between them having reached its climax, both parties drew weapons and fired. Howard was killed and Nichols wounded, though not fatally, as was at first thought. The tragedy—the cause of which was never generally known—made a profound impression.

The work of extending water mains along Fort, Spring and other streets progressed steadily until the Los Angeles Water Company struck a snag which again demonstrated the city's dependence. Difficulty in coupling pipes called a halt, and the management had to send all the way to San Francisco for a *complete set of plumbers' tools!*

In the spring, Tileston, Emery & Company, a Los Angeles and San Gabriel firm, brought south the first steam separator seen here and took contracts to thrash the farmers' grain. On June 3d they started the machine, and many persons went out to see it work. Among features pointed out were precautions against fire from the engine, which the contractors declared made "everything perfectly safe."

From its inception, Wilmington sought, in one way or another, to rival Los Angeles, and in April threw down the gauntlet. A. A. Polhamus, a workshop engineer of the Los Angeles & San Pedro Railroad, (in 1887, a manufacturer of straw wrapping paper somewhere between here and Wilmington,) had built a velocipede; and no sooner was it noised about than John Goller set to work to eclipse the achievement. About one o'clock, therefore, on April 25th one of Goller's apprentices suddenly appeared ready to make the first experiment. The streets were soon crowded and interest was at fever heat. The young fellow straddled the wheels, moved about half a block, and then, at the junction of Main and Spring streets, executed a first-class somersault! Immediately, however, other intrepid ones tried their skill, and the velocipede

Loebau Market Place, near the House in which Harris Newmark was Born

Street in Loebau, Showing (right) Remnant of ancient City Wall

Robert M. Widney

Dr. Joseph Kurtz

Isaac N. Van Nuys

Abraham Haas

was voted a successful institution of our young and progressive city.

By the first week in May, the velocipede craze had spread, crowds congregating daily on Main Street to see the antics of the boys; and soon H. F. Laurence announced the opening in Stearns's Hall, on May 14th, of a Velocipede School, where free instruction would be given: afternoons to *ladies* and evenings to men; and to further stimulate interest, Laurence announced a raffle on May 15th of "a splendid velocipede." By May 22d, J. Eastman had obtained permission of the Common Council to build a velocipede track on the historic old Plaza; but evidently he did not make use of the privilege, for a newspaper writer was soon giving vent to the following sarcasm:

Our City Fathers tried to make a little coin by leasing the Plaza as a velocipede circle or square; but, so far, the velocipedist has failed to connect. I dare say the cost of cleaning up the place of weeds backed the poor soul out!

It happened in 1869 that Judson, the financier, and Belshaw, a practical miner, began working their lead mines in Cerro Gordo, in the Owens River country; and as the handling of the ore necessitated a great many wagons, Remi Nadeau obtained the contract for the transportation of the ore brought down to Wilmington and then shipped by boat to San Francisco. Remi had returned here about 1866, after having been in San Francisco for four or five years; and eventually he built the Nadeau Hotel at the corner of Spring and First streets, where A. Bouelle, father of Frank A. Bouelle, had formerly kept a little grocery store in an adobe. This ore was loaded on to very large wagons, each drawn on level stretches by twelve or fourteen mules, but requiring as many as twenty or more mules while crossing the San Fernando Mountains—always regarded as one of the worst places on the route. In order not to return with empty wagons, Nadeau purchased supplies of every description, which he sold to people along the route;

25

and in this way he obtained the best financial results. This was about the same time that Victor Beaudry (Prudent's brother, who came in 1855, to mine at San Gabriel) opened a store at Camp Independence, Inyo County, and became a stockholder in the Cerro Gordo mines. In the early eighties, Beaudry was interested with his brother in local real estate movements. He died in Montreal in 1888.

After a time, the mines yielded so much ore that Nadeau found himself short of transportation facilities; but with the assistance of Judson & Belshaw, as well as H. Newmark & Company, he was enabled to increase his capacity until he operated thirty-two teams. Los Angeles was then the southern terminus of his operations, although, during the building of the numerous Southern Pacific tunnels, his headquarters were removed to San Fernando, and still later, on the completion of the railroad, to Mojave. Nadeau's assistant, Willard G. Halstead, son-in-law of H. K. W. Bent, handled most of the business when Nadeau was absent; A. E. Lott was foreman of teams and continually rode up and down the line of operations; while Thomas O'Brien was station-agent at Cerro Gordo. The contract had been very profitable to Judson & Belshaw; yet when the agreement expired on January 1st, 1872, they wished to renew it at a lower figure. Nadeau, believing that no one else could do the work satisfactorily, refused the new terms offered; whereupon Judson & Belshaw entered into an arrangement with William Osborn, a liveryman, who owned a few teams.

The season of 1871–72 was by no means a good one and barley was high, involving a great expense to Nadeau in feeding four or five hundred animals; and right there arose his chief difficulty. He was in debt to H. Newmark & Company and therefore proposed that he should turn his outfit over to us; but as we had unlimited confidence both in his integrity and in his ability, we prevailed on him to keep and use his equipment to the best advantage. The suggestion was a fortunate one, for just at this time large deposits of borax were discovered in the mountains at Wordsworth, Nevada, and Nadeau commenced operations there with every promise of success. In his work of hauling between Cerro Gordo and Los Angeles, Nadeau had always been very regular, his teams with rare exceptions arriving and leaving on schedule time; and even when, occasionally, a wagon did break down, the pig-lead would be unloaded without delay, tossed to the side of the trail and left there for the next train; a method that was perfectly safe, since thieves never disturbed the property. Osborn, on the other hand, soon proved uncertain and unreliable, his wagons frequently breaking down and causing other accidents and delays. To protect themselves, Judson & Belshaw were compelled to terminate their contract with him and reopen negotiations with Nadeau; but the latter then rejected their advances unless they would buy a half-interest in his undertaking and put up one hundred and fifty thousand dollars for the construction and maintenance of the numerous stations that had become necessary for the proper development of his business. Nadeau also made it a condition that H. Newmark & Company be paid. The stations already constructed or proposed were Mud Springs, Lang's Station, Mojave, Red Rock, Panamint, Indian Wells, Little Lake, Haiwee Meadows and Cartago. Before these were built, the teamsters camped in the open, carrying with them the provisions necessary for man and beast. Cartago was on the south side of Owens Lake, Cerro Gordo being on the north side, eighteen miles opposite; and between these points the miniature side-wheeler *Bessie*, of but twenty tons capacity, operated.

An interesting fact or two in connection with Owens Lake may be recorded here. Its water was so impregnated with borax and soda that no animal life could be sustained. In the winter, the myriads of wild duck were worth talking about; but after they had remained near the lake for but a few days, they were absolutely unpalatable. The teamsters and miners operating in the vicinity were in the habit of sousing their clothes in the lake for a few minutes, and when dried, the garments were found to be as clean as if they had passed through the most perfect laundry. Even a handful of the water applied to the hair would produce a magnificent lather and shampoo.

Judson & Belshaw were compelled to accept Nadeau's terms; and Nadeau returned from Nevada, organized in 1873 the Cerro Gordo Freighting Company, and operated more extensively than ever before until he withdrew, perhaps five years after the completion of the Southern Pacific Railroad and just before the petering out of the Cerro Gordo Mines. In their palmy days, these deposits were the most extensive lead-producers of California; and while the output might not have been so remarkable in comparison with those of other lead mines in the world, something like eighty-five to ninety bars, each weighing about one hundred pounds, were produced there daily. Most of this was shipped, as I have said, to San Francisco; and for a while, at least, from there to Swansea, Wales.

Nadeau at one time was engaged in the industry of raising sugar-beets at the Nadeau *rancho*, near Florence, now Nadeau Station; and then he attempted to refine sugar. But it was bad at best, and the more sugar one put in coffee, the blacker the coffee became.

On April 24th, 1869, under Mayor Joel Turner's administration, the Los Angeles Board of Education came into existence.

In the early sixties, the City authorities promised to set out trees at the Plaza, providing neighboring property-owners would fence in the place; but even though Governor Downey supplied the fence, no trees were planted, and it was not until the spring of 1869 that any grew on the public square. This loud demand for trees was less for the sake of the usual benefits than to hide the ugliness of the old water tank.

On May 9th, F. G. Walther issued the first number of the *Los Angeles Chronik*, a German weekly journal that survived scarcely three months.

The tenth of May was another red-letter day for the Pacific Coast, rejoicing, as it did, in the completion of the Central Pacific at Promontory Point in Utah. There, with a silver hammer, Governor Stanford drove the historic gold spike into a tie of polished California laurel, thus consummating the vast work on the first trans-continental railroad. This event recalls the fact that, in the railway's construction, Chinese labor was extensively employed, and that in 1869 large numbers of the dead bodies of Celestials were gathered up and shipped to Sacramento for burial.

William J. Brodrick, after wandering in Peru and Chile, came to Los Angeles in 1869 and started as a stationer; then he opened an insurance office, and still later became interested in the Main Street Railway and the water company. On May 8th, 1877, Brodrick married Miss Laura E., daughter of Robert S. Carlisle. On October 18th, 1898, Brodrick died, having been identified with many important activities.

Hacks and omnibuses first came into use in 1869. Toward the end of May of that year, J. J. Reynolds, who had long been popular as a driver between Los Angeles and Wilmington, purchased a hack and started in business for himself, appealing to his "reputation for good driving and reliability" as a reasonable assurance that he would bring his patrons right side up to their scattered homes; and so much was he in demand, both in the city and its suburbs, that a competitor, J. Hewitt, in the latter part of June ordered a similar hack to come by steamer. It arrived in due time and was chronicled as a "luxurious vehicle." Hewitt regularly took up his stand in the morning in front of the Lafayette Hotel; and he also had an order slate at George Butler's livery-stable on Main Street.

During the sixties, Dr. T. H. Rose, who had relinquished the practice of medicine for the career of a pedagogue, commenced work as Principal of the Boys' Grammar School on Bath Street, and in 1869 was elected Superintendent of City Schools. He held this office but about a year, although he did not resign from educational work here until 1873. During his incumbency, he was Vice-Principal of the first Teachers' Institute ever held here, contributing largely toward the founding of the first high school and the general development of the schools prior to the time when Dr. Lucky, the first really professional teacher, assumed charge. On leaving Los Angeles, Dr. Rose became Principal of the school at Healdsburg, Sonoma

County, where he married a Mrs. Jewell, the widow of an old-
time, wealthy miner; but he was too sensitive and proud to live
on her income and, much against her wishes, insisted on teaching to support himself. In 1874, he took charge of the high
school at Petaluma, where the family of Mrs. Rose's first husband had lived; and the relationship of the two families probably lead to Rose and his wife separating. Later, Dr. Rose
went to the Sandwich Islands to teach, but by 1883, shortly
before he died, he was back in Los Angeles, broken in health
and spirit. Dr. Rose was an excellent teacher, a strict dis-
ciplinarian and a gentleman.

The retirement of Dr. Rose calls to mind a couple of years
during which Los Angeles had no City School Superintendent.
While Rose was Principal, a woman was in charge of the girls'
department; and the relations between the schoolmaster and the
schoolmistress were none too friendly. When Dr. Rose became
Superintendent, the schoolma'am instantly disapproved of the
choice and rebelled; and there being no law which authorized
the governing of Los Angeles schools in any other manner than
by trustees, the new Superintendent had no authority over
his female colleague. The office of Superintendent of City
Schools, consequently, remained vacant until 1873.

Dr. James S. Crawford had the honor, as far as I am aware,
of being one of the first regular dentists to locate in Los Angeles. As an itinerant he had passed the winters of 1863, 1864
and 1865 in this city, afterward going east; and on his return
to California in 1869 he settled in the Downey Block at Spring
and Main streets, where he practiced until, on April 14th,
1912, he died in a Ventura County camp.

In 1864, the California Legislature, wishing to encourage the
silk industry, offered a bounty of two hundred and fifty dollars
for every plantation of five thousand mulberry trees of two years'
growth, and a bounty of three hundred dollars for each one
hundred thousand salable cocoons; and in three years an enormous number of mulberry trees, in various stages of growth, was
registered. Prominent among silk-growers was Louis Prévost,
who rather early had established here an extensive mulberry-

tree nursery and near it a large cocoonery for the rearing
of silk worms; and had planned, in 1869, the creation of a
colony of silk-worms whose products would rival even those
of his native *belle France*. The California Silk Center Association
of Los Angeles was soon formed, and four thousand acres of
the *rancho* once belonging to Juan Bandini, fourteen hundred and
sixty acres of the Hartshorn Tract and three thousand one
hundred and sixty-nine acres of the Jurupa, on the east side
of the Santa Ana River, were purchased.   That was in June
or July; but on August 16th, in the midst of a dry season, Louis
Prévost died, and the movement received a serious setback.
To add to the reverses, the demand for silk-worm eggs fell off
amazingly; while finally, to give the enterprise its death-blow,
the Legislators, fearful that the State Treasury would be depleted through the payment of bounties, withdrew all State
aid.

The Silk Center Association, therefore, failed; but the Southern California Colony Association bought all the land, paying
for it something like three dollars and a half an acre.   To
many persons, the price was quite enough: old Louis Robidoux
had long refused to list his portion for taxes, and some one had
described much of the acreage as so dry that even coyotes,
in crossing, took along their canteens for safety! A town
called at first Jurupa, and later Riverside, was laid out; a
fifty thousand-dollar ditch diverted the Santa Ana River to a
place where Nature had failed to arrange for its flowing; and
in a few months a number of families had settled beside the
artificial waterway.   Riversiders long had to travel back and
forth to Los Angeles for most of their supplies (a stage, still
in existence, being used by ordinary passengers), and this made
a friendly as well as profitable business relation with the older
and larger town; but experiments soon showing that oranges
could grow in the arid soil, Riverside in course of time had
something to sell as well as to buy.

Who was more familiar both to the youth of the town and to
grown-ups than Nicolás Martinez, in summer the purveyor of
cooling ice cream, in winter the vender of hot *tamales!* From

morning till night, month in and month out during the sixties
and seventies, Martinez paced the streets, his dark skin made
still swarthier in contrast to his white costume—a shirt, scarcely
tidy, together with pantaloons none too symmetrical and
hanging down in generous folds at the waist.   On his head, in
true native fashion, he balanced in a small hooped tub what he
had for sale; he spoke with a pronounced Latin accent, and
his favorite method of announcing his presence was to bawl
out his wares.   The same receptacle, resting upon a round board
with an opening to ease the load and covered with a bunch
of cloths, served both to keep the *tamales* hot and the ice
cream cool; while to dispense the latter, he carried in one hand
a circular iron tray, in which were holes to accommodate three
or four glasses.   Further, for the convenience of the exacting
youth of the town, he added a spoon to each cream-filled glass;
and what stray speck of the ice was left on the spoon after the
youngster had given it a parting lick, Nicolás, bawling anew
to attract the next customer, fastidiously removed with his
tobacco-stained fingers!

CHAPTER XXVII

COMING OF THE IRON HORSE

1869

THE Los Angeles & San Pedro Railroad continued in 1869 to be the local theme of most importance, although its construction did not go on as rapidly as had been promised. The site for a depot, it is true, had been selected; but by June 14th, only six miles were finished. Farmers were loud in complaints that they had been heavily taxed, and in demanding that the road be rushed to completion, in order to handle the prospectively-large grain crop. Additional gangs were therefore employed, and by the twentieth of July, seven more miles of track had been laid. In the meantime, the Sunday School at Compton enjoyed the first excursion, the members making themselves comfortable on benches and straw in some freight cars.

As the work on the railroad progressed, stages, in addition to those regularly running through from Los Angeles to Wilmington, began connecting with the trains at the temporary terminus of the railroad. People went down to Wilmington to see the operations, not merely on the track, but in the machine shops where the cars for freight, express, baggage, smoking and passenger service (designed by A. A. Polhamus, the machinist) were being built under the superintendence of Samuel Atkinson, who had been brought West by the San Francisco & San José Valley Railroad, because of a reputation for railroad experience enjoyed by few, if by any other persons on the Coast. The Company also had a planing mill and wheelwright shop under the charge of George W. Oden.

By the first of August, both the railroad and connecting stages were advertising Sunday excursions to the beach, emphasizing the chance to travel part of the way by the new means of transit. Curiously, however, visitors were allowed to enjoy the sea-breezes but a short time: arriving at Wilmington about ten or half-past, they were compelled to start back for Los Angeles by four in the afternoon. Many resorters still patronized the old service; and frequently the regular stages, racing all the way up from the steamer, would actually reach the city half an hour earlier than those transferring the passengers from the railway terminus which was extended by August 1st to a point within four miles of town.

When eighteen miles had been finished, it was reported that General Stoneman and his post band would make an excursion on the first train, accompanied by General Banning and leading citizens of the town; but strong opposition to the Company laying its tracks through the center of "The Lane," now Alameda Street, having developed, the work was stopped by injunction. The road had been constructed to a point opposite the old Wolfskill home, then "far from town," and until the matter was settled, passengers and freight were unloaded there.

Great excitement prevailed here shortly after sundown on Wednesday evening, August 21st, when the mail-stage which had left for Gilroy but a short time before came tearing back to town, the seven or eight passengers excitedly shouting that they had been robbed. The stage had proceeded but two miles from Los Angeles when four masked highwaymen stepped into the road and ordered, "Hands up!" Among the passengers was the well-known and popular Ben Truman who, having learned by previous experience just what to do in such a ticklish emergency and "being persuaded that the two barrels of cold steel had somewhat the porportions of a railway tunnel," sadly but promptly unrolled one hundred and eighty dollars in bills, and quite as sadly deposited, in addition, his favorite chronometer. The highwayman picked up the watch, looked it over, shook his head and, thanking Ben, returned it, expressing the hope that, whatever adversity might overwhelm him, he should never be discovered with such a timepiece! All in all, the robbers secured nearly two thousand dollars; but, strange to relate, they overlooked the treasure in the Wells Fargo chest, as well as several hundred dollars in greenbacks belonging to the Government. Sheriff J. F. Burns and Deputy H. C. Wiley pursued and captured the robbers; and within about a week they were sent to the Penitentiary.

On the same evening, at high tide, the little steamer christened *Los Angeles* and constructed by P. Banning & Company to run from the wharf to the outside anchorage, was committed to the waters, bon-fires illuminating quite distinctly both guests and the neighboring landscape, and lending to the scene a weird and charming effect.

In a previous chapter I have given an account of Lady Franklin's visit to San Pedro and Los Angeles, and of the attention shown her. Her presence awakened new interest in the search for her lamented husband, and paved the way for the sympathetic reception of any intelligence likely to clear up the mystery. No little excitement, therefore, was occasioned eight years later by the finding of a document at San Buenaventura that seemed "like a voice from the dead." According to the story told, as James Daly (of the lumber firm of Daly & Rodgers) was walking on the beach on August 30th, he found a sheet of paper a foot square, much mutilated but bearing, in five or six different languages, a still legible request to forward the memoranda to the nearest British Consul or the Admiralty at London. Every square inch of the paper was covered with data relating to Sir John Franklin and his party, concluding with the definite statement that Franklin had died on June 11th, 1847. Having been found within a week of the time that the remnant of Dr. Hall's party, which went in search of the explorer, had arrived home in Connecticut with the announcement that they had discovered seven skeletons of Franklin's men, this document, washed up on the Pacific Coast, excited much comment; but I am unable to say whether it was ever accepted by competent judges as having been written by Franklin's associates.

In 1869, the long-familiar adobe of José António Carrillo was razed to make way for what, for many years, was the leading hotel of Los Angeles. This was the Pico House, in its decline known as the National Hotel, which, when erected on Main Street opposite the Plaza at a cost of nearly fifty thousand dollars, but emphasized in its contrasting showiness the ugliness of the neglected square. Some thirty-five thousand dollars were spent in furnishing the eighty-odd rooms, and no little splurge was made that guests could there enjoy the luxuries of both gas and baths! In its palmy days, the Pico House welcomed from time to time travelers of wide distinction; while many a pioneer, among them not a few newly-wedded couples now permanently identified with Los Angeles or the Southland, look back to the hostelry as the one surviving building fondly associated with the olden days. Charles Knowlton was an early manager; and he was succeeded by Dunham & Schieffelin.

Competition in the blacking of boots enlivened the fall, the Hotel Lafayette putting boldly in printer's ink the question, "Do You Want to Have Your Boots Blacked in a Cool, Private Place?" This challenge was answered with the following proclamation:

Champion Boot-Black! Boots Blacked Neater and Cheaper than Anywhere Else in the City, at the *Blue Wing* Shaving Saloon by D. Jefferson.

Brickmaking had become, by September, quite an important industry. Joe Mullally, whose brickyard was near the Jewish Cemetery, then had two kilns with a capacity of two hundred and twenty-five thousand; and in the following month he made over five hundred thousand brick.

In course of time, the Los Angeles & San Pedro Railroad was completed to the Madigan lot, which remained for several years the Los Angeles terminus; and justly confident that the difficulty with the authorities would be removed, the Company pushed work on their depot and put in a turn-table at the foot of New Commercial Street. There was but one diminutive locomotive, though a larger one was on its way around the Horn from the East and still another was coming by the Continental Railway; and every few days the little engine would go out of commission, so that traffic was constantly interrupted. At such times, confidence in the enterprise was somewhat shaken; but new rolling stock served to reassure the public. A brightly-painted smoking-car, with seats mounted on springs, was soon the "talk of the town."

I have spoken of J. J. Reynolds's early enterprise and the competition that he evoked. Toward the end of July, he went up to San Francisco and outdid Hewitt by purchasing a handsome omnibus, suitable for hotel service and also adapted to the needs of families or individuals clubbing together for picnics and excursions. This gave the first impetus to the use of hotel 'buses, and by the first Sunday in September, when the cars from Wilmington rolled in bringing passengers from the steamer *Orizaba*, the travelers were met by omnibuses and coaches from all three hotels, the Bella Union, the United States and the Lafayette; the number of vehicles, public and private, giving the streets around the railroad depot a very lively appearance.

Judge W. G. Dryden, so long a unique figure here, died on September 10th and A. J. King succeeded him as County Judge.

A notable visit to Los Angeles was that of Secretary William H. Seward who, in 1869, made a trip across the Continent, going as far north as Alaska and as far south as Mexico, and being everywhere enthusiastically received. When Seward left San Francisco for San Diego, about the middle of September, he was accompanied by Frederick Seward and wife (his son and daughter-in-law), General W. S. Rosecrans, General Morton C. Hunter, Colonel Thomas Sedgwick and Senator S. B. Axtell; and the news of their departure having been telegraphed ahead, many people went down to greet them on the arrival of the steamer *Orizaba*. After the little steamer *Los Angeles* had been made fast to the wharf, it was announced, to everyone's disappointment, that the Secretary was not coming ashore, as he wished to continue on his way to San Diego.

Meanwhile, the Common Council had resolved to extend the hospitality of the City to the distinguished party; and by September 19th, posters proclaimed that Seward and his party were coming and that citizens generally would be afforded an opportunity to participate in a public reception at the Bella Union on September 21st. A day in advance, therefore, the Mayor and a Committee from the Council set out for Anaheim, where they met the distinguished statesman on his way, whence the party jogged along leisurely in a carriage and four until they arrived at the bank of the Los Angeles River; and there Seward and his friends were met by other officials and a cavalcade of eighty citizens led by the military band of Drum Barracks. The guests alighted at the Bella Union and in a few minutes a rapidly-increasing crowd was calling loudly for Mr. Seward.

The Secretary, being welcomed on the balcony by Mayor Joel H. Turner, said that he had been laboring under mistakes all his life: he had visited Rome to witness celebrated ruins, but he found more interesting ruins in the Spanish Missions (great cheers); he had journeyed to Switzerland to view its glaciers, but upon the Pacific Coast he had seen rivers of ice two hundred and fifty feet in breadth, five miles long and God knows how high (more cheers); he had explored Labrador to examine the fisheries, but in Alaska he found that the fisheries came to him (Hear! hear! and renewed applause); he had gone to Burgundy to view the most celebrated vineyards of the world, but the vineyards of California far surpassed them all! (Vociferous and deafening hurrahs, and tossing of bouquets.)

The next day the Washington guests and their friends were shown about the neighborhood, and that evening Mr. Seward made another and equally happy speech to the audience drawn to the Bella Union by the playing of the band. There were also addresses by the Mayor, Senator Axtell, ex-Governor Downey and others, after which, in good old American fashion, citizens generally were introduced to the associate of the martyred Lincoln. At nine o'clock, a number of invited guests were ushered into the Bella Union's dining-room where, at a bounteous repast, the company drank to the health of the Secretary. This brought from the visitor an eloquent response with interesting local allusions.

Secretary Seward remarked that he found people here agitated upon the question of internal improvements—for everywhere people wanted railroads. Californians, if they were patient, would yet witness a railroad through the North, another by the Southern route, still another by the Thirty-fifth parallel, a fourth by the central route, and lastly, as the old plantation song goes, one "down the middle!" California needed more population, and railroads were the means by which to get people.

Finally, Mr. Seward spoke of the future prospects of the United States, saying much of peculiar interest in the light of later developments. We were already great, he affirmed; but a nation satisfied with its greatness is a nation without a future. We should expand, and as mightily as we could; until at length we had both the right and the power to move our armies anywhere in North America. As to the island lying almost within a stone's throw of our mainland, ought we not to possess Cuba, too?

Other toasts, such as "The Mayor and Common Council," "The Pioneers," "The Ancient Hospitality of California," "The Press," "The Wine Press" and "Our Wives and Sweethearts," were proposed and responded to, much good feeling prevailing notwithstanding the variance in political sentiments represented by guests and hosts; and everyone went home, in the small hours of the morning, pleased with the manner in which Los Angeles had received her illustrious visitors. The next day, Secretary Seward and party left for the North by carriages, rolling away toward Santa Bárbara and the mountains so soon to be invaded by the puffing, screeching iron horse.

Recollecting this banquet to Secretary Seward, I may add an amusing fact of a personal nature. Eugene Meyer and I arranged to go to the dinner together, agreeing that we were to meet at the store of S. Lazard & Company, almost directly opposite the Bella Union. When I left Los Angeles in 1867, evening dress was uncommon; but in New York I had become accustomed to its more frequent use. Rather naturally, therefore, I donned my swallowtail; Meyer, however, I found in a business suit and surprised at my query as to whether he intended going home to dress? Just as we were, we walked across the street and, entering the hotel, whom should we meet but ex-Mayor John G. Nichols, wearing a grayish linen duster, popular in those days, that extended to his very ankles; while Pio and Andrés Pico came attired in blue coats with big brass buttons. Meyer, observing the Mayor's outfit, facetiously asked me if I still wished him to go home and dress according to Los Angeles fashion; whereupon I drew off my gloves, buttoned up my overcoat and determined to sit out the banquet with my claw-hammer thus concealed. Mr. Seward, it is needless to say, was faultlessly attired.

The Spanish archives were long neglected, until M. Kremer was authorized to overhaul and arrange the documents; and even then it was not until September 16th that the Council built a vault for the preservation of the official papers. Two years later, Kremer discovered an original proclamation of peace between the United States and Mexico.

Elsewhere I allude to the slow development of Fort Street. For the first time, on the twenty-fourth of September street lamps burned there, and that was from six to nine months after darkness had been partially banished from Nigger Alley, Los Angeles, Aliso and Alameda streets.

Supplementing what I have said of the Los Angeles & San Pedro Railroad depot: it was built on a lot fronting three hundred feet on Alameda Street and having a depth of one hundred and twenty feet, its situation being such that, after the extension of Commercial Street, the structure occupied the southwest corner of the two highways. Really, it was more of a freight-

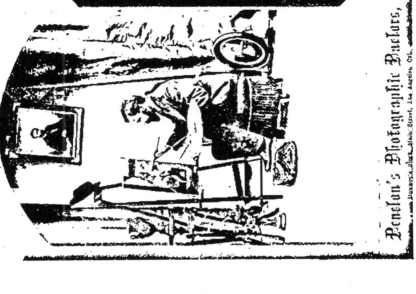

Henri Penelon, in his Studio

Phineas Banning, about 1869

Carreta, Earliest Mode of Transportation

Alameda Street Depot and Train, Los Angeles & San Pedro Railroad

shed than anything else, without adequate passenger facilities; a small space at the North end contained a second story in which some of the clerks slept; and in a cramped little cage beneath, tickets were sold. By the way, the engineer of the first train to run through to this depot was James Holmes, although B. W. Colling ran the first train stopping inside the city limits.

About this time the real estate excitement had become still more intense. In anticipation of the erection of this depot, Commercial Street property boomed and the first realty agents of whom I have any recollection appeared on the scene, Judge R. M. Widney being among them. I remember that two lots—one eighty by one hundred and twenty feet in size at the north-west corner of First and Spring streets, and the other having a frontage of only twenty feet on New Commercial Street, adjacent to the station—were offered simultaneously at twelve hundred dollars each. Contrary, no doubt, to what he would do to-day, the purchaser chose the Commercial Street lot, believing that location to have the better future.

Telegraph rates were not very favorable, in 1869, to frequent or verbose communication. Ten words sent from Los Angeles to San Francisco cost one dollar and a half; and fifty cents additional was asked for the next five words. After a while, there was a reduction of twenty-five per cent. in the cost of the first ten words, and fifty per cent. on the second five.

Twenty-four hundred voters registered in Los Angeles this year.

In the fall, William H. Spurgeon founded Santa Ana some five miles beyond Anaheim on a tract of about fifty acres, where a number of the first settlers experimented in growing flax.

It is not clear to me just when the rocky Arroyo Seco began to be popular as a resort, but I remember going there on picnics as early as 1857. By the late sixties, when Santa Monica Cañon also appealed to the lovers of sylvan life, the Arroyo had become known as Sycamore Grove—a name doubtless suggested by the numerous sycamores there—and Clois F.

Henrickson had opened an establishment including a little "hotel," a dancing-pavilion, a saloon and a shooting-alley. Free lunch and free beer were provided for the first day, and each Sunday thereafter in the summer season an omnibus ran every two hours from Los Angeles to the Sycamores. After some years, John Rumph and wife succeeded to the management, Frau Rumph being a popular *Wirtin;* and then the Los Angeles Turnverein used the grove for its public performances, including gymnastics, singing and the old-time sack-racing and target-shooting.

James Miller Guinn, who had come to California in November, 1863 and had spent several years in various counties of the State digging for gold and teaching school, drifted down to Los Angeles in October and was soon engaged as Principal of the public school at the new town of Anaheim, remaining there in that capacity for twelve years, during part of which time he also did good work on the County School Board.

Under the auspices of the French Benevolent Society and toward the end of October, the corner-stone of the French Hospital built on City donation lots, and for many years and even now one of the most efficient institutions of our city, was laid with the usual ceremonies.

On October 9th, the first of the new locomotives arrived at Wilmington and a week later made the first trial trip, with a baggage and passenger car. Just before departure a painter was employed to label the engine and decorate it with a few scrolls; when it was discovered, too late, that the artist had spelled the name: LOS ANGELOS. On October 23d, two lodges of Odd Fellows used the railway to visit Bohen Lodge at Wilmington, returning on the first train, up to that time, run into Los Angeles at midnight.

October 26th was a memorable day, for on that date the Los Angeles & San Pedro Railroad Company opened the line to the public and invited everybody to enjoy a free excursion to the harbor. Two trains were dispatched each way, the second consisting of ten cars; and not less than fifteen hundred persons made the round trip. Unfortunately, it was very warm and dusty, but such discomforts were soon forgotten in the novelty of the experience. On the last trip back came the musicians; and the new Los Angeles depot having been cleared, cleaned up and decorated for a dedicatory ball, there was a stampede to the little structure, filling it in a jiffy.

Judge H. K. S. O'Melveny, who first crossed the Plains from Illinois on horseback in 1849, came to Los Angeles with his family in November, having already served four years as a Circuit Judge, following his practice of law in Sacramento. He was a brother-in-law of L. J. Rose, having married, in 1850, Miss Annie Wilhelmina Rose. Upon his arrival, he purchased the southwest corner of Second and Fort streets, a lot one hundred and twenty by one hundred and sixty-five feet in size, and there he subsequently constructed one of the fine houses of the period; which was bought, some years later, by Jotham Bixby for about forty-five hundred dollars, after it had passed through various hands. Bixby lived in it for a number of years and then resold it. In 1872, O'Melveny was elected Judge of Los Angeles County; and in 1887, he was appointed Superior Judge. H. W. O'Melveny, his second son, came from the East with his parents, graduating in time from the Los Angeles High School and the State University. Now he is a distinguished attorney and occupies a leading position as a public-spirited citizen, and a patron of the arts and sciences.

In his very readable work, *From East Prussia to the Golden Gate*, Frank Lecouvreur credits me with having served the commonwealth as Supervisor. This is a slight mistake: I was an unwilling candidate, but never assumed the responsibilities of office. In 1869, various friends waited upon me and requested me to stand as their candidate for the supervisorship; to which I answered that I would be glad to serve my district, but that I would not lift a finger toward securing my election. H. Ábila was chosen with six hundred and thirty-one votes, E. M. Sanford being a close second with six hundred and sixteen; while five hundred and thirty-seven votes were cast in my favor.

Trains on the new railway began to run regularly on November 1st; and there still exists one of the first time-tables, bearing at the head, "Los Angeles & San Pedro Railroad" and a little picture of a locomotive and train. At first, the train scheduled for two stated round trips a day (except on steamer days, when the time was conditioned by the arrival and departure of vessels) left Wilmington at eight o'clock in the morning and at one o'clock in the afternoon, returning at ten in the morning and four in the afternoon. The fare between Los Angeles and Wilmington was one dollar and fifty cents, with an additional charge of one dollar to the Anchorage; while on freight from the Anchorage to Los Angeles, the tariff was: dry goods, sixteen dollars per ton; groceries and other merchandise, five dollars; and lumber, seven dollars per thousand feet.

After the formal opening of the railroad, a permanent staff of officers, crew and mechanicians was organized. The first Superintendent was H. W. Hawthorne, who was succeeded by E. E. Hewitt, editor of the *Wilmington Journal*. N. A. McDonald, was the first conductor; Sam Butler was the first and, for a while, the only brakeman, and the engineers were James McBride and Bill Thomas. The first local agent was John Milner; the first agent at Wilmington, John McCrea. The former was succeeded by John E. Jackson, who from 1880 to 1882 served the community as City Surveyor. Worthy of remark, perhaps, as a coincidence, is the fact that both Milner and McCrea ultimately became connected in important capacities with the Farmers & Merchants Bank.

The first advertised public excursion on the Los Angeles & San Pedro Railroad after its opening was a trip to Wilmington and around San Pedro Harbor, arranged for November 5th, 1869. The cars, drawn by the locomotive *Los Angeles* and connecting with the little steamer of the same name, left at ten and returned at three o'clock in the afternoon. Two dollars was the round-trip fare, while another dollar was exacted from those who went out upon the harbor.

In the late seventies, a Portuguese named Fayal settled near what is now the corner of Sixth and Front streets, San Pedro; and one Lindskow took up his abode in another shack a block away.   Around these rude huts sprang up the neighborhoods of Fayal and Lindville, since absorbed by San Pedro.

Probably the first attempt to organize a fire company for Los Angeles was made in 1869, when a meeting was called on Saturday evening, November 6th, at Buffum's Saloon, to consider the matter.   A temporary organization was formed, with Henry Wartenberg as President; W. A. Mix, Vice-President; George M. Fall, Secretary; and John H. Gregory, Treasurer. An initiation fee of two dollars and a half, and monthly dues of twenty-five cents, were decided upon; and J. F. Burns, B. Katz, Emil Harris, George Pridham, E. B. Frink, C. D. Hathaway, P. Thompson, O. W. Potter, C. M. Small and E. C. Phelps were charter members.   A committee appointed to canvass for subscriptions made little progress, and the partial destruction of Rowan's American Bakery, in December, demonstrating the need of an engine and hose cart, brought out sharp criticism of Los Angeles's penuriousness.

About the middle of November, Daniel Desmond, who had come on October 14th of the preceding year, opened a hat store on Los Angeles Street near New Commercial, widely advertising the enterprise as a pioneer one and declaring, perhaps unconscious of any pun, that he proposed to fill a want that had "long been felt."   The steamer *Orizaba*, which was to bring down Desmond's goods, as ill luck would have it left half of his stock lying on the San Francisco pier; and the opening, so much heralded, had to be deferred several weeks. As late as 1876, he was still the only exclusive hatter here. Desmond died on January 23d, 1903, aged seventy years, and was succeeded by his son, C. C. Desmond.   Another son, D. J. Desmond, is the well-known contractor.

Toward the close of November, Joseph Joly, a Frenchman, opened the Chartres Coffee Factory on Main Street opposite the Plaza, and was the pioneer in that line.   He delivered to both stores and families, and for a while seemed phenomenally successful; but one fine morning in December it was discovered that the "Jolly Joseph" had absconded, leaving behind numerous unpaid bills.

The first marble-cutter to open a workshop in Los Angeles was named Miller. He came toward the end of 1869 and established himself in the Downey Block. Prior to Miller's coming, all marble work was brought from San Francisco or some source still farther away, and the delay and expense debarred many from using that stone even for the pious purpose of identifying graves.

With the growth of Anaheim as the business center of the country between the new San Gabriel and the Santa Ana rivers, sentiment had been spreading in favor of the division of Los Angeles County; and at the opening of the Legislature of 1869–70, Anaheim had its official representative in Sacramento, ready to present the claims of the little German settlement and its thriving neighbors. The person selected for this important embassy was Major Max von Stroble; and he inaugurated his campaign with such sagacity and energy that the bill passed the Assembly and everything pointed to an early realization of the scheme. It was not, however, until Los Angeles awoke to the fact that the proposed segregation meant a decided loss, that opposition developed in the Senate and the whole matter was held up.

Stroble thereupon sent posthaste to his supporters for more cash, and efforts were made to get the stubborn Senate to reconsider. Doubtless somebody else had a longer purse than Stroble; for in the end he was defeated, and the German's dream did not come true until long after he had migrated to the realms that know no subdivisions. One of the arguments used in favor of the separation was that it took two days's time, and cost six dollars, for the round trip to the Los Angeles Courthouse; while another contention then regarded as of great importance was that the one coil of hose pipe owned by the County was kept at Los Angeles! Stroble, by-the-way, desired to call the new county Anaheim.

Major von Stroble was a very interesting character. He was a German who had stood shoulder to shoulder with Carl Schurz and Franz Sigel in the German Revolution of 1848, and who, after having taken part in the adventures of

Walker's filibustering expedition to Nicaragua, finally landed in Anaheim, where he turned his attention to the making of wine. He soon tired of that, and in 1867 was found boring for oil on the Brea Ranch, again meeting with reverses where others later were so successful. He then started the movement to divide Los Angeles County and once more failed in what was afterward accomplished. Journalism in Anaheim next absorbed him ard, having had the best of educational advantages, Stroble brought to his newspaper both culture and the experience of travel.

The last grand effort of this adventurous spirit was the attempt to sell Santa Catalina Island. Backed by the owners, Stroble sailed for Europe and opened headquarters near Threadneedle Street in London. In a few weeks he had almost effected the sale, the contract having been drawn and the time actually set for the following day when the money—a cool two hundred thousand pounds—was to be paid; but no Stroble kept tryst to carry out his part of the transaction. Only the evening before, alone and unattended, the old man had died in his room at the very moment when Fortune, for the first time, was to smile upon him! Eighteen or twenty years later, Catalina was sold for much less than the price once agreed upon.

CHAPTER XXVIII

THE LAST OF THE VIGILANTES

1870

AS I have somewhere related, I began buying hides as far back as 1855, but it was not until 1870 that this branch of our business assumed such importance as to require more convenient quarters. Then we bought a place on the southeast corner of Alameda and Commercial streets, facing sixty feet on Alameda and having a depth of one hundred and sixty-five feet, where we constructed a hide-house and erected a press for baling. We paid P. Beaudry eleven hundred dollars for the lot. The relatively high price shows what the Los Angeles & San Pedro Railroad depot had done for that section. In the days when hides were sent by sailing-vessels to the East, a different method of preparing them for shipment was in vogue. The wet hides having been stretched, small stakes were driven into the ground along the edge of, and through the skins, thus holding them in place until they had dried and expanding them by about one-third; in this condition they were forwarded loose. Now that transportation is more rapid and there are tanneries in California, all hides are handled wet.

In 1870, business life was centered on Los Angeles Street between Commercial and Arcadia; and all the hotels were north of First Street. Fort Street ended in a little bluff at a spot now between Franklin and First streets. Spring Street was beginning to take on new life, and yet there was but one gas lamp along the entire roadway, though many were the appeals to add another lamp, "say, as far as First Street!"

Sometime in January, a number of ladies of this city met and, through the exertions of Mrs. Rosa Newmark, wife of Joseph Newmark, formed the Ladies' Hebrew Benevolent Society. Mrs. Newmark, as was once pointed out in a notable open-air meeting of women's clubs (to which I elsewhere refer), never accepted any office in the Society; but for years she was untiring in her efforts in the cause of charity. The first officers were: President, Mrs. W. Kalisher; Vice-President, Mrs. Harris Newmark; Treasurer, Mrs. John Jones; Secretary, Mrs. B. Katz; and Collector, Mrs. A. Baer. Three Counselors—Henry Wartenberg, I. M. Hellman and myself—occasionally met with the ladies to advise them.

Aside from the fact of its importance as the pioneer ladies' benevolent organization instituted in Los Angeles, the Society found a much-needed work to do. It was then almost impossible to obtain nurses, and the duty devolved on members to act in that capacity, where such assistance was required, whether the afflicted were rich or poor. It was also their function to prepare the dead for interment, and to keep proper vigil over the remains until the time of burial.

During the year 1869 or 1870, as the result of occasional gatherings in the office of Dr. Joseph Kurtz, the Los Angeles Turnverein was organized with eleven members—Emil Harris leading in the movement, assisted by Dr. Kurtz, Ed. Preuss, Lorenzo Leck, Philip and Henry Stoll, Jake Kuhrts, Fred Morsch, C. C. Lips and Isaac Cohn. Dr. Kurtz was elected President. They fraternized for a while at Frau Wiebecke's Garden, on the west side of Alameda near First Street, about where the Union Hardware and Metal Company now stands; and there, while beer and wine were served in the open air, the Teutons gratified their love of music and song. Needing for their gymnastics more enclosed quarters, the Turnverein rented of Kalisher & Wartenberg the barn on Alameda Street between Ducommon and First, used as a hide-house; and in that rough-boarded shack, whose none too aromatic odors are still a souvenir to many a pioneer resident, the *Turners* swung and vaulted to their heart's content. Classes were soon arranged for boys; and the envy of all was the lad who, after numerous risks to limb and neck, proudly topped the human pyramid. Another garden of this period often patronized by the Turnverein was Kiln Messer's, on First Street between Alameda and the river.

The Post Office was moved this year from the corner of North Main and Market streets to the middle of Temple Block, but even there the facilities were so inadequate that Wells Fargo & Company, in June, put up a letter-box at the corner of Main and Commercial streets which was emptied but once a day, at four o'clock in the afternoon, save on steamer days when letters were taken out at half-past nine. One other box was at the sole railroad depot, then at the corner of Alameda and Commercial streets. The Post Office at that time was also so miserably illuminated that citizens fumbled about to find their letter-boxes, and ladies were timid about entering the building at night. Postmasters were allowed small reserves; and, for some time in 1870 the Los Angeles Post Office was entirely out of one- and two-cent stamps.

In February, the way was prepared for the first city directory when the houses of Los Angeles were ordered to be numbered, a public discussion of the need for a directory having taken place the previous December. When the collaborators began to collect names and other data, there were many refusals to answer questions; but the little volume of seventy pages was finally published in 1871.

Until 1870 Los Angeles had no bookbinder, all binding having had to be sent to San Francisco; and a call was then sent out to induce a journeyman to settle here.

On the fourteenth of February, Phineas Banning was married to Miss Mary, daughter of Colonel J. H. Hollister—the affair being the consummation of a series of courtly addresses in which, as I have related, it was my pleasurable privilege to play an intermediary part. As might be expected of one who was himself an experienced and generous entertainer, the wedding was a social event to be long and pleasantly remembered by the friends of the bride and groom. Mrs. Banning, who for years maintained an attractive home on Fort Hill, is now living on Commonwealth Avenue.

About this time, Colonel Isaac R. Dunkelberger came to Los Angeles to live, having just finished his fifth year in the army in Arizona, following a long service under Northern banners during the Civil War. While here, the Colonel met and courted Miss Mary Mallard, daughter of Judge Mallard; and on February 26th, 1867, they were married. For eight years, from March, 1877, Dunkelberger was Postmaster. He died on December 5th, 1904, survived by his widow and six children. While writing about this estimable family, it occurs to me that Mary, then a little girl, was one of the guests at my wedding.

Frank Lecouvreur, who was Surveyor of Los Angeles County from 1870 until 1873, was a native of East Prussia and like his predecessor, George Hansen, came to California by way of the Horn. For a while, as I have related, he was my bookkeeper. In 1877, he married Miss Josephine Rosanna Smith who had renounced her vows as a nun. Ten years later he suffered a paralytic stroke and was an invalid until his death, on January 17th, 1901.

Once introduced, the telegraph gradually grew in popularity; but even in 1870, when the Western Union company had come into the field and was operating as far as the Coast, service was anything but satisfactory. The poles between Los Angeles and San Francisco had become rotten and often fell, dragging the wires with them, and interrupting communication with the North. There were no wires, up to that time, to Santa Bárbara or San Bernardino; and only in the spring of that year was it decided to put a telegraph line through to San Diego. When the Santa Bárbara line was -proposed, the citizens there speedily subscribed twenty-two hundred and forty-five dollars; it having been the company's plan always to get some local stockholders.

As the result of real estate purchases and exchanges in the

late sixties and early seventies between Dr. J. S. Griffin, Phineas Banning, B. D. Wilson, P. Beaudry and others, a fruit-growing colony was planned in April, when it was proposed to take in some seventeen hundred and fifty acres of the best part of the San Pasqual *rancho*, including a ten-thousand-dollar ditch. A company, with a capital stock of two hundred thousand dollars divided into four thousand shares of fifty dollars each, was formed to grow oranges, lemons, grapes, olives, nuts and raisins, John Archibald being President; R. M. Widney, Vice-President; W. J. Taylor, Secretary; and the London & San Francisco Bank, Treasurer. But although subscription books were opened and the scheme was advertised, nothing was done with the land until D. M. Berry and others came from Indiana and started the Indiana Colony.

A rather uncommon personality for about thirty years was Fred Dohs, who came from Germany when he was twenty-three and engaged in trading horses. By 1870 he was managing a barber shop near the Downey Block, and soon after was conducting a string band. For many years, the barber-musician furnished the music for most of the local dances and entertainments, at the same time (or until prices began to be cut) maintaining his shop, where he charged two bits for a shave and four bits for a hair-cut. During his prosperity, Dohs acquired property, principally on East First Street.

The first foot-bridge having finally succumbed to the turbulent waters of the erratic Los Angeles River, the great flood of 1867–68 again called the attention of our citizens to the necessity of establishing permanent and safe communication between the two sides of the stream; and this agitation resulted in the construction by Perry & Woodworth of the first fairly substantial bridge at the foot of the old Aliso Road, now Macy Street, at an outlay of some twenty thousand dollars. Yet, notwithstanding the great necessity that had always existed for this improvement, it is my recollection that it was not consummated until about 1870. Like its poor little predecessor carried away by the uncontrolled waters, the more dignified structure was broken up by a still later flood, and the pieces of timber once so carefully put together by a confident and satisfied people were strewn for a mile or two along the river banks.

'Way back in the formative years of Los Angeles, there were suddenly added to the constellation of noteworthy local characters two jovial, witty, good-for-nothing Irishmen who from the first were pals. The two were known as Dan Kelly and Micky Free. Micky's right name was Dan Harrington; but I never knew Kelly to go under any other appellation. When sober, which was not very frequent, Dan and Micky were good-natured, jocular and free from care, and it mattered not to either of them whether the morrow might find them well-fed and at liberty or in the jail then known as the Hotel de Burns: "sufficient unto the day is the evil thereof" was the only philosophy they knew. They were boon companions when free from drink; but when saturated, they immediately fought like demons. They were both in the toils quite ten months of the year, while during the other two months they carried a hod! Of the two, Micky was the most irredeemable, and in time he became such a nuisance that the authorities finally decided to ship him out of the country and bought him a ticket to Oregon. Micky got as far as San Pedro, where he traded his ticket for a case of delirium tremens; but he did something more—he broke his leg and was bundled back to Los Angeles, renewing here the acquaintance of both the bartender and the jailer. Some years later, he astonished the town by giving up drink and entering the Veterans's Home. When he died, they gave him a soldier's honors and a soldier's grave.

In 1870, F. Bonshard imported into Los Angeles County some five or six hundred blooded Cashmere goats; and about the same time or perhaps even earlier, J. E. Pleasants conducted at Los Nietos a similar enterprise, at one time having four or five hundred of a superior breed, the wool of which brought from twenty-five to thirty-five cents a pound. The goat-fancying Pleasants also had some twelve hundred Angoras.

On June 1st, Henry Hamilton, who two years before had

resumed the editorship of the Los Angeles *Star*, then a weekly, issued the first number of the *Daily Star*. He had taken into partnership George W. Barter, who three months later started the *Anaheim Gazette*. In 1872, Barter was cowhided by a woman, and a committee formally requested the editor to vamose the town! Barter next bought the *Daily Star* from Hamilton, on credit, but he was unable to carry out his contract and within a year Hamilton was again in charge.

At the beginning of this decade, times in Arizona were really very bad. H. Newmark & Company, who had large amounts due them from merchants in that Territory, were not entirely easy about their outstanding accounts, and this prompted Kaspare Cohn to visit our customers there. I urged him to consider the dangers of the road and to abandon his project; but he was determined to go. The story of the trip, in the light of present methods and the comparative safety of travel, is an interesting one, and I shall relate his experiences as he described them to me.

He started on a Saturday, going by stage (in preference to buckboard) from Los Angeles to San Bernardino, and from there rode, as the only passenger, with a stage-driver named Brown, passing through Frink's Ranch, Gilman's, White River, Agua Caliente, Indian Wells, Toros, Dos Palmas, Chuckawalla, Mule Springs and Willow Springs. H. Newmark & Company had forwarded, on a prairie schooner driven by Jesse Allen of Los Angeles, a considerable amount of merchandise which it was their intention should be sold in Arizona, and the freighting charge upon which was to be twelve and a half cents per pound. In Chuckawalla, familiarly called Chucky Valley, the travelers overtook Allen and the stock of goods; and this meeting in that lonesome region was the cause of such mutual rejoicing that Kaspare provided as abundant an entertainment as his limited stores would permit. Resuming their journey from Chuckawalla, the driver and his companion soon left Allen and his cumbersome load in the rear.

It was near Granite Wash, as they were jogging along in the

evening, that they noticed some Indian fire signals. These
were produced by digging a hole in the ground, filling it with
combustible material, such as dry leaves, and setting fire to it.
From the smoldering that resulted, smoke was emitted and
sparks burst forth. Observing these ticklish warnings, the
wayfarers sped away and escaped—perhaps, a tragic fate.
Arriving at Ehrenberg on a Tuesday morning, Kaspare remained there all night. Still the only passenger, he left the
next day; and it may be imagined how cheering, after the
previous experience, was the driver's remark that, on account
of the lonesome character of the trip, and especially the danger
from scalping Apaches, he would never have departed without
some company!

Somewhere between Granite Wash and Wickenberg, a
peculiar rattling revealed a near-by snake, whereupon Kaspare
jumped out and shot the reptile, securing the tail and rattles.
Changing horses or resting at Tyson's Wells, McMullen's and
Cullen's Station, they arrived the next night at Wickenberg, the
location of the Vulture Mines, where Kaspare called upon the
Superintendent—a man named Peoples—to collect a large
amount they owed us. Half of the sum was paid in gold bars,
at the rate of sixteen dollars per ounce, while the other half
we lost.

A niece of M. Kremer lived in Wickenberg, where her
husband was in business. She suffered a great deal from
headaches, and a friend had recommended, as a talisman, the
possession of snake rattles. Kaspare, with his accustomed
gallantry, produced the specimen which he had obtained and
gave it to the lady; and it is to be hoped that she was as permanently relieved of her pain as so many nowadays are cured
of imaginary troubles by no more substantial superstitions.

Making short stops at Wilson's Station, Antelope Station,
Kirkland Valley, Skull Valley and Mint Valley, Kaspare reached
Prescott, some four hundred and thirty miles from San Bernardino, and enquired after Dan Hazard, the ex-Mayor's
brother and one of our customers—who died about the
middle of the eighties—and learned that he was then on his

way to St. Louis with teams to haul back freight for Levi Bashford who, in addition to being an important trader, was Government Receiver of Public Moneys. Kaspare decided to remain in Prescott until Hazard returned; and as Jesse Allen soon arrived with the merchandise, Kaspare had ample time to sell it. Bashford, as a Government official, was not permitted to handle such goods as matches and cigars, which bore revenue stamps, but Kaspare sold him quantities of lard, beans, coffee, sugar and other supplies. He sold the revenue-stamped articles to Buffum & Campbell, the former of whom had once been a well-known resident of Los Angeles. He also disposed of some goods to Henderson Brothers, afterward prominent bankers of Tucson and Globe, Arizona. In the meantime, Dan Hazard returned and settled his account in full.

Kaspare remained in Prescott nearly four weeks. Between the collections that he made and the money which he received for the consigned merchandise, he had about thirteen thousand dollars in currency to bring back with him. With this amount of money on his person, the return trip was more than ever fraught with danger. Mindful of this added peril, Kaspare kept the time of his departure from Prescott secret, no one, with the exception of Bashford, being in his confidence. He prepared very quietly; and at the last moment, one Saturday afternoon, he slipped into the stage and started for California. Brown was again his companion as far as Ehrenberg. There he met Frank Ganahl and Charles Strong, both soon to become Southern Californians; and knowing them very well, their companion-ship contributed during the rest of the trip not only pleasure but an agreeable feeling of security. His arrival in Los Angeles afforded me much relief, and the story of his adventures and success added more than a touch of interest.

The first street-sprinklers in Los Angeles were owned and operated about the middle of July by T. W. McCracken, who was allowed by the Council to call upon residents along the route for weekly contributions to keep the water wagon going.

I have told of the establishing of Hellman, Temple & Company as bankers. In September, the first-named bought out his partners and continued, until 1871, as Hellman & Company.

With the commencement of autumn, when the belief prevailed that little or nothing could be done toward persuading the Common Council to beautify the Plaza, a movement to lay out and embellish the five-acre tract bounded by Hill and Olive, and Fifth and Sixth streets, met with such favor that, by the first week in October, some eight hundred dollars had been subscribed for the purpose. On November 19th a public meeting was held, presided over by Prudent Beaudry, Major H. M. Mitchell serving as Secretary; and it was suggested to call the proposed square the Los Angeles Park, and to enclose it, at a cost of about five hundred dollars, with a fence. Another two hundred dollars was soon made up; and the services of L. Carpenter, who offered to plow the land prior to sowing grass-seed, were accepted in lieu of a subscription. Both George Lehman and Elijah Workman showed their public spirit by planting what have since become the largest trees there. Sometime later, the name was changed to Central Park, by which it is still known.

The first hackney coach ever built in Los Angeles was turned out in September by John Goller for J. J. Reynolds —about the same time that the Oriental Stage Company brought a dozen new Concord coaches from the East—and cost one thousand dollars. Goller was then famous for elaborate vehicles and patented spring buggies which he shipped even to pretentious and bustling San Francisco. Before the end of November, however, friends of the clever and enterprising carriage-maker were startled to hear that he had failed for the then not insignificant sum of about forty thousand dollars.

Up to the fall of the year, no connection existed between Temple and First Streets west of Spring; but on the first day of September, a cut through the hill, effected by means of chain-gang labor and continuing Fort Street north, was completed, to the satisfaction of the entire community.

About the middle of October, a petition was presented to the

Common Council calling attention to the fact that the Los Angeles Water Company two years before had agreed to erect a fountain on the Plaza; and declaring that the open place was little short of a " scarecrow for visitors." The Company immediately replied that it was ready to put up the fountain; and in November the Council ordered the brick tank taken away. At the beginning of August, 1871, the fountain began playing.

During the second marshalship of William C. Warren, when Joe Dye was one of his deputy officers, there was great traffic in Chinese women, one of whom was kidnaped and carried off to San Diego. A reward of a hundred dollars was offered for her return, and she was brought back on a charge of theft and tried in the Court of Justice Trafford, on Temple Street near Spring. During the trial, on October 31st, 1870, Warren and Dye fell into a dispute as to the reward; and the quarrel was renewed outside the courtroom. At a spot near the corner of Spring and Temple streets Dye shot and killed Warren; and in the scrimmage several other persons standing near were wounded. Dye was tried, but acquitted. Later, however, he himself was killed by a nephew, Mason Bradfield, whose life he had frequently threatened and who fired the deadly bullet from a window of the New Arlington Hotel, formerly the White House, at the southeast corner of Commercial and Los Angeles streets. Mrs. C. P. Bradfield, Bradfield's mother and a teacher, who came in 1875, was the author of certain text-books for drawing, published by A. S. Barnes & Company of New York.

Failures in raising and using camels in the Southwest were due, at least partially, to ignorance of the animal's wants, a company of Mexicans, in the early sixties, overloading some and treating them so badly that nearly all died. Later, Frenchmen, who had had more experience, secured the two camels left, and by 1870 there was a herd of no less than twenty-five on a ranch near the Carson River in Nevada, where they were used in packing salt for sixty miles or more to the mills.

On October 31st, the first Teacher's Institute held in Los Angeles County was opened, with an attendance of thirty-five, in the old Bath Street schoolhouse, that center being selected because the school building at Spring and Second streets, though much better adapted to the purpose, was considered to be too far out of town! County Superintendent W. M. McFadden was President; J. M. Guinn was Vice-President; and P. C. Tonner was Secretary; while a leader in discussions was Dr. Truman H. Rose, who there gave a strong impetus to the founding of the first high school.

Soon after this Institute was held, the State Legislature authorized bonds to the amount of twenty thousand dollars for the purpose of erecting another schoolhouse; and the building was soon to be known as the Los Angeles High School. W. H. Workman, M. Kremer and H. D. Barrows were the building committee.

Mentioning educators, I may introduce the once well-known name of Professor Adams, an instructor in French who lived here in the early seventies. He was so very urbane that on one occasion, while overdoing his polite attention to a lady, he fell off the sidewalk and badly broke his leg!

In a previous chapter I have spoken of a Frenchman named Lachenais who killed a fellow-countryman at a wake, the murder being one of a succession of crimes for which he finally paid the penalty at the hands of a Vigilance Committee in the last lynching witnessed here.

Lachenais lived near where the Westminster Hotel now stands, on the northeast corner of Main and Fourth streets, but he also had a farm south of the city, adjoining that of Jacob Bell who was once a partner in sheep-raising with John Schumacher. The old man was respectable and quiet, but Lachenais quarreled with him over water taken from the zanja. Without warning, he rode up to Bell as he was working in his field and shot him dead; but there being no witnesses to the act, this murder remained, temporarily, a mystery. One evening, as Lachenais (to whom suspicion had been gradually directed), was lounging about in a drunken condition, he let slip a remark as to the folly of anyone looking for

Bell's murderer; and this indiscretion led to his arrest and incarceration.

No sooner had the news of Lachenais's apprehension been passed along than the whole town was in a turmoil. A meeting at Stearns's Hall was largely attended; a Vigilance Committee was formed; Lachenais's record was reviewed and his death at the hands of an outraged community was decided upon. Everything being arranged, three hundred or more armed men, under the leadership of Felix Signoret, the barber—Councilman in 1863 and proprietor of the Signoret Building opposite the Pico House—assembled on the morning of December 17th, marched to the jail, overcame Sheriff Burns and his assistants, took Lachenais out, dragged him along to the corral of Tomlinson & Griffith (at the corner of Temple and New High streets) and there summarily hanged him. Then the mob, without further demonstration, broke up; the participants going their several ways. The reader may have already observed that this was not the first time that the old Tomlinson & Griffith gate had served this same gruesome purpose.

The following January, County Judge Y. Sepúlveda charged the Grand Jury to do its duty toward ferreting out the leaders of the mob, and so wipe out this reproach to the city; but the Grand Jury expressed the conviction that if the law had hitherto been faithfully executed in Los Angeles, such scenes in broad daylight would never have taken place. The editor of the *News*, however, ventured to assert that this report was but another disgrace.

CHAPTER XXIX

THE CHINESE MASSACRE

1871

H. NEWMARK & COMPANY enjoyed associations with nearly all of the most important wool men and *rancheros* in Southern California, our office for many years being headquarters for these stalwarts, as many as a dozen or more of whom would ofttimes congregate, giving the store the appearance of a social center. They came in from their ranches and discussed with freedom the different phases of their affairs and other subjects of interest. Wheat, corn, barley, hay, cattle, sheep, irrigation and kindred topics were passed upon; although in 1871 the price of wool being out of all proportion to anything like its legitimate value, the uppermost topic of conversation was wool. These meetings were a welcome interruption to the monotony of our work. Some of the most important of these visitors were Jotham, John W. and Llewellyn Bixby, Isaac Lankershim, L. J. Rose, I. N. Van Nuys, R. S. Baker, George Carson, Manuel Dominguez, Domingo Amestoy, Juan Matías Sanchez, Dan Freeman, John Rowland, John Reed, Joe Bridger, Louis Phillips, the brothers Garnier, Remi Nadeau, E. J. Baldwin, P. Banning and Alessandro Repetto. There was also not a weather prophet, near or far, who did not manage to appear at these weighty discussions and offer his oracular opinions about the pranks of the elements; on which occasions, one after another of these wise men would step to the door, look at the sky and broad landscape, solemnly shake his head and then render his verdict to the speculating circle within.   According as the moon emerged "so that one could hang something upon it," or in such a manner that "water would run off" (as they pictured it), we were to have dry or rainy weather; nor would volumes of talk shake their confidence.   Occasionally, I added a word, merely to draw out these weather-beaten and interesting old chaps; but usually I listened quietly and was entertained by all that was said.   Hours would be spent by these friends in chatting and smoking the time away; and if they enjoyed the situation half as much as I did, pleasant remembrances of these occasions must have endured with them.   Many of those to whom I have referred have ended their earthly careers, while others, living in different parts of the county, are still hale and hearty.

A curious character was then here, in the person of the reputed son of a former, and brother of the then, Lord Clanmorris, an English nobleman.   Once a student at Dr. Arnold's famous Rugby, he had knocked about the world until, shabbily treated by Dame Fortune, he had become a sheepherder in the employ of the Bixbys.

M. J. Newmark, who now came to visit us from New York, was admitted to partnership with H. Newmark & Company, and this determined his future residence.

As was natural in a town of pueblo origin, plays were often advertised in Spanish; one of the placards, still preserved, thus announcing the attraction for January 30th, at the Merced Theater:

TEATRO MERCED
LOS ANGELES
Lunes, Enero 30, de 1871

Primero Función de la Gran Compañia Dramática, De Don Tomás Maguire, El Empresario Veterano de San Francisco, VEINTE Y CUATRO Artistas de ambos sexos, todos conocidos como ESTRELLAS de primera clase.

In certain quarters of the city, the bill was printed in English.

Credit for the first move toward the formation of a County

Medical Society here should probably be given to Dr. H. S. Orme, at whose office early in 1871 a preliminary meeting was held; but it was in the office of Drs. Griffin and Widney, on January 31st, that the organization was effected, my friend Griffin being elected President; Dr. R. T. Hayes, Vice-President; Dr. Orme, Treasurer; and Dr. E. L. Dow, Secretary. Thus began a society which, in the intervening years, has accomplished much good work.

Late in January, Luther H. Titus, one of several breeders of fast horses, brought from San Francisco by steamer a fine thoroughbred stallion named *Echo*, a half-brother of the celebrated trotter *Dexter* which had been shipped from the East in a Central Pacific car especially constructed for the purpose—in itself something of a wonder then. Sporting men came from a distance to see the horse; but interest was divided between the stallion and a mammoth turkey of a peculiar breed, also brought west by Titus, who prophesied that the bird, when full grown, would tip the beam at from forty-five to fifty pounds.

Early in February, the first steps were taken to reorganize and consolidate the two banking houses in which Downey and Hellman were interested, when it was proposed to start the Bank of Los Angeles, with a capital of five hundred thousand dollars. Some three hundred and eighty thousand dollars of this sum were soon subscribed; and by the first week in April, twenty-five per cent. of the capital had been called in. John G. Downey was President and I. W. Hellman was Cashier; their office was in the former rooms of Hellman, Temple & Company. On the tenth of April the institution was opened as the Farmers & Merchants Bank; and on July 10th, J. G. Downey, Charles Ducommun, O. W. Childs, I. M. Hellman, George Hansen, A. Glassell, J. S. Griffin, José Mascarel and I. W. Hellman were chosen Trustees. From the first the Bank prospered, so that when the crisis of 1875 tested the substantiability of the financial institutions here, the Farmers & Merchants rode the storm. In April, 1871, Hellman inaugurated a popular policy when he offered to pay interest on time deposits, for it brought many clients who had previously been accustomed to do their banking in San Francisco; and before long the Bank advertised one hundred thousand dollars to lend on good security.

On February 14th, Stephen Samsbury, known as Buckskin Bill, and a man named Carter murdered the twin brothers Bilderback who had taken up some land very close to Verdugo—now incorporated in Glendale—and were engaged in chopping wood; the murderers coveting the land and planning to sell the fuel. Deputy Sheriff Dunlap went in pursuit of the desperadoes, and noticing some loose earth in the roadbed near by, he thrust a stick into the ground and so uncovered the blood-stained end of a blanket which led to the finding of the bodies.

J. F. Burns, who, at eighty-three years of age, still manifests his old time spirit, being then Sheriff, pursued Buckskin Bill until the twenty-fourth of June. A young soldier on the way to Fort Yuma met Burns at San Pedro, and having agreed to sell him certain information about the fugitive, revealed the fact that Bill had been seen near Tecate, mounted on a horse, with his squaw and infant riding a mule. The chase had previously taken the Sheriff from Verdugo Cañon to White Pine, Nevada, and back to Los Angeles; and acting on this new clue, Burns obtained a requisition on the Mexican Governor from Judge Ygnácio Sepúlveda, and went to Lower California where, with Felipe Zarate, a Mexican officer, he located the man after two or three days' search. About twenty miles north of Real Castillo, the Sheriff found the fugitive, and in the ensuing fight Samsbury accidentally shot himself; and so terribly did the wounded man suffer that he begged Burns to finish him at once. The Sheriff, refusing, improved the opportunity to secure a full confession of Bill's numerous crimes, among which figured the killing of five other men—besides the Bilderback brothers—in different parts of California.

After Samsbury died, Burns cut off his foot—known to have six toes—and placed it in *mescal*, a popular and strongly-intoxicating beverage of the Mexicans; and when later the

Sheriff presented this trophy to the good citizens of California, it was accepted as abundant proof that the man he had gone after had been captured and disposed of. The Legislature promptly paid Burns nearly five thousand dollars; but Los Angeles County, which had pledged two hundred dollars' reward, refused to recompense the doughty Sheriff and has never since made good its promise. In 1889, Burns was Chief of Police, with Emil Harris as his Captain.

The earliest move toward the formation of a Los Angeles Board of Trade was made, not in 1883, nor even in 1873—when the first Chamber of Commerce began—but in 1871, a fact that seems to be generally forgotten. Late in February of that year, a number of leading shippers came together to discuss Coast trade and other interests; and B. L. Peel moved that a Board of Trade be organized. The motion was carried and the organization was effected; but with the waning of enthusiasm for the improvements proposed or, perhaps, through the failure of its members to agree, the embryonic Board of Trade soon died.

In February, B. L. Peel & Company installed the telegraph in their commission office—probably the first instance of a private wire in local business history.

At the outset of the somewhat momentous decade of the seventies, Hellman, Haas & Company was established, with H. W. Hellman, Jacob Haas and B. Cohn partners; their first store being on the east side of Los Angeles Street opposite H. Newmark & Company's. Abraham Haas, who came in December, 1873, had a share in his brother's venture from the start; but it was not until 1875, when he bought out Cohn's interest, that he became a partner. Ten years after the firm commenced business, that is, in 1881, Jacob Baruch, who had come to California with J. Loew, and with him had made his start at Galatin, was admitted to partnership; and in 1889, a year after Jacob Haas's death, Haas & Baruch bought out H. W. Hellman. Then it was that Haas, Baruch & Company, a name so agreeably known throughout Southern California, first entered the field, their activity—immediately felt—permitting very little of the proverbial grass to grow under one's feet. On January 7th, 1909, Jacob Baruch died. Haas since December 12th, 1900 has been a resident of San Francisco.

This year the United States Government began the great work of improving Wilmington or San Pedro Harbor. The gap between Rattlesnake and Dead Man's islands was closed by means of a breakwater, creating a regular current in the channel; and dredging to a depth of seventeen or eighteen feet first made it possible for vessels of size to cross the bar at low tide. Among those active in preparing documents for Congress and securing the survey was Judge R. M. Widney, of whose public services mention has been made; while Phineas Banning, at his own expense, made trips to Washington in behalf of the project.

A genuine novelty was introduced in 1871, when Downs & Bent late in February opened a roller-skating rink at Teutonia Hall. Twenty-five cents was charged for admission, and an additional quarter demanded for the use of skates. Ladies and gentlemen flocked to enjoy the new sensation; a second rink was soon opened in Los Angeles and another in El Monte; and among those who became proficient skaters was Pancho Coronel, one of the social lions of his day. In time, however, the craze waned, and what had been hailed as fashionable because of its popularity in the great cities of the East, lost in favor, particularly among those of social pretensions.

In March, a call for a meeting to organize an Agricultural Society for the Counties of Los Angeles, Santa Bárbara, San Bernardino, Kern and San Diego brought together a large number of our citizens. L. J. Rose and his neighbor L. H. Titus, Dr. J. S. Griffin, Colonel J. J. Warner, Judge H. K. S. O'Melveny, Judge A. J. King, John G. Downey, F. N. Slaughter and many others including myself became actively interested, and then and there started the Southern District Agricultural Society which, for years, contributed so much to advance the agricultural interests of Southern California. Annual trotting races, lasting a week, lent impetus to the breeding of fine stock, for which this part of the State became famous. L. J. Rose was the moving spirit in this enterprise; and he it was who induced me and other friends to participate.

Even the first ice machine, in March, did not freeze the price below four cents per pound.

Edited by Henry C. Austin, the *Evening Express* made its first appearance on March 27th.   It was started by the printers, George and Jesse Yarnell, George A. Tiffany, J. W. Paynter and Miguel Verelo; but James J. Ayers—in 1882 State Printer —who was one of the founders of the San Francisco *Morning Call*, succeeded Austin in 1875, and then the Yarnells and Verelo retired.

L. V. Prudhomme, better known as Victor Prudhomme— a name sometimes, but probably incorrectly, spelled Prudhon— who is said to have come from France about the middle of the thirties, died here on May 8th.   His wife was a Spanish woman and for a while they resided on the east side of Main Street between Requena and First, not far from my brother's store. As a rather active member of the French Colony, he was a man in good standing, and was engaged, it seems to me, in the wine industry.   He also owned some land near San Bernardino and was continually visiting that place.

On May 27th, S. J. Millington, announced as "the pioneer dancing master of California," opened a dancing academy at Stearns's Hall, and it at once sprang into social favor.   He had morning classes for children and evening classes for adults. I happen to recall the circumstances more clearly for I was one of his committee of patrons.   Dances, by the way, were given frequently, and were often attended in costume and even in disguise.   I remember such an occasion in the early seventies when elaborate toilettes and variety of dress marked an advance in these harmless diversions.   Conspicuous among the guests was John Jones, elderly and seldom given to frivolity, who appeared in the character of the Father of his Country.

In early June, a Chinese junk, cruising in search of *abalones*, attracted no little attention at San Pedro as a primitive and clumsy specimen of marine architecture.

The sudden and abnormal demand for the *abalone* shell offered such large returns as to tempt men to take desperate chances in hunting for them among the rocks. Sometime in the seventies, a Chinaman, searching near San Diego, thrust his hand into an open shell and the *abalone* closed upon his wrist with such an irresistible grip that the unfortunate shell-hunter was held fast until overtaken by the rising tide and drowned.

For many years Los Angeles booklovers were supplied by merchants who sold other things, or who conducted a limited loan library in conjunction with their business. Such a circulating collection Samuel Hellman displayed in February, 1871. The first exclusively book and periodical store was opened in the same year, by Brodrick & Reilly, adjoining the Post Office on Spring street.

Albert Fenner Kercheval, who took up his residence in 1871 on the west side of Pearl Street near the end of Sixth, on what was formerly known as the Gelcich Place, first came to California—Hangtown—in 1849 and experienced much the same kind of mining adventure as inspired Bret Harte. On his second visit to the Coast, Kercheval raised strawberries and early tomatoes, for which he found a ready sale in San Francisco; and in his spare moments he wrote poems—collected and published in 1883 under the title of *Dolores*—some of which rather cleverly reflect California life.

On June 19th, the Teutonia-Concordia society merged with the Los Angeles Turnverein, forming the Turnverein-Germania; and about the same time, the original home of the *Verein*, a frame building on South Spring Street, was erected. In that year, also, the first German school was founded— the sessions being conducted at the old Round House.

Having had no fitting celebration of the Fourth of July for years, a number of citizens in 1871 called a meeting to consider the matter, and A. J. Johnston, L. Lichtenberger, W. H. Perry, J. M. Griffith, John Wilson, O. W. Childs and myself were appointed to make arrangements. A list of forty or fifty leading merchants willing to close their places of business

(Standing) Lorenzo Leck   Louis Mesmer   William Nordholt
(Sitting) Henry C. G. Schaeffer   Henry Hammel   John Schumacher

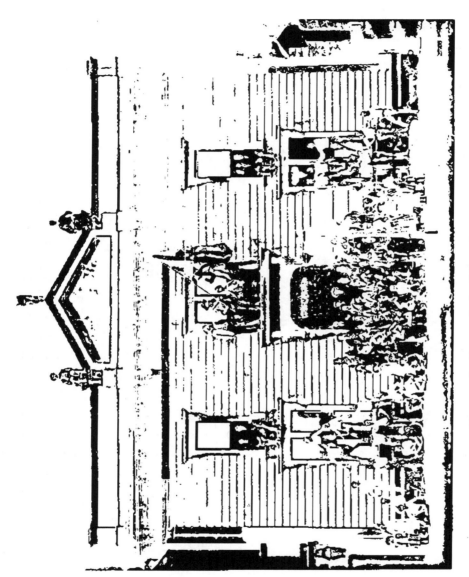

Turnverein–Germania Building, Spring Street

on Independence Day was drawn up; a program was easily prepared; and the music, display of flags and bunting, and the patriotic addresses awakened, after such a neglect of the occasion, new and edifying emotions.

Slight regard was formerly paid by officers to the safety or life of the Indian, who had a persistent weakness for alcohol; and when citizens did attend to the removal of these inebriates, they frequently looked to the Municipality for compensation. For instance: at a meeting of the Common Council, in July, Pete Wilson presented a bill of two dollars and a half "for the removal of a nuisance," which nuisance, upon investigation, was shown to have been a drunken squaw whom he had retired from the street! The Council, after debating the momentous question of reimbursement, finally reached a compromise by which the City saved just—twenty-five cents.

Alexander Bell died on July 24th, after a residence of twenty-nine years in Los Angeles.

Beginning with the seventies, attention was directed to Santa Monica as a possible summer resort, but it was some years before many people saw in the Bay and its immediate environment the opportunities upon which thousands have since seized. In the summer of 1871 less than twenty families, the majority in tents, sojourned there among the sycamore groves in the Cañon where J. M. Harned had a bar and "refreshment parlor." The attractions of beach and surf, however, were beginning to be appreciated, and so were the opportunities for shooting—at Tell's and elsewhere; and on Sundays two or three hundred excursionists frequently visited that neighborhood, Reynolds, the liveryman, doing a thriving business carrying people to the beach.

Speaking of this gradual awakening to the attractions of Santa Monica, I recall that school children of the late sixties held their picnics at the Cañon, going down on crowded stages where the choicest seats were on the box; and that one of the most popular drivers of that period was Tommy O'Campo. He handled the reins with the dexterity of a Hank Monk, and before sunrise Young America would go over to the corral, there to wait long and patiently in order to get an especially desirable seat on Tommy's stage.

With the completion of the Los Angeles & San Pedro Railroad, excursions to Catalina began to be in vogue; but as the local population was small, considerable effort was needed sometimes to secure enough patrons to make the trips pay. Thus an excursion for Sunday, August 13th, was advertised by the skipper of the steamer *Vaquero*, a couple of dollars for the round trip being charged, with half price for children; but by Saturday morning the requisite number of subscribers had not been obtained, and the excursion was called off.

Otto J. and Oswald F. Zahn, sons of Dr. Johann Carl Zahn who came here about 1871, were carrier-pigeon fanciers and established a service between Avalon and Los Angeles, fastening their messages, written on tissue paper, by delicate wire to the birds' legs. For some time the Catalina Pigeon Messengers, as they were called, left Avalon late in the afternoon, after the last steamer, bringing news that appeared in the Los Angeles newspapers of the following morning. Usually the birds took a good hour in crossing the channel; but on one occasion, *Blue Jim*, the champion, covered the distance of forty-eight miles in fifty minutes.

On the evening of August 23d, the announcement came over the wires of Don Abel Stearns's death in San Francisco, at five o'clock that afternoon, at the Grand Hotel. Late in October, his body was brought to Los Angeles for final interment, the tombstone having arrived from San Francisco a week or two previously. Awesome indeed was the scene that I witnessed when the ropes sustaining the eight hundred pound metallic casket snapped, pitching the coffin and its grim contents into the grave. I shall never forget the unearthly shriek of Doña Arcadia, as well as the accident itself.

With the wane of summer, we received the startling news of the death, through Indians, of Frederick Loring, the young journalist and author well known in Los Angeles, who was with the United States Exploring Expedition to Arizona as a correspondent of *Appleton's Journal*. "Bootless, coatless and everything but lifeless," as he put it, he had just escaped perishing in Death Valley, when the stage party was attacked by Apaches, and Loring and four other passengers were killed.

In September, during Captain George J. Clarke's administration as Postmaster, foreign money-orders began to be issued here for the first time, payable only in Great Britain and Ireland, twenty-five cents being charged for sending ten dollars or less; and shortly afterward, international money-orders were issued for Germany and some other Continental countries. Then five or six hundred letters for Los Angeles County were looked upon as rather a large dispatch by one steamer from San Francisco and the North; and the canceling of from twelve to fifteen dollars' worth of stamps a day was regarded as "big business."

Vincent Collyer—the Peace Commissioner sent out with General O. O. Howard by the Government in 1868—who eventually made himself most unpopular in Arizona by pleading the cause of the scalping Apaches in the fall of 1871, put up at the Pico House; when public feeling led one newspaper to suggest that if the citizens wished "to see a *monster*," they had "only to stand before the hotel and watch Collyer pass to and fro!"

In the fall, tidings of Chicago's awful calamity by fire reached Los Angeles, but strange to say, no public action was taken until the editor of the Los Angeles *News*, on October 12th, gave vent to his feelings in the following editorial:

Three days ago the press of this City called upon the public generally to meet at a stated hour last evening, at the County Courtroom, to do something towards alleviating the sufferings of the destitute thousands in Chicago. The calamity which has overtaken that unfortunate City has aroused the sympathy of the world, and the heart and pulse of civilized humanity voluntarily respond, extending assistance in deeds as well as in words. From all parts of the globe, where the name of Chicago is known, liberal donations flow into a common treasury. We had hoped to be able to add the name of Los Angeles among the list, as having done its duty. But in whatever else she may excel, her charity is a dishonorable exception. Her bowels are absolute strangers to sympathy, when called upon to practically demonstrate it. At the place of meeting, instead of seeing the multitude, we were astonished to find but three persons, viz: Governor Downey, John Jones, and a gentleman from Riverside, who is on a visit here. Anything more disgraceful than this apathy on the part of her inhabitants she could not have been guilty of. For her selfishness, she justly deserves the fearful fate that has befallen the helpless one that now lies stricken in the dust. Let her bow down her head in shame. Chicago, our response to your appeal is, *Starve! What do we care?*

This candid rebuke was not without effect; a committee was immediately formed to solicit contributions from the general public, and within an hour a tidy sum had been raised. By October 18th the fund had reached over two thousand dollars, exclusive of two hundred and fifty dollars given by the Hebrew Benevolent Society and still another hundred dollars raised by the Jewish ladies.

About the twenty-first of October a "war" broke out near Nigger Alley between two rival factions of the Chinese on account of the forcible carrying off of one of the companies' female members, and the steamer *California* soon brought a batch of Chinamen from San Francisco, sent down, it was claimed, to help wreak vengeance on the abductors. On Monday, October 23d some of the contestants were arrested, brought before Justice Gray and released on bail. It was expected that this would end the trouble; but at five o'clock the next day the factional strife broke loose again, and officers, accompanied by citizens, rushed to the place to attempt an arrest. The Chinese resisted and Officer Jesus Bilderrain was shot in the right shoulder and wrist, while his fifteen-year-old brother received a ball in the right leg. Robert Thompson, a citizen who sprang to Bilderrain's assistance, was met by a Chinaman with two revolvers and shot to death. Other shots from Chinese barricaded behind some iron shutters wounded a number of bystanders.

News of the attacks and counter-attacks spread like wildfire, and a mob of a thousand or more frenzied beyond control, armed with pistols, guns, knives and ropes, and determined to avenge Thompson's murder, assembled in the neighborhood of the disturbance.   While this solid phalanx was being formed around Nigger Alley, a Chinaman, waving a hatchet, was seen trying to escape across Los Angeles Street; and Romo Sortorel, at the expense of some ugly cuts on the hand, captured him. Emil Harris then rescued the Mongolian; but a detachment of the crowd, yelling "Hang him! shoot him!" overpowered Harris at Temple and Spring streets, and dragged the trembling wretch up Temple to New High street, where the familiar framework of the corral gates suggested its use as a gallows.   With the first suspension, the rope broke; but the second attempt to hang the prisoner was successful.   Other Chinamen, whose roofs had been smashed in, were rushed down Los Angeles Street to the south side of Commercial, and there, near Goller's wagon shop, between wagons stood on end, were hung. Alarmed for the safety of their cook, Sing Ty, the Juan Lanfrancos hid the Mongolian for a week, until the excitement had subsided.

Henry T. Hazard was lolling comfortably in a shaving saloon, under the luxurious lather of the barber, when he heard of the riot; and arriving on the scene, he mounted a barrel and attempted to remonstrate with the crowd.   Some friends soon pulled him down, warning him that he might be shot.   A. J. King was at supper when word was brought to him that Chinese were slaughtering white people, and he responded by seizing his rifle and two revolvers.   In trying one of the latter, however, it was prematurely discharged, taking the tip off a finger and putting him *hors de combat*.   Sheriff Burns could not reach the scene until an hour after the row started and many Chinamen had already taken their celestial flight. When he arrived, he called for a *posse comitatus* to assist him in handling the situation; but no one responded.   He also demanded from the leader of the mob and others that they disperse; but with the same negative result.   About that time, a party of rioters started with a Chinaman up Commercial

28

Street to Main, evidently bent on hanging him to the Tomlinson & Griffith gate; and when Burns promised to attempt a rescue if he had but two volunteers, Judge R. M. Widney and James Goldsworthy responded and the Chinaman was taken from his tormentors and lodged in jail.   Besides Judge Widney, Cameron E. Thom and H. C. Austin displayed great courage in facing the mob, which was made up of the scum and dregs of the city; and Sheriff Burns is also entitled to much credit for his part in preventing the burning of the Chinese quarters. All the efforts of the better element, however, did not prevent one of the most disgraceful of all disturbances which had occurred since my arrival in Los Angeles.   On October 25th, when Coroner Joseph Kurtz impanelled his jury, nineteen bodies of Chinamen alone were in evidence and the verdict was: "Death through strangulation by persons unknown to the jury."   Emil Harris's testimony at the inquest, that but one of the twenty-two or more victims deserved his fate, about hits the mark and confirms the opinion that the slight punishment to half a dozen of the conspirators was very inadequate.

At the time of the massacre, I heard a shot just as I was about to leave my office, and learned that it had been fired from that part of Chinatown facing Los Angeles Street; and I soon ascertained that it had ended Thompson's life.   Anticipating no further trouble, however, I went home to dinner.   When I returned to town, news of the riot had spread, and with my neighbors, Cameron E. Thom and John G. Downey, I hurried to the scene.   It was then that I became an eye-witness to the heroic, if somewhat comical parts played by Thom and Burns. The former, having climbed to the top of a box, harangued the crowd, while the Sheriff, who had succeeded in mounting a barrel, was also addressing the tumultuous rabble in an effort to restore order.   Unfortunately, this receptacle had been coopered to serve as a container, not as a rostrum; and the head of the cask under the pressure of two hundred pounds or more of official avoirdupois suddenly collapsed and our Worthy Guardian of the Peace dropped, with accelerated speed, clear through to the ground, and quite unintentionally, for the moment at least, turned grim tragedy into grotesque comedy.

Following this massacre, the Chinese Government made such a vigorous protest to the United States that the Washington authorities finally paid a large indemnity. During these negotiations, Chinese throughout the country held lamentation services for the Los Angeles victims; and on August 2d, 1872, four Chinese priests came from San Francisco to conduct the ceremonies.

In 1870, F. P. F. Temple, who had seen constructed two sections of the building now known as Temple Block, made the fatal blunder of accepting the friendly advice that led him to erect the third section at the junction of Spring and Main streets, and to establish therein a bank under the name of Temple & Workman. The building, costing in the neighborhood of one hundred and fifty thousand dollars, was all that could have been desired, proving by long odds the most ornamental edifice in the city; and when, on November 23d, 1871, the bank was opened in its comfortable quarters on the Spring Street side of the block, nothing seemed wanting to success. The furnishings were elaborate, one feature of the office outfit being a very handsome counter of native cedar, a decided advance in decoration over the primitive bare or painted wood then common here. Neither Temple, who had sold his fine ranch near Fort Tejón to embark in the enterprise, nor Workman had had any practical experience in either finance or commerce; and to make matters worse, Workman, being at that time a very old man, left the entire management to his son-in-law, Temple, in whom he had full confidence. It soon became evident that anybody could borrow money with or without proper security, and unscrupulous people hastened to take advantage of the situation. In due season I shall tell what happened to this bank.

In the preceding spring when the Coast-line stage companies were still the only rivals to the steamers, a movement favoring an opposition boat was started, and by June leading shippers were discussing the advisability of even purchasing a competitive steamer; all the vessels up to that time having been owned by companies or individuals with headquarters in the Northern metropolis. Matthew Keller was then in San Francisco; and having been led to believe that a company could be financed, books were opened for subscriptions in Los Angeles, Santa Bárbara, San Luis Obispo and elsewhere. For lack of the necessary support, this plan was abandoned; but late in July a meeting was held in the Bella Union to further consider the matter. Among those present was George Wright, long engaged in coast shipping; and he proposed to sell the control of the *Olympia*.

H. Newmark & Company being considerably interested in the movement, declared themselves ready to coöperate in improving the situation; for which reason great surprise was expressed when, in December, 1871, B. L. Peel, the commission merchant, made an attack on us, openly charging that, although "the largest shippers in the city," we had revoked our pledge to sustain the opposition to high freight rates, and so had contributed toward defeating the enterprise! It is true that we finally discouraged the movement, but for a good and sufficient reason: Wright was in the steamship business for anything but his health. His method was to put on a tramp steamer and then cut passenger and freight rates ridiculously low, until the regular line would buy him out; a project which, on former occasions, had caused serious disturbances to business. When therefore Wright made this offer, in 1871, H. Newmark & Company forthwith refused to participate. I shall show that, when greater necessity required it, we took the lead in a movement against the Southern Pacific which, for lack of loyalty on the part of many of the other shippers, met not only with disastrous failure but considerable pecuniary loss to ourselves.

On December 18th, 1871, Judge Murray Morrison died. Three days later, his wife, Jennie, whom we knew as the attractive daughter of Dr. Thomas J. White, also breathed her last.

CHAPTER XXX

THE WOOL CRAZE

1872–1873

AS already stated, the price of wool in 1871 was exceedingly high and continued advancing until in 1872 when, as a result, great prosperity in Southern California was predicted. Enough wool had been bought by us to make what at that time was considered a very handsome fortune. We commenced purchasing on the sheep's back in November, and continued buying everything that was offered until April, 1872, when we made the first shipment, the product being sold at forty-five cents per pound. As far as I am aware, the price of wool had never reached fifty cents anywhere in the world, it being ordinarily worth from ten to twelve cents; and without going into technicalities, which would be of no interest to the average reader, I will merely say that forty-five cents was a tremendously high figure for dirty, burry, California wool in the grease. When the information arrived that this sale had been effected, I became wool-crazy, the more so since I knew that the particular shipment referred to was of very poor quality.

Colonel R. S. Baker, who was living on his ranch in Kern County, came to Los Angeles about that time, and we offered him fifty cents a pound for Beale & Baker's clip amounting to one hundred and seventy-five thousand pounds. His reply was that it would be impossible to sell without consulting Beale; but Beale proved as wool-crazy as I, and would not sell. It developed that Beale & Baker did not succeed in effecting a sale in San Francisco, where they soon offered their product, and that they concluded to ship it to Boston; the New England metropolis then, as now, being the most important wool-center in the United States. Upon its arrival, the wool was stored; and there it remained until, as Fate would have it, the entire shipment was later destroyed in the great Boston fire of 1872. As a result of this tremendous conflagration, the insurance company which carried their policy failed and Beale & Baker met with a great loss.

The brothers Philip, Eugène and Camille Garnier of the Encino Ranch—who, while generally operating separately, clubbed together at that time in disposing of their product—had a clip of wool somewhat exceeding one hundred and fifty thousand pounds. The spokesman for the three was Eugène, and on the same day that I made Colonel Baker the offer of fifty cents, I told Eugène that I would allow him forty-eight and a half cents for the Garnier product. This offer he disdainfully refused, returning immediately to his ranch; and now, as I look back upon the matter, I do not believe that in my entire commercial experience I ever witnessed anything demonstrating so thoroughly, as did these wool transactions, the monstrous greed of man. The sequel, however, points the moral. My offer to the Garnier Brothers was made on a Friday. During that day and the next, we received several telegrams indicating that the crest of the craze had been reached, and that buyers refused to take hold. On Monday following the first visit of Eugène Garnier, he again came to town and wanted me to buy their wool at the price which I had quoted him on Friday; but by that time we had withdrawn from the market. My brother wired that San Francisco buyers would not touch it; hence the Garnier Brothers also shipped their product East and, after holding it practically a full year, finally sold it for sixteen and a half cents a pound in currency, which was then worth eighty-five cents on the dollar. The year 1872 is on record as the most disastrous wool season in our history, when millions were lost; and H. Newmark & Company suffered their share in the disaster.

It was in March that we purchased from Louis Wolfskill, through the instrumentality of L. J. Rose, the Santa
Anita *rancho*, consisting of something over eight thousand
acres, paying him eighty-five thousand dollars for this beautiful domain.   The terms agreed upon were twenty thousand
dollars down and four equal quarterly payments for the
balance.   In the light of the aftermath, the statement that
our expectations of prospective wool profits inspired this purchase seems ludicrous, but it was far from laughable at the
time; for it took less than sixty days for H. Newmark & Company to discover that buying ranches on any such basis was
not a very safe policy to follow and would, if continued, result
in disaster.   Indeed, the outcome was so different from our
calculations, that it pinched us somewhat to meet our obliga-
tions to Wolfskill.   This purchase, as I shall soon show, proved
a lucky one, and compensated for the earlier nervous and
financial strain.   John Simmons, who drove H. Newmark &
Company's truck and slept in a barn in my back yard on Main
Street, was so reliable a man that we made him overseer of the
ranch.   When we sold the property, Simmons was engaged
by Lazard Frères, the San Francisco bankers, to do special
service that involved the carrying of large sums of money.

When we bought the Santa Anita, there were five eucalyptus
or blue gum trees growing near the house.   I understood at
the time that these had been planted by William Wolfskill from
seed sent to him by a friend in Australia; and that they were
the first eucalyptus trees cultivated in Southern California.
Sometime early in 1875, the Forest Grove Association started
the first extensive tract of eucalyptus trees seen in Los
Angeles, and in a decade or two the eucalyptus had become
a familiar object; one tree, belonging to Howard & Smith,
florists at the corner of Olive and Ninth streets, attaining,[1] after
a growth of nineteen years, a height of one hundred and thirty-
four feet.

On the morning of March 26th, Los Angeles was visited
by an earthquake of sufficient force to throw people out of bed,

[1] Blown down, in a wind-storm, on the night of April 13th, 1915.

many men, women and children seeking safety by running out in their night-clothes. A day or two afterward excited riders came in from the Owens River Valley bringing reports which showed the quake to have been the worst, so far as loss of life was concerned, that had afflicted California since the memorable catastrophe of 1812.

Intending thereby to encourage the building of railroads, the Legislature, on April 4th, 1870, authorized the various Boards of Supervisors to grant aid whenever the qualified voters so elected. This seemed a great step forward, but anti-railroad sentiment, as in the case of Banning's line, again manifested itself here. The Southern Pacific, just incorporated as a subsidiary of the Central Pacific, was laying its tracks down the San Joaquin Valley; yet there was grave doubt whether it would include Los Angeles or not. It contemplated a line through Tehachepi Pass; but from that point two separate surveys had been made, one by way of Soledad Pass *via* Los Angeles, through costly tunnels and over heavy grades; the other, straight to the Needles, over an almost level plain along the Thirty-fifth parallel, as anticipated by William H. Seward in his Los Angeles speech. At the very time when every obstacle should have been removed, the opposition so crystallized in the Legislature that a successful effort was made to repeal the subsidy law; but thanks to our representatives, the measure was made ineffective in Los Angeles County, should the voters specifically endorse the project of a railroad.

In April, 1872, Tom Mott and B. D. Wilson wrote Leland Stanford that a meeting of the taxpayers, soon to be called, would name a committee to confer with the railroad officials; and Stanford replied that he would send down E. W. Hyde to speak for the company. About the first of May, however, a few citizens gathered for consultation at the Board of Trade room; and at that meeting it was decided unanimously to send to San Francisco a committee of two, consisting of Governor Downey and myself, there to convey to the Southern Pacific Company the overtures of the City. We accordingly visited Collis P. Huntington, whose headquarters were at the Grand

Hotel; and during our interview we canvassed the entire situation. In the course of this interesting discussion, Huntington displayed some engineer's maps and showed us how, in his judgment, the railroad, if constructed to Los Angeles at all, would have to enter the city. When the time for action arrived, the Southern Pacific built into Los Angeles along the lines indicated in our interview with Huntington.

On Saturday afternoon, May 18th, 1872, a public meeting was held in the Los Angeles Court-house. Governor Downey called the assembly to order; whereupon H. K. S. O'Melveny was elected President and Major Ben C. Truman, Secretary. Speeches were made by Downey, Phineas Banning, B. D. Wilson, E. J. C. Kewen and C. H. Larrabee; and resolutions were adopted pledging financial assistance from the County, provided the road was constructed within a given time. A Committee was then appointed to seek general information concerning railroads likely to extend their lines to Los Angeles; and on that Committee I had the honor of serving with F. P. F. Temple, A. F. Coronel, H. K. S. O'Melveny, J. G. Downey, S. B. Caswell, J. M. Griffith, Henry Dalton, Andrés Pico, L. J. Rose, General George Stoneman and D. W. Alexander. A few days later, Wilson, Rose and W. R. Olden of Anaheim were sent to San Francisco to discuss terms with the Southern Pacific; and when they returned, they brought with them Stanford's representative, Hyde. Temple, O'Melveny and I were made a special committee to confer with Hyde in drawing up ordinances for the County; and these statutes were immediately passed by the Supervisors. The Southern Pacific agreed to build fifty miles of its main trunk line through the County, with a branch line to Anaheim; and the County, among other conditions, was to dispose of its stock in the Los Angeles & San Pedro Railroad to the Southern Pacific Company.

When all this matter was presented to the people, the opposition was even greater than in the campaign of 1868. One newspaper—the *Evening Express*—while declaring that "railway companies are soulless corporations, invariably selfish, with a love for money," even maintained that "because they

are rich, they have no more right to build to us than has
Governor Downey to build our schoolhouses." Public addresses were made to excited, demonstrative audiences by
Henry T. Hazard, R. M. Widney and others who favored the
Southern Pacific. On the evening of November 4th, or the
night before the election, the Southern Pacific adherents held
a torchlight procession and a mass-meeting, at the same time
illuminating the pueblo with the customary bonfires. When
the vote was finally counted, it was found that the Southern
Pacific had won by a big majority; and thus was made the
first concession to the railroad which has been of such paramount importance in the development of this section of the
State.

In 1872, Nathaniel C. Carter, who boasted that he made for
the Government the first American flag woven by machinery,
purchased and settled upon a part of the Flores *rancho* near
San Gabriel. Through wide advertising, Carter attracted
his Massachusetts friends to this section; and in 1874 he
started the Carter excursions and brought train-loads of people
to Los Angeles.

Terminating a series of wanderings by sea and by land,
during which he had visited California in 1849, John Lang,
father of Gustav J. (once a Police Commissioner), came to Los
Angeles for permanent residence in 1872, bringing a neat little
pile of gold. With part of his savings he purchased the five
acres since known as the Laurel Tract on Sixteenth Street, where
he planted an orchard, and some of the balance he put into a
loan for which, against his will, he had to take over the lot on
Spring Street between Second and Third where the Lang Building now stands. Soon after his advent here, Lang found himself
one of four persons of the same name, which brought about such
confusion between him, the pioneer at Lang's Station and two
others, that the bank always labelled him "Lang No. 1," while
it called the station master "Lang No. 2." In 1866, Lang
had married, in Victoria, Mrs. Rosine Everhardt a sister of
Mrs. Kiln Messer; and his wife refusing to live at the lonesome
ranch, Lang bought, for four hundred dollars, the lot on Fort

Street on which Tally's Theater now stands, and built there a modest home from which he went out daily to visit his orchard. Being of an exceedingly studious turn of mind, Lang devoted his spare time to profitable reading; and to such an extent had he secluded himself that, when he died, on December 9th, 1900, he had passed full thirty years here without having seen Santa Monica or Pasadena. Nor had he entered the courtroom more than once, and then only when compelled to go there to release some property seized upon for taxes remaining unpaid by one of the other John Langs. Regarded by his family as idealistic and kind-hearted, John Lang was really such a hermit that only with difficulty were friends enough found who could properly serve as pall-bearers.

On June 2d, B. F. Ramirez and others launched the Spanish newspaper, *La Cronica*, from the control of which Ramirez soon retired to make way for E. F. de Celis. Under the latter's leadership, the paper became notable as a Coast organ for the Latin race. Almost simultaneously, A. J. King and A. Waite published their City Directory.

On the seventeenth of July our family circle was gladdened by the wedding festivities of Kaspare Cohn and Miss Hulda, sister of M. A. Newmark. The bride had been living with us for some time as a member of our family.

I have spoken of the attempt made, in 1859, to found a Public Library. In 1872, there was another agitation that led to a mass-meeting on December 7th, in the old Merced Theatre on Main Street; and among others present were Judge Ygnácio Sepúlveda, General George H. Stoneman, Governor John G. Downey, Henry Kirk White Bent, S. B. Caswell, W. J. Brodrick, Colonel G. H. Smith, W. B. Lawlor and myself. The Los Angeles Library Association was formed; and Downey, Bent, Brodrick, Caswell and I were appointed to canvas for funds and donations of books. Fifty dollars was charged for a life membership, and five dollars for yearly privileges; and besides these subscriptions, donations and loans of books maintained the Library. The institution was established in four small, dark rooms of the old Downey Block on Temple and

Spring streets, where the Federal Building now stands, and where the *Times*, then the youngest newspaper in Los Angeles, was later housed; and there J. C. Littlefield acted as the first Librarian.   In 1874, the State Legislature passed an enabling act for a Public Library in Los Angeles, and from that time on public funds contributed to the support of the worthy undertaking.

On January 1st, 1873, M. A. Newmark, who had come to Los Angeles eight years before, was admitted into partnership with H. Newmark & Company; and three years later, on February 27th, he married Miss Harriet, daughter of J. P. Newmark.   Samuel Cohn having died, the associates then were: Kaspare Cohn, M. J. Newmark, M. A. Newmark and myself.

On February 1st, 1873, two job printers, Yarnell & Caystile, who had opened a little shop at 14 Commercial Street, began to issue a diminutive paper called the *Weekly Mirror*, with four pages but ten by thirteen inches in size and three columns to the page; and this miniature news-sheet, falling wet from the press every Saturday, was distributed free.   Success greeted the advertising venture and the journal was known as the smallest newspaper on the Coast.   A month later, William M. Brown joined the firm, thenceforth called Yarnell, Caystile & Brown.   On March 19th, the publishers added a column to each page, announcing, rather prophetically perhaps, their intention of attaining a greatness that should know no obstacle or limit.   In November, the *Mirror* was transferred to a building on Temple Street, near the Downey Block, erected for its special needs; and there it continued to be published until, in 1887, it was housed with the *Times*.

Nels Williamson, to whom I have referred, married a native Californian, and their eldest daughter, Mariana, in 1873 became the wife of António Franco Coronel, the gay couple settling in one of the old pueblo adobes on the present site of Bishop & Company's factory; and there they were visited by Helen Hunt Jackson when she came here in the early eighties. In 1886, they moved opposite to the home that Coronel built on the southwest corner of Seventh Street and Central Avenue.

Educated here at the public and the Sisters' schools, Mrs. Coronel was a recognized leader in local society, proving very serviceable in the preparation of *Ramona* and receiving, in return, due acknowledgment from the distinguished authoress who presented her with the first copy of the book published.

Daniel Freeman, a Canadian who came in 1873, was one of many to be attracted to California through Nordhoff's famous book. After looking at many ranches, Freeman inspected the Centinela with Sir Robert Burnett, the Scotch owner then living there. Burnett insisted that the ranch was too dry for farming and cited his own necessity of buying hay at thirty dollars a ton; but Freeman purchased the twenty-five thousand acres, stocked them with sheep and continued long in that business, facing many a difficulty attendant upon the dry seasons, notably in 1875–76, when he lost fully twenty-two thousand head.

L. H. Titus, who bought from J. D. Woodworth the land in his San Gabriel orchard and vineyard, early used iron water-pipes for irrigation. A bold venture of the same year was the laying of iron water-pipes throughout East Los Angeles, at great expense, by Dr. John S. Griffin and Governor John G. Downey. About the same time, the directors of the Orange Grove Association which as we shall later see founded Pasadena, used iron pipe for conducting water, first to a good reservoir and then to their lands, for irrigating. In 1873 also, the Alhambra Tract, then beginning to be settled as a fashionable suburb of Los Angeles, obtained its water supply through the efforts of B. D. Wilson and his son-in-law, J. De Barth Shorb, who constructed large reservoirs near the San Gabriel Mission, piped water to Alhambra and sold it to local consumers.

James R. Toberman, destined to be twice rechosen Mayor of Los Angeles, was first elected in 1873, defeating Cristóbal Aguilar, an honored citizen of early days, who had thrice been Mayor and was again a candidate. Toberman made a record for fiscal reform by reducing the City's indebtedness over thirty thousand dollars and leaving a balance of about twenty-five thousand in the Treasury; while, at the same time, he caused the tax-rate during his administration to dwindle, from one dollar and sixty cents per hundred to one dollar. Toberman Street bears this Mayor's name.

In 1873, President Grant appointed Henry Kirk White Bent, who had arrived in 1868, Postmaster of Los Angeles.

The several agitations for protection against fire had, for a long time no tangible results—due most probably to the lack of water facilities; but after the incorporation of the Los Angeles Water Company and the introduction of two or three hydrants, thirty-eight loyal citizens of the town in April organized themselves into the first volunteer fire company, popularly termed the 38's, imposing a fee of a dollar a month. Some of the yeomen who thus set the ball a-rolling were Major Ben C. Truman, Tom Rowan, W. J. Brodrick, Jake Kuhrts, Charley Miles, George Tiffany, Aaron Smith, Henry T. Hazard, Cameron E. Thom, Fred Eaton, Matthew Keller, Dr. J. S. Crawford, Sidney Lacey, John Cashin and George P. McLain; and such was their devotion to the duty of both allaying and producing excitement, that it was a treat to stand by the side of the dusty street and watch the boys, bowling along, answer the fire-bell —the fat as well as the lean hitched to their one hose-cart. This cart, pulled by men, was known as the *jumper*—a name widely used among early volunteer firemen and so applied because, when the puffing and blowing enthusiasts drew the cart after them, by means of ropes, the two-wheeled vehicle jumped from point to point along the uneven surface of the road. The first engine of the 38's, known as Fire Engine No. 1, was housed, I think, back of the Pico House, but was soon moved to a building on Spring Street near Franklin and close to the City Hall.

About 1873, or possibly 1874, shrimps first appeared in the local market.

In 1873, the Los Angeles *Daily News* suspended publication. A. J. King had retired on the first of January, 1870, to be succeeded by Charles E. Beane; on October 10th, 1872, Alonzo Waite had sold his interest and Beane alone was at the helm when the ship foundered.

To resume the narrative of the *Daily Star*. In July, Henry

Hamilton sold both the paper and the job-printing office for six thousand dollars to Major Ben C. Truman, and the latter conducted the *Star* for three or four years, filling it brimful of good things just as his more fiery predecessor had done.

John Lang—"number two"—the cultivator of fruit on what was afterward Washington Gardens, who established Lang's Station and managed the sulphur springs and the hotel there, in July killed a bear said to have been one of the grizzliest grizzlies ever seen on the Coast. Lang started after Mr. Bruin and, during an encounter in the San Fernando range that nearly cost his life, finally shot him. The bear tipped the beam—forbid it that anyone should question the reading of the scales!—at two thousand, three hundred and fifty pounds; and later, as gossip had it, the pelt was sold to a museum in Liverpool, England. This adventure, which will doubtless bear investigation, recalls another hunt, by Colonel William Butts, later editor of the *Southern Californian*, in which the doughty Colonel, while rolling over and over with the infuriated beast, plunged a sharp blade into the animal's vitals; but only after Butts's face, arms and legs had been horribly lacerated. Butts's bear, a hundred hunters in San Luis Obispo County might have told you, weighed twenty-one hundred pounds—or more.

Dismissing these bear stories, some persons may yet be interested to learn of the presence here, in earlier days, of the ferocious wild boar. These were met with, for a long time, in the wooded districts of certain mountainous land-tracts owned by the Ábilas, and there wild swine were hunted as late as 1873.

In the summer, D. M. Berry, General Nathan Kimball, Calvin Fletcher and J. H. Baker came to Los Angeles from Indianapolis, representing the California Colony of Indiana, a coöperative association which proposed to secure land for Hoosiers who wished to found a settlement in Southern California. This scheme originated with Dr. Thomas Balch Elliott of Indianapolis, Berry's brother-in-law and an army surgeon who had established the first grain elevator in Indiana and whose wife, now ill, could no longer brave the severe winters of the middle West.

Soon after their arrival, Wall Street's crash brought ruin to many subscribers and the members of the committee found themselves stranded in Los Angeles. Berry opened a real estate office on Main Street near Arcadia, for himself and the absent Elliott; and one day, at the suggestion of Judge B. S. Eaton, Baker visited the San Pasqual *rancho*, then in almost primeval glory, and was so pleased with what he saw that he persuaded Fletcher to join Dr. Elliott, Thomas H. Croft of Indianapolis and himself in incorporating the San Gabriel Orange Grove Association, with one hundred shares at two hundred and fifty dollars each. The Association then bought out Dr. J. S. Griffin's interest, or some four thousand acres in the ranch, paying about twelve dollars and a half per acre, after which some fifteen hundred of the choicest acres were subdivided into tracts of from fifteen to sixty acres each.

The San Pasqual settlement was thus called for a while the Indiana Colony, though but a handful of Hoosiers had actually joined the movement; and Dr. and Mrs. Elliott, reaching Los Angeles on December 1st, 1874, immediately took possession of their grant on the banks of the Arroyo Seco near the Frémont Trail. On April 22d, 1875, The Indiana Colony was discontinued as the name of the settlement; it being seen that a more attractive title should be selected. Dr. Elliott wrote to a college-mate in the East for an appropriate Indian name; and *Pasadena* was adopted as Chippewa for "Crown of the Valley." Linguists, I am informed, do not endorse the word as Indian of any kind, but it is a musical name, and now famous and satisfactory. Dr. Elliott threw all his energy into the cultivation of oranges, but it was not long before he saw, with a certain prophetic vision, that not the fruit itself, but the health-giving and charming qualities of the San Pasqual climate were likely to prove the real asset of the colonists and the foundation of their prosperity. Pasadena and South Pasadena, therefore, owe their existence largely to the longing of a frail Indiana woman for a less rigorous climate and her dream that in the sunny Southland along the Pacific she should find health and happiness.

M. J. Newmark was really instrumental, more than any-one else, in first persuading D. M. Berry to come to California. He had met Berry in New York and talked to him of the possibility of buying the Santa Anita *rancho*, which we were then holding for sale; and on his return he traveled homeward by way of Indiana, stopping off at Indianapolis in order to bring Berry out here to see the property. Owing to the high price asked, however, Berry and his associates could not negotiate the purchase, and so the matter was dropped.

Lawson D. Hollingsworth and his wife, Lucinda, Quakers from Indiana, opened the first grocery at the crossroads in the new settlement, and for many years were popularly spoken of as Grandpa and Grandma Hollingsworth. Dr. H. T. Hollingsworth, their son, now of Los Angeles, kept the Post Office in the grocery, receiving from the Government for his services the munificent sum of—twenty-five cents a week.

The summer of 1873 was marked by the organization of a corporation designed to advance the general business interests of Los Angeles and vicinity. This was the Chamber of Commerce or, as it was at first called, the Board of Trade; and had its origin in a meeting held on August 1st in the old Court-House on the site of the present Bullard Block. Ex-Governor John G. Downey was called to the chair; and J. M. Griffith was made Secretary *pro tem*. Before the next meeting, over one hundred representative merchants registered for membership, and on August 9th, a constitution and by-laws were adopted, a board of eleven Directors elected and an admission fee of five dollars agreed upon. Two days later, the organization was incorporated, with J. G. Downey, S. Lazard, M. J. Newmark, H. W. Hellman, P. Beaudry, S. B. Caswell, Dr. J. S. Griffin, R. M. Widney, C. C. Lips, J. M. Griffith and I. W. Lord, as Directors; and these officers chose Solomon Lazard as the first President and I. W. Lord as the first Secretary. Judge Widney's office in the Temple Block was the meeting-place. The Chamber unitedly and enthusiastically set to work to push forward the commercial interests of Southern California; and the first appropriation by Congress for the survey and improvement of San Pedro Harbor was effected mainly through the new society's efforts. Descriptive pamphlets setting forth the advantages of our locality were distributed throughout the East; and steps were taken to build up the trade with Arizona and the surrounding territory. In this way the Chamber of Commerce labored through the two or three succeeding years, until bank failures, droughts and other disasters, of which I shall speak, threw the cold blanket of discouragement over even so commendable an enterprise and for the time being its activities ceased.

On October 3d, C. A. Storke founded the *Daily and Weekly Herald*, editing the paper until August, 1874 when J. M. Bassett became its editor. In a few months he retired and John M. Baldwin took up the quill.

In the autumn of 1873, Barnard Brothers set in operation the first woolen mill here, built in 1868 or 1869 by George Hansen and his associates in the Canal and Reservoir Company. It was located on the ditch along the *cañon* of the Arroyo de Los Reyes—now Figueroa Street; and for fifteen years or more was operated by the Barnards and the Coulters, after which it was turned into an ice factory.

In March of the preceding year, I sent my son Maurice to New York, expecting him there to finish his education. It was thought best, however, to allow him, in 1873, to proceed across the ocean and on to Paris where he might also learn the French language, at that time an especially valuable acquisition in Los Angeles. To this latter decision I was led when Zadoc Kahn, Grand Rabbi of Paris and afterward Grand Rabbi of France, and a brother-in-law of Eugene Meyer, signified his willingness to take charge of the lad; and for three years the Grand Rabbi and his excellent wife well fulfilled their every obligation as temporary guardians. How great an advantage, indeed, this was will be readily recognized by all familiar with the published life of Zadoc Kahn and his reputation as a scholar and pulpit orator. He was a man of the highest ideals, as was proved in his unflinching activity, with Émile Zola, in the defense and liberation of the long-persecuted Dreyfus.

Sometime in December, L. C. Tibbetts, one of the early colonists at Riverside, received a small package from a friend at Washington, D. C., after having driven sixty-five miles to Los Angeles to get it; and he took it out of the little express office without attracting any more attention than to call forth the observation of the clerk that some one must care a lot about farming to make so much fuss about two young trees. "'Tis nothing, says the fool!" The package in question contained two small orange' trees from Bahia, Brazil, brought to the United States by the Agricultural Department and destined to bestow upon Tibbetts the honor of having originated the navel orange industry of California.

In 1873, Drum Barracks at Wilmington were offered by the Government at public auction; and what had cost a million dollars or so to install, was knocked down for less than ten thousand dollars to B. D. Wilson, who donated it for educational purposes.

During the winter of 1873-74, the Southern Pacific commenced the construction of its Anaheim branch; and the first train from Los Angeles to the thriving, expectant German settlement made the run in January, 1875.

Max Cohn, a nephew, arrived in Los Angeles in 1873 and clerked for H. Newmark & Company for a number of years. In December, 1885, when I retired from the wholesale grocery business, Max became a full partner. In 1888, failing health compelled him, although a young man, to seek European medical advice; and he entered a sanatorium at Falkenstein, in the Taunus Mountains where, in 1889, he died.

CHAPTER XXXI

THE END OF VASQUEZ

1874

ALTHOUGH a high school had been proposed for Los Angeles as early as 1860, it was not until 1873, during Dr. W. T. Lucky's superintendency and under his teaching, that high-school courses were inaugurated here. Then the more advanced students were accommodated in the schoolhouse on Pound Cake Hill, where the Court-house now stands; and from this humble beginning the present high-school system of Los Angeles has been evolved. Later, under Dr. T. H. Rose's leadership, the grammar departments were removed to the other school buildings and the High School was conducted as an independent institution.

In 1874, S. Lazard & Company dissolved, Eugene and Constant Meyer succeeding, on June 15th, under the firm name of Eugene Meyer & Company or, as the store was better known, the City of Paris.

Charles H., or Charley White, long prominent in the passenger department of the Southern Pacific, entered the service of the Los Angeles & San Pedro Railroad in 1874, as John Milner's assistant, and soon became the regular ticket-agent here. After forty years of invaluable service, he is still with the Southern Pacific occupying the important position of Chief Clerk of the General Passenger Office.

George H. Peck, County Superintendent of Schools between 1874 and 1876, was a Vermonter who came in 1869 and bought five hundred acres of land near El Monte. On his

Vasquez and his Captors.

Vasquez and his Captors

(*Top*) D. K. Smith,
William R. Rowland,
Walter E. Rodgers.

(*Middle*) Albert Johnson,
Greek George's Home,
G. A. Beers.

(*Bottom*) Emil Harris,
Tibúrcio Vasquez,
J. S. Bryant.

Greek George

Nicolás Martínez

first visit to the Coast, Peck handled hay in San Francisco when it was worth two hundred dollars a ton; then he mined a little; and subsequently he opened the first public school in Sacramento and the first industrial school in San Francisco.

Andrew A. Weinschank, a veteran of the Battle of Vera Cruz who came to Los Angeles in 1856, died on February 16th, 1874. For a while, he sold home-made sauerkraut, pickles and condiments, and was one of a well-known family in the German pioneer group here. Carrie, one of Weinschank's daughters, married a circus man named Lee who made periodical visits to Los Angeles, erecting a small tent, at first somewhere in the neighborhood of the present *Times* Building, in which to conduct his show. Later, Polly Lee became a rider in the circus and with her father electrified the youth of the town when Lee, in the character of *Dick Turpin*, and mounted on his charger, *Black Bess*, carried off the weeping Polly to his den of free-booters. A son, Frank A. Weinschank, was a pioneer plumber.

In the early seventies, while the Southern Pacific Railway was building from San Francisco to San José, some twelve or fifteen bandits, carousing at a country dance in the Mexican settlement, Panamá (about six miles south of Bakersfield) planned to cross the mountains and hold up the pay-car. They were unsuccessful; whereupon, they turned their attention to the village of Tres Pinos, robbed several store-keepers and killed three or four men. They were next heard of at little Kingston, in Tulare County, where they plundered practically the whole town. Then they once more disappeared.

Presently various clues pointed to the identity of the chief *bandido* as one Tibúrcio Vasquez, born in Monterey in the thirties, who had taken to the life of an outlaw because, as he fantastically said, some *Gringos* had insolently danced off with the prettiest girls at *fandangos*, among them being his sweet-heart whom an American had wronged. With the exception of his Lieutenant, Chavez, he trusted no one, and when he moved from place to place, Chavez alone accompanied him. In each new field he recruited a new gang, and he never slept in camp with his followers.

Although trailed by several sheriffs, Vasquez escaped to Southern California leading off the wife of one of his associates—a bit of gallantry that contributed to his undoing, as the irate husband at once gave the officers much information concerning Vasquez's life and methods. One day in the spring of 1874, Vasquez and three of his companions appeared at the ranch of Alessandro Repetto, nine miles from town, disguised as sheep-shearers. The following morning, while the inmates of the ranch-house were at breakfast, the highwaymen entered the room and held up the defenceless household. Vasquez informed Repetto that he was organizing a revolution in Lower California and merely desired to borrow the trifling sum of eight hundred dollars. Repetto replied that he had no money in the house; but Vasquez compelled the old man to sign a check for the sum demanded, and immediately dispatched to town a boy working for Repetto, with the strict injunction that if he did not return with the money alone, and soon, his master would be shot.

When the check was presented at the Temple & Workman Bank, Temple, who happened to be there, became suspicious but could elicit from the messenger no satisfactory response to his questions. The bank was but a block from the Courthouse; and when Sheriff Rowland hurriedly came, in answer to a summons, he was inclined to detain the lad. The boy, however, pleaded so hard for Repetto's life that the Sheriff agreed to the messenger's returning alone with the money. Soon after, Rowland and several deputies started out along the same trail; but a lookout sighted the approaching horsemen and gave the alarm. Vasquez and his associates took to flight and were pursued as far as Tejunga Pass; but as the cut-throats were mounted on fresh horses, they escaped. Even while being pursued, Vasquez had the audacity to fleece a party of men in the employ of the Los Angeles Water Company who were doing some work near the Alhambra Tract. The well-known Angeleño and engineer in charge, Charles E. Miles, was relieved of an expensive gold watch.

In April, 1874, Sheriff Rowland heard that Vasquez

had visited the home of "Greek George"—the Smyrniot camel-driver to whom I have referred—and who was living about ten miles from Los Angeles, near the present location of Hollywood. Rowland took into his confidence D. K. Smith and persuaded him to stroll that way, ostensibly as a farmer's hand seeking employment; and within two weeks Smith reported to Rowland that the information as to Vasquez's whereabouts was correct. Rowland then concluded to make up a *posse*, but inasmuch as a certain clement kept Vasquez posted regarding the Sheriff's movements, Rowland had to use great precaution. Anticipating this emergency, City Detective Emil Harris—four years later Chief of Police—had been quietly transferred to the Sheriff's office; in addition to whom, Rowland selected Albert Johnson, Under Sheriff; B. F. Hartley, a local policeman; J. S. Bryant, City Constable; Major Henry M. Mitchell, an attorney; D. K. Smith; Walter Rodgers, proprietor of the Palace Saloon; and G. A. Beers, a correspondent of the *San Francisco Chronicle*. All these were ordered to report, one by one with their horses, shortly after midnight, at Jones's Corral on Spring Street near Seventh. Arms and ammunition, carefully packed, were likewise smuggled in. Whether true or not that Vasquez would speedily be informed of the Sheriff's whereabouts, it is certain that, in resolving not to leave his office, Rowland sacrificed, for the public weal, such natural ambition that he cannot be too much applauded; not even the later reward of eight thousand dollars really compensating him for his disappointment.

By half-past one o'clock in the morning, the eight members of the *posse* were all in the saddle and silently following a circuitous route. At about daybreak, in dense fog, they camped at the mouth of Nichols's Canyon—two miles away from the house of Greek George—where Charles Knowles, an American, was living. When the fog lifted, Johnston, Mitchell, Smith and Bryant worked their way to a point whence they could observe Greek George's farm; and Bryant, returning to camp, reported that a couple of gray horses had been seen tied near the ranch-house. Shortly thereafter, a four-horse empty wagon, driven by two Mexicans, went by the *cañon* and was immediately stopped and brought in.   The Mexicans were put in charge of an officer, and about the same time Johnston came tearing down the ravine with the startling statement that Vasquez was undoubtedly at Greek George's!

A quick consultation ensued and it was decided by the *posse* to approach their goal in the captured vehicle, leaving their own horses in charge of Knowles; and having warned the Mexicans that they would be shot if they proved treacherous, the deputies climbed into the wagon and lay down out of sight. When a hundred yards from the house, the officers stealthily scattered in various directions.   Harris, Rodgers and Johnston ran to the north side, and Hartley and Beers to the west. Through an open door, Vasquez was seen at the breakfast table, and Harris, followed by the others, made a quick dash for the house.   A woman waiting on Vasquez attempted to shut the officers out; but Harris injected his rifle through the half-open door and prevented her.   During the excitement, Vasquez climbed through a little window, and Harris, yelling, "There he goes!" raised his Henry rifle and shot at him.   By the time Harris had reached the other side of the house, Vasquez was a hundred feet away and running like a deer toward his horse.   In the meantime, first Hartley and then the other officers used their shotguns and slightly wounded him again.   Vasquez then threw up his hands, saying: "Boys, you've done well! but I've been a damned fool, and it's my own fault!"   The identity of the bandit thus far had not been established; and when Harris asked his name, he answered, "Alessandro Martinez."[1]   In the meantime, captors and prisoner entered the house; and Vasquez, who was weakened from his wounds, sat down, while the young woman implored the officers not to kill him.   At closer range, a good view was obtained of the man who had so long terrorized the State.   He was about five feet six or seven inches in height, sparely built, with small feet and hands— in that respect by no means suggesting the desperado—with

[1] Not the Spanish Alejandro; a variation doubtless suggested by the Italian Repetto's forename.

a low forehead, black, coarse hair and mustache, and furtive, cunning eyes.

By this time, the entire *posse*, excepting Mitchell and Smith (who had followed a man seen to leave Greek George's), proceeded to search the house. The first door opened revealed a young fellow holding a baby in his arms. He, the most youthful member of the organization, had been placed on guard. There were no other men in the house, although four rifles and six pistols, all loaded and ready for use, were found. Fearing no such raid, the other outlaws were afield in the neighborhood; and being warned by the firing, they escaped. One of Vasquez's guns, by the way, has been long preserved by the family of Francisco Ybarra and now rests secure in the County Museum.

Underneath one of the beds was found Vasquez's vest containing Charley Miles's gold watch, which Harris at once recognized. The prisoner was asked whether he was seriously hurt and he said that he expected to die, at the same time admitting that he was Vasquez and asking Harris to write down some of his bequests. He said that he was a single man, although he had two children living at Elizabeth Lake; and he exhibited portraits of them. He protested that he had never killed a human being, and said that the murders at Tres Pinos were due to Chavez's disobedience of orders.

The officers borrowed a wagon from Judge Thompson—who lived in the neighborhood—into which they loaded Vasquez, the boy and the weapons, and so proceeded on their way. When they arrived near town, Smith and Mitchell caught up with them. Mitchell was then sent to give advance notice of Vasquez's capture and to have medical help on hand; and by the time the party arrived, the excitement was intense. The City Fathers, then in session, rushed out pellmell and crowds surrounded the Jail. Dr. K. D. Wise, Health Officer, and Dr. J. P. Widney, County Physician, administered treatment to the captive. Vasquez, in irons, pleaded that he was dying; but Dr. Widney, as soon as he had examined the captive, warned the Sheriff that the prisoner, if he escaped, would still be game for a long day's ride. Everybody who could, visited him and I was no exception. I was disgusted, however, when I found Vasquez's cell filled with flowers, sent by some white women of Los Angeles who had been carried away by the picturesque career of the *bandido;* but Sheriff Rowland soon stopped all such foolish exuberance.

Vasquez admitted that he had frequently visited Mexicans in Los Angeles, doing this against the advice of his lieutenant, Chavez, who had warned him that Sheriff Rowland also had good friends among the Mexicans.

Among those said to have been in confidential touch with Vasquez was Mariano G. Santa Cruz, a prominent figure, in his way, in Sonora Town. He kept a grocery about three hundred feet from the old Plaza Church, on the east side of Upper Main Street, and had a curiously-assorted household. There on many occasions, it is declared, Vasquez found a safe refuge.

Five days after the capture, Signor Repetto called upon the prisoner, who was in chains, and remarked: "I have come to say that, so far as *I* am concerned, you can settle that little account with God Almighty!" Vasquez, with characteristic flourishes, thanked the Italian and began to speak of repayment, when Repetto replied: "I do not expect that. But I beg of you, if ever you resume operations, never to visit *me* again." Whereupon Vasquez, placing his hand dramatically upon his breast, exclaimed: "Ah, Señor, I am a cavalier, with a cavalier's heart!"—*¡Señor Repetto, yo soy un caballero, con el corazón de un caballero!*

As soon as Vasquez's wounds were healed, he was taken by Sheriff Rowland to Tres Pinos and there indicted for murder. Miller & Lux, the great cattle owners, furnished the money, it was understood, for his defense—supposedly as a matter of policy. His attorneys asked for, and obtained, a change of venue, and Vasquez was removed to San José. There he was promptly tried, found guilty and, in March, 1875, hanged.

Many good anecdotes were long told of Vasquez; one of which was that he could size up a man quickly, as to whether he was a native son or not, by the direction in which he would roll a cigarette—toward or away from himself! As soon as the long-feared bandit was in captivity, local wits began to joke at his expense. A burlesque on Vasquez was staged late in May at the Merced Theater; and the day the outlaw was captured, a merchant began his advertisement: "Vasquez says that Mendel Meyer has the Finest and Most Complete Stock of Dry Goods and Clothing, etc."

In the spring of 1874, Charles Maclay, with whom were associated George K. and F. B. Porter, purchased the San Fernando *rancho* which consisted of fifty-six thousand acres and embraced the old Spanish Mission; and on April 20th, Maclay invited fifty of his friends to a picnic on his newly-acquired possession. During the day some one suggested founding a town there. The name of the new settlement was to be decided by a vote of the participants, and almost unanimously they selected the title of San Fernando. Within a couple of weeks, hundreds of lots were sold and the well-known colony was soon on the way to prosperity. Boring for petroleum commenced in the San Fernando Mountains about that time, and the new town became the terminus of the Southern Pacific until the long tunnel was completed. Maclay, who was a native of Massachusetts, came to California at about the same time as I did; he was at first a tanner in Santa Cruz, but later came south and, entering into politics in addition to his other activities, became State Senator, in which position he attained considerable local prominence.

A charming home of the seventies was that of Dr. and Mrs. Shaw, pioneers situated, as I recollect, on San Pedro Street perhaps as far south as what is now Adams. They conducted a diversified nursery, including some orange trees, to obtain which Shaw had journeyed all the way to Nicaragua.

Toward the end of April, 1874, General E. F. Beale and Colonel R. S. Baker, representing themselves and New York capitalists, sought support for a new railroad project—a single-track line to run from this city to Shoo-Fly Landing, located, I think, near the present Playa del Rey and considerably north of San Pedro; where a town, Truxton—doubtless named after the General's son—was to be founded. The proposed railway was to be known as the Los Angeles & Truxton Railroad, with a route from the western part of the city in the direction of Ciénega and the Rincon de los Bueyes, and along a corner of the Ballona. The estimated length of the line was fourteen miles, and the projectors claimed that it would enable the Angeleño to reach San Francisco within thirty hours, with but one night at sea, and so add to the comfort, convenience and cheapness of passenger travel. A new harbor and an additional pier stretching far into the ocean were to be features of the enterprise; but for some reason or other, nothing grew out of the movement. As late as the following September, the promoters were still interviewing councilmen and ranch-owners; but the Los Angeles & Truxton Railroad remained a mere fancy of the financier and engineer.

For a resort that never came to be settled by a community, Truxton acquired some fame in the early seventies, a rumor also being current in the summer of 1874 that a fine sea-shore hotel was to be built there. A clipping before me of the same date even says that "the roads to Santa Monica, Truxton and Will Tell's are in splendid order—the former being the finest natural highway on the Pacific Coast."

F. X. Eberle and wife, Marsetes, came here in 1874, bought six or seven acres on the corner of San Pedro and the present Eighth streets, and fitted up the City Gardens, with bowling alleys, swings, lawns and bowers, erecting there also a picturesque windmill.

I have expressed the surprise that I felt, when, upon my return from New York in 1868, I observed that the approaches to the hills were dotted here and there with little homes. This extension of the residence area, together with the general lack of street and sidewalk improvements making travel to and from the town somewhat inconvenient, suggested, I have no doubt, the need of the first street railroad here. In 1869, Judge R. M. Widney, together with his associates, obtained a fifty-year franchise; and by 1874, the little Spring and Sixth Street

line—in time bought by S. C. Hubbell and J. E. Hollenbeck—had been built and was in operation. It is my recollection that this line (partly paid for by subscriptions from
property owners along the selected route, each of whom contributed fifty cents per running foot) began at the Plaza and
extended as far out as Pearl and Sixth streets by way of Main,
Spring, First, Fort, Fourth, Hill, Fifth and Olive; and that it
was at the Sixth and Pearl Street terminus that the almost
miniature wooden barn was put up. For the convenience
of the traveling public, two bob-tailed, one-horse cars with a
small platform at each end were used over a single track
approximately but two and a half miles in length; and to
permit these cars to pass each other when they met halfway
along the line, a turnout or side-track was constructed.
Many a time at such a siding have I wasted precious minutes
awaiting the arrival of the other, belated car; and the annoyance of these delays was accentuated when, in winter, the cars
stuck in the mud and often required an hour or more to make
the run from one end of the line to the other. Indeed, the ties
having been laid almost on the surface of the streets, service in
bad weather was sometimes suspended altogether. Each car
was in charge of a driver who also acted as conductor and was
permitted to stop as often as he pleased to take on or let off
passengers; and while the single horse or mule jogged along
slowly, the driver, having wound his reins around the handle
of the brake, would pass through the never-crowded vehicle
and take up the fares. Single rides cost ten cents; four tickets
were sold for two bits; and twenty tickets were given for a
dollar. So provincial was the whole enterprise that passengers
were expected to purchase their tickets either at W. J. Brodrick's book store or of Dr. Fred. P. Howard, the druggist. At a
later period, a metal box with a glass front was installed, into
which the passenger was required to drop his coin or ticket.

In those modest days, small compensation in public utility
enterprises—if such they could be called—was quite acceptable;
and since the Spring and Sixth Street line had proven rather
profitable, it was not long before W. J. Brodrick, Governor

Downey, O. W. Childs, Dave Waldron, I. W. Hellman and others inaugurated a second horse-railway. This was popularly known as the Main Street line and extended straight down Main Street from Temple Block to Washington Gardens. Much the same kind of equipment was used, one horse or mule poking along with a bob-tailed car in tow, seating at most eight or ten passengers; but the fare for adults was ten cents, and for children five. At night, the motor power and the couple of cars were housed in a barn at either Main or Washington Street.

Soon after this line was in running order, it was extended from Washington south to Jefferson, out Jefferson to Wesley (now University) Avenue, and thence to the race-track at Agricultural Park; and there the shed for this section was erected. Still later, a branch was built out Washington Street to Figueroa, and down Figueroa to Jefferson, where it connected with the first extension. No formal transfers were made, transfer-tickets first coming into vogue in Los Angeles about 1889. Two routes for the cars were arranged, both running between Temple Block and the race-track. The entire system was controlled by the Main Street & Agricultural Park Railroad Company, with which W. J. Brodrick was associated as its first President, continuing in that office until his death in 1898. In 1877, Colonel John O. Wheeler, the quondam journalist, was Manager. Later, E. M. Loricke was Superintendent—the same Loricke who built the line between Oakland and Berkeley, and was finally killed by one of his own cars. James Gallagher, who went to work for the Main Street & Agricultural Park Railroad Company in October, 1888, and who had charge also of one of the first electric cars run here, is still a street-car conductor pleasantly known, with the longest record for service of any conductor in the city. As I have said, travel in winter was anything but expeditious and agreeable; and it was not uncommon for passengers, when a car left the track, to get out and assist in the operation of putting it back. Notwithstanding these drawbacks, however, the mule-car novelty became popular with some; and one Spanish girl in particular, whose father amply supplied her with pocket-money, was a frequent passenger, riding back and forth, from hour to hour, for months. As late as 1887, there were no cars before six o'clock in the morning or after ten o'clock at night; and in that same year, serious complaint was made that, despite a city ordinance forbidding any street railway company to carry more than forty persons in a car drawn by a single horse, the ordinance was shamefully disregarded. Another regulation then frequently disobeyed was supposed to limit smoking to the rear end of street cars.

The same year, D. V. Waldron bought about thirty-five acres on the southwest corner of Main and Washington streets, soon known as the Washington Gardens, later Chute's Park. These Gardens, among the most popular pleasure resorts here, were served by the Main Street cars which ran direct to the gate. In addition to a Sunday afternoon variety show that held forth in a small pavilion and secured most of its talent from Wood's Opera House, there was also dancing for those who wished to indulge. I may add that this so-called opera house was nothing more than a typical Western song and dance resort, the gallery being cut up into boxes where the actresses, between the acts, mingled with the crowd. Patrons indulged in drinking and smoking; and the bar in front did a thriving business. An insignificant collection of animals—one of which, an escaping monkey, once badly bit Waldron—attracted not only the children, but their elders as well; and charmingly-arranged walks, amid trees and bowers, afforded innocent and healthful means of recreation. Waldron later went to Alaska, where a tragic death closed his career: alone and in want, he was found, in May, 1911, dead in his hut.

Waldron and Eberle's prosperity may have influenced George Lehman's fortunes; but however that was, he always maintained his popularity. Many a joke was cracked at his expense; yet everybody had a good word for him. Here is a newspaper note of '74:

Round House George is making great improvements in his property at Fort and Sixth streets. He has already, at great expense, *set out a post and whitewashed a cactus plant!*

The popularity of the 38's Fire Company soon inspired a second group of the good men of Los Angeles; and in 1874 or 1875, George Furman, George E. Gard, Joe Manning, John R. Brierly, Bryce McClellan and others started Confidence Engine Company No. 2, obtaining a steamer known as an Amoskeag, which they installed in a building on Main Street near First, on what was later the site of Childs' Opera House. It soon developed, as in the days of the San Pedro stages when the most important feature of the trip was the race to town, that a conflagration was a matter of secondary importance, the mad dash, in rivalry, by the two companies being the paramount object. This was carried to such an extent that the day following a fire was largely given to discussing the race, and the first thing that everybody wished to know was, who got there first? Indeed, I believe that many an alarm was sounded to afford the boys around town a good chance to stake their bets! All this made the fire-laddies the most popular groups in the pueblo; and in every public parade for years the volunteer fire companies were the chief attraction. In 1876, Walter S. Moore, an arrival of 1875, became the Confidence Engine Company's Secretary, that being the commencement of his career as a builder of the department. In 1877, Moore was elected President, occupying that office till 1883 when he was made Chief Engineer of the Los Angeles Fire Department.

On May 13th, 1874, the Los Angeles *Daily Star* contained the following reference to Mr. and Mrs. Joseph Newmark and an event of particular interest to me and my family:

Mr. Newmark, *père* and wife, were among the passengers for San Francisco by the *Senator* yesterday. This well-known and highly-esteemed couple go to attend the marriage of their son, Judge M. J. Newmark, which event occurs on the seventh proximo, as announced in the Star some time ago.

Eugene Meyer and myself attended the wedding, leaving Los Angeles by stage and completely surprising the merry company a few moments before the groom's father performed the

Benjamin S. Eaton

Henry T. Hazard

Fort Street Home, Harris Newmark, Site of Blanchard Hall; Joseph Newmark
at the Door

Calle de los Negros (Nigger Alley), about 1870

Second Street, Looking East from Hill Street, Early Seventies

ceremony. The fair bride was Miss Sophie Cahen, and the occasion proved one of the very agreeable milestones in an interesting and successful career. The first-born of this union, Henry M. Newmark, now of Morgan & Newmark, has attained civic distinction, being President of the Library Board.

The reason we journeyed north by stage was to escape observation, for since the steamer-service had been so considerably improved, most of our friends were accustomed to travel by water. The Pacific Mail Steamship Company at that time was running the *Senator*, the *Pacific*, the *Orizaba* and the *Mohongo*, the latter being the gunboat sold by the Government at the end of the War and which remained on the route until 1877; while the line controlled by Goodall, Nelson & Perkins or Goodall, Nelson & Company had on their list the *Constantine*, the *Kalorama*, the *Monterey* and the *San Luis*, sometimes also running the *California*, which made a specialty of carrying combustibles. A year later, the *Ancon* commenced to run between San Francisco and San Diego, and excepting half a year when she plied between the Golden Gate and Portland, was a familiar object until 1884.

The Farmers & Merchants Bank, on June 15th, 1874, moved to their new building on the west side of Main Street, opposite the Bella Union.

On July 25th, 1874, Conrad Jacoby commenced in the old Lanfranco Building the weekly *Sued-Californische Post;* and for fifteen years or more it remained the only German paper issued in Southern California. Jacoby's brother, Philo, was the well-known sharpshooter.

Henry T. Payne, the early photographer, was probably the first to go out of town to take views in suburbs then just beginning to attract attention. Santa Monica was his favorite field, and a newspaper clipping or two preserve the announcements by which the wet-plate artist stimulated interest in his venture. One of these reads:

Mr. Payne will be at Santa Monica next Sunday, and take photographic views of the camp, the ocean, the surrounding scenery, and such groups of campers and visitors as may see fit to arrange themselves for that purpose;

while another and rather contradictory notice is as follows:

To make photographs of *moving* life, such as Mr. Payne's bathing scenes at Santa Monica next Sunday, *it is absolutely necessary that everybody should keep perfectly still* during the few seconds the plate is being exposed, for the least move might completely spoil an otherwise beautiful effect. Santa Monica, with its bathers in nice costume, sporting in the surf, with here and there an artistically-posed group basking in the sunshine, ought to make a beautiful picture.

As late as 1874, Fort Street—not yet called Broadway—was almost a plain, except for the presence of a few one-story adobe houses. J. M. Griffith, the lumberman, put up the first two-story frame dwelling-house between Second and Third streets, and Judge H. K. S. O'Melveny the second; shortly after which Eugene Meyer and myself built our homes in the same block. These were put upon the lots formerly owned by Burns & Buffum. Within the next two or three years, the west side of Fort Street between Second and Third was the choicest residence neighborhood in the growing city, and there was certainly not the remotest idea at that time that this street would ever be used for business purposes. Sometime later however, as I was going home one day, I met Griffith and we walked together from Spring Street down First, talking about the new County Bank and its Cashier, J. M. Elliott—whom Griffith had induced four years previously to come to Los Angeles and take charge of Griffith, Lynch & Company's lumber yard at Compton. We then spoke of the city's growth, and in the course of the conversation he said: "Newmark, Fort Street is destined to be the most important business thoroughfare in Los Angeles." I laughed at him, but Time has shown the wisdom of Griffith's prophecy.

The construction of this Fort Street home I commenced in the spring, contracting with E. F. Keysor as the architect, and with Skinner & Small as the builders. In September, we moved in; and I shall never forget a happy compliment paid us the first evening. We had already retired when the sound of music and merriment made it unmistakable that we were being serenaded. Upon opening the door, we saw a large group of friends; and having invited them into the house, the merrymakers remained with us until the early morning hours.

In July, 1874, the Los Angeles County Bank was started with a capital of three hundred thousand dollars, its first directors being R. S. Baker, Jotham Bixby, George S. Dodge, J. M. Griffith, Vincent A. Hoover, Jonathan S. Slauson and H. B. Tichenor, with J. M. Elliott as Cashier. Its first location was the room just rented by the Farmers & Merchants Bank adjoining the Bella Union, the County Bank's step in that direction being due, no doubt, to a benevolent desire to obtain some of its predecessor's business; and in July, 1878, it moved into the Temple & Workman banking-room, after the latter's failure. For a while the County Bank did both a commercial and a savings business; but later it forfeited the savings clause of its charter, and its capital was reduced to one hundred thousand dollars. In time, John E. Plater, a well-known Angeleño, became a controlling factor.

About the end of 1874, Edward F. Spence, who had come to California by way of the Nicaragua route a year earlier than myself, reached Los Angeles. In 1884, Spence was elected Mayor on the Republican ticket. In the course of time, he withdrew somewhat from activity in Los Angeles and became a heavy investor in property at Monrovia.

In 1874 or 1875, there appeared on the local scene a man who, like his second cousin, United States Senator Mallory of Florida, was destined to become a character of national renown; a man who as such could and, as a matter of fact, did serve his constituents faithfully and well. That man was Stephen M. White. He was born in San Francisco a few weeks before I saw that harbor city, and was, therefore, a Native Son, his parents having come to the Coast in 1849. While a youth, he was sent to Santa Clara where, in June, 1871, he graduated from the well-known college; he read law at Watsonville and later at Santa Cruz; and having been admitted to the Bar in 1874, he shortly afterward came to the Southland.

Arriving in Los Angeles, White studied law with John D. Bicknell, who afterward took him into partnership; and he soon proved to be a brilliant lawyer. He was also an orator of the first magnitude; and this combination of talent made him not only prominent here, but attracted great attention to him from beyond the confines of city and county. Standing as a Democrat in 1882, he was elected District Attorney by a large majority and in that capacity served with distinction, in the end declining renomination. In 1886 he was elected State Senator and soon became President of the Senate, and then acting Lieutenant Governor. After a phenomenal career both in his profession and in the public service—during which he was one of three counsel elected by the California Legislature to maintain the Scott Exclusion Act before the United States Supreme Court and thus conclude the controversy in the Chae Chan Ping case—he was elected to the United States Senate, and there, too, his integrity and ability shone resplendent.

The zeal with which White so successfully entered the conflict against C. P. Huntington in the selection of a harbor for Los Angeles was indefatigable; and the tremendous expenditures of the Southern Pacific in that competition, commanding the best of legal and scientific service and the most powerful influence, are all well known. Huntington built a wharf—four thousand six hundred feet long—at Port Los Angeles, northwest of Santa Monica, after having obtained control of the entire frontage; and it was to prevent a monopoly that White made so hard a fight in Congress in behalf of San Pedro. The virility of his repeated attacks, his freedom from all contaminating influence and his honesty of purpose—these are some of the elements that contributed so effectively to the final selection of San Pedro Harbor. On February 21st, 1901, Senator White died. While at his funeral, I remarked to General H. G. Otis, his friend and admirer, that a suitable monument to White's memory ought to be erected; and on December 11th, 1908, the statue in front of the County Courthouse was unveiled.[1]

Hotel competition was lively in 1874. Charles Knowlton concluded his advertisement of the Pico House with a large index-finger and the following assurance:

The unpleasant odor of gas has entirely disappeared since the building of the new sewer!

Hammel & Denker announced for the United States (commonly known as the U. S.):

We have all *Spring Beds* at this Hotel!

Fluhr & Gerson—the latter long a popular chap about town—claimed for the Lafayette:

The Eating Department will be conducted with especial care;

and this was some of the bait displayed by the Clarendon, formerly the Bella Union:

Carriages are kept standing at the door for the use of the guests, and every effort is being made by COL. B. L. BEAL, the Present Manager, to render the guests comfortable and happy.

A couple of years later, the name of the Clarendon was changed to the St. Charles; next to which, during the Centennial year, the Grand Central, pretentious of name though small of dimension, opened with a splurge. Hammel & Denker continued to manage the United States Hotel. The Lafayette in time became, first the Cosmopolitan and then the St. Elmo.

Octavius Morgan, a native of the old cathedral town of Canterbury, England, came to Los Angeles in 1874 and

[1] Executive Committee of the Memorial Fund: M. P. Snyder, Chairman; Joseph Scott, Secretary; James C. Kays, Treasurer; F. W. Braun, A. B. Cass, R. F. Del Valle, I. B. Dockweiler, W. J. Hunsaker, M. H. Newmark and H. G. Otis.

associated himself with the architect, E. F. Keysor, the two forming the firm of Keysor & Morgan. They were charter members of the Southern California Architects Association, and for many years Morgan and his associates have largely influenced the architectural styles of Los Angeles.

A really picturesque old-timer even now at the age of nearly seventy, and one who, having withstood the lure of the modern automobile, is still daily driving a "one-hoss" buggy to the office of the Los Angeles Soap Company, is J. A. Forthman. In 1874, he brought a small stock of groceries from San Francisco and started a store at what is now Sixth and Olive streets; but at the end of three months, having sold out at a loss, he bought a quarter interest in a little soap plant conducted by C. W. Gibson. Soon thereafter, vats and fat were moved to their present site on First Street. In 1875, W. B. Bergin and in 1879, Gideon Le Sage joined Forthman and Gibson; and in 1887, the latter sold out to his associates. J. J., a brother of W. B. Bergin, was added to the force in 1895. For many years the concern dealt in hides, and this brought us into close business relations. I have referred to the death of four children. Edith, a child of six, was taken from us on October 15th, 1874.

While William F. Turner, son of the miller, was busy in his little store near the Puente Mills about three miles from El Monte, on the third of June, 1874, a Californian named Romo, who lived at Pio Pico's *Ranchito*, entered and bought some goods, also asking to be shown a pair of boots. Turner stooped to reach the articles, when the stranger drew a pruning-knife across his throat. In defense, the storekeeper caught hold of the sharp blade with both hands and thereby crippled himself for the rest of his days.

Turner had been in the habit of closing before dark on account of the rough element near by; and when he did not return home at the accustomed hour, Mrs. Turner, taking with her a little five-shooter, set out to find him and arrived in the midst of the murderous assault. Her pistol missed fire, but she succeeded in seizing the assassin and dragging him away from her husband; after which, the Mexican shot her

just as Turner, bleeding, fell in the road. The explosion aroused
a neighbor who reached the scene after Romo had fled with
some boots—mostly for one foot!—and seventy dollars in cash.

When the news passed from mouth to mouth in El Monte,
a *posse* started out to hunt for the Mexican; but after two
days' unsuccessful search, they gave up the job. Then Fred
Lambourn, who had a share in Turner's business, rushed in on
Jake Schlesinger, shouting excitedly, "By God, Jake, I know.
where the fellow is!" and Jake and others responded by saddling
their horses and hurrying to a rendezvous at Durfee's farm.
The party of nineteen, including John Broaded and Bill Cooper,
broke up into divisions of one or two and in time found themselves wading in and out of the San Gabriel River and the
Puente Creek. Soon old Dodson spied their quarry floundering
across stream; and when Schlesinger took a pop at him, the
culprit cried out, "Don't shoot!" and agreed to come ashore.
Of the money stolen, all but a few dollars was found on the
prisoner; nevertheless, the captors told him that, as soon as
Turner should identify him, he would be hung and that there
was not much time for foolishness. Romo said that he had
assaulted the storekeeper in order to get money with which, on
the following Sunday, to marry; that his immediate need was a
cigar; and that, if he must die, he would like to have his friends
notified, that they might bury him. Jake handed the doomed
man his only weed; and soon after, five or six masked men rode
up and announced that they would care for the criminal.
Then they drove under a tree on the bank of the river and
there, in short order, the cutthroat was hanged.

Pio Pico soon heard of the lynching and sent Jake and the
El Monte boys word that he would come over and "kill the
whole damned lot" of them; in reply to which, El Monte forwarded to the last of the Mexican governors a cordial invitation to come, at the same time pledging to receive him in true
California style—with due hospitality and warmth. This was
contemporaneous with the Vasquez excitement, and Romo was
probably bent on imitating the outlaw.

CHAPTER XXXII

THE SANTA ANITA *RANCHO*

1875

UNTIL near the end of the seventies, there was very little done toward the laying of sewers, although the reader will remember that a private conveyor connected the Bella Union with the *zanja* running through Mellus's Row.. Los Angeles Street from First to Second, in 1873, had one of brick and wood; and in 1875, a brick sewer was built from the corner of Main and Arcadia streets down to Winston and thence to Los Angeles Street. It must have been in the early seventies that a wooden sewer was constructed on Commercial Street from Los Angeles to Alameda, and another on New High Street for about one block. In 1879, one of brick was laid from Los Angeles and Commercial as far north as Arcadia, and connecting with the Main Street sewer. At about the same time, vitrified clay was used on a portion of Temple Street. My impression is that there was no *cloaca* laid on Spring Street until after 1880, while it was still later that Fort, Hill and Olive streets were served. As late as 1887, Hope Street had no sewer and very little conduit-building, if any, had been undertaken south of Seventh or west of Flower.

In January, 1875, the Commercial Bank, that was to change five years later into the First National, began business. Most of the incorporators were San Diego men—among them being Captain Henry Wilcox—although four—L. J. Rose, S. H. Mott, R. M. Town and Edward Bouton—were from Los Angeles. M. S. Patrick, of Chicago, was President; and

Edward F. Spence was Cashier. Their room was on Main
Street between Commercial and Requena. J. E. Hollenbeck,
who was succeeded by Spence, was the first President of the
National Bank. J. M. Elliott, made Cashier in 1885, has for
years well filled the office of President. A pillar of strength
in this institution is Vice-president Stoddard Jess.

Captain Wilcox, owner of the Colorado Steam Navigation
Company, who finally sold out to the Pacific Mail Steamship
Company, brought to California, on his own vessel in 1848,
the first light-houses. He married Señorita María Antónia
Arguello, the granddaughter of an early Governor of Califor-
nia. One of his daughters became the wife of Lieutenant
Randolph Huntington Miner, and another married Lieutenant
J. C. Drake. Captain Wilcox had induced E. F. Spence to
come from San Diego to Los Angeles, and thereby gave a
decided impetus to the starting of the Commercial Bank.

Milton Lindley, formerly an Indiana saddle-maker and
Treasurer of Los Angeles County in 1879, arrived here in 1875,
accompanied by Walter, the physician; Henry, the banker,
who settled at Whittier; Albert, an attorney; and Miss Ida B.,
a teacher. In the eighties, he was twice Supervisor. Dr.
Walter Lindley, once a Minnesota schoolmaster, so soon established himself that in 1878 he was elected health officer and,
in 1880, a member of the Board of Education. The following
year, he was President of the County Medical Society. With
Dr. Widney, he contributed to the literature setting forth
California's natural attractions; and with his brother-in-law,
Dr. John R. Haynes, he took a leading part in organizing the
California Hospital. Both Lindley and Haynes have identified
themselves with many other important local institutions and
movements.

Madame Caroline Severance, already distinguished as
the founder, in 1868, of the first woman's club in America—
the New England, of Boston—took up her residence in Los
Angeles in 1875 and soon made her home, *El Nido*, the
center of many notable sociological and philanthropic activities.
Especially active was she in promoting the free kindergarten,

working in coöperation with Mrs. Grover Cleveland and Kate Douglas Wiggin, the California author who was her *protégée* and resided for some time at *El Nido* when she was first becoming famous as a story-writer.

On March 27th, the *Weekly Mirror* was again enlarged and a subscription rate of one dollar a year was charged. By the beginning of 1876, a bindery was established in connection with the printery; and a Potter cylinder press—one of the first operated west of the Rockies—was installed.

E. J. Baldwin bought the Santa Anita *rancho*, in April, from H. Newmark & Company—a transaction recalled thirty-eight years later when, in 1913, the box which had been sealed and placed in the corner-stone of the Trinity Methodist Episcopal Church, at about the time of the sale, was brought forth from its long burial. Baldwin had just sold his controlling interest in the Ophir mine of the Comstock district for five million, five hundred thousand dollars. In the same year, we purchased of the Vejar estate the splendid vineyard of fifty acres commencing at Washington Street, on the south and a little east of Main Street, and taking in many important sections of to-day; selling it, in the early eighties, to Kaspare Cohn who, in turn, disposed of it during the boom of that decade. George Compère, somewhat noted as a local entomologist, cared for this vineyard while we owned it. Baldwin died on March 1st, 1909.

The sale of the Santa Anita is not without an incident or two, perhaps, of exceptional interest. On "Lucky" Baldwin's first visit, he offered us one hundred and fifty thousand dollars for the property; but learning that we wanted two hundred thousand dollars, he started off in a huff. Then Reuben Lloyd, the famous San Francisco attorney who accompanied him, said on reaching the sidewalk, "Lucky, go back and buy that ranch, or they'll raise the price on you!" and Baldwin returned, carrying under his arm a tin-box (containing several million dollars) from which he drew forth twelve thousand, five hundred, tendering the same as a first payment.

One can hardly refer to Baldwin without recalling H. A.

Unruh, in the late sixties in the employ of the Central Pacific.
It is my impression that I first met him at the Baldwin Hotel
in San Francisco. This meeting may have occurred nearly
thirty-five years ago; and after his removal to the Santa Anita
Ranch, where he took charge of Baldwin's interests in the
Southland, he transacted a large amount of business with H.
Newmark & Co. In 1887, Unruh was also in partnership at
La Puente with a man named Carroll, the firm advertising as
"Agents for Baldwin's Grain Warehouse, Wells Fargo & Co.'s
Express and Postmaster." When Baldwin died, his will named
Unruh executor; Bradner W. Lee being the attorney.

Ravenna, on the Southern Pacific, was a town of the
middle seventies, at whose start James O'Reilly, an Irishman
of medium build, with reddish hair and a pug nose decidedly
indented at the bridge, turned up with a happy-go-lucky air.
Always slovenly, he wore a big, black slouch hat on the back
of his head, as well as a good-natured expression, in days of
prosperity, on his comical face. He had a grocery, famed for a
conglomeration of merchandise not at all improved by age and
hard usage; and this he sold to a none too fastidious clientele.
He also cooked for himself, bragging that he was sufficiently
adroit to throw a slapjack up the chimney and catch it in
the pan, *outside the shanty* on its flop or turn! When Jim
took to working a couple of claims known as the New York
and Parnell Mines, his tribulations began: he spent more in
the development of his property than he ever recovered, and
claim-jumpers bothered him to death. In truth, once ascrib-
ing debatable motives to a man prowling there, he took aim
at the intruder and—shot off an ear! Later, he married; but
his wife soon divorced him. In time, his troubles affected his
mind; and having lost everything and come to fancy himself
an alchemist, he would sit for hours in the burning sun (his
temples plastered with English mustard) industriously stirring
a pestle and convinced that he could bring about a transmuta-
tion of the mortarful of mud. In the end, this good-natured
Son of Erin was one day found dead in his little shanty.

J. A. Graves arrived in Los Angeles on June 5th and soon

entered the office of Brunson & Eastman, lawyers. The following January he was admitted to practice before the Supreme Court and then became a member of the firm of Brunson, Eastman & Graves, dissolved in 1878. Practicing alone for a couple of years, Graves, in 1880, formed a partnership with J. S. Chapman. On the dissolution of this firm, in 1885, Graves joined, first H. W. O'Melveny and then J. H. Shankland; Graves, O'Melveny & Shankland continuing until January, 1904. On June 1st, 1903, Graves became Vice-president of the Farmers & Merchants National Bank. In the fall of 1879, the young attorney married Miss Alice H., daughter of J. M. Griffith, and for nine years they lived at the corner of Fort and Third streets. In 1888 they removed to Alhambra, where they still live. In 1912, Graves published some entertaining reminiscences entitled, *Out of Doors California and Oregon.*

Colonel W. E. Morford, a native of New Jersey and, late in the eighties, Superintendent of Streets, returned to Los Angeles in 1875, having previously been here. Morford had been assistant to Captain Sutter; and when he left San Francisco on March 14th, 1849, to return East, he carried the first gold taken from the diggings in the exciting era of 1848. This gold was sent by Frank Lemon, a member of Stevenson's Regiment, to his brother William, a partner of John Anderson, the New York tobacco merchant; and Morford liked to tell how, when the strange find was displayed on August 22d, in a little window of the well-known jewelry store of Benedict at 7 Wall Street near a high-hatted guard, the narrow thoroughfare was soon beyond hope of police control, thousands of curious, excited people struggling to get a glimpse of the California treasure.

Moses Langley Wicks was a Mississippian who for some years had a law office at Anaheim until, in 1877 or 1878, he removed to Los Angeles and soon became an active operator in real estate. He secured from Jonathan S. Slauson—who organized the Azusa Land and Water Company and helped lay out the town—the Dalton section of the San José Ranch.

Spring Street Entrance to Garden of Paradise

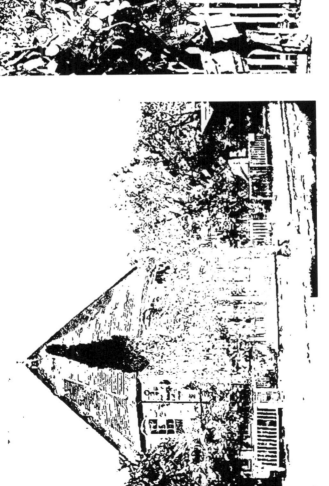

Round House, with Main Street Entrance

Temple Street, Looking West from Broadway, about 1870

Pico House, soon after Completion

Wicks was also active in locating the depot of the Santa Fé Railroad, carrying through at private expense the opening of Second Street from Main almost to the river. A brother, Moye Wicks, long an attorney here, later removed to the State of Washington.

Southern California was now prospering; in fact, the whole State was enjoying wonderful advantages. The great Comstock mines were at the height of their prosperity; the natural resources of this part of the country were being developed; land once hard to sell, at even five dollars an acre, was being cut up into small tracts; new hamlets and towns were starting up; money was plentiful and everybody was happy.

About this time my brother, J. P. Newmark, and I made a little tour, visiting Lake Tahoe—an unusual trip in that day— as well as the mines of Nevada. Virginia City, Gold Hill and other mining-camps were the liveliest that I had ever seen. My friend, General Charles Forman, was then Superintendent of the Overman and Caledonia Mines, and was engaged in constructing a beautiful home in Virginia City. After the collapse of the Nevada boom in the early eighties, he transported this house to Los Angeles, at a freight expense of eleven hundred and thirty-five dollars and a total cost of over six thousand, and located it on ten acres of land near the present site of Pico and Figueroa streets, where Mr. and Mrs. Forman, still residents of Los Angeles, for years have enjoyed their home.

Miners were getting high wages and spending their money lavishly, owners of buildings in Virginia City receiving from four to eight per cent. a month on their investments. W. C. Ralston, President of the Bank of California at San Francisco, was largely responsible for this remarkable excitement, for he not only lent money freely but he lent it regardless of conservative banking principles. He engaged in indiscriminate speculation, for a time legitimatizing illegitimacy, and people were so incited by his example that they plunged without heed. All of Nevada's treasure was shipped to San Francisco, whose prosperity was phenomenal. From San Francisco the excitement spread throughout the State; but these conditions, from the nature of things, could not endure. From Bull to Bear is but a short step when the public is concerned, and it happened accordingly, as it so frequently does, that the cry of "Save yourself, if you can!" involved California in a general demoralization. One day in October, 1875, when Ralston's speculation had indeed proven disastrous, the Bank of California closed its doors; and a few days after this, Ralston, going a-swimming in the neighborhood of the North Beach at San Francisco, was drowned—whether a suicide or not, no one knows. In the meantime, the recessional frenzy extended all over the State, and every bank was obliged to close its doors. Those of Los Angeles were no exception to the rule; and it was then that Temple & Workman suspended. I. W. Hellman, who was on a European trip at the time, forthwith returned to Los Angeles, re-opened the doors of the Farmers & Merchants Bank and resumed business just as if nothing had happened. Following this panic, times became dreadfully bad; from greatest prosperity, we dropped to the depths of despair. Specie disappeared from circulation; values suffered, and this was especially true of real estate in California.

Temple & Workman's Bank, for reasons I have already specified, could not recover. Personally, these gentlemen stood well and had ample resources; but to realize on these was impossible under conditions then existing. They applied to E. J. Baldwin, a Monte Cristo of that period, for a loan. He was willing to advance them two hundred and ten thousand dollars, but upon two conditions: first, that they would give him a blanket-mortgage on their combined real estate; secondly, that their intimate friend, Juan Matías Sanchez, would include in the mortgage his splendid tract consisting of twenty-two hundred acres of the finest land around the Old Mission. Sanchez, who transacted a good deal of business with H. Newmark & Company, came to me for advice. I felt convinced that Temple & Workman's relief could be at best but temporary, although I am sure that they themselves believed it would be permanent, and so I strenuously urged Sanchez to refuse; which he finally promised me to do. So impressive was our interview that I still vividly recall the scene when he dramatically said: "*¡No quiero morir de hambre!*"—"I do not wish to die of hunger!" A few days later I learned, to my deep disappointment, that Sanchez had agreed, after all, to include his lands. In the course of time, Baldwin foreclosed and Sanchez died very poor. Temple also, his pride shattered—notwithstanding his election in 1875 to the County Treasurership—died a ruined man; and Workman soon committed suicide. Thus ended in sorrow and despair the lives of three men who, in their day, had prospered to a degree not given to every man, and who had also been more or less distinguished. Baldwin bought in most of the land at Sheriff's sale; and when he died, in 1909, after an adventurous career in which he consummated many transactions, he left an estate of about twenty millions. A pathetic reminder of Sanchez and his one-time prosperity is an *azador* or meat toaster, from the old Sanchez homestead, now exhibited at the County Museum.

In 1874, Senator John P. Jones came south and engaged with William M. Stewart, his senatorial colleague (once an obscure lawyer in Downieville, and later a Nevada Croesus), in mining at Panamint, purchasing all their supplies in Los Angeles. About the same time, Colonel R. S. Baker, who had shortly before bought the San Vicente *rancho*, sold a two-thirds interest in the property to Jones; and one of their first operations was the laying out of the town of Santa Monica. After the hotel and bath-houses had been built, an auction sale of lots took place on July 16th, 1875, and was attended by a large number of people, including myself; prospective buyers coming from as far as San Francisco to compete with bidders from the Southland. Tom Fitch, already known as the "Silver-tongued Orator," was the auctioneer and started the ball rolling with one of his most pyrotechnical efforts. He described the place about to be founded as "The Zenith City by the Sunset Sea," and painted a gorgeous vista of the day when the white sails of commerce would dot the placid waters of the harbor, and the products of the Orient would crowd those of the Occident at the great wharves that were to stretch far out into the Pacific!

Then Tom turned his attention and eloquence to the sale of the lots, which lay along Ocean Avenue, each sixty by one hundred and fifty feet in size. Calling for a bid, he announced the minimum price of three hundred dollars for sites along the ocean front. Several friends—I. M. Hellman, I. W. Hellman, Kaspare Cohn, Eugene Meyer and M. J. Newmark—had authorized me to act for them; and I put in the first bid of three hundred dollars. Fitch accepted, and stated that as many more of these lots as I wanted could be had at the same price; whereupon I took five, located between Utah and Oregon avenues. These we divided among us, each taking fifty feet front, with the expectation of building summer homes; but strange to say, none of us did so, and in the end we sold our unimproved ground. Some years later, I bought a site in the next block and built a house which I still occupy each year in the summer season.

Three early characters of Santa Monica had much to do with the actual starting of the place.. The one, L. G. Giroux, a Canadian, walked out to Santa Monica one day in 1875, to get a glimpse of the surf, and came back to town the owner of a lot on which he soon built the second permanent house there —a small grocery and liquor shop. In the eighties, Giroux did good public service as a Supervisor. The second, Billy Rapp, also came in 1875 and built a small brick house on the west side of Second Street somewhere between Utah and Arizona avenues. There, after marrying a German *Frau*, he opened a saloon; and pleasure-seekers visiting Santa Monica on Sundays long remembered Billy's welcome and how, on the arrival of the morning train from Los Angeles, he always tapped a fresh keg of lager. After a while, he closed his saloon and sold the little building for a town hall. Hard times in later years rapped at Billy's door, forcing him to work on the public streets until 1899, when he died. The third settler was George Boehme, who landed with the first steamer and, within an hour or two, invested in lots. His family is there to-day.

Another pioneer Santa Monica family was that of William D. Vawter who, with his sons, W. S. and E. J., originally members of the Indiana Colony at Pasadena, removed to the beach in 1875. My relations with these gentlemen were quite intimate when they conducted a general merchandise business, that being but one of their numerous enterprises. Of late years, W. S. Vawter has twice been Postmaster at Santa Monica.

In 1875, Paul Kern, who had come to Los Angeles in 1854 and was for years a baker, set to work to improve a piece of property he owned at the junction of South Main and Spring streets, between Eighth and Ninth. At the end of this property he erected a two-story brick building—still to be seen—in the lower part of which he had a grocery and a saloon, and in the upper part of which he lived.

Toward the middle of the seventies, A. Ulyard, the baker, embarked in the carrying of passengers and freight between Los Angeles and Santa Monica, sending a four-horse stage from here at half-past seven every morning, and from Santa Monica at half-past three in the afternoon, and calling at all four Los Angeles hotels as well as at the private residences of prospective patrons. One dollar was the fare charged.

Ralph Leon had the only regular cigar store here in the late sixties, occupying a part of the United States Hotel; and he was very prosperous until, unable to tolerate a nearby competitor—George, a brother of William Pridham—he took up a new stand and lost much of his patronage. Pridham opened the second cigar store, about 1872 or 1873, next to the hotel; and Leon moved to a shop near the Farmers & Merchants Bank.

The names of these early dealers remind me of an interesting custom especially popular with Captain Thom, Billy Workman and other lovers of the aromatic weed. Instead of buying cigars by the piece, each of these inveterate smokers purchased a box at a time, wrote his name on the lid and left it on a shelf of the dealer; and from time to time they would slip in by a rear door and help themselves—generally from their own or, occasionally, from their neighbor's supply. When Leon discovered that the patron's box was empty, he would have it refilled.

3ɪ

In the autumn, Temple & Workman were obliged to suspend. After closing temporarily, they made an effort to resume, but a run on the Bank deprived them of all reserves and they finally had to close their doors. It was the worst of all bank failures here, the creditors losing everything. Some idea of the disaster may be gathered from the fact that the Receiver finally sold worthless securities to the extent of about three hundred thousand dollars for the paltry sum of thirty dollars.

On the sixth of November, 1875, Mrs. Joseph Newmark, my wife's mother, died here surrounded by her nearest of kin.

During the construction of the Southern Pacific Railway, Sisson, Wallace & Company, who furnished both labor and supplies, brought M. Dodsworth to Los Angeles and like many of their employees, he remained here after the railroad was completed. He engaged in the pork-packing business, for a long period prospered and built a residence on the southwest corner of Sixth and Main streets, opening it with a large reception. He was an honorable man and had a host of friends; but about 1887, when the Santa Fé had been built to Los Angeles, the large Eastern packers of hog products sent agents into Southern California and wiped Dodsworth out of business.

S. J. Mathes came in 1875, helped enlarge the *Mirror* and was identified with the *Times;* but failing health, forcing him to abandon office work, led him in the eighties to conduct Pullman excursions, in which undertaking he became a pioneer, bringing thousands of tourists to the Southland. He also toured the country with a railway car exhibit known as "California on Wheels," pointing the way of exploitation to later Chambers of Commerce.

Toward the end of the year, when attention was being centered on the coming exposition at Philadelphia, I was asked by the Chamber of Commerce to assist in editing a report on the resources, conditions, population, climatic advantages and mercantile interests of the city and county of Los Angeles. The aim of the Board was to make the report truthful and helpful, and to distribute it gratis, particularly at the Centennial. Ben C. Truman wrote about cities, towns and climate; Judge R. M. Widney reported on railroads; H. McClellan, the steamship agent (who preceded Willis Parris, the present representative and once a competent bill-clerk in the employ of H. Newmark & Company) and brother of Bryce and George F. McClellan, told of ocean navigation; Dr. J. E. Fulton, of Fulton Wells, discussed farming; Dr. J. P. Widney described our harbor; D. M. Berry argued for real estate; Governor Downey presented banks and banking; M. Keller and L. J. Rose treated of vine culture; J. de B. Shorb looked after semi-tropical fruits and nuts, and T. A. Garey—himself the owner of a charming place on San Pedro Street, where his spiritualistic tendencies kept him up at night awaiting the arrival of spooks—considered other fruits and nurseries; W. J. Brodrick stated our advance in trades, professions, churches and societies; E. C. French summed up about stock; Captain Gordon recounted our prospects for beet culture; while H. D. Barrows and I prepared data as to the commerce of Southern California. Thus compactly put together, this booklet certainly led many Easterners to migrate West and to settle in Los Angeles and vicinity.

In the early seventies, Grange Stores, brought into existence by a craze for coöperation, were scattered throughout the State, and Milton H. La Fetra in February, 1875 helped to organize one here. In time, this establishment became known, first as Seymour & Company and then as Seymour, Johnson & Company, their location being on Main Street near First.

W. H. Northcraft's activity as an auctioneer began about the middle of the seventies. For a while, he had an office in Temple Block, but about 1880 moved to the east side of Los Angeles Street near Requena; later to the Signoret Building, and still later to the Baker Block. In 1879, Thomas B. Clark, still well known "in the profession," came to Los Angeles and, marrying Northcraft's daughter, joined his father-in-law in partnership. C. L. Northcraft, a son, was added to the firm. Alonzo B. Cass came to Los Angeles in 1888, accompanied by his brothers, and soon after, as Cass Brothers' Stove Company, they started a hardware store on Third Street, purchasing some of Northcraft & Clark's stock of merchandise. A. B. Cass, who served as President of the Chamber of Commerce in 1901, has freely given of his time to public movements. As President of the Home Telephone & Telegraph Company, he has had much to do with their local success. E. W. Noyes was also a popular, old-time auctioneer, remaining in harness until he was seventy-five years old or more.

The mention of these names recalls the auction of past decades, such a familiar feature of Los Angeles life. In few respects were the methods of early days at all like those of our own: there were no catalogues, no neatly-arranged store-rooms and but little expert service; noise and bluff constituted a good, even important portion of the necessary auctioneering talent; household effects were usually offered at homes; horses—and these constituted the objects of most early auctioneering activities—were trotted up and down Los Angeles Street for display and sale.

CHAPTER XXXIII

LOS ANGELES & INDEPENDENCE RAILROAD

1876

ONCE Santa Monica's boom had been launched, the town developed as had few other suburbs of Los Angeles. Within nine or ten months a thousand inhabitants pointed with satisfaction to one hundred and sixty houses and perhaps half as many tents. Senator Jones built a wharf and pushed to completion the Los Angeles & Independence Railroad; and the road was opened to the public on Wednesday, December 1st, 1875, with a depot on San Pedro Street near Wolfskill Lane. Two trains a day were run—one leaving Los Angeles for Santa Monica at half-past nine in the morning and another at a quarter after four in the afternoon; the trains from Santa Monica for Los Angeles departing at half-past seven in the morning and half-past two in the afternoon. On January 5th, 1876, the Railroad Company offered sixty single commutation tickets for ten dollars; and a few days later, the conductor and other train employees appeared in uniform, each wearing on his cap what was then considered an innovation, the badge of his office. Captain Joseph U. Crawford was Superintendent and Chief Engineer.

From the start the Road did a thriving freight business, although passenger traffic was often interfered with. Early in January, 1876, for instance, the train from Santa Monica failed to make its appearance, the engineer having spied a bit of ground suspiciously soft in the *ciénaga*—locally spelled *ciénega*—refused, despite the protests of passengers, to proceed!

There were also inconveniences of travel by steamer such as arose from the uncertainty whether a vessel running between San Francisco and San Diego would put in at San Pedro or Santa Monica. According to conditions, or perhaps through the desire to throw a little trade one way or the other, the captain might insist on stopping at one port, while friends had assembled to greet the traveler at the other. A single car, with such objects of wonder as air brakes and Miller couplers drew Sunday crowds; and when, about the middle of January, the Company carried down ten car-loads of people on a single day and brought them back safely, substantial progress, it was generally felt, had been made.

In February, the Santa Monica Land Company was pushing its sales of real estate, and one of its announcements began with the headlines:

SANTA MONICA!
The Wonderful Young City and Seaport of
Southern California!
The Future Terminus of the Union & Texas Pacific Railroad!

the advertisement winding up with the declaration that several hundred vessels, including the largest boats of the Pacific Mail Steamship Company, had already loaded and discharged at the wharf in all weathers!

My memory is obscure as to just when Senator Jones built his splendid mansion at the corner of Ocean and Nevada avenues, but I think it was about 1890. I certainly recollect that it was then considered the most extensive and elaborate home in the vicinity of Los Angeles.

Rather late in January, H. Newmark & Company had their first experience with burglars who scaled the wall behind the store one Saturday night, cut away enough brick to enable them to throw back the bolt of the door, then barricaded the front doors by means of crowbars and proceeded to open the safe, which was of the old Tilton & McFarland pattern. The face was forced off, but the eight hundred dollars in the safe remained intact and undisturbed, the burglars making a total haul of only five dollars.   Other merchants also suffered at this time from the depredations of cracksmen.

Following this futile attack, we sent for a new safe of the Hall type.   Scarcely had a month elapsed, however, when a second attempt was made in much the same way.   Then the burglars went to work in real earnest and soon effected an entrance into the money-drawers.   But, alas! the entire contents secured would not have provided half a dozen *tamales!*   This fact, probably, aroused the ire of the rascals, for they mutilated the front of the prettily-decorated safe before leaving, and tried to destroy the combination.   The best excuse—and perhaps not such a bad one—that the police had to offer for not furnishing Los Angeles Street better protection, was that the night was dark, the street and sidewalks flooded and that a policeman, who had tried the beat, had been nearly drowned!

In February, trains on the Los Angeles & Independence Railroad began to leave Los Angeles at ten o'clock in the morning and five o'clock in the afternoon, and Santa Monica at eight and four o'clock, the Company deeming it a sufficient inducement to allow excursionists five or six hours to bathe, fish or picnic.   Round-trip tickets, good for the day and date only, were sold at a dollar each; and the management reserved the right, on steamer days, to change the schedule to fit the sailings.   When a fourth passenger coach was added to the equipment, the Company declared that the accommodations between this city and Santa Monica were "equal to those on any road along the entire Coast;" but the high-water mark of effort was reached when it was announced that the "splendid palace car dubbed *Santa Monica*, which had carried Senator Jones to Washington," was then being sent south from San Francisco for the convenience of the Company's patrons.   In March, while the San Pedro Street Railway was being built, another official announcement said that "in the course of a few days the people of this city will have the *honor* and delight of seeing a *palace* car standing on a railroad track near the Pico House;" and about the end of March printer's ink displayed this appeal to the expectant public:

Go, by all means,·to the grand seaside excursion to Santa Monica on Friday, for among the objects of interest will be Senator Jones's magnificent new palace-car now being completed by the tailors (*sic*) which will have three *salons*, supplied with tables and all the usual comforts, and two private compartments, the whole sumptuously furnished and partly upholstered with crimson velvet!

On February 14th, General Andrés Pico died at his residence, 203 Main Street, and was buried from his home on the following day.

On March 1st, work was commenced on the San Pedro Street Railway, which in time was extended from the Santa Monica station to the Plaza, *via* San Pedro, Los Angeles, Arcadia and Sanchez streets. The gauge was that of the Los Angeles & Independence Railway, thus permitting freight cars to be hauled to the center of the city; on which account business men looked upon the new road as a boon. Passenger cars soon ran from the depot to the Pico House; and as the fare was but five cents, or thirty tickets for a dollar, this line was rewarded with a fair patronage. At the end of 1876, four street railways were in operation here.

In March, also, two hundred pleasure-seekers, then considered a generous outpouring, went down to Santa Monica on a single Sunday; and within the first three months of the year, the Land Company there gathered in about seventy-three thousand dollars—selling a lot almost every day. South Santa Monica was then looked upon as the finer part of the growing town, and many of my friends, including Andrew Glassell, Cameron E. Thom, General George Stoneman, E. M. Ross, H. M. Mitchell, J. D. and Dr. Frederick T. Bicknell and Frank Ganahl, bought sites there for summer villas.

Micajah D. Johnson, twice City Treasurer, was a Quaker who came here in 1876. He built at Santa Monica a hotel which was soon burned; and later he became interested in the colony at Whittier, suggesting the name of that community.

In 1876, the City purchased a village hook-and-ladder truck in San Francisco which, drawn by hand in the vigorous old-fashioned way, supplied all our needs until 1881.

In 1876, the Archer Freight and Fare Bill, which sought to regulate railroad transportation, engrossed the attention of commercial leaders, and on March 9th, President S. Lazard called together the Directors of the Chamber of Commerce at the office of Judge Ygnácio Sepúlveda. Besides President Lazard, there were present R. M. Widney, W. J. Brodrick, M. J. Newmark, E. E. Hewitt and I. W. Lord. Little time was lost in the framing of a despatch which indicated to our representatives how they would be expected to vote on the matter. Several speeches were made, that of M. J. Newmark focusing the sentiment of the opposition and contributing much to defeat the measure. Newmark expressed surprise that a bill of such interest to the entire State should have passed the Lower House apparently without discussion, and declared that Southern Californians could never afford to interfere with the further building of railroads here. Our prosperity had commenced with their construction, and it would be suicidal to force them to suspend.

In a previous chapter I have spoken of the rate—ten dollars per thousand—first charged for gas, and the public satisfaction at the further reduction to seven dollars and a half. This price was again reduced to six dollars and seventy-five cents; but lower rates prevailing elsewhere, Los Angeles consumers about the middle of March held a public meeting to combat the gas monopoly. After speeches more lurid, it is to be feared, than any gas flame of that period, a resolution was passed binding those who signed to refrain from using gas for a whole year, if necessary, beginning with the first of April. Charles H. Simpkins, President of the Los Angeles Gas Company, retorted by insisting that, at the price of coal, the Company could not possibly sell gas any cheaper; but a single week's reflection, together with the specter of an oil-lamp city, led the Gas Company, on March 21st, to grant a reduction to six dollars a thousand.

Will Tell was a painter in 1869 and had his shop in Temple Block, opposite the Court House. Early in 1876 he opened a lunch and refreshment house at the corner of Fourth Street and Utah Avenue in Santa Monica, where he catered to excursionists, selling hunting paraphernalia and fishing tackle, and providing "everything, including fluids." Down at what is now Playa del Rey, Tell had conducted, about 1870, a resort on a lagoon covered with flocks of ducks; and there he kept eight or ten boats for the many hunters attracted to the spot, becoming more and more popular and prosperous. In 1884, however, raging tides destroyed Tell's happy hunting grounds; and for fifteen or twenty years, the "King's Beach" was more desert than resort. Tell continued for a while at Santa Monica and was an authority on much that had to do with local sport.

On Sunday, April 9th, the Cathedral of Sancta Vibiana, whose corner-stone had been laid in 1871 on the east side of Main Street south of Second, was opened for public service, its architecture (similar to that of the Puerto de San Miguel in Barcelona, Spain) at once attracting wide attention. As a matter of fact, the first corner-stone had been placed, on October 3d, 1869, on the west side of Main Street between Fifth and Sixth, when it was expected that the Cathedral was to extend to Spring Street. The site, however (and oddly enough,) was soon pronounced, "too far out of town," and a move was undertaken to a point farther north. In more recent years, efforts have been made to relocate the bishop's church in the West End. A feature of the original edifice was a front railing, along the line of the street, composed of blocks of artificial stone made by Busbard & Hamilton who in 1875 started a stone factory, the first of its kind here, in East Los Angeles.

Victor Dol, who arrived here in the Centennial year and became the Delmonico of his day, kept a high-grade restaurant, known as the Commercial in the old Downey Block, about one hundred and fifty feet north of the corner of Spring

and Temple streets. The restaurant was reached through a
narrow passageway that first led into an open court paved with
brick, in the center of which a fountain played. Crossing this
court, the interested patron entered the main dining-room, where
an excellent French dinner was served daily at a cost of but
fifty cents, and where the popular *chef* furnished many of the
notable banquets of his time. Dol also had a number of private
dining-rooms, where the epicures of the period were wont to
meet, and for the privilege of dining in which there was an
additional charge. Dol's Commercial was a popular institution
for more than a quarter of a century.

Dol then had in his employ an uncle, who was a rather mysterious individual, and who proved to be a French anarchist.
It was said that his pet scheme for regulating the government of
Louis Philippe met with such scant approval that, one fine
day, he found himself in jail. Escaping in course of time from
the anxious and watchful authorities, he made his way to the
outside world and finally located here. After the Franco-
Prussian War of 1870–71, he was supposed to have returned to his
native land, where he once more satisfied his peculiar propensity
for patriotic activity by tearing down and burning, in company
with other so-called Communists, some of the most beautiful
buildings in all Paris.

In the spring of 1876, Los Angeles boasted of another
French restaurant, a dining place called the Oriental and conducted by a Frenchman, C. Casson and a German, H. Schmitt.
It was on Main Street opposite the Pico House, and much ado
was made of the claim that everything was "in European
style" and that it was "the largest and most commodious
restaurant south of San Francisco."

Human nature—at least of the feminine type—was much
the same, thirty-five or forty years ago, as it is to-day. Such a
conclusion, at least, the reader may reach after scanning an
Easter advertisement of Miss Hammond, an 1876 milliner
who had a little shop at 7 North Spring Street and who then
made the following announcement to those of her fashion-
loving sex:

Miss Hammond, who has just received a splendid lot of new styles of hats, bonnets, silks, ribbons, etc., invites the ladies of Los Angeles to call at her place of business before purchasing elsewhere. One glance into her show-window will be enough to project any modern heart into a state of palpitation.

Elsewhere I have mentioned the salt works near Redondo's site. Dr. H. Nadeau (who came here in 1876, had an office in the Grand Central Hotel and was soon elected Coroner) was once called there and started with a constable and an undertaker—the latter carrying with him a rough board coffin for the prospective "subject." Losing their way, the party had to camp for the night on the plains; whereupon the Coroner, opening the coffin, crawled in and "slept like a brick!"

John Edward Hollenbeck, who in 1888 built the Hollenbeck Hotel, returned to Los Angeles in the spring of 1876—having been here in 1874, when he made certain realty investments—secured land on the east side of the Los Angeles River, spent a large sum of money for improvements and soon built a residence exceptionally fine for that time. And in this beautiful home, in close proximity to Boyle Avenue, he lived until his death, on September 2d, 1885, at the age of fifty-six years. Succeeding A. C. Bilicke in 1903, John S. Mitchell, long a prominent Angeleño, is still controlling this busy hostelry.

I have spoken of an adobe on ten acres of land I once purchased to secure water for my flock of sheep. After Hollenbeck had built his home on Boyle heights, he was so disturbed by a company of Mexicans who congregated in this adobe that, in sheer desperation, he asked me in 1882 to sell him the land. I did so, and we agreed upon six hundred and twenty-five dollars as a price for the entire piece.

Hollenbeck then made another noteworthy investment. H. C. Wiley owned a lot, one hundred and twenty feet by one hundred and sixty-five, on the southeast corner of Fort and Second streets, where he lived in a small cottage. He had mortgaged this property for six thousand dollars; but since, under his contract, Wiley was not required to pay interest, the mortgagee tired of the loan. Hollenbeck bought the mortgage and made a further advance of four thousand dollars on the property. He finally foreclosed, but at the same time did the handsome thing when he gave Mrs. Wiley, a daughter of Andrés Pico, a deed for the forty feet on Fort Street upon which the cottage stood. These forty feet are almost directly opposite Coulter's dry goods store.

So many ranchers had again and again unsuccessfully experimented with wheat in this vicinity that when I. N. Van Nuys, in 1876, joined Isaac Lankershim in renting lands from the company in which they were interested, and in planting nearly every acre to that staple grain, failure and even ruin were predicted by the old settlers. Van Nuys, however, selected and prepared his seed with care and the first season rewarded them with a great harvest, which they shipped to Liverpool. Thus was inaugurated the successful cultivation of wheat in Southern California on a large scale. In 1878, the depot of the Southern Pacific at the corner of Alameda and Commercial streets had become too small for the Company's growing business, compelling them to buy on San Fernando Street; and Lankershim and his associates purchased the old structure from the Company for the sum of seventeen thousand, five hundred dollars, and there erected a flour mill which they conducted until the ranch was sold, a few years ago.

One of the very interesting cases in the Los Angeles courts was that which came before Judge H. K. S. O'Melveny on May 15th when Mrs. Eulalia Perez Guillen, one hundred and thirty years old according to the records of the church at San Gabriel, claimed the right to exhibit herself at the Centennial Exposition in Philadelphia as a California curiosity. .She was accompanied to court by a daughter, Mariana and their counsel, F. P. Ramirez; but there was also present another daughter, Mrs. de White, who brought Attorney Stephen M. White to assist in opposing the visionary scheme. Mariana admitted that she had not the means to humor the old lady in her hobby, while Mrs. de White objected that her mother was in her dotage and could not travel as far as Philadelphia.

The Judge granted the old lady liberty to live with either daughter, but required of Mariana a bond of five hundred dollars as a guarantee that she would not take her mother out of the county.

On May 17th, William Workman was gathered to his fathers, later being buried near the little chapel at La Puente, side by side with John Rowland, his early comrade and life-long friend.

An early and popular educator here was Miss E. Bengough who, about 1870, had started her "Select School for Young Ladies and Children," and who on June 5th had one of her "commencements" in the Spring Street school house. At the beginning of the eighties, the Bengough school was at No. 3 Third Street. Miss Bengough died, a number of years ago, after having been for some years at the Hollenbeck Home.

Glowing descriptions of the Centennial Exposition first attracted the attention of Madame Helena Modjeska, the Polish lady eventually so famous, and the presence here of a small Polish colony finally induced her and her husband, Charles Bozenta Chlapowski, to make the dubious experiment of abandoning the stimulation of Old World culture and committing themselves to rustic life near the bee ranch of J. E. Pleasants in Santiago Cañon. Heaps of cigarettes, books and musical instruments were laid in to help pass the hours pleasantly; but disaster of one kind or another soon overtook the idealists who found that "roughing it" in primeval California suggested a nightmare rather than a pleasant dream. Forced to take up some more lucrative profession, Madame Modjeska, in July, 1877, made her *début* in San Francisco as *Adrienne Lecouvreur* and was soon starring with Booth. This radical departure, however, did not take the gifted lady away for good: her love for California led her to build, near the site of their first encampment and in what they called the Forest of Arden, a charming country home to which she repaired when not before the footlights. Still later, she lived near Newport. More than one public ovation was tendered Madame Modjeska in Los Angeles, the community looking upon her as their own; and I remember a reception to her at O. W. Childs's home when I had a better opportunity for noting her unostentatious and agreeable personality. Modjeska Avenue is a reminder of this artist's sojourn here.

In June, W. W. Creighton started the *Evening Republican;* but during the winter of 1878–79 the paper, for lack of support, ceased to be published.

Andrew W. Ryan, a Kilkenny Irishman commonly called Andy, after footing it from Virginia City to Visalia, reached Los Angeles on horseback and found employment with Banning as one of his drivers. From 1876 to 1879, he was County Assessor, later associating himself with the Los Angeles Water Company until, in 1902, the City came into control of the system.

CHAPTER XXXIV

THE SOUTHERN PACIFIC

1876

BEFORE the completion of the San Fernando tunnel, a journey East from Los Angeles by way of Sacramento was beset with inconveniences. The traveler was lucky if he obtained passage to San Fernando on other than a construction train, and twenty to twenty-four hours, often at night, was required for the trip of the Telegraph Stage Line's creaking, swaying coach over the rough road leading to Caliente—the northern terminal—where the longer stretch of the railroad north was reached. The stage-lines and the Southern Pacific Railroad were operated quite independently, and it was therefore not possible to buy a through-ticket. For a time previously, passengers took the stage at San Fernando and bounced over the mountains to Bakersfield, the point farthest south on the railroad line. When the Southern Pacific was subsequently built to Lang's Station, the stages stopped there; and for quite a while a stage started from each side of the mountain, the two conveyances meeting at the top and exchanging passengers. Once I made the journey north by stage to Tipton in Tulare County, and from Tipton by rail to San Francisco. The Coast Line and the Telegraph Line stage companies carried passengers part of the way. The Coast Line Stage Company coaches left Los Angeles every morning at five o'clock and proceeded *via* Pleasant Valley, San Buenaventura, Santa Bárbara, Guadalupe, San Luis Obispo and Paso de Robles Hot Springs, and connected at Soledad with the Southern Pacific Railroad bound for San Francisco by way of Salinas City, Gilroy and San José; and this line made a speciality of daylight travel, thus offering unusual inducements to tourists. There was no limit as to time; and passengers were enabled to stop over at any point and to reserve seats in the stage-coaches by giving some little notice in advance.

In 1876, I visited New York City for medical attention and for the purpose of meeting my son, Maurice, upon his return from Paris. I left Los Angeles on the twenty-ninth of April by the Telegraph Stage Line, traveling to San Francisco and thence east by the Central Pacific Railroad; and I arrived in New York on the eighth of May. My son returned, June 29th, on the steamer *Abyssinia;* and a few days later we started for home. While in Brooklyn, on June 4th, I attended Plymouth Church and heard Henry Ward Beecher preach on "Serve Thy Master with a Will." His rapid transition from the pathetic to the humorous, and back to the pathetic, was most effective.

Our itinerary brought us to the Centennial Exhibition in Philadelphia, on the Fourth of July; and aside from the peculiar satisfaction at being present on historic ground upon that anniversary, I recall, with pleasure, many experiences and impressions new and interesting, notwithstanding the inconvenience caused by the great crowds. At the Exhibition, which had a circumference of only three and a half miles, I saw California's small but very creditable display; and I remember my astonishment at seeing a man seated before an apparatus, apparently in the act of printing letters. He was demonstrating an early typewriter, and I dictated to my wife half a dozen lines which he rapidly typed upon paper. Of the various nations, the Japanese and the Chinese attracted me most. Machinery Hall, with its twelve hundred machines all run by one huge Corliss engine, was as noisy as it was interesting. The New York *Herald* and the *Times* were printed there daily. In the Art Gallery there was one marble figure so beautifully draped that a young lady, passing by, said: "Father, why don't they remove that lace shawl from the statue?" During the evening, on the balconies of the Union League Club, we enjoyed a torchlight parade never to be forgotten.

On our way West we stopped at Salt Lake City; and as we had been informed that Brigham Young would be at the Opera House that evening, we attended the performance. I have forgotten the name of the play, but Rose Eytinge was the star. Brigham sat in his private box with two of his wives; and as it was a very hot night in July and the building was packed with people, his wives were both fanning him assiduously and otherwise contributing to his comfort. The following day we called at his residence to see him, expecting to renew an acquaintanceship established years before; but to our regret he was ill and could not receive us. A few months later, he died.

Leaving Salt Lake City early in August, we traveled by the Central Pacific to San Francisco where several days were very pleasantly spent with my brother and his family, and from there we left for Los Angeles, taking the Southern Pacific to its terminus at Lang's Station. Proceeding over the mountain by stage, we arrived at what is now the south end of the long tunnel and there boarded the train for this city.

Among others who went from Los Angeles to the Philadelphia Centennial was Ben C. Truman. He took with him specimens of choice California plants, and wrote letters, from various stations on the way, to his paper, the *Star*. Governor and Mrs. Downey, whom I met in New York in June, were also at the Exhibition.

Ben Truman's visit recalls the enterprise of preparing a booklet for circulation at the exposition setting forth the advantages of Los Angeles, and the fact that the *Star* was the first to propose sending copies of the local newspapers to Philadelphia, at the same time agreeing to contribute its share. In that connection, it also referred to a previous, similar experiment, endorsed by Truman, in these words:

This City has never been so prosperous as when the Chamber of Commerce sent fifty papers each week for one year of the *Herald, Express* and *Star*, to the leading hotels and libraries throughout the country, a movement inaugurated and carried out by Mr. M. J. Newmark. Those few papers, distributed where they would do the most good, filled our hotels and boarding houses, and sent joy to the hearts of the real estate dealers. It's a most trifling thing to do, and "there's millions in it."

Another interesting experiment in early advertising, by means of the stereopticon, was made in 1876 when the Los Angeles photographer, Henry T. Payne, exhibited at Philadelphia a fine selection of views designed to inform the spectator about Southern California and to attract him hither. Toward the end of May, Payne left for the East, taking with him a first-class stereopticon and nearly a thousand lantern slides of the old wet-plate process, the views being the product of Payne's own skill and labor.

For some time prior to 1876, the suitable observance here of the anniversary of the Nation's independence had been frequently discussed, and when James J. Ayers called a meeting of citizens in the County Court House, on the evening of April 29th, and another on May 6th, it was decided to celebrate the Fourth of July in a manner worthy of the occasion. Committees were appointed to arrange the details; and when the eventful day arrived, the largest throngs in the City's history assembled to give vent to their patriotism.

The procession—led by Grand Marshal H. M. Mitchell, assisted by Marshals Eugene Meyer, Francisco Guirado, John F. Godfrey and Otto von Ploennies, mounted on the best-groomed steeds of the Fashion Stables—formed towards ten o'clock and was half an hour in passing the corner of Temple, Spring and Main streets. The Woods Opera House Band, the Los Angeles Guard and the Los Angeles Rifleros assisted. The parade wended its tortuous way from the Aliso Mills in the northeast to the Round House in the south.

An interesting feature of the march was the division of Mexican War Veterans. Forty-two of these battle-scarred soldiers, a number of whom had become prominent in civic life, lined up, among them General George Stoneman, Captain

William Turner, Dr. J. S. Griffin, Major Henry Hancock, S. C.
Foster, John Schumacher, L. C. Goodwin, D. W. Alexander
and A. W. Timms.   Another feature worthy of note was the
triumphal chariot of the French Benevolent Society, in which
three young ladies represented respectively the Goddess of Liberty, France and America.   ·Fire Engine Company No. 38,
Confidence Engine Company No. 2 and the Hook and Ladder
Company formed another division, followed by several societies and secret orders.   In one float thirteen young ladies
represented the thirteen original colonies and in another
twenty-five damsels portrayed the rest of the States.   There
were also the Forty-niners, the butchers and the other tradesmen; while George and Martha Washington accompanied the
Philadelphia Brewery!

For this local celebration of the Centennial, streets, public buildings, stores and private residences were beautifully
decorated, portraits of Washington being everywhere.   Hellman, Haas & Company, S. C. Foy, the Los Angeles Social
Club and H. Newmark & Company were among those who
especially observed the day.   There was a triple arch on Main
Street, with a center span thirty feet wide and thirty feet
high, and statues of Washington, Grant and others.   The railroad depots and trains were also fittingly adorned; and at the
residence and grounds of Consular Agent Moerenhaut, the
Stars and Stripes, with the French tricolor, were displayed
under the legend, "Friends Since One Hundred Years."   The
Pico House was perhaps the most elegantly adorned, having
a column, a flagstaff and a Liberty cap, with the enthusiastic
legends:

1776. 1876. Now for 1976!
To the patrons of the Pico House: May you live 100 years!
No North, no South, no East, no West!

The Round House gardens having been reached, the literary
and musical program began.   The band played *Hail Columbia!*
and General Phineas Banning, the presiding officer, introduced
the Rev. T. T. Packard who delivered the opening prayer.

William Pridham

Benjamin Hayes

Isaac Lankershim

Rabbi A. W. Edelman

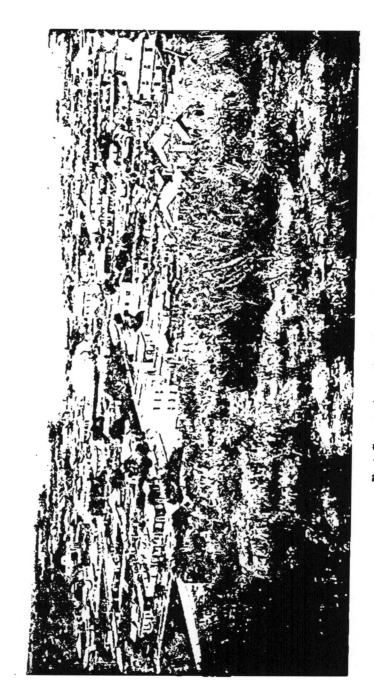

Fort Street, from the Chaparral on Fort Hill

Banning then made a short patriotic address; *America* was sung by several church choirs of the city; Professor Thomas A. Saxon read the *Declaration of Independence;* the choirs sang the *Red, White and Blue;* and J. J. Ayers, as poet of the occasion, read an original poem. *Yankee Doodle* came after that; and then James G. Eastman, as orator of the day, delivered the address, reviewing the civilization and wonders of every age, and tickling the hearers' vanity with perorations such as this:

When the mournful zephyrs, passing the plain where Marathon once stood, shall find no mound to kiss; when the arch of Titus shall have been obliterated; the Colosseum crumbled into antique dust; the greatness of Athens degenerated into dim tradition; Alexander, Cæsar and Napoleon forgotten; the memories of Independence Hall shall still bloom in imperishable freshness!

At the conclusion of the oration, Jacob A. Moerenhout, the venerable French representative, spoke very appropriately of the relation of France to America in our great Revolutionary struggle; after which the Rev. A. W. Edelman concluded the exercises by pronouncing the benediction. The celebration had a soul in it and no doubt compensated in patriotic sincerity for what it may have lacked in classical elegance.

Incidental to this commemoration, the Literary Committee having in charge the exercises had named Don J. J. Warner, Judge Benjamin Hayes and Dr. J. P. Widney a sub-committee to compile the most interesting data about the old town from the Spanish occupancy by the founding of the Mission at San Gabriel; and on the Fourth of July, or within less than two months after their appointment, the historians produced their report—to which I have already referred—a document, known as *An Historical Sketch of Los Angeles County, California*, which, in spite of the errors due to the short period allotted the editors, is still interesting and valuable; portraying, as it does, various characteristics of early life in the Southland and preserving to posterity many names and minor facts.

In the summer of 1875, fifteen hundred men began to dig their way into the San Fernando Mountains; and about the end of the first week in September, 1876, the long tunnel was completed—a bore six thousand nine hundred and forty feet in length, beginning twenty-seven miles from Los Angeles. During the course of construction, vast quantities of candles, generally the best, were employed to furnish light for the workmen, H. Newmark & Company supplying most of the illuminants.

Some of the facts concerning the planning, building and attendant celebration of this now famous tunnel should be peculiarly interesting to the Angeleño of to-day, as also to his descendants, for not only do they possess intrinsic historical importance, but they exemplify as well both the comparative insignificance of Los Angeles at the time when this great engineering feat was so successfully undertaken and the occasional futility of human prophecies, even when such prophecies are voiced by those most fitted at the time to deliver them.

I have already mentioned the interview which Governor Downey and I had with Collis P. Huntington, in San Francisco, when we presented the arguments of Los Angeles for the extension of the Southern Pacific Railroad to this point. The greatest difficulty, from an engineering standpoint, was the boring and finishing of the San Fernando tunnel, and the then small town of Los Angeles was compelled to pass through much discouragement before she became the Southern terminus of the road, a selection of the most vital importance to her future prosperity and growth. In the first place, a Mr. Rice, whose office was in Temple Block, represented the Railroad Company in telling the citizens of Los Angeles that if they did not appropriate toward the undertaking two hundred and fifty thousand dollars—then an enormous sum of money—Los Angeles would be left out of the line of travel and the railroad would be built so as to pass several miles inland, compelling our city to make a choice between putting in a branch to connect with the main line or resigning any claim she might have to become a railroad center. In fact, this is precisely what occurred in the case of Visalia and a number of other towns; that is to say: they are to-day the termini of railroad feeders, instead of a part of the main line as they perhaps might have been.

When this threat or warning was delivered, an agitation immediately set in, both to collect the money that the Company demanded and to influence its management to include Los Angeles on the main line. Judge R. M. Widney was one of the prominent figures in the local campaign. The Chamber of Commerce, through its President, Solomon Lazard, also buckled on its armor in behalf of Los Angeles and entered the lists. Notably it sent a telegram to the United States Senate—the railroad, as is well known, having received land-grants of inestimable value from Congress and being considered, therefore, susceptible to influence; and this telegram was penned with such classical eloquence that it poured seventy-five dollars into the coffers of the telegraph company. The net result of the campaign was the decision of the Railroad Company to include Los Angeles among the favored stations.

The politics of the situation having thus been satisfactorily settled, the engineering problems began to cast their shadows. General Stoneman stated that the tunnel bore could not be effected, an opinion which was by no means uncommon at that time. Others again said that people would never be induced to travel through so long a tunnel; still another set of pessimists stated that the winter rains would cause it to cave in, to which Senator Stanford laconically replied that it was "too damned dry in Southern California for any such catastrophe." This railroad and the tunnel, however, were fortunately to become one of those happy instances in which the proposals of man and the disposals of the Lord are identical, for in course of time both found their completion under the able direction of railroad genius, assisted in no small way by the gangs of thousands of Orientals who did the hard road-work.

As in the case with practically every Southern Californian enterprise, the finishing of this great undertaking was accompanied by a rather elaborate celebration. A delegation of San Francisco citizens, one of whom was my brother, met at

Newhall a delegation from Los Angeles including S. Lazard[1] and myself, and I thus have the pleasant recollection of having been among the very first who went through the tunnel on that initial trip.   Having arrived at Newhall, the citizens of the Northern and Southern cities symbolized, by fraternal handshaking, the completion of this new and strongest bond between them.   Amidst general rejoicing, and with thousands of Chinamen lined up on either side of the track, each at full attention and all presenting their—*shovels!*—General D. D. Colton drove the golden spike which bound the rails from the North with the rails from the South.   After considerable speech-making and celebrating, most of the company boarded the train for Los Angeles, where the jollification was concluded with a banquet, a ball, illuminations and other festivities.   Possibly due to the great increase in Chinese brought to Southern California through railroad work, repeated demonstrations against the Mongolians were made here at meetings during the summer.

Shortly after the completion of the Southern Pacific Railroad the people of Los Angeles became very much dissatisfied with the Company's method of handling their business, and especially with the arbitrary rulings of J. C. Stubbs in making freight rates.   On one occasion, for example, a shipper approched Stubbs and asked for a rate on a carload of potatoes from San Francisco to Tucson.   Stubbs asked him how much he expected to pay for the potatoes and what he would get for them; and having obtained this information, he allowed the shipper a small profit and took the balance for freight.   This dissatisfaction on the part of an enterprising community accustomed to some liberality found in time such an open expression that Charles F. Crocker, one of the original promoters of the Central, and one of the owners of the Southern Pacific, who had occasionally visited Los Angeles, came down to confer with the City Council at a public meeting.

Crocker, as President of the Central Pacific Railroad Company, was a very important man, and I felt at the time that he

[1] Died, January 13, 1915, in the ninetieth year of his age.

was most discourteously received by those with whom he had come to discuss the situation. The meeting, which I attended, was held in the small Council Room, and I well remember the oppressive closeness. The place was, indeed, packed; people were smoking and chewing tobacco; and the reader may perhaps imagine the extreme condition of both the atmosphere and the floor. This, however, was not all: when one of the Councilmen—out of regard, I suppose, for the railroad President's other engagements—asked that Mr. Crocker be permitted to address the City Fathers, J. S. Thompson, a revolutionary Councilman, stood up and declared that the San Francisco magnate would be heard when his time came and—not before! How this lack of consideration impressed the visitor may be seen from the conclusion of my story.

After a while, Crocker was allowed to speak; and in the course of his remarks he stated that the Southern Pacific Railroad Company had invested a great amount of money, and that it was necessary to realize proper interest on their expenditure. Thereupon, Isaac W. Lord, one of the spectators, after whom Lordsburg was named, arose and begged to tell a little story. An ambitious individual, he said, who had once built a hotel on the desert at a cost of one hundred and fifty thousand dollars, was without a guest until, one day, a lone traveler rode across the burning sands and put up for the night at the hostelry. Next morning, the stranger was handed a bill for seventy-five dollars; and upon inquiring why so much had been charged, the proprietor explained that he had spent one hundred and fifty thousand dollars in building the hotel; that the stranger was, thus far, the first and only guest; and that, therefore, he must pay his part of the interest on the investment.

The story, to Mr. Crocker's discomfiture, brought a loud laugh; and it was then, before the laughter had died out, that the famous railroad man, resuming the debate, made his memorable threat:

"If this be the spirit in which Los Angeles proposes to deal with the railroad upon which the town's very vitality must depend, *I will make grass to grow in the streets of your city!*"

And, considering the fate that has befallen more than one community which coldly regarded the proposals of these same California railroads, Crocker's warning was not without significance.

The Crocker incident having left matters in a worse state than before, Colonel Eldridge E. Hewitt, agent for the Southern Pacific, brought Governor Stanford to my office and introduced him. Stanford stated that his road would soon be in operation and expressed the hope that H. Newmark & Company would patronize it. I told Stanford that our relations with the steamship company had always been very pleasant, but that we would be very glad to give his line a share of our business, if rates were made satisfactory. At the same time, the Southern Pacific Railroad Company, having secured control of the Los Angeles & San Pedro Railroad, issued circulars announcing that steamer freight would henceforth be classified. As this was a violent departure from established precedents, it foreshadowed trouble; and, sure enough, rates moved upward from eight to as high as thirty dollars a ton, according to classification.

H. Newmark & Company and Hellman, Haas & Company, who were the heaviest shippers in Los Angeles, together with a number of other merchants, decided to charter a steamer or sailing vessel. James McFadden, of Santa Ana, owned the tramp steamboat *Newport* which plied between San Francisco and Newport Landing, in an irregular lumber-trade; and this, after some negotiations, we engaged for three years, on the basis of three dollars per ton. Having made this contract, we entered valiantly into the contest; and, in order suitably to impress the Southern Pacific Railroad Company with our importance, we loaded the vessel, on her initial trip, to the gunwales. Now cargo, on arriving at Wilmington at that time, used to be loaded into cars, brought to Los Angeles and left in the freight shed until we removed it at our convenience; but when the *Newport* arrived, the vessel was unloaded and the merchandise put into the warehouse at Wilmington, where it was held several days before it was reshipped. On its arrival in Los Angeles, the Railroad Company gave notice that removal must be effected within twenty-four hours, or demurrage would be charged; and since, with the small facilities in those days at our command, so prompt a withdrawal of an entire cargo was a physical impossibility, our expenses were straightway heavily increased.

Subsequent to this first shipment, we adopted a more conservative policy, in spite of which our troubles were to multiply. The Southern Pacific Railroad Company named a rate of three dollars a ton in less than carload lots between San Francisco and way-stations, and this induced many of our country customers to trade in that city. At the same time, the Company carried many lines between San Francisco and Los Angeles free of charge, potatoes and other heavy items being favored. The mask was now discarded, and it became evident that we were engaged in a life-and-death struggle.

Had there been a united front, the moral effect might have sustained us in the unequal contest; but unfortunately, H. Newmark & Company were abandoned by every shipper in Los Angeles except Hellman, Haas & Company, and we soon found that fighting railroad companies recalled the adage, "The game's not worth the candle." At the end of ten months of sacrifices, we invoked the assistance of my former partner and friend, Phineas Banning, who was then associated with the Southern Pacific; and he visited the officials in San Francisco in our behalf. Stanford told him that the Railroad Company, rather than make a single concession, would lose a million dollars in the conflict; but Banning finally induced the Company to buy the *Newport*, which brought to a close the first fight in Los Angeles against a railroad.

In the winter of 1876–77, a drought almost destroyed the sheep industry in Southern California. As a last resort, the ranchers, seeing the exhausted condition of their ranges, started to drive their sheep to Arizona, New Mexico or Utah; but most of them fell by the way.

Again, we had the coincidence of drought and a fatal epidemic of smallpox, not only leaving death in its wake, but incidentally damaging business a good deal. Mrs. Juan Lanfranco was one of those who died; Mr. and Mrs. Solomon Lazard lost a son, and a grocer by the name of Henry Niedecken, who had a little frame store where the Angelus Hotel now stands, as well as many others, succumbed.

CHAPTER XXXV

THE REVIVAL OF THE SOUTHLAND

1877–1880

THE late seventies were marked by an encouraging awakening of national energy and a growing desire on the part of the Angeleño, notwithstanding the excessive local dullness, to bring the outside world a pace or two nearer; as a result of which, things began to simmer, while there was an unmistakable manifestation on the part of those at places more or less remote to explore the almost unknown Southwest, especially that portion bordering on the Pacific.

I have already noted, with varying dates, the time when patents to land were issued. These dates remind me of the long years during which some of the ranch owners had to wait before they received a clear title to their vast estates. Although, as I have said, the Land Commission was in session during the first decade of my residence here, it was a quarter of a century and more, in some cases, after the Commissioners had completed their reports before the Washington authorities issued the desired patents confirming the Mexican grants; and by that time, not a few of those who had owned the ranches at the beginning of the American occupancy were dead and buried.

William Mulholland, who was really trained for navigation and had followed the sea for four or five years, steered for Los Angeles in 1877 and associated himself with the Los Angeles Water Company, giving his attention especially to hydraulic engineering and passing as it were in 1902, with the rest of the water-plant, to the City when it bought the Company out.

On March 22d, the Common Council changed the name of Nigger Alley, in the adobe days known as Calle de los Negros, to that of Los Angeles Street; and thus faded away a designation of Los Angeles' early gambling district long familiar to old settlers. The same year, the City marshalship, which J. J. Carrillo had held during 1875–76, was discontinued, and J. F. Gerkins was appointed the first Chief of Police.

Part of the property included in the blanket mortgage given by Temple & Workman to E. J. Baldwin was Temple Block; and when this was sold at sheriff's sale in 1877, H. Newmark & Company decided to acquire it if they could. Dan Freeman, acting for Baldwin, was our only competitor; and after a somewhat spirited contest, the property was knocked down to us. In 1909, we sold Temple Block to the City of Los Angeles. Quite a large contribution of money was then made by adjoining landowners, with the understanding that the site would form the nucleus for a civic center; but thus far this solemn promise remains unfulfilled—more's the shame, especially since the obligation is precisely coincidental with the City's needs.

In 1877, Colonel R. S. Baker erected the block bearing his name on the site of the historic adobe home of Don Abel Stearns, the walls of which structure, when demolished, killed two of the workmen. This building, the most modern of that period, immediately became the scene of much retail activity; and three wide-awake merchants—Eugène Germain, George D. Rowan and Rev. B. F. Coulter—moved into it. Germain was the first of these to arrive in Los Angeles, coming in 1870 and, soon after, establishing several trading posts along the line of the Southern Pacific during its construction through Arizona. One day, while inspecting branches in this wild and woolly region, Germain ran into a party of cowboys who were out gunning; and just for a little diversion, they took to peppering the vicinity of his feet, which attention persuaded him into a high-step less graceful than alert. Germain came to occupy many positions of trust, being appointed, in 1889, Commissioner from California to the Paris Exposition, and later American Consul at Zurich, Switzerland. Next among the tenants was George D. Rowan, who opened a grocery store in the Strelitz Block, opposite the old Jail, remaining there until the completion of Baker's building; thus supplying another illustration of the tendency then predominating to gravitate toward the extreme northern end of the town. In several enterprises, Rowan was a pioneer: he brought from Chicago the first phaeton seen on our streets; and in conjunction with Germain, he inaugurated the shipping of California products, in carload lots, to the Eastern market. He was also one of the first to use pennies here. Withdrawing from the grocery trade, in 1882, he busied himself with real estate until 1892, when he retired. A public-spirited man, he had the greatest confidence in the future of Los Angeles, and was instrumental in subdividing much important acreage, including the block between Sixth, Seventh, Hill and Olive streets, which he sold in sixty-foot lots at prices as low as six hundred dollars each. He was a prime mover in having the name of Fort Street altered to that of Broadway, certainly a change of questionable propriety considering the origin of the old name. Rowan died on September 7th, 1901. His sons, R. A. and P. D. Rowan, constitute the firm of R. A. Rowan & Company. Reverend Coulter, father of Frank M. Coulter,[1] brought his family to Los Angeles on September 17th, 1877, and after a short association in the hardware firm of Harper & Coulter, he entered the dry goods field as B. F. Coulter, now the Coulter Dry Goods Company. In 1878, Coulter bought the woolen mills on Pearl Street near Fifth. Coulter was a man of genial temperament and great integrity; and I shall have occasion to speak of him again.

R. F. Del Valle was born in December, 1854, at the Plaza ancestral home, where, before the family's removal to Camulos *rancho*, I frequently saw him playing when I attended the political councils at his father's home. By the by, I believe that

[1] Died on October 27th, 1915.

J. L. Brent had his law office there, which may account for those gatherings. Del Valle's boyhood days were spent in and around Los Angeles. He studied law in San Francisco and returned to Los Angeles in 1877, a promising young orator and attorney. Since that period he has been in public life practically all of the time. For some time past he has been a member of the Water Board. He has been frequently honored by the Democratic party, especially in 1880, when as elector he was instructed to vote for our former fellow-townsman, General W. S. Hancock. In 1890, Del Valle married Mrs. Helen Caystile, widow of Thomas Caystile and daughter of Caleb E. White, a Pomona horticulturist and sheepman.

A murder case of the late seventies was notable on account of the tragic fate of two indirect participants. On October 10th, G. M. Waller, custodian of the land company's bath-house at Santa Monica, detected Victor Fonck, who had been warned to keep off the premises, in the act of erecting a private bath-house on the beach, and shot him in the leg, from which wound, after two days, Fonck died. In his defense, Waller claimed that, as watchman, he was acting under orders from E. S. Parker, the land company's agent. Waller was found guilty of involuntary homicide and sentenced on January 25th, 1878, to one year in the Penitentiary. Parker, on the other hand, was convicted of murder in the second degree, and on March 8th was sentenced to ten years' imprisonment. This severe and unexpected punishment caused a mental excitement from which Parker soon died; and, but a few days later, his broken-hearted wife fell dead.

Annual public fairs were centers of social life as late as the middle of the seventies, one being held, about 1876 or 1877, in the old Alameda Street depot, which, decorated with evergreens and flowers, had been transformed into a veritable garden. With succeeding years, these displays, for some time in Horticultural Hall on Temple Street, came to be more and more enchanting. Still later, one or more flower festivals were held in Hazard's Pavilion on Fifth Street, near Olive, that of 1889 in particular attracting, in the phraseology of a local newspaper, "one of the largest and most brilliant gatherings in the history of the city." It is indeed a pity that these charming exhibitions, requiring but the mere bringing together of some of the flowers so bountifully supplied us, have been abandoned.

On February 1st, 1878, twenty-three years after the Odd Fellows first organized here, their newly-constructed hall in the Oxarart Block at 108 North Spring Street was dedicated with elaborate ceremonies.

About 1878, Captain George J. Clarke, who had been Postmaster from 1866 to 1873, and who lived well out of town, offered me sixty feet adjoining my home on Fort Street, a site now occupied by the J. W. Robinson Company. He asked one hundred dollars a foot for the Fort Street frontage alone, but as only sixteen dollars a foot had been paid for the full depth to Hill Street of the piece I already owned, I refused to purchase; nor was I persuaded even when he threatened to erect a livery stable next to my house.

Another item respecting land values, and how they impressed me: in 1878, Nadeau purchased, for twenty thousand dollars, the site of the Nadeau Hotel, whereupon I told him that he was crazy; but later events proved him to have been a better judge than I.

Sometime in the late seventies, Jerry Illich started a chophouse on North Main Street and prospered so well that in time he was able to open a larger and much finer establishment which he called the Maison Dorée. This restaurant was one of the best of the time, and became the *rendezvous* of men about town. In 1896, Jerry moved again, this time to Third Street opposite the Bradbury Block; and thither went with him his customers of former days. When Illich died in December, 1902, he had the finest restaurant in the city.

In April the Public Library was transferred to the care of the City. In the beginning, as I have stated, a fee of five dollars was charged to patrons; somewhat later, it is my recollection, a legislative enactment permitted a small addition to the tax-rate for the partial support of this worthy enterprise, and this municipal assistance enabled the directors to carry the

33

work along even though the annual membership fee was reduced to four dollars, payable quarterly.

On September 25th, General John C. Frémont arrived in Los Angeles on his way to Arizona, of which Territory he had been appointed Governor; and accompanied by his wife and daughter, he was driven at once to the St. Charles Hotel. There, in response to a demonstration by the citizens, he referred to the great changes which had taken place here during his absence of thirty years. Two days later, General Frémont and family left for Yuma, the explorer traveling that route by means of the iron horse for the first time

Benjamin Franklin Taylor, the lecturer and author, visited Los Angeles, in 1878, and wrote the sympathetic book, *Between the Gates*, full of just discrimination and hopeful views respecting the Southland.

Some new ordinances regulating vegetable venders having been passed in the winter of 1878–79, the Chinese peddlers went on a strike, and for some time refused, to the inconvenience of their dependent customers, to supply any truck-farm products.

During the Postmastership of Colonel Isaac R. Dunkelberger, the Post Office was moved, in 1879, to the Oxarart Block on North Spring Street near First. There it continued for eight years, contributing much toward making the neighborhood an important commercial center.

M. J. Newmark, having sold to his partners his interest in the firm of H. Newmark & Company, left Los Angeles, in 1879, for San Francisco, after building a residence on Spring Street next to the southwest corner of Spring and Seventh and adjoining the dwellings owned by Kaspare Cohn and M. A. Newmark. Each of these houses stood on a sixty-foot lot; and to protect themselves from possibly unpleasant neighbors, the holders had bought the corner of Seventh and Spring streets for four hundred and twenty-five dollars. On his departure, M. J. Newmark committed his affairs to my care, desiring to dispose of his place; and I offered it to I. N. Van Nuys for seven thousand five hundred dollars, which represented the cost of the house alone. Times were quite hard in Los Angeles at this period; and when Van Nuys said that he would give six thousand five hundred dollars for it, I accepted his offer and induced the owners to sell to him the corner lot for four hundred and seventy-five dollars. This is the earlier history of the corner now occupied by the I. N. Van Nuys Building, in which the First National Bank conducts its affairs.

Long before there was any necessity for cutting Sixth Street through, east of Main, George Kerckhoff (who, in 1879, had brought his family from Indiana) bought the six acres formerly belonging to the intrepid pioneer, J. J. Warner, and, in the midst of this pretty orchard, built the home in which he continued to reside until 1896, when he died. William G. Kerckhoff, a son, came with his father and almost immediately engaged in the lumber business with James Cuzner. An ordinary man might have found this enterprise sufficient, especially as it expanded with the building up of our Southland communities; but this was not so with the younger Kerckhoff, who in 1892 entered the ice business, after which effort, within ten years, he evolved the San Gabriel Electric Company. Henry E. Huntington then associated himself with this enterprise, somewhat later buying that part of the Kerckhoff property on which the Huntington Building, opposite the Kerckhoff, now stands; and as a result of the working together of two such minds, huge electrical enterprises culminated in the Pacific Light and Power Company.

The year 1879 was tragic in my family. On the 20th of January, our son Philip, only nine years of age, died of diphtheria; and a trifle more than three weeks later, on February 11th, Leo, a baby of three years, succumbed to the same treacherous disease. Barely had the grave closed on the second, when a daughter became seriously ill, and after her recovery, in a fit of awful consternation we fled the plague-infected house and the city, taking with us to San Francisco, Edward, a son of five years. But alas! hardly had we returned to town, when he also died, on March 17th, 1879.

In May, Judge R. M. Widney broached to the Rev. A. M.

Hough, Rev. M. M. Bovard, E. F. Spence, Dr. J. P. Widney and G. D. Compton his project for the first Protestant institution of higher learning in Southern California; and meeting with their encouragement, certain land in West Los Angeles, consisting of three hundred and eight acres, was accepted in trust as a gift from I. W. Hellman, J. G. Downey and O. W. Childs, forty acres being later added. In 1880, the first building was put up on Wesley Avenue; and on the sixth of October the college was opened. Most of the projectors were Methodists; and the institution, since known as the University of Southern California, became a Methodist college. The beginning of the institution has been odd: its first department of arts was built, in 1883, at Ontario; while two years later its theological school was opened at San Fernando. Recently, under the energetic administration of President F. D. Bovard, the University has made much progress.

A. B. Chapman, about 1879, joined C. T. Paul in opening a hardware store at 12 Commercial Street, with a little tin-shop opposite; and they soon introduced here the first gasoline stoves, to which the insurance companies at once seriously objected.

Probably the earliest Los Angeles newspaper published in French was a weekly, *L'Union Nouvelle*, which commenced in 1879 with P. Ganée as editor.

Exceeding the limits of animated editorial debate into which the rival journalists had been drawn in the heated campaign of 1879, William A. Spalding, a reporter on the *Evening Express*, waited for Joseph D. Lynch, the editor of the *Herald*, at about eleven o'clock in the morning of August 16th, and peppered away with a bull-dog pistol at his rival, as the latter, who had just left the Pico House, was crossing Spring Street from Temple Block to go to the *Herald* office. Lynch dropped his cane, and fumbled for his shooting-iron; but by the time he could return the fire, A. de Celis and other citizens had thrust themselves forward, making it doubly perilous to shoot at all. Spalding sent the bullet which wounded, not his adversary, but a bystander, L. A. Major of Compton.

Colonel G. Wiley Wells arrived in 1879, after a Civil War career in which his left arm was permanently crippled. He also served as United States District Attorney in Mississippi, where he prosecuted many of the Ku-Klux Klan, and as United States Consul-General to China, where he had a varied experience with men and affairs. With A. Brunson, he formed the law partnership of Brunson & Wells, having offices in the Baker Block. The next year, Bradner W. Lee, a nephew of Wells, who had arrived here in 1879, was added to the firm. After fifteen years' practice in the local courts, during which time Wells became a noted figure, he retired to private life at Santa Monica, disposing of his extensive law library, consisting of some six thousand volumes, to his successors, Works & Lee.

Henry Milner Mitchell, to whom I have referred as assisting to run down Vasquez, reached Los Angeles by way of Nicaragua in 1868, and was successively a surveyor, a reporter, a law student and, finally, from 1878 to 1879, Sheriff. In 1879, he was admitted to practice before the Supreme Court of California, and in the same year, he married the eldest daughter of Andrew Glassell. Eventually he met a very tragic death: while hunting near the scene of Vasquez's capture, he was shot by a friend who mistook him for a deer.

Colonel Henry Harrison Markham, a New Yorker, pitched his tent in Los Angeles and Pasadena in 1879, and was elected to Congress from the Sixth District, defeating R. F. Del Valle. He succeeded in getting one hundred and fifty thousand dollars for a public building and appropriations for Wilmington and other harbors; and he also aided in establishing army head-quarters at Los Angeles for Arizona, New Mexico and Southern California.

Carl Seligman left Germany for America in 1879 and spent a year in San Francisco, after which he removed to Tucson, Arizona. And there he remained, engaged in the wholesale and retail grocery business until, on December 6th, 1885, he married my daughter Ella, following which event he bought an interest in the firm of M. A. Newmark & Company.

The early eighties witnessed a commercial development so marked as to remind one of the proverbial grass that could be heard to grow.   During an entire century, business (centered, like social life, more or less about the Plaza) had crawled southward to First Street, a distance of but three or four blocks; and now, in five or six years, trade passed First, extended along both Main and Spring streets and reached almost to, or just beyond Second.   At this time, the Baker Block, at the corner of North Main and Arcadia streets, which contained the first town ticket-office of the Southern Pacific Railroad, was still the center of the retail trade of Los Angeles.

And yet some idea of the backwardness of the city, even then, may be obtained from the fact that, in 1880, on the southwest corner of Spring and Second streets where the Hollenbeck Hotel was later built, stood a horse corral; while the old adobe on the lot at the corner of First and Spring streets, which was torn down later to make room for the Hotel Nadeau, was also still there.

Obadiah Truax Barker settled in Los Angeles in 1880 and, with Otto Mueller, started a furniture and carpet business, known as Barker & Mueller's, at 113 North Spring Street. Strange as it seems, however, the newcomers found themselves too far from the business district; and, on Mueller's retiring, O. T. Barker & Sons moved to a store near the Pico House. Now the firm is Barker Brothers.

In fond recollection, the homely cheerfulness of the old-time adobe recurs again and again.   The eighties, however, were characterized by another form of dwelling, fashionable and popular; some examples of which, half-ruined, are still to be seen.   This was the frame house, large and spacious with wide, high, curving verandas, semicircular bay-windows, towers and cupolas.   Flower-bordered lawns generally encircled these residences; there were long, narrow hallways and more spare bedrooms than the less intimate hospitality of to-day suggests or demands.

On January 1st, 1880, the District Court of Los Angeles was abolished to give way to the County Court; on which occasion

Don Ygnácio Sepúlveda, the last of the District Court judges, became the first County Judge.

The first cement pavement in the city was laid on Main Street north of First by a man named Floyd. Having bought Temple Block, we were thinking of surrounding it with a wooden sidewalk. Floyd recommended cement, asking me, at the same time, to inspect a bit of pavement which he had just put down. I did so, and took his advice; and from this small beginning has developed the excellent system of paving now enjoyed by Los Angeles.

In 1880, there visited Southern California a man who not only had a varied and most interesting past, but who was destined to have an important future. This was Abbot Kinney, a blood relation of Emerson, Holmes and old General Harrison, and a student of law and medicine, commission merchant, a botanical expert, cigarette manufacturer and member of the United States Geological Survey; a man, too, who had traveled through, and lived long in Europe, Asia and Africa; and who, after seeing most of our own Northwest, was on his way to settle in Florida in search of health. While in San Francisco he heard of the recently-formed Sierra Madre Colony, whither he made haste to go; and after a month or two there, he liked it so well that he decided to remain on the gentle slope, found there a home and lay out a farm. At that time we had a customer by the name of Seabury, who owned one hundred and sixty acres along the foothills; and this land he had mortgaged to us to secure a note. When Kinney came, he bought a place adjoining Seabury's, and this led him to take over the mortgage. In due season, he foreclosed and added the land to his beautiful property, which he named *Kinneloa.*

All Kinney's combined experience was brought to bear to make his estate pleasurable, not only to himself but for the casual visitor and passer-by; and in a short time he became well known. He also was made a Special Commissioner of the United States to examine into the condition of the Mission Indians of Southern California; and on this commission he served with Helen Hunt Jackson, so famous as *H. H.* or, especially in California, as the author of *Ramona*, visiting with her all the well-known Indian *rancherias* between San Diego and Monterey, in addition to the twenty-one Franciscan Missions.

Toward the end of April, F. P. F. Temple passed away at the Merced Ranch and was buried in the family burying-ground at La Puente. This recalls to mind that, in early days, many families owned a hallowed acre where, as summoned one by one, they were laid side by side in rest eternal.

On May 16th, John W. Bixby died, at his Long Beach estate. About 1871 he had entered his brother Jotham's service, supervising the sheep ranch; and to John Bixby's foresight was attributed, first the renting and later the purchase of the great ranch controlled, through foreclosure of mortgage, by Michael Reese. A year or two before Bixby's death, five thousand acres were set aside for the town of Los Alamitos, but John never saw the realization of his dream to establish there a settlement.

It was on the eighteenth of the same month that my brother found it necessary to visit Carlsbad for the benefit of his health, and the decision occasioned my removal to San Francisco to look after his affairs. What was expected to be a brief absence really lasted until September, 1882, when he and his family returned to America and San Francisco, and I came back to Los Angeles, with which, of course, I had continued in close communication. During our absence, my wife's father, Joseph Newmark, died rather suddenly on October 19th, 1881.

Reference has been made to the movement, in 1859, for the division of California into two states. In the spring of 1880, John G. Downey republished the original act and argued that it was still valid; and Dr. J. P. Widney contended that the geographical, topograhical, climatic and commercial laws were all working for the separation of California into two distinct civil organizations. Not long after, at a mass-meeting in Los Angeles called to forward the improvement of Wilmington

Antonio Franco and Mariana Coronel

From an oil painting in the Coronel Collection

Fourth Street, Looking West from Main

Timms Landing

From a print of the late fifties

Santa Catalina, in the Middle Eighties

harbor, an Executive Committee consisting of J. G. Downey, W. H. Perry, E. F. Spence, Dr. J. P. Widney, A. B. Moffitt and J. G. Estudillo was named to see what could be done; and this Committee appointed a Legal Committee, consisting of Henry T. Hazard, R. M. Widney, George H. Smith, C. E. Thom, A. Brunson, S. C. Hubbell and H. A. Barclay. The latter Committee endorsed Downey's view that Congress could admit the new State; and it arranged for a convention which met on September 8th, 1881. There the gist of the sentiment was that State division was a necessity, but that the time was not yet ripe!

In 1880, Jotham Bixby & Company sold four thousand acres of their celebrated Cerritos Ranch to an organization known as the American Colony, and in a short time Willmore City, named after W. E. Willmore and the origin of Long Beach, was laid out and widely advertised. Willmore, a teacher, had been fairly successful as a colonizer in Fresno County; but after all his dreaming, hard work and investments, he lost all that he had, like so many others, and died broken-hearted. The earliest recollection I have of a storekeeper at Long Beach was my customer, W. W. Lowe.

At an early period in the development of Santa Monica, as we have seen, Senator Jones built a wharf there; but the Los Angeles & Independence Railroad, expected to become the outlet on the Pacific Coast of a supposedly great mining district in Inyo County, never reached farther east than Los Angeles. The Southern Pacific Railroad Company, desiring to remove this competition, obtained possession of the new road, razed the warehouse and condemned and half dismantled the wharf; and by setting up its terminus at Wilmington, it transferred there the greater part of its shipping and trade. By 1880, Santa Monica, to-day so prosperous, had shrunk to but three hundred and fifty inhabitants.

Competition compelled us, in 1880, to put traveling salesmen into the field—an innovation we introduced with reluctance, involving as it did no little additional expense.

Near the end of August, a Citizens' Committee was appointed to receive and entertain President Rutherford B. Hayes, whose visit to Los Angeles, as the first President to come here, caused quite a stir. His stay was very brief. During the few hours that he was here, he and his party were driven around the neighborhood in open hacks.

In the midst of his successive Greenback campaigns, General Ben. F. Butler sojourned for a few days, in 1880, in Los Angeles and was the recipient of many attentions.

At the beginning of this decade, the Los Angeles & San Pedro Railway was extended to Timms' Landing, the well-known old shipping point; and San Pedro then began to grow in earnest, both on the bluff and in the lowlands bordering on the bay. Wharves were projected; and large vessels, such as would have startled the earlier shippers, yet none too large at that, made fast to their moorings. ' But the improvement of yesterday must make way for that of to-day, and even now the Harbor Commissioners are razing historic Timms' Point. Penning again this familiar cognomen, I am reminded of what, I dare say, has been generally forgotten, that the Bay of Avalon was also once called Timms' Landing or Cove—after A. W. Timms, under-officer in the United States Navy —and that the name was changed prior to the Bannings' purchase of Catalina.

Frequent reference has been made to those who, in one way or another, sought to infuse new commercial life here and more rapidly to expand the city; but, after all, George Lehman, of whom I have already spoken, was perhaps *the* pioneer local boomer before that picturesque word had become incorporated in the Angeleño's vocabulary. Nor were his peculiarities in this direction entirely confined to booming, for he did considerable buying as well. Lehman's operations, however, most unfortunately for himself, were conducted at too early a period, and his optimism, together with his extensive, unimproved holdings, wrought his downfall. Besides the Round House and gardens, he owned real estate which would now represent enormous value, in proof of which I have only to mention a few of his possessions at that time: the southwest corner of Sixth and Spring streets; the northeast corner of Sixth and Hill streets; large frontages and many other corners on Main, Spring, Fort and Hill streets. Practically none of this property brought any income, so that when the City began to grade and improve the streets, Lehman's assessments compelled him to give a fifteen thousand dollar blanket mortgage to Lazard Frères of San Francisco.

Lehman soon found himself beyond his depth and defaulted in the payment of both principal and interest. Not only that, but with a complacency and a confidence in the future that were sublime, he refused to sell a single foot of land, and Lazard Frères with a worthy desire, natural to bankers, to turn a piece of paper into something more negotiable, foreclosed the mortgage, in 1879, and shut the gates of the Garden of Paradise forever; and a sheriff's sale was advertised for the purpose of concluding this piece of financial legerdemain. I attended the sale, and still distinctly remember with much amusement some of the incidents.

The vociferous auctioneer mounted the box or barrel provided for him and opened the program by requesting an offer for the corner of Hill and Second streets, a lot one hundred and twenty by one hundred and sixty feet in size. Nor did he request in vain.

One of the heroes of the occasion was Louis Mesmer, a friend of Lehman, whose desire it was to take a talking part in the proceedings, force up the prices and so help the latter. Amidst the familiar, "Going, going, going!" accordingly, the bidding began and, under the incentive of Mesmer's bullish activities, the figures soon reached four hundred dollars, the last bidder being Eugene Meyer, local agent for the mortgagee. At this juncture Mesmer, in his enthusiasm, doubled the bid to eight hundred dollars, expecting, of course, to induce someone to raise the price, already high for that day, still higher.

But "the best-laid schemes o' mice an' men gang aft a-gley." How eagerly Mesmer awaited the fruition of his shrewd manipulation! how he listened in hopeful anticipation to the repeated, "Going, going, going!" of the auctioneer! In vain, however,

he waited, in vain he listened.   To his mortification and embarrassment, his astounded ear was greeted with the decisive,
"Gone!—for eight hundred dollars! Sold to Louis Mesmer!"

Mesmer had bought, for more than it was worth, a piece of
property which he did not want, a catastrophe realized as well
by all the others present as it was patent to the victim himself.
The crowd relished keenly the ludicrous situation in which
Mesmer found himself, encumbered as he was with an investment which he had had no intention of making; and throughout the remainder of the contest he was distinguished only by
his silence.

Poor old George!   His vision was accurate: Los Angeles *was*
to become great, but her splendid expansion was delayed too
long for him to realize his dreams.   When Lehman died, he
was buried in a pauper's grave; and toward the end of the
eighties, the adobe Round House, once such a feature of
George Lehman's Garden of Paradise, was razed to make way
for needed improvements.

I have spoken of the intolerable condition of the atmosphere
in the Council Chamber when Charles Crocker made his
memorable visit to Los Angeles to consult with the City Fathers.
In the eighties, when the Common Council met in the southeast corner of the second floor of Temple Block, the same
objectionable use of tobacco prevailed, with the result that
the worthy Aldermen could scarcely be distinguished twenty-
five feet away from the rough benches on which sat the equally
beclouded spectators.

Doubtless the atmosphere of the court room was just as
foul when the Mayor, as late at least as 1880, passed judgment
each morning, sitting as a Justice, on the crop of disorderlies of
the preceding night.   Then not infrequently some neighbor
or associate of the Mayor himself, caught in the police drag-
net, appeared among the drowsy defendants!

CHAPTER XXXVI

CENTENARY OF THE CITY—ELECTRIC LIGHT

1881–1884

THE year 1881 opened with what, for Los Angeles, was a curious natural phenomenon—snow falling in February and covering the streets and plains with a white mantle. So rare was the novelty that many residents then saw the oddly-shaped flakes for the first time. It was about that time, according to my recollection, that another attempt was made to advertise Los Angeles through her far-famed climate, an effort which had a very amusing termination. Prominent men of our city invited the California Editorial Association, of which Frank Pixley of the *Argonaut* was President, to meet in Los Angeles that year, with the far-sighted intention of having them give wider publicity to the charms and fame of our winters. During this convention, a banquet was held in the dining-room of the St. Elmo Hotel, then perhaps called the Cosmopolitan. After a fine repast and a flow of brilliant eloquence, principally devoted to extolling our climatic wonders, the participants dispersed. But what was the surprised embarrassment of the Los Angeles boomers, on making their exit, to find pieces of ice hanging from all points of vantage and an intense cold permeating and stiffening their bones. Thus ended, amid the few icicles Los Angeles has ever known, the first official attempt to extend the celebrity of our glorious and seductive climate.

In February, Nathaniel C. Carter, to whom I have referred as a pioneer in arranging railroad excursions for tourists coming

to California, bought from E. J. Baldwin some eleven hundred
acres of the Santa Anita Ranch, comprising the northern and
wilder portion which sloped down from the base of the Sierra
Madre Mountains. This he subdivided, piping water from
the hills; and by wide advertising he established Sierra Madre,
appropriating the name already selected by a neighboring
colony.

In 1881, J. M. Guinn, who for a decade or more had been
Principal of the schools at Anaheim, was made Superintendent
of Los Angeles City Schools.

A tragedy attracted unusual attention in the early eighties,
owing, in part, to the social connections of the persons involved.
Francisco, or Chico Forster, as he was popularly called, the
sporting son of Don Juan Forster, had been keeping company
with a Señorita Abarta, a young woman of superb stature,
whose father was French and mother was Mexican; and having
promised to marry her, he betrayed her confidence. Her insist-
ence that Forster should keep his word had its *dénouement*
when, one day, at her behest, they visited the Plaza church;
but Forster so far endeavored to postpone the ceremony that
he returned to the carriage, in which he had left her, declaring that no priest could be found. Then they drove around
until they reached the corner of Commercial and Los Angeles
streets, half a block from H. Newmark & Company's. There
the young woman left the carriage, followed by Forster; and
on reaching the sidewalk, she said to him in Spanish,
"*¿Chico, que vas hacer?*" ("What are you going to do?")
Forster gave some evasive answer, and Señorita Abarta shot
him dead. She was arrested and tried; but owing to the expert
evidence in her behalf given by Dr. Joseph Kurtz she was ex-
onerated, to the satisfaction of nearly the entire community.
Among those who followed the proceedings closely with a view
to publishing the dramatic story was George Butler Griffin,
traveler and journalist, who, having recently arrived, had joined
the staff of the *Express*, later becoming somewhat noted as a
student of local history.

At a meeting in Turnverein Hall, on March 24th, the.

German Ladies' Benevolent Society of Los Angeles, so long known for its commendable work, was organized. Mrs. John Milner was elected President; Mrs. D. Mahlstedt, Vice-President; Mrs. John Benner, Secretary; and Mrs. Jacob Kuhrts, Treasurer.

Savarie J., *alias* Professor Brewster, was a simple-minded freak of the freakish eighties, who dropped into Los Angeles —as such characters generally do—without anyone knowing much about his origin. It was during the time that walking matches were much in vogue, and whenever one of these took place, Savarie J. was sure to participate. He was the only man in town that took Savarie J. seriously, and I assume that he was generally entered rather to attract spectators than for any other purpose. One day the Professor disappeared and no clue to his whereabouts could be discovered until his dead body was found far out on the desert. He had walked once too often and too far!

Fabian was a Frenchman and a jack-at-all-trades doing odd jobs around town, whose temperament and out-spoken way of expressing himself used to produce both amusement and surprise. On one occasion, when he took offense at the daughter of a prominent family for whom he was working, he sought out the lady of the house and said to her: "Madam, your sons are all right, but *your daughters are no good!*"

Two other names not forgotten by householders of an earlier day in Los Angeles are John Hall and Henry Buddin. The former, whose complexion was as black as his soul was white, came to Los Angeles a great many years ago. He was a whitewasher by trade and followed this calling for a livelihood, later giving it up to run an express wagon; and I can still see John plying about town and driving in summer between Los Angeles and Santa Monica, his wagon piled high with household effects, as our good citizens moved from one dwelling to another or went on their way to the shore of the sea. I remember, also, that one day some unnatural parent left a newborn, white infant on John Hall's steps. He was never able to locate the mother of the little fellow, and therefore took the foundling into his home and raised him as his son. Moses was the name John very appropriately bestowed upon the baby; and the white lad grew into manhood in the midst of this negro family. Like Fabian, Buddin proved himself handy in doing odd jobs of carpentering and upholstering, and was in frequent demand.

On September 5th, at the conclusion of the City's first century, or, more strictly speaking, one hundred years and a day after the founding of Los Angeles, a noteworthy celebration was undertaken. A population of about twelve thousand was all that Los Angeles then boasted; but visitors added greatly to the crowd, and the town took on a true holiday appearance. Main Street was decorated with an arch, bearing the inclusive figures, *1781–1881*; and the variegated procession, under the grand marshalship of General George Stoneman, was made up of such vehicles, costumed passengers and riders as suggested at once the motley but interesting character of our city's past. There were old, creaking *carretas* that had seen service in pioneer days; there were richly-decorated saddles, on which rode gay and expert horsemen; and there were also the more up-to-date and fashionable carriages which, with the advent of transcontinental railroading, had at last reached the Coast. Two Mexican Indian women—one named Benjamina—alternately scowling and smiling, and declared to be, respectively, one hundred and three and one hundred and fourteen years old, formed a feature of the procession. Clouds of dust, from the crowding auditors, greeted the orators of the day, who spoke not only in English and Spanish, but also in French; there were festal games and sports characteristic of the olden time; and the celebration concluded with a Spanish *baile*, at which dancing was continued until the following morning.

One of the musical celebrities of her time, and a native of Los Angeles of whom the city was justly proud, was Miss Mamie Perry, daughter of Mr. and Mrs. William H. Perry. In 1880, she went to Italy and studied under Sangiovanni and in September, 1881, made her *début*, singing in Milan, Florence,

Mantua and Bologna the title *rôle* of Petrella's opera, *Contessa d'Amalfi.* In other cities, she attained further distinction. A musical career was interrupted by her marriage, in 1883, to Charles W. Davis; but, after his untimely death in 1889, Mrs. Perry-Davis returned to Italy, a notable *musicale* in Turnverein Hall being given, as a farewell honor, on April 22d. Still later, she returned to Los Angeles and married C. Modini Wood.

When the funeral of President Garfield took place at Washington, on September 27th, his memory was also honored in Los Angeles. A procession started at two o'clock from Spring Street and marched to the Plaza, Colonel John O. Wheeler acting as Grand Marshal and George E. Gard, Chief of Police, leading the way. A catafalque, draped with black, star-bedecked silk and green smilax, and surmounted by a shrouded eagle and a little child—Laura Chauvin, daughter of A. C. Chauvin, the grocer—kneeling and representing Columbia lamenting the loss of the martyred chief, was drawn by six horses, followed by the honorary pallbearers and by civic and official bodies. Judge Volney E. Howard, as President, introduced Dr. J. P. Widney, who read the resolutions of condolence, after which A. Brunson delivered the eulogy. Mrs. Garfield, the President's widow, who first came to winter in California in 1899, finally built her own winter home in Pasadena, in October, 1904.

S. A. and M. A. Hamburger, who were engaged in business in Sacramento, concluded they would do better if they secured the right opening in the Southland; and having persuaded their father, Asher Hamburger, to join them in the new enterprise, they came to Los Angeles in November, 1881, and established their present business, under the firm name of A. Hamburger & Sons. D. A. Hamburger, who had been reading law, joined them in January, 1883. For years, until his death on December 2d, 1897, the elder Hamburger participated actively in all the affairs of the concern. They first opened on Main Street near Requena—close to the popular dry-goods store of Dillon & Kenealy, conducted by Richard Dillon & John

34

Kenealy—what was known as the People's Store, occupying a one-story building with a room containing not more than twenty-five hundred square feet; but having outgrown this location, they moved to the Bumiller Block. Again obliged to seek more room, the Phillips Block, at the corner of Spring and Franklin streets, was built for their use on the site of the old City and County Building and the Jail. In 1908, the Hamburgers moved to their extensive building on Broadway and Eighth Street.

Owen Brown, son of the famous John Brown of Ossawatomie, and long the only survivor of the little party that seized the arsenal at Harpers Ferry, came West late in 1881 and settled with his brother Jason, already at Pasadena. A horseback trail up one of the neighboring mountains still leads the traveler to speak in friendly spirit of this late pioneer, who died in 1889 and is buried near the foothills. Five years later, Jason Brown returned to Ohio.

The *Daily Times*, a Republican sheet started by Nathan Cole and James Gardiner, began on December 4th to be issued six days in the week. Both publishers within a month were succeeded by Yarnell, Caystile & Mathes, owners of the *Mirror*. So successful was the paper that it soon grew to be a nine-column folio.

In the height of the Winter season of 1881–82, when the semi-tropical glory of Southern California was most appealing, Helen Hunt Jackson, exploring the Southwest for materials of value in the study of the Indian, came to Los Angeles and met, as I have already related, Abbot Kinney, himself a student of the aborigines. She also met Don Antónío F. and Doña Mariana Coronel; and finding in the latter a highly intelligent and affable lady, she passed some hours each day at the hospitable Coronel mansion, driving out there from her hotel and reclining under the broad palm trees. When Mrs. Jackson first came, with her pencils and note-books, the retiring Señora (as she used to tell me), having little comprehension of the Eastern lady's ambitious plans, looked with some suspicion on the motives of her enthusiastic visitor; but fortunately this half-

Main Street, Looking North from Sixth, Probably in the Late Seventies

High School, on Pound Cake Hill, about 1873

First Street, Looking East from Hill

Temple Court House, after Abandonment by the County

distrust was dispelled by the warmth of the author's geniality, and Doña Mariana, opening both her house and heart, contributed inestimably to the success of the now famous *Ramona*, most of the rough notes for which were written at a little table on the Coronel veranda. On Doña Mariana's advice, Mrs. Jackson selected the Del Valle ranchhouse at the Camulos, as the best-preserved and most typical place for a background; although, disappointed in not finding the Del Valles at home, and consequently seeing the imagined headquarters of Ramona for but an hour or two, she was compelled to rely upon her Los Angeles hostess for many of the interesting and singularly accurate details. On departing from Southern California, Mrs. Jackson wrote for the *Century Magazine* a charming description of life at the old Coronel adobe, whence she never departed without a carriageful of luscious fruit. She also added her tribute to the attractions of the San Gabriel and San Fernando valleys. Now the world at large has been made more conversant with the poetical past of Los Angeles for the most part through the novel *Ramona*.

In 1882, the telephone was first introduced here, H. Newmark & Company so early subscribing for the service that they were given 'phone No. 5, the old River Station having No. 1. But it may amuse the reader to know that this patronage was not pledged without some misgivings lest the customary noises around the store might interfere with hearing, and so render the curious instrument useless!

On January 20th, Don Juan Forster died at his Santa Margarita rancho, in San Diego County; followed to the grave but a few months later by Mrs. Forster, a sister of Pio Pico.

As rugged as the climate of his native State of Maine, A. T. Currier, after the usual hazardous life of the pioneer on the plains and in mines, proved his good judgment when, in the late sixties, after riding through California in search of the best place to found a home, he selected a ranch close to that of Louis Phillips. For years, I had pleasant relations with Currier; and I must confess that it was not easy to decide, in 1882, when two such friends as he and Billy Rowland were the opposing candidates, how I should vote for Sheriff. Currier was elected.

The Arroyo Vista—later and more correctly named the Vista del Arroyo—kept by Mrs. Emma C. Bangs, was the only hotel in the Pasadena settlement in 1882, and not infrequently passengers who journeyed there by the narrow, stuffy stage, running every day except Sunday, found on arriving that they could not be accommodated. So small, in fact, was the hostelry that it became necessary to advertise when all the rooms had been taken. The stage left for Los Angeles at nine o'clock in the morning and returned at three; and the driver, who was a student of the classics from the East, doled out to the passengers both crossroad data and bits of ancient lore.

Fire having destroyed the State Normal School at San José, in 1880, then the only institution of its kind in California, the Legislature, on March 14th, 1881, provided for the establishing here of a branch; and the following March George Gephard, a German who had come in 1875, raised eight thousand dollars to purchase the orange grove at Bellevue Terrace, near Fifth Street and Charity, for a site. On August 29th, 1882, the school was opened with Charles H. Allen of San Francisco as first Principal, two other teachers and sixty-one students. In 1883, Allen was succeeded by President Ira More and the school became an independent institution. Edward T. Pierce, who followed Professor More, retired in 1904. An instructor there for twenty-two years was Professor Melville Dozier, who made for California, by way of Panamá, in 1868. Largely through the devotion of these pioneer teachers, as well as through those qualities which have marked the administration of Dr. Jesse F. Millspaugh, scholar and pedagogue, for nearly the last decade, this Normal School has grown, each year, from a very humble beginning until now it sends out hundreds of men and women into one of the noblest of all professions.

A commencement of the Los Angeles High School of par-

ticular interest to me was celebrated in June in the old
Turnverein Hall, on Spring Street—Superintendent James
M. Guinn presenting the diplomas—when my daughter Ella
graduated. Among her instructors had been Mrs. Chloe P.
Jones, for three years Principal of the school and for one year
Superintendent (having been the last incumbent, at the same
time, of both offices), and the late Mrs. Anna Averill, a noted
club woman. Mrs. Jones came to California from Ohio in
1873, taught for a while in Santa Rosa and, after a year of grade
work here, began to instruct in the new high school; and there,
after a service of nearly four decades, she is still a highly esteemed member of the staff. Mrs. Averill was the first woman
to enter the Board of Education; and in her honor a bell was
placed on the Mission Road, El Camino Real, to celebrate her
seventieth birthday.

Colonel Harrison Gray Otis, who had been a farmer's boy,
printer, Union soldier, foreman of the Government printing
office, newspaper correspondent and editor, and had first visited
Los Angeles late in 1874 or 1875 to familiarize himself with
local conditions, on August 1st, 1882 joined the firm of Yarnell,
Caystile & Mathes, thereupon assuming the management
of both the *Times* and the weekly *Mirror*. In October, 1883,
Yarnell and Mathes retired. A year later, the Times-Mirror
Company was incorporated with a capital stock of forty
thousand dollars.

Notwithstanding the failure of the *Evening Republican*, in
1878–79, Nathan Cole, Jr. started another afternoon daily,
the *Evening Telegram*, on August 19th. It was very neatly
printed; was delivered by carrier at sixty-five cents a month;
and was a pioneer here in inserting free advertisements for
those desiring situations.

In the spring of 1882, my attention had been called to the
public need of proper facilities for obtaining a drink of good
water; and no one else having moved in the matter, the following communication was sent, during the heated summer, to the
City authorities:

LOS ANGELES,
August 25, 1882.

To the Honorable,
     The Council of Los Angeles City:

GENTLEMEN:—
     The undersigned hereby tender to the city a drinking
fountain, as per the accompanying cut, to be placed on that
portion of Temple Block fronting the junction of Main and
Spring streets, for the free use of the public, and subject to the
approval of your honorable body.

Respectfully,
H. NEWMARK & CO.

About the same time Stephen H. Mott, Secretary of the
Los Angeles City Water Company, promised enough drinking
water, free of charge, to supply the fountain.

The unpretentious gift having been accepted, the fountain
was installed. The design included an iron pedestal and
column, surmounted by a female figure of attractive proportions; while below, the water issued from the mouth of a lion's
head. Though but seven feet in height and not to be
compared with more ambitious designs seen here later, the
fountain may have given some incentive to city service and
adornment.

It has been shown that Remi Nadeau bought the southwest
corner of Spring and First streets at what I then considered
a ridiculously high price. On that site, in 1882, he commenced building the Hotel Nadeau—the first four-story structure in town. This fact is not likely to escape my memory,
since he acquired the necessary funds out of the profit he
made in a barley speculation involving the sale, by H.
Newmark & Company, of some eighty thousand bags of
this cereal; his gain representing our loss. It thus happened
that I participated in the opening festivities (which began
with a banquet and ended with a ball) to a greater extent
than, I dare say, the average guest ever suspected. For

many years thereafter, the Nadeau, now comparatively so deserted, was the center of social and business life in Los Angeles.

On October 11th occurred the death of Don Manuel Dominguez, his wife surviving him but a few months.

In 1882, F. H. Howland, representing the Brush Electric Lighting Company, made an energetic canvass in Los Angeles for the introduction of the electric light; and by the end of the third week in August, forty or more arc lamps had been ordered by business houses and private individuals. He soon proposed to light the city by seven towers or spliced masts—each about one hundred and fifty feet high—to be erected within an area bounded by the Plaza, Seventh, Charity and Main streets, and supplied from a power-house at the corner of Banning and Alameda streets. The seven masts were to cost seven thousand dollars a year, or somewhat more than was then being paid for gas. This proposition was accepted by the Council, popular opinion being that it was "the best advertisement that Los Angeles could have;" and when Howland, a week later, offered to add three or four masts, there was considerable satisfaction that Los Angeles was to be brought into the line of progress. On the evening of December 31st, the city was first lighted by electricity when Mayor Toberman touched the button that turned on the mysterious current. Howland was opposed by the gas company and by many who advanced the most ridiculous objections: electric light, it was claimed, attracted bugs, contributed to blindness and had a bad effect on—ladies' complexions!

In 1883, Herman Flatau came to Los Angeles from Berlin and soon entered the employ of H. Newmark & Company. His first duty was to bale hides; in a year, he was a porter in the grocery department; and by another year he had advanced to a place in the billing-office. Since then, he has risen step by step until he is now a stockholder in M. A. Newmark & Company and is taken into the most confidential and important councils of that firm. On the nineteenth of February, 1888, Flatau married Miss Fanny Bernstein, a lady distinguished as the first girl graduate of a Los Angeles high school to enter the State University, receiving therefrom the Ph.B. degree.

Dr. Elizabeth A. Follansbee registered in Los Angeles in February, 1883, and as one of the earliest women physicians here soon secured an enviable position in the professional world, being called to the chair for diseases of children in the College of Medicine of the University of Southern California.

J. W. Robinson in 1833 established a small dry goods shop at the corner of Temple and Spring streets, which he named the Boston Dry Goods Store.[1] A couple of years later he moved into the Jones Block opposite the Court House, the growth of his business having warranted such a change. In 1895 the block next to Blanchard Hall was built by this firm, and this he has occupied ever since. In March, 1896, the present manager, J. M. Schneider, became associated with the Boston Dry Goods Co., which was incorporated in 1891. N. B. Blackstone, a kinsman of Robinson, once in business with him, in time withdrew and set up for himself, under his own name, on Broadway.

One of the most shocking railroad accidents in the history of California blotted the calendar for January 20th, when over twenty persons were killed and sudden grief was brought to several happy Los Angeles circles. About three o'clock on a cold wintry night, an express train, bound south, stopped at the Tcháchepi Station, near the summit; and while the engineer and fireman on the detached locomotive and tender were busy loading water and fuel, and the conductor was in the office making his report, the brakeman, with what proved to be uncalculating gallantry, was hastening to escort a young lady from the car to the railway station. In his hurry, he had forgotten to apply the brakes; and before he could return, the entire train, started by a heavy gale, had begun to move away

[1] May 1st, 1914, the J. W. Robinson Dry Goods Co. contracted to move to Seventh Street between Grand Avenue and Hope Street. This is one of the notable examples of leapfrog that real estate operators have played in Los Angeles, to the detriment perhaps, at times, of the town itself.

—at the outset slowly, then dashing, with ever-increasing momentum, down the heavy mountain grade!

The conductor, upon leaving the depot, was the first to discover that the cars had started away; the disappearing lights having become so faint as to be scarcely visible. The passengers, too, had noticed nothing unusual until too late; when the train, plunging along at fearful velocity, leaped the track and fell in a heap to the ravine below. The old-fashioned lamps and stoves set fire to the *débris;* with the result that those who were not crushed were burned. The dead and wounded were brought to Los Angeles as quickly as possible; but the remains of some were never identified. Governor Downey, who was on the train, was rescued, though for years he suffered from the nervous shock; but among those lost was his charmimg wife.

Marshall & Henderson established themselves, in 1883, in the wholesale iron and wagon-supply trade; whereupon we sold that branch of our business to them. Shortly after, we vacated the storerooms in the Arcadia Block, which we had continuously occupied since the establishing of H. Newmark & Company in 1865, and moved to the two-story Amestoy Building on Los Angeles Street, north of Requena, but a few paces from the corner on which I had first clerked for my brother.

At a meeting in the office of the Los Angeles Produce Exchange, in the Arcadia Block on Los Angeles Street on March 9th, presided over by C. W. Gibson when J. Mills Davies acted as Secretary, the Board of Trade of Los Angeles was organized, M. Dodsworth, C. W. Gibson, A. Haas, J. M. Davies, Eugène Germain, J. J. Mellus, John R. Mathews, Walter S. Maxwell, I. N. Van Nuys and myself being the incorporators. Six directors—Gibson, Van Nuys, Haas, Dodsworth, Mathews and Newmark—were chosen. On March 14th, 1883, the Board was formally incorporated for fifty years. After a while the Board met in the Baker Block, and still later it assembled in a two-story brick structure at the northwest corner of Fort and First streets. In October, 1906, the Board of Trade and the Wholesalers' Board of Trade were consolidated, the new organization becoming known as the Wholesalers' Board of Trade. This move was initiated by Herman Flatau.

The republication, in the Los Angeles *Express* of March 23d, 1908, under the caption, "Twenty-five Years Ago To-day," of several paragraphs, savoring of village gossip such as the following—

Some very fine nugas [*nougats?*] are to be seen at Dol's Commercial Restaurant. They are meant for the silver-wedding feast at Mr. Newmark's—

calls to mind an event of March 21st, when my wife and I celebrated our silver wedding at our home on Fort Street. At half-past six in the evening, all of my employees sat down at dinner with us, having come in a body to tender their congratulations. A reunion of three generations of the Newmarks, some of whom then saw one another for the first time, came to a close a week or two later.

As the anniversary approached, I prepared a surprise for my wife, arranging that her brother, Abraham Newmark of St. Louis, should be present in Los Angeles for the occasion. His visit, however, had a grievous termination: while in San Francisco on his way home from Los Angeles, death came to him suddenly in the home of a friend.

In May, the Los Angeles Board of Education sold the northwest corner of Spring and Second streets—a lot one hundred and twenty by one hundred and sixty-five feet, where the City, in 1854, had built the first schoolhouse—to the city authorities for thirty-one thousand dollars; and the next year the Council erected on the inside sixty feet the first municipal building of consequence. When the Boom was at its height in 1887, the City sold the balance of the lot with its frontage on Spring Street and a depth of one hundred and five feet for one hundred and twenty thousand dollars, to John Bryson, Sr., an arrival of 1879 and ten years later Mayor of Los Angeles; and George H. Bonebrake (who came a year earlier than Bryson, and was in his day a prominent financier) opened, if my memory serves me correctly, the first agency for Eastern vehicles. Together, they built the Bryson Block.

This sale and purchase reminds me that when the lot was cleared to make way for the new City Hall, ten or twelve fine black locust trees were felled, much to the regret of many old-timers. These were the same shade trees for the preservation of which Billy McKee, the early schoolmaster, had risked bodily encounter with the irate waterman.

When the Board of Education sold this lot, it bought another, which extended from Fort Street to Spring between Fifth and Sixth streets and had a frontage of one hundred and twenty feet on each street. The price paid was twelve thousand five hundred dollars. This is the lot now known as Mercantile Place, whose retention or sale has been so much debated and which, with its many small stores, reminds the traveler not a little of those narrow but cosy, and often very prosperous, European streets and alleys on both sides lined with famous shops.

August 22d was the date of the City ordinance creating Elysian Park, the act leading the early settler back to pueblo days when the land in question passed from Mexican to American control and remained a part of the City lots, already described, and never subdivided and sold.

The last companies of volunteer firemen were organized in 1883, one being in the Morris Vineyard, a district between what is now Main, Hill, Fifteenth and Sixteenth streets, and the other in East Los Angeles, where a hose company was formed.

During September or October, a party of distinguished German bankers and statesmen, who had come to the United States to investigate certain branches of business, visited Los Angeles. The most important of this commission was Dr. Edward Lasker of the German Reichstag, other eminent members being Henry Villard, President of the Northern Pacific Railroad, and Judge Siemens, President of the German Bank of Berlin. A committee, consisting of I. W. Hellman, C. C. Lips,

M. Morris, A. W. Edelman, Conrad Jacoby, Dr. Joseph Kurtz and myself took charge of these gentlemen, as well as a number of others, whose names I forget.   Dr. Lasker, during his brief stay, accepted the hospitality of my home, and there received considerable honor at the hands of his German admirers, a large body of enthusiasts serenading him.   Even while with us, it was evident that Dr. Lasker was an ailing man; and on the fifth of the following January, while riding in a carriage in Galveston, he suddenly died.

General George H. Stoneman, when he retired from the army in 1871, settled near San Gabriel; and continuing more or less in public life, he was elected in 1883 Governor of California.

In December, 1883, Eugene Meyer sold out to Nathan Cahn and Leon Loeb, his partners in the City of Paris store, and engaged in banking with Lazard Frères, in San Francisco, in which enterprise he continued until 1892, when he moved to New York and became one of the managing partners of the same institution in that city, retiring from active business nearly a decade later.

When Meyer left, he sold his home on Fort Street, which had originally cost him six thousand, to Moses L. Wicks for sixteen thousand dollars; and his friends told him that so successful a sale proved the Meyer luck.   Wicks in time resold it to John D. Bicknell, whose heirs still own it.

With the coming at Christmas in 1883 of Robert N. Bulla, began a career that has made itself felt in local legal, political, commercial, social and scientific circles.   In 1884, he joined the law firm of Bicknell & White; nine years later, he was representing his district in the State Assembly; in 1897, he was a State Senator; and his efficient activity as a director of the Chamber of Commerce, together with his forensic talent, lead one to anticipate his rise to further distinction in that body. As a director of the Southwest Museum, Bulla performs another of his services to the community.

After an unsuccessful canvass made by Judge Noah Levering, which resulted in the attendance of just four persons, the

Historical Society of Southern California was finally organized at meetings in Temple Block, in November and December, 1883. J. J. Warner was the first President; H. D. Barrows, A. F. Coronel, J. G. Downey and John Mansfield, the Vice-Presidents; J. M. Guinn, Treasurer; and C. N. Wilson, Secretary. For a time, the Society's meetings were held in the City Council room, after that in the County Court room; and later at the houses of the members. On February 12th, 1891, the Society was incorporated.

Le Progrès, a seven-column paper, was started here, in 1883, as the organ of the French population, some rather prominent citizens of Gallic origin becoming the stockholders. Dr. Pigné du Puytren was the first editor, and he was succeeded, in a year or two, by Georges Le Mésnager, the wine-grower.

On February 18th, another flood of unusual proportions, continuing until May, devastated the Southland. Following several days of heavy rain, the river rose and fifty houses and large sections of vineyards and orchards in the low-lying portions of the city were carried away by the mad waters; several lives being lost. In that year, the Santa Ana cut its new channel to the sea, deviating from the old course from one to three miles, but still holding to the southwest, a direction apparently characteristic of rivers in this vicinity.

Speaking of rains, reminds me that, in 1884, one of the difficulties in the way of solving the water problem was removed in the purchase, by the City of Los Angeles, for fifty thousand dollars, of Colonel Griffith J. Griffith's right to the water of the Los Angeles River.

Charles F. Lummis, long a distinguished and always a picturesquely-recognizable resident, walked across the continent "for fun and study," from Cincinnati to Los Angeles, by a roundabout route of 3507 miles in one hundred and forty-three days, in 1884, having made an arrangement with the Los Angeles *Times* to which he contributed breezy letters on the way. The day after his arrival he became city editor of that newspaper, and in the last Apache campaign, in 1886, he was its war correspondent. In 1887 a stroke of paralysis sent him

to New Mexico; and recovering, he spent several years exploring and studying Spanish-America from Colorado to Chile,
becoming acknowledged here and abroad as an authority on the
history and the peoples of the lands he visited. In 1893, returning from Peru, he edited for a dozen years the *Land of
Sunshine* magazine (later *Out West*); after that founding the
Landmarks Club to which we owe the preservation, from utter
ruin, of several of the old Missions. This club has lately been
reorganized to care for all of the twenty-one Missions of the
State. Later Lummis incorporated the Sequoya League which
has so much bettered the condition of thousands of California
Indians—securing, in particular, for the evicted Warner's
Ranch Indians a better reservation than that from which they
were driven. From 1905 to 1911 he was Librarian of the Los
Angeles Public Library. In 1903 he founded the Southwest
Society of the Archæological Institute of America which conducted many scientific expeditions in Arizona, New Mexico
and Guatemala, acquired valuable collections and maintained
the first free public exhibits of science in Southern California.
In 1907 he and others incorporated the Southwest Museum,
whereupon the Society conveyed to it all its collections, a
twenty-acre site and the fifty thousand dollars bequeathed
by Mrs. Carrie M. Jones for the first buildings. Besides other
and many literary activities, Lummis has published over a
dozen notable books on the Southwest and Spanish America.[1]
Clad in corduroys from Barcelona—coat and trousers, with
very wide wales, of olive or green—wearing no vest, but having
a shirt of heavy drawn-work of the Pueblo Indians (with whom
he dwelt six years), a red-and-white *faja* or waist-band made
by the same people, and a grey *sombrero* banded with Mexican
braided horse-hair, Lummis roams the desert or is welcome at
the most exclusive functions; having already been a guest many
times at the White House and the palaces of Diaz and other
presidents in Spanish America. "I don't change my face for

[1] In 1915, in recognition of historical work, the King of Spain conferred upon
Lummis the dignity of a Knight Commander of the Royal Order of Isabel la
Católica.

company," he says, "then why my garb—so long as both are clean?" An interesting figure at scientific meetings and on the lecture platform, Lummis is equally so at home where, after twenty years' work with his own hands, he is still building his stone "castle," *El Alisal;* and as his house is a rendezvous for artists, musicians, authors and scientists, his guests often find him toiling as either carpenter or mason. The *Alisal,* by the way, is built around the huge sycamore under which Greek George camped with his camels on his first arrival in Los Angeles nearly sixty years ago.

In 1884, Colonel H. Z. Osborne—always a foremost citizen of the town and in 1912 a most energetic President of the Chamber of Commerce—and E. R. Cleveland bought· the *Express;* and two years later they organized the Evening Express Company, J. Mills Davies, once Secretary of the Board of Trade, becoming business manager. In 1897, Colonel Osborne was appointed United States Marshal for the Southern California District, whereupon Charles Dwight Willard became general manager of the paper, to be succeeded by J. B. Abell. For a short time in 1900, the *Express* fell into the hands of a group of men, of whom John M. Miller acted as President and Richard Beebe served as Secretary.

O. W. Childs opened his new theater known as Childs' Opera House, on Main Street south of First, in what was then the center of the city, on May 24th, when the *School for Scandal* was given, Mlle. Rhea taking the leading part. This, the first theater of real consequence built in Los Angeles, had a seating capacity of eighteen hundred; and for some time, at least, an entertainment was booked there for every night of the week. Frequently, too, whenever anything of moment was going to happen there, Childs sent me an invitation to occupy his private box.

An interesting personality for many years was C. P. Switzer, a Virginian, who came in 1853 with Colonel Hollister, W. H. Perry and others. Switzer became a contractor and builder; but in 1884, in search of health, he moved to an eminence in the Sierras, where he soon established Switzer's Camp, which gradually became famous as a resort generally reached on bur-ros. A few years ago, "Commodore" Switzer—or Sweitzer as he was also called—retired, but the camp, more than ever popular, has been continued as "Switzer's."

Toward the middle of the eighties, excitement among citrus growers throughout Southern California gave way to deep depression due to the continued ravages of the fluted scale, a persistent insect whose home, according to research, is Austra-lia, and which had found its way, on Australian plants (and especially on *Acacia latifolia*) into South Africa, New Zealand and California, arriving on the Pacific Coast about 1868. This particular species, known to the scientist as the *Icerya pur-chasi*, resisted and survived all insecticide sprayings, washes and fumigation, and for a while it seemed that one of the most important and growing industries of the Southland was abso-lutely doomed. Indeed, not until 1889, when the result of Albert Koebele's mission to Australia, as a representative of the Department of Agriculture, was made known, did hope among the citrus orchardists revive. In that year, the tiny ladybird—styled by the learned the *Novius cardinalis*, but more popularly spoken of as the ladybug—the most effective enemy of the fluted scale, was introduced here, the Govern-ment establishing, among other stations, an experimental laboratory on the Wolfskill ranch under the charge of Professor D. W. Coquillett; and so rapidly was this tiny favorite of children propagated and disseminated, that the dreaded scale was exterminated and the crops were saved. Wolfskill, by the way, though he fought hard with the assistance of his foreman, Alexander Craw, to save his noted trees, lacked the coöpera-tion of his neighbors; and the injury then inflicted largely influenced him to subdivide his famous citrus property.

With the arrival on March 1st, 1887, of J. O. Koepfli, a man came on the scene who during the next twenty-five years was to be not only one of the real forces in the development of the city, but, as a whole-souled gentleman, was to surround himself, through his attractive personality, with a large circle of representative and influential friends. As President of the

Merchants' Association, his record was such that in 1896 he was elected a director of the Chamber of Commerce where, during twelve years, he performed valiant service on all the important committees. His work in behalf of the harbor and the Owens River aqueduct is especially memorable. He was President of the Chamber in 1905 and 1906. With such men as C. D. Willard and R. W. Burnham, he founded the Municipal League, whose President he was for seven years. His efforts were always free from the taint of personal aggrandizement, and he thus had the public confidence. He is a member of the well-known firm of Bishop & Company.

Among the present social organizations of the city, the Los Angeles Athletic Club takes second place in point of age. . It was organized in 1879 by forty young men, among whom were Fred Wood, Bradner W. Lee, Mark G. Jones, Frank M. Coulter, Frank A. Gibson, John S. Thayer, M. H. Newmark, W. G. Kerckhoff, Alfredo Solano, J. B. Lankershim, W. M. Caswell, James C. Kays, Joseph Binford, and Samuel Dewey. The initial meeting took place in Wood's office in the McDonald Block, and a hall in the Arcadia Building was the Club's earliest headquarters. J. B. Lankershim was the first President. A few years later, the Club moved to the Downey Block; and there the boys had many a merry bout. In the course of time, the gymnasium was located on Spring Street, between Fourth and Fifth; now it occupies its own spacious and elaborate building on Seventh Street, at the corner of Olive, the Club's quarters being among the finest of their kind in America.

35

CHAPTER XXXVII

REPETTO AND THE LAWYERS

1885–1887

TEN or twelve months after the starting of the first cable railway here, Los Angeles, in 1885, resumed the march of progress, this time with an electric street car line. Poles—with huge arms stretching out into the middle of the street and often spoken of derisively as gallows-poles—and wires were strung along Los Angeles and San Pedro streets, down Maple Avenue to Pico Street and thence westward to what was known as the Electric Homestead Tract, just outside of the city limits. A company owned much land not likely to be sold in a hurry, and to exploit the same rapidly, the owners built the road. F. H. Howland, who introduced the electric light here, was a prime mover in this project, but ill fortune attended his efforts and he died a poor man.

On January 11th, my wife and I left for a trip to the City of Mexico, where we spent four or five days and were pleasantly entertained, before going to the New Orleans Exposition, by our old friend, Judge Ygnácio Sepúlveda and his wife. Previous to crossing the border, we stored our trunks in El Paso and received them upon our return, strapped as before. Some valuables, however, which I had hidden away in the linen were missing when I reopened the trunk, and have never been recovered. Among other companions on this outing were Fred, son of J. M. Griffith, and James S., son of Jonathan S. Slauson. By the bye, James himself has had an honorable public career,

546

having served in one of his activities as President of the Chamber of Commerce.

Early in March, I believe, sewing was first introduced into the public schools of Los Angeles, the Board of Education consenting to it only as an experiment.

Two celebrities divided the honors in the spring and summer in local circles: United States Senator John Sherman, who visited Los Angeles on May 8th, 1885, and Sir Arthur Sullivan, the distinguished English composer, of *Pinafore* and *Mikado* fame, who tarried near the ocean in the hot days of August.

About 1885, a Dr. Sketchley, who enjoyed some reputation for his work in the natural history field and had been a traveler through many remote countries, brought to Los Angeles quite a collection of ostriches and opened, about where Tropico lies, an amusement resort known as "The Ostrich Farm." Having provided a coach to connect with the end of the Temple Street cable cars and advertised the strange peculiarities of his finely-feathered animals, the Doctor soon did a thriving business, notwithstanding the task of caring for the birds in their new environment. Later, Sketchley removed from Los Angeles to Red Bluff; but there he failed and lost all that he had.

Soon after Dr. Sketchley arrived here with his ostriches and three or four men and one woman from Madras, Edwin Cawston, an Englishman now retired and living in Surrey, happening (while on a tour through America) to glance at an article in *Harper's Magazine* pointing out the possibilities of successfully raising ostriches, returned to London, secured the necessary capital and in 1887 began shipping these camel-birds from South Africa to Los Angeles. Many of the easily-affected creatures died at sea; yet forty, as good luck would have it, survived, and with them Cawston and a partner named Fox opened a second "ostrich farm" at Washington Gardens. In time, Cawston transferred his establishment to La Habra, associating with himself E. H. Rydall as publicity agent; and in 1908 the Cawston Ostrich Farm, between Los Angeles and Pasadena, was incorporated.

Quite naturally with the advent of the settler from the East and the Middle West, the *zanjas*, in early years so serviceable both for domestic and irrigation purposes and, therefore, more or less venerable, came to be looked upon as mere surface-conveyers and public nuisances; a sign, in 1883, at the corner of Sixth and Olive streets warning teamsters against crossing the ditch. By 1885, such opposition had developed that most of the *zanjas* were condemned, the one extending from Requena Street to Adams *via* Figueroa being, if I am right, one of the last that was buried from view.

For some time, East Los Angeles maintained its character as a village or small town, and in 1885 the *East Side Champion*, started and edited by Edward A. Weed, voiced the community's interests.

This year was marked by the demise of a number of well-known Angeleños. On the second of March, John Schumacher, a man esteemed and beloved by many, died here of apoplexy, in the seventieth year of his age. Six days later, General Phineas Banning, who had been sick for several months, expired at San Francisco, his wife and daughters being with him; and on March 12th, he was buried in Rosedale Cemetery. In his declining years, illness often compelled General Banning to remain at home in Wilmington; and when needing the services of his physician, Dr. Joseph Kurtz, he would send a locomotive to fetch him. On June 5th, Dr. Vincent Gelcich, the pioneer surgeon, died here at the age of fifty-six years.

In 1885, the first medical school in Los Angeles was founded in the house once occupied by Vaché Frères, the wine-makers, on Aliso Street between Lyons and Center. For years the school was conducted as a part of the University of Southern California, and Dr. J. P. Widney was Dean.

In the fall of 1885 Dr. M. Dorothea Lummis, a graduate in medicine of the Boston University, settled in Los Angeles and in time became President of the Los Angeles County Homeopathic Medical Society. Distinguished in her profession, Dr. Lummis became a leader in humane endeavor, reorganizing here the Society for the Prevention of Cruelty to Animals

and founding the Society for the Prevention of Cruelty to
Children.

The first train of the Santa Fé Railroad to enter the city
of Los Angeles ran from Colton over the rails of the Southern
Pacific, on November 29th, the two corporations having come
to an agreement to use the one set of tracks until the spring
of 1887, when the Santa Fé finished building from San Bernardino to its junction with the Los Angeles & San Gabriel
Valley Railroad. The locomotive bore the name, *L. Severy*—
a prominent director in the Company, and the father of the
well-known resident of Pasadena—and the number *354.*

After twenty years' association with the wholesale grocery
business, I withdrew, on December 5th, 1885, from H. Newmark & Company, and on that day the business was absorbed
by M. A. Newmark, M. H. Newmark, Max Cohn and Carl
Seligman, and continued as M. A. Newmark & Company.
This gave me the opportunity of renewing my association with
one of my earliest partners, Kaspare Cohn, the new firm becoming K. Cohn & Company; and the change in my activities
found me once again shipping hides and wool.

Looking through the haze of years, many are the recollections—often vague, it is true—of those with whom I had
business relations. In the picturesque adobe days, the majority
of my customers were simple-mannered natives such as
Manuel Carizosa, on South Alameda Street; José María
Dávila, in Sonora Town next door to José María Fuentes,
his competitor; and M. G. Santa Cruz, in the same district.
Jordan Brothers, Americans, kept store on Aliso Street opposite
the Aliso Mill, and G. Ginnochio, father-in-law of James Castruccio, on Macy Street, near the river; while Bernardino Guirado, Mrs. John G. Downey's brother, and Max Schwed supplied
the wants of Los Nietos.   J. B. Savarots, who went to South
America when he sold out to J. Salaberri & Company—a firm
composed of two Basques, Juan Salaberri and Domingo Oy-
harzabel—was in general merchandise in San Juan Capistrano.
Hippolyte Cahen (whose widow is a member of the Lazarus
Stationery Company,) had an up-to-date general store at

Anaheim; and Simon Cahen, son-in-law of Bernard Cohn, was similarly occupied in the Azusa district. Others of about the same period, were Dominico Rivara, who established himself on Main Street near Commercial, shortly to be succeeded by Vignolo & Sanguinetti, in whose store—known as La Esperanza and near Castruccio Brothers' La Mariposa—Jim Moiso bought an interest. Two more Main Street merchants were A. C. Chauvin, who conducted his El Dorado Store in the Lanfranco Building, and his neighbor, Joe Lazarowich. And near them Francisco Vassallo had his little fruit stand. The erratic Lucas Sciscisch, who terminated his life as a suicide, attended diligently to business on First Street, near Los Angeles; and not so very far away Thomas Strohm was laying the foundation, in his grocery trade, for that popularity which caused him, in the eighties, to be chosen Chief of the Fire Department. António Valle, who built on the northeast corner of First and Los Angeles streets (calling the block in honor of his five sons, the Five Brothers), for a number of years had a grocery store on Main Street near Requena and not far from the butcher shop of Vickery & Hinds.

In view of the ravages of time among the ranks of these old-timers, it is a satisfaction to observe that at least some of those who were active before I retired are still in the trade. The first-comer was George A. Ralphs, who, reaching Los Angeles as a boy, learned brick-masonry and was known as the Champion Bricklayer of California until, while on a hunting expedition, he lost an arm.[1] With a man named Francis, he started, in 1877, the Ralphs & Francis Grocery, on the old Georgetown corner. This was the beginning of the Ralphs Grocery Company. In February, 1882, Hans Jevne, a Norwegian by birth, who had been associated with his brother in Chicago, came to Los Angeles, and a few months later he opened a small grocery store in the Strelitz Block at 38 and 40 North Spring Street. In less than no time, so to

[1] On June 21st, 1914, Mr. Ralphs lost his life in a deplorable accident in the San Bernardino Mountains, being crushed by a huge bowlder; although his wife escaped by springing from the rolling rock.

speak, the good housewives of the town were able to secure the rarest tidbits from all the markets of the world; and not only that, but Jevne, since his advent here, has been identified with most important steps in the evolution of the city. W. F. Ball for thirty years or more has been a tobacconist, and for thirty years, or somewhat less, has occupied the same premises on Spring Street, north of First. The Williams family came from England in 1882, and George soon established his grocery business out in what was then known as the University district, where he bought a block of land. George has given of his time for the public weal, having been for several terms a City Councilman. Another Los Angeles merchant who has attained success is Albert Cohn; and while his start in life, in an independent career, began a couple of years after my retirement, he had been in my employ as a clerk almost from the time of his arrival, in 1882. Marius Bellue has been located on South Alameda Street so long that it seems as though he must have arrived here in the Year One.

So much for the merchants of the city; among such tradesmen in the districts outside of Los Angeles, I can recall but three active in my day and still active in this. Alphonse Weil, a native of the sunny slopes of France, has grown up with the town of Bakersfield. John R. Newberry opened his doors in 1882, and, after moving to Los Angeles in 1893, commenced that meteoric career, during which he established stores throughout Los Angeles and its suburbs. George A. Edgar, about thirty-one years ago, brought a stock of groceries and crockery to Santa Ana and deposited the contents of his cases in the same location, and on the same shelves, from which he still caters to his neighbors.

The great flood of 1886 reached its first serious state on January 19th. All of Los Angeles between Wilmington Street and the hills on the east side was inundated; levees were carried off as if they were so much loose sand and stubble; and for two or three weeks railway communication with the outside world was impossible.

During this inundation on January 19th, Martin G. Aguirre,

who was a deputy under Sheriff George E. Gard, gave an exhibition of great courage. So rapidly had the waters risen that many persons were marooned; and it was only by throwing himself on the back of his favorite horse that Aguirre, at very great risk, rescued twenty or more people from drowning, the number including many children. In the last attempt, Aguirre nearly lost his own life. Somewhat of a hero, in November, 1888, he was elected Sheriff, defeating Tom Rowan for that office.

Rebecca Lee Dorsey, another of the early women practitioners of medicine, came to Los Angeles in January, 1886, a graduate both of Eastern colleges and of a leading Vienna hospital. Peddling vegetables as a child, later working as a servant and hiring out as a nurse while finishing her course in Europe, Dr. Dorsey was of a type frequently found among the early builders of the Southwest.

Largely to a board of Commissioners, consisting of Mayor E. F. Spence, H. Sinsabaugh and the ever-ready Jake Kuhrts, appointed in 1886 when provision was made for a paid fire department, is due the honor of having successfully arranged the present excellent system in Los Angeles.

It was in 1886 that we bought the Repetto *rancho*, under circumstances of such interest that it may be well to tell something about the owner and his connections. Alessandro Repetto was an Italian of such immense size that he was compelled, when standing, to shift the weight of his body from one leg to the other. He was miserly in the extreme, but this was compensated for by his honesty and uprightness of character. He was also far from being neat, and I remember the way in which he dispensed hospitality when I visited his ranch to buy wool. He would bring out some very ordinary wine and, before serving it, would rinse out the glasses with his fat fingers; and it was courtesy alone that prompted me to partake of what he offered. He lived on his ranch, but when attacked by his last illness, he took a room at the New Arlington Hotel, formerly the White House, on the southeast corner of Commercial and Los Angeles streets.

There, finding him alone and neglected, I advised him to go to the Sisters' Hospital on Ann Street; but the change did not save him and after a few days he died. A fellow Italian named Scotti, a knave of a chap who was with him in his last moments, knowing that I was Repetto's executor, soon brought to my house a lot of papers which he had taken from the dead man's pockets.

Repetto being a recluse somewhat on the misanthropic order, I had difficulty in getting pallbearers for his funeral, one of my applications being to James Castruccio, President of the Italian Benevolent Society and then Italian Consul, who said that Repetto had never helped anyone, but that if I would give, in his name, five hundred dollars to charity, the attendants would be supplied. To this I demurred, because Repetto had made no such provision in his will; and Castruccio giving me no satisfaction, I went to Father Peter, explained to him that Repetto had bequeathed six thousand dollars to the Church, and stated my needs; whereupon Father Peter arranged for the bearers. All the provisions for the funeral having been settled, I cabled to his brother and heir, then living in the mountains near Genoa, whose address I had obtained from Castruccio. Repetto had really hated this brother and, in consequence, he had very unwillingly bequeathed him his large estate.

In due season, the brother, a hunchback, appeared on deck as an intimate with Scotti, and I found him to be an uncouth, ignorant fellow and a man who had probably never handled a ten-dollar gold piece or its equivalent in his life. He had on shoes that an elephant might have worn, a common, corduroy suit, a battered hat and plenty of dirt. Wishing to take him to Stephen M. White, my lawyer, I advised the purchase of new clothes; but in this, as in other matters, I appealed in vain. So miserly was he indeed, that one day, having purchased a five-cent loaf of bread in Sonora Town, he was seen to hide himself behind a building while he ate it, doubtless fearful lest someone might ask him for a bite.

Alessandro Repetto had lived with an Indian woman by

whom he had a son; and a Los Angeles attorney soon had himself appointed guardian, declaring that the property belonged, not to the brother, but to the boy. This, because the woman had never left her husband, was blackmail, pure and simple; besides Repetto had willed the lad some property in San Gabriel. Stephen M. White was the attorney for the estate; but when this lawsuit started, Scotti advised the unsophisticated brother to take other lawyers. Two men, accordingly, one named Robarts and the other Jim Howard, suddenly appeared at the trial; and when I asked why they were there, they replied that they had been engaged by Repetto's brother. Four hundred and seventy-five dollars settled this extortion, the lawyers taking all but twenty-five dollars, which was paid to the mother of the boy.

Early in the morning, a few days later—either on Christmas or New Year's—there was a knock at my door; and when the girl answered the call, the Sheriff was found there with the interesting news that Repetto had been arrested and that he wished me to bail him out! I learned that Robarts and Howard had presented him with a bill for three thousand five hundred dollars, for services; and that, since the money was not immediately forthcoming, they had trumped up some sort of a charge and had had the foreigner incarcerated. White advised a settlement, and after much difficulty we succeeded in having their bill reduced to three thousand dollars, which we paid.

Repetto's troubles now seemed at an end; but just as he was ready to leave for Italy, Scotti put in an appearance with a claim for benefits bestowed, which the much-fleeced Italian refused to pay. Scotti, knowing along which road the unfortunate man would travel, was early at San Gabriel with the Sheriff, to intercept Repetto and return him to limbo; and the Genoese being brought back, he again appealed to me. It was now my turn, as executor, to have an interesting inning with Scotti. While I was settling the estate, I was made aware that Repetto had loaned another Italian named G. Bernero, on his note, some three thousand dollars; but this document

I missed, and it was only by accident that I traced it to Scotti. He had abstracted it from the papers found in Repetto's pocket, carried it to the borrower, and sold it back to him, for four hundred dollars! I recovered this note and collected the balance due; nevertheless, when Scotti had Repetto arrested, I threatened the former with prosecution on the charge of stealing and selling the note, with the result that Scotti did not press his suit and Repetto was released.

In connection with this move by Scotti, Robarts and Howard reappeared to defend Repetto, notwithstanding his previous announcement that he would have nothing more to do with them; and to bolster up their claim, they drew forth a paper certifying that Repetto had engaged them to attend to any law business he might have while he was in this country! Repetto, now really alarmed, once more quickly settled; but the crafty Robarts and Howard had another bill up their sleeves, this time for three or four thousand dollars, and poor Repetto was obliged to pay that, too!

Kaspare Cohn, J. D. Bicknell, I. W. Hellman and S. M. White, in conjunction with myself, bought the Repetto Ranch from the brother, before he left for Italy, for sixty thousand dollars. All in all, the heir, who survived the date of his windfall but a few years, carried away with him the snug sum of one hundred thousand dollars.

This fine domain, lying between Whittier and Los Angeles, was apportioned long before 1899, among the five purchasers. In that year, Kaspare Cohn and I, on the advice of William Mulholland, developed water on our undivided share, meeting with as great a success as has attended all of the operations of that eminent engineer. After an abundance of water was secured, we sold the property in five-acre and smaller lots, locating the town site of Newmark near the tracks of the San Pedro, Los Angeles & Salt Lake Railroad, and naming the entire settlement Montebello.

It was in the spring of 1886 that Colonel H. H. Boyce, who had been business manager of the Times-Mirror Company, was bought out by Colonel H. G. Otis and became editor-in-chief

556 Sixty Years in Southern California [1885-

and general manager of the Los Angeles *Tribune*, conducting the paper, during his short association, with some vigor.

One more reference to the *Times-Mirror* publishing house. On April 8th, the company was reorganized, with Colonel H. G. Otis as President and General Manager, Albert McFarland as Vice-President and Treasurer and William A. Spalding as Secretary. About the middle of July, the company bought the corner of Fort and First streets, and in the following May moved to its new home erected there. On February 1st, 1887, the *Times* began to appear seven days in the week.

After grinding away for ten years as the sole owner of the Los Angeles *Herald*, J. D. Lynch, in 1886, took into partnership his former associate, James J. Ayers, and once more the alliance of these puissant forces made of the paper a formidable bulwark for the Democracy.

Colonel John Franklin, or plain J. F. Godfrey as he was known in those days, was rather a prominent attorney in his time; and I knew him very well. About 1886, as chairman of a Democratic committee, he headed the delegation that invited me to become a candidate for Mayor of Los Angeles; but a contemplated European trip compelled me to decline the honor.

In the spring of 1886, a falling out between the Southern Pacific and the Santa Fé railroads brought on a rate-war, disastrous enough to those companies but productive of great benefit to Los Angeles. Round-trip tickets from points as far east as the Missouri River were hammered down to fifteen dollars, and for a few days, Charley White (who then conducted the Southern Pacific office in the Baker Block, and had full authority to make new fares) defied the rival road by establishing a tourist rate of just one dollar! When normality again prevailed, the fare was advanced to fifty dollars for first-class passage and forty dollars for second-class. The low rate during the fight encouraged thousands of Easterners to visit the Coast, and in the end many sacrificed their return coupons and settled here; while others returned to their Eastern homes only to prepare for permanent removal West. In a sense, therefore, this railroad war contributed to the Boom of a year or two later.

Freight as well as passenger rates were slashed during this spasmodic contest, and it was then that the ridiculous charge of one dollar per ton permitted me to bring in by rail, from Chicago, several carloads of coal, which I distributed among my children. Such an opportunity will probably never again present itself to Los Angeles.

Another interesting shipment was that of a carload of willow-ware from New York, the freight-bill for which amounted to eight dollars and thirty-five cents. These goods ordinarily bear a very high tariff; but competition had hammered everything down to a single classification and rate. I remember, also, that M. A. Newmark & Company brought from New York a train-load of Liverpool salt, then a staple commodity here, paying a rate of sixty cents per ton.

Stimulated, perhaps, through the setting aside of Elysian Park by the City Council, another pleasure-ground, then known as East Los Angeles Park, was assured to the public toward the middle of the eighties; the municipal authorities at the same time spending about five thousand dollars to improve the Plaza, one of the striking features of which was a circular row of evergreens uniformly trimmed to a conical shape.

On October 14th, H. T. Payne and Edward Records published the initial number of the Los Angeles *Tribune*, this being the first newspaper here to appear seven days in the week. The following January, a company was incorporated and for years the *Tribune* was well maintained.

Charles Frederick Holder, the distinguished naturalist, came to California in search of health,[1] in 1886, and settled in Pasadena, where he was appointed Professor of Zoölogy in the Throop Institute. An enthusiastic admirer of the Southland and an early explorer of its islands and mountain ranges, Professor Holder has devoted much attention to Pasadena and the neighboring coast. As early as 1891, he published *Antiquities of Catalina;* later he wrote his spirited Southern California book on *Life and Sport in the Open;* and with his

[1] Died on October 10th, 1915.

gift for popularizing, probably no other scientific writer has contributed more to make known, both in America and abroad,
this attractive portion of our great State.

Prudent and Victor Beaudry bought considerable land on
the west side of New High Street, probably in 1887, including
the site of one of the old *calabozos;* and as some of the purchase
was a hill, he spent about one hundred thousand dollars grading
the property, excavating fifty thousand or more cubic feet of
earth and building the great retaining wall, finished in 1888,
four hundred and sixty-five feet long and fifty feet high, and
containing two hundred thousand cubic feet of stone.   When
he was ready, Beaudry began to advertise the superior merits of
his land; and I still have in my possession one of the flaring
circulars, printed in red ink, including such headlines as
these:

NOW IS THE TIME !

DON'T SHUT YOUR EYES AND TURN YOUR BACK!

and the following:

Have a Home on the Hills!   Stop paying rent in the Valleys!
View from your own home the broad Pacific, the green hills and
the model city!   Best water supply.   Drainage perfect.   Best
sunny exposures.   Pure air, and away from fogs!
Have a Home on the line of the great Cable Railway system!
Mark your Catálogue before the day of sale!
February 15, 16 and 17, at 10 o'clock each Day.

Bear in mind that this property is on the HILLS, and on
the line of the Cable Railway System!   No such opportunity
has ever been offered to the people of Southern California.
Public School and Young Ladies' Seminary in the immediate
vicinity.

Four years after he had built the Nadeau Block, Remi

Nadeau died here, at the age of sixty-eight, on January 15th. The same month, another man of marked enterprise, Llewellyn J., brother of Reese and William Llewellyn, founded the Llewellyn Iron Works, attaining a success and fame very natural considering that the Llewellyns' father, David, and uncle, Reese before them had acquired a reputation as ironworkers both in Wales and San Francisco.

In January, Fred W. Beau de Zart and John G. Hunsicker established *The Weekly Directory*, whose title was soon changed to that of *The Commercial Bulletin*. Under the able editorship of Preston McKinney, the *Bulletin* is still fulfilling its mission.

Phineas, son of J. P. Newmark, my brother, came to Los Angeles in 1887 and associated himself with M. A. Newmark & Company. In July, 1894, he bought out the Southern California Coffee and Spice Mills, and in the following September, his younger brother, Samuel M. Newmark, also came to Los Angeles and joined him under the title of Newmark Brothers. On December 26th, 1910, the city suffered a sad loss in the untimely death of the elder brother. Sam's virility has been amply shown in his career as a business man and in his activity as a member of the Municipal League directorate.

Among the hotels of the late eighties were the Belmont and the Bellevue Terrace, both frame buildings. The former, at the terminus of the Second Street Cable Railway, was known for its elevation, view, fresh air and agreeable environment of lawn and flower-bed, and the first floor was surrounded with broad verandas. For a while it was conducted by Clark & Patrick, who claimed for it "no noise, dirt or mosquitoes." The latter hotel, on Pearl Street near Sixth, was four stories in height and had piazzas extending around three of them; both of these inns were quite characteristic of Southern California architecture. The Bellevue Terrace, so full of life during the buoyant Boom days, still stands, but alas! the familiar old pile has surrendered to more modern competitors.

The Tivoli Opera House, on Main Street between Second and Third, was opened by McLain & Lehman in 1887, and for a time it was one of the attractions of the city. It presented a curious mixture of Egyptian, East Indian and Romanesque styles, and was designed by C. E. Apponyi, an architect who had come to the Coast in 1870. The stage was the largest, except one—that of the San Francisco Grand Opera House—on the Coast, and there were eight proscenium boxes. The theater proper stood in the rear of the lot, and entrance thereto was had through the building fronting on the street; and between the two structures there was a pretty garden, with grottos and fountains, and a promenade gallery above.

In February, the Postmaster packed the furniture and other outfit—only two or three good loads—and moved the Post Office to the Hellman Building, at the corner of North Main and Republic streets; but it was soon transferred to an office on Fort Street, south of Sixth, a location so far from the center of the city as to give point to cards distributed by some wag and advertising rates for sleeping accommodations to the new office. In that year, the sum-total of the receipts of the Los Angeles Post Office was not much over seventy-four thousand dollars. During the twelve months of the Boom, mail for over two hundred thousand transients was handled; and a familiar sight of the times was the long column of inquirers, reminding one of the famous lines in early San Francisco when prospectors for gold paid neat sums for someone else's place nearer the general delivery window.

I have told of some incidents in the routine of court proceedings here, in which both judge and counselor played their parts. Now and then the juror also contributed to the diversion, as was evidenced in the late eighties when a couple of jurymen in a San Gabriel Cañon water case created both excitement and merriment through a practical joke. Tiring of a midnight session, and bethinking himself of the new invention to facilitate speaking at a distance, one of the jurors telephoned police headquarters that rioters were slashing each other at a near-by corner; whereupon the guardians of the peace came tearing that way, to the merriment of the "twelve good men and true" peeking out from an upper window. The police having traced the telephone message, the jury was duly haled before the judge; and the latter, noting the reticence of the accused, imposed a fine of twenty-five dollars upon each member of the box for his prank.

William H. Workman, who had repeatedly served the City as Councilman, was elected Mayor of Los Angeles in 1887. During Workman's administration, Main, Spring and Fort streets were paved.

About 1887, Benjamin S. Eaton, as President, took the lead in organizing a society designed to bring into closer relationship those who had come to California before her admission to the Union. There were few members; and inasmuch as the conditions imposed for eligibility precluded the possibility of securing many more, this first union of pioneers soon ceased to exist.

Professor T. S. C. Lowe, with a splendid reputation for scientific research, especially in the field of aëronautics—having acquired his first experience with balloons, as did also Graf Ferdinand Zeppelin, by participating in the Union army maneuvers during our Civil War—took up, in the late eighties, the business of manufacturing gas from water, which he said could be accomplished beyond any doubt for eight cents a thousand feet. C. F. Smurr, the capable Los Angeles agent of the Southern Pacific Railroad Company, as well as Hugh Livingston Macniel, son-in-law of Jonathan S. Slauson and then Cashier of the Main Street Savings Bank, became interested with Lowe and induced Kaspare Cohn and me to participate in the experiment.

Accordingly, we purchased six acres of land on the southeast corner of Alameda and Seventh streets for fifteen thousand dollars, and there started the enterprise. We laid pipes through many of the streets and, in the course of a few months, began to manufacture gas which it was our intention to sell to consumers at one dollar per thousand feet. The price at which gas was then being sold by the Los Angeles Gas Company was one dollar and fifty cents per thousand, and we therefore considered our schedule reasonable. Everything at the outset looked so plausible that Smurr stated to his associates that he would resign his position with the railroad and assume the management of the new gas works; but to our chagrin, we found that gas was costing us more than one dollar per thousand, and as one discouragement followed another, Smurr concluded not to take so radical a step.   Yet we remained in business in the hope that the Los Angeles Gas Company would rather buy us out than reduce their price fifty cents a thousand feet, and sure enough, it was not so very long before they did.   The large gas tank now standing at the corner of Seventh and Alameda streets is the result of this transaction.

Late in the spring, Senator Stanford and a party of Southern Pacific officials visited Los Angeles with the view of locating a site for the new and "magnificent railroad station" long promised the city, and at the same time to win some of the popular favor then being accorded the Santa Fé.   For many years, objection had been made to the tracks on Alameda Street, originally laid down by Banning; and hoping to secure their removal, Mayor Workman offered a right of way along the river-front.   This suggestion was not accepted.   At length the owners of the Wolfskill tract donated to the railroad company a strip of land, three hundred by nineteen hundred feet in size, fronting on Alameda between Fourth and Sixth streets, with the provision that the company should use the same only for railroad station purposes; and Stanford agreed to put up a "splendid arcade," somewhat similar in design to, but more extensive and elaborate than, the Arcade Depot at Sacramento. Soon after this, the rest of that celebrated orchard tract, for over fifty years in the possession of the Wolfskill family, was subdivided, offered at private sale and quickly disposed of.

The old-fashioned, one-horse street car had been running on and off the tracks many a year before the City Railroad, organized, in the middle eighties, by I. W. Hellman and his associates, W. J. Brodrick, John O. Wheeler and others, made its more pretentious appearance on the streets of Los Angeles. This, the first line to use double tracks and more modern cars with drivers and conductors, followed a route then considered very long.   Starting as it did at Washington Street and leading north on Figueroa, it turned at Twelfth Street into Olive and thence, zigzagging by way of Fifth, Spring, First, Main, Marchessault, New High, Bellevue Avenue, Buena Vista, College, Upper Main and San Fernando streets, it passed River Station (the Southern Pacific depot on San Fernando Street), and ran out Downey Avenue as far as the Pasadena Railroad depot.

The year 1885 saw the addition of another Spanish name to the local map in the founding of Alhambra, now one of the attractive and prosperous suburbs of Los Angeles.

Sometime in the spring of 1885, or perhaps a little earlier, the Second Street Cable Railway was commenced when Isaac W. Lord turned a spadeful of earth at the corner of Second and Spring streets; and within a few months cars were running from Bryson Block west on Second Street over Bunker Hill along Lakeshore Avenue and then by way of First Street to Belmont Avenue, soon bringing about many improvements on the route. And if I am not mistaken, considerable patronage came from the young ladies attending a boarding school known as Belmont Hall. Henry Clay Witmer was a moving spirit in this enterprise. In course of time the cable railway connected with the steam dummy line, landing passengers in a watermelon patch—the future Hollywood.

Unlike Sierra Madre, so long retarded for want of railway facilities, Monrovia—founded in May, 1886, by William N. Monroe, at an altitude of twelve hundred feet, and favored by both the Santa Fé and the Southern Pacific systems—rapidly developed, although it did not attain its present importance as a foothill town until it had passed through the usual depression of the late eighties, due to the collapse of the Boom, of which I am about to speak.

CHAPTER XXXVIII

THE GREAT BOOM

1887

NOT as impulsively perhaps as on previous occasions, I left Los Angeles for Europe on April 30th, 1887, accompanied by my wife and our two children, Marco and Rose. Mrs. Eugene Meyer, my wife's youngest sister, and her daughter joined us at San Francisco and traveled with us as far as Paris. We took passage on the French ship *Normandie*, departing from the Morton Street Pier in New York on May 14th, and nine days later we landed at Havre, from which port we proceeded to the French capital.

On this trip we visited France, England, Scotland, Ireland, Belgium, Holland, Denmark, Germany, Austria—including Bohemia—and Italy. We also touched at points in Sweden, although we did not "do" that country thoroughly until a later voyage. While in Germany, where I met my nephew Leo—son of J. P. Newmark—then a student in Strassburg, I was impressed with the splendid hotels and State highways, and the advantage taken of natural resources; and from Ems on July 22d, I wrote a letter on the subject to Kaspare Cohn, which I later found had been published by one of the Los Angeles dailies. During this journey we traveled with M. J. Newmark and his family. It was also on this tour, on June 10th, that I returned to my native town of Loebau, both to visit the graves of my parents and once more to see some relatives and a few old friends.

In Paris we had an exciting experience as observers of a conflagration that might have terminated seriously for us. We had been thinking of going to the Opéra Comique in the evening, but instead had accepted an invitation to dinner at the residence of Alexander Weil, the well-known international banker, formerly of San Francisco; and only on our return to the Hôtel du Helder, a comfortable family hostelry in the Rue du Helder (within a couple of blocks of the theater), did we learn of a disastrous fire in the opera house which caused the loss of many lives. For blocks around, streets and sidewalks were roped in and great was the confusion everywhere. The following day a number of solicitous inquiries arrived from friends in America.

In connection with our departure for this tour of Europe, I am reminded of a unique gift to my wife of a diary in eight volumes, tastefully bound in Russian leather—the whole neatly encased for traveling. With almost painful regularity my wife entered there her impressions and recollections of all she saw, refusing to retire at night, as a rule, until she had posted up her book for the day. Glancing over these pages written in her distinct, characteristically feminine hand, I note once more the intellectual vigor and perspicuity displayed by my companion in this, her first contact with European life and customs.

It was during my absence, on May 2d, that Erskine Mayo Ross was appointed, by President Cleveland, Judge of the new United States District Court just established. He was then in partnership with Stephen M. White. A native of Belpré, Virginia, he had come to Los Angeles in 1868 to study law with his uncle, Cameron E. Thom. Soon admitted to the Bar, he was elected in 1879, at the age of thirty-four, to the Supreme Bench of the State. The Judge, with whom I have been on friendly terms since his arrival, is still living in Los Angeles, a familiar and welcome figure in club circles.

Speaking of this esteemed Judge, I am reminded of a visit here, in 1887, of Justice Stephen J. Field, when he sat with Judge Ross in the United States Circuit Court, the sessions of which were then held over the Farmers & Merchants National Bank at the corner of Main and Commercial streets. On that occasion the members of the Bar, irrespective of party, united to do him honor; and Justice Field, in turn, paid a warm tribute to Los Angeles and her hospitality.

D. W. Hanna, a Michigan pedagogue who had come to Los Angeles in 1884 to open Ellis College on Fort Street near Temple —burned in 1888—established on September 2d, 1885, the Los Angeles College, a boarding school for girls, in a couple of buildings at the corner of Fifth and Olive streets. In 1887 Hanna, having formed a stock company, erected a new school structure at the southwest corner of Eighth and Hope streets, where eighteen teachers soon instructed some two hundred and fifty students. But the institution failed, and the building, still standing, was finally bought by Abbot Kinney and named the Abbotsford Inn.

In a note regarding the life and accomplishments of Mme. Severance, I have referred to the distinguished *rôle* played by this Angeleña in the early advocacy of the kindergarten for America. It took three years, however, for the educational authorities here to awake to the significance of the departure, for it was not until 1887 that Froebel's plan was admitted for experiment into the Los Angeles schools.

A group of Presbyterian clergymen from Los Angeles and vicinity in 1887 joined in establishing Occidental College—now, as developed under John Willis Baer, one of the promising institutions of the Southwest—locating its site east of the city between First and Second streets, both lots and acreage having been donated with the usual Southern California liberality. There, the following year, the main college building was erected; but in 1896 that structure and most of its contents were destroyed by fire.

Early in June, as ex-Mayor E. F. Spence was about to leave for Europe, some enthusiasm was created in educational circles by the announcement that he would deed certain property, including the lot at the corner of Pearl and Sixth streets (on which the Gates Hotel now stands), to the University of Southern California for the establishing of a telescope on Mount Wilson. The matter had been communicated to President M. M. Bovard, who ordered a glass from the celebrated Cambridge

Spring Street, Looking North from First, about 1885

Cable Car, Running North on Broadway (Previously Fort Street), near Second

Early Electric Car, with Conductor James Gallagher (still in Service)

grinders, Alvan Clark & Sons. When President Bovard died, Spence was too ill to arrange the details necessary to the further carrying out of his plans; the property that he had promised to give remained part of his estate; and the great glass, when ground, had to be resold, the University of Chicago becoming the lucky purchaser. As all the scientific world knows, the Carnegie Foundation at Washington some years later established, to the extension of California's fame, the celebrated Wilson telescopes on the mountain Spence once had in view.

Early in June, also, Smith & McPhee issued a directory of Los Angeles. But two weeks afterward, George W. Maxwell published another book of addresses with more than *five thousand* additional names! The second directory listed over eighteen thousand adults, from which fact it was estimated that Los Angeles then had a population of quite sixty thousand.

In 1887, Mrs. Charlotte LeMoyne Wills, wife of the attorney, John A. Wills, and daughter of Dr. Francis Julius LeMoyne (who in 1876 erected at Washington, Pennsylvania, the first modern crematory in the world, notwithstanding that he was denied permission by the cemetery authorities there and was compelled to construct the furnace on his property outside of the town), inspired the establishing here of what is said to have been the second crematory in the United States and certainly the first built west of the Rocky Mountains. It was opened at Rosedale Cemetery by the Los Angeles Crematory Society, which brought to the Coast an incinerating expert. Dr. W. LeMoyne Wills, a son, was one of the leading spirits in the enterprise and among the first directors of the local organization. The first cremation occurred in June; and the first body so disposed of was that of the wife of Dr. O. B. Bird, a homeopathic physician. The experiment stirred up a storm of adverse, as well as of favorable criticism.

The brothers Beaudry were interested, doubtless through their undeveloped hill-property, in organizing the Temple Street Cable Railway, running from the foot of Temple Street at Spring out Temple as far west as Union Avenue, with cars operated every ten minutes. The Company had an office at

No. 10 Court Street, and the Directors were: Prudent Beaudry, Victor Beaudry, Walter S. Maxwell, E. T. Wright, the surveyor, Octavius Morgan, Ralph Rogers, Thomas Stovell, John Milner and E. A. Hall.

About July, the trustees of James Lick sold Santa Catalina Island to George R. Shatto (who founded Avalon[1]—at first giving it his name—and after whom Shatto Street is called), the price fixed upon being one hundred and fifty thousand dollars, Shatto making a partial payment; whereupon the latter agreed to resell the island to an English syndicate. Failure to find there the store of minerals they expected, however, led the English bankers to refuse the property; and in 1892, after a friendly suit had reëstablished the title of the Lick trustees, they disposed of that part of the estate (for about the same price offered Shatto), to William, J. B. and Hancock Banning—sons of my old friend, Phineas Banning—the three forming the Santa Catalina Island Company. Several years later, George S. Patton was admitted as a partner. Little by little Catalina became a favorite resort, although it was years before there was patronage enough to warrant a daily steamer service. In the summer of 1887, for example, at the height of the Boom, William Banning, manager of the Wilmington Transportation Company, ran the steamer *Falcon* (whose Captain was J. W. Simmie) only once every seven or eight days. Then the vessel used to leave San Pedro wharf at one o'clock in the afternoon and return the next day in time to connect with the three o'clock train for Los Angeles. The fare for the round trip was four dollars.

The year 1887 witnessed the completion of the Arcadia Hotel at Santa Monica, named after Doña Arcadia, wife of Colonel R. S. Baker. It was built on a bluff, was four stories high and had a great veranda with side wings; and with its center tower and cupola was more imposing than any hotel there to-day. Under the proprietorship of J. W. Scott, the Arcadia became one of the first fine suburban hotels in Southern California.

As late as 1887 there was no passenger service between the

[1] Largely destroyed by fire, November 29th, 1915.

city and Santa Monica from six to seven o'clock in the evening, though I cannot say just how many trains ran during the day. I am sure, however, that there were not many. Merchants spending their summers at the beach were more inconvenienced through this lack of evening service than at any other time; and after repeated complaints, a coach was hooked onto a freight train. Later, the Board of Trade objected to this slow method, and arrangements were made for another passenger train.

Speaking of Santa Monica in the late eighties, I am reminded of a gravity railroad, somewhat on the principle of the present-day roller-coaster, which was opened near the Arcadia Hotel and as a novelty was a great success. The track was not more than fifteen feet above the ground at its highest point of elevation—just sufficient to give the momentum necessary for an undulating movement.

As the final sequence to the events of three or four preceding years, Los Angeles, at the time when I left for Europe, had already advanced beyond the threshold of her first really violent "boom;" and now symptoms of feverish excitement were everywhere noticeable in Southern California. The basis of real estate operations, heretofore sane enough, was quickly becoming unbalanced, a movement that was growing more and more intensified, as well as general; and as in the case of a mighty stream which accumulates overwhelming power from many feeders, there was a marshalling, as it were, in Los Angeles of these forces. The charms of climate and scenery (widely advertised, as I have said, at the Philadelphia Centennial and, later, through the continuous efforts of the first and second Chambers of Commerce and the Board of Trade), together with the extension of the Southern Pacific to the East and the building of the Santa Fé Railroad, had brought here a class of tourists who not only enjoyed the winter, but ventured to stay through the summer season; and who, having remained, were not long in seeking land and homesteads. The rapidly-increasing demand for lots and houses caused hundreds of men and women to enter the local real-estate field, most of whom were inexperienced and without much responsibility. When, therefore, the news of their phenomenal activity got abroad, as was sure to be the case, hordes of would-be speculators—some with, but more without knowledge of land-manipulation, and many none too scrupulous—rushed to the Southland to invest, wager or swindle. Thousands upon thousands of Easterners swelled the number already here; dealers in realty sprang up like mushrooms. It was then that the demand for offices north of First Street, exceeding the supply, compelled many an agent unwillingly to take accommodations farther south and brought about much building, even to—Second Street! It also happened that a dozen or more competitors occupied a single store-room. Selling and bartering were carried on at all hours of the day or night, and in every conceivable place; agents, eager to keep every appointment possible, enlisted the services of hackmen, hotel employees and waiters to put them in touch with prospective buyers; and the same properties would often change hands several times in a day, sales being made on the curbstone, at bars or restaurant tables, each succeeding transfer representing an enhanced value. Although I was abroad during the height of this period, psychologically so interesting, newspapers, letters and photographs from home—supplemented, on my return, by the personal narratives of friends—supplied me with considerable information of the craze.

As I have already remarked, the coming of the Santa Fé—as well as the ensuing railroad war—was a very potent factor in this temporary growth and advance in values; and soon after the railroad's advent, a dozen towns had been laid out on the line between Los Angeles and San Bernardino, the number doubling within a few months. Indeed, had the plan of the boomers succeeded, the whole stretch between the two cities would have been solidly built up with what in the end proved, alas! to be but castles in the air. Wherever there was acreage, there was room for new towns; and with their inauguration, thousands of buyers were on hand to absorb lots that were generally sold on the installment plan. More frequently than otherwise, payments became delinquent and companies "went broke;" and then the property reverted to acreage again. This

sometimes led to serious complications, especially when the contract between the landowner and the so-called syndicate allowed
the latter to issue clear title to those who paid for their lots.
In such cases, the acreage when recovered by the original owner
would be dotted here and there with small possessions; and to re-
instate his property was, as a rule, no easy task.   This, of course,
refers to the failures of which there were more than enough; on
the other hand, many of the towns inaugurated during the
Boom period not only have survived and prospered, but have
become some of our most attractive and successful neighbors.

If every conceivable trick in advertising was not resorted
to, it was probably due to oversight.   Bands, announcing
new locations, were seen here and there in street cars, hay and
other wagons and carriages (sometimes followed by fantastic
parades a block long); and for every new location there was
promised the early construction of magnificent hotels, theaters
or other attractive buildings that seldom materialized.   When
processions filled the streets, bad music filled the air.   Elephants
and other animals of jungle and forest, as well as human freaks
—the remnants of a stranded circus or two—were gathered into
shows and used as magnets; while other ingenious methods were
often invoked to draw crowds and gather in the shekels.   The
statements as to climate were always verified, but in most other
respects poor Martin Chuzzlewit's experience in the Mississippi
town of Eden affords a rather graphic story of what was frequently in progress here during the never-to-be-forgotten days
of the Boom.   As competition waxed keener, dishonest methods
were more and more resorted to; thus schemers worked on the
public's credulity and so attracted many a wagon-load of people
to mass-meetings, called ostensibly for the purpose of advancing
some worthy cause but really arranged to make possible an
ordinary sale of real estate.   An endless chain of free lunches,
sources of delight to the hobo element in particular, drew not
only these chronic idlers but made a victim of many a worthier
man.   Despite all of this excitement, the village aspect in some
particulars had not yet disappeared: in vacant lots not far from
the center of town it was still not unusual to see cows content-

edly chewing their cud and chickens scratching for a living. In 1889, however, the Council governed this feature of domestic life by ordinance, and thenceforth there was less of the "cock's shrill clarion."

Extraordinary situations arose out of the speculative mania, as when over-ambitious folks, fearful perhaps lest they might be unable to obtain corner- and other desirably-situated lots, stationed themselves in line two or three days before the date of anticipated land-sales; and even though quite twenty selections were frequently the limit to one purchase, the more optimistic of our boomers would often have two or three substitutes waiting in a line extending irregularly far down the sidewalk and assuming at night the appearance of a bivouac. I have heard it said that as much as a hundred dollars would be paid to each of these messengers, and that the purchaser of such service, apprehensive lest he might be sold out, would visit his representative many times before the eventful day. Later, this system was improved and official place-numbers were given, thus permitting people to conduct their negotiations without much loss of time.

So little scientific consideration was given to actual values that they were regulated according to calendar and clock; lots in new subdivisions remaining unsold were advertised to advance to certain new prices at such and such an hour, on such and such a day. After these artificial changes, investors would gleefully rub their hands and explain to the downcast outsider that they had "just gotten in in time;" and the downcast outsider, of whom there were many, yielding after repeated assaults of this kind, would himself become inoculated with the fever and finally prove the least restrained boomer of them all. From what I read at the time and heard after my return, I may safely declare that during the height of the infection, two-thirds of our population were, in a sense, more insane than sane.

Syndicates, subdivisions and tracts: these were the most popular terms of the day and nearly everybody had a finger in one or the other pie. There were enough subdivisions to accommodate ten million people; and enough syndicates to handle the

affairs of a nation.   And talking about syndicates: the disagree-
ment of members themselves as to values frequently prevented
the consummation of important sales and resulted in the loss of
large profits to the objectors as well as to their associates.   In
many a well-authenticated case, the property remained on the
owners' hands until it became almost worthless.

Wide-awake syndicates evolved new methods, one of which
—the lottery plan—became popular.   A piece of land would
be prepared for the market; and after the opening of streets, as
many chances would be sold as there were lots in the tract.
On the eventful day, the distribution took place in the presence
of the interested and eager participants, each of whom made
a selection as his number was drawn.   To increase the at-
tractiveness of some of these offers, cottages and even more
elaborate houses were occasionally promised for subsequent
erection on a few lots.   The excitement at many of these events,
I was informed, beggared description.   Among others sold in
this manner at the beginning, or possibly even just before the
Boom, were the Williamson Tract, beginning at the corner of
Pico and Figueroa streets and once the home-place of the For-
mans, and the O. W. Childs orchard on the east side of Main
Street and running south from what is now about Eleventh.
Both of these drawings took place in Turnverein Hall, and the
chances sold at about three hundred and fifty dollars each.

Tricksters, of whom at such times there are always enough,
could exercise their mischievous proclivities; and the unwary one,
who came to be known as the tenderfoot, was as usual easily
hoodwinked.   Land advertised as having "water privileges"
proved to be land *under water* or in dry creeks; land described as
possessing scenic attractions consisted of—mountains and
chasms!   So situated were many of these lots that no use whatever could be made of them; and I presume that they are without value even now.   One of the effects of subdividing a good
part of the ten thousand or more acres of agricultural land in the
city then irrigated from the *zanjas* was both to reduce the calls
for the service of the city *Zanjero*, and to lessen considerably
the importance and emoluments of his office.

Advertisers tried to outdo themselves and each other in original and captivating announcements; with the result that, while many displayed wit and good humor, others were ridiculously extravagant.   The Artesian Water Company came onto the market with three hundred acres of land near Compton and the assurance that "while the water in this section will be stocked, the stock will not be watered."   Alvan D. Brock, another purveyor of ranches, declared:

I mean business, and do not allow any alfalfa to grow under my feet.

A. F. Kercheval, the poet, to whom I have already referred, relieved himself of this exuberance regarding the Kercheval Tract (on Santa Fé Avenue, between Lemon and Alamo streets):

HE OR SHE
That Hesitates is Lost!
An axiom that holds good in real estate, as well as in
affairs of the heart.
Selah!

Another advertisement read as follows:

HALT! HALT! HALT!
Speculators and Homeseekers, Attention!
$80,000—Eighty Thousand Dollars—$80,000
Sold in a Day at the Beautiful
McGarry Tract
Bounded by Ninth and Tenth and Alameda Streets.
Come Early, before they are All Gone!

Still another was displayed·

Boom!   Boom!

ARCADIA!

Boom!   Boom!

And now and then, from a quarter to a full page would be taken to advertise a new town or subdivision, with a single word—the name of the place—such as

RAMIREZ!

Vernon and Vernondale were names given to subdivisions on Central Avenue near Jefferson Street. Advertising the former, the real-estate poet was called into requisition with these lines:

> Go, wing thy flight from star to star,
> From world to luminous world as far
> As the universe spreads its flaming wall,
> Take all the pleasure of all the spheres,
> And multiply each through endless years,
> One Winter at Vernon is worth them all!

while, in setting forth the attractions of the Lily Langtry Tract, the promoter drew as follows from the store of English verse:

> Sweet Vernon, loveliest village of the plain,
> Where health and plenty cheers the laboring swain,
> Where smiling Spring its earliest visit paid,
> And parting Summer's lingering blooms delayed;

concluding the announcement with the following lines characteristic of the times:

> Catch on before the whole country rushes to Vernondale!
> Every man who wishes a home in Paradise should locate in this,
> the loveliest district of the whole of Southern California.

This is where the orange groves are loveliest!
This is where the grapes are most luxuriant!
This is where the vegetation is grandest!
This is where the flowers are prettiest!

With the Boom affecting not only Los Angeles but also each acre of her immediate vicinity, Pasadena and the district lying between the two towns took on new life. Five thousand inhabitants boasted a million dollars in deposits and a couple of millions invested in new buildings; while "gilt-edged Raymond," a colony surrounding the Raymond Hotel, became a bustling center. In March, George Whitcomb laid out Glendora, naming it (with the use of a couple of additional letters) after his wife, Ledora; and at the first day's sale, he auctioned off three hundred lots. In December, the old-established town of Pomona was incorporated. Whittier, started by Quakers from Indiana, Iowa and Illinois, and christened in honor of the New England poet, began at this time with a boom, two hundred thousand dollars' worth of property having been sold there in four months. This prosperity led one newspaper to say with extreme modesty:

Whittier is the coming place! It will dwarf Monrovia and eclipse Pasadena. Nothing can stop it! The Quakers are coming in from all over the United States;

and another journal contained an advertisement commencing as follows:

WHITTIER! WHITTIER!! WHITTIER!!!
Queen of the Foothills and Crown of the San Gabriel Valley.

I. W. Lord established Lordsburg—or at least an elaborate hotel there, for in those days a good hotel was half of a town; and when Lordsburg slumped, he sold the building to a colony of Dunkers for a college. Nadeau Park was projected as a town at the junction of the Atchison, Topeka & Santa Fé's Ballona road and the Southern Pacific. Santa Ana, too, after its sale in June of over eighty thousand dollars' worth of land, came forward in the summer with this confident salutation:

THIS IS PURE GOLD!!!

Santa Ana,

The Metropolis of Southern California's Fairest Valley!

Chief Among Ten Thousand, or the One

Altogether Lovely!

Beautiful! Busy! Bustling! Booming! It

Can't be Beat!

The town now has the biggest kind

of a big, big boom.

A Great Big Boom!   And you

Can Accumulate Ducats by Investing!

Fullerton was started in July, when ninety-two thousand dollars changed hands within half a day; and conditions favoring the young community, it survived.   Rivera, in the Upper Los Nietos Valley, also then came into being.   The glories of Tustin (founded in 1867 by Columbus Tustin, but evidencing little prosperity until twenty years later) were proclaimed through such unassuming advertisements as this:

TUSTIN

THE BEAUTIFUL

Unexcelled in charm and loveliness.

An Earthly Eden Unsurpassed in

Wealth of Flower and Foliage.

However, Imagination Cannot Conceive It:

It must be seen to be realized,

supplemented by the following versification:

When the Angel of Peace to Earth first descended,
To bless with his presence the children of men,
'Mid the fairest of scenes his pathway e'er tended,
And unto his smile the glad earth smiled again.

He joyed in the fragrance of orange and roses,
And loved 'mid their glances to linger or roam,
And he said: "Here in Tustin, where Beauty reposes,
I also will linger or build me a home!"

In April, Jonathan S. Slauson and a company of Los Angeles capitalists laid out and started the town of Azusa, on a slope eight hundred feet high in a rich and promising country. Not so far away was Palomares, announced through the following reassuring poster:

Grand Railroad Excursion and Genuine

AUCTION SALE!

No Chenanekin!!

Thursday, June 7, 1887.

Beautiful Palomares, Pomona Valley!

Lunch, Coffee, Lemonade, and Ice Water Free!

Full Band of Music.

And here it may not be without interest to note the stations then passed in making such an excursion from Los Angeles to the new town: Commercial Street, Garvanza, Raymond, Pasadena, Lamanda Park (named, Henry W. O'Melveny tells me, after Amanda, wife of L. J. Rose), Santa Anita, Arcadia, Monrovia, Duarte, Glendora, San Dimas and Lordsburg. Providencia *rancho*, consisting of seventeen thousand acres of mountain and valley, was opened up in 1887 and the new town of Burbank was laid out; J. Downey Harvey, J. G. Downey's heir, and David Burbank, the good-natured dentist and old-timer, then living on the site of the Burbank Theater (once the orchard of J. J. Warner), being among the directors. About the same time, twelve thousand acres of the Lankershim-*rancho*, adjoining the Providencia, were disposed of. Sixty-five dollars was asked for a certificate of stock, which was exchangeable later for an acre of land. Glendale was another child of the Boom, for the development of which much dependence was placed on a new motor railroad. Rosecrans and its Addition were two other tracts relying on improved facilities for communicating with Los Angeles. Under the caption, *Veni, Vidi, Vici!* a motor road was promised for service within ninety days; and lots, from one hundred dollars up, were then to be advanced five hundred per cent! Excursions, accompanied by Colonel Bartlett's Seventh Infantry Band, to "magnificent Monte Vista, the Gem of the Mountains! the Queen of the Valley!" near San Fernando, fifteen miles from Los Angeles, were among the trips arranged.

Speaking of the Boom, I recall an amusing situation such as now and then relieved the dark gloom of the aftermath. When a well-known suburb of Los Angeles was laid out, someone proposed that a road be named Euclid Avenue; whereupon a prominent citizen protested vigorously and asked *what Mr. Euclid had ever done for Southern California?*

During 1887, and at the suggestion of George E. Gard, many neighboring towns—a number of which have long since become mere memories—donated each a lot, through whose sale a Los Angeles County exhibit at the reunion of the Grand Army of the Republic was made possible; and among these places were Alosta, Gladstone, Glendora, Azusa, Beaumont, Arcadia, Raymond, San Gabriel, Glendale, Burbank, Lamar's Addition to Alosta, Rosecrans, St. James, Bethune, Mondonville, Olivewood, Oleander, Lordsburg, McCoy's[1] Addition to Broad Acres, Ivanhoe, New Vernon, Alta Vista, Nadeau Park, Bonita Tract, San Dimas, Port Ballona, Southside, Ontario, Walleria and Ocean Spray. When the lots were sold at Armory Hall, some ten thousand dollars was realized—twelve hundred and seventy-five dollars, paid by Colonel Banbury for a piece of land at Pasadena, being the highest price brought. Not even the celebrity given the place through the gift of a lot to the Grand Old Man of England saved Gladstone; and St. James soon passed into the realms of the forgotten, notwithstanding that one hundred and fifty vehicles and five hundred people were engaged, in June, in caring for the visitors who

[1] Bearing the name of Frank McCoy, who died on March 4th, 1915.

made their way to the proposed town-site, five miles from Anaheim, and bought, when there, forty thousand dollars' worth of property in a few hours.

Ben E. Ward—a good citizen whose office was in the renovated municipal adobe—operated with Santa Monica realty during the Boom, somewhat as did Colonel Tom Fitch in the cradle days of the bay city. He ran private trains and sold acre and villa lots, and five- and ten-acre farms, for ten per cent. of the price "at the fall of the hammer;" the balance of the first quarter payable on receipt of the agreement, and the other payments in six, twelve and eighteen months. On one occasion in June, Ward was advertising as follows:

HO, FOR THE BEACH!
To-morrow,   To-morrow!
Grand Auction Sale at
Santa Monica.
350—Acres—350

One of the Grandest Panoramic Views the Human Eye ever rested upon, including Ballona, Lake and Harbor, with its outgoing and in-coming vessels, the Grand Old Pacific, the handsome new Hotel Arcadia, while in the distance may be seen Los Angeles, the Pride of All, and the coming city of two hundred thousand people.

Long Beach came in for its share of the Boom. In July, H. G. Wilshire (after whom, I believe, Wilshire Boulevard was named), as general manager of the new hotel at that place, offered lots at one hundred and fifty dollars and upward, advertising under the caption, "Peerless Long Beach!" and declaring that the place was "no new settlement, but a prosperous town of two thousand people," to be "reached without change of cars." The hotel was to be doubled in size, streets were to be sprinkled and bathhouses—with hot and cold water—were to be built. One of the special attractions promised was even a billiard-room for ladies! But the hotel was afterward destroyed by fire, and Long Beach dwindled away until, in 1890, it had scarcely a population of five hundred.

Besides the improving of Santa Monica and the expanding of San Pedro, several harbor projects were proposed in the days of the Boom. About the first of June, 1887, Port Ballona—formerly Will Tell's—began to be advertised as "The Future Harbor of Southern California" and the ocean terminus of the California Central Railroad, which was a part of the Atchison, Topeka & Santa Fé system. In August, thousands of people assembled at the beach to celebrate the opening of La Ballona Harbor. The enterprise had been backed by Louis Mesmer, Bernard Mills, Frank Sabichi and others; and Mesmer, General Nelson A. Miles, ex-Governor Stoneman, Eugène Germain and J. D. Lynch were among the speakers. A syndicate, headed by J. R. Tuffree, which purchased the Palos Verdes *rancho*, announced its intention of creating the harbor of Catalina at Portuguese Bend. The syndicate was to build there a large hotel named Borromea, while a Mr. Kerckhoff, encouraged by the prospect of a railroad around Point Firmin, was to erect another huge hotel and lay out a watering place.

As the Boom progressed and railroads continued to advertise Los Angeles, the authorities began to look with consternation on the problem of housing the crowds still booked to come from the East; and it was soon recognized that many prospective settlers would need to roost, for a while, as best they could in the surrounding territory. The Hotel Splendid, an enterprise fostered by Hammel & Denker, proprietors of the United States Hotel, was then commenced on Main Street, between Ninth and Tenth, though it was never completed. Numerous capitalists and business houses encouraged the proposition; yet the site was sold, but a single generation ago, to O. T. Johnson, a local philanthropist, for about twenty-five thousand dollars—a conservative estimate placing its present value at not much less than two and a half millions.

But there are other indications of the strength, or perhaps the weakness, of the Boom. In 1887, the total assessment of the young City and County was three million dollars, or about one-third that recorded for the longer-developed City and County of San Francisco. In one day in July, real estate valued at $664,000 was transferred; on another day in the same month, $730,000 worth; and soon after, in one day, property to the value of $930,000 changed hands. From forty million dollars in March, 1886, the wealth of the county jumped, in just two years, to one hundred and three millions. So many, indeed, were the purchasers of real estate in Los Angeles at that time who soon left the town and were seldom or never heard of again, and so many were the sales effected by proxy, that even in August of 1887 one of the newspapers contained over three pages of taxes listed on property whose possessors were unknown.

During this wild excitement, few men of position or reputation who came to town escaped interrogation as to what they thought of the Boom. "Phil" D. Armour, head of the Armour Packing Company, was one who arrived late in July, and whose opinion was immediately sought; and his answer indicated the unbounded confidence inspired in the minds of even outsiders by the unheard-of development of land values. "Boom—will it break soon?" repeated Armour and proceeded to answer his own query. "There is no boom to break! This is merely the preliminary to a boom which will so outclass the present activities that its sound will be as thunder to the cracking of a hickory nut!" Nor was Armour the only one who was so carried away by the phenomena of the times: San Francisco watched Los Angeles with wonder and interest, marveling at all she heard of the magic changes south of the Teháchepi, and asking herself if Los Angeles might not be able to point the way to better methods of city-building?

I have thus endeavored to give a slight idea of the lack of mental poise displayed by our good people in the year 1887, when the crop of millionaires was so great that to be one was no distinction at all. But alas! the inevitable collapse came and values tumbled fully as rapidly as they had advanced, finding many (who but a short period before had based their worth on investments figured at several times their value)

loaded with overwhelming debts and mortgages quite impossible
of liquidation. Indeed, readjustments took years and years
to accomplish; and so it happened that many an imaginary
Crœsus then became the bidder, often unsuccessful, for humble
employment. Just as is always the case, too, in periods such
as I have described, the depression, when it came was correspondingly severe and sudden. Many of our greatest boomers
and speculators lost all hope; and more than one poor suicide
so paid the price of his inordinate craving for wealth.

To be sure, some level-headed people, acting more conserva-
tively than the majority, in time derived large profits from
the steady increase in values. Those who bought judiciously
during that period are now the men of wealth in Los Angeles;
and this is more particularly true as to ownership in business
sections of the city. Even at the height of the Boom but
little property on any of the streets south of Fifth was worth
more than two hundred dollars a foot. Following the Boom,
there was an increase of building, much of it doubtless due to
contracts already entered into.

Incidental to the opening of the Southern Pacific Railroad's
route between the North and South by way of the coast, on
August 20th, a great railway *fête* was held at Santa Bárbara, the
first through trains from San Francisco and Los Angeles meeting at that point. A procession, illustrating the progress in
transportation methods from the burro pack and stage coach
to the modern train of cars, filed about the streets of the
old Spanish town. On the return of the Los Angeles excursion train, however, a defective culvert near the Camulos
Ranch caused the cars, with one hundred and fifty passengers, to plunge down an embankment—luckily with but few
casualties.

L. E. Mosher, who had much literary ability and is still
remembered as the author of the poem, *The Stranded Bugle*,
joined the *Times* staff in August and became prominently
identified with the conduct of that newspaper. Later, he left
journalism and entered on a business career in New York; but
experiencing reverses, he returned to Los Angeles. Failing

here, he at length committed suicide, to the deep regret of a large circle of friends.

Late in August, the paving of Main Street, the first thoroughfare of Los Angeles to be so improved, was begun, much to the relief of our townspeople who had too long borne the inconvenience of dusty and muddy roadways, and who, after heavy rains the winter before, had in no uncertain fashion given utterance to their disgust at the backward conditions. This expression was the result of a carefully and generally organized movement; for one morning it was discovered that all of the principal streets were covered with mounds of earth resembling little graves, into each of which had been thrust imitation tombstones bearing such inscriptions as the following:

BEWARE OF QUICKSAND!
FARE FOR FERRYING ACROSS, 25 CENTS.
NO DUCK-HUNTING ALLOWED IN THIS POND!
BOATS LEAVE THIS LANDING EVERY HALF-HOUR.
REQUIESCAT IN PACE!

This year, the *Sued-Californische Post*, which had been established in 1874, began to appear as a daily, with a weekly edition, the Germans in Los Angeles in the eighties representing no mean portion of the burgher strength.

In 1887, the Turnverein-Germania sold to L. J. Rose and J. B. Lankershim, for removal and renovation, the frame structure on Spring Street which for so many years had served it as a home, and erected in its place a substantial brick building costing about forty thousand dollars. Six or seven years afterward, the society resold that property—to be used later as the Elks' Hall—for one hundred thousand dollars; then it bought the lot at 319 and 321 South Main Street, and erected there its new stone-fronted Turner Hall. On the occasion of the cornerstone laying, on August 14th, 1887, when the Turnverein-Germania, the Austrian Verein and the Schwabenverein joined hands and voices, the Germans celebrated their advancement by festivities long to be remembered, ex-Mayor Henry T. Hazard making the chief address; but I dare say that the assembly particularly enjoyed the reminiscences of the pioneer President, Jake Kuhrts, who took his hearers back to the olden days of the Round House (that favorite rendezvous which stood on the very spot where the new building was to rise) and pointed out how Time had tenderly and appropriately joined the associations of the Past with those of the Present. Turner Hall, with its restaurant, brought our German citizens into daily and friendly intercourse, and long served their rapidly-developing community.

How true it is that a man should confine himself to that which he best understands is shown in the case of L. J. Rose, who later went into politics, and in 1887 was elected State Senator. Neglecting his business for that of the public, he borrowed money and was finally compelled to dispose of his interest in the New York house. Indeed, financially speaking, he went from bad to worse; and the same year he sold his magnificent estate to an English syndicate for $1,250,000, receiving $750,000 in cash and the balance in stock. The purchasers made a failure of the enterprise and Rose lost $500,000. He was almost penniless when on May 17th, 1899, he died— a suicide.

Rose was an indefatigable worker for the good of the community, and was thoroughly interested in every public movement. For years he was one of my intimate friends; and as I write these lines, I am moved with sentiments of sadness and deep regret. Let us hope that, in the life beyond, he is enjoying that peace denied him here.

The Los Angeles & San Gabriel Valley Railroad, begun the previous year by J. F. Crank and destined to be absorbed by the Santa Fé, was opened for traffic to Pasadena on September 17th by a popular excursion in which thousands participated.

With the increase in the number and activity of the Chinese here, came a more frequent display of their native customs and ceremonies, the joss house and the theater being early instituted. On October 21st, a street parade, feast and theatrical performance with more or less barbarous music marked a celebration that brought Mongolians from near and far.

On October 24th, Cardinal Gibbons made his first visit to Los Angeles—the most notable call, I believe, of so eminent a prelate since my settling here.

One of the numerous fires of the eighties that gave great alarm was the blaze of October 28th, which destroyed the Santa Fé Railroad depot and with it a trainload of oil. The conflagration proved obstinate to fight, although the good work of the department prevented its spread. A host of people for hours watched the spectacular scene.

The Raymond Hotel, commonly spoken of as belonging to Pasadena although standing just inside the city to the south, was completed in November; and catering exclusively to tourists, its situation on an eminent knoll overlooking the towns and orange-groves contributed to make it widely famous. In April, 1895, it was swept by fire, to be rebuilt on larger and finer lines. The hotel La Pintoresca, on Fair Oaks Avenue, burned four or five years ago, was another Pasadena hostelry, where I often stopped when wishing to escape the hurly-burly of city life. Now its site and gardens have been converted into a public park.

In November, following the efforts made by the Board of Trade to secure one of the veterans' homes projected by Congress, the managers of the National Home for Disabled Volunteer Soldiers visited Los Angeles. A committee, representing business men and the Grand Army, showed the visitors around; and as a result of the coöperation of General Nelson A. Miles, Judge Brunson (representing Senator Jones) and others, three hundred acres of the old San Vicente *rancho* were donated by the Jones and Baker estates and the Santa Monica Land and Water Company, as were also three hundred acres of the Wolfskill Tract. Orchards were laid out, and barracks, chapel, hospital and extra buildings for a thousand men erected. Near this worthy institution, housing as it now does more than two thousand veterans, has developed and prospered—thanks to the patronage of these soldiers and their families—the little town of Sawtelle.

In November, local Democratic and Republican leaders,

wishing to draft a new charter for Los Angeles, agreed on a non-partisan Board consisting of William H. Workman, Cameron E. Thom, I. R. Dunkelberger, Dr. Joseph Kurtz, Walter S. Moore, Jeremiah Baldwin, General John Mansfield, P. M. Scott, J. H. Book, José G. Estudillo, Charles E. Day, Thomas B. Brown, W. W. Robinson, A. F. Mackey and George H. Bonebrake; and the following 31st of May the Board was duly elected. Workman was chosen Chairman and Moore, Secretary; and on October 20th the result of their deliberations was adopted by the City. In January, 1889, the Legislature confirmed the action of the Common Council. The new charter increased the number of wards from five to nine, and provided for the election of a councilman from each ward.

As the result of an agitation in favor of Los Angeles, the Southwest headquarters of the United States Army were transferred from Whipple Barracks, Arizona, about the beginning of 1887, the event being celebrated by a dinner to Brigadier-General Nelson A. Miles, at the Nadeau Hotel. Within less than a year, however, General Miles was transferred to San Francisco, General B. H. Grierson succeeding him at this post.

CHAPTER XXXIX

PROPOSED STATE DIVISION

1888-1891

BY agreement among property owners, the widening of Fort Street from Second to Ninth began in February, 1888. This was not accomplished without serious opposition, many persons objecting to the change on the ground that it would ruin the appearance of their bordering lots. I was one of those, I am frank to say, who looked with disfavor on the innovation; but time has shown that it was an improvement, the widened street (now known as Broadway), being perhaps the only fine business avenue of which Los Angeles can boast.

Booth and Barrett, the famous tragedians, visited Los Angeles together this winter, giving a notable performance in Child's Opera House, their combined genius showing to greatest advantage in the presentation of *Julius Cæsar* and *Othello*.

Toward the end of the seventies, I dipped into an amusing volume, *The Rise and Fall of the Mustache*, by Robert J. Burdette—then associated with the *Burlington Hawkeye*—little thinking that a decade later would find the author famous and a permanent resident of Southern California.[1] His wife, Clara Bradley Burdette, whom he married in 1899 and who is well known as a clubwoman, has been associated with him in many local activities.

George Wharton James, an Englishman, also took up his residence in Southern California in 1888, finally settling in

[1] Dr. Burdette died on November 19th, 1914.

Pasadena, although seven years previously he had been an interested visitor in Los Angeles. James has traveled much in the Southwest; and besides lecturing, he has written ten or twelve volumes dealing in a popular manner with the Spanish Missions and kindred subjects.

Through the publication by D. Appleton & Company of one of the early books of value dealing with our section of the State, progress was made, in the late eighties, in durably advertising the Coast. This volume was entitled, *California of the South;* and as a scientifically-prepared guide was written by two fellow-townsmen, Drs. Walter Lindley and J. P. Widney.

Very shortly after their coming to Los Angeles, in April, 1888, I had the pleasure of meeting Mr. and Mrs. Tomás Lorenzo Duque with whom I have since been on terms of intimacy. Mr. Duque, a Cuban by birth, is a broad-minded, educated gentleman of the old school.

Frederick William Braun established on May 1st, at 127 New High Street, the first exclusively wholesale drug house in Southern California, later removing to 287 North Main Street, once the site of the adobe in which I was married.

The same season my brother, whose health had become precarious, was again compelled to take a European trip; and it was upon his return in September, 1890, that he settled in Los Angeles, building his home at 1043 South Grand Avenue, but a few doors from mine.

The coast-line branch of the Santa Fé Railroad was opened in August between Los Angeles and San Diego.

W. E. Hughes has been credited with suggesting the second and present Chamber of Commerce, and J. F. Humphreys is said to have christened it when it was organized on October 15th. E. W. Jones was the first President and Thomas A. Lewis the first Secretary. In addition to these, S. B. Lewis, Colonel H. G. Otis, J. V. Wachtel (a son-in-law of L. J. Rose), Colonel I. R. Dunkelberger and William H. Workman are entitled to a great deal of credit for the movement. So well known is this institution, even internationally, and so much has been written about it, that I need hardly speak of its remarkable and honorable part in developing Southern California and all of the Southland's most valuable resources.

Late in the fall the Los Angeles Theater, a neat brick edifice, was opened on Spring Street, between Second and Third. At that time, other places of amusement were the Childs or Grand Opera House, Mott Hall, over Mott Market—an unassuming room without stage facilities, where Adelina Patti once sang, and where Charles Dickens, Jr., gave a reading from his father's books—and Hazard's Pavilion at Fifth and Olive, built on the present site of the Temple Auditorium by Mayor H. T. Hazard and his associate, George H. Pike. During the Boom especially and for a few years thereafter (as when in 1889, Evangelist Moody held forth), this latter place was very popular; and among celebrities who lectured there was Thomas Nast, *Harpers'* great cartoonist, who had so much to do with bringing Boss Tweed to justice. As Nast lectured, he gave interesting exhibitions of his genius to illustrate what he had to say; and many of his sketches were very effective. Doubtless alluding to the large audience gathered to do him honor, the artist said: "Ladies and Gentlemen, I will now show you how to draw a big house," whereupon he rapidly sketched one.

On the morning of October 21st, the *Los Angeles Times* created one of the most noted surprises in the history of American politics, making public the so-called Murchison letters, through which the British diplomat Lord Sackville West, caught strangely napping, was recalled in disgrace from his eminent post as British Minister to Washington. In 1882, George Osgoodby located at Pomona. Though of English grandparents, Osgoodby possessed a strong Republican bias; and wishing to test the attitude of the Administration toward Great Britain, he formed the scheme of fathoming Cleveland's purpose even at the British Minister's expense. Accordingly, on September 4th, 1888—in the midst of the Presidential campaign—he addressed Lord West, signing himself Charles F. Murchison and pretending that he was still a loyal though naturalized Englishman needing advice as to how to vote. "Murchison" reminded his lordship that, just as a small

State had defeated Tilden, so "a mere handful of naturalized countrymen might easily carry California." The British Minister was betrayed by the plausible words; and on September 13th he answered the Pomona farmer, at the same time indicating his high regard for Cleveland as a friend of England. Osgoodby gave the correspondence publicity through the *Times;* and instantly the letters were telegraphed throughout America and to England, where they made as painful an impression as they had caused jubilation or anger in this country. How, as a consequence, diplomatic relations between America and England were for a while broken off, is familiar history.

During the winter of 1888–89, Alfred H. and Albert K. Smiley, twin brothers who had amassed a fortune through successful hotel management at summer-resorts in the mountains of New York, came to California and purchased about two hundred acres near Redlands, situated on a ridge commanding a fine view of San Timoteo Cañon; and there they laid out the celebrated Cañon Crest Park, more popularly known as Smiley Heights. They also gave the community a public library. On account of their connections, they were able to attract well-to-do settlers and tourists to their neighborhood and so contribute, in an important way, to the development and fame of Redlands.

The City Hall was erected, during the years 1888–89, on the east side of Broadway between Second and Third streets on property once belonging to L. H. Titus. As a detail indicating the industrial conditions of that period, I may note that John Hanlon, the contractor, looked with pride upon the fact that he employed as many as thirty to forty workmen and all at one time!

Another effort in the direction of separating this part of California from the northern section was made in December, 1888 and here received enthusiastic support. General William Vandever, then a representative in Congress from the Sixth District, introduced into that body a resolution providing for a State to be called South California. Soon after, a mass meeting was held in Hazard's Pavilion, and a campaign was opened with an Executive Committee to further the movement; but—California is still, and I hope will long continue to be, a splendid undivided territory.

On January 1st, 1889, Pasadena held her first Rose Tournament. There were chariot races and other sports, but the principal event was a parade of vehicles of every description which, moving along under the graceful burden of their beautiful floral decorations, presented a magnificent and typically Southern California winter sight. The tournament was so successful that it has become an annual event participated in by many and attracting visitors from near and far. It is managed by a permanent organization, the Tournament of Roses Association, whose members in 1904 presented Tournament Park, one of the City's pleasure-grounds, to Pasadena.

Once outdistanced by both Main and Spring streets, and yet more and more rising to importance as the city grew, Fort Street—a name with an historical significance—in 1889 was officially called Broadway.

Fred L. Baker, who reached Los Angeles with his father, Milo Baker in 1874, designed in 1889, and when he was but twenty-four years of age, the first locomotive built in Los Angeles. It was constructed at the Baker Iron Works for the Los Angeles County Railroad, and was dubbed the *Providencia;* and when completed it weighed fifteen tons.

On February 16th, Jean Louis Sainsevain, everywhere pleasantly known as Don Louis, died here, aged seventy-three years.

I have spoken of L. J. Rose's love for thoroughbred horses. His most notable possession was *Stamboul,* the celebrated stallion, which he sold for fifty thousand dollars. At Rose Meade, toward the end of the eighties, there were about a hundred and twenty pedigreed horses; and at a sale in 1889 fifty of these brought one hundred and ninety thousand dollars. This reminds me that early in April, the same year, Nicolás Covarrúbias (in whose stable on Los Angeles Street, but a short time before, nearly a hundred horses had perished by fire) sold *Gladstone* to L. H. Titus for twenty-five hundred dollars.

General Volney E. Howard died in May, aged eighty years, just ten years after he had concluded his last notable public service as a member of the State Constitutional Convention.

One of those who well illustrate the constant search for the ideal is Dr. Joseph Kurtz. In the spring of 1889 he toured Europe to inspect clinics and hospitals; and inspired by what he had seen, he helped, on his return, to more firmly establish the Medical College of Los Angeles, later and now a branch of the University of California.

In 1889, I built another residence at 1051 South Grand Avenue, and there we lived for several years. As in the case of our Fort Street home, in which four of our children died, so here again joy changed to sorrow when, on November 18th, 1890, our youngest daughter, Josephine Rose, was taken from us at the age of eight years.

The Los Angeles Public Library was once more moved in July from the Downey Block to the City Hall where, with some six thousand books and about one hundred and thirty members, it remained until April, 1906, when it was transferred by Librarian Charles F. Lummis to the Annex of the Laughlin Building. It then had over one hundred thousand volumes. In the fall of 1908, it was removed to the new Hamburger Building.

Colonel James G. Eastman, who arrived in Los Angeles during the late sixties, associated himself with Anson Brunson in the practice of law and, as a cultured and aristocratic member of the Bar, became well known. For the centennial celebration here he was chosen to deliver the oration; yet thirteen years later he died in the County Poorhouse, having in the meantime sunk to the lowest depths of degradation. Drinking himself literally into the gutter, he lost his self-respect and finally married a common squaw.

The early attempts to create another county, of which Anaheim was to have been the seat, are known. In 1889, the struggle for division was renewed, but under changed conditions.

Santa Ana, now become an important town and nearer the heart of the proposed new county, was the more logical center; but although Anaheim had formerly strongly advocated the separation, she now opposed it. The Legislature, however, authorized the divorce, and the citizens chose Santa Ana as their county seat; and thus on August 1st, Orange County began its independence.

Although the cable lines on Second and Temple streets were not unqualified successes, J. F. Crank and Herman Silver in 1887 obtained a franchise for the construction of a double-track cable railway in Los Angeles, and in 1889 both the Boyle Heights and the Downey Avenue lines were in operation. On August 3d, 1889, the Boyle Heights section of the Los Angeles Cable Railway was inaugurated with a luncheon at the Power House—invitations to which had been sent out by the Boyle Heights Board of Trade, William H. Workman, President—preceded by a parade of cars; and on November 2d, the official opening with its procession of trains on the Downey Avenue line culminated, at noon, with speech-making at the Downey Avenue Bridge, and in the evening with a sham battle and fireworks. Some old-timers took part in the literary exercises, and among others I may mention Mayor Henry T. Hazard, Dr. J. S. Griffin, General R. H. Chapman and the Vice-President and Superintendent of the system, J. C. Robinson. The East Los Angeles line started at Jefferson Street, ran north on Grand Avenue to Seventh, east on Seventh to Broadway, north on Broadway to First, east on First to Spring, north on Spring to the Plaza, down San Fernando Street, then on the viaduct built over the Southern Pacific tracks and thence out Downey Avenue. The Boyle Heights line started on Seventh Street at Alvarado, ran along Seventh to Broadway, up Broadway to First and east on that street to the junction of First and Chicago streets. Quite a million dollars, it is said, was invested in the machinery and tracks—so soon to give way to the more practicable electric trolley trams—to say nothing of the expenditures for rolling stock; and for the time being the local transportation problem seemed solved, although the cars first used

George W. Burton

Ben C. Truman

Charles F. Lummis

Charles Dwight Willard

Grand Avenue Residence (left), Harris Newmark, 1889

were open, without glass windows, and the passengers in bad weather were protected only by curtains sliding up and down. To further celebrate the accomplishment, a banquet was given Colonel J. C. Robinson on December 18th, 1889. Herman Silver, to whom I have just referred, had not only an interesting association as a friend of Lincoln, but was a splendid type of citizen. He achieved distinction in many activities, but especially as President of the City Council.

On November 4th, Bernard Cohn, one of the originators of Hellman, Haas & Company (now Haas, Baruch & Company, the well-known grocers), and a pioneer of 1856, died. During the late seventies and early.eighties, he was a man of much importance, both as a merchant and a City Father, sitting in the Council of 1888 and becoming remarkably well-read in the ordinances and decrees of the Los Angeles of his day.

Like Abbot Kinney, Dr. Norman Bridge, an authority on tuberculosis, came to Sierra Madre in search of health, in 1890; lived for a while after that at Pasadena, and finally settled in Los Angeles. Five or six years after he arrived here, Dr. Bridge began to invest in Californian and Mexican oil and gas properties. Despite his busy life, he has found time to further higher culture, having served as Trustee of the Throop Institute and as President of the Southwest Museum, to both of which institutions he has made valuable contributions; while he has published two scholarly volumes of essays and addresses.

Thomas Edward Gibbon who, since his arrival in 1888, has influenced some of the most important movements for the benefit of Los Angeles, and whose activities have been so diversified, in 1890 bought the *Daily Herald*, becoming for several years the President of its organization and its managing editor. During his incumbency, Gibbon filled the columns with mighty interesting reading.

After living in Los Angeles thirty years and having already achieved much, I. W. Hellman moved to San Francisco on March 2d, 1890, and there reorganized the Nevada Bank. Still a resident of the northern city, he has become a vital part of its life and preëminent in its financial affairs.

Judge Walter Van Dyke was here in the early fifties, although it was some years before I knew him; and I am told that at that time he almost concluded a partnership with Judge Hayes for the practice of law. He was Judge of the Superior Court when the City of Los Angeles claimed title—while I was President of the Temple Block Company—to about nine feet of the north end of Temple Block. The instigator of this suit was Louis Mesmer, who saw the advantage that would accrue to his property, at the corner of Main and Requena streets, if the square should be enlarged; but we won the case. A principal witness for us was José Mascarel, and our attorneys were Stephen M. White and Houghton, Silent & Campbell. My second experience with Judge Van Dyke was in 1899, when I bought a lot from him at Santa Monica. This attempt to enlarge the area at the junction reminds me of the days when the young folks of that neighborhood used to play tag and other games there. Baseball, here called town-ball, was another game indulged in at that place.

Temple Block came to be known as Lawyer's Block because the upper floors were largely given over to members of that profession; and many of the attorneys I have had occasion to speak of as being here after our acquisition of the building had their headquarters there. Thus I became acquainted with Judge Charles Silent who, like his partner, Sherman Otis Houghton, hailed from San José in 1886, or possibly 1885, the two doubtless coming together. Judge Houghton brought with him a reputation for great physical and moral courage; and the two friends formed with Alexander Campbell the law firm of Houghton, Silent & Campbell. Judge Charles Silent, a native of Baden, Germany (born Stumm, a name Englished on naturalization), father of Edward D. Silent and father-in-law of Frank J. Thomas, once served as Supreme Court Judge in Arizona, to which office he was appointed by President Hayes; and since his arrival here, he has occupied a position of prime importance, not only on account of his qualifications as an attorney but also through the invaluable service he has always rendered this community. The judge now possesses a splendid orange orchard near the foothills, where he is passing his declining years. In the same way I had pleasant relations with the barrister, C. White Mortimer, for a long time the popular English Vice-consul, who came from Toronto. Among other attorneys whom it was a pleasure to know were Aurelius W. Hutton; John D. Bicknell (once a partner of Stephen M. White); J. H. Blanchard; Albert M. Stephens; General John Mansfield (who, by the way, was the first Lieutenant-Governor under the Constitution of 1879); Thomas B. Brown, District Attorney from 1880 until 1882; Will D. Gould; Julius Brousseau; J. R. Dupuy, twice District Attorney; and General J. R. McConnell. Most of these gentlemen were here before 1880. On the twentieth of January, 1889, M. L. Graff, a practicing attorney, reached Los Angeles, and until my family broke up housekeeping, he was a regular and welcome visitor in my home.

Ferdinand K. Rule came to Southern California in 1890 and soon after associated himself with the old Los Angeles Terminal Railroad. He was a whole-souled, generous man, and was henceforth identified with nearly every movement for the welfare of his adopted city.

Charles Dudley Warner, the distinguished American author, revisited Los Angeles in May, 1890, having first come here in March, three years before, while roughing it on a tour through California described in his book, *On Horseback*, published in 1888. On his second trip, Warner, who was editor of *Harper's Magazine*, came ostensibly in the service of the Harpers, that firm later issuing his appreciative and well-illustrated volume, *Our Italy*, in which he suggested certain comparisons between Southern California and Southern Europe; but the Santa Fé Railroad Company, then particularly desirous of attracting Easterners to the Coast, really sent out the author, footing most if not all of the bills. Mrs. Custer, widow of the General, was another guest of the Santa Fé; and she also wrote about Southern California for periodicals in the East.

News of the death, in New York City, of General John C. Frémont was received here the day after, on July 14th, and caused profound regret.

In the fall, Henry H. Markham stood for the governorship of California and was elected, defeating ex-Mayor Pond of San Francisco by a majority of about eight thousand votes— thereby enabling the Southland to boast of having again supplied the foremost dignitary of the State.

After several years of post-graduate study in higher institutions of learning in Germany, Leo Newmark, son of J. P. Newmark, in 1887 received his degree of Doctor of Medicine from the University of Strassburg. He then served in leading European hospitals, returning in 1890 to his native city, San Francisco, where he has attained much more than local eminence in his specialty, the diseases of the nerves.

The public pleasure-grounds later known as Hollenbeck Park were given to the City, in 1890–91, by William H. Workman and Mrs. J. E. Hollenbeck, Workman donating two-thirds and Mrs. Hollenbeck one-third of the land. Workman also laid out the walks and built the dam before the transfer to the City authorities. Mrs. Hollenbeck suggested the title, Workman-Hollenbeck Park; but Billy's proverbial modesty led him to omit his own name. At about the same time, Mrs. Hollenbeck, recognizing the need of a refuge for worthy old people, and wishing to create a fitting memorial to her husband (who had died in 1885), endowed the Hollenbeck Home with thirteen and a half acres in the Boyle Heights district; to maintain which, she deeded, in trust to John D. Bicknell, John M. Elliott, Frank A. Gibson, Charles L. Batcheller and J. S. Chapman, several valuable properties, the most notable being the Hollenbeck Hotel and a block on Broadway near Seventh.

More than once I have referred to the Chino Ranch, long the home of pioneer Isaac Williams. In his most extravagant dreams, he could not have foreseen that, in the years 1890–91 there would grow on many of his broad acres the much-needed sugar-beet; nor could he have known that the first factory in the Southland to extract sugar from that source would be erected in a town bearing the name of Chino. The inauguration of this important activity in Southern California was due to Henry T. and Robert Oxnard, the last-named then being engaged in cane-sugar refining in San Francisco. Henry T., who had previously ventured in the beet-sugar field in Nebraska, while on the Coast was impressed with the possibilities in our soil and climate; and after a survey of the State, he reached the conclusion that of all California the South offered the conditions most favorable to his plans. Accordingly, he entered into negotiations with Richard Gird, then the owner of the Chino Ranch, who made some preliminary experiments; and the outcome was the factory started there in the season of 1890–91, under the superintendency of Dr. Portius, a German agricultural chemist. In this initial enterprise the Oxnards met with such success that they extended their operations, in 1898 establishing a second and larger factory in Ventura County, in what soon came to be called Oxnard, Dr. Portius again taking charge.

Five or six years after the Oxnards opened their Chino factory, J. Ross Clark and his brother, Senator William A. Clark, commenced the erection of a plant at Alamitos; and in the summer of 1897, the first beets there were sliced, under the superintendency of G. S. Dyer, now in Honolulu. Since then, under a protective policy, several more refineries have started up in the neighborhood of Los Angeles.

In January, 1891, the Home of Peace Society was organized by the Hebrew ladies of Los Angeles, largely through the exertions of Mrs. M. Kremer, who was the first to conceive the idea of uniting Jewish women for the purpose of properly caring for and beautifying the last resting-place of their dead.

Amos G. Throop, of Chicago, more familiarly known among his friends and fellow-citizens as Father Throop, founded at Pasadena in 1891 the institution at first called Throop University and now known as the Throop College of Technology, giving it two hundred thousand dollars and becoming its first President. The next year, when it was decided to specialize in manual training and polytechnic subjects, the name was again changed—remaining, until 1913, Throop Polytechnic Institute.

The Southern California Science Association, later called the Southern California Academy of Science, was organized in 1891 with Dr. A. Davidson as its first President, and Mrs. Mary

E. Hart as Secretary.   For five years, it struggled for existence; but having been reorganized and incorporated in 1896, it has steadily become a factor for intellectual progress.

The Friday Morning Club began its existence in April, 1891, as one of the social forces in the city, many of the leading lecturers of the country finding a place on its platform; and in 1899 the Club built its present attractive home on Figueroa Street.

As far as I was familiar with the facts, I have endeavored in these recollections to emphasize the careers of those who from little have builded much, and quite naturally think of William Dennison Stephens whom I came to know through his association as a salesman from 1891 until 1902 with M. A. Newmark & Company, after which he engaged with J. E. Carr on Broadway, between Sixth and Seventh streets, in the retail grocery business.   Much of his success I attribute to honest, steady purpose and a winning geniality.   By leaps and bounds, Stephens has advanced—in 1907 to the presidency of the Chamber of Commerce; in 1908 to the grand commandership of Knights Templars in California; in 1909 to the mayoralty of Los Angeles; and in 1910 to one of the advisory committee for the building of the aqueduct.   At present, he is the Congressman from the Tenth Congressional District.

Three years before Congressman Stephens entered the employ of the Newmarks, Robert L. Craig had just severed his relations with them to form, with R. H. Howell of Louisiana, the third wholesale grocery house to come to Los Angeles. In the course of a few years, Howell & Craig sold out; but Craig, being young and ambitious, was not long in organizing another wholesale grocery known as Craig & Stuart, which was succeeded by R. L. Craig & Company.   At Craig's untimely death, Mrs. Craig, a woman of unusual mental talent, took the reins and, as one of the few women wholesale grocers in the country, has since guided the destinies of the concern; still finding time, in her arduous life, to serve the public as a very wide-awake member of the Board of Education.

Four other names of those once associated with my successors and who have been instrumental in establishing important commercial houses here are, P. A., a brother of M. A. Newmark; E. J. Levy; Frank Humphreys, now deceased; and D. Wiebers. The first-named, for some years connected with Brownstein, Newmark & Louis—now Brownstein & Louis—inaugurated and is at the head of P. A. Newmark & Company; while Levy, Humphreys and Wiebers incorporated the Standard Wooden Ware Company.

In 1891, the Terminal Railroad was completed from Los Angeles to East San Pedro, and rapid connection was thus established between Pasadena and the ocean, the accomplishment being celebrated, on November 14th, by an excursion. The road ran *via* Long Beach and Rattlesnake, later known as Terminal Island—a place that might become, it was hoped, the terminus of one of the great transcontinental railroads; and since the island is now the end of the San Pedro, Los Angeles & Salt Lake Railroad, that hope has been realized. It was in connection with this railway enterprise that Long Beach made the great mistake of giving away the right of thoroughfare along her ocean front.

CHAPTER XL

1892–1897

ACCOMPANIED by my family, I traveled to Alaska, in 1892, going as far as Muir Glacier and visiting, among other places, Metlakahtla (where we met Father William Duncan, the famous missionary and *Arctander*), Sitka, Juneau and the Treadwell Mines, near which the town of Treadwell has since developed. To-day, the tourist starts from Seattle; but we left Tacoma, sailing north about the seventh of July. I found much to inspire me in that rather extreme portion of the globe, where I was profoundly impressed with the vast forests and colossal rivers of ice, so emblematic of Nature's law of eternal change. Our party was especially fortunate in witnessing the rare sight of huge masses of ice as, with sound of thunder, they broke from the glacier and floated away, brilliantly-tinted bergs, to an independent, if passing, existence.

Having arrived in the Bay of Sitka, our ship, the *Queen of the Pacific*, struck a submerged rock. Instantly excitement and even frenzy prevailed. Levi Z. Leiter, a member of the firm of Field, Leiter & Company of Chicago, was so beside himself with fear that he all but caused a panic, whereupon the Captain ordered the First Mate to put the Chicagoan and his family ashore. Leiter, however, was shamed by his daughter, Miss Mary Victoria—afterward Lady Curzon and wife of the Viceroy of India—who admonished him not to make a scene; and having no desire to be left for a protracted stay in Sitka, he came to his senses and the commotion somewhat abated.

Meantime, not knowing how much damage had been done to the vessel, I hastily proceeded to gather our party together, when I missed Marco and only after considerable trouble found the boy in the cabin—such is the optimism of youth—with a huge sandwich in his hand, not in the least excited over the possible danger nor in any mood to allow a little incident of that kind to dissipate his appetite. When it became evident that the ship had sustained no vital damage, the Captain announced that as soon as a higher tide would permit we should proceed on our way.

In 1892, Abbot Kinney and F. G. Ryan, disregarding the craze for property along the bluffs of old Santa Monica, gave practical evidence of their faith in the future of the sand dunes hereabouts by buying an extensive strip of land on the ocean-front, some of it being within the town of Santa Monica but most of it stretching farther south. They induced the Santa Fé to lay out a route to Ocean Park as the new town was to be called; and having erected piers, a bath house and an auditorium, they built numerous cottages. Hardly was this enterprise well under way, however, when Ryan died and T. H. Dudley acquired his share in the undertaking. In 1901, A. R. Fraser, G. M. Jones and H. R. Gage purchased Dudley's half interest; and the owners began to put the lots on the market. One improvement after another was made, involving heavy expenditures; and in 1904, Ocean Park was incorporated as a city.

E. L. Doheny and a partner had the good luck to strike some of the first oil found in quantities within the city limits. They began operations in February on West State Street, in the very residence section of the town; and at about one hundred and sixty feet below the surface, they found oil enough to cause general excitement. Mrs. Emma A. Summers, who had been dealing in real estate since she came in 1881, quickly sank a well on Court Street near Temple which in a short time produced so lavishly that Mrs. Summers became one of the largest individual operators in crude oil. She is now known as the Oil Queen.

At the suggestion of Mrs. M. Burton Williamson, an interesting open-air meeting of the Los Angeles Historical Society was held on the evening of March 28th at the residence of Don António and Doña Mariana Coronel, near the corner of Central Avenue and Seventh Street.   Three hundred guests assembled to enjoy the proverbial Spanish hospitality of this distinguished couple, and to hear reports of the activities of various Los Angeles societies.   Don António possessed, as is well known, valuable historical and ethnological collections; and some of his choicest curios were that evening placed at the service of his guests.   Professor Ira More participated, presiding at a table once used by the first Constitutional Governor, Echeandia, and I still recall the manner in which António· chuckled when he told us how he had swapped "four gentle cows" for the piece of furniture; while, instead of a gavel, Señora Coronel had provided a bell long used to summon the Indians to Mission service.

As early as the height of the great Boom, Professor T. S. C. Lowe (to whom I have referred in the story of an experiment in making gas) advocated the construction of a railroad up the mountain later officially designated Mt. Lowe; and almost immediately financiers acted on the proposal and ordered the route surveyed.   The collapse of the Boom, however, then made the financing of the project impossible; and the actual work of building the road was begun only in 1892.   On the Fourth of July of the following year, the first car carrying a small party of invited guests successfully ascended the incline; and on August 23d the railway was formally opened to the public, the occasion being made a holiday.   In 1894, the Mt. Lowe Astronomical Observatory was built.   At one time, the railway was owned by Valentine Peyton, my agreeable neighbor and friend then and now residing on Westlake Avenue.

In June, 1893, the Los Angeles Post Office was moved from its location at Broadway near Sixth Street to the National Government Building at the southeast corner of Main and Winston streets, which had just been completed at a cost of one hundred and fifty thousand dollars.

Seized with the same desire that animated many thousands

who journeyed to Chicago, I visited the World's Fair in the fall of 1893. Everywhere I was impressed with the extraordinary progress made, especially by Americans, since the display in Philadelphia; and I was naturally proud of the exhibits from California in charge of my fellow-townsman, Ben Truman.

Russell Judson Waters, a well-known banker and member of Congress from the Sixth District between 1899 and 1903, came from Redlands in 1894 and is another Southern Californian who has turned his attention to literary endeavor: his novel, *El Estranjero*, dealing with past local life.

Joseph Scott, who has risen to distinction in the California legal world, alighted in Los Angeles in June, having tried without success to obtain newspaper work in Boston, in 1887, although equipped with a letter of introduction from John Boyle O'Reilly. In New York, with only two dollars in his pocket, he was compelled to shoulder a hod; but relief came: as Scott himself jovially tells the story, he was carrying mortar and brick on a Tuesday in February, 1890, and but two days later he faced a body of students at St. Bonaventura's College in Allegany, New York, as instructor in rhetoric! Within ten months after Scott came to Southern California, he was admitted to practice at the Los Angeles Bar; and since then he has been President of the Chamber of Commerce. He is now a member of the Board of Education, and all in all his services to the commonwealth have been many and important.

The existence of the Merchants' Association, which was organized in 1893 with W. C. Furrey as President and William Bien (succeeded the following year by Jacob E. Waldeck, son-in-law of Samuel Hellman) as Secretary, was somewhat precarious until 1894. In that year, Los Angeles was suffering a period of depression, and a meeting was called to devise ways and means for alleviating the economic ills of the city and also for attracting to Los Angeles some of the visitors to the Midwinter Fair then being held in San Francisco. At that meeting, Max Meyberg, a member of the Association's executive committee, suggested a carnival; and the plan being enthusiastically endorsed, the coming occasion was dubbed *La Fiesta de*

Los Angeles. Meyberg was appointed Director-General; and the following persons, among others, were associated with him in the undertaking: Mayor T. E. Rowan, F. W. Wood, R. W. Pridham, H. Jevne, J. O. Koepfli, Leon Loeb, H. T. Hazard, Charles S. Walton and M. H. Newmark.

The *Fiesta* lasted from the 10th to the 13th of April and proved a delightful affair. The participants marched in costume to the City Hall during a meeting of the Council, usurped the Government, elected a Queen—Mrs. O. W. Childs, Jr.— to preside over the destinies of the City during the *Fiesta* and communicated to everybody a spirit of uncontrollable enthusiasm based on a feeling of the most' genuine patriotic sentiment. The result was thoroughly successful, the carnival bringing out the real Californian fellowship—whole-souled and ringing true. Indeed, it is conceded by all who have seen Los Angeles grow, that this first *Fiesta* and the resulting strengthening of the Association have been among the earliest and, in some respects, the most important elements contributory to the wonderful growth and development of our city. A few evenings after the conclusion of the celebration, and while the streets were brilliantly illuminated with Bengal fire, the leaders again marched in a body, this time to the hall over Mott Market, where they not only laid plans for the second *Fiesta*, but installed J. O. Koepfli as President of the Merchants' Association.

So enthusiastic had the citizens of Los Angeles really become that in the years 1895 and 1896 the *Fiesta* was repeated and many prominent people supported the original committee, assisting to make the second festival almost equal to the first. Among these patrons were John Alton, Hancock Banning, W. A. Barker, A. C. Bilicke, L. W. Blinn, W. C. Bluett, R. W. Burnham, John M. Crawley, James Cuzner, J. H. Dockweiler, T. A. Eisen, J. A. Foshay, John F. Francis, A. W. Francisco, H. W. Frank, Dan Freeman, Mrs. Jessie Benton Frémont, W. M. Garland, T. E. Gibbon, J. T. Griffith, Harley Hamilton, R. H. Howell, Sumner P. Hunt, A. Jacoby, General E. P. Johnson, John Kahn, F. W. King, Abbot Kinney, E. F. C. Klokke, J. Kuhrts, Dr. Carl Kurtz, J. B. Lankershim, General

C. F. A. Last, S. B. Lewis, H. Lichtenberger, Charles F. Lummis, Simon Maier, D. C. McGarvin, John R. Mathews, James J. Mellus, L. E. Mosher, Walter S. Newhall, J. W. A. Off, Colonel H. Z. Osborne, Colonel H. G. Otis, Madison T. Owens, W. C. Patterson, Niles Pease, A. Petsch, John E. Plater, R. W. Pridham, Judge E. M. Ross, F. K. Rule, Frank Sabichi, J. T. Sheward, Colonel W. G. Schreiber, John Schumacher, Professor P. W. Search, Edward D. Silent, Alfredo Solano, George H. Stewart, Frank J. Thomas, D. K. Trask, Ben C. Truman, I. N. Van Nuys, K. H. Wade, Stephen M. White, Frank Wiggins, C. D. Willard, Dr. W. Le Moyne Wills, W. B. Wilshire, H. J. Woollacott and W. D. Woolwine.

This second *Fiesta* brought into the local field two men then unknown, but each destined to play an important part in the affairs of Los Angeles. J. O. Koepfli, President of the Merchants' Association, and M. H. Newmark, Chairman of the Finance Committee, selected Felix J. Zeehandelaar (a reporter for the Los Angeles *Herald* during the short ownership of John Bradbury) as financial and publicity agent; with the result that more than thirty thousand dollars was collected and valuable advertising was secured. At that time, the Finance Committee also discovered the undeveloped talent of Lynden Ellsworth Behymer, since so well known as the impresario, who, in managing with wonderful success the sale of tickets for the various events, laid the foundation for his subsequent career. Commencing with Adelina Patti, there have been few celebrities in the musical world that Behymer's enterprise has not succeeded in bringing to Los Angeles; his greatest accomplishment in recent seasons being the booking of the Chicago Grand Opera Company, in February, 1913, under a guarantee of eighty-eight thousand dollars.

Second in chronological order among the larger societies of women, and doubtless equal to any in the importance of its varied activities, the Ebell Club was organized in 1894, in due time providing itself with a serviceable and ornate home, within which for years broad courses of departmental study have been prosecuted with vigor.

After worshiping for more than fifteen years in the old Synagogue on Fort Street, and five years more after that name was changed to Broadway (during which period, from 1881 until I started, in 1887, on my second European trip, it was my privilege to serve as President of the Congregation), the reformed Jews of Los Angeles built, in 1894, the Temple B'nai B'rith on the corner of Hope and Ninth streets. In the meantime, following the resignation of Dr. A. W. Edelman, in 1886, Dr. Emanuel Schreiber for two years occupied the pulpit; and then Reverend A. Blum came from Galveston to succeed him. From the early part of 1895, Rabbi M. G. Solomon held the office until 1899. It was during his administration, it may be interesting to observe, and while Herman W. Hellman was President, that the present Temple was consecrated.

In 1894, Homer Laughlin, of Ohio, during a visit purchased from Mrs. Mary A. Briggs the property on Broadway between Third and Fourth streets, where she had lived. Three years later, he moved to Los Angeles and began the erection of the Homer Laughlin fire-proof building, adding to the same, in 1905, a reinforced concrete annex.

At midnight, on April 17th, Don António Franco Coronel died at his home in Los Angeles, aged seventy-seven years. In less than four months, his life-long friend, Don Pio Pico died here—on September 11th, aged ninety-three years.

The Belgian hare aberration was a spasmodic craze of the nineties and when I remember what the little rabbit did to our judgment then, it brings to mind the black-tulip bubble of Holland though, in point of genuine foolishness, I should award the prize to the former. A widely-copied newspaper article, claiming for the flesh of the timid Belgian rodent extraordinary qualities and merit, led first hundreds, then thousands, to rig up hare-coops for the breeding of the animal, expecting to supply the world with its much-lauded meat. Before long, people abandoned profitable work in order to venture into the new field, and many were those who invested thousands of dollars in Belgian hare companies. During the wild excitement attention was also given to the raising of hares for exhibition, and fancy prices were paid for the choicest specimens. At last, the bubble burst: the supply far exceeded the now-diminishing demand and the whole enterprise collapsed.

A lively election in 1895 was that which decided the immediate future of a suburb of Los Angeles where, on April 27th of the same year, Don Juan Warner, who had lived there with his daughter, Mrs. Rúbio, went to his rest. This was University Place, in 1880 a mere hamlet, though three years later it had a post office of its own. In 1895, an effort was made to annex the community, with Vernon, Rosedale and Pico Heights; but the measure was defeated, and only on June 12th, 1899 was the college district annexed to Los Angeles. For some years, the boundary line of the town at that point followed such a course through house-lots that residents there, still at home, often ate in the county and slept within the city!

The early nineties were full of the spirit of accomplishment, and notwithstanding the failure of the Electric Homestead Tract Association and its street car line, already described, a successful electric railway system for Los Angeles was at length installed. In 1892, a route was laid out to Westlake Park, the company having been encouraged by a subsidy of fifty thousand dollars pledged by owners of property most likely to be affected by the service; and by 1895 the electric traction system was so general that even the bob-tailed cars on Main Street gave way to the new order of things. At this early stage in the application of electricity to street cars, some of the equipment was rather primitive. Wooden poles, for example, were a part of the trolley; and as they were easily broken, conductors were fined a dollar for any accident to the rod with which they might have to do! Electricity—when it was forthcoming at all—was only harnessed to impel the vehicle; but there were no devices for using the current to warm the car, and instead of an electric light, an *oil* lamp, hung onto the dashboard, faintly illuminated the soft roadbed of the irregular tracks. The most active promoters of the improvements of 1895 were the two brothers, William Spencer and Thomas J. Hook, who operated mainly in the southwestern part of the city, developing that rather sparsely-settled district and introducing what was the best and most handsome rolling stock seen here up to that time.

B. F. Coulter, who from 1881 to 1884 had preached here as a clergyman of the Christian Church, in 1895 built a place of worship at his own expense, on Broadway near Temple Street, costing twenty thousand dollars—no inconsiderable sum for that time.

Sometime in March appeared the first issue of the *Los Angeles Record*, a one-cent evening paper started by E. W. Scripps as "the poor man's advocate." It was really another one of the many enterprising Scripps newspapers scattered throughout the country and championing, more or less, Socialistic principles; in accordance with which Scripps, from the outset, distributed some of the stock among his working associates. At the present time, W. H. Porterfield is the editor-in-chief, and W. T. Murdoch the editor.

Thomas J. Scully, a pioneer school teacher who came to Los Angeles the same year that I did, died here in 1895. For some time Scully was the only teacher in the county outside of the city, but owing to the condition of the public treasury he actually divided his time between three or four schools, giving lessons in each a part of the year. After a while, the schoolmaster gazed longingly upon a lovely vineyard and its no less lovely owner; and at last, by marrying the proprietress, he appropriated both. This sudden capture of wife and independence, however, was too much for our unsophisticated pedagogue: Scully entered upon a campaign of intemperance and dissipation; his spouse soon expelled him from his comfortable surroundings, and he was again forced to earn his own living with birch and book.

Inoffensive in the extreme, yet with an aberration of mind more and more evident during twenty years, Frederick Merrill Shaw, a well-informed Vermonter born in 1827, shipped for California as cook on the brig *Sea Eagle* and arrived in San Francisco in September, 1849, where he helped to build, as he always claimed, the first three-story structure put up there.

Well-proportioned and standing over six feet in height, Shaw presented a dignified appearance; that is, if one closed an eye to his dress.   Long ago, he established his own pension bureau, conferring upon me the honor of a weekly contributor; and when he calls, he keeps me well-posted on what he's been doing. His weary brain is ever filled with the phantoms of great inventions and billion-dollar corporations, as his pocketful of maps and diagrams shows; one day launching an aerial navigation company to explore the moon and the next day covering California with railroad lines as thick as are automobiles in the streets of Los Angeles.

On September 21st, my brother, J. P. Newmark, to whom I am so indebted, and who was the cause of my coming to California, died at his home, in the sixty-ninth year of his age; his demise being rather sudden.   During the extended period of his illness, he was tenderly nursed by his wife, Augusta; and I cannot pay my sister-in-law too high a tribute for her devoted companionship and aid, and her real self-sacrifice.   Mrs. Newmark long survived her husband, dying on January 3d, 1908 at the age of seventy-four.

The reader will permit me, I am certain, the privilege of a fraternal eulogy: in his acceptance and fulfillment of the responsibilities of this life, in the depth and sincerity of his feeling toward family and friend, my brother was the peer of any; in his patient, silent endurance of long years of intense physical suffering and in his cheerfulness, which a manly courage and philosophical spirit inspired him to diffuse, he was the superior of most; and it was the possession of these qualities which has preserved his personality, to those who knew him well, far beyond the span of natural existence.

In May, 1896, the Merchants' Association consolidated with the Manufacturers' Association (of which R. W. Pridham was then President), and after the change of name to the Merchants & Manufacturers' Association, inaugurated the first local exhibit of home products, using the Main Street store of Meyberg Brothers for the display.   On August 1st, 1897, Felix J. Zeehandelaar, later also Consul of the Netherlands, became the stalwart, enthusiastic and now indispensable Secretary, succeeding, I believe, William H. Knight.

This same year Major Ben. C. Truman, formerly editor of the *Star*, together with George D. Rice & Sons established the *Graphic*, which is still being published under the popular editorship of Samuel T. Clover. In 1900, Truman was one of the California Commissioners to the Paris Exposition. After his foreign sojourn, he returned to Los Angeles and, with Harry Patton, started a weekly society paper called the *Capitol*. Rather recently, by the advantageous sale of certain property early acquired, Ben and his good wife have come to enjoy a comfortable and well-merited degree of prosperity. Clover came to Los Angeles in 1901; was editor and publisher of the *Express* for four years; and in 1905 started the *Evening News*, continuing the same three years despite the panic of 1907. A year previously, he purchased the *Graphic*, more than one feature of which, and especially his "Browsings in an Old Book Shop," have found such favor.

W. A. Spalding, whose editorial work on Los Angeles newspapers—dating from his association with the *Herald* in 1874, and including service with both the *Express* and the *Times*—in 1896 assumed the business management of his first love, the *Herald*. After again toiling with the quill for four years, he was succeeded by Lieutenant Randolph H. Miner.

The magnificent interurban electric system of Los Angeles is indebted not a little to the brothers-in-law, General M. H. Sherman and E. P. Clark—the former a Yankee from Vermont, and the latter a Middle Westerner from Iowa—both of whom had settled in Arizona in the early seventies. While in the Territory, Sherman taught school and, under appointment by Governor Frémont as Superintendent of Instruction, laid the foundation of the public school system there. Both came to Los Angeles in 1889, soon after which Sherman organized the Consolidated Electric Railway Company. In 1896, the old steam railroad—which about the late eighties had run for a year or so between Los Angeles and the North Beach, by way of Colegrove and South Hollywood—was equipped with electrical

motor power and again operated through the enterprise of
Eli P. Clark, President of the Los Angeles Pacific Railroad
Company.   Together, Sherman and Clark built an electrical
road to Pasadena, thus connecting the mountains with the
sea.

In 1896, I dissolved partnership with Kaspare Cohn, taking
over the hide business and, having fitted up a modest office
under the St. Elmo Hotel, revived with a degree of satisfaction
the name of H. Newmark & Company.

A notable career in Los Angeles is that of Arthur Letts who
in 1896 arrived here with barely five hundred dollars in his
pocket and, as it would appear, in answer to a benign Providence.   J. A. Williams & Company, after a brief experience,
had found the corner of Broadway and Fourth Street too far
south, and their means too limited, to weather the storm; so
that their badly-situated little department store was soon in
the hands of creditors.   This was Letts' opportunity: obtaining some financial assistance, he purchased the bankrupt
stock.   His instantaneous success was reflected in the improvement of the neighborhood, and thereafter both locality and
business made rapid progress together.

Meredith P. Snyder, who became a resident in 1880 and
started business by clerking in a furniture store, in 1896 was
elected to the office of mayor, on a municipal water-works
platform.

During the presidential campaign of 1896, when the West
went wild over "16 to 1," and it looked as if W. J. Bryan
would sweep aside all opposition here, an organization known
as the Sound Money League undertook to turn the tide.
George H. Stewart was elected President, the other members of
the Executive Committee being John F. Francis, Frank A. Gibson, R. W. Burnham and M. H. Newmark.   So strenuous was
the campaign, and so effective was the support by the public,
that when the sun set on that memorable Tuesday in November,
Los Angeles was found to be still strong for sound principles.
Perhaps the most remarkable outpouring in the political history of the city took place during this period when business

men, regardless of previous party affiliations, turned out to hear Tom Reed, the "Czar" of the House of Representatives.

It was in the Christmas season of 1896 that Colonel Griffith J. Griffith so generously filled the stocking of Los Angeles with his immensely important gift of Griffith Park, said to be, with its three thousand and more diversified acres, magnificent heights and picturesque roadways—some of which, with their dense willow growth, remind me of the shaded lanes described in earlier chapters—the second largest pleasure ground in the world.

On July 1st, 1897, the Atlantic & Pacific Railroad was absorbed by the Santa Fé; Charles W. Smith, the receiver, having brought order out of chaos after the former road in 1895 had met with disaster.

Dr. Henry S. Orme, H. W. O'Melveny, J. M. Griffith, J. W. Gillette, A. L. Bath, J. M. Guinn, M. Teed, J. M. Elliott and W. A. Spalding on August 2d met in the office of the *Daily Herald*, in the Bradbury Block on Third Street, to consider the organization of an Old Settlers' Society. At that meeting a committee, consisting of Dr. J. S. Griffin, Henry W. O'Melveny, Benjamin S. Eaton, H. D. Barrows, J. M. Guinn, Dr. H. S. Orme, J. W. Gillette and myself was appointed to direct the movement. On August 10th, we selected the Los Angeles County Pioneers of Southern California as the name of the society and decided that eligibility should be limited to those who had resided in the county twenty-five years. A public meeting was held at the Chamber of Commerce on September 4th, 1897 and the twenty-five persons present signed the roll. The first President chosen was Benjamin S. Eaton and the first Secretary, J. M. Guinn.

Dr. William F. Edgar, who had resided here continuously for over thirty years, died on August 23d, at the age of seventy-three; a sword given to him by General Phil Kearney resting among the floral tributes. The tenth of the following November witnessed the death of George Hansen, the surveyor, whose body (in accordance with his expressed wish) was cremated. On the same day, J. J. Ayers died.

This year, when the town was full of unemployed, hundreds of men were set at work to improve Elysian Park, a move suggested by Judge Charles Silent.

Frank Walker, who had been here for a while in the middle of the eighties and had gone away again, returned to Los Angeles about 1897 and set himself up as a master builder. While contracting for certain unique bungalows, his attention was directed to the possibility of utilizing the power of the sun, with the result that he soon patented a solar heater, similar to those now extensively built into Southern California residences, and organized a company for exploiting the invention.

CHAPTER XLI

THE SOUTHWEST ARCHÆOLOGICAL SOCIETY

1898–1905

A CLOUD, considerably larger than a man's hand, flecked the skies at the dawn of 1898 and troubled many who had been following the course of events in Cuba. So, too, like the thrill sent through the nation at the firing on Fort Sumter, the startling intelligence of the destruction of the United States battleship *Maine* electrified and united the people. Along the Coast, intense excitement scarcely permitted Westerners to keep themselves within bounds; and instant was the display of patriotic fervor, Southern Californians willingly shouldering their share of the unavoidable war burdens.

On January 22d, John G. Nichols, several times Mayor of Los Angeles and always a welcome figure on the streets, died here at the age of eighty-five years.

Colonel Harrison Gray Otis, soldier, Union officer, Government official in Alaska and President of the Los Angeles *Times* publishing company, was appointed by President McKinley, on May 27th, a Brigadier-General of the United States Volunteers, following which he was assigned to a command in the Philippines, where he saw active service until honorably discharged in 1899, after the fall of Malolos, the insurgent capital. During General Otis's absence, his influential son-in-law, the large-hearted, big man of affairs, Harry Chandler, Vice-President of the corporation, was general manager of the *Times;* while L. E. Mosher was managing editor. In 1897, Harry E. Andrews joined the *Times* staff, in 1906 becoming manag-

Isaias W. Hellman

Herman W. Hellman

Cameron E. Thom

Ygnácio Sepúlveda

Main Street, Looking North, Showing First Federal Building, Middle Nineties

First Santa Fé Locomotive to Enter Los Angeles

ing editor and infusing into the paper much of its characteristic vigor. In 1899, Hugh McDowell, who had entered the employ of the *Times* four years before, began his long editorship of the *Times'* magazine, a wide-awake feature which has become more and more popular. During many years, Mrs. Eliza A. Otis, the General's gifted wife, now deceased, also contributed to both the *Times* and the *Mirror*. From the beginning, the paper has been Republican and in every respect has consistently maintained its original policies. Especially in the fight for San Pedro harbor, it was an important element and did much to bring the energetic campaign to a successful termination.

Paul De Longpré, the French artist who made his mark, when but eleven years old, in the Salon of 1876, was a distinguished member of a little group of Frenchmen arriving in the late nineties. In 1901, he bought a home at Hollywood and there surrounded himself with three acres of choicest gardens—one of the sights of suburban Los Angeles—which became an inspiration to him in his work as a painter of flowers. De Longpré died in Hollywood, on June 29th, 1911.

On August 23d, my excellent friend, Dr. John Strother Griffin, for nearly fifty years one of the most efficient and honored residents of Los Angeles, died here.

A career such as should inspire American youth is that of Henry T. Gage (long in partnership with the well-known bibliophile, W. I. Foley,) a native of New York who in 1877, at the age of twenty-four, began the practice of law in Los Angeles, to be elected, twenty-one years later, Governor of California. A handsome man, of splendid physique—acquired, perhaps, when he started as a sheep-dealer—he is also genial in temperament, and powerful and persuasive in oratory; qualifications which led to his selection, I dare say, to second the nomination at Chicago, in 1888, of Levi P. Morton for the Vice-Presidency. Ex-Governor Gage's wife was Miss Fannie V., daughter of John Rains and granddaughter of Colonel Isaac Williams.

April 27, 1899 was printed large and red upon the calendar

for both Los Angeles and San Pedro, when the engineers, desiring to commence work on the harbor in true spectacular fashion, brought a load of quarried rock from Catalina to dump on the breakwater site. President McKinley sent an electric spark from the White House, intended to throw the first load of ballast splashing into the bay; but the barge only half tilted, interfering with the dramatic effect desired. Nevertheless, the festivities concluded with the usual procession and fireworks.

Movements of great importance making for a municipal water-system occurred in 1899, the thirty years' contract with the assigns of John S. Griffin, P. Beaudry, S. Lazard and others having expired on July 22d, 1898. An arbitration committee, consisting of Charles T. Healey for the Company and James C. Kays—long a citizen of importance and Sheriff from 1887 to 1888—for the City, failed to agree as to the valuation of the Los Angeles City Water Company's plant, whereupon Colonel George H. Mendell was added to the board; and on May 12th, 1899, Kays and Mendell fixed their estimate at $1,183,591, while Healey held out for a larger sum. In August, the citizens, by a vote of seven to one, endorsed the issuing of two million dollars of City bonds, to pay the Water Company and to build additional equipment; and the water-works having been transferred to the municipality, five commissioners were appointed to manage the system.

During August, 1899, the Reverend Dr. Sigmund Hecht of Milwaukee took into his keeping the spiritual welfare of Los Angeles Reformed Jewry; and it is certainly a source of very great satisfaction to me that during his tenure of office his good fellowship has led him, on more than one occasion, to tender the altar of the Jewish temple for Christian worship. Scholarly in pursuits and eloquent of address, Dr. Hecht for sixteen years has well presided over the destinies of his flock, his congregation keeping pace with the growth of the city.

Incursions of other jobbing centers into Los Angeles territory induced our leading manufacturers and wholesalers to combine for offensive as well as defensive purposes; and on

October 11th, 1899, in answer to a call, an enthusiastic meeting was held in Room 86, Temple Block, attended by J. Baruch, J. O. Koepfli, J. Saeger, R. L. Craig, L. Kimble, L. C. Scheller, George H. Wigmore, F. W. Braun, C. C. Reynolds, I. A. Lothian, W. S. Hunt, A. H. Busch, M. H. Newmark and others, who elected Baruch, President; Koepfli, First Vice-President; Reynolds, Second Vice-President; Scheller, Treasurer; and Braun, Secretary. A couple of weeks later, A. M. Rawson was named Secretary, Braun having resigned to accept the Third Vice-Presidency; and on November 3d, the Associated Jobbers of Southern California, as the organization was called, was re-christened the Associated Jobbers of Los Angeles. Meanwhile at a quiet luncheon, Koepfli and Newmark had entered into negotiations with Charles D. Willard, with the result that, when Rawson withdrew on February 28th, 1900, Willard assumed the duties of Secretary, holding the office for years, until compelled by sickness, on January 18th, 1911, to relinquish the work. On February 21st, 1900, Baruch having resigned, M. H. Newmark began a service of twelve years as President. The strength of the organization was materially increased when, in March, 1908, F. P. Gregson, well up in the traffic councils of the Atchison, Topeka & Santa Fé Railroad, assumed the management of the recently-established traffic bureau.

On April 10th, 1908, after many years of hardship, financial trouble and disappointment, during which the Executive Committee and Secretary Willard had frequent conferences with J. C. Stubbs and William Sproule (then Stubbs's assistant) of the Southern Pacific, and W. A. Bissell, of the Atchison, Topeka & Santa Fé Railroad, it became evident that more equitable rates for shippers into the San Joaquín Valley and elsewhere could not peaceably be obtained. A promised readjustment, lowering Los Angeles rates about twenty per cent., had been published; but at the request of the San Francisco merchants, the new tariff-sheet was repudiated by the transportation companies. A rehearing was also denied by them. The Associated Jobbers then carried the case before

the newly-created Railroad Commission and obtained conces-
sions amounting to fifty per cent. of the original demands.
Guided by their astute Traffic Manager, F. P. Gregson, the
jobbers, not satisfied with the first settlement, in 1910 renewed
their activity before the Commission; and on the 15th of the
following February, still further reductions were announced.
The last rates authorized in 1912 are still in effect.

In 1899, James M. Guinn, after some years of miscellaneous
work in the field of local annals, issued his *History of Los Angeles
County*, following the same in 1907 with a *History of California
and the Southern Coast Counties*. As I write, he has in preparation a still more compendious work to be entitled, *Los Angeles
and Environs*.

At half-past four o'clock on the morning of December
25th, a slight shock of earthquake was felt in Los Angeles;
but it was not until some hours later that the telegraph reported the much greater damage wrought at San Jacinto,
Riverside County. There, walls fell in heaps; and a peculiar
freak was the complete revolution of a chimney without the disturbance of a single brick! Six squaws, by the falling of their
adobes at the Reservation some miles away, were instantly
killed. When day dawned and the badly-frightened people
began to inspect the neighborhood, they found great mountain-
crevices, into some of which even large trees had fallen.

Toward the end of the nineties, Henry E. Huntington
sold much or all of his large holdings in the San Francisco
railways and began both to buy up Los Angeles railway stocks
and to give his personal attention to the city's traffic-problems.
At the same time, he bent his energies to the crowning work of
his life—the development of the various interurban electric
systems focusing in Los Angeles. In 1902, the road to Long
Beach was completed; and in the following year electric cars
began to run to Monrovia and Whittier. In 1903, the seven-
story Huntington or Pacific Electric Building at the corner of
Main and Sixth streets was finished. The effect of these
extensive improvements on local commerce and on the value
of real estate (as well as their influence on the growth of popula-

tion through the coming of tourists seeking the conveniences and pleasures of social life) cannot, perhaps, be fully estimated —a fact which the people of this city should always remember with gratitude.

During the winter of 1899–1900, business cares so weighed upon me that I decided temporarily to cast off all worry and indulge myself with another visit to the Old World. This decision was reached rather suddenly and, as my friends insist, in a perfectly characteristic manner: one morning I hastened to the steamship office and bought the necessary tickets; and then I went home leisurely and suggested to my wife that she prepare for a trip to Europe!

About the first of January, therefore, we left Los Angeles, reached Naples on February 1st and traveled for nine months through Great Britain, France, Germany, Italy, Switzerland, Norway, Sweden and Denmark. I returned to my birthplace, Loebau, which in my youth had appeared of such importance; but although somewhat larger than it used to be, it now nevertheless seemed small and insignificant.

While making this tour of Europe, I revisited Sweden and renewed my acquaintance with the families that had been so kind to me as a boy. Time had lamentably thinned the ranks of the older generation, but many of the younger, especially those of my own age, were still there. Those only who have had a similar experience will appreciate my pleasure in once again greeting these steadfast friends. I also reviewed numerous scenes formerly so familiar. It is impossible to describe my emotions on thus again seeing this beautiful country, or to convey to the reader the depth of my respect and affection for her intelligent, thrifty and whole-souled people, especially when I remembered their liberal encouragement of my father about forty years before.

Thanks to the indefatigable labors of Mrs. A. S. C. Forbes of Los Angeles, the beautiful ceremony of strewing flowers upon the restless ocean waters in honor of the naval dead was first observed at Santa Monica on Memorial Day in 1900, and bids fair to become an appropriate national custom.

Señora Antónío F. Coronel entrusted to the Chamber of Commerce, on June 6th, the invaluable historical souvenirs known as the Coronel Collection; and now [1] for years these exhibits, housed in the Chamber of Commerce Building, have been one of the sights of the city, a pleasure and a stimulation alike to tourist and resident.

A good anecdote as to the transfer of this collection is related on the authority of Miss Anna B. Picher, President of the Boundary League and the lady who made the first move to secure the interesting League mementos now preserved and displayed at the County Museum. When the matter of making the Coronel heirlooms more accessible to the public was brought to Señora Coronel's attention, she not only showed a lively interest, but at once agreed to make the donation. She imposed, however, the condition that Miss Picher should bring to her M. J. Newmark and John F. Francis, then directors, in whose integrity and acumen she had great confidence. This was done; and these gentlemen having pledged their personal attention and sponsorship, the Señora committed the historic objects to the Chamber of Commerce for the benefit, forever, of all the people.

The Los Angeles *Herald*, on July 7th, passed into the hands of a group of stockholders especially interested in petroleum, Wallace R. Hardison being President and General Manager, and R. H. Hay Chapman, Managing Editor. At the same time the newspaper's policy became Republican.

The Harvard School was opened, on September 25th by Grenville C. Emery and was the first notable military academy for youth in Los Angeles. After many terms of successful work under Congregational auspices, the School has passed to the control of the Rt. Reverend J. H. Johnson, as trustee for the Episcopal Church, which has acquired other valuable school properties in the Southland; Professor Emery remitting fifty thousand dollars of the purchase price in consideration of a promise to perpetuate his name.

A tunnel was put through Bunker Hill—by the way, one of

[1] Installed, of late, in the County Museum.

the highest of downtown elevations—from Hill Street to Hope on Third, in 1901, bringing the western hill district into closer touch with the business center of the town and greatly enhancing the value of neighboring property.   The delay in cutting through First and Second streets, which would afford so much relief to the municipality, is a reproach against the good sense of the City.

The Los Angeles *Express*, which enjoys the honor of being the oldest daily newspaper still published in Los Angeles, and which, for fifteen years, has been so well managed by H. W. Brundige, was sold in January to Edwin T. Earl, who moved the plant to a building erected for it on Fifth Street between Broadway and Hill.   Earl came to Los Angeles in 1885, having previously for years packed and shipped fruit on a large scale.   In 1890, as a result of the obstacles handicapping the sending of fresh fruit to the East, Earl invented a new refrigerator car with ventilating devices; and unable to get the railroads to take over its construction, he organized a company for the building of the conveyors.   On selling out to the Armours, Earl made large investments in Los Angeles real estate.   A few years ago, the *Express* was moved to Hill Street near Seventh. Possibly owing to the renewed interest in local historical study, the *Express*, in 1905, commenced the republication of news items of "Twenty-five Years Ago To-day"—a feature of peculiar pleasure to the pioneer.

William F. Grosser, who died on April 15th, was long active in Los Angeles Turnverein circles, having popularized science before institutions and lecture-courses existed here for that purpose.   A native of Potsdam, Prussia, Grosser came to Southern California *via* Panamá, and on settling in Los Angeles, laid out the Grosser Tract.   Having been an advanced student of astronomical science and microscopy, and possessing a good-sized portable telescope, he was soon in demand by societies and schools, for which he lectured without financial remuneration.   One of Grosser's sisters, Mrs. A. Jelinek— whose husband, a Boston cabinet-maker, had an interesting part in the carving of the chair made from "the spreading chestnut tree" and presented to the poet Longfellow by the school children of Cambridge—has been for years an honored resident of Ocean Park, where she was one of the early investors. A granddaughter is Fräulein Elsa Grosser, the violinist.

On April 24th, Samuel Calvert Foy died, aged seventy-one, survived by his wife and six children.

A little town in Ventura County, bearing the name of the famous student and author, recalls the death near here in July of Charles Nordhoff, whose pioneer book, *California: For Health, Pleasure and Residence*, published in the early seventies, did more, I dare say, than any similar work to spread the fame of the Southland throughout the East.

Charles Brode, who died in August, first saw Los Angeles in 1868, when he came here to nurse Edward J., my wife's brother, in his last illness. He then opened a grocery store at South Spring Street near Second, and was active in Turnverein and Odd Fellow circles. The mention of Brode recalls the name of one who has attained distinction here: even as a messenger boy at the California Club in the eighties, Oscar Lawler gave promise of an important future. He had come from Iowa as a child, and his personality, ability and ambition soon brought him prominently before the Bar and the people. He served as United States Attorney for this district from 1906 until 1909, when he became Assistant to the Attorney-General of the United States. He is high in Masonic circles, being Past Grand Master of the Masonic Grand Lodge of California. In 1901, he married Miss Hilda, daughter of Charles Brode.

Catalina Island, in the summer of 1902, established wireless connection with the mainland, at White's Point; and on August 2d, the first messages were exchanged. On March 25th of the following year began the publication of the Catalina newspaper known as the *Wireless*.

After graduating from the University of California in 1902, my son Marco attended for a while the University of Berlin; after which he returned to Los Angeles and entered the house of M. A. Newmark & Company.

The women of California, in the late eighties, wishing to

pay Mrs. John C. Frémont an appropriate tribute, presented her with a residence at the northwest corner of Hoover and Twenty-eighth streets, Los Angeles where, on December 27th, 1902, at the age of seventy-eight years, she died.   Mrs. Frémont was a woman of charming personality and decidedly intellectual gifts; and in addition to having written several meritorious works, she was engaged, at the time of her death, on her autobiography.   Her ashes were sent East to the banks of the Hudson, to be interred beside those of her distinguished husband; but her daughter, Miss Elizabeth Benton Frémont, has continued to reside here in the family homestead.

On the site of one of my early homes, the corner-stone of the new Chamber of Commerce was laid on March 28th with impressive Masonic ceremonies.   The principal address was made by Jonathan S. Slauson.   Ferdinand K. Rule was then President of the Chamber; and the Building Committee consisted of M. J. Newmark, Chairman; A. B. Cass, Homer Laughlin, F. K. Rule, H. S. McKee and James A. Foshay— the latter for sixteen years, beginning with the middle nineties, having demonstrated his efficiency as Superintendent of City Schools.

Early in 1903, G. A. Dobinson, a Shakespearian student and teacher of elocution, induced me to build a hall on Hope Street near Eleventh, connected with a small theater; and there, in the spring of 1904, he opened the well-known Dobinson School, which he conducted until 1906.   Then the Gamut Club, an organization of 1904—whose first President was Professor Adolph Willhartitz,[1] the artistic German pianist —moved in.

The pioneer experiments with the navel orange have already been referred to; a late episode associates the luscious fruit with a President of the United States.   On May 6th, amid great festivity participated in by all Riverside, Theodore Roosevelt replanted, in front of Frank Miller's Mission Inn, one of the original, historic trees.

William K. Cowan came to Los Angeles as a jeweler in

[1] Died on January 12th, 1915, aged seventy-eight years.

1887, later embarked in the bicycle trade and was one of the first men in Los Angeles to sell automobiles, at length building in 1903 at 830 South Broadway the first large garage here.

Some months later, if I recollect aright, witnessed the advent on our streets of a number of horseless carriages, and I was seized with a desire to possess not one, but two. My acquisitions were both electric, and soon I was extending, right and left, invitations to my friends to ride with me. On the first of these excursions, however, one of the machines balked and the second also broke down; and to make a long story short, no mechanic in town being sufficiently expert to straighten out the difficulty, I soon disposed of them in disgust for about seven hundred dollars.

In 1903, a notable change was made, and one decidedly for the better interests of the public schools, when one hundred citizens, pursuant to a change in the City's charter, selected a non-partizan Board of Education consisting of John D. Bicknell, Joseph Scott, J. M. Guinn, Jonathan S. Slauson, Charles Cassatt Davis, Emmet H. Wilson and W. J. Washburn.

On October 23d the Southwest Society was founded here by Charles F. Lummis with Jonathan S. Slauson as its first President; Charles F. Lummis, Secretary and W. C. Patterson, Treasurer. Associated with these officers were J. O. Koepfli, M. A. Hamburger, General H. G. Otis, Henry W. O'Melveny, Major E. W. Jones, J. A. Foshay, the Right Reverend Thomas J. Conaty, J. D. Bicknell and others. In the beginning, it was a branch of the Archæological Institute of America; but so rapid was the Society's growth that, in three years, it had fifty per cent. more members than belonged to the thirty-year-old parent organization in Boston, with which it remained affiliated until 1913 when it withdrew in order that all its funds might go toward the maintenance of the Southwest Museum, a corporation founded in 1907 as the result of the Southwest Society's labors.

The first plant of the Los Angeles *Examiner*, a newspaper owned by William Randolph Hearst, was installed in 1903 by Dent H. Robert, then and now publisher of the San Francisco

Examiner. The paper, illustrated from the start, made its first appearance on December 12th and sprang into immediate favor. R. A. Farrelly was the first managing editor. The office of the paper was on the west side of Broadway near Fifth Street, where it remained for ten years, during which it rendered valuable service to the community, notably in conducting a successful campaign for the sale of seven hundred and twenty thousand dollars' worth of school bonds which had hitherto proven unmarketable. In the meantime, Robert had been succeeded, first by a Mr. Strauss, and then by Henry Lowenthal and William P. Leech, while Farrelly was followed by Foster Coates, Arthur Clark and W. P. Anderson. In 1908, the enterprising Maximilian F. Ihmsen assumed the responsibilities of publisher, and at the same time Frederick W. Eldridge became the efficient managing editor. Under the able direction of these experienced men, this morning daily has attained its highest prosperity, marked by removal in the fall of 1913 to the *Examiner* Building at Broadway and Eleventh Street.

Abbot Kinney, foreseeing a future for the tide-flats and lagoons south of Ocean Park, in 1904 purchased enough acreage whereon to build the now well-known Venice, which, as its name implies, was to be adorned with canals, bridges and arcades. Through Kinney's remarkable spirit of enterprise, a wonderful transformation was effected in a single year. Such in fact was the optimism of this founder of towns that, in order to amply supply the necessary funds, he closed out important city holdings including the Flat Iron Square, lying between Eighth and Ninth, and Main and Spring streets, the Abbotsford Inn property and the large southeast corner of Spring and Sixth streets, at present occupied by the Grosse Building. Kinney's foresight, courage and persistence have been rewarded, the dreams of his prime becoming the realities of his more advanced age.

The task of building here a King's Highway—El Camino Real—intended to connect all the missions and *presidios* between San Diego and Sonoma was undertaken in the troublous days of Don Gaspar de Portolá and Father Junípero Serra;

but time in a measure obliterated this landmark. Since 1904, however, such kindred spirits as Miss Anna B. Picher—for nearly twenty years a zealous toiler for the preservation of our historic monuments, and whose zeal in behalf of the royal road was paramount—Mr. and Mrs. A. S. C. Forbes, Dr. Milbank Johnson, R. F. Del Valle, Mrs. C. R. Olney of Oakland and Frank Ey, Mayor of Santa Ana, have so caused the work to prosper that at the present time much of the original highway is about to be incorporated with the good State roads of California. The first bell for one of the mission-bell guide posts (designed, by the way, by Mrs. Forbes) was dedicated at the Plaza Church on August 15th, 1906; and since then some four hundred of these indicators have been placed along the Camino Real.

An interesting attempt to transplant a small Eastern town to California was made in 1904 when Alfred Dolge, the founder of Dolgeville, New York (and the author of the elaborate work, *Pianos and their Makers*, published in 1911 at little Covina), established Dolgeville in Los Angeles County, opening there, with three hundred or more operatives, a felt works for piano fixtures. The experiment had been undertaken because of expected advantages in the supply of wool; but changes in the tariff ruined the industry, and after some years of varying prosperity, Dolgeville was annexed to Alhambra.

A syndicate, styled the Los Angeles Herald Company, whose President was Frank G. Finlayson, in 1904 bought the *Herald*, at that time under the editorial management of Robert M. Yost.

Future generations will doubtless be as keen to learn something about the preserving of albacore, commonly spoken of as tuna, as I should like to know how and by whom sardines were first successfully put into cans. The father of this industry is Albert P. Halfhill, a Minnesotan drawn here, in 1892, through the opportunities for packing mackerel on this southern coast. In 1894, we find him organizing the California Fish Company, soon to be known as the Southern California Fish Company. In 1904, Halfhill, while experimenting with various western sea-foods, accidentally discovered the extraordinary quality of the albacore, a briny-deep heavyweight so interesting to the angler and so mysterious to the scientist. As a mere bit of gossip, Halfhill's assurance that M. A. Newmark & Company purchased the first canned tuna is entitled to mention.

The Turnverein-Germania took a notable step forward this year by buying a lot, one hundred by three hundred feet, on South Figueroa, between Pico and Fifteenth streets; and on September 3d, 1905, the new club building and gymnasium were formally opened.

William H. Workman in 1904 was elected Treasurer of the City of Los Angeles for the third time, his first term of office having begun in 1901. This compliment was the more emphatic because Workman was a Democrat and received four thousand five hundred votes more than his opponent—and that, too, only a month after Roosevelt had carried Los Angeles by a majority of thirteen thousand.

In a previous chapter, I have described the vender of *tamales* and ice-cream, so familiar through his peculiar voice as well as his characteristic costume. About 1905, another celebrity plying a trade in the same line, and known as Francisco, appeared here and daily made his rounds through the more fashionable Westlake district. He had a tenor voice of rare quality and power, and used it, while exquisitely rendering choice *arias*, to advertise his wares. Such was his merit that lovers of music, as soon as his presence was known, paused to listen; with the natural result that business with Francisco was never dull. Whenever a grand opera company came to town, the Italian was there, in a front seat of the gallery; and so great was his enthusiastic interest in the performance of those whose voices were often inferior to his own, that he could be seen, with gaze fixed on the proscenium, passionately beating time as if to direct the orchestra. Seven or eight years ago, the long-favorite Francisco was foully murdered, and under strange circumstances; leading many to believe that, having perhaps degraded himself from his former estate and fleeing, an alien, to an unknown land, he had fallen at last the victim of a *vendetta*.

In 1905, I took part in a movement, headed by Joseph Mesmer, to raise by subscription the funds necessary to buy the old Downey Block—fronting on Temple and North Main streets, and extending through to New High—for the purpose of presenting it to the National Government for a Federal Building site. Unusual success attended our efforts, and the transfer to Uncle Sam was duly made. In the meantime, an appropriation of eight hundred thousand dollars had been secured for the building, and it was with no little surprise and disappointment when the bids for construction were opened, in May, 1906, that the lowest was found to be nearly a million dollars. This delayed matters until the following fall. In October, the site at the corner of Main and Winston streets was sold for three hundred and fourteen thousand dollars; and the deficiency having thus been supplied, it was not long before the new building was in course of construction.

Desiring to celebrate the fifty years which had elapsed since, perched upon an ox-cart, he rode into Los Angeles for the first time, William H. Workman on January 21st gave a banquet to five hundred pioneers in Turnverein Hall, the menu being peculiarly *mejicano*. The reminiscences, speeches and quips were of the friendliest and best; and the whole affair was one that recalled to both host and guests the *dolce far niente* days of dear old Los Angeles.

On February 21st, the San Pedro, Los Angeles & Salt Lake Railroad was completed—the fourth transcontinental line, with its connections, to enter Los Angeles.

In the spring, A. C. and A. M. Parson bought a tract of land on Alamitos Bay and there, at the mouth of the San Gabriel River, founded Naples, with features somewhat similar to those at Venice; but unlike the latter town, the new Naples has never developed into a crowded resort.

Arriving in California in 1869, at the age of seven, Frank Putnam Flint, a native of Massachusetts concerning whom much of importance might be related, was elected in 1905

United States Senator from California. His brother, Motley H. Flint, high in Masonic circles, has also enjoyed an important career, having long been associated with many local public movements.

An optimist of optimists, still young though having passed more than one milestone on the road to success, Willis H. Booth came to Los Angeles a mere lad and is a product of the Los Angeles High School and the State University. Before, while and since filling the office of President of the Chamber of Commerce, Booth has been identified with nearly everything worth while here and gives promise of an important and interesting future. He is now one of the Vice-Presidents of the Security Trust and Savings Bank.

In August, Juan B. Bandini, second son of the famous Don Juan, died at Santa Monica. Two of Bandini's daughters were noted Los Angeles belles—Arcadia, who became the wife of John T. Gaffey, of San Pedro; and Dolores, who married into the well-known literary family, the Wards, of London.

Strenuous efforts were made in 1905 to house the Historical Society of Southern California, which, incorporated on February 12th, 1891, boasts of being the oldest organization of its kind on the Coast and the only one doing State work; and the Legislature appropriated one hundred and twenty-five thousand dollars for a building. Governor Pardee, however, vetoed the bill— an act which later contributed to the endowment, by the State, of the comely County Museum in which the Historical Society now has its home.

In the spring of 1905, the then eight-year-old town of Redondo, with her large hotel and busy wharf, and famed for her fields of carnations, became the scene of one of those infrequent, but typically American, real estate frenzies which come suddenly, last a few days and as suddenly depart. This particular attack, not to say epidemic, was brought on by one or two newspaper headlines announcing to the breakfasting reader that Henry E. Huntington had decided to spend millions of dollars in making immense railroad and other improvements in the seaside town, and that this would at once raise Redondo from the humble status of a village to almost metropolitan dignity. In about as little time as is required to relate it, the astonished beach-dwellers found themselves overwhelmed by a surging mass of humanity struggling for the privilege of buying lots. The real estate offices were soon surrounded by hundreds of people, fighting, pushing and shoving, all possessed of but the one idea—to buy.

And they bought. They bought corners and they bought in the middle of the blocks; they bought heaps of sand and holes in the ground; they bought in one breath and sold in the next; they bought blindly and sold blindly. Redondo had become a huge, unregulated stock exchange, lots instead of stocks for five days becoming the will-o'-the-wisps of the fated bidders, until the boom collapsed leaving hundreds with lots they had never seen and which, for the time being, they could not sell at any price.

Huntington did not spend his millions—at least then and there. Redondo did not suddenly become a big center. Yet, in passing through the experience of many a town, Redondo has gradually grown in population and importance, even developing something of a suburb—Clifton-by-the-Sea. Such was the famous boom of 1905; and such will probably be the story of similar California booms to come.

CHAPTER XLII

1906–1910

ON January 1st, 1906, after more than half a century of commercial activity—with some things well done, and some poorly enough—during which it has never been my ambition to better myself at the expense of others, I retired from business to enjoy the moderate but sufficient affluence which years of varying fortune had bestowed upon me.

Rather early in the morning of April 18th, news was received here of the awful calamity that had befallen San Francisco; and with lightning rapidity the report spread throughout the city. Newspaper and telegraph offices were besieged for particulars as to the earthquake, which, strange to say, while it also affected even San Diego, was scarcely felt here; and within a couple of hours, more than a thousand telegrams were filed at one office alone, although not a single message was despatched. Thousands of agitated tourists and even residents hastened to the railroad stations, fearing further seismic disturbance and danger, and bent on leaving the Coast; and soon the stations and trains were so congested that little or nothing could be done with the panic-stricken crowds. Meanwhile, more and more details of the widespread disaster poured in; and Los Angeles began to comprehend how paralyzing to her sister cities must have been the wreck and ruin following, first, the shaking of the earth, and then the much more serious fires and explosions. Soon, too, refugees from the North commenced flocking into our city; and these thousands, none with complete and few with decent

633

attire, each pleading pathetically for assistance, told the sad tale much more frankly than could the noisy newsboy, with his flaring headlines and shrill, intermittent *Extra!*

Long before much information was secured as to just what had happened, public-spirited men and women, some under the banners of regular organizations, some acting independently, moved energetically to afford relief. The newspapers led off with large subscriptions, while the Chamber of Commerce, Board of Trade and the Merchants & Manufacturers' Association swelled the amount. Eventually some two hundred and fifty thousand dollars was raised. At the same time, and within two or three hours after the terrifying news had first been received, the Directors of the Chamber of Commerce met and appointed various committees headed by Francis Quarles Story, a patriotic and indomitable citizen who arrived in 1883; and having the valuable coöperation of Frank Wiggins, who served as Secretary, they went actively to work to render the most practical assistance possible. A Supply Committee, of which M. H. Newmark was chairman, by five o'clock the same afternoon had assembled fourteen carloads of goods, partly donated and partly sold to the Committee at cost, to go by rail, and nine carloads to go from San Pedro by water. This train full of necessaries was the first relief of its kind that reached San Francisco; other shipments of supplies followed daily; and with the first relief train went a corps of surgeons, under the chairmanship of Dr. L. M. Powers, Health Officer, who established a hospital in the Jefferson Square Building, treating two thousand patients in less than three weeks. Among the chairmen of the several committees were: J. O. Koepfli, J. Baruch, R. W. Burnham, Niles Pease, Perry Weidner, John E. Coffin, J. J. Fogarty, W. L. Vail, D. C. McGarvin, W. A. Hammel, F. Edward Gray, Mrs. R. M. Widney and D. J. Desmond; while H. B. Gurley, long identified with Frank Wiggins in Chamber of Commerce work, was Assistant Secretary.

In this way was our sister-city laid low; but only, as it were, for a moment. While the flames were yet consuming the old San Francisco, her children were courageously planning the new; and supported by that well-nigh superhuman spirit which community misfortune never fails to inspire—the spirit that transforms weakness into strength, and transmutes, as by an altruistic alchemy, the base metal of "eachness" into the pure gold of "allness"—this stricken people built and built until, to-day, less than a decade after that memorable night, there stands by the Golden Gate a finer and more beautiful city than the one from which it sprang.   And, as if to emphasize to other nations the fulness of San Francisco's accomplishment, her invincible citizens are now organizing and triumphantly carrying out a great world's exposition.

One incident of this period of excitement and strain is perhaps worthy of record as evidence of the good fellowship existing between Los Angeles and the prostrate city.   On May 2d the Executive Committee[1] of the Associated Jobbers passed resolutions discouraging any effort to take advantage of San Francisco's plight, and pledging to help restore her splendid commercial prestige; whereupon Samuel T. Clover made this editorial comment in the Los Angeles *Evening News:*

We commend the reading of these expressions of kindly good will to every pessimist in the country, as an evidence that all commercial honor is not wiped out in this grossly materialistic age.   The resolutions, as passed, are an honor to the Jobbers' Association in particular, and a credit to Los Angeles in general.   The *Evening News* desires to felicitate President Newmark and his associates on the lofty attitude they have taken in the exigency.   We are proud of them.

Among the many who at this time turned their faces toward Los Angeles is Hector Alliot, the versatile Curator of the Southwest Museum.   Born in France and graduating from the University of Lombardy, Dr. Alliot participated in various important explorations, later settling in San Francisco.   Losing

---

[1] President, M. H. Newmark; First Vice-President, J. O. Koepfli; Second Vice-President, C. C. Reynolds; Third Vice-President, F. W. Braun; Treasurer, L. C. Scheller; Secretary, Charles Dwight Willard; Directors: H. R. Boynton, J. Baruch, P. A. Benjamin, A. Douglass, I. A. Lothian and D. Wiebers.

in the earthquake and fire everything that he possessed, Alliot came south and took up the quill, first with the *Examiner* and then the *Times.*[1]

Mr. and Mrs. M. Kremer, on April 9th, celebrated their golden wedding; less than a year later, both were dead. Mrs. Kremer passed away on March 5th, 1907, and her husband followed her two days later—an unusual dispensation.

In July, I was seized with an illness which, without doubt, must have precluded the possibility of writing these memoirs had it not been for the unselfish attendance, amounting to real self-sacrifice, of Lionel J. Adams. From that time until now, in fair weather or foul, in good health or ill, Adams uncomplainingly and, indeed cheerfully, has bestowed upon me the tender care that contributed to the prolongation of my life; and it affords me peculiar pleasure to record, not only the debt of gratitude that I owe him and the sincere friendship so long marking our relations, but also his superior character as a man.

J. M. Griffith, for years a leading transportation agent and lumber merchant, died here on October 16th. Griffith Avenue is named after him. Just two weeks later, William H. Perry passed away—a man of both influence and affluence, but once so poor and tattered that when he arrived, in February, 1854, he was unable to seek work until he had first obtained, on credit, some decent clothes.

Sometime about 1907, Major Ben C. Truman, both a *connoisseur* of good wines and an epicure, figured in an animated controversy as to the making of mint-julep, the battle waging around the question whether a julep's a julep, or not a julep, with the mint added before or after a certain stage in the concocting!

In an exceedingly informal manner, at the Westlake Avenue residence of my daughter, Mrs. L. Loeb, my wife and I on the 24th of March, 1908 celebrated our golden wedding anniversary,

[1] One of Dr. Alliot's most recent accomplishments is a comprehensive *Bibliography of Arizona*, recently published—the result of Dr. J. A. Munk's liberal provision.

Harris and Sarah Newmark, at Time of Golden Wedding

Summer Home of Harris Newmark, Santa Monica

the occasion being the more unusual because both the nuptials and the silver wedding festivity had occurred in Los Angeles.[1] Our pleasure on that occasion was intensified by the presence of friends with whom, during most of our married life, we had maintained unbroken the most amicable relations.

Many years after spur-track switching charges had been abolished throughout other industrial districts of the United States, the Western railroads continued to assess this charge in Los Angeles, to the extent that, as was estimated, our merchants were paying through this tribute alone an amount not less than $250,000 a year. In August, 1908, however, or shortly after F. P. Gregson became identified with the Associated Jobbers, suit was filed by M. H. Newmark, as President, before the Interstate Commerce Commission; and on May 7th, 1910, a decision was rendered in favor of local shippers. But unfortunately this decision was reversed on July 20th, 1911, by the Commerce Court.[2] Joseph P. Loeb and Edward G. Kuster, young attorneys, handled the case in a manner recognized among men of their profession as being unusually brilliant; while Gregson brought together a mass of valuable facts. This was probably the most notable of all the cases of its kind in the commercial history of Los Angeles. The other directors at the time the suit was brought were: J. O. Koepfli, C. C. Reynolds, F. W. Braun, L. C. Scheller, H. R. Boynton, A. Douglass, D. Wiebers, W. H. Joyce, W. E. Hampton and E. H. Greppin.

Not the least interesting step forward in providing Los Angeles with a harbor was the acquisition of a strip of land known as the Shoe String connecting Los Angeles with San Pedro and Wilmington. This practical idea made possible in 1909

[1] On July 5th, 1915, Mr. and Mrs. S. Lazard celebrated their golden wedding, Mrs. Lazard being the third daughter of Mr. and Mrs. Joseph Newmark to enjoy the privilege—almost unique in a single family, and that will become the more remarkable if Mrs. Eugene Meyer (the fourth daughter) and her husband live to commemorate, on the 20th of November, 1917, the fiftieth anniversary of their marriage.

[2] The Supreme Court of the United States, on June 8th, 1914, affirmed the decision of the Interstate Commerce Court, and thus was obliterated this very iniquitous charge.

the unhampered consolidation of the three places; and before the beginning of April their various civic bodies had been considering the formation of committees to bring this about.   On Saturday, April 3d, the Los Angeles appointees met at the rooms of the Chamber of Commerce for permanent organization.   They were William D. Stephens, Mayor of Los Angeles; Stoddard Jess; Homer Hamlin, City Engineer; F. W. Braun; J. A. Anderson, Attorney for the Harbor Commission and ex-member of the Board of Public Works; Leslie R. Hewitt, City Attorney; Frank Simpson; Joseph Scott, President of the Board of Education; M. H. Newmark, President of the Associated Jobbers; J. M. Schneider, President of the Merchants and Manufacturers' Association; A. P. Fleming, Secretary of the Harbor Commission; ex-Mayor M. P. Snyder, H. Jevne, O. E. Farish, President of the Realty Board; and F. J. Hart. Jess was elected President; Fleming, Secretary; and to the admirable manner in which they conducted the campaign, much of the ultimate success of the movement must be attributed. The delegates from San Pedro and Wilmington refused to go on until the Associated Jobbers had pledged themselves to obtain for the harbor districts, after consolidation was effected, the same freight advantages enjoyed by Los Angeles.   This promise was given and fulfilled.   Various other pledges were outlined in the Committee's report and adopted by the City Council; but many of these assurances have not thus far been carried out by the authorities.   Then a vigorous campaign was projected, as a result of which both elections—that of Wilmington and Los Angeles on August 5th, and the other, of San Pedro and Los Angeles, on August 12th—resulted in handsome majorities for consolidation.   These substantial victories were fittingly celebrated throughout the consolidated cities; and on February 13th, 1910, the port became officially known as Los Angeles Harbor.

In April, 1906, the one hundred thousand books of the Los Angeles Public Library, then under the administration of Charles F. Lummis, were moved from the City Hall to the Laughlin Building.   With the opening of September, 1908, the Library was again moved by the same Librarian, this time to the Hamburger Building.[1]

On the evening of October 11th, 1909, I attended a banquet tendered to President Taft by the City of Los Angeles, at the Shrine Auditorium. Every honor was shown the distinguished guest, and his stay of two or three days was devoted to much sight-seeing, to say nothing of the patriotic efforts of many politicians whose laudable desire was to whisper in the Presidential ear *à propos* of government employment.

The election of George Alexander as Mayor on November 10th, 1909 was largely responsible for the later success of the Progressive party—with whose Socialistic policies I am not in sympathy. W. C. Mushet, the more acceptable candidate, ran on a ticket endorsed by business-men organized under the chairmanship of M. H. Newmark, while George A. Smith was the Republican candidate. Alexander's campaign was managed by Meyer Lissner, an arrival of 1896 who had a brief experience as a jeweler before he turned his attention to law. He possessed much political sagacity, and was therefore quick to turn the Alexander success to the advantage of Hiram Johnson who was soon elected Governor. George N. Black, who came here a child in 1886, and graduated from the Los Angeles High School, later being President of the California State Realty Confederation and Grand President of the Independent Order B'nai B'rith of this district, directed Smith's campaign.

On January 29th, 1910, the citizens of Los Angeles, under the leadership of Max Meyberg, tendered to D. A. Hamburger (Chairman), Perry W. Weidner, Fred L. Baker, William M. Garland, M. C. Neuner, Dick Ferris and F. J. Zeehandelaar, the committee in charge of the first Aviation Meet here, a banquet at the Alexandria Hotel. The contests had occurred a few days before at Dominguez Field, on a part of the once famous *rancho;* and to see the aërial antics of the huge man-

---

[1] On June 1st, 1914, the Library—directed by Everett R. Perry, who came to Los Angeles in the fall of 1911, from the staff of the New York Public Library—was removed to the Metropolitan Building at the northwest corner of Broadway and Fifth Street, its shelves, a month later, holding 227,894 volumes.

made birds, as they swiftly ascended and descended, was no less nerve-racking, at least to me, than it was interesting.

Litigation having established a clear title to the property once held by the Sixth District Agricultural Association, and the State, the declared owner, having agreed to lease the ground to the County and the City for fifty years, decisive steps were taken in January, 1910, by the Historical Society of Southern California to provide the Museum building now such a source of civic pride. Other bodies, including the Fine Arts League, the Southern California Academy of Science and a branch of the Cooper Ornithological Society, were invited to coöperate, each being promised a place in the park and museum plans; and by the middle of February, the supervisors had agreed to vote the necessary building funds. On July 11th, 1910, in the presence of a large and representative gathering at Exposition Park, ground was broken for the building, although the corner-stone was not laid until the 10th of December.

In the dark hours of the night of April 25th, 1910, after an illness of four days and almost entirely free from suffering, she who had shared with me the joys and sorrows of over half a century was called to her reward. She passed from this life as she had passed through it—gently and uncomplainingly. I was left in the midst of a gloom that I thought would be for-ever black; for six out of our eleven children had preceded their mother, whose spirit on that night was reunited with theirs. I was soon to find, however, how true it is that "The Lord tempers the wind to the shorn lamb." Common misfortune and common memories made but stronger the tie, always strong, between my children and myself. Time has performed his kindly offices: he has changed the anguish of grief to the solace of recollection; and in assisting me to realize that I was permitted so long and so happy a companionship, he has turned my heart from its first bitterness to lasting gratitude.

CHAPTER XLIII

RETROSPECTION

1910–1913

AT one o'clock in the morning of October 1st, 1910, occurred the most heinous crime in the history of Los Angeles. This was the dynamiting, by the evil element of union labor, of the building and plant of the Los Angeles *Times*, resulting in the sudden extinction of no less than twenty human lives and the destruction of the property of the corporation. The tragedy, lamented in obsequies of the most impressive kind ever witnessed in this city, was followed by the construction, on the same site and at the earliest moment, of the present home of the *Times*. The trial of some of those deemed responsible for this disaster brought to the fore John D. Fredericks, District Attorney[1] in 1900, 1902, 1906 and 1910.

Not the least of the many and far-reaching losses entailed through the ruin of this printery was a *History of the Medical Profession of Southern California* by Dr. George H. Kress, with an introduction by Dr. Walter Lindley—a work of extended research almost ready for publication. After all such material as could be saved from the ruins had been assembled, an abridged edition of the volume once planned was issued.

In strong contrast to this annihilation of man by his brother, were the peaceful exercises marking the afternoon of the previous Sunday, June 19th, when the Kaspare Cohn Hospital, on Stephenson Avenue, was dedicated; a worthy charity made

---

[1] In 1914, Fredericks was the Republican candidate for the Governorship of California.

possible through the munificence, several years before, of the pioneer after whom the hospital is named.

As Superintendent of City Schools here for four years beginning in 1906, C. E. Moore laid the foundation for that national reputation which, in July, 1910, led to his being called as a professor to Yale University.

Jacob A. Riis, the famous Danish-American sociologist, who was so instrumental in cleaning up New York's tenement districts, visited Los Angeles for the fourth time, on March 10th, 1911, lecturing at the Temple Auditorium on "The Battle with the Slum."

The City Council having created a Harbor Board, Mayor George Alexander, in October, 1909, appointed Stoddard Jess, Thomas E. Gibbon and M. H. Newmark as Commissioners. In March, 1911, at a popular election, the Board was made a charter body, and Mayor Alexander reappointed the gentlemen named. Owing, however, to the numerous difficulties thrown in the way of the Commissioners in the accomplishment of their work, M. H. Newmark resigned in December, 1911 and Stoddard Jess in January, 1912; while Thomas E. Gibbon, for many years one of the most formidable advocates of a free harbor, met with such continued obstacles that he was compelled, in the summer of 1912, to withdraw.

Having left Los Angeles, as I have said, in 1879, Myer J. Newmark made San Francisco his home until December, 1894, at which time he returned here and became associated with Kaspare Cohn. In December, 1905, he once more took up his abode in San Francisco where, on May 10th, 1911, he died at the age of seventy-two years.

The first issue of the Los Angeles *Tribune*, a wide-awake sheet projected by Edwin T. Earl, owner of the *Express*, appeared on July 4th, flying the banner of the Progressive party, but making its strongest appeal for support as the first one-cent morning newspaper on the Coast, and a readable journal advocating the moral uplift of the community. Like all the other newspapers of this period, the *Tribune* was illustrated with photo-engravings.

In 1911, William R. Hearst, of national newspaper fame, bought the Los Angeles *Daily Herald*, making it at the same time an evening newspaper and placing it under the management of Guy B. Barham. The latter had come to Southern California with his father, Richard M. Barham, who located in 1873 at Anaheim, conducting there the old Planters' Hotel. After school was out, Guy did chores. Graduating, he worked for Hippolyte Cahen, the Anaheim merchant; then he kept books for Eugene Meyer & Company, and in time became Deputy Internal Revenue Collector. For some years he has been a Custom House broker, in which activity, in addition to his newspaper work, he is still successfully engaged.

The Federal Telegraph Company, which had established itself in Los Angeles in the fall of 1910, inaugurated in July, 1911 a wireless service with San Francisco and other Coast cities; and just a year later it effected communication with Honolulu, although oddly enough at first, owing to atmospheric conditions, it was necessary to flash all messages across the waste of waters during the night. For some years, the giant steel masts erected by the Company in the southwestern part of the city have puzzled the passer-by.

At half-past three o'clock on November 28th, I turned the first spadeful of earth in the breaking of ground for the Jewish Orphans' Home of Southern California. This privilege was accorded me because, in response to the oft-expressed wish of my wife to assist those dependent children bereft of their natural protectors, I had helped, in a measure, shortly after her demise, to assure the success of the proposed asylum.

Sixteen years after Colonel Griffith J. Griffith agreeably surprised Los Angeles in the presentation of Griffith Park, his munificent bounty again manifested itself in another Christmas donation, that of one hundred thousand dollars for the construction of an observatory on Mount Hollywood, the highest point in Griffith Park. Incidental to the making of this gift, due official recognition of the Colonel's large-heartedness was displayed at a public meeting in the City Hall, in which I had the honor of participating.

M. A. Newmark & Company in February, 1912 removed to their present quarters on Wholesale Street—a building (it may some day be interesting to note) five stories high with a floor space of one hundred and thirty thousand square feet.

In common with the rest of the civilized world, Los Angeles, on April 15th, was electrified with the news of the collision between an iceberg and the great ocean steamer *Titanic* which so speedily foundered with her 1535 helpless souls. For a day or two, it was hoped that no one with Los Angeles connections would be numbered among the lost; but fate had decreed that my nephew, Edgar J. Meyer, a son of Mr. and Mrs. Eugene Meyer, should perish. He was one of those who heroically hastened to the aid of the women and children; nor did he rest until he saw his wife and child placed in one of the lifeboats. They were saved, but he went down, with other gallant men, among whom I may mention Walter M. Clark, son of J. Ross Clark, of this city.

Nor can I refrain, while mentioning this awful catastrophe, from alluding to another example of courage and conjugal devotion[1] than which, perhaps, neither song nor story portrays one more sublime. As the huge liner was sinking into the dark abyss, one frail woman declined to become the beneficiary of that desperate command, "*Women and children first!*" The wife of Isadore Straus, unafraid though face to face with Death and Eternity, still clung to her loyal husband, refusing, even in that terrible moment, to leave him. She chose rather to die by his side; and as the black sea roared out its chill welcome, it received one who, in the manner of her going, left a precious heritage for all mankind.

Through a high school friendship of my son Marco I came to know quite well one who, though physically handicapped, acquired much international fame. I refer to Homer Lea, a native of Denver, who came to Los Angeles in 1890, at the age

[1] Even while this manuscript is being revised, the name of another Angeleño—that of the lamented A. C. Bilicke, a self-made man of large accomplishments, who perished on May 7th, 1915, in the awful destruction of the *Lusitania*—is added to the scrolls of the ill-starred.

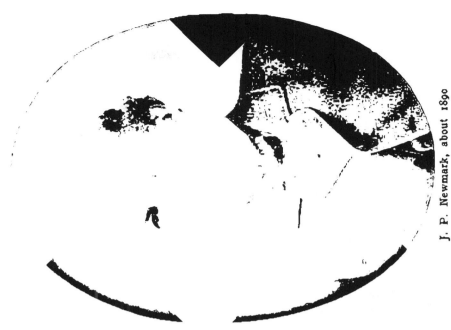

J. P. Newmark, about 1890

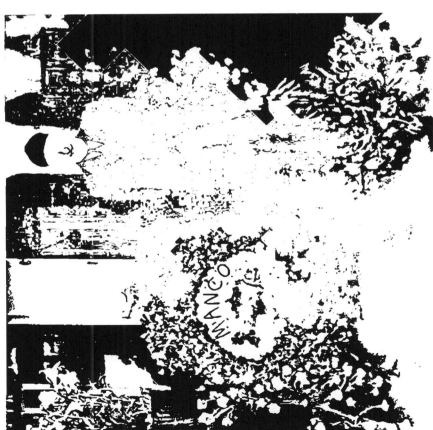

Harris Newmark, at the Dedication of M. A. Newmark & Co.'s Establishment, 1912

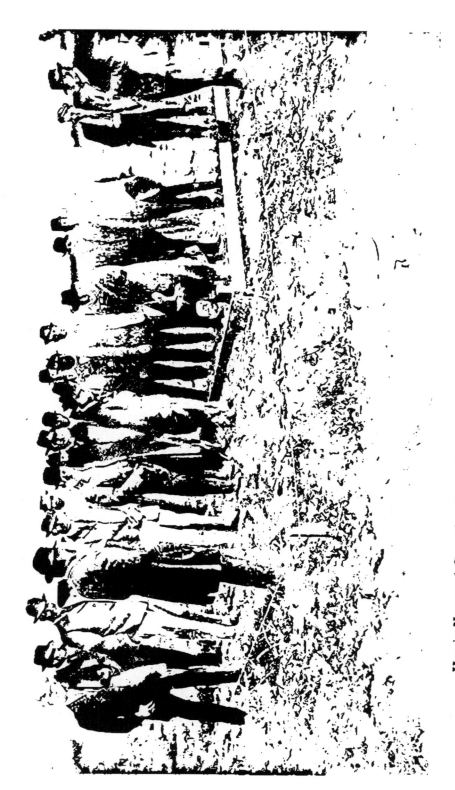

Harris Newmark Breaking Ground for the Jewish Orphans' Home, November 28th, 1911

of fourteen, studied at the High School, Occidental College and
at Stanford, and then conceived the monumental idea of freeing
the Chinese from the despotism of the old Manchurian dynasty.
Making his first trip to China in 1900, he took an active part
in a revolutionary campaign; and returning to America a
Lieutenant-General and a force in the Chinese Republican party,
he devoted himself to drilling Chinese troops, and to literary
work, some of his writings, notably *The Valor of Ignorance*, when
widely translated, bringing him repute as a military strategist.
Having married Mrs. Ethel Powers, General Lea, late in 1911,
joined Dr. Sun Yat Sen, the Chinese leader, and proceeded with
him from London to Shanghai, only to arrive there after the
revolution had actually started. Even then success was not
to crown his labors; during the convention called to establish
the Republic, General Lea was stricken with paralysis and his
public career was at an end. He returned to Southern California; and at Ocean Park on November 1st, 1912, while looking
out toward the land that he loved so well, Homer Lea yielded up
his soul. He was not destined to see the fulfillment of his
dream; but when the people for whom he labored shall some day
have established a true democracy, his name will loom large in
their history.

In December, the Museum of History, Science and Art, so
favorably situated in Exposition Park, was informally opened[1]
to the public under the scholarly administration of Dr. Frank S.
Daggett, who had been appointed Director the year previous;
and during the few months following, Professor Daggett, backed
by the Board of Supervisors, carried forward with such enterprise
the excavations of the pits at La Brea *rancho* that, before the
ornate building was ready to receive the finds, a unique collection of fossils invaluable for the study of California fauna
had been assembled. The discovery of these evidences of
primeval animal life, already concentrating the attention of the
scientific world, may well be regarded with pride by every
Southern Californian; while the proper housing here of precious
souvenirs recalling those whose lives have contributed so much

[1] The formal dedication took place on November 5th, 1913.

to making Los Angeles what it was and is, will permanently
add to the attractions of the Southland.

Pluckily resisting the inroads of an insidious disease, yet
cheerful under all the discouraging circumstances and as deeply
interested as ever in the welfare of this community, Charles
Dwight Willard has been confined to his home for many months.
On my last visit I found him very feeble,[1] though still fired with
a resistless enthusiasm; the power of his mind asserting itself
over the flesh in forcible, if quiet, expression. We sat in a
comfortable little bower at his home on San Rafael Heights,
with Mrs. Willard, his faithful companion; and after he had
uttered an earnest desire to see these memoirs published, we
chatted about his life and his activities here. Born in Illinois
and graduating from the University of Michigan, an affection
of the lungs, brought on by an attack of typhoid fever, induced
him in 1888 to come to Los Angeles in search of a milder climate.
His first occupation here was to serve as a reporter for the
Times, and then for the morning *Herald*. In 1891, he was
elected Secretary of the Chamber of Commerce; and during the
six years of his incumbency he raised the membership from
one hundred and fifty to a thousand, at the same time contributing in a powerful manner to the leading part played by this
organization in the fight for a free harbor. During that period
also, in conjunction with Frank A. Pattee and Harry Brook
(both well-known wielders of the pen), he started the *Land of
Sunshine* (six months later taken over by Charles F. Lummis,
as editor, and in 1902 renamed the *Out West Magazine;*) while
in 1897 he assumed the management of the Los Angeles *Express*,
from which he resigned two years later. In 1892, he organized
with others the Municipal League, serving it ever since as either
Secretary or Vice-President, and in the same energetic way in
which he toiled as Secretary of the Associated Jobbers. In
his literary capacity, Willard has been equally efficient, being
the author of a compact *History of Los Angeles*, a *History of
the Los Angeles Chamber of Commerce*, *The Free Harbor Contest*

---

[1] During the night of January 21st, 1914, Willard died—on the anniversary of
his birth.

and a high school text-book on city government, all of which, as well as contributions to the San Francisco *Argonaut*, have been favorably received by a discerning public.

Frank Wiggins' name is considered by many of his friends a synonym for that of the Chamber of Commerce. Like his predecessor, Charles D. Willard, Wiggins came to California for his health; and upon its restoration, identified himself with the Chamber of Commerce on September 17th, 1889, becoming Secretary in 1897. Although ferociously bewhiskered, he is the mildest and best-natured man in town. He has had charge, in all parts of the country, of many exhibits so unique and so successful that he is known from coast to coast.

On May 24th, 1913, while many thousand people were assembled at Long Beach for a Southern California celebration of Empire Day, one of the worst of local catastrophes occurred through the caving-in of the defective floor of a crowded dancing pavilion. Medical and police aid were at once despatched from Los Angeles; but the result of the accident, the death of forty persons and injury to many more, cast a deep spell over the two cities.

Dr. Charles F. Lummis, assisted by other public-spirited men and women of Los Angeles including Lieutenant-General Adna R. Chaffee[1] (the first President), Joseph Scott, Mrs. Clara B. Burdette, Miss Mary E. Foy, M. H. Newmark and William Lacy, on the last day of 1907 incorporated the Southwest Museum.[2] On the 1st of March, 1910, Dr. Lummis, celebrating his fifty-first birthday, conveyed to the Museum his priceless collection of *Americana*. A sightly eminence of seventeen acres near Sycamore Grove was secured; and on November 16th, 1912, ground was broken with the formalities usual to such events, the first spadeful being turned by Miss Elizabeth Benton Frémont, daughter of the Pathfinder, followed by General

[1] Died on November 1st, 1914.

[2] The present officers are: President, Dr. Norman Bridge; Vice-Presidents, Mrs. Clara B. Burdette, Joseph Scott and J. S. Torrance; Founder Emeritus, Charles F. Lummis; Treasurer, Stoddard Jess; Curator, Hector Alliot; Directors, Dr. Norman Bridge, Robert N. Bulla, Mrs. Clara B. Burdette, E. P. Clark, Charles F. Lummis, Dr. J. A. Munk, M. H. Newmark, Joseph Scott and J. S. Torrance.

Chaffee and Dr. Lummis.   An inspiring feature of the day was
the raising by Miss Frémont and General Chaffee of the same
flag that on August 16th, 1842 General Frémont had unfurled on
the crest of the Rocky Mountains.   On this occasion Henry W.
O'Melveny presented a certified check for fifty thousand dollars,
the bequest of Mrs. Carrie M. Jones.   This auspicious beginning
was followed, on July 9th, 1913, by the pouring of the first concrete.[1]   How broadly and well those have built who planned
this much-needed institution may be seen from both the distinguishing architectural features of the structure, including the
caracole tower of cement, and the location—one of the most
notable occupied by any museum in the United States.

Dr. J. A. Munk, an Ohioan, to whom I have just referred,
has not been in Los Angeles as long as many others, having
arrived only in 1892, but he is known among his friends for his
charming personality, and among historians and scientists for
his splendid collection of *Arizoniana*—commenced on his first
trip to Arizona in 1884—all of which has been given to the
Southwest Museum.

Among the features of the Southwest Museum is the
large square, or so-called Torrance Tower, the funds for which
were generously provided by Jared S. Torrance, whose residence in Pasadena dates from 1887.   In that year he came from
the Empire State; and ever since he has been an active par-
ticipator in the development of Southern California.   The
town of Torrance is an example of his enterprise.

My sixty years' residence in Los Angeles has been by no
means free from the ordinary family cares, vicissitudes and
sorrows, and it seems proper that I should refer to the physicians
who, in times of illness, have ministered to the comfort of my
home and its inmates.   Our first doctor was John S. Griffin,
and he continued in that capacity until I left for New York.
Shortly before 1873, Dr. Griffin, whose advancing age compelled

[1] On December 6th, 1913, the corner-stone for the building already looming
large was laid by the Rt. Reverend Thomas J. Conaty—the broad-minded,
scholarly and much-respected Bishop of Monterey and Los Angeles, who died
on September 18th, 1915—and by General Chaffee.

him to withdraw from general practice, had been calling Dr. Joseph Kurtz into consultation; and it was then that the latter became my family physician. For a short time, I consulted Dr. Charles A. H. De Szigethy, a relic of the old school, whose nauseating doses were proverbial; and then Dr. John R. Haynes, now well known as an advocate of Socialism, who had arrived from Philadelphia in May, 1887, assumed the responsibility. Again a long period elapsed before events caused a change. In the year 1897, my nephew, Dr. Philip Newmark, came to Los Angeles from Berlin and succeeded Dr. Haynes.

Notwithstanding these mutations and cares, my friends have often insisted that I am quick and perhaps even sprightly for my age, and have more than once asked to what I attribute this activity and alertness. It is due, I think, first, to the inheritance from my parents of a strong constitution; and, secondly, to the preservation of my health by a moderate, though never over-abstemious, manner of living.

To begin with, ever since I traveled with my father in Sweden, I have kept my mind healthfully employed, while I have never long deprived myself of rest. I have also always used tobacco and liquor in moderation; and in this connection I can testify that, although wine and beer were at the free disposal of my children, they have grown up to use it either most temperately or not at all. This fact I ascribe to liberal views on such subjects; for it has always been my belief that to prohibit is to invite, whereas to furnish a good example and at the same time to warn, is to insure rational restriction and limitation. In short, in preparation for a vigorous old age, I have followed as closely as I could the ancient ideal, "A sound mind in a sound body."

At the age of nineteen, I came to Los Angeles; and after a lapse of exactly sixty years—that is, on October 21st, 1913—I find myself completing these reminiscences, ruminating on the past, and attempting a prophecy for the future.

A battle of eighty years with the world cannot, in the nature of human affairs, leave any man or woman unscarred; but I have learned many things, and among them the consolations of philosophy. It would be presumption on my part to make complaint against the inscrutable decrees of that Providence which guides the destinies of us all; I dwell, rather, on the manifold blessings which have been my lot in this life—the decision of Fate which cast my lines in the pleasant places of Southern California; the numerous excellent and estimable friends whom I have met on life's highway; the many years of happiness vouchsafed me to enjoy; and, finally, whatever degree of success has attended my more serious efforts.

When I came, Los Angeles was a sleepy, ambitionless adobe village with very little promise for the future. The messenger of Optimism was deemed a dreamer; but time has more than realized the fantasies of those old village oracles, and what they said would some day come to pass in Los Angeles, has come and gone, to be succeeded by things much greater still. We possessed however, even in that distant day, one asset, intangible it is true, but as invaluable as it was intangible—the spirit popularly called "Western," but which, after all, was largely the pith of transferred Eastern enterprise. This characteristic seized upon a vast wilderness—the same which Daniel Webster declared, in the Senate of the United States, unworthy of membership in the sisterhood of States; and within this extensive area it builded great cities, joined its various parts with steel and iron, made great highways out of the once well-nigh impassable cattle-paths, and from an elemental existence developed a complex civilization. Nor is there to-day in all this region a greater or finer city than fair Los Angeles.

Many of us saw it grow; none of us foresaw that growth, even from decade to decade.

"Westward the course of empire takes its way." When Bishop Berkeley so poetically proclaimed this historic truth, even he could hardly have had in mind the shores of the Pacific; but here we have an empire, and one whose future is glorious. This flourishing city stands, in fact, with its half million or more human beings and its metropolitan activities, at the threshold of a new era. The operations of Nature change so slowly as to show almost no change at all: the Southern California of the coming years will still possess her green hills and vales, her life-giving soil, her fruits, flowers and grain, and the same sun will shine upon her with the same generous warmth, out of the same blue sky, as ever. The affairs of men, on the other hand, change rapidly. After gigantic labor initiated but ten short years ago, the Panamá Canal is dedicated to the use of mankind, and through its crowded waters will come the ships of every nation, bringing to the marts of Los Angeles choice products to be exchanged for our own. For this and other reasons, I believe that Los Angeles is destined to become, in not many years, a world-center, prominent in almost every field of human endeavor; and that, as nineteen hundred years ago the humblest Roman, wherever he might find himself, would glow with pride when he said, "I am a Roman!" so, in the years to come, will the son of the metropolis on these shores, wheresoever his travels may take him, be proud to declare,

"I AM A CITIZEN OF LOS ANGELES!"

INDEX

A

Abalones, 427; shells as jewelry, 261; gatherer trapped, 428
Abarca, Luis (Louis), 63
Abarta, Señorita, 526
Abbotsford Inn, 566, 627
Abbott, William and Mrs. (née Garcia), 186
Abell, J. B., 543
Abila, Francisco, 100
Abila, H., 403
Abila, José María and Señora, 100
Abila ranch, 447; springs, 210
Abolitionists, 296, 308
Acacia latifolia, 544
Acapulco, 359
Acorns, as Indian food, 203
Acqueduct, Owens River, 50
Active, U. S. ship, 251
Adams, Lionel J., 636
Adams, Professor, 419
Adams Street, 459
Adams & Co., 242
Ada Hancock, disaster to steamer, 75, 109, 132, 154, 295, 300, 316, 319, 329
Adelsdorfer Bros., 120
Adler, Adelaide (later Mrs. Samuel Hellman), 142
Adler, Caroline (later Mrs. I. M. Hellman), 142
Adobe, municipal and county, 36, 40, 41, 209, 256, 324, 338, 530
Adobes, 31, 32, 38, 61, 62, 63, 65, 66, 67, 73, 76, 78, 80, 81, 94, 97, 99, 100, 101, 103, 104, 109, 113, 115, 119, 121, 124, 134, 147, 165, 167, 193, 197, 202, 220, 256, 257, 263, 293, 317, 335, 343, 347, 372, 376, 396, 444, 466, 492, 510, 518, 620
Adrienne Lecouvreur, Modjeska in, 494
Advertisements, 137, 151, 177, 281, 292, 297, 396, 422, 465, 469, 486, 492, 558; pictures in, 356
Advertising, freak, 571; boom—, 573 ff.
Æneas, xiii
Africa, 193, 211
Agricultural Park, 462, 640; —Society, 426
Agua Caliente, 50, 92, 414
Aguardiente, 134, 278
Aguilar, Casildo, 147
Aguilar, Cristóbal, 66, 98, 100, 120, 366, 445
Aguilar, José María, 210
Aguirre, José Antónío, 174
Aguirre, Martin O., 551
Alameda Street, 63, 112, 187, 197, 201, 304, 383, 394, 400, 408, 493, 562
Alamitos, Los, 599, 520
Alamitos Bay, 374, 630
Alamitos ranch, 166, 329
Alaska, 397, 463, 602
Albacore, 628
Albino, exhibition of, 186
Albuquerque, 222
Alder, 197

Alder, Captain, 251
Alexander, David W., 23, 35, 38, 43, 61, 64, 74, 120, 218, 343, 350, 445, 500; Mrs.— (formerly Mrs. Francis Mellus), 227;—& Banning, 218;—& Mellus, 62, 151
Alexander, Frank, 206
Alexander, George, 639, 642
Alexander, George C., 74, 194, 297
Alexander, Henry N., 39, 241, 260; Mrs.—, 39
Alexander, Ramón (Raimuudo), 59, 64, 193
Alexandria Hotel, 77, 639
Alfilaria, 126
Alhambra and A. Tract, 445, 454, 563, 628
Alisal, El, 543
Aliso, El, 198
Aliso, meaning of, 197
Aliso Mill, 198, 218, 303, 499
Aliso Road, 198, 412;—Street, 71, 112, 197, 198, 238, 288, 292, 400
Aliso Vineyard, 197, 198
Allanson, Horace S., 62, 256
Allen Block, 372
Allen, Charles H., 532
Allen, Gabriel, 221
Allen, Jesse, 414, 416
Alliot, Hector, 635, 636, 647
Alosta, 579; Lamar's Addition to, 579
Alta California, 270
Altadena, 178, 337
Alta Vista, 579
Alton, John, 606
Altschul, Richard, 230
Alvarado house, the, 115
Alvitre, Felipe, 139
Alvitre, José Claudio, 147
Amat, Thaddeus, 189, 279
America, foreign ideas as to, 361
America, steamship, 149
American Bakery, 405
American boy, first born here, 33
American Colony, 521
American Express Co., 234
American Fork, 155
Amestoy, Domingo, 310, 421;—Building, 537
Amigo del Pueblo, El, 308
Amigos, Los dos, 64
Amo, Dr. del, 174
Amusements, 102, 124, 135, 161, 182, 183, 186, 192, 229, 263, 282, 286, 318, 352, 372, 381, 383, 384, 409, 422, 463, 488, 547, 569, 592, 596, 605
Anaheim, 177, 212, 309, 329, 376, 398, 401, 406, 441, 451, 526, 580, 593
Anaheim, proposed County of, 406, 593
Anaheim Gazette, 414
Anaheim Landing, 366
Anchorage, 404
Ancon, steamer, 465
Anderson, D., 83, 297
Anderson, J. A., 638
Anderson, John, 476
Anderson, W. P., 627
Andersonville, 295

Index

Made in the USA
Middletown, DE
24 May 2015